CANADA AT WAR AND PEACE, II

A Millennium of Military Heritage

VOLUME II

IN DEFENCE OF OTHERS: 1920-2000

**WORLD WARRIORS
AND PEACEKEEPERS**

ESPRIT DE CORPS BOOKS
1066 Somerset St. W., Suite 204
Ottawa, ON, Canada
K1Y 4T3
Tel: (613) 725-5060

EDITOR-IN-CHIEF
Scott Raymond Taylor

SENIOR EDITOR
Dr. Bill Twatio

PRODUCTION MANAGER
LAYOUT AND DESIGN
Cathy Hingley

EDITOR, ILLUSTRATIONS AND PHOTO RESEARCH
Julie Simoneau

EDITORS
Norman Shannon
Les Peate
Bruce Poulin
Strome Galloway
Howard Michitsch

SALES AND PROMOTION
Katherine Taylor

COVER ILLUSTRATION
Raymond Taylor

COPY ASSISTANTS
Michèle Simoneau
Anne Trinneer
Joyce Peate
Dr. Roy Rempel

CONTRIBUTORS
James G. Scott
Andrew Moxley
Ian McCulloch
Brian Reid
Mike McNorgan
Stephen Prince
Paul Culliton
David Smart
Steven Gavard
Roy Thomas
Brian Nolan
Cathy Hingley
Tom Brooks
W.B.S. Sutherland
Hugh Jones
David Muralt
R.T. Walsh
Larry Mitiuk
George Orsyk
G. Jaxon
Phil Lancaster
James Steele
E.C. Meyers
Denis Whitaker
Shelagh Witaker
Peter Stursberg
Paul Burden
Harry V. Smith
David Smart
L.H. Packard
Steve Hewitt
John Coffey
David Batten
John de Chastelain
Daniel G. Skuka
Victor Suthren
Howard Michitsch
Warren Ferguson
Chris Champion
Howard Ripstein
Ralph Patton
Fred Gaffen
Paul Richards
David Deere

ACKNOWLEDGEMENTS
CANADA AT WAR AND PEACE: A Millennium of Military Heritage, was designed and produced by the staff of Esprit de Corps, Canadian Military Magazine. This publication would not have been possible without the generous financial donations and contributions received from FM, MB, PH and the Taylor family. In addition, the publishers wish to thank the legion of volunteers who dedicated their time and talent to this project.

CANADIAN CATALOGUING IN PUBLICATION DATA
Main entry under title: Canada at war and peace, II: a millennium of military heritage.

2nd edition. Includes indexes.
Editor-in-chief: Scott R. Taylor
Contents: v.1. Forged in fire, 1000-1919 -- v.2. In defence of others, 1920-2000
ISBN 1-895896-12-6 (set) – ISBN 1-895896-14-2 (v.1)
ISBN 1-895896-16-9 (v.2)

1. Canada--History, Military.
FC226.C32 2001 971 C00-901289-3
F1028.C32 2001

Printed and bound in Canada by Gilmore Printing.

CANADA AT WAR AND PEACE, II

A Millennium of Military Heritage

VOLUME II

IN DEFENCE OF OTHERS: 1920-2000

WORLD WARRIORS AND PEACEKEEPERS

Following the Great War, Canada took her first independent steps on the world stage. As a signatory on the Versailles Treaty "...to end all wars," our fledgling nation accepted an immense global responsibility to protect the peace beyond our own shores. In the subsequent eight decades, Canada has answered the call on numerous occasions – fighting when necessary and peacekeeping where possible.

WORLD WARRIORS & PEACEKEEPERS 1920-2000

1920-1939 – BETWEEN THE ACTS

1939 – WAR AGAIN!

1940 – CANADA ANSWERS THE CALL

WEAPONS AND UNIFORMS

1941 – THE WIDENING CONFLICT

1942 – THE RISING AXIS TIDE

1943 – REVERSAL OF FORTUNES

1944 – THE BEGINNING OF THE END

258

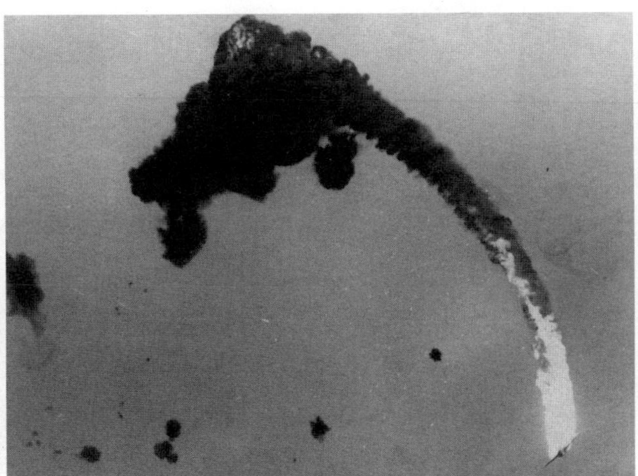

BETWEEN THE ACTS, 1920 - 1939

Throughout the 'Roaring Twenties,' Canada's military was reduced to a pittance and woefully neglected: A generation came to believe they had fought the "war to end all wars." Faced with the economic crisis of the Great Depression, the major powers failed to recognize the re-emergence of German nationalism under the guidance of a fanatical dictator named Adolf Hitler. War weary and bankrupt, British and French politicians adopted a policy of "appeasement" towards Hitler rather than confront his aggression.

1925 The Treaty of Locarno is signed and the Allies agree to abandon their occupation of the Rhineland by 1930, provided Germany keeps her troops from re-entering this territory.

1929 The stock market crashes on Wall Street, plunging the world into a financial crisis. The next decade is labelled the Great Depression.

1933 Adolf Hitler becomes the Chancellor of Germany and the Nazi party has its first taste of power.

1935 Italian fascist dictator Benito Mussolini attempts to restore the glory of the Roman Empire by launching an invasion of Abyssinia. The League of Nations protests but does not take any action.

1936 On 27 February Hitler correctly gambles that Britain and France will not oppose his re-occupation of the Rhineland.

During the spring and summer, local clashes in Spain develop into a full-scale civil war. Volunteers from around the world (including Canada) volunteer to fight the fascists.

15 MARCH 1938 Hitler delivers an ultimatum and then annexes Austria into his Third Reich. Britain and France protest.

12 SEPTEMBER 1938 Hitler stages the Nuremburg rally and announces his intention to annex Czechoslovakia.

29 SEPTEMBER 1938 After initial protests, Britain and France "appease" Hitler by sanctioning his seizure of Czechoslovakia. Britain's Prime Minister leaves the Munich summit and proclaims he has negotiated "peace in our time."

LEFT: *In 1937, Mackenzie King, a strong supporter of appeasement, met with Adolf Hitler in Berlin to promote "friendly relations" with Nazi Germany. In his diary, King sized up Hitler as "one who truly loves his fellow man...." History would prove how inaccurate King was in his first impression of Hitler.* (NAC/PA 119013)

RIGHT:
The extreme drought suffered in the Prairies worsened the Depression in the west. Saskatchewan's provincial income decreased by 90 per cent in just two years and forced 66 per cent of its rural population onto government relief, while the other western provinces were technically bankrupt as of 1932. (SASKATCHEWAN WHEAT POOL)

CANADA: THE YEARS BETWEEN

Having become Prime Minister in 1921, Mackenzie King believed public debate could resolve any dispute.

ALTHOUGH THE UNITED STATES was a latecomer to WWI action, President Wilson dominated the peace talks and the formation of the League of Nations which followed. Tucked away among many articles of covenant was an early-day peacekeeping clause which proclaimed that members should go to war to protect another member if necessary. Ironically, Wilson was defeated at home and the U.S. sank into isolationism and never did join the League while failure to enforce Article 10 led to another World War.

Mackenzie King, who became Canadian Prime Minister in 1921, was quick to fight for a Canadian voice at the League of Nations but when he got it he had nothing to say. Shaken by the trauma of the conscription issue of 1917, King was determined to steer clear of international affairs in order to avoid a breach with Quebec. He considered the League to be a civilized debating society and strongly opposed any attempts at collective security arrangements.

His Government believed that public debate could resolve any dispute, an attitude which set the tone for a pathetic military situation. Following the war the permanent force melted to some 5,000. During the conflict, Canadian officers showed strong leadership and Canadian troops were considered the best in Europe, but with the Armistice most of this resource went to Civvie Street. Little of the keen grasp of modern warfare was evident in Canada's army of the 1920's.

In scattered depots across Canada, training was often restricted to the troop or squadron level and instructors seemed to be reading manuals from the Boer War days. In spite of limited use and high casualties in WWI, the cavalry charge was back in style as the Royal Canadian Dragoons underwent summer training. The working army found duty at home maintaining peace in a strife torn decade as they policed strikes at Winnipeg, Quebec and Sydney.

SCENARIOS DEVELOPED

Meanwhile, at National Defence Headquarters, Buster Brown and his associates pursued a course of fiction which challenged the best of H.G. Wells. Colonel Brown, the Director of Military Intelligence, was convinced that America's grand design was to occupy Canada. So he and his associates spent months developing scenarios whereby Canada would launch a preemptive strike against our southern cousins. They roamed the northern U.S. from Vermont to Washington drawing up attack plans, confident that a fictitious 300,000 militiamen would seize key positions such as Glen Falls, N.Y. and hold them until the British came to our rescue.

The toothless League of Nations began to show its true colours in 1931 when Japan invaded Manchuria. Hitler attacked the disarmament provisions of the Treaty of Versailles and withdrew from the League in 1935 but there was no response. That same year Mussolini invaded Ethiopia and Canada's representative to the World Security Conference – Dr. Walter Riddell – proposed strong oil sanctions against Italy. It was the first occasion when the League of Nations showed the courage to confront. An infuriated Mussolini promised retaliation against any country which followed Dr. Riddell's proposal. As this was happening, the Bennett government was defeated by King who immediately withdrew the resolution and told the media that Riddell deserved a "good spanking."

While Mussolini conquered Ethiopia and the world watched, Canada cast an ironic glance backwards to 1917 and Vimy Ridge. In 1922 the French Government ceded to Canada in perpetuity some 250 acres on the crest of the disputed ridge. The Canadian Battlefields Memorial Commission later selected a magnificent design for a memorial by Walter Allward of Toronto. It took 11 years to complete the project, unveiled at the summit of Hill 145. Among the 10,000 Canadian veterans who attended was a lady who lost eight sons. Mrs. Wood personified Canada's past sacrifices while Prime Minister Mackenzie spoke for the naiveté of the times when he returned from Germany after meeting Hitler. Within 36 months of war, King decided that the Führer was a simple sort of peasant who was "not very intelligent and no serious danger to anyone."

***AUTHOR**: Norman Shannon*

OPPOSITE PAGE:
The official unveiling ceremonies for the Canadian War Memorial atop Vimy Ridge on 26 July 1936. France ceded 250 acres of land, in perpetuity, to Canada to commemorate the 40,000 soldiers (of them 3598 killed and some 7000 wounded), who succeeded in April 1917 in regaining this land from the Germans. (NAC/PA 803934)

RIGHT:
During the First World War, Turkey was Germany's ally and was the site of several key campaigns, including Gallipoli and the Dardanelles. By 1922, the Treaty of Sèvres, which Britain and Canada had signed with defeated Turkey, was in tatters as most of the country lay in the hands of nationalist forces. British occupation troops were pinned down at Chanak (now Canakkale). Britain found itself alone when the Dominions did not readily respond to the Empire's plea for solidarity against the Turks. (ROBERT HUNT PICTURE LIBRARY)

WHEN CANADA SAID "NO" TO BRITAIN

King's refusal to respond with a "Ready! Aye Ready!" when Britain beckoned made 1922 Chanak Crisis a benchmark in Canada's evolution as an independent nation.

ON THE STROKE OF midnight (London time) 4 August 1914, the British Empire, then the world's only superpower, went to war against Germany. At precisely the same moment, Canada, part of an empire which comprised one quarter of the world's population and one quarter of its land mass, joined them. In 1914 the empire spoke with one voice and that voice came from London. One fourth of the world was under the Union Jack, and Great Britain also controlled the wold's oceans. "Rule Britannia, Britannia rule the waves," was the command. And Britannia did. (Not until decades later would anyone rule the air, or space.)

Twenty-five years later, on 3 September 1939, Great Britain went to war against Germany once more – but Canada did not. The intervening quarter century had brought Canada new status. It was no longer a colony whose Motherland spoke for it, but an adult nation capable of speaking for itself. Its voice was Prime Minister Mackenzie King and the answer he mouthed came from the Canadian parliament. However the people of Canada stood loyally behind their Motherland. Between 3 and 10 September the people, the Press and Parliamentarians loudly demanded that Canada join the war. The country's pacifist prime minister had no option. So Canada declared war against Germany one week after Great Britain had. Canada went to war, but by its own declaration. This time, not as a subordinate, but rather as a partner.

Ever since Toronto-born Alexander Dunn won the Victoria Cross in the historic Charge of the Light Brigade during the Crimean War of the 1850s, Canada and Canadians had responded to Great Britain's call to arms. A small contingent of volunteers took part in the Nile expedition of 1884. Fifteen years later more than 7000 of all arms fought beside the British Army in the Boer War, a three-year struggle that proved the Empire's last war of conquest. In 1914 and again in 1939, Canadians in their hundreds of thousands streamed across the Atlantic to fight under the Union Jack. More than a 100,000 never came back. Others garrisoned far-flung outposts of the empire to relieve British regulars for the battlefield. In the Second World War one of these outposts was Hong Kong. Finally, in 1951 and in the ensuing three years, some 22,000 Canadians fought under British command in the Commonwealth Division, which operated as a United Nations force against the Chinese communists in Korea.

Only once did Canada refuse to answer Great Britain's call to arms. That was in September 1922, when Canada said "No!" – in the voice of Prime Minister Mackenzie King. Yet, 17 years later, almost to the day, King agreed to joining Great Britain in its war against Nazi Germany! The 1922 affair was called the Chanak Crisis.

MUSTERING TO FIGHT

The Chanak Crisis was a hang-over from the First World War. Turkey, having fought on Germany's side, was occupied by the Allies. The Greeks occupied the port of Chanak as well as that of Smyrna and made it known they intended to incorporate them as Greek territory. A certain belligerent Turk, under an up-and-coming national leader

RIGHT:
Sitting atop his trusty steed, this Royal Canadian Dragoon cavalryman is equipped with riding breaches and spurs. (ROYAL CANADIAN DRAGOONS)

named Mustapha Kemal, later known as Kemal Ataturk, "the father of modern Turkey," found the Greek position unacceptable and began mustering to fight the Greeks. This was embarrassing for the other allies occupying other parts of Turkey, including Great Britain. It looked as though all-out war between Turkey and Greece was to take place. For although Turkey was occupied in certain strategic areas, most of its soil was unoccupied and huge numbers of recently discharged war veterans were eager to strike back at their wartime enemy. They rallied to Kemal's call and Great Britain decided that their former ally, Greece, must be supported. When the call for troops went out to the British dominions, New Zealand responded immediately, while Australia and South Africa hesitated. But Canada's "No" ended the indecision and also ended Great Britain's aggressive attitude. War never came. Greece did not keep Chanak or Smyrna. The allied forces withdrew and Turkey became a modern nation under its most dynamic leader, Ataturk. It even adopted the Western alphabet in place of its centuries-old Arabic script.

One slight Canadian connection reveals itself. Among the British occupation troops on Turkish soil was the 1st Battalion Irish Guards, commanded by Lieutenant Colonel Harold Alexander, later to become a Second World War Field Marshal and Governor General of Canada from 1946 to 1952.

Although Canada turned down this 1922 call to arms, many Canadians were unhappy over the negative response. The leader of the Opposition, Arthur Meighen, attempted to electrify Canada's parliament with the war cry of "Ready, Aye Ready!" It didn't work. To many Conservatives, it was in Canada's interest to support British prestige. But Canada was war weary and most people, and the press of the country, supported the Prime Minister.

TREATY OF VERSAILLES

For many, the Chanak Crisis became the real benchmark of Canada's maturity as a nation independent of British foreign policy. Canada could choose its own course of action. It said "No" in 1922, but it said "Yes" in 1939, and through the same mouth – that of Prime Minister Mackenzie King. Its stand in 1922 was a direct result of the Treaty of Versailles which ended the First World War. For the first time Canada signed a treaty for itself. Thanks to Prime Minister Sir Robert Borden, who fought at the peace conference for this right, the objection of the United States of America was overcome.

The USA strove to confine the British Empire to one signature as being one national entity. It feared that in future international conferences it could be out-voted if the British Empire was not seen as one nation and limited to one vote. But the British recognized that Canada's contribution to the winning of the war had been of such a greater proportion than that of the United States, that to deny its nationhood was unthinkable.

The Chanak Crisis is almost a totally forgotten piece of Canadian history. The writer, seven years old at the time, remembers living in Melville, Saskatchewan, a railway divisional point, where the going and coming of trans-Canada trains was always an interesting event. One September evening my family witnessed a troop train refilling its boilers. The soldiers were stretching their legs up and down the platform. What fine fellows they looked to a seven-year old! They were either cavalry, or artillery, or perhaps signal corps, for they wore riding breeches and spurs, and had highly-polished leather ammunition bandoleers over their right shoulder. They also had snow-white lanyards around their left shoulder, attached to hoof-picks in their breast pocket. (The hoof picks were to remove stones lodged in their horses' hooves.) In 1922 the army was not yet mechanized.

ALL THAT MATTERED

Whether these troops were members of the Permanent Force going back to their Winnipeg barracks after summer camp at Sarcee or some such place, or militiamen also returning home after a camp outing I have no idea.

As we drove away from the station into the Saskatchewan sunset slanting over the surrounding prairie, our McLaughlin Master-Six with the yellow wooden spokes rolling along the twin ruts that served as a road, my Mother said to my Father, "If there is going to be another war, those poor chaps will soon be going overseas again." As it happened, they didn't go overseas, because Mackenzie King said no to Great Britain's call. Seventeen years later I went overseas, because he said "Yes."

REPRINTED FROM:
Esprit de Corps, *Volume 4 Issue 4*
AUTHOR:
Strome Galloway

LEFT: *Much of Canada's forests were mapped for timber resources and patrolled for fires by the Curtiss seaplane. These bush planes were a key element in summer, but were useless in winter.* (ILLUSTRATION BY ROBERT W. BRADFORD, NATIONAL AVIATION MUSEUM)

DICKINS CRASHED ON ICE AT AKLAVIK, SMASHING HIS PROP AND WIPING OUT THE LANDING GEAR ON THE FOKKER UNIVERSAL. HE AND HIS CO-PILOT BUILT A NEW UNDERCARRIAGE FROM BITS OF SCRAP METAL FOUND IN THE LUGGAGE COMPARTMENT, AND FLEW OUT.

AN INDUSTRY GROWS IN WAR'S PROPWASH

The dramatic development of bush flying in Canada came in the propwash of wartime aviation. Ironically, the men who had been ignored by their own country for most of the war formed the dedicated nucleus that opened it up to its full potential.

JIMMY AND HENRY HOFFAR of Vancouver were part of an early breed of do-it-yourself aircraft builders who sprang up across Canada in the years following the Wright brothers' manned flight. In 1917, the Hoffars switched from building boats long enough to produce a sleek seaplane. Self-taught pilot Jimmy Hoffar took a daring reporter aloft for a look at Vancouver, but a few weeks after the successful flight the seaplane hit a log while taxiing in the harbour and sank.

The Hoffars went on to build a flying boat which caught the attention of the British Columbia government, which was considering using it for forestry patrols. Victor Bishop, an RAF pilot home on leave, took the flying boat up on a test in September 1918. The engine cut out at 1500 feet over Vancouver's west end, and Bishop made an unexpected house call on Dr. J.C. Farish. Much of the flying boat – then on lease to the BC government – was splattered over the roof and Bishop ended up in the Farish's bathroom. Unfortunately, the incident convinced the BC government that the day of forestry patrols had not arrived. But things were different in Eastern Canada.

AIRCREW RETURNS TO CANADA

Within a year of the Armistice, an estimated 12,500 Canadian aircrew had returned to Canada. One of the first was Stu Graham, who had flown with the Royal Naval Air Service. Upon his return to Canada, he soon went to work for Ellwood Wilson, the chief forester with the Laurentide Lumber Company which operated out of Quebec's St. Maurice Valley. Wilson had bought two surplus Curtiss flying boats from the Yanks who had flown them out of Halifax and Sydney for the last few months of the war. In June 1919, Graham cranked up the old Curtiss and took off from Dartmouth Harbour to become the world's first bush pilot. Four days later, he touched down at Lac à la Tortue and the 645-mile trip became the longest in Canada up to that date.

Soon the two Curtiss flying boats were flying forestry patrols in which they mapped timber resources and searched for forest fires. The patrols instantly became a key element in forestry operations. But as costs escalated, Laurentide Lumber became reluctant to continue underwriting the operation, and Laurentide Air Services became a separate operation in 1922. The world's first bush charter flew 688 hours, and carried 310 passengers that summer.

Ontario employed the company to map 20,000 square miles of timber, a job that would have taken six years on the ground but was done in just 160 hours. The government was so impressed that it decided to form the Ontario Provincial Air Service (OPAS) and lured several key Laurentide Air personnel. Three years later, Laurentide Air Services closed down.

MUSHING TO RED LAKE

Geologist, mining engineer and former RFC pilot Doc Oaks was among the OPAS pilots who flew some 170,000 patrol miles and spotted 600 fires in 1924. When gold was discovered at Red Lake the next year, Oaks and pilot Tommy Thompson quit their jobs and mushed a dogteam to Red Lake where they established a claim. They later sold their claim to buy a Curtiss Lark and started

Patricia Airways; they were soon flying freight, passengers and mail out of Sioux Lookout to Red Lake. With financial backing from James Richardson of Winnipeg, Oaks expanded the operation which became Western Canada Airways. When the Canadian government planned to build a railway terminal a Churchill, Oaks carried eight tons of equipment and 14 engineers some 280 miles in the first major airlift. "There has been no more brilliant operation in the history of commercial aviation," the government acknowledged.

CANADIAN AIR FORCE

The government got into the licensing and control business in 1919 when it formed the Air Board. With a surplus of gift aircraft in crates at Borden and Halifax, it also formed a Canadian Air Force which was primarily an auxiliary unit providing refresher courses for pilots who had flown with the British. Then, in 1924, the Royal Canadian Air Force was formed. For over a decade, most of its flying was civilian in nature and RCAF pilots were soon winging North on a variety of assignments. While not in overt competition with civilian operators, the widely-based operation and government resources became a major element in developing the North.

Mining became the great impetus to the development of aviation. Doc Oaks branched out and formed a company designed to transport prospectors anywhere from the Rockies to Hudson Bay. The Fairchild, with its enclosed cockpit, became his all-season bush plane of choice with a range enhanced by 33 fuel caches along the Barrens. Northern Aerial Minerals Exploration became another victim of success; as operational costs mounted, it went into bankruptcy.

Punch Dickins returned from France with seven victories and joined the CAF in 1921. Posted to Edmonton, he specialized in winter flying and joined Western Canada in 1926. He flew a party on an exploratory mining flight which covered 4,000 miles in less than two weeks. He initiated a mail run to Fort Simpson and made regular flights to the Northwest Territories. Dickins crashed on ice at Aklavik, smashing his prop and wiping out the landing gear on the Fokker Universal. He and his co-pilot then spent five days cutting eight inches off each tip of the propeller and pounding it into a new shape. They built a new undercarriage from bits of scrap metal found in the luggage compartment, and flew out.

ABOVE: *Captain Don MacLaren, seated at left with members of 1 Squadron, founded Pacific Airlines.* (NATIONAL ARCHIVES)

Don MacLaren – the third ranking Canadian ace with 54 victories – started Pacific Airways in 1921 and flew forestry and fishery patrols for the BC government. An interesting element in the fisheries patrol, lacking today, was the fact that flying boats landed and taxied up to suspicious boats and the crews performed inspections.

USELESS IN WINTER

Much of the bush pilot's life was a struggle with hostile, uncharted terrain, and cruel, cold and monotonous hours of flying or attempting to fly in sub-zero temperatures. It involved mapping, forest patrols, fishery patrols, mining and oil exploration, airmail and just plain transportation. While flying boats had relatively safe passage on thousands of lakes in summer, they were useless in winter. Aircraft using skis or floats often came to misery during a spring breakup or an early autumn freeze. Floats were constantly damaged by sunken logs, and whiteouts or glassy landings on summer still lakes haunted pilots. Engineers were haunted by weather. Anti-freeze solutions were unknown then, and the engineer drained the oil on landing and sometimes, even took the battery to bed with him as temperatures dropped to -50° Farenheit. For at least two hours before take-off, the engineer would warm the oil and then heat the engine with a gasoline burner, known as a blowpot. These were the daily challenges faced by bush pilots and engineers, although some of the more spectacular episodes caught the public's attention.

Wop May – who was Baron Richthofen's target the day *he* was killed – was an instructor at the Edmonton Flying Club when word came through that the settlement of Little Red River was threatened by a diphtheria epidemic and toxin was needed immediately. At -40°, May and Vic Horner took off in an Avro Avian with open cockpits. Numb from cold, with faces cracked and bleeding from frostbite, they landed on a lake when darkness set in, knowing that if they didn't get off in the morning nobody would ever find them. But they did get off, and delivered the toxin to Fort Vermillion. May was later involved in tracking the mad trapper of Rat River. He followed the tracks of killer Arthur Johnson for days. Johnson kept backtracking and evading the ground party until May's direction led to a shootout in which Johnson was killed. Then May landed and picked up the body.

The dramatic development of bush flying in Canada came in the propwash of wartime aviation. Ironically, the men who had been ignored by their own country for most of the war formed the dedicated nucleus which opened it up to its full potential. Then, with the advent of WWII, many came out of the bush to act as instructors as the British Commonwealth Air Training Plan got underway.

REPRINTED FROM:

Esprit de Corps, *Volume 8 Issue 3*

AUTHOR: *Norman Shannon*

RIGHT: *Once the United States joined the war effort, Joe Boyle (fourth from the left) found a friend in Herbert Hoover, who chose Joe to head up missions to Russia and Rumania.*

JOE BOYLE: HERO OF THE CENTURY?

The audacity of Joe Boyle (1867-1923) saw him through life as a fight manager, peacemaker, diplomat, negotiator, fundraiser, spy, thief – and possibly even a seducer of royalty.

KLONDIKE JOE BOYLE CAME in from the creeks in 1916 and told his wife Elma to wait as he went outside on business. She never saw him again. Joe's "business" took him to Russia where he got caught up in a revolution, and Rumania where he was made a Duke and became known as "the saviour of Rumania." And, while there is no actual proof, there is also a fair possibility that the bigger-than-life hero was bedding Queen Marie of Rumania.

Born in Toronto in 1867, Joe grew up in Woodstock where his father raised horses. He ran off to sea at 17 and later became part owner of a ship. By the time he was 20, Joe dropped anchor in New York, marrying his brother's girlfriend three days after meeting her and went into the feed and freighting business. His wife Millie's expensive taste drove them to a separation in 1896 and Joe became manager of Australian heavyweight Frank Slavin.

Slavin thirsted for John L. Sullivan's crown but they toured Toronto, Quebec and Montreal with limited success. Their moment of near-greatness came overseas at the opening of London's Crystal Palace. The Prince of Wales looked on as Joe worked Slavin's corner for ten rounds. Slavin had piled up a nice lead in early rounds but failed to show much in the ninth and tenth. He grinned when the bell rang for the 11th but was unable to stand. Boyle had been mixing booze with his water.

NIGHTLY DEAD COUNT

Slavin was promised $5000 to fight Jack Johnson in San Francisco, but when they got there Johnson refused to meet Slavin. Boyle and Slavin headed north to Skagway by the summer of 1897, drawn not by news of gold but by a dream of making a fortune in the fight game. At Skagway there was a dead count virtually every night and a friendly bartender challenged Boyle's plan of staging fights. He wanted to know why anyone would pay to watch two guys fighting in the ring when they could see a fight in his bar two or three times a night for nothing… and with knives.

They were broke in Skag when Joe found a discarded banjo. A singer at ship's concerts, Joe worked the crowd preparing for the trek to the goldfields, while Slavin passed the hat. A month later they had enough money to move on and blazed a trial over White Pass, a route which thousands of prospectors, and the Whitehorse Railway, would follow.

Joe's drive and perception soon made him a successful businessman but he and Slavin parted on the square in 1899 when the Slasher still felt the call of the bell. Joe became a major stockholder in the Canadian Klondike Mining Company and brought 1700 tons of steel over White Pass to set up the largest dredge in the territory.

STANLEY CUP CHALLENGE

In 1905, prosperous citizen Boyle led a hockey team, the Klondike Wanderers, 312 miles through the snow to Whitehorse and then to Ottawa in the great Stanley Cup Challenge. Ottawa won the first game before a capacity crowd at Dey's arena. Joe telegraphed a report to the *Dawson Daily News*, predicting victory. His team set a record for goals scored against as, in the final game, Ottawa scored 23 points to their two.

By 1914, the prominent Joe Boyle brought a new wife to the Klondike and five months after the outbreak of war raised a company of 52 men, 72 horses and four machine guns which he turned over to the government. Then in 1916, he told wife Elma to stay put while he went "outside" on business.

After a brief stop in Ottawa, he turned up in London wearing a Savile Row uniform with gold Yukon shoulder flashes. Militia Minister Sam Hughes had made him an honourary colonel in the militia, and for nine months, Joe Boyle's Klondike pure gold shoulder flashes dazzled London society as he looked for an assignment. but nobody had a job for a 49-year old sourdough until the United States got into the war.

Boyle's old friend Herbert Hoover selected Joe to head up a mission to Russia for the American committee of Engineers. The mission's objective was to improve rail service which was in a state of chaos like everything else.

With no credentials from the British War Office or the Canadian Army, Boyle used his gold insignia and natural brass to infiltrate the Russian hierarchy as a communications expert. He was given a private railway car and was soon roaming Russia like a troubleshooting Scarlet Pimpernel. It was a land on the brink of revolt and, when Nicholas II abdicated, Joe had an escape plan for him, but the Tsar insisted on staying.

The people of Moscow faced starvation because rail transportation to the city had come to a virtual standstill as some 10,000 cars stood idle. Boyle infiltrated the top Bolshevik echelons and was given the job of breaking the gridlock. The change in government meant little to Boyle, whose main interest was keeping an army in the field against Germany.

He went down to the tracks where sullen workers wanted to talk politics instead of work. Boyle took off his tunic and grabbed a pickaxe. The sight of a big, foreign, dandy-dancer in fancy clothing wielding the pickaxe stunned the workers, who then responded to the challenge with a vigour which broke the Moscow traffic knot in 48 hours.

RAILROAD INSPECTOR

Boyle later inspected railroads in Rumania which were also in such an appalling state that a corner of the country faced starvation. He confronted the Brigadier General responsible and started a backlash in diplomatic channels. After months of diplomatic notes, Canada's Governor-General issued the recall of the upstart Joe Boyle. But Boyle was so often on the move nobody knew where to send the recall.

With Civil War, Boyle became disenchanted with the Bolsheviks. The Rumanian government asked for his services with relief work and Joe went to Paris where he convinced Hoover, Chairman of Red Cross Relief, to divert two shipments of food to Rumania. He then went to London and negotiated $25 million in Canadian aid.

Rumanian national treasures had been sent to Moscow for safekeeping early in the war. With the Bolsheviks in control, the Rumanians decided it would take more than a diplomatic note to get them back. They called on Boyle and master spy George Hill who developed a plan of invading the Kremlin to recover the treasures and smuggle them out of Russia. Hill later reported that the Crown Jewels were part of the treasures but this has never been publicly confirmed. The shipment involved at least $20 million in currency and archival material.

A BLISTERING TIRADE

In unlocking it, Boyle's greatest weapon was a fat briefcase full of letters of reference, passes and documents which would browbeat any bureaucrat if presented with enough aplomb. They got into the Kremlin where they bundled the treasures into 36 Red Cross packages. At the station, the station master refused to hook Boyle's coaches onto the first train to Kiev. Although he spoke no Russian, Boyle delivered such a blistering tirade the stationmaster changed his mind.

Fifty miles out of Moscow, Boyle's party of five fought off an ambush and later made an unscheduled stop at a blazing vodka factory. The purloined vodka came in handy when they were intercepted by a Bolshevik detachment. Dressed in his Savile Row uniform, Boyle met the officer in command and explained that he was from the Republic of Canada and that the car was Canadian territory. He then invited the officer in for a vodka but asked that the men remain outside the rolling embassy.

The pair later hijacked an engine at Kiev which Hill took over when the engineer lost

OPPOSITE PAGE, LEFT: *Strong-willed and ambitious, Queen Marie strove for a "Greater Rumania." Finding a confidante in Joe Boyle – his negotiations with the Bolsheviks resulted in the release of Rumanian hostages – their friendship would continue until his death on 14 April 1923.* ***OPPOSITE PAGE, RIGHT:*** *Dawson was the gold rush capital of the Klondike and many were lured by dreams of prosperity. Joe Boyle made his fortune in the north – from his talents as a busker and some wise investments.* (RCMP ARCHIVES) ***RIGHT:*** *A romanticized version of the Bolshevik takeover of Petrograd's Winter Palace in November 1917. Once the centre of Tsarist Russia, Petrograd became the hub of the peoples' revolution.*

his nerve as they crashed through a barricade at the Bessarabian border. Jassy, the temporary Rumanian capital, celebrated the return of the treasures days before relations with the Bolsheviks turned into war, and Joe Boyle had another assignment.

A number of prominent Rumanians were held as hostages aboard a ship at Odessa. Boyle flew to Odessa, boarded the ship and negotiated with the Bolshevik crew for two weeks. Boyle was no linguist and details of how he arranged the return of the hostages are vague. The Royal view was that the big Canadian waved a magic wand and he became a national hero.

A REASONABLE TREATY?

The next assignment for Boyle and Hill was to seek a reasonable treaty with the Bolsheviks which they achieved by 9 March. Allied military missions were forced to leave Rumania but Boyle stayed. Queen Marie sat with Boyle as they waited for the others to leave the station. "I poured out my heart to him during those hours he sat with me," she wrote. It was the start of a strange liaison which may or may not have been sexual but soon engulfed both the sourdough and the Queen. Boyle became a frequent visitor at her cottage and Marie found a strength in the Canadian which was lacking in her husband, Ferdinand.

Boyle was soon exerting a tremendous influence over Rumanian affairs, and when he suffered a stroke Marie brought him to Bicaz where she had a summer home and became a frequent visitor to his cottage. When she made him the Duke of Jassy, a backlash developed among Rumanian politicians who resented the Canadian's influence in Rumanian affairs. Boyle was also a loose cannon with no official status in either the Canadian or British armies.

The backlash, from many quarters, was intensified when Boyle saved the royal dynasty. Prince Carol had married a commoner and renounced his claim to the throne which meant the dynasty would be broken. Boyle managed to bring the wayward Prince onside and the marriage was annulled. This so aroused political leaders that they insisted Queen Marie ask Boyle to leave.

ROYAL ORDERS

While Boyle was being attacked in Rumania, both the British War office and the Canadian government demanded that he take off his uniform. It was now two years after the Armistice and the War Office had a point when they questioned the propriety of negotiating oil land deals in uniform, which was what Boyle was then doing. Boyle thought the uniform lent a certain class to such negotiations and refused to take it off. He scuppered the bureaucrats by insisting that King George V once instructed him to wear the uniform and would not take it off unless ordered to do so by the King. He was finally given an extension until September 1921 but left Bucharest in the fall of 1920.

Boyle returned to England where his health deteriorated. He saw Marie once although they continued to correspond. He later refused to return to Rumania saying, "I want you to remember the man I was."

He died at Hampton Hill in 1923 and the Queen made several pilgrimages to his grave. She wrote in her diary, "You are still somewhere quite near – you know it – you know you cannot die in my heart."

In 1983, Boyle's remains were returned to Woodstock where a monument marks his grave. Delegations of Rumanian-Canadians have gathered there to honour the King of the Klondike and the saviour of their native country. Although Boyle was awarded a Distinguished Service Order, A Croix de Guerre and a chestful of Rumanian awards, Canadian officialdom still hasn't recognized one of our greatest heroes of the 20th century because Joe Boyle marched to the sound of his own drum in a soldier suit from Savile Row.

AUTHOR: *Norman Shannon*

GENERAL CURRIE – THE LAST GREAT BATTLE

The ghost of a vindictive Sam Hughes haunts Currie for a decade, reaching its climax in a court battle.

LEFT: *Considered Canada's most distinguished field commander, General Arthur Currie would face undue criticism for his actions in WWI.* (IMPERIAL WAR MUSEUM)

GENERAL SIR ARTHUR CURRIE fought his final battle of the First World War, not in the ravaged countryside of France, but in the courthouse of the peaceful Canadian town of Port Hope, Ontario. Between 12 April and 1 May 1928, forces of the long dead Sir Sam Hughes (d. 1921), Canada's wartime defence minister, engaged Canada's greatest general and World War One's best strategist – on either side – in a bitterly fought contest dubbed appropriately, 'The Third Battle of Mons.' Though Currie emerged victorious, the ordeal probably hastened his death for his health began an almost immediate decline. He was to live but another five and a half years.

Arthur William Currie, born near Strathroy, Ontario on 5 December 1875, was a second generation Canadian, the third of seven children. As a student, a talent emerged which would shape his life: he possessed an analytical mind. In school debates he learned never to rush headlong into argument. Researching his subject, giving attention to every detail, he analyzed the situation, speaking only when his course of action was determined.

THE POWER TO ANALYZE

This trait determined his character. From his first job as teacher in Sydney, BC, to real estate broker in Victoria, to the battlefields at Ypres, Vimy and Passchendale, to his superb administration of McGill University, Currie's leadership stemmed from an ability to correctly analyze any situation.

Currie's military genius became the envy of German and Allied officers alike. One captured German general requested to meet the Canadian officer who moved troops so stealthily that the point of attack was often miles from the expected site. The Canadian victory at Vimy Ridge so stunned General Erich Ludendorff, Germany's Chief of Staff, that when the war ended he requested, and received, the battle plan Currie had conceived. Field Marshal Haig, Commander-in-Chief of all British forces, so respected Currie his admiration overrode resentment of Currie's criticism of British strategy, criticism that history has justified.

PERFECTING THE CREEPING BARRAGE

Currie, contrary to popular belief, did not invent the "creeping barrage" used so successfully at Vimy. British and French armies had used it previously without success and abandoned the idea as useless. Currie, putting his analytical mind to the subject, perfected the tactic still used by modern armies.

Currie's successes earned him knighthood in 1917. Had the war continued into 1919 he would undoubtedly have replaced Haig as Commander-in-Chief.

About 08:00 hours, 11 November 1918, Currie's Canadians moved to liberate the town of Mons, scene of two previous, vicious battles. By 08:45 hours the town was secured. This final action of the Great War would return to haunt him nine years later.

HUGHES UNSTABLE

When the war ended, Currie returned to Canada to find himself idolized by the majority of ordinary citizens and ignored by Ottawa. Despite the fact that he had been granted Britain's highest honors, that France had awarded him two Croix de Guerre (one *avec palme*) and the Légion d'Honneur de la France, that Belgium named him Grand Officer of the Ordre de la Couronne to accompany their Croix de Guerre and the Americans awarded him their Distinguished Service Medal, the Canadian government offered only criticism. The most vocal critic was Sir Sam Hughes. Though no longer minister and undeniably mentally unbalanced, Hughes still carried influence in Parliament. It was enough to deny Currie official recognition.

Currie, despite Ottawa's ingratitude, stayed with the Army as inspector-general until 1920 when he resigned to accept the principalship of McGill University at Montreal, the position he held until he died.

Currie was stunned by the first shot fired in what was dubbed The Fifty Thousand Dollar Lawsuit by the press and The Third Battle of Mons by the Canadian Legion.

THE OPENING ROUND

That opening round was an article published 13 June 1927 in the Port Hope *Evening Guide*, a tiny newspaper owned and edited by Frederick W. Wilson. The article, written by William T.R. Preston, was titled, simply, *MONS*.

Commenting on a ceremony held in Mons to honour Canadian war dead, Preston contended that Currie deserved no honour because, seeking personal glory, he had sent troops into a bloodbath knowing the official armistice was but hours away. Currie's action, the article alleged, caused the needless deaths of Canadian soldiers simply to glorify the Headquarters Staff which, of course, included himself.

ABOVE RIGHT: *Sam Hughes, having had a long-standing dislike for Currie, had been one of his most vocal critics. Although no longer a serving member of Parliament, he still carried enough influence to prevent Currie from receiving due recognition.* (NAC/PA 202394)

ABOVE LEFT: *In November 1918, General Arthur Currie, on horseback, salutes as 1500 Canadians marched by the Grand Place in Mons. The Belgians showed their gratitude to the soldiers who liberated their city from the Germans. Canada would not be so quick to honour one of her greatest soldiers.* (NAC/PA 3547)

The article was unabashed nonsense, similar to that which Sam Hughes had periodically spouted in the House of Commons. Hughes, insane but not stupid, took care to confine his comments to the House which gave protection from libel laws. Preston and Wilson had no such aegis.

CURRIE SUES

Currie, hurt and furious, initiated a libel suit against Preston and Wilson. Currie felt a talk with Wilson would likely gain a retraction so he invited Wilson to Montreal. The two met at McGill. Currie detailed the operation's cautious progress, how the town had been secured with no casualties whatever because the Germans, already withdrawing to demarcation lines, gave no resistance. Mons had been occupied, not attacked.

Wilson returned to Port Hope to discuss the meeting with Preston whom, it appears, wanted to retract. Wilson, however, refused. He recalled that in March 1919 Hughes, in Parliament, had declared that Canadians had "...been blown up by the hundreds..." while liberating Mons. Wilson perhaps was unaware that Hughes, already senile and blissfully unconcerned with reality, had interpolated a 1917 battle at Cambrai with the liberation of Mons. Wilson, unfortunately, based his decision on this incoherent speech. Dead soldiers, he told Preston, would have their say. He would be their voice. Wilson, by refusing to retract, forced Currie to launch his suit.

TRIAL BEGINS

The trial, under the watchful eye of Mr. Justice Hugh Rose, commenced on 12 April 1928. Jurors (ten civilians and two ex-soldiers) were chosen to decide if Sir Arthur Currie, plaintiff, had been slandered by Frederick Wilson and William Thomas Rochester Preston, co-defendants. They would also decide if Currie should receive damages in the amount of $50,000 plus costs, the amount he was demanding in the suit. The jurors were then introduced to the lawyers: William N. Tilley acting for Currie; Frank Regan representing Wilson. Preston made a mistake by representing himself.

One by one the many witnesses were called and the next three weeks were busy with examination and cross-questions. The tiny courtroom was packed daily with onlookers and reporters exceeding any to have covered a previous trial in Canada.

Daily William Tilley dismantled the defendants' case. Preston emerged as a political hack relying on patronage when the Liberals controlled Ottawa, and by his wits during the Conservative years. Wilson emerged a gullible small-town businessman duped by Preston and friends of Sam Hughes into believing that Currie, negligent and bumbling, had led his troops to slaughter.

OUTCOME IN DOUBT

But Regan was also a skillful lawyer. He did his utmost to unravel Tilley's case. When one of the witnesses stated that 39 dead Canadians had been seen in Mons, Regan pounced. For several days this statement placed the outcome in doubt.

Tilley played his trump card – Major George Kilpatrick, senior chaplain of the Third Division. Kilpatrick confirmed the presence of the dead soldiers but testified that they had been killed five days before. The townspeople, in gratitude for liberation, had ventured into the countryside with wagons. Collecting all the bodies they could find – 39 – they brought the fallen soldiers to the town where they placed them in the finest coffins available. The soldiers were then given a proper funeral. Not one had fallen in the liberation of Mons because the day had seen no casualties.

TWISTING TESTIMONY

Regan, frustrated, turned his attack on Currie. Quoting the speeches of Sam Hughes, and twisting witnesses' statements, he insisted that Currie had risked his men by acting recklessly in a showboat attack against a highly fortified position which had withstood months of British and French attacks. The ghost of Sam Hughes was hard at work in the person of Frank Regan. Regan, however, harmed his case with such implications. Justice Rose, wearying of the pointless tirades, overruled Regan at almost every turn.

On 30 April, Tilley, Regan and Preston made final addresses to the jury. The following morning, a sunny Tuesday, Judge Rose made his statement to the jury. Carefully summarizing the proceedings he reviewed the 53 exhibits, including battle diaries and maps, and the testimony of over 70 witnesses.

The morning had but 15 minutes remaining when the 12 men retired to consider their verdict. Three and a half hours later the jury returned an 11-1 verdict in favor of Currie. It is perhaps ironic that the dissenting juror was one of the soldiers, a man named Mouncey. The jurors, feeling $50,000 was an amount neither Wilson nor Preston could ever pay, awarded $500. Mr. Justice Rose made the addendum that court costs be added making the award nearly $5,800.

APPEAL DENIED

Preston never paid a dime. Wilson eventually paid just over $5,200. Tilley's fees, nearly $15,000, were paid by Currie's friends. Who paid Regan remains a mystery as does the identity of who paid for the appeal, an extremely costly process, launched on Wilson's behalf. The appeal was denied.

The jury's decision exorcised Sam Hughes' ghost from Currie's life. His remaining few years, though busy, were peaceful. Ottawa, however, continued to deny him the recognition he so richly deserved. Sam Hughes' ghost still prowled the halls of Parliament exerting influence against his favorite target.

After the Armistice was signed, Canada initially committed two divisions to the Allied occupation force of Germany. Marching past General Arthur Currie, a battalion of Canadian soldiers cross the Rhine to Bonn where they will occupy one of two bridgeheads. ***(NAC/PA 3776)***

Currie continued to serve his country. Instrumental in the formation of the Canada Pension Board which saw to the welfare of veterans, he worked tirelessly with the Legion practicing the philosophy of his own words in which he summed up the efforts of Canadians who had died in the Great War: "They served till death - why not we?"

"ROYAL" FUNERAL

Sir Arthur died in Montreal on 30 November 1933. Tributes from around the world poured in. On 4 December, 1933 (exactly 58 years from the day of his birth) he was laid to rest with a dual military/civil funeral befitting a monarch. The cortege moved slowly from Christ Church Cathedral to the Mount Royal Cemetery through streets crowded with thousands paying last respects. Cavalry and infantry units escorted the gun carriage. The 2nd Montreal Regiment fired a 17 gun salute and Sir Arthur Currie, Canada's greatest general, was laid to rest.

The funeral, reported live by CBC Radio, was also covered by American and other foreign papers. In London that same day a memorial service, attended to overflowing by commoners and nobility alike, was held in Westminster Abbey, another of the many honours Britons had extended to the man they recognized as the greatest General of the war.

RECOGNITION, FINALLY

Canadians, sad though it is, have never appreciated their heroes while they live. Not until Sir Arthur Currie was safely dead did official Canadian honors come in. In 1935 Ottawa awarded $50,000 to the Currie estate which allowed his family to keep their holdings. (Parliament passed the grant without a dissenting voice, indicating the ghost of Sam Hughes had finally moved on). In 1936 a monument was erected at the gravesite by former members of the Canadian Corps. The sprawling army camp near Calgary, built in 1937, was named Currie Barracks. McGill University honored him with a building. A military cemetery in Point Claire PQ, The Field of Honour, erected a granite cross as a memorial to his name.

Sir Arthur Currie, years after his passing, lives in memory. The great Canadian educator and writer, Stephen Leacock, may well have described General Currie best when he eulogized him thus:

"There, was a man!"

REPRINTED FROM:
Esprit de Corps, *Volume 3 Issue 12*
AUTHOR:
E.C. Meyers

RIGHT: As the years passed, the shortages of equipment and supplies plaguing the Forces increased to the point where mechanized brigades, such as the 8th New Brunswick Hussars, had to rent vehicles in order to carry out training exercises.
(8TH CANADIAN HUSSARS MUSEUM)

Horse harnesses were the only item in plentiful supply as the Canadian forces mouldered away.

BETWEEN THE ACTS

THE PEACETIME PERMANENT Force was a pale reflection of the Canadian Corps that had fought the Great War. The General Staff had envisaged a force of twenty to thirty thousand and 15 militia divisions kept up to strength by conscription. That was a nonstarter and fewer than 5,000 now served in the ranks and every unit was under strength. Pay was poor, promotion was slow and modern equipment woefully lacking. The war had been known as "the war to end all wars" and Canadians had had enough of conflict. Most would agree with the editorial which appeared in the *Farmer's Sun* in 1920:

"The Ottawa authorities may as well realize, first and last, that Canada is not going to stand for the wholesale expenditure of large sums of money for military and naval purposes. The people of this country do not propose to submit to the god of militarism. We have just fought a five years' war in order to make wars to cease."

The following year, when the Minister of Militia presented his estimates calling for a small increase in defence appropriations, Mackenzie King, the leader of the Opposition, advanced an argument which became all too familiar throughout the 20s and 30s:

"The Minister seems to think that at the present time we ought to vote an amount at least equal to amounts that were being voted prior to the war. That is where I take issue with him. Conditions are wholly different today; there is no world menace. Where does the Minister expect invasion from? The Minister says that this expenditure is needed for the defence of Canada - defence against whom?"

THE LATE GREAT ARMY

The once proud army which had held against gas attack at Ypres, stormed Vimy Ridge, slogged through the mud at Passchendaele and triumphed at Mons, mouldered away. By the late thirties its equipment, apart from rifles, consisted of five mortars, four anti-aircraft guns, ten Bren guns, two light tanks and enough ammunition to last for little more than an hour in battle. Horse harnesses were the only item in plentiful supply.

Farley Mowat, a 19-year old reserve officer, "a playtime soldier," with the Hastings and Prince Edward Regiment in Picton, Ontario, would later write:

"The army dwindled away until it became hardly more than a pile of dusty papers – dusty names. In the whole-country that bordered on three oceans, there were three-infantry battalions under arms. For a nation 5,000 miles across, there were a few dozen antiquated aircraft that the few serving pilots hardly dared to taxi on the ground. And for those three oceans, there was a pitiful handful of little ships – a navy that the Swiss could very nearly have out matched.

"Once a week a handful of men in civilian clothes, or in bits of last-war uniforms gathered in an old garage, a packing shed, or if they were lucky, in an armoury that echoed emptily to the sound of their few feet. And as they came to the evening drill they were sometimes sneered at by the loungers in the streets.

"Thanks to 20 years of governmental neglect, the militia had no uniforms, modern weapons, or anything much else of a military nature. One had to be inventive, and I was. Out of lengths of pipe I manufactured '3-inch mortars' that fired shells consisting of empty condensed milk cans exploded by giant firecrackers. I also got hold of a photograph of a Bren – the new standard light machine gun, of which there were reportedly six in all of Canada – and had a dozen wooden imitations made up in a local furniture factory. These, together with a few score condemned Ross rifles of World War One vintage provided our armament."

NO HORSES, NO WAGONS

One militia officer gave lectures in the dining room of his home. Another begged for used Post Office vans for his artillery regi-

***LEFT**: The Great Depression of the 1930s resulted in economic and social disaster as thousands found themselves without work. One in five Canadians depended upon government assistance.* (UNIVERSITY OF WINNIPEG) ***MAIN**: After WWI, the Regular Force was reduced to 5000 all ranks. The result was undermanned companies with little training beyond the troop or platoon level. In August 1930, this was the Lord Strathcona's Horse at full strength.* (LDSH MUSEUM)

ment. A captain of a Horse Transport Company recalled that his troops "were trained to take the harness apart, put it back together and hang it up in the Quartermaster's Store. That's about as far as it went. We never did have a horse. We never did have a wagon."

And yet, the Department of National Defence called on officers and men to improve themselves. "It is realized that you have a fair amount of time on your hands," a directive from Headquarters stated. "Is it employed in working up your efficiency, or is it wasted in Bridge, Mah-Jong or Poker? Do you read? ...No one is looking for geniuses, but all expect a good showing both in a military and intellectual way from men who chose soldiering for their profession." Officers were encouraged to read the *Times* as "unfortunately, few if any Canadian publications give all the news of the world and it is practically necessary to rely on the English ones. This is perhaps a good thing as they are written in the best of English."

THE ENEMY WITHIN

From time to time, the army was called out to intervene in labour disputes. Troops quelled disturbances in St. Catharines and Stratford, Ontario and Quebec City. In the summer of 1923, 1100 were called in, mostly from other military districts, when Cape Breton coal miners went out on strike. Mackenzie King complained that "the demonstration of force seems to have exceeded all bounds of necessity or prudence." Senior officers, however, were obsessed with the idea of internal subversion and seemed to consider every strike to be the work of foreign agitators and a threat to the social order. "The principal peril confronting us at the present time," the General Staff proclaimed in 1919, "is the danger of the overthrow of Law and Order in our own Country." On the eve of the Winnipeg General Strike, an internal document stated:

"In the period preceding the War, immigration was unrestricted, with the result that we have taken into Canada large numbers of foreigners, who in many instances have preserved their original nationality; who have not absorbed our civilization and national ideals; and who see in 'bouleversement' an opportunity for personal gain. In certain districts in the West the number of aliens exceeds the citizens of Canadian nationality. The Bolshevik revolution in Russia and such organizations as the International Workers of the World (I.W.W.) have created large funds and organizations for the spread of ideals and aims contrary to our own, and they find this foreign element a fruitful soil on which to work ...The contagion begun by the foreign element spreads to the less intelligent of our citizens and is creating a very dangerous and unhealthy state of affairs."

WORK CAMPS ESTABLISHED

During the Depression, the fear of subversion led the Bennett Government to establish work camps for single, unemployed men administered by the army. Known as the "Royal Twenty-Centers," they were paid 20 cents a day to clear bush, build roads, bridges and airfields and restore historic sites. Many would come to hold the army in contempt. Many more, long-term "breadliners," would enlist in 1939 out of desperation. "I wasn't patriotic," a graduate of the camps explained. "None of my buddies were. I just wanted some good clothes and hot showers and three decent meals a day and a few dollars for tobacco and beer in my pocket, and that's about all I wanted ...It was funny, lining up for days to get into a war, to get yourself killed.

Discouraged and stung by mounting criticism of the army and the camps, General McNaughton, the Chief of Staff, resigned in 1935 to accept an appointment as president of the National Research Council. Before his departure, he presented the gov-

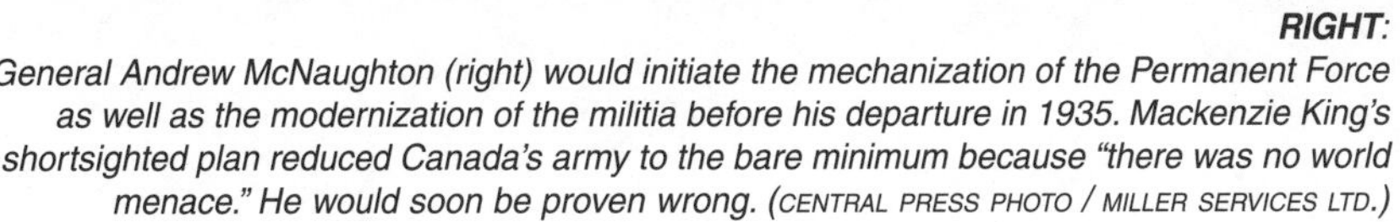

RIGHT:
General Andrew McNaughton (right) would initiate the mechanization of the Permanent Force as well as the modernization of the militia before his departure in 1935. Mackenzie King's shortsighted plan reduced Canada's army to the bare minimum because "there was no world menace." He would soon be proven wrong. (CENTRAL PRESS PHOTO / MILLER SERVICES LTD.)

ernment with a memorandum, "The Defence of Canada," in which he discussed the matter of equipment:

"As regards reserves of equipment and ammunition, the matter is shortly disposed of. Except for rifles and rifle ammunition, partial stocks of which were inherited from the Great War there are none.

"As regards equipment, the situation is almost equally serious, and to exemplify it I select a few items from the long list of deficiencies on file at National Defence Headquarters:

"(i) There is not a single modern anti-aircraft gun of any sort in Canada.

"(ii) The stocks of field gun ammunition on hand represents 90 minutes' fire at normal rates for the field guns inherited from the Great War and which are now obsolescent.

"(iii) The coast defence armament is obsolescent and, in cases defective in that a number of the major guns are not expected to be able to fire more than a dozen or so rounds. To keep some defence value in these guns, which are situated on the Pacific coast, we have not dared for some years to engage in any practice firing.

"(iv) About the only article of which stocks are held is harness, and this is practically useless. The composition of a modern land force will include very little horsed transport.

"(v) There are only 25 aircraft of service type in Canada, all of which are obsolescent except for training purposes; of these, 15 were purchased before 1931 and are practically worn out... Not a single machine is of a type fit to employ in active operations.

"(vi) Not one service air bomb is held in Canada."

BUSTER BROWN'S DEFENCE SCHEME NUMBER ONE

Military planners still assumed that the main external threat to Canada would come from the United States. Defence Scheme Number I, developed by Colonel James Sutherland "Buster" Brown, an officer afflicted with virulent anti-Americanism, envisaged a war between Britain and the United States in which Canada would be the main battleground. In the event of hostilities, Pacific Command would move to occupy Spokane, Seattle and Portland, Oregon. Flying columns from the Prairies would take Fargo, North Dakota and then advance in the direction of Minneapolis and St. Paul. Great Lakes Command would remain on the defensive while Quebec Command launched an offensive on both sides of the Adirondacks converging on Albany, and Maritime Command struck into Maine.

In the autumn of 1922, Brown and Colonels Hodgins and Prower, disguised as tourists, crossed the border to scout out potential invasion routes. A period photograph shows the intrepid trio sitting on a farm fence in Vermont grinning for the camera.

Mackenzie King, an accomplished fence-sitter himself, would provide little leadership as Prime Minister in countering the very real threat posed by Hitler and Mussolini in the 1930's. Hitler he dismissed as a "simple peasant" and although he assured the British that he would stand by them in the event of war, he quickly backtracked when Germany absorbed Czechoslovakia in March 1939, telling the House of Commons:

"The idea that every 20 years this country should automatically and as a matter of course take part in a war overseas for democracy or self-determination of other small nations ...to save, periodically, a continent that cannot run itself and to these ends risk the lives of its people and bankruptcy and political disunion, seems to many a nightmare of sheer madness."

Many more, then and now considered Canada's unpreparedness a nightmare of madness. A recurring nightmare.

AUTHOR: *Bill Twatio*

Long before the world was swept into the Second World War, Canadians fought fascism in Spain (from 1937 to late 1938). Of the 1250 volunteers, 385 would die for the cause.

CANADIANS IN SPAIN

ABOVE:
In 1935, men from western unemployment relief camps began their march towards the capital on their "On to Ottawa Trek." Travelling by train from Vancouver and picking up more strikers along the way, they were stopped in Regina by the RCMP with orders from Prime Minister Bennett to prevent them from continuing eastward. (PUBLIC ARCHIVES OF CANADA)

BY THE MID-1930s the industrialized world was still in the grips of a great economic depression. Millions of homeless and destitute men were on the move, picking up jobs here and there as they tried to support themselves or their families.

In Europe, communists and fascists were at each others throats. German fascists under Adolf Hitler and his Nazis were flexing their nationalistic muscles while Mussolini's Italy was trying to regain the world stage by building a new African empire via a reign of terror. The League of Nations was in disarray.

In Canada the Depression had virtually crippled the industrialised base, throwing tens of thousands of men out in the streets. To add to the plight of the Canadians a drought had swept across the prairies leaving abandoned farms and broken homes in its wake.

To the masses of unemployed workers the Bennett government seemed to be steering a rudderless ship of state. Worse, the destitute believed the government did not care.

WORK CAMPS

In 1932 the Unemployment Relief Camps came into being. Overseen by the Department of National Defence these work camps existed from 1932 to 1936. One hundred and seventy thousand men, earning 20 cents per day, would eventually pass through this system. The camps became the perfect breeding grounds for the communist inspired Workers Unity League which blamed the worker's ills on the Capitalists and Fascists of the world.

In 1935 the workers in the British Columbia camps went on strike then began their great trek to Ottawa. They halted in Regina and soon riots broke out between the trekkers and the RCMP. To the by now indoctrinated workers, this use of police force was confirmation of the government's lack of concern to their plight.

A change in government occurred in 1936 but the unemployed saw no immediate change of fortune.

In far off Spain the flames of a nationalistic rebellion erupted. With the ousting of the monarchy in 1931 the Spanish Republic had been formed. In 1936 a coalition of leftist parties won the general election and formed the New Republican government. Immediate land reform acts, reorganisation of the army and the demise of traditional powers put the fear into the Right.

The right wing military uprising began in Spanish Morocco on 17 July 1936 and successfully spread to Spain. In September General Franco was proclaimed the head of the nationalist armies, government and state.

Hitler agreed to aid Franco while Mussolini began despatching aircraft and troops to the Nationalist. The legally elected Republican government was soon under siege. The West declared a stand of non-intervention. Moscow funnelled cash and supplies to the Republicans. The League of Nations did not want to discuss Spain.

UNEMPLOYED SIGN UP

In Canada, as well as other Western nations, news of the war in Spain struck the conscience of many of the unemployed. Seeing the Nationalist revolution as a war of the Fascist Right on the working class they soon

began to offer their services to the Spanish Republican armies.

For Canadian volunteers the Foreign Enlistment Act of 1937 made it illegal for a citizen to enlist in any foreign state at war.

Disregarding this act, the Canadians, for the most part, made their way to Toronto and into the United States where they boarded ships to France. Landing at LeHavre, they made their way to Paris where contacts at the trade union complex supplied them with meal tickets until they could make their way to Spain.

THE PYRENNES

The trip across France had to be done in a clandestine manner because of the strict non intervention rule. Nearing the Spanish border there was the fear of being reported by Spanish Nationalist sympathisers or spies. When they reached the border one final obstacle had to be broached before they stood on Spanish soil – the Pyrennes mountains. Crossing these by foot, usually during the night, could take up to 16 hours.

By mid-1937 almost 500 Canadian volunteers, infantrymen, artillerymen and medical units made up of men and women, had taken the field in Spain. Some had taken part in the early siege of Madrid while others had fought with the XVth International Brigade during the epic battles of the Jarama River Valley.

The XVth International Brigade had been formed in February 1937 and consisted mainly of English speaking battalions. Most Canadians had been fighting with the Abraham Lincoln Battalion, the George Washington Battalion or the British Battalion but near the end of June the Canadian Mackenzie-Papineau Battalion was formed. Though Canadian in name, the ranks were usually augmented with a majority of American volunteers.

MUDDLED TIMING

The "Mac-Paps'" first engagement came on 13 October 1937. Their task was to turn the Nationalist troops out of the village of Fuentes de Ebro situated along the Ebro River in north east Spain. To reach Fuentes they had to cross approximately one mile of open field. The battle took on all appearances of the First World War – muddled timing, lack of communication, poor cooperation and lack of firepower.

The attack was a disaster. Individual heroism could not help hold any gains that were made and soon the men were driven back to their original assembly trenches.

ABOVE: *General Franco was proclaimed Chief of the Insurgent Forces when he accepted the leadership of the rebel forces.* (ILLUSTRATED LONDON NEWS)

TOP LEFT: *In July 1936, civil unrest erupted into a vicious war which pitted General Franco's Fascists against the communist-backed Republican government. Some 1300 Canadians served in the Mackenzie-Papineau Battalion as part of the International Brigade. Only 35 men remained when the Mac-Paps withdrew from the Spanish Civil War in September 1938.* (NAC C 67469)

TOP RIGHT: *The RCMP was called in to clear out the rioters after a sit-down strike by relief camp workers.* (VANCOUVER PUBLIC LIBRARY)

ABOVE LEFT: *As the Depression deepened, with thousands out of work, the situation was ripe for displays of political extremism on both the left and right.* (UNIVERSITY OF WINNIPEG)

ABOVE RIGHT: *Dr. Norman Bethune accepted the challenge of offering aid to the wounded. He also organized the first mobile blood transfusion unit.* (PAC/PA 114788)

Here they dug in with the rest of the XVth International Brigade and remained in those positions for a further few weeks. The attack on the 13th had cost the Mackenzie-Papineau Battalion over 250 casualties, 60 of them fatal.

After two weeks of holding the line near Fuentes de Ebro the XVth International Brigade was placed in reserves where all units were brought up to strength with the arrival of more volunteers. Over two months of intensive training would ensue before the Mac-Paps and the XVth would move to the front again.

CANADIANS IN THE LINE

By January 1938 Franco's army was on a counter-offensive. As he prepared to assault the town of Teruel the Canadians were put in the line on the valley floor just west of the town.

On 17 January the Nationalists launched an all-out attack on the Republican defences. The Canadian machine gunners, though being pounded by the Nationalist Artillery, held their ground and drove them off. Franco kept up the offensive in this area but could not fully break through the Republican lines. After two weeks in the valley the XVth was pulled out.

Though the Mac-Paps would be involved in two more extremely bloody battles, culminating once again at the Ebro River, for the most part they were on the retreat which would last until the withdrawal of the Internationals in October 1938.

SECOND TO NONE

In the time that they had been in Spain the Canadians had made a well respected name for themselves. Not only the frontline infantry men, but the gunners and the medics were all considered second to none. Dr. Norman Bethune, who had also served with the Communists in China, had proven his method of battlefield blood transfusions which altered forever the plight of the wounded soldier.

About 1250 Canadian volunteers (no definitive figure is available) fought in Spain. Three hundred and eighty-five were killed in action.

By early 1939 most of the surviving Canadian volunteers had returned to Canada. Only their peers gave them a welcome home. Their government totally ignored them.

On 1 April General Franco proclaimed the defeat of the Republicans and declared the end of the civil war. On 1 September 1939 Hitler and Stalin invaded Poland and the world went to war again.

Many of the battle-hardened Canadians who fought fascism in Spain immediately volunteered their services to the Canadian government. Some, because of their politics, and because they had broken the foreign enlistment law, were refused enlistment. Others would fight fascism once again but on the battlefields of Italy and north-west Europe.

When they again returned to their homes the welcome from the public was far different than that of 1939. However, with the chill of the cold war descending upon the West these veterans would always be regarded as suspect by their government and its agencies. There would be no justice for these men and women who, as they saw it, had volunteered to fight the evils of fascism long before the world was swept into the cataclysm of World War II.

REPRINTED FROM:
Esprit de Corps, *Volume 4 Issue 9*
AUTHOR: *James Steele*

WAR AGAIN!

Having secretly built-up his military and signed a "non-aggression" pact with the Soviet Union, Adolf Hitler felt confident that he could add Poland to his Third Reich without any serious opposition. When the German Wehrmacht and Luftwaffe unleashed their Blitzkrieg offensive on 1 September 1939, Britain and France did honour their commitment to defend Polish neutrality. However, their declarations of war and belated mobilizations could not provide any timely military support for Poland. In anticipation of possible hostilities, Canada had begun to mobilize on 1 September. A formal declaration of war was not issued until nine days later.

3 APRIL Hitler unveils plans to his military commanders for an attack on Poland code-named "Case WHITE."

7 MAY Germany and Italy sign a military alliance known as The Pact of Steel.

23 AUGUST Hitler and Stalin sign a non-aggression pact which outlines the partitioning of Poland by Germany and Russia.

25 AUGUST Poland and Britain sign a pact of "mutual assistance" – which is a formal guarantee of military intervention to protect Polish neutrality against German/Soviet aggression.

31 AUGUST "Negotiations" between Polish ambassador and Germany's foreign minister are broken off.

1 SEPTEMBER Germans launch massive airstrikes and a blitzkrieg ground assault into Poland.

3 SEPTEMBER Britain and France declare war on Germany.

4-12 SEPTEMBER France launches an abortive offensive into the Saarland which fails to divert German forces from their Polish offensives.

10 SEPTEMBER Canada declares war on Germany.

17 SEPTEMBER Soviet troops enter Poland from the east.

27 SEPTEMBER Warsaw surrenders.

5 OCTOBER Last Polish resistance ends with the surrender of 17,000 Poles at Kock.

***BELOW LEFT**: Not wishing to let go, a mother says goodbye to her son, a member of the Winnipeg Grenadiers.* (UNIVERSITY OF WINNIPEG)
***BELOW**: The first contingent of the 1st Canadian Division boards their troopship bound for England from Halifax on 18 December 1939.* (NAC/C 24717)

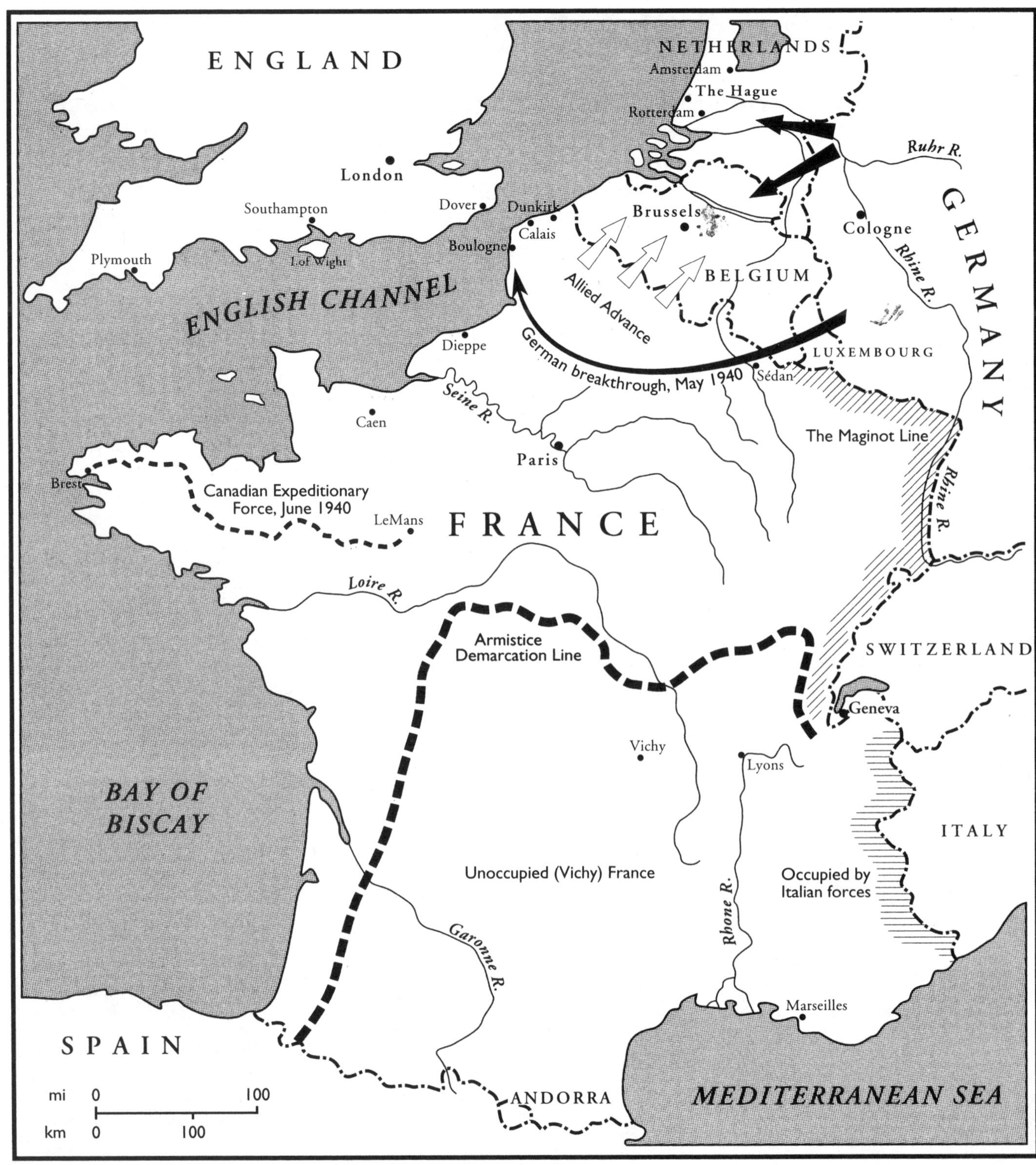

ENGLAND
NETHERLANDS
Amsterdam
The Hague
Rotterdam
Ruhr R.
London
Southampton
Dover
Dunkirk
Calais
Boulogne
Brussels
Cologne
GERMANY
Plymouth
I. of Wight
BELGIUM
Rhine R.
ENGLISH CHANNEL
Allied Advance
German breakthrough, May 1940
Dieppe
LUXEMBOURG
Sédan
Seine R.
Caen
The Maginot Line
Paris
Brest
Canadian Expeditionary Force, June 1940
LeMans
FRANCE
Rhine R.
Loire R.
Armistice Demarcation Line
SWITZERLAND
Geneva
Vichy
Lyons
BAY OF BISCAY
ITALY
Unoccupied (Vichy) France
Occupied by Italian forces
Rhone R.
Garonne R.
Marseilles
SPAIN
mi 0 100
km 0 100
ANDORRA
MEDITERRANEAN SEA

WAR AGAIN!

DURING THE SUMMER OF 1936, 6000 Canadian veterans returned to France for the unveiling of the Vimy Memorial. It was a fitting and sincere tribute to some 61,000 of their comrades who died during the Great War. But even as the veterans took pictures of the statue of Canadian motherhood brooding over the plains of Douai, the world was moving towards another war.

When Adolf Hitler saw that the League of Nations did little about Benito Mussolini's rape of Abyssinia, he became increasingly aggressive. He occupied the Rhineland, in conflict with the Treaty of Versailles, and then initiated construction on the Siegfried Line on Germany's western border. The Rome-Berlin Axis was formed within weeks of the Vimy Pilgrimage and German troops were major players in the Spanish Civil War. Spain had become a convenient proving ground for equipment and tactics and in the three brief years following the Vimy ceremony a misguided British Prime Minister talked about "peace in our time."

Peace ran out on 1 September when Hitler's 53 divisions crashed into Poland. The world saw the results of the experiments in Spain, as the blitzkrieg covered 50 miles in 36 hours. Two days later Britain declared war on Germany and the news reached Canada on a Sunday morning. In what obviously was a political gesture to Quebec, the Mackenzie King Government waited a week before declaring war.

The resources Canada brought to bear were meagre, as the regular army numbered only 4500 men. Unlike 1914, there were few bands or heroic celebrations yet five days after mobilization started, the Active Service Force numbered almost 23,000. This figure jumped to over 58,000 by the end of September.

Because of the deference to Hitler – which persisted throughout the winter of the phoney war – the evils of Naziism were relatively unknown. The original response was not a crusade against evil but probably the result of a decade of depression and the hopes of three square meals a day.

Canada backed into an Air Force after WWI when Britain delivered some 100 war surplus machines as a gift. By 1924 the RCAF establishment consisted of 68 officers and 307 men. Most of the operational flying in the lean decade which followed consisted of survey work, but in the late 1930s, with war imminent, budgets were dramatically increased. When mobilization came, the RCAF had grown to 20 squadrons with a strength of some 4000 personnel. But the paper tiger only had 102 remotely operational aircraft and 235 pilots.

The RCN didn't even fare as well as the RCAF during the interwar years. It suffered from an appalling lack of public interest, or at least positive interest. According to Rear Admiral L.W. Murray, most Canadians would have been pleased if somebody had taken the entire navy to sea and scuttled it.

TOP:
When Germany invaded Poland in 1939, it did so with 60 tactical units – roughly 1.8 million soldiers – equipped with 10,000 cannons and mortars.

BOTTOM:
When it was announced that Canada would join Britain in defending her interests from the Nazis, Canadians lined up to join in the fight.
(UNIVERSITY OF WINNIPEG)

When war arrived, the RCN had six destroyers and five minesweepers. With a permanent force of 1800 and 1700 reservists, the RCN was escorting the first convoy of 18 merchant ships out of Halifax within a week of hostilities. The ships were the first of some 25,000 which would sail under Canadian escort.

AUTHOR: *Norman Shannon*

1939 – THE STAGE IS SET

After the Blitzkrieg had successfully over-run Poland, the Allies continued to build up their forces while simultaneously striving to avoid provoking a German reaction. At sea the U-boats scored a number of early victories over British warships, while the German surface-raiders had only mixed success. Canadians flooded to recruiting centers to enlist, many of them simply eager to have a job after a decade of unemployment.

1 SEPTEMBER German troops unleash a Blitzkrieg offensive into Poland.

3 SEPTEMBER Britain and France declare war in support of Polish neutrality – within hours U-boat 30 sinks the *Athenia.*

10 SEPTEMBER Canada formally declares war on Germany and begins a full-scale mobilization.

17 SEPTEMBER HMS *Courageous*, a British aircraft carrier, is torpedoed and sunk by U-29 in the Bristol Channel.

14 OCTOBER U-boat 29 enters the British fleet anchorage at Scapa Flow and destroys the HMS *Royal Oak*.

30 NOVEMBER Soviet aircraft launch a surprise attack against tiny Finland, sparking the Russo-Finnish war.

15 DECEMBER Canada and Britain establish a $600 million plan to train Commonwealth pilots in Canada.

18 DECEMBER The German pocket battleship *Graf-Spee* is scuttled following a battle (River Plate) with three British cruisers.

BELOW: *The German pocket battleship* Admiral Graf Spee *is scuttled off Montevideo, Uruguay. British Prime Minister Winston Churchill hailed the Royal Navy's success as a major victory.*

RIGHT: *The Rhineland had been demilitarized by the Treaty of Versailles and, by signing the 1925 Locarno Treaty, Germany agreed to maintain this area free of troops. However, in 1936 German troops crossed the bridges into the Rhineland thereby violating both treaties and placing France in danger.* *(NAC/C 24958)*

A STANDING START

When Hitler added Poland to his victims of aggression, Britain and France were finally aroused to a cautious standing start.

THE FAILURE OF THE League of Nations to halt aggression during the 1930s and the lack of preparedness by most allied nations came to a head in 1938 when Germany invaded Czechoslovakia and occupied the Sudetenland. Prime Minister Chamberlain of Britain and France's Premier Daladier later blessed the action in an agreement signed at Munich. The so-called agreement surrendered to Hitler over 11,000 square miles of Czech territory, some three million people and most of Czechoslovakia's mineral wealth and electric power. Chamberlain personified the era of neglect and deceit as he returned from Munich and waved a sheet of paper while announcing, "peace in our time."

PACT OF STEEL

Although the allied world drifted along on the current of illusion, Hitler signed the Pact of Steel with Mussolini in the spring of 1939. If either country got into a war, the other would provide assistance. Hitler had already decided that Germany needed more living space (or *lebensraum)* and this meant invading other countries. Mussolini was quick to renege on the treaty, but Hitler's next move was the invasion of Poland in spite of the fact that both Britain and France had previously pledged assistance if Poland were invaded.

When the attack on Poland came on 1 September, 21 German submarines were already in position around the British Isles, as they were ordered to sea on 19 August. As disaster loomed, Canada virtually ignored the impending crisis.

HARMLESS PEASANT?

Mackenzie King had met Hitler and regarded him as a harmless peasant. The crisis mounted as Hitler and Stalin signed a ten-year non-aggression pact on 25 August 1939, but media interest in Canada was subdued. Two days before Hitler invaded Poland, The *Toronto Star's* banner headline concerned a father and son fending off three thugs.

About seven hours after Britain declared war on Germany, Captain Fritz Lemp of the U-30 was running on the surface some 250 miles west of the Irish coast. Lookouts spotted a ship on the horizon and ordered the crew to dive. The submarine then closed on the 14,000-ton British passenger liner bound for Montréal. The ship was two days out and Captain James Cook of the *Athenia* had spent a stressful afternoon explaining to 1103 passengers that England was now at war but insisting that his ship was protected from submarine attack by international law.

TOP: *Mackenzie King saw no real threat in Germany when he addressed the League of Nations in 1936, stressing the need for appeasement and peaceful resolution of conflicts between European nations.* (NAC/PA 16787) ***ABOVE:*** *After the death of Hindenburg, Adolf Hitler ruled his country and demanded unconditional obedience from his troops.* (NAC/PA 130023)

ATHENIA IS HIT

Standing at the periscope, Lemp waited until *Athenia* crossed his sights at close range. Then he launched two torpedos, one of which caught the liner on the port side, trapping a number of passengers in the lower decks. Although mortally wounded, the ship died a slow death, enabling the radio operator to get off an SOS.

Lemp surfaced and fired two shots at the radio masts before leaving. When rescue ships arrived, 118 of the 1300 on board were dead or missing. Among these were 28 Americans and a number of Canadians. News of the disaster reached North America on virtually the same radio broadcast as the declaration of war, and the sea war became part of the Canadian experience from the first day.

CONSCRIPTION UNNECESSARY

Prime Minister Mackenzie King called Parliament on 8 September and the ghost of conscription haunted three days of speeches. Finally, King declared that conscription was unnecessary and would not be introduced by his administration. The

ABOVE**:** *More than 120,000 Nazi stormtroopers stand at attention before Adolf Hitler in the Luitpold Arena of Nuremburg in 1938. (ILLUSTRATED LONDON NEWS)*

proclamation was signed and delivered to Buckingham Palace by 10 September and Canada was now officially at war.

Mobilization had started on 1 September and the response was overwhelming. In less than a month, there were over 70,000 men technically "under arms." What arms existed were of a 1914-18 vintage and Canada's response to the blitzkrieg would be 16 ancient tanks. Most disconcerting, during the early days of enlistment, was the fact that uniforms and clothing were lacking.

The colonel of a regiment in Saint John got a frantic call from his company sergeant-major on a Sunday night. A recent recruit had taken to his bunk because he did not have boots, and a major inspection of visiting brass was scheduled for the next morning. According to the reluctant warrior, the army had failed to provide clothing, and, as a consequence, he had signed a separate peace.

The sight of a man refusing to soldier on without boots was not calculated to improve the regiment's performance rating. So the colonel, who owned the store, had the CSM accompany the bootless warrior to the store in a taxi, in what was probably one of the strangest clothing parades in army history. Yet the incident personified Canada's war effort because, after a standing start, the new boots went marching up the gangplank to war.

AUTHOR: *Norman Shannon*

BRITISH COMMONWEALTH AIR TRAINING PLAN

MACKENZIE KING AND HIS OUIJA BOARD

When Canada went to war in 1939, policy was influenced by the Prime Minister's ouija board, but no system is perfect.

IS IT POSSIBLE THAT the most significant of Canada's wartime developments came as a result of the right vibes on a ouiji board? Don't knock it. Mackenzie King's dog, his ouija board and dead parents had a profound effect on his decisions. All were communicating with the Prime Minister during the bizarre weeks and months that preceded the announcement of the British Commonwealth Air Training Plan.

Although the RCAF was formed in 1924, most of its 235 pilots were involved in flying forest patrols, aerial mapping or in training. There was little military about RCAF operations until the eve of the war.

FLEXIBLE CONCEPT

Robert Leckie, a distinguished Canadian airman in WWI, went back to the RAF and, in 1936, became assistant to the Director of Training, Air Commodore Arthur Tedder. Leckie came up with a plan for training pilots in Canada and Tedder was enthusiastic. The concept was flexible: the plan could be run jointly, by the RAF or with major Canadian input.

The Canadian Cabinet rejected the plan primarily because Mackenzie King could not risk the wrath of Quebec if he set up British training schools in Canada. The British returned with another variation of the program but King was adamant. He either misunderstood or deliberately misinterpreted the British view that Canadians as well as British aircrew would be trained. Once again he rejected the proposal.

The Prime Minister was not unduly alarmed by all the crisis talk early in September because 24 hours before England went to war, King's dead father had told him a Pole would shoot Hitler, and his mother chimed in with news from the other side that war would be averted. Alas! That was not the way things worked out. The next day King got a wire from British Prime Minister Neville Chamberlain which urged immediate expansion of Canadian training facilities.

The prospect of air operations over Europe raised immediate fears of manpower shortages in the RAF and soon a need for 8000 pilots was predicted.

Perhaps it was the manner in which the Royal Flying Corps arbitrarily initiated a training program in Canada in 1917 or perhaps it was his fear of Quebec's reaction. In any event, King did nothing for over two weeks.

***ABOVE**: These BCATP students make their way toward WWI-vintage Fleet Finch biplanes at an elementary flying school in Windsor Mills, Quebec. (NAC/PL 2039)*

NO AUTHORIZATION

Vincent Massey, Canadian High Commissioner to London, backed into what could have been a major political mess without any authorization. With his Australian counterpart, he went to Colonial Secretary Anthony Eden with the idea of an air training plan in Canada for all Commonwealth aircrew.

King was furious with Massey but later offered to host a conference on the subject at which there was much haggling but little detail. But the concept of a $600 million plan was agreed upon by mid-December. There is no record of what King's ouija board advised, but from incredible political confusion a remarkable structure developed which played a major part in the final victory.

AUTHOR:

Norman Shannon

***ABOVE**: A graduate of Toronto's Curtiss Flying School, Robert Leckie was a major contributor to the RCAF's growth. The first to shoot down a Zeppelin in the First World War, he was given the task of setting up BCATP schools during WWII. (PL 117339)*

***OPPOSITE PAGE, RIGHT**: Students enrolled with the BCATP not only learned to fly, but also became familiar with radio operations. (NAC/PA 140653)*

CANADA ANSWERS THE CALL - 1940

The phoney war ended with explosive fury as Germany unleashed offensives in Norway, Belgium, Luxembourg and France. On all fronts the Blitzkrieg tactics scored major victories. The British were driven from Dunkirk and the French capitulated. Canadian pilots were among the few who first successfully challenged the Luftwaffe's heretofore invincibility in the skies above Britain. U-boats prowled the Atlantic and Canada's fledgling navy was beginning to suffer their first losses.

JANUARY-MARCH All across the western front there is a period of inactivity dubbed the "Phoney War," as both sides avoid confrontation. The Germans man the defences of the Siegfried Line, while French soldiers bunker down in their Maginot Line fortresses.

12 MARCH Russo-Finnish war concludes with the tiny Finnish army capitulating. In the David vs. Goliath conflict, the Finns inflicted enormously disporportionate casualties on the Russians – but they could not help but be overwhelmed by the sheer weight of Soviet superiority.

9 APRIL Germany launches an attack on Norway and simultaneously occupies Denmark. British and French forces deploy to Norway, but are later withdrawn.

10 MAY Blitzkrieg is launched across Europe as German troops invade Luxembourg, Belgium, Holland and France.

14 MAY The Dutch capitulate.

3 JUNE The defeated remainder of the British Expeditionary Force is withdrawn from Dunkirk's beaches.

14 JUNE Paris is occupied by the Germans.

25 JUNE HMCS *Fraser* is sunk after colliding with the British cruiser *Calcutta.* Forty-seven sailors perish.

1 AUGUST The Luftwaffe begins the first air raids against England – the Battle of Britain begins.

13 SEPTEMBER Italians launch an offensive against British in North Africa.

15 SEPTEMBER German losses in Battle of Britain are so severe, a seaborne invasion (Operation Sea Lion) is cancelled.

22 OCTOBER Following a collision, *HMCS Margaree* is sunk with a loss of 142 sailors.
28 OCTOBER 1940 Mussolini invades Greece.

22 NOVEMBER Greek victory at Korista culminates a successful defensive campaign against Italians.

9 DECEMBER British launch a major counter offensive in North Africa.

RIGHT: *On 17 April 1940 contingents of French chasseurs-alpins and British troops (13,000 strong), were ferried by Norwegian fishing boats and coasters from their troopships to Narvik, Namsos and Andalsnes. (IWM)*
FAR RIGHT: *After the disastrous assault on the beaches of Dunkirk, troops of the British Expeditionary Force await evacuation. (IWM)*

LEFT: *A corporal of the Permanent Force (as the Army was called between WWI and WWII). Note the WWI style load-bearing equipment, or "webbing" and Short Magazine Lee-Enfield (SMLE) rifle. This soldier is dressed for summer duty as indicated by his shorts and pith helmet. Between the wars, a malaise settled over the military as tens of thousands of Canadian soldiers had died in the "war to end all wars," and the population as a whole put the issue of war preparedness out of mind. This would have dire consequences in 1939.*
(ILLUSTRATION BY KATHERINE TAYLOR)
RIGHT: *A soldier of WWII sporting typical battle dress, with his gas cape pulled back. Early in the war it was anticipated that poison gas would be used, just as it was in the First World War, so the small pack held a gas mask for quick use. Thankfully, no deliberate gas attacks were perpetrated by either the Allies of the Axis powers.*
("PORTRAIT OF A CANADIAN SOLDIER," BY LILIAS TORRANCE NEWTON, CWM 14250)
BOTTOM: *In the years leading up to D-Day, the Canadian Army continued to grow and equip itself. As it was a monumental task to create a field army, extensive training was required in England before the Canadians were committed to action. Seen here are Ram tanks of the 5th Canadian Armoured Division, HQ Squadron (6th Duke of Connaught's Royal Canadian Hussars), in Ashdown Forest, Sussex, in September 1942.*
("CANADIAN TANKS MANOEUVRING" BY WILL OGILVIE, COURTESY THE NATIONAL GALLERY OF CANADA)

WAR AGAIN

WEAPONS AND UNIFORMS

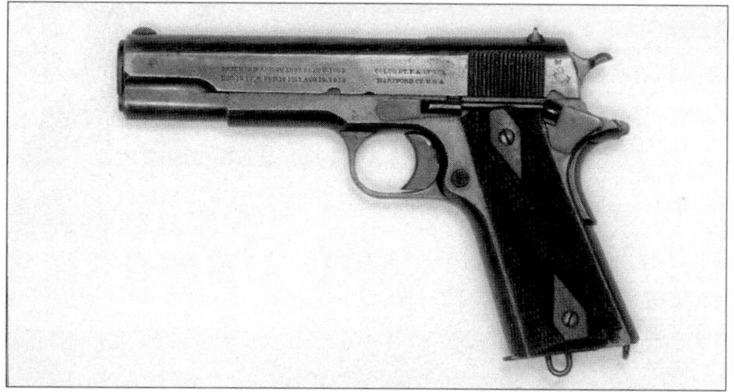

LEFT: *This .45 calibre, M1911 pistol was a Camp X favorite. It is commonly considered a solely American-issued pistol, but M1911A1s can be found in Canadian military collections. John M. Browning designed the M1911 in response to the U.S. Army's need for a pistol with greater knock down power following the American experience during the Phillippine Insurrection (1899-1901). The M1911A1 is an improved variant as the pistol is a magazine-fed, semi-automatic, recoil-operated, single action handgun. It uses a .45 calibre rimless cartridge in a seven-round magazine. It fires one round each time the trigger is squeezed, and once the hammer is cocked by prior action of the slide or thumb. This design is referred to as single action and makes shooting much easier when compared to the double action only revolvers commonly issued to Commonwealth forces during WWII. Plus, reloading can be done infinitely faster than any revolver and saves lives in combat.*

MIDDLE LEFT: *In this detail from Charles Comfort's "The Hitler Line," the "Tommy Gun" is seen. Although American, it had a limited role with Canadian troops. The older 1928A1 Thompson was a delayed blowback submachine gun, issued chiefly to armoured and reconnaissance units. It was selective for either semi- or fully-automatic fire. It fired a .45 calibre cartridge in 20- or 30-round magazines, or a 50-round drum. It featured a complex leaf with aperture notch battle sight. The rate of fire was 600-725 rounds per minute (rpm). This model had a removable buttstock, most had a horizontal fore grip, but some had a vertical fore grip. The submachine gun, M1/M1A1 Thompson, was introduced to simplify the M1928A1 and save money. It was now a blowback submachine gun. Again, it was select fire and used the 20- or 30-round .45 calibre magazines, but not the drum. Its rate of fire was 700 rpm. The M1 had a permanently attached buttstock. The M1 had a simple, fixed aperture rear sight. (CWM 12296)*

OPPOSITE PAGE, BOTTOM LEFT: *The battle for control of the Mediterranean island of Malta heated up in the summer of 1942 as both the Italians and British saw strategic value in its possession. Here, a Spitfire fighter tries to get an Me-109 in its sights while approaching from above.* (*"*BATTLE OVER MALTA,*"* BY DENIS A. BARNHAM, IWM) ***OPPOSITE PAGE, BOTTOM RIGHT:*** *Prisoners of war (POWs) taken in the European campaigns were routinely shipped to Canada for internment. Most were employed in the agricultural sector, providing manual labour to farmers short of manpower due to enlistments in the armed forces. Canadian WWI veterans served in their home guard, often guarding POWs or internees.* (*"*RETURNING FROM NIGHT DUTY,*"* BY JACK SHADBOLDT, CWM 14284) ***RIGHT:*** *During the Battle of the Atlantic, the corvette HMCS* Ville de Quebec *rammed German submarine U-224 on 13 January 1943 when it surfaced in her path, throwing one man overboard as he rushed towards his gun on the conning tower.* Ville de Quebec *would serve on many WWII convoy missions before being paid off on 6 July 1945.* (HAROLD BEAMENT, CWM) ***BOTTOM:*** *The Dieppe raid on 19 August 1942 proved to be a disaster of major proportions. The reasons why this debacle occurred are still debated today. In total, 65 per cent of the troops in the six assault battalions were casualties. The 2nd Infantry Division was said to be "destroyed" at Dieppe.* (*"*DIEPPE RAID*"* BY CHARLES COMFORT, CWM 12276)

***LEFT**: The British Commonwealth Air Training Program (BCATP) conducted by Canada was a major contributing factor to winning the war in the skies. This very successful program ran from 1939 to 1945. There were 131,553 aircrew trained in Canada for the RAF, RCAF, RNZAF and the RAAF. Unfortunately there were 856 training fatalities. Pictured is an Avro Anson Canada training aircraft at No. 3 Flying Training School in Calgary, Alberta. ("CONTROL TOWER" BY PETER WHYTE, NATIONAL GALLERY OF CANADA)*

***BOTTOM:** At its peak, the strength of the armed forces of Canada was 779,000. During the war, servicemen were required to wear their uniforms at all times. Trains, being the best mode of transport, carried servicemen to postings across the country. Scenes such as this played themselves out countless times as civilian and military personnel spent innumerable hours in transit. Here, airmen, sailors and soldiers ride a train bound for Gander, Newfoundland. Selected in 1935 as a refueling point for trans-Atlantic flights because it is fog-free, Gander developed into a key base during the Second World War. Established by the RCAF in 1940, Gander served as a strategic link in North America's defence, and in the development of Ferry Command, as planes built in North America would refuel in Gander before continuing to Britain. ("POSTED TO NEWFIE" BY PAUL A. GORANSON, CWM 11430)*

***OPPOSITE PAGE, TOP LEFT:** A corporal of the Princess Patricia's Canadian Light Infantry clothed in summer dress during the hot Sicilian campaign. The plan called for an assault on two fronts with the U.S. Seventh Army landing on the southwest coast of the island and the British 8th Army, of which the Patricias were a part, covering the southern tip of Sicily. The landings, early on the morning of 10 July 1943, were very successful and within 24 hours the Patricia's were 22 miles inland. (ILLUSTRATION BY KATHERINE TAYLOR)* ***OPPOSITE PAGE, BOTTOM LEFT:** A different kind of war art, heroic depictions of armed forces personnel were pervasive in Canada throughout the war. Seen here is a poster exhorting Canadians to help finance the war by buying war bonds. Posters such as this were also used to caution people. The "loose lips sink ships" slogan warned Canadians about inadvertently divulging critical information that could have helped the enemy. (NAC)*

BELOW: *Halifax became a bustling city and the home port for the Royal Canadian Navy's Atlantic fleet. Merchant ships would head for ocean meeting points to be escorted across the ocean by the Western Approaches Force. Along with escort ships such as the River class destroyers (HMCS* St. Laurent, *depicted), air cover was provided by RAF and RCAF aircraft from both sides of the Atlantic and Iceland. ("CANADIAN DESTROYERS," BY E.H. HOLGATE, NATIONAL GALLERY OF CANADA)*

BOTTOM, RIGHT: *HMCS* Drumheller *at St. John's Harbour in Newfoundland.* Drumheller *was a Flower class corvette, her design based on Arctic whaling vessels. Armed with a four-inch gun forward, anti-aircraft guns, and a load of depth charges, the corvettes were excellent convoy escorts. HMCS* Drumheller *was commissioned in Montreal on 13 September 1941 and on 11 December she headed out on her first convoy. On 13 May 1943,* Drumheller, *HMS* Logan, *and a Sunderland aircraft together sank* U-456. *Paid off on 11 July 1945 at Sydney, Nova Scotia, she was broken up for scrap in 1949 at Hamilton, Ontario. (PAINTING BY TOM WOOD, CWM)*

LEFT:
The North Atlantic has some of the roughest waters in the world in the winter. These corvettes fought not only the German Kriegsmarine, but the foul weather as well during their convoy escort duties. Early in the war there were not enough ships to escort the merchantmen for the entire trip. As a stopgap measure, the RCN and RN developed a handover procedure for the mid-Atlantic. The RN would assume control of the east-bound loaded convoys, and the RCN would take over control of the west-bound convoys. (PAINTING BY ROWLEY P. MURPHY, CANADIAN WAR MUSEUM)

BOTTOM:
A Lancaster bomber crew prepares for their nightly bombing run into German airspace. The bombing of Berlin caused the Luftwaffe to change its strategy from attacking British airfields to that of attacking the city of London. This change in strategy gave the RAF a chance to regroup, and eventually led to Germany's failure to win the Battle of Britain. (PAINTING BY DAME LAURA KNIGHT, IMPERIAL WAR MUSEUM)

OPPOSITE PAGE, TOP LEFT:
An American squadron of Boeing B-17 Flying Fortress bombers is accompanied by the distinctive twin-boomed Lockheed P-38 fighters as they make their way towards Berlin on a daylight bombing raid. Excessive damage to many German industrial cities was caused by both day and night bombing missions. Under the overall command of Sir Arthur Harris, Bomber Command conducted its air campaign on Germany throughout the war. Following the Casablanca Conference of January 1943, the bombing campaign became a crucial prerequisite for a land campaign. The long-range fighter escorts accompanied the bombers, offering them some protection from German fighters. Britain favoured nighttime area bombing raids, believing them safer for the crews and aircraft. The Americans contended that daylight "precision" bombing would have higher success rates – hitting precise targets – than blind night bombing. (PAINTING BY JOHN LAVALLE, U.S. AIR FORCE ART COLLECTION)

OPPOSITE PAGE, TOP RIGHT:
This Lancaster heavy bomber was hit by a Junkers JU-88 German night-fighter while on a bombing sortie. This aerial second front caused German forces to dedicate more and more of their resources to the defence of their homeland. The Lancasters were introduced in 1942, and carried the heaviest bombloads of any bomber to fly in the war. They were also the first to carry such defensive counter-measures as "window" and deceptive jamming. (PAINTING BY DON CONNOLLY)

OPPOSITE PAGE, MIDDLE RIGHT:
A crew prepares its armoured car during the First Special Serve Force's deployment to the Aleutian Island of Kiska in 1943. Armoured personnel carriers (APCs) were developed to give the ground soldier mobility and versatility on a changing battlefield. Although the Japanese had withdrawn prior to the assault, there were 24 casualties from mines, booby traps and friendly fire. The operation did, however, help prepare the SSF for the arduous Italian campaign. ("ARMOURED CAR IN WHITE" BY EDWARD JOHN HUGHES, CWM 12739)

MIDDLE, LEFT:
The battle for Ortona was ferocious, and was in marked contrast to the battles fought in the open space of North Africa. Characteristic of fighting in a built-up area is the damage to buildings, infrastructure and agriculture. Seen in this painting is a damaged 17-pound anti-tank gun used by the 90th Anti-Tank Battalion of the 1st Canadian Division. Also, in the middle ground is a destroyed German Tiger tank, a most formidable weapon that outgunned the Canadian Sherman tanks. In the background, artillery rounds can be seen descending upon the already burning city.
("BATTLEGROUND NEW ORTONA, ITALY, 1943" BY LAWREN P. HARRIS, CWM)

RIGHT:
Canadian soldiers advance across the German defences known as the Hitler Line, in Italy. This hard-fought battle began on 23 May 1944. The First Canadian Corps finally breached the Line after months of heavy fighting through Germany's other defence, the Gustav Line. On 24 May 1944, a bridgehead was consolidated and the Allies advanced on Rome.
("THE HITLER LINE" BY CHARLES COMFORT, CWM 12296)

ABOVE, LEFT: *In order to maintain the momentum of the attack on Ortona in December 1943, the Allies required air superiority over the battle area. Although the Luftwaffe's assets were being depleted, it tried to keep up the pressure on the advancing Canadians. Pictured observing the duel in the sky is the crew of a 40-mm Bofors anti-aircraft gun. Later in the Italian campaign, the Germans retreated from the skies. This left the artillery's anti-aircraft regiments with little to do. As there had been a dearth of infantrymen, many of the gunners, much to their chagrin, were re-roled to infantry or "groundpounders."("DOGFIGHT OFF ORTONA, ITALY," BY LAWREN P. HARRIS, CWM)*

ABOVE, RIGHT: *Troops on the advance in Italy would take whatever shelter was available wherever they were. Countless villages, centuries-old abbeys and churches, and beautiful palaces were used by Canadian soldiers as messes and sleeping quarters. Most of the young men in the Army had never seen such grand accommodations. These junior ranks are using an ornate baronial hall as their mess and dining facility. Note the mess tins the soldier in the foreground has tucked under his arm. ("SPLENDID QUARTERS, ITALY" BY CAMPBELL TINNING, CWM)*

LEFT: *In the spring of 1944, the 1st Canadian Corps, under command of the British Eighth Army, began its punch up the west side of Italy. The drive to relieve the Anzio beachhead and then head north to Rome was blocked by the enemies' defensive lines – Gustav and Hitler. Canadian tanks helped crack the Gustav Line, then the First Canadian Corps was given the task of breaking the Hitler Line. The battle lasted four days and cost 900 lives. (ILLUSTRATION BY KATHERINE TAYLOR)*

Even before their country became "officially" involved in WWII (1939) Canadians were fighting – and dying – in Europe.

THE WINTER OF THE PHONEY WAR

ABOVE: *Germany's swift invasion of Denmark and Norway in April 1940 brought an end to the phoney war. German minesweepers (left) escorted the high-speed troop transports to their northern destination.* (ILLUSTRATION BY ADOLF BOCK, U.S. NAVY COMBAT ART COLLECTION)

CANADA ENTERED INTO THE war in 1939 with little official enthusiasm as Prime Minister MacKenzie King issued a perplexing statement that his government would seek authority to co-operate with the United Kingdom. King faced reluctance from the Canadian Commonwealth Federation (CCF) which was for home defence, bundles for Britain but no Canadians abroad, and some of his senior ministers made the point that Quebec members would never endorse conscription.

Ten days after Canada did declare war, Quebec Premier Duplessis called for an election while his Union Nationale held a 75-15 seat majority. King sent four of his ministers to Quebec to fight the corrupt regime and turned back the Union Nationale with an upset victory for the Liberals. While he was so engaged, Canada's entry into the war moved in slow motion. This created a breach between the federal government and Ontario's Premier Mitch Hepburn who was concerned about the state of preparedness.

PROPAGANDA WAR

There was something to be said for Hepburn's concern. The army had 4500 men, the navy 1800 and the Royal Canadian Air Force (RCAF) had a total of 4000. As for training, most had never seen an aircraft, a tank or a ship. Yet newsreels soon had them in the back of trucks, singing: "We're going to hang our washing on the Siegfried Line." The propaganda war preceded reality by about five years. While Canada appeared to be slow in coming to grips with war in 1939, this was by no means unique among Allied nations. Prime Minister Neville Chamberlain, who had a way with words, left a meeting with Hitler in 1938 and proclaimed peace in our time.

When Hitler, in collusion with the Soviet Union, raped Poland, lines were drawn elsewhere, but they had little military backing. Most of Europe agreed to support democracy but did not wish to incite Hitler.

RAID ON BASE

However, some Canadians were involved in the war before Canada got around to making its participation official. Al Prince was killed over Wilhelmshaven five days before his country declared war, and Alfred Thompson was a prisoner of war by 8 September. Although Canadians flying with the RAF died from the outset, they were also victims of the phoney war. Flight Officer Max Aitken – son of Lord Beaverbrook – led Blenheims on the first raid against a seaplane base at Borkum. Like all crews, they were restrained by a Bomber Command edict: "The greatest care is to be taken not to injure the civilian population. The intention is to destroy the German fleet. There is no alternative target."

In mid-December, Squadron Leader Archibald Guthrie led one of three Wellington Squadrons against shipping at Wilhelmshaven and Shillig Roads. They were hit with intense flak and 80 fighters. Guthrie's Wimpys circled Wilhelmshaven unable to bomb because ships were tied at docks and presented a danger to civilians. In the air battle which followed, 12 of 22 Wellingtons were lost including those of fellow Canadians Guthrie and John Challes. Another, William McCrae, survived this incident but was killed two months later.

ALLIED TIMIDITY

The war that winter was characterized by Allied timidity, as well as desire to not antagonize the Nazis. There was a pervasive illusion that, somehow, peace was about to break out. When the Russians attacked Finland in November, the Finns resisted gallantly and, while Britain and France made noises about assistance, their strategy in aiding Finland included a bid to get at Swedish iron ore. The projected route was across Norway, down to the Swedish iron coast and across to Finland. Finland fell before the plan was executed.

Historically, the Germans invaded Norway on 9 April, but the fact that it was the Germans and not the British was poor timing by the latter. On 8 April, the British and French informed the Norwegians three mine fields had been laid off their coast. As Fleet Air Arm pilot Charles Lamb put it: "Our mine-laying was in nightly demand, generally at the request of sinister little men in bowler hats, carrying dispatch cases."

ABOVE:
When war was declared on Germany by France and Britain on 3 September 1939, experts had predicted immediate action by the Germans, but none came. Although troops were enlisted and sent to France, they had little to do beyond patrolling and guard duty.
(IMPERIAL WAR MUSEUM)

FORCED TO WITHDRAW

The Norwegians had little time to worry about the British declaration as, within minutes, Oslo got word that a Norway-bound German transport had been sunk by a Polish submarine. The Germans took Denmark, virtually without firing a shot. In Norway, the Germans took airdromes at Stavanger, Trondheim and Oslo, and a stream of Ju-52 transports brought in thousands of airborne troops. Although the British and French put 12,000 troops ashore on either side of Trondheim, they were forced to withdraw within ten days.

Air support for this operation was provided in part by 263 Squadron of the RAF. Led by Squadron Leader Baldy Donaldson, the ancient Gladiators took off in a snowstorm from the heaving deck of HMS *Glorious*. They landed on a lake south of Trondheim and, by patrol time next morning, carburetors were frozen and tires were locked into ice. Relays of Ju-88's and He-111's hit throughout the morning while ground-crew fought to get two aircraft off the ground. By noon 10 of 18 Gladiators were destroyed and, although survivors brought down many enemy machines in the afternoon, only five Gladiators remained and the ice was like the residual from a cocktail party.

ESCAPE TO SCOTLAND

The shattered squadron withdrew to another area and flew a sortie the next morning from which only three of five aircraft returned. By noon the second day, one Gladiator remained – without fuel. The squadron escaped to Scotland where it regrouped and returned about a month later. In deplorable weather, three machines ploughed into a mountain; the others turned back to HMS *Furious* in an Arctic storm to face their first carrier landing.

They got ashore the next day and flew 50 sorties in the Narvik area. With a Hurricane squadron, they fought off heavy air attacks and logged 80 sorties as the British operation became an evacuation. Canadians Alvin Williams and Phil Purdy were among the pilots who later flew back to HMS *Glorious*. The following day, the *Glorious* was among three ships attacked by the *Scharnhorst*, *Gneisenau* and the *Hipper*. It went down and the pilots of 263 Squadron disappeared without a trace.

ONLY A FIASCO

The original British plans for the defence of Narvik encouraged General Andrew McNaughton to commit battalions of the Princess Patricia's and the Loyal Edmontons to the operation. They were shipped to Scotland where they waited in vain as a potential disaster was downgraded to a fiasco.

To the south, during the winter of the phony war, Holland and Belgium clung to the hope of neutrality and did little to provoke Germany. This posed problems for RAF crews en route to Germany on leaflet raids. James Miller was an observer whose aircraft strayed over Dutch air space and was shot down by Dutch fighters. He is buried in Rotterdam.

France strutted behind a useless pile of cement called the Maginot Line and refurbished faded images of Verdun. Five British divisions hunkered down, hampered by conflicting directives issued by General Maurice Gamelin. One of these prohibited the RAF's Advanced Air Striking Force from bombing German troops unless they were on allied territory. They soon were and the phoney war came to an abrupt end.

HODGE-PODGE OF ARMIES

Early on 10 May, Hitler sent 2.5 million well-equipped, well-trained men against a hodge-podge of armies whose leaders were hardly on speaking terms. Belgian and Dutch military leaders had done little consulting with the British or French for fear of provoking Hitler. When the attack came, Field Marshal von Rundstedt's plan was to drive his armour through the Ardennes and split the Allies. He almost did it again in 1944.

Parachutists swept down on Rotterdam and The Hague, seizing vital bridges and, within four days, Holland collapsed while the Belgians also fell back. Von Rundstedt blasted a 50-mile gap in the French line and his troops rolled towards the coast under intense air cover. In 11 days, German armour severed Allied forces as it reached the coast.

As this was happening, Canadians were assigned to restore communications with the retreating BEF near Calais. The 1st Canadian Infantry Brigade was on ship at Dover when orders were cancelled. France had lost the will to fight and 337,000 soldiers were drawn from Dunkirk on 5 June. Although French leaders later accused the British of abandoning them, 100,000 of those snatched from Dunkirk were French.

The new British Prime Minister, Winston Churchill, then made the questionable gesture of sending troops to France. The 1st Canadian Division and the 52nd Lowland Division sailed on a ship known as *Forlorn Hope* to southern France. They were moving on to Le Mans when the War Office reasoned that with the surrender of Paris and the lack of any organized resistance, it was mission impossible. The disgruntled Canadians returned to England where they became one of the few units capable of meeting an enemy. France fell and the Canadians waited and waited. The phoney war was over but the Canadian army in England had to endure that long period during which its birth rate exceeded its death rate.

REPRINTED FROM:
Esprit de Corps,
Volume 5 Issue 5
AUTHOR: *Norman Shannon*

RIGHT:
A key element in Germany's planned invasion of Norway was the use of paratroopers in securing airfields followed by the rapid reinforcement by infantry units.

The news media lends credence to the adage that the first casualty of war is truth.

THE PHONEY WAR AND CANADIANS INVADE NORWAY

SOME OF US MAY recall the news reports of April 1940 stating Canadian units were fighting alongside British and French *Chasseurs Alpins* forces against the Germans in Norway. These reports also stated a Canadian had even been killed in action. The Germans, for their part, boasted they had captured several Canadians near Lillehammer. The only problem with these reports, however, was that they were all false. Canadian units were neither part of the actions nor were they captured by the Germans. This propensity for mendacity, on both sides but especially by the free and democratic Canadian press, has since given rise to the belief, in some Canadian circles, that the Canadian media and not the Canadian soldier suffered the most devastating effects during the "Phoney War."

On 28 March 1940, the Anglo-French Supreme War Council decided to mine the inshore passages of the Norwegian coast. This order, known as Operation Wilfred, was carried out on 8 April 1940. The Germans responded by shattering the relative calm of the Phoney War and launched Operation Weserubung – the invasion and subsequent occupation of Denmark and Norway on 9 April 1940. While the Danish government surrendered within hours, the Norwegian and Anglo-French response was another matter. Here the Allies wished to draw German forces to a remote theatre of war where they would find it easier than the Germans would to supply their forces. The invasion of Norway also afforded the Allies an opportunity as well as a chance to exploit their maritime supremacy.

FLOTILLA LAUNCHED

The German invasion of Norway prompted the Anglo-French Supreme War Council to launch a British destroyer flotilla against German forces in Narvik on 10 April. The next day, the Canadian newspaper, *The Toronto Star*, reported: "While officials remained silent, military circles in London confirmed an earlier report that Canadian troops were among the forces Britain has sent to fight in Norway. It is possible that some Canadians saw action yesterday when Allied troops and marines drove the Germans out of Narvik." This attack was soon followed by an Allied landing at Namsos on 14 April. This force was commanded by British Major General Carton de Wiart.

On 16 April the Canadian newspaper *The Journal* reported, "There is no comment whatever from the Department" regarding reports of Canadian troop involvement in the British Expeditionary Force in Norway. On the evening of 16 April 1940, however, the BBC "officially confirmed that Canadian troops are with the British and French forces in Norway." *Reuters* also issued a report stating it

ABOVE: *German destroyers and supply ships suffered heavy losses at Narvik. After recapturing the town, the Allied troops withdrew on 7 June 1940 as a result of Germany's victory in France.* (IWM)

"understands that a number of Canadian troops are included in the British Expeditionary Force in Norway." The *Ottawa Citizen* picked up on the story the next day stating, "A fully equipped force with tanks and guns – including Canadians...was hurriedly concentrated at various eastern ports of the United Kingdom, placed in convoy and secretly carried 400 miles across the North Sea."

Notwithstanding the dearth of information supporting the presence of Canadian troops on Norwegian soil, *Reuters* confirmed, on 20 April 1940, that Canadian troops had taken part in an Allied landing off Andalsnes, Norway on 18 April and "fighting is expected to break out shortly in this region..." By 23 April 1940, the media (the Canadian Press Association and the French news agency *Havas*) reported that Canadian troops along with French *chasseurs alpins* had formed the "spearhead of an Allied army driving southward along the railway running from Namsos to German-held Trondheim."

BOASTFUL PROPAGANDA

Soon thereafter, Germany's ministry of propaganda also began to boast about Canadian troops in Norway. On 24 April 1940, Nazi officials informed Canadian Press (CP) Berlin that "Canadian troops had been taken prisoner in the fighting in the Lillehammer area northwest of Hamar."

Interestingly, this same CP report also noted, "Apparently these sources (German) had not at that time learned – as officially announced in Ottawa and London that there are no Canadian units in Norway." Although it may not have been planned for at the time, the German announcement followed by the Canadian denial was a major coup for the German propaganda machine because it compelled the enemy to forego its lies and "tie himself up in denials."

By 25 April 1940, confusion about the presence of Canadian troops in Norway was reaching alarming proportions and several Canadian media outlets began voicing their dismay, much to the satisfaction of the German propaganda machine. *The Journal*, for example, stated, "this is all part of an extraordinary picture we do not understand and cannot explain."

KEEP THE ENEMY GUESSING

When confronted with this dichotomy, one military official in London stated, "any information about Canadian troop movements will be given when it is safe to do so – not before. Composition of the British Expeditionary Force in Norway must for the present remain a closely guarded secret. Furthermore, it isn't a bad idea to keep the enemy guessing until such time as our troops are firmly established and ready for the next stage."

Still, while Power claimed there were no Canadian troops in Norway, and several media outlets were voicing their dismay, the *Globe and Mail* reported on 26 April 1940 that a Canadian soldier had died while serving in Norway. Harry B. Wilson of the PPCLI, was believed to have been killed in action somewhere near Lillehammer, Norway the day before.

DEARTH OF EVIDENCE

When the media spoke with Wilson's father in Albuquerque, New Mexico, however, he did not "know where the word came from." He said he presumed it came from the British War Office but there was no information about what unit Wilson had belonged to. Wilson's parents had divorced, and his

RIGHT: *German machine-gunners defend the port of Narvik from their skyline position atop the ridge.*

mother now lived somewhere in California. Notwithstanding the dearth of evidence to support the death of Harry B. Wilson, the *Globe and Mail* printed the story.

On 10 May 1940, Germany officially ended the Phoney War when the Wehrmacht launched its western offensive known as operation "Sichelschnitt" (Sickle Stroke) against Belgium, Holland and France. The offensive, combined with the Norwegian fiasco, also lead to the resignation of British Prime Minister Neville Chamberlain on that same day.

Only with the end of the Norwegian campaign in sight, combined with the resignation of the British Prime Minister and the collapse of the Allied front in France, did the media begin reporting on Canada's actual contribution to the Norwegian campaign. On 20 May 1940, *The Journal* reported that privates Arni Johannson and Gustav Hansen, both from the Saskatoon Light Infantry (M.G.) had volunteered to serve as interpreters and they had been detailed to an anonymous British unit (later revealed to be the 1st Battalion of the King's Own Yorkshire Light Infantry) to fight in Norway.

FALSE INTERPRETATION

These Canadian military interpreters claimed to have actually landed in Andalsnes and served for approximately ten days in Norway before being evacuated along with the British unit. They also claimed, while they were fighting in Norway, they "were subjected to heavy shelling. Many of the explosions gave off large puffs of yellow coloured vapour which floated towards us. We were not close enough to ascertain whether or not this was gas." They also admitted that the "main language difficulty they had met was in understanding Yorkshire English."

The Allied Expeditionary Force in Norway eventually withdrew from both Namsos and Andalsnes on 3 May and began to withdraw from all of Norway on 24 May. The Norwegian Government, for its part, decided to end hostilities on Norwegian soil on 7 June 1940.

BRITISH CENSORSHIP

In a commentary designed to rationalise its reporting of the Canadian involvement in Norway, *The Journal* stated "...that all these reports were permitted by British censorship and indeed encouraged by official quarters with the deliberate purpose of deceiving the enemy, for reasons at which we can only guess.

"If that happens to be true it is pretty rough on the newspapers and the relatives of the Canadian troops overseas."

Although no Canadian units ever took part in the British Expeditionary Force invasion of Norway, there may have been some Canadian nationals serving in the all-British expedition force as well as the Royal Air Force, the British Home Fleet and perhaps various North Sea trawlers. This fact, however, only came to light several weeks later when it was revealed that Major General R.H. Dewing, British Director of Military Operations at the War Office had approached then Brigadier H.D.G. Crerar at Canadian Military Headquarters, for forces on 16 April 1940, "in view of the lack of other trained troops in the United Kingdom." Two Canadian units, some 1,300-strong and under command of Colonel E.W. Sansom, were even selected. They were the Princess Patricias and the Loyal Edmonton Regiment.

These units were chosen because they were considered, "...the most advanced units in training...." After they had been selected, they were "fitted with winter gear, piped aboard trains at Aldershot (evening of 18 April), drawn up before waiting ships in Scotland (Dunfermline) – then sent back to Aldershot, their mission cancelled."

In conclusion, the Canadian contribution of two interpreters was a far cry from Canadian troops spearheading the assault by an Allied Army on Trondheim. Yet even this admission of Canada's true involvement in Norway was cushioned with a suggestion the Germans may be resorting to gas attacks reminiscent of World War One. This assertion of a potential use of gas only confirmed many critics who had suggested that, during the Phoney War, the Canadian media, like many other news mediums, contributed to one of the war's first casualties – truth!

REPRINTED FROM:
Esprit de Corps, *Volume 7 Issue 1*
AUTHOR: *George Orsyk*

SIGNED WITH THEIR HONOUR

Outnumbered but never outfought, a heroic group of airmen turn back Hitler's preliminary to the invasion of England.

Me110 flies over the white cliffs of Dover. The long-range two-seater heavy fighter proved to be a disappointment when challenged by the RAF as deficiencies in speed and manoeuvrability revealed themselves in close combat. (IWM)

"Born of the sun they travelled a short while towards the sun,
And left the vivid air signed with their honour."

STEPHEN SPENDER

ON 10 JULY 1940, TWO weeks after the fall of France, RAF Fighter Command scrambled five squadrons to intercept 64 enemy aircraft over Dover. They destroyed 12 and lost three in what is considered to be the first encounter in the Battle of Britain. Hitler had set a timetable of two months during which the Luftwaffe was to break the back of the RAF. Invasion would then follow. Duncan Hewitt of Saint John, New Brunswick, was killed attacking a Dornier 17 the next day over Portland, and became the first of 20 Canadians to die in the air battle which decided the course of history.

Göring's *Luftwaffe* made 34 attacks on shipping in as many days. Most of the 261 aircraft lost fell to Air Vice-Marshal Keith Park's fighters from 11 Group. Because of its location, Park's group would later bear the brunt of airfield attacks and the defence of London.

BRITAIN STANDS ALONE

Air Chief Marshal Hugh Dowding, the crusty chief of Fighter Command, sighed with relief although Britain now stood alone. He had seen enough of allied entanglements during the confusion in France, leaving him with an estimated 750 Spitfires and Hurricanes to counter 2,800 enemy machines. He had an additional 150 Blenheims and Defiants which were unfit to fly in the company of the Messerschmidt-109.

After losing 261 aircraft, Hitler tried to give the battle a new spin by declaring 13 August Eagle Day; predicting the new attacks, directed at airfields, would cripple the RAF and pave the way for an invasion within two months. At the time there were some 80 Canadian fighter pilots in Britain; 26 were with the newly arrived RCAF No. 1 Squadron and 16 flew with the badly mangled No. 242 Squadron (which lost 14 pilots over France two months earlier). The others were products of the "cattle-boat brigade," volunteers who had gone to England before the war and were scattered throughout the RAF.

ALTHOUGH 250 PILOTS PASSED THROUGH OPERATIONAL TRAINING UNITS IN AUGUST, INEXPERIENCED 'SPROGS' BECAME COLD MEAT IN ACTION.

EAGLE DAY

Eagle Day opened with 1485 enemy sorties against ports and assaults on Detling and Eastchurch airfields, and for the next two days, airfields and radar stations were hit. Joe Laricheliere, from Montreal, became an instant ace when he destroyed six machines in two days, but on the third day was killed. The day after his death, Harry Mitchell of Port Hope downed three for a hat trick.

Kenley airfield became a major target on 18 August as 36 bombers approached from height while nine Dorniers, unseen on radar, skimmed the channel bound for the same field. A second group of 60 bombers and 150 fighters followed. Kenley was knocked out of action for two days and 60 bombers hit Biggin Hill which remained operational.

Over 100 Stuka dive-bombers hit radar stations on the south coast from Gosport to Ford. The field at Ford was put out of action in the engagement which cost the Luftwaffe 24 aircraft. In four days of such raids, the Germans lost 180 aircraft.

As August progressed, British losses increased. In a ten day period prior to 6 September, Fighter Command lost 248 machines with 231 pilots killed or wounded, who were very difficult to replace. Although 250 pilots passed through Operational Training Units in August, inexperienced 'sprogs' became cold meat in action.

ALCOHOLIC RESUSCITATION

No. 1 Squadron, RCAF, had arrived from

Canada after the evacuation from Dunkirk. In the first Wing take-off from Northolt, a certain shambles prevailed. RCAF No. 1 Squadron, Polish No. 303 Squadron and RAF No. 1 were at dispersals when orders came to scramble. Orders were either faulty or misinterpreted because 44 aircraft thundered around perimeter tracks, all heading for the same spot. According to Paul Pitcher, the only casualty was the Station Commander who had to be helped to the mess for "alcoholic resuscitation."

Squadron Leader Ernie McNabb led the squadron into its first action against the enemy on 26 August. As the 12 Canadians attacked 30 Dorniers, McNabb saw one victim burst into flames just as his own aircraft was hit, forcing him to land. R. Edwards shot the tail off another Dornier before he was killed. In its first contact with the enemy, the squadron destroyed three and damaged four bombers.

Ernie McNabb led by example. By October he was the RCAF's first ace and was awarded the first Distinguished Flying Cross. Gordon McGregor, 38, was the oldest Canadian but one of the first to score a victory. He shot down a Dornier over Biggin Hill late in August and later accounted for five enemy aircraft.

RAF "ORPHANS"

Among the Canadians orphaned to the RAF was Johnnie Kent, a veteran of the campaign in France who became a flight leader with Polish No. 303 Squadron. By mid-October, "Kentowski" had four victories and within a year – when posted to non-operational duties – his score stood at 13. Hilly Brown flew with RAF No. 1 Squadron which he commanded by November when he had 14 personal victories and several shared.

While fighting over France, No. 242 Squadron had lost 14 pilots but Canadian veterans provided a high level of leadership for replacements. Willie McKnight went into the Battle of Britain with eight victories while Stan Turner had six and two probables. Robert Grassick, Noel Stansfeld and John Latta were other veterans whose drive to have at the enemy matched that of their new leader, Douglas Bader. The impatient squadron was scrambled on 30 August and ran into about 100 bombers over North Weald. Willie McKnight accounted for two of the 12 aircraft destroyed.

The outcome of the entire war may have hinged on an accident when stray German bombs fell on London on 24 August. In retaliation, the RAF bombed Berlin and Hitler's act of retaliation was to turn the wrath of the Luftwaffe against London.

THE BATTLE OF BRITAIN SEGUED TO THE BLITZ AS 300 BOMBERS FELL OVER ENGLAND IN OCTOBER... AND IN MID-NOVEMBER, 500 BOMBERS HIT COVENTRY, KILLING OVER 550 PEOPLE

JAWS OF VICTORY

He probably snatched defeat from the jaws of victory. According to Winston Churchill: "Extensive damage had been done to five of 911 Group's forward airfields. If the enemy had persisted...the whole intricate organization of Fighter Command might have broken down."

Against the advice of his senior commanders, Göring switched tactics. London became a target and more fighters were brought into play hoping to now destroy the RAF in the air. Some 950 aircraft hit London on 7 September and returned that evening, leaving the city in flames. But before the flames died, day bombers were back to set the pattern for the next week.

Fighter Command was caught off guard by the change of tactics, and for at least three days heavy cloud also prevented ground observers from tracking enemy formations. Fighter Command's brief failure to respond with its customary aggressiveness led Göring to misread the situation and mount a 1700-plane raid on 15 September.

Designed to break the back of Fighter Command, the operation started shortly after midnight with attacks which went on for two hours. Then, after noon, fighter bombers struck in the first of five major raids. That evening, at about 2000 hours, the night-side took over with the first of ten raids.

EXAGGERATED NUMBERS

Lazy contrails chalked the high blue that Sunday as Britons looked up trying to decipher their fate in the tracings. The next day, The *Daily Express* announced that 175 enemy aircraft had been shot down, a number which later checked out at about 56. The same issue of the paper had a story of lawns being set on fire at Buckingham Palace. Keith Ogilvie, of Ottawa, was credited with bringing down the Dornier responsible.

Two days later, Hitler postponed his Operation Sea Lion invasion plans, which were later cancelled. But the air battle continued and, on 27 September, RCAF No. 1 downed eight invaders.

Days shortened and nights gave way to bombing, sending some seven million Londoners to shelters or subways. A million children were taken from their homes and sent around the world. The battle of Britain segued to the Blitz as 300 bombers fell over England in October. Liverpool, Southampton, Portsmouth became designated targets and in mid-November, 500 bombers hit Coventry, killing over 550 people.

INCREDIBLE DETERMINATION

The young men in the Spitfires and Hurricanes showed incredible determination in winning the Battle of Britain, but Bomber Command also contributed by flying several missions against invasion barges in channel ports. Members of the Women's Auxiliary Air Force were also key figures under fire at isolated radar posts as well as busy airfields.

But it was the fortitude of the average citizen who won the blitz. By the spring of 1941, 43,000 civilians were killed and 51,000 seriously injured. Their spirit of resistance paraphrased Churchill's promise to fight on the beaches and never surrender. As for weapons, they were determined to fight to the last bottle – the last empty bottle.

REPRINTED FROM:
Esprit de Corps, *Volume 2 Issue 5*
AUTHOR: *Norman Shannon*

RIGHT:
Carrying vital supplies, the merchant ship Ohio *along with her naval escort, came under heavy attack as she approaches Malta. Although badly damaged, she successfully docked at Valletta and unloaded most of her cargo before sinking.*
(PAINTING BY NORMAN WILKINSON, NATIONAL MARITIME MUSEUM)

Disaster at Dunkirk brings Italy into the war with massive air attacks on Malta.

FAITH, HOPE AND... NOT MUCH CHARITY

A FEW WEEKS BEFORE Hitler's Panzers rolled across Europe in 1940, the HMS *Glorious* steamed out of Malta and left four packing cases on the wharf. Curious longshoremen eventually investigated and found the crates contained four ancient Gloster Gladiator aircraft. The RAF then breathed life into three of the Fleet Air Arm aircraft which became Malta's sole air defence.

When France fell, Italy declared war on Britain. Prime Minister Winston Churchill greeted the treachery with relief. He allowed that it was only fair that Germany have the Italians as allies in this war because Britain had them as allies in the last one.

Churchill's sense of fair play notwithstanding, Mussolini's bombers struck at Malta the next evening and all that rose to meet them were three old Gladiators.

BULLETS SNAPPING

Timber Woods and two companions drove the first wave back out to sea but the second formation closed on the Port of Valetta. Woods got a burst at a bomber which sped away leaving his biplane a sitting duck for enemy fighters. Bullets snapped around Woods' ears and he threw the machine into a tight bank which brought him onto the tail of a Macchi-Castolldi 200, the best of Italy's fighters. A quick burst sent the enemy into a steep dive and a trail of smoke marked its passage. It was the opening engagement in Malta's 30 months of agony.

MALTA WAS A ROCK IN THE MIDDLE OF THE MEDITERRANEAN WHICH HAD BEEN WRITTEN OFF AS BEING UNDEFENDABLE BY BRITISH CHIEFS OF STAFF.

Malta was a rock — actually five rocks — in the middle of 2,000 miles of Mediterranean which had been written off as being undefendable by British chiefs of staff. But Churchill saw it as vital to protecting some 4.5 million square miles of the Middle East – including the Suez Canal – and the tiny island about the size of London became critical to both British defence and attacks on Axis shipping as the war spread across North Africa.

As the Italians continued to pound the island from bases in Sicily – some 60 miles away – with raids of 200 aircraft, they were met by three Gladiator biplanes from another era. When they were able, Faith, Hope and Charity — as they became known — intercepted 72 formations and shot down 37 hostiles. After three weeks, Italy declared a somewhat premature victory. Wanting to make the most of the victory, the Germans asked for a photo for propaganda. A reconnaissance aircraft was sent out to oblige and was promptly shot down.

The Gladiators were joined by four Hurricanes. Considering down-time for maintenance, for two months they met odds of ten to one. Later that summer, an additional 12 Hurricanes flew in from the aircraft carrier *Argus* but the second batch of reinforcements met with disaster.

SHODDY WEATHER REPORT

The *Argus* slipped through Gibraltar but stood off a maximum distance from Malta because of possible enemy action. The fighters were escorted by a Fleet Air Arm machine and pilots had been briefed on a weather report which was sadly out of date. What should have been a tail-wind became a head-wind and long before they reached Malta, fighters had exhausted fuel and were falling into the sea. Nine machines and pilots were lost.

The Battle of Britain was about to begin, yet demand for fighters was critical in North Africa. During 1940, assorted aircraft bound for other parts were seconded, diverted or otherwise assigned to Malta but it was June,

RIGHT:
One of three Gloster Gladiators – affectionately known as Faith, Hope and Charity – that, for three weeks in June 1940, protected the rocky Mediterranean island of Malta from Italian bombers.
(IMPERIAL WAR MUSEUM)

1941, before a squadron of Blenheims added to Malta's offensive punch.

Disaster dogged British efforts to launch fighters from aircraft carriers. In June 1941, the *Ark Royal* and *Victorious* sent 48 Hurricanes off their decks. They took-off at maximum distance and the RAF pilots used statute miles to compute distance to Malta while Fleet Air Arm escorts used nautical miles. The formations flew south of Malta and this time 36 pilots and fighters were lost.

ENEMY SHIPPING HIT HARD

Meanwhile, RAF and Fleet Air Arm aircraft took a heavy toll on enemy shipping during the summer of 1941, sinking over 160,000 tons or about 50 per cent of enemy sailings. By fall, Beauforts and Sunderland flying-boats were observing and photographing enemy ports. Aircraft from Malta provided the fleet with final details of enemy strength at Taranto on 11 November. The harbour sheltered six battleships, 14 cruisers and 27 destroyers.

Swordfish strikes from some 170 miles out sank three battleships, two auxiliaries and left two cruisers listing. Taranto was a major defeat for the Italian navy which never again ventured out to sea in force.

Days after the attack, a Japanese observer visited Taranto to assess the damage of the first carrier-based airstrike. He was greatly impressed, and his report became a primer for the 7 December 1941 attack on Pearl Harbour.

By early 1942, the Luftwaffe was flying ten to 15 attacks a day on the four Malta airfields, and by February the island the size of London suffered from 2,000 enemy sorties.

THE CONFECTIONER

Two months later, the *USS Wasp* loaded 48 Spitfires in England and sailed through the Straits of Gibraltar to within 600 miles of Malta. The *Wasp* turned into the wind and Martlet fighters provided cover as the Spits prepared to take-off. The first machine to attempt it was flown by an officer known as "the Confectioner" because he considered anything a piece of cake. On this particular take-off, his role was to show the others how it was done. His Spit trembled as he applied full boost. Then, when he released the brakes, a sudden torque, which went uncorrected, hit the machine. It slewed 90° and jumped over the edge. Somewhere in the 60 feet to the water, "the Confectioner" managed to gain air speed, but the other 47 machines took the long way down the runway.

Although 46 Spitfires reached Malta, they landed amid dust from a recent air raid and within 72 hours every machine was either destroyed or unserviceable. The battle for Malta now reached critical proportions as a major allied convoy failed to get through and fuel had to be brought in by submarine.

SURVIVAL OF MALTA

The survival of Malta was dependent on the growth of an air defensive and offensive force; the resolution of the Maltese to resist; and the ability of the merchant navy to provide essentials for survival, including food.

In August, one such convoy fought its way through attacks by submarines, E-boats and dive-bombers. All 14 ships were seriously damaged and nine were sunk. The exploits of the tanker *Ohio* puts things into perspective. Early on the morning of 12 August, a torpedo blasted a 24 by 27 foot hole in her side and seconds later the engine room was ablaze. Part of the extensive damage was to the instruments and steering but the engines were still growling and the captain eventually managed to close on the distant ships of the convoy.

After daybreak next day, the *Ohio* was sailing in line with a merchantman who was hit by a bomb and blew up. It spread a lake of flame across the Mediterranean which a second ship ploughed through. Thirty-four members of its confused crew jumped into the sea of flame, thinking their ship had been hit. The *Ohio* was so close that one of its kerosene tanks was set ablaze.

THE *OHIO* TAKES A LICKING

Within an hour, a second wave of Ju-87s struck, and this time the *Ohio* took a 500-pounder in the bow. About half an hour later, the crew shot down a Ju-88 which hit the water nearby and bounced onto the foredeck. Two sticks of bombs from another aircraft straddled the wounded *Ohio*, lifting it out of the water. It rocked, rattled and rolled but continued towards Malta. Then a second Ju-88 hit the sea and bounced aboard the poopdeck. This time two boilers blew out and the engines ground to a halt.

The *Ohio* underwent further bombing for two hours and attempts to take her in tow failed because of her damaged steering gear and severe structural damage. She drifted for three hours, down to the bows in the water, listing sharply, engine room flooding six inches an hour and, to add further to the danger, water mixing with kerosene. Some 70 miles from Malta, the tanker was near death when three ships took her in tow. Further air attacks were met by Spitfires from Malta, but a 1000 pound bomb pitched the *Ohio* out of the water where her screws were torn out of alignment and the plates began to buckle. One final attempt to tow the wreck was successful and she and her cargo arrived at Malta on 16 August.

PILOT STATS

A number of Canadian pilots had arrived in Malta by the summer of 1942 and at one point about one-quarter of all pilots on the island were Canadian. Wing Commander Hilly Brown commanded fighter operations until he was shot down by anti-aircraft fire in a raid on a German field in Sicily. At the time of his death, he had scored 20 victories. Wally McLeod got 13 victories in 18 weeks and Buck McNair fulfilled the promise shown in the Battle of Britain. Although Buzz Buerling showed few of the leadership qualities of the above, his deadly ability at deflection shooting enabled him to score 29 victories in four months before being shot down and rehabilitated.

By the winter of 1942, the siege of Malta had been lifted. Some 5,715 bombs killed 1500 civilians and destroyed 25,000 buildings. At times, the lack of oil made it impossible to operate water pumps as buildings burned. The four airfields were pitted and suffered such extensive damage that returning fighters were sometimes unable to land for smoke and dust. But the people persevered and the navy endured brutal convoy action as the RAF built up its defensive and offensive strength. Malta then emerged as a key base which dominated the central Mediterranean and became an important element in eventual victory, a victory inspired by Faith, Hope and Charity and the men who flew them.

REPRINTED FROM:
Esprit de Corps, *Volume 6 Issues 8 & 9*
AUTHOR: *Norman Shannon*

THE BRIDGE GROWS WINGS

ABOVE: *Goose Bay, Labrador, became the first step for ferry runs across the Atlantic to bases in Greenland and Iceland. Before this Hudson makes the journey, a service crew gives it a major overhaul.* (NAC/PA 153982)

Hattie's Camp, Newfoundland, sees the start of Ferry Command, an operation which delivers 10,000 aircraft at high cost.

WHEN THE RAF FORMED Transport Command 50 years ago, it was officialdom's second attempt to give a wild and wonderful bunch of adventurers a new look. There were other motives, such as developing a world-wide transport network and the new command performed well in this role. But somehow the men in their neat blue uniforms lacked the colour of the mackinaws, parkas and whipcord breeches of the civilian crews who built an air bridge across the Atlantic in the darkest days of the war.

As if the fall of France wasn't bad enough, 1940 brought the Battle of Britain, a new war in North Africa and heavy strikes against allied shipping in the Atlantic. In spite of allied convoys, U-boat attacks on shipping grew in intensity and effectiveness. Only one of 13 RAF Coastal Command squadrons was equipped with Hudsons, a machine capable of long patrols and packing a deadly punch. Most of the other RAF machines simply could not cope with the demands of long-range patrol.

NEED FOR BOMBERS

When Churchill appointed Lord Beaverbrook to head up the Ministry of Aircraft Production, he stressed the need for bombers and turned his eyes to North America. The concept of regular flights across the Atlantic was not unknown, but until 1941 nobody gave it much serious thought – nobody with the authority to do anything about it. British Overseas Airways flew survey flights in 1937 but the RAF seemed to have little interest in the prospect. When George Woods-Humphrey, former managing director of Imperial Airways,was given the job of putting together a team to fly aircraft to England, few dreamed that the civilian undertaking with such humble beginnings would contribute some 10,000 Atlantic crossings to the war effort.

The new operation was adopted by the CPR which provided office space and other facilities in Montreal. Woods-Humphrey, who had flown 1937 survey flights with Imperial, recruited his old team of five pilots, the sixth was then in the RCAF and a flurry of paper work was necessary to set him free. While the first group of crews was being assembled,"Punch" Dickins, the legendary bush pilot and WWI veteran, spread

ABOVE: *A Lockheed Hudson from No. 11 Squadron patrols the waters off Halifax in 1940. The Hudson was used primarily for maritime reconnaissance and as an anti-submarine aircraft. Initially, the aircraft served as a navigational trainer.* (DND PHOTO)

his net across North America. The word went out to bush pilots, mail pilots, airline pilots, the last of the barnstormers; anybody with experience and guts. The prize was $1,000 a month. Dickins, an employee in CPR's air service, became operations manager of the new group and soon was selecting an incredible cross-section of talented adventurers.

The response from pilots was good but wireless operators were harder to get. Many of the original group were drawn from air lines. Jim Howard, a former Imperial Airways man, did a stretch in the RAF. He escaped from a sinking flying boat in a Norwegian fjord and then spent some time on standby in Scotland to fly important people out in case Britain fell. When things subsided, he traded the uniform for 'civvies' and reported to Montreal.

THE MONEY OFFERED RCAF PILOTS [$1,000 PER MONTH] WAS A PRINCELY SUM, CONSIDERING THAT A NEW RAF PILOT PROBABLY MADE $165. YET SOMEHOW THE DISPARITY IN PAY WAS NOT A CAUSE FOR TENSION...

HATTIE'S CAMP

The first leg of the plan called for a 950-mile trip to Hattie's Camp in Newfoundland. After crossing on the Sydney ferry to Cape-Aux-Basques and a wearisome train ride across Newfoundland, David Powell found that the air terminal which cost $4 million had runways but little else. There was a small hangar, a control tower and a few construction shacks. Powell had railway cars brought into a siding and these became living quarters and offices for crews. Then for some reason Hattie's Camp became Gander.

D.T. Bennett, a former Imperial Airways captain, was to lead the first group overseas. The first step was getting aircraft to fly and Bennett and R.H. Page went to Burbank to pick up two Hudsons. Some peculiar interpretation of the U.S. neutrality law made it necessary to fly to North Dakota as passengers and then have the aircraft towed across the border by horses. For a period of months a horse or an old Ford truck hauled aircraft to isolated border points without incurring the wrath of Hitler.

The men recruited by Dickins were under contract at $1,000 a month for pilots, with lesser amounts for other aircrew. The money offered pilots was a princely sum, considering that a new RAF pilot probably made $165. Yet somehow the disparity in pay was not a cause for tension when RAF and RCAF pilots later came on stream. If there was complaint, the pilot was usually reminded of all the advantages he derived from being in the service. Whereupon, not wishing to appear obtuse, he would nod in agreement.

THE SKIRL OF PIPES

Just before nightfall on 10 November, seven Lockheed Hudsons were assembled at Hattie's Camp. Light snow scudded across the runway as two engineers hauled the starter trolley from ship to ship. Engines were run up and then tanks were topped. By departure time at eight o'clock, the Hudsons took off to the skirl of pipes.

Colonel Blackadder of the Queen's Own Rifles, or his bandmaster, had a strange sense of history as the planes flew into darkness but it was just as well the 22 men on board didn't hear the band which played "Nearer My God to Thee."

As Capt Bennett led nine Americans, six Brits and six Canadians out over the Atlantic, they flew in formation. Not the most desirable thing for such a time and flight but not all pilots had sufficient navigation experience. In North America many had been flying radio ranges which gridded most air routes. When the machines went into darkness that night, acceptable losses were calculated at as high as 50 per cent.

The need for aircraft in the U.K. was so great that half of the crews could go missing yet the project would continue. But ten and a quarter hours later all Hudsons were touching down near Belfast and the ferry operation became a reality. By mid-December three groups had safely flown the Atlantic.

ROUTES EXPANDED

Suddenly the idea of ferrying aircraft exploded. Routes expanded to accommodate a variety of aircraft and increased numbers resulting from U.S. lend-lease in March

Amazingly, the crew and passengers of this return ferry service Liberator survived the 9 February 1943 crash just ten miles short of the Gander runway. (NAC/PA 191279)

ABOVE: *A Douglas Dakota returns after a successful 1944 supply mission to Burma. The Dakota was also used to ferry troops. (PL 60123)*

WHEN THE FLIGHTS STARTED PILOTS RETURNED FROM THE UNITED KINGDOM BY SHIP. BUT IN MID-1941 BOAC INITIATED RETURN FLIGHTS. THREE LIBERATOR CRASHES KILLED 47 RETURNING AIRCREW.

1941. A Bermuda-based operation delivered 51 Catalina flying boats by the end of May.

Increased traffic meant more crews, more maintenance and more training. The Atlantic Ferry Organization (ATFERO) moved from St. Hubert into new quarters at Dorval. The civilian nature of ATFERO made it extremely efficient because it ignored red tape and Dorval became a symbol for an operation which soon was spanning the globe. With the entry of the United States into the war, Americans became active partners in developing ferry routes. On the Atlantic run, Goose Bay became the first stepping stone to bases in Greenland and Iceland. The distance of 800 nautical miles between bases meant that aircraft of much shorter range than Hudsons with extra tanks could now fly the new route. Liberators, Hudsons and B-17's flew the old route from Gander while Bostons, Dakotas and the popular Mitchell bombers took the new one. A network of inland routes was also linked to these Altantic bridges. Closer to the west coast, routes were developed for flying aircraft to Russia but this became primarily an American function.

The routes moved south as 50 Marauders and Mitchells were delivered on an ad hoc basis to West Africa where the Desert Air Force was in dire need. This led to an air lift with ammunition and fighters in crates flown into West Africa. The aircraft were reassembled and flown across Africa where both aircraft and ammunition were major factors in the October 1942 Second Battle of El Alamein.

U.S. BECOMING BIG PLAYER

By this time ATFERO had become RAF ferry command primarily because the U.S. was now a big player and the Americans insisted on their pilots delivering aircraft to another military organization. Then in 1943, ferry command was absorbed by Air Transport Command. It was viewed with apprehension by some as "attempting to mix oil with water" but, considering the needs created by global war, it was inevitable. At about the same time the Canadian government hauled an old Lancaster out of Malton and established the Canadian Government Transatlantic Air Service which flew four VIP's and five tons of mail to England twice a week. Jack Barclay and George Lothian, who had been on loan to Ferry Command, became the first to fly what became Trans-Canada's Atlantic schedule.

The first Hudson loss occurred on 20 February 1941, when Joe Mackey, less than an hour out of Gander, turned back with engine trouble. He kept losing height and the heavily laden machine crashed on a frozen lake. Mackey survived with injuries but Sir Frederick Banting, en route to England on scientific work for the government, was killed along with two crew members.

When the flights started pilots returned from the UK by ship. But in mid-1941 BOAC initiated return flights. Three Liberator crashes killed 47 returning aircrew. The cost of building a bridge with wings over the Atlantic never reached anything like the losses originally considered acceptable. But 320 aircrew were killed, including a quarter of all contract pilots. On the plus side they delivered almost 10,000 aircraft of over a dozen varieties to the U.K. and other theatres of operation at a time when they were needed most.

REPRINTED FROM:
Esprit de Corps, *Volume 2 Issue 8*
AUTHOR: *Norman Shannon*

WHEN THE *JERVIS BAY* PROMISED TO DO ITS BEST

Outgunned, the armed merchantman shot it out with a pocket battleship.

The journey for Atlantic convoys was most dangerous at night, when German ships, especially U-boats, could prowl the surface unseen. On 5 November 1940, the merchant ship Jervis Bay *took on the pocket battleship* Admiral Scheer *and lost.* (IMPERIAL WAR MUSEUM)

HALIFAX, 28 OCTOBER 1940. Commander Richard Oland was pleased that the convoy conference went so well. For the 37 merchant captains of HX 84 it was not only an essential briefing session but their presence in the board room also introduced the human factor to the parade of ships which would soon be leaving Halifax harbour. The masters were not foreign names now but people. Towards the end of the conference, Captain Fogarty Fegen, skipper of the RN's armed merchant cruiser *Jervis Bay,* concluded his remarks: "Should we have the unlikely bad luck to cross the path of a pocket battleship, I can only promise to do my best."

The *Cornish City* led the procession past Sambro lighthouse and radio silence descended as the convoy challenged the Atlantic where 217 merchant ships had been sunk since July. The silence was maintained until 5 November when a messenger rushed to Oland's office with the message: *"Cornish City being gunned. Latitude 52 30 N 32 W."* As other messages trickled in the profile of a disaster and extreme heroism took shape.

Arctic twilight was descending at the point on the map which was 275 miles southwest of Greenland when Fogerty Fegen moved the *Jervis Bay* to the head of the convoy while laying smoke that the convoy could scatter. Fegen then ordered the *Jervis Bay* towards a spot on the horizon which became the German pocket battleship *Admiral Scheer*. The armed merchantman had just received a refit in Saint John. Some 30 of the crew were Canadians and Newfoundlanders.

One of the crew, Bob Squires, later remembered taking his position at one of the *Bay's* seven guns. "We didn't know what ship we were going to engage," Squires recalled years later. "The convoy scattered and we tried to get as close as possible to the enemy. The guns we had were made in 1899 or 1900." The *Bay* carried seven six-inch guns while the *Sheer* mounted six 11-inch guns and several smaller ones.

"But Captain Fegen took on the German battleship and the enemy fired three salvoes of armour-piercing shells. One hit under the gun I was on and put it out of action." The *Jervis Bay* was soon burning amidships. Squires didn't see the skipper again. Fegen's arm was blown off but he refused to go below.

Squires remembers a burning ship on a dark sea but the men stayed at their post until the ship sank. "I was all sweating and hot with the ship all afire – everything was happening so fast and the thing that scared most of us was the water – the cold water. There were too many men on the raft... I couldn't get on so I just hung onto the ropes." There were originally 80 men on the raft but only 30 were picked up alive.

The Swedish freighter *Stureholm* had escaped in the smoke screen laid by the *Jervis Bay.* At 2100 hours the crew saw an SOS coming from a flashlight and two hours later picked up 20 men from the *Jervis Bay* raft.

ABOVE: *Life on the North Atlantic was a wet, cold, uncomfortable one. A messenger waits in the radio room of a merchant ship, hoping that no wireless message needed to be taken to the bridge until he thaws out.* (PAINTING BY TOM WOOD, CANADIAN WAR MUSEUM)

There were 13 Canadians among the survivors. Throughout the night recurring gunfire and pillars of burning fuel marked the passing of merchantmen but the heroic stand of the *Jervis Bay* had kept casualties down to five of the 37 merchantmen. Captain Fegen won a posthumous Victoria Cross and the sacrifice of the *Jervis Bay* was a tremendous factor in bringing the war home to Atlantic Canada.

AUTHOR: *Norman Shannon*

1941 - THE WIDENING CONFLICT

Despite some initial setbacks in North Africa and the Mediterranean, the Axis forces continued to expand their conquests and appeared invincible. By mid-summer German forces had captured Yugoslavia and Greece with relative ease. and launched a massive offensive deep into Russia. U-boat wolf packs threatened Britain's Atlantic lifeline and Rommel reigned supreme in the desert. On 7 December, the Japanese attacked the United States fleet at Pearl Harbour and the Pacific was soon engulfed in conflict.

5 FEBRUARY British forces take Benghazi and capture 20,000 Italian troops, culminating a succesful offensive to Libya.

8 FEBRUARY Germany deploys the first Panzer division, under General Rommel, to North Africa.

6 APRIL Germany invades Greece and Yugoslavia. Six days later Belgrade is captured and by month's end all British troops have been pushed out of Greece.

20-28 MAY German paratroops assault Crete and after heavy fighting capture the Island.

26 MAY The Royal Navy's hunt for Germany's *Bismarck* ends in the sinking of the great battleship.

22 JUNE Three million German (and Axis) troops launch Operation Barbarossa into Russia. Within four months the Germans captured over one million prisoners, occupied Smolensk, besieged Leningrad and were threatening Moscow.

19 AUGUST British attempt to relieve the Garrison in Tobruk after Rommel's Afrika Korps encircled it.

2 OCTOBER Germans launch major offensive to capture Moscow Within two weeks they are 40 miles from Russian capital.

30 OCTOBER Canadian contingent sails for Hong Kong to garrison the remote British colony.

6 DECEMBER After German offensive falters, Russians launch counter-attacks outside Moscow.

7 DECEMBER Pearl Harbour is attacked by Japanese bombers. The United States Pacific fleet is crippled – but America is now at war.

10 DECEMBER Japanese troops besiege Hong Kong.

25 DECEMBER Hong Kong surrenders.

RIGHT:
The final fight of the Bismarck. *After sinking the battleship HMS* Hood, *the "unsinkable" Bismarck was hunted by the entire British home fleet.*

FAR RIGHT:
German paratroops land on the Island of Crete. This operation was one of the largest airborne assault of the war.

BARBAROSSA

BELOW: *Although Germany's invasion of Russia would not be the success Hitler hoped for, by September 1940 Germans claimed the destruction of four Russian armies and the taking of over 600,000 prisoners, their vehicles and guns.*

Hitler's invasion of Russia was named after a German king who led his knights to the Crusades.

HISTORY'S MOST MASSIVE INVASION was named after the German hero of the Middle Ages. Barbarossa was the popular name of Frederick I who led Teutonic knights against Moslem armies in the Holy Land. Ominously for modern-day German warriors, Barbarossa never reached his destination, but drowned somewhere in Asia Minor.

From the outset, the nature of this campaign was dictated by the megalomaniacal leaders on either side. Hitler was puffed up by the surprisingly easy victories in the West and refused to entertain any hint of restraint or realism on the part of his generals. He also failed to make clear what the specific objectives of the offensive would be, and instead modified them on an ongoing basis, sowing further confusion and error. As a result of his racist views, any sympathy that the Wermacht might have naturally engendered among the disgruntled Ukranians, was turned to revenge by the brutality of the SS.

REINS OF POWER

Like Hitler, Stalin had the reins of power firmly in his grasp. While this may have been efficient for making decisions, it prevented the input of wiser counsel. Stalin had a wealth of information on his desk revealing precisely what the Germans were up to and when it would occur. But, either through wishful thinking or some unfathomable dark design, he studiously ignored it all. His generals were prevented from taking even the most rudimentary preventive measures. The NKVD (secret police) made everyone too nervous to even hint that Stalin might be wrong.

At 0300 hours on 22 June 1941, the Luftwaffe attacked the Red navy base at Sevastopol, Crimea. German bombers followed, destroying neatly arrayed Soviet planes on the ground. German artillery erupted along the entire front and, at daybreak, 162 divisions (3 million men), poured across a 2000 mile front that stretched from northern Finland to the Black Sea.

The size of the offensive is difficult to comprehend even today. For Stalin, who had ignored all warnings of impending attack, and his shaken government, the difficulty had to be overcome for the sake of survival. Until noon that day, Soviet radio continued to play "keep fit" music while shells and bombs dropped on front line villages and towns. By the time the Kremlin announced that Russia was at war, the Red air force had lost 1200 planes, and German panzers were driving their pincers deep into Soviet territory. By the end of July, Army Group Centre, under Field Marshal Feder von Bock, would capture Smolensk and accept the surrender of 390,000 prisoners, 4500 tanks and 3300 guns. Army Group North (Leeb) and South (Runstedt) had similar success.

Some German officers, however, realized that the victories did not destroy Russia's potential, and every mile gained only made the supply lines longer, the troops more tired, and the limitless front dangerously wider.

AUTHOR: *James G. Scott*

THE ORDEAL OF SC-42

Moving at a vulnerable five knots per hour, a slow convoy of 64 ships leaves Sydney, Nova Scotia, and is spread over 25 miles of ocean when attacked. Their heavy losses set the pattern for months to come.

AN EXPLOSION RIPPED THE BELLY OUT OF THE TANKER *MUNERIC* AND SHE SANK WITH ALL HANDS.

ABOVE LEFT:
Known for the monocle he sported, Commander J.S.D. Prentice is on record for the first submarine kill by a member of the Canadian Forces in the Second World War. (DND)

ABOVE RIGHT:
Seeing rocket flares in the distance, HMCS Chambly *(left) quickly came to the aid of SC-42. The* Chambly *would go on to have one of the best fighting records in the Royal Canadian Navy during WWII.* (DND)

AFTER SUCCESSIVE CANADIAN governments had chosen to base their defence policies on financial, rather than strategic considerations, the version of the Royal Canadian Navy which ventured forth to contest the North Atlantic sea lanes was deficient in numbers, equipment, training and time. Their role in this epic struggle did not allow for the luxury of a long careful build-up and meticulous preparation. The RCN had to join the battle in the condition she found herself, but like the merchantmen she shepherded across that murderous ocean, one thing she had in great abundance was courage.

It was certainly not pay that kept men crossing the icy bridge from the New Word to the Old. Canadian merchantmen received $75 per month and $44.50 as war risk bonus. The conditions and dangers could never be compensated for, and would only slowly be mitigated by the development of the navy.

SLOW CONVOY

In September of 1941 that development was still a long way off and the escort of Slow Convoy-42 (SC-42) had its work cut out for it. Among the three corvettes and the destroyer that made up the escort, there was no radar, and one corvette, HMCS *Kenogami*, was brand new.

The destroyer, HMCS *Skeena*, under Lieutenant Commander Jim Hibbard, led the 64 ship convoy out of Sydney, Nova Scotia on 30 August. The assembly spread over 25 square miles in 12 columns and averaged a stately five knots. For a quiet week the great mass of ships wallowed along without incident, until the evening of 9 September.

TRAGIC MOMENT

HMCS *Skeena* led the way with *Kenogami*, *Orillia* and *Alberni* at the quarter stations. Suddenly, an explosion ripped the belly out of the tanker *Muneric* and she sank with all hands. *Kenogami* turned first and narrowly missed the same fate. She sighted a U-boat at 1000 yards and fired her deck gun, but she was recalled because of another sighting. Commander J.S.D. Prentice was desperately signalling evasive manoeuvres as a third U-boat slashed between columns. A second and third ship erupted in flames and a tragic moment of decision had arrived.

Overhead a glaring moon outlined doomed ships, and any attempt to stop and rescue drowning comrades would only aid the enemy. The escorts gave what assistance they could, but no sooner would one ship be torn asunder than another geyser of flame and shattered metal would mark the desperate struggles of another crew. Before a cloud bank gave shelter of darkness, seven ships would end their journey in the icy black water off the Greenland coast. HMCS *Orillia* left the convoy with the tanker *Tahchee* in tow. Though torpedoed, she was still afloat and every ship and her cargo was worth the chance in those desperate days.

ABOVE:
In an attempt to force the marauding U-boat to rise or sink, the first two in a pattern of depth charges are launched. Each heavy drum had a 300-pound charge and fired at pre-set depths. The explosion created a tremendous concussion wave which could crack open the pressure hulls of a submarine. (DND)

A LUMBERING HULK

HMCS *Skeena*, meanwhile, had been alerted to one of the raiders by a merchantman's machine guns blazing at a conning tower. The U-boat was between the rows of ships and *Skeena* raced off in pursuit. The U-boat cut across one column and slithered down the next, passing *Skeena* in the opposite direction. At this point the convoy proceeded to execute a turn and the destroyer found her erstwhile charges bearing down on her instead. From the gloom a lumbering hulk was only avoided by "full astern" and some expert seamanship. *Skeena* danced free only to witness another explosion and smoky cenotaph raised over the Atlantic.

The next day gave all too short a breathing space to count losses. *Tahchee* was still underway to Iceland with *Orillia*, but the *Muneric, Empire Springbuck, Baron Pentland, Winterswijk, Stargaard,* and others were no more. *Thistleglen* went down at noon. *Skeena, Alberni* and *Kenogami* joined in depth charging over an asdic contact, but only a "probable kill" was recorded. Two more ships were lost before the escort was reinforced.

THE LARGE NUMBER OF LOSSES OF LATE 1941 WERE NOT THE FIRST FOR THE ALLIED NAVIES NOR THE LAST. TWO MORE YEARS OF STRUGGLE AND TRAGEDY WOULD PASS BEFORE THE SEA ADVANTAGE WAS GAINED.

TRAINING CRUISE

Engaged in a training cruise off Greenland, the two corvettes, HMCS *Chambly* and *Moose Jaw* would get a chance to use their training sooner than they expected. *Chambly*, under Commander J.D. Prentice made for two white rockets on the horizon. As *Moose Jaw*, under Lieutenant Fred Grubb, made speed to follow along, two more rockets, signalling a torpedoed ship, rose from the ocean surface.

Within minutes, *Chambly* picked up an asdic echo and dropped a pattern of depth charges. A second pattern proved unnecessary as U-501 broke the surface and crossed *Moose Jaw*'s bow at 400 yards. Guns blazing, the little corvette bore down on the sub in preparation for ramming, but this also seemed unnecessary. U-501 stopped dead in the water. *Moose Jaw* came along side and the German captain leapt from his bridge to the ship's deck.

TOO GOOD TO PASS UP

The sub's crew was now on deck and refused to accompany the boarding party back down below, even at gunpoint. It was obvious that the sub was rigged for scuttling, but the prize seemed too good not to at least take a look inside. As the Canadians searched the interior for intelligence data, the sub lurched and settled, sending the party scrambling for the exits. All escaped except stoker W.I. Brown who drowned with 11 of the German crew.

The battle for survival of SC-42 was still on, and the reinforcements provided little help. After midnight, SS *Stonepool* went down, then the *Berury*. Between 02:00 and 02:30 hrs, the *Scania, Empire Crossbill* and *Garm* joined their unfortunate compatriots. U-85 was depth-charged by *Kenogami*, but escaped, as did the remainder of the eight-boat wolf pack who feasted on SC-42. Not until British escorts and air cover from Iceland arrived did the survivors sail freely into port.

HMCS *LEVIS* SUNK

The same month, on 19 September, the RCN lost its first corvette. HMCS *Levis*, part of the escort for SC-44, was struck on the port side by a torpedo and split down her side. Forty survivors were picked up by *Mayflower* and *Agassiz*.

The losses of late 1941 were not the first for the Allied navies nor the last, and two years of struggle and tragedy in that most unforgiving front of the war would pass before the advantage was gained. After December, the Americans would officially be in the war, (their navy was barely active in the Atlantic at first), but they would learn lessons similar to the RCN. Without keeping up-to-date equipment, training, and technology the price paid far exceeded the dollars saved.

REPRINTED FROM:
Esprit de Corps, *Volume 1 Issue 5*
AUTHOR: *James G. Scott*

LEFT: *Raymond Collishaw was a fighter pilot ace in WWI, and in WWII he added to his reputation by commanding successful air operations in North Africa.*

A major challenge to Richthofen's Jastas, 24 years later Raymond Collishaw crippled the Italian Air Force...

COMBAT AND COMMAND

"NEVER BEFORE IN THE field of human conflict has one man done so much and is remembered by so few." The quote says volumes about Raymond Collishaw, the virtually unknown Canadian airman who was credited with at least 60 victories and commanded a squadron in WWI. By the fall of 1940, Air Commodore Collishaw was at the point in another war as he commanded ten RAF squadrons in North Africa which literally crippled the Italian Air Force.

Ray Collishaw left his job on the Fisheries Protection Service on the west coast and came to Toronto to learn to fly at the Curtiss School during the summer of 1915. The school closed for the winter before he got off the ground. Fortunately the Royal Navy worked out a deal whereby candidates for the Royal Naval Air Service were assigned to *HMCS Niobe* until they could be accommodated overseas.

By August 1916, Collishaw was assigned to Three Wing where he flew a Sopwith 1.1/2 strutter to Luxeuil. The base was located in south-eastern France where delivery of aircraft was slow, and operations long delayed.

OCTOBER RAID

Collishaw took part in a raid on Oberndorf in October and, shortly afterwards, was ferrying a Sopwith to a new base without a gunner when jumped by six enemy fighters. Their initial blast shattered his cockpit instruments and goggles. Semi-blind, he flung the Sopwith about and one overly enthusiastic enemy pilot crashed into a tree as he pursued the Canadian deeper into Germany. Eventually the enemy scouts abandoned the chase and Collishaw turned for home, using the sun to navigate.

When his eyes cleared, he saw an airfield and decided to put down for gasoline and directions. As he touched down the row of aircraft in front of a tent hanger became more familiar because they bore black crosses on their fuselage. The Sopwith picked up speed and, with a few eager bumps, sought a more convivial portion of the wild blue yonder.

Collishaw had goggle trouble again some three months later. By then he was flying on the Western Front with Squadron Commander Redford Mulock's Naval Three. In an engagement with enemy fighters at 17,000 feet his gun jammed – a regular occurrence at the time – and once again enemy bullets shattered his goggles. He reached around the windscreen while trying to clear the guns and froze his face.

Bloody April had reached its zenith before Collishaw was released from hospital and became a flight commander with Naval Ten.

ABOVE: *Known as the Queen of the Battlefield because her 78 mm armour was invulnerable to the Italians' artillery, the Matildas ruled the desert until the arrival of powerful German anti-tank guns. (IWM)* **OPPOSITE PAGE:** *General Sir Richard O'Connor commanded the 8th Army in North Africa. Collishaw provided tactical air support to O'Connor's successful offensive.*

CHILLY DIP

According to Collishaw, the action on the Western Front came as a bit of a shock to the pilots who considered themselves to be "slightly hot stuff." His book, *Air Command,* says the transition was "like plunging into an ice-cold bath after paddling about in a heated swimming pool."

But they adapted quickly on Naval Ten where 13 of 15 squadron pilots were Canadians who flew the Sopwith Triplane, and Collishaw scored his fifth victory on their first patrol out of the Dunkirk area.

Nowhere did the image of Canadian fighter pilots find greater expression than in the Black Flight which moved into Droglandt. As a reaction to the brightly coloured aircraft of Richthofen's circus, Collishaw's all-Canadian flight was satisfied to paint portions of their aircraft black and become known as the Black Flight. Collishaw had *Black Maria* stencilled below the rim of his cockpit. Ellis Reid was *Black Roger;* John Sharman became *Black Death* while Gerry Nash flew *Black Sheep* and Mel Alexander reigned as *Black Prince.*

BLACK FLIGHT

On 6 June the Black Flight engaged 17 enemy aircraft and, in a 35-minute duel, destroyed five and sent five down out of control. That month Collishaw added 16 enemy aircraft to his total. Gerry Nash was shot down by German ace Karl Allmenroder on 24 June and taken prisoner. Three days later Nash heard church bells ring in the village where he was being held.

A guard told Nash the bells were ringing for Allmenroder's funeral. The German pilot had been shot down by Collishaw. Oddly enough, Collishaw had fired a distant burst at an Albatros on 27 June. It staggered and went into a long glide but Collishaw did not pursue nor claim a victory.

On 6 July Collishaw led his flight into a battle in which some 30 of Richthofen's fighters were attacking half a dozen Fe2D's. The Fee two-seaters had circled the wagons and were giving a good account of themselves. The only thing tougher than the aircraft were the men who flew them. Observer Albert Woodbridge was such a man. "I fired my forward and aft guns until they were hot – jumping from one to another," he recalled. He had knocked down four aircraft when two more approached. "Two of them came at us head-on and I think the first one was Richthofen.... I could see my tracers splashing along the barrels of his Spandeaus and I knew the pilot was sitting right behind them."

Richthofen was hit on the head and tumbled blindly downward, enduring the agony of death without its release. He recovered in time to land behind his lines but the experience would haunt him for the rest of his numbered days. Meanwhile, Collishaw's flight swept down and Collishaw got six hostiles while Mel Alexander and Ellis Reid each got two. The air war intensified as the ground war bogged in the mud of Passchendaele, and pilots were on call or in the air from dawn until dusk. Naval Ten accounted for 79 machines in six weeks and, according to Collishaw, the summer had become "strictly a war of attrition and it was simply a question of who was going to give out first…"

RAYMOND COLLISHAW TOOK COMMAND OF NAVAL THREE IN LATE JANUARY 1918. IN SPITE OF THE ADMINISTRATIVE DUTIES WHICH THE COMMAND IMPOSED, HE MANAGED TO SCORE 19 MORE VICTORIES BEFORE THE ARMISTICE TO BRING HIS TOTAL UP TO 59.

Collishaw took command of Naval Three in late January 1918. In spite of the administrative duties which the command imposed, he managed to score 19 more victories before the Armistice to bring his total up to 59. While on duty in Russia in 1919, Collishaw was credited with a Red machine.

NORTH AFRICA

He remained in the RAF and the day Italy struck at the British in North Africa, Air Commodore Collishaw commanded what later became the Desert Air Force. He had set up his headquarters at Maaten Baggush, some 160 miles from the Libyan border. His role essentially was to provide an advanced defence network for Alexandria, Cairo and the Suez Canal.

He had nine squadrons of Blenheims, Gladiators and Lysanders while the Italians in Libya had some 400 aircraft on well-serviced stations near Tripoli, Benghazi and Tobruk. After Italy's treacherous declaration of war on the allies on 10 June 1940, Collishaw launched a strike on El Adem, an airfield near Tobruk. One squadron reported that their bombs fell on a parade ground while a ceremonial parade celebrating Italy's entry into the war was in progress. There was little ceremony about the way the parade dissolved. Next day Collishaw's aircraft struck Tobruk harbour and seriously damaged the cruiser *San Giordo* which was mother ship to Italian submarines.

The following day, Victoria native Woody Woodward shot down his first bomber and then a fighter; he would round out his string at 20 destroyed and five probables. Woodward was a member of the cattleboat brigade who joined the RAF in the late 30's and Collishaw had many of them in his command. Collishaw's superior, Air Chief Marshal Sir Arthur Longmore, was responsible for 4.5 million square miles of territory with very limited resources. Collishaw had sustained some losses during the first few days and Longmore asked him to fight a less aggressive war because he saw little chance of replacing parts, aircraft and, above all, crews. Collishaw's pilots took a dim view of being muzzled and Collishaw then embarked on a campaign of psychological warfare and deception to outfox the enemy and maintain morale.

BOMBAY BOMBERS

When somebody found a store of ancient fragmentation bombs, Colly had them put in boxes and loaded them onto lumbering Bombay Transports for nightly excursions over enemy encampments. Each aircraft had 200 unstable bombs which had to be fused in flight. They were then tossed out one bomb at a time, and. The entire process took about four hours which meant the aircraft had to be refuelled in flight. The empty fuel drums where then tossed overboard and the consensus grew that the drums did more damage to the enemy than the bombs. But the operation kept the enemy awake and the offensive spirit alive.

An ancient Hurricane called "Colly's Battleship" was dragged from field to field and left exposed to the lens of Italian reconnaissance cameras. Collishaw also started a cottage industry among Jewish settlers in Palestine who built a host of wooden aircraft to be scattered around advanced airfields.

Marshal Graziani moved some 215,000 Italian troops 60 miles closer and the British retired an equal distance, losing several forward landing strips. But instead of pursuing the attack, Graziani spent three months building substantial fortifications. On the allied side of the line, the army commander, General Sir Richard O'Connor, and Collishaw occupied adjacent huts and developed a strong rapport.

ABOVE:
When Italy entered the war, the Royal Air Force had but a few Gloster Gladiator fighters available to cover the north African desert in 1940, plus some Blenheim light bombers, and Wellington and Bombay medium bombers.
(IMPERIAL WAR MUSEUM)

NEW WARFARE

The relationship between the two men established a new level of army-airforce cooperation and set the tone for a new form of warfare which later became the 2nd Tactical Air Force. Both remembered the lessons of 1918 when close air support almost enabled the Germans to break through to the coast. One of the major reasons the enemy drive failed was because airfields did not advance with the troops and air support suffered. Both commanders agreed that their drive to dislodge Graziani would be a drive to re-establish the airfields lost in the British retreat. The plan for OPERATION COMPASS – a major British thrust at Graziani – became a war for airdromes.

OPERATION COMPASS

The night before O'Connor's ground attack, Collishaw borrowed a page from 1918 when the Australians and Canadians broke out of Amiens as bombers drowned out the sound of assembling tanks. Collishaw had Bristol Bombays pounding a beat where O'Connor's Matilda tanks were being assembled. The tanks swept through Graziani's encampments and drove the Italians back 250 miles to Bengazi and beyond. Collishaw's bombers struck Italian airfields while fighters screened the battle area and swept the way ahead for advancing troops.

On the opening day of the attack, George Keefer, of Charlottetown, shot down his first enemy and would add 17 more during his 400 operational hours.

O'Connor destroyed 10 Italian Divisions in two months and 1,100 Italian aircraft were abandoned or destroyed. Collishaw's meagre forces crippled the Italian Air Force for a loss of 26 aircraft from all causes, but it should be remembered that O'Connor's rampaging troops were a big factor in Italian aircraft losses.

The supreme moment in RAF-Army cooperation was short lived. Although O'Connor ended up 200 miles beyond Tobruk, he didn't get the support he needed to deliver a knock-out punch.

Churchill had long been thirsting for a foothold in Greece but Greek Premier Mextaxas refused to accept troops because he feared German retaliation, but he did accept five squadrons which came from Collishaw's group. Mextaxas died of a heart attack a month later, and Churchill convinced his successor to take troops which were drawn from O'Connor's meagre 40,000.

With a victory within his grasp, O'Connor was forced to break off without securing Tripoli. General Erwin Rommel's troops had just arrived in Tripoli and he and his officers failed to understand why the British had not been more aggressive.

Greece continued to drain away Collishaw's squadrons. In April, he was given command of a new group formed back at Maaten Baggush where his Wellingtons became involved in the milkrun to Benghazzi. Although Collishaw left North Africa in 1942, his rapport with the army commander and his determination to provide for army needs set a standard which was later evidenced as airpower became a major factor in driving Rommel out of Africa, and the 2nd Tactical Air Force blasted the Falaise Gap closed.

REPRINTED FROM:
Esprit de Corps, *Volume 7 Issue 10*
AUTHOR:
Norman Shannon

THE RAID ON SPITZBERGEN

Canadian troops escape the boredom of inactivity in England when they stage a raid on enemy-held territory to destroy coal and petroleum supplies.

ABOVE:
Codenamed Operation GAUNTLET, soldiers and engineers from Canada, Britain and Norway were sent to the remote archipelago of Spitzbergen to destroy mine machinery and radio stations, burn coal stocks and evacuate 2800 residents. (DND PHOTO)

THE SUMMER OF 1941 was a fateful one in North Africa and the Ukraine, but for the thousands of Canadians doing yeoman's duties in England, their inactivity was a blow to their pride and enthusiasm. The aborted plan to send Canadians to Norway in April, and the mad dash to Brest in June of 1940, only made those young men more eager to prove their martial mettle.

The opportunity to do so would not come for another year, but the operation to evacuate Spitzbergen, and deny its use to the enemy, offered some small consolation.

The island was located 760 kilometres northwest of Norway, and of limited strategic value. Originally, the British intended to establish a naval anchorage from which they could support the Murmansk convoys and harass German forces sent to disrupt them. General Andrew McNaughton and the Canadian Corps were asked to supply a brigade (minus one battalion) and supporting services, including two 50-bed field hospitals, a company of engineers and signals section. The major units would be from the Princess Patricia's Canadian Light Infantry and the Loyal Edmonton Regiment.

BRITISH DOUBTS

On 5 and 6 August this force was transported from Surrey to Glasgow, and thence to the Combined Training Centre at Inverary aboard the *Empress of Canada*. However, before this stage was completed, the British Chiefs of Staff Committee began to have doubts about the entire operation. A reconnaissance report by Rear Admiral Philip Vian ruled out the possibility of a base on lonely Spitzbergen. He confirmed his opinion in person on 9 August, and the general assessment was that placing a garrison, even for the four-month period originally planned, had no military value.

On 11 August, Canadian troops were saved from a complete disappointment when the War Office indicated that a reduced operation would still be carried out. McNaughton and his subordinates, Brigadiers A.E. Potts and J.C. Murchie, were informed on 16 August that the priority would be the simple destruction of the coal stocks and mines. Wireless and meteorological stations would be wrecked, Russian miners repatriated, and the Norwegian inhabitants brought back to the U.K.

REMAINING FORCE

The remaining force under Potts consisted of 46 officers and 599 other ranks. To facilitate translation, the Norwegians were represented by a detachment of 25 under Captain Aubert. The British contributed 93 all ranks, mostly Royal Engineers. The remainder were Canadians from the Edmonton Regiment under Major Bury, 3rd Field Company RCE under Major Walsh and a detachment from the Saskatoon Light Infantry (M.G.).

On the morning of 19 August, the *Empress of Canada* steamed from the Clyde on her way to the frozen north. By evening, she joined Force A under Admiral Vian, and the cruisers *Nigeria* and *Aurora*, with destroyers *Anthony, Antelope* and *Icarus*, headed to Iceland to refuel. It was not until 22 August that the Canadian troops were told their destination. To prairie troops on the open ocean, the destination was of little concern as long as it did not roll under their feet.

IMMEDIATE CO-OPERATION

While there is no evidence that the Germans ever intended to exploit Spitzbergen, there was the potential for one million tons per year of coal to fall into their hands and the regular weather reports from the island were an aid to intelligence. In any case, "Force III" approached West Spitzbergen in the early hours of 25 August with prudence. Two Walrus amphibious aircraft reconnoitred the Isfjord (Ice Sound), an inlet which led to the main settlements. At 04:30 hrs, Canadians and Norwegians landed at Kap Linne to secure the communication station. The occupants welcomed their new land-

Canadian sappers stoke the fires on a 150,000 ton pile of coal. (DND)

lords and immediately set to co-operating in the mission. Normal broadcasts continued uninterrupted with the additional information that the area was fogged in; thereby discouraging air reconnaissance by the enemy. These bogus transmissions resulted in the capture of three colliers, a tug, two sealers and a whaling vessel, which were lured into harbour.

Not all Norwegians were pleased at the evacuation and destruction to come. For them the war was distant and they were content to carry on their activities as if nothing extraordinary was happening beyond their shores. However, they were eventually convinced to accept the new plan.

EXCESS FRIENDLINESS

The Russian inhabitants appeared to have had no qualms whatsoever. This was one of the few times that Canadians got to meet their allies and relationships seem to have been friendly to the point of excess. Canadian soldiers were almost embarrassed by the generosity of their new friends, though their chief had some trouble convincing the Russian consul at Barentsburg that there was no time to load heavy machinery along with personal stores.

SPITZBERGEN WAS A GREAT SUCCESS; COMPLETED WITHOUT THE LOSS OF A MAN OR SHIP, AND WITHOUT THE ENEMY'S KNOWLEDGE AT ANY POINT.

The *Empress* sailed away from the land force with *Nigeria* and the three destroyers. *Aurora* was left to defend the remaining craft. One and a half days later, 1955 Russians with 250 tons of baggage and stores, disembarked at Archangel.

In the meanwhile, sappers got busy destroying 450,000 tons of coal and 275,000 gallons of petroleum products (by burning and sea-dumping; wartime apparently mitigates any ecological sense). Demolitions took care of the mine shafts, transportation, machinery and radio masts. Several small craft were sunk in harbour and anything of possible use to the enemy was either disabled or destroyed. Even 600 pigs, in addition to some horses and cattle, fell to the butcher's knife.

Wholly unintended was the fire that destroyed the empty town of Barentsburg near the end of the expedition. An earlier fire had been extinguished, but on 1 September, aided by a steady wind and coal-dust impregnated wooden buildings, a second fire raged out of control and levelled the town.

CANADIANS SAIL FOR ENGLAND

After ten days, the exhausted Canadian troops packed up the remaining Norwegians and set sail for England. Aboard the *Empress* were an additional 186 French soldiers who had escaped German prisoner of war camps, to Russia, where they had been interned.

In the grand scheme of the Second World War, Spitzbergen does not rate much more than a footnote, at least in the strategic view. Tactically, it was a great success; the mission was carried out completely, without the loss of a man or ship, and without the enemy's knowledge at any point. It was not quite like slogging it out toe-to-toe with the *Wehrmacht*, but there would be plenty of time for that.

REPRINTED FROM:
Esprit de Corps, *Volume 1 Issue 4*
AUTHOR:
James G. Scott

SOLDIERING IN BRITAIN, 1940-1945

LEFT: *Men of the Canadian Scottish take a smoke break during a house clearing exercise in England. The endless hours of training would soon prove invaluable.* (NAC/PA 162246)

Endless exercises and route marches in the English countryside would pay off years later in Italy, Normandy and Holland... In the meantime, Canadians griped.

NOT ALL THOSE SERVING in the Canadian armed forces experienced the same wartime Britain between 1939 and 1945. Over the six years of war, Canada's armed forces' build-up on that island fortress was a slow process. The 13th Infantry Brigade, for example, did not arrive in Britain until mid-1944, four and a half years after the 1st, 2nd and 3rd Brigades. By then, these three brigades which comprised the 1st Infantry Division, had been fighting in Sicily and Italy for almost a year, their three and a half years in Britain almost a distant memory.

THINGS WERE DIFFERENT THEN...

For the earliest arrivals of Canada's navy and air force, things had been different. They had seen action in the skies over Europe or on the High Seas while their comrades in khaki sweated it out on gruelling training exercises and lengthy route marches that criss-crossed Surrey, Sussex and Kent, or in barrack life in Aldershot and other reinforcement depots.

Only the 1st Division and elements of the 2nd Division experienced the Battle of Britain, which raged among the clouds from August to October in 1940. By the time the 3rd, 4th and 5th Divisions arrived from Canada with two armoured brigades, the Battle of Britain and the winter blitz on London and other urban centres were memories. The 3rd and 4th Divisions and 2nd Armoured Brigade did in early 1944 experience the V1 and V2 strikes, unlike the 1st and 5th Divisions and the 1st Armoured Brigade did not, which by then were in the Mediterranean.

The year 1940 was an exciting one for the 1st Division. Twice, elements were rushed off to ports for embarkation. One such flurry occurred when a planned attack on Norway was stopped midway, the second when the Canadians were asked to cross to Calais and help hold a shrinking perimeter. That time Canada's General McNaughton landed in France, assessed the situation, and said "No!"

A few days later the 1st Brigade actually landed in France as part of a British force which hoped to block the German advance on Paris. It was too late and, after destroying their vehicles and other equipment, the Canadians crammed on to available ships at Brest and returned to England. The Royal Canadian Horse Artillery managed to save their guns.

Then came the aerial campaign against southern England called the Battle of Britain. Canadian troops were camped directly below this sky war and were bombed and machine-gunned and suffered casualties. With this phase of the war over, and Germany's fighter wings defeated by the RAF's Hurricanes and Spitfires, the enemy turned to the massive night bombing of London and sporadic daylight raids. By May 1941 after one tremendous assault on London during which heavy losses were suffered, the Germans turned their fury on Poland and Russia and life became quite hum-drum in Britain. Occasionally, German planes machine-gunned coastal towns or dropped land mines, but the aerial war was virtually at an end.

DIEPPE RAID

Late Canadian arrivals, either in formed units or in the reinforcement stream, may

ABOVE:
Canadian troops of 1st Division spent the majority of their time on training exercises and route marches in southern England upon their arrival. (NAC/PA 177678)

have found their new environment somewhat exciting, but the 1st Division found 1941, 1942 and the first half of 1943 boring from a military standpoint. Two brief periods of commando-type training in Scotland gave a bit of renewed enthusiasm as it indicated that action somewhere was likely. Of course, 1942 was not dull for the 2nd Division, or the more recently arrived armoured brigade. They trained hard for a given task and in August they carried it out – the disastrous raid on Dieppe. The raid was an epic for those who took part in it, but for the other Canadians it was only someone else's moment in history.

HOME GUARD?

Apart from leave periods, 48-hour passes and absence without leave, life in H-huts, Nissen huts, 19th Century barracks, and under canvas, was enough to brown anybody off. Of course there was pub life, girl friends and recently acquired English and Scottish wives to alleviate the boredom for some. But training had become repetitively boring and General McNaughton's boast that the Canadian Army in Britain was "a dagger pointed at the heart of Berlin" became a joke. The Canadians were sometimes taunted at being no more than a Home Guard. Englishmen, not even in the forces when the first Canadians arrived on their shores, had been fighting and dying in the Western Desert, Crete, Greece, Singapore, Burma and Tunisia for months and even years. So one could hardly blame the average British citizen for wondering why Canada's khaki contribution was playing at soldiers year after year, when obviously fears of a German invasion were long over. Most Canadians were becoming acutely embarrassed.

WAITING JUSTIFIED

Italy, Normandy and the victory campaign in Holland eventually justified the long years of waiting in Britain. These experiences blotted out many memories of the sojourn in England, of the tiring exercises with their 35-mile route marches, or the ten-day vehicle manoeuvres. But some memories remained indelibly in the mind, particularly for those who had become part of the local community, or saw their leave periods as an opportunity to travel the length and breadth of the land, including Scotland. Some enjoyed joining in village life, or acquiring additional "culture" by visiting castles, cathedrals and places of literary or historic interest.

DIVERSIONARY PUB CRAWLS

For those who liked to live a little more wildly there were always the temptations of Piccadilly and Soho. Further afield were Liverpool and Glasgow with their delights for the daring. Coming from a country where at the time liquor laws were strict and drinking looked upon as a vice, Canadian innocents found pub crawls a favourite diversion from camp and barrack life.

I recall in the summer of 1941 taking a junior leader's course at a stately home called Shillinglee Park. Every evening after classes we would walk a couple of miles to the Crown Inn at Chiddingford, an allegedly 600-year old establishment where we were always welcome and the beer was good. Some contacts with civilians were not always pleasant. Farmers particularly did not like to see us cutting down their trees to get "fields of fire," or digging slit trenches in their lawns and gardens, or moving into their outbuildings during tactical exercises, turning them into temporary headquarters and cookhouses. By 1941 most people were convinced that Hitler would never attempt an invasion of England as he was too involved with Russia. However, the military high command was not so sure and, being charged with the defence of their island, they continued to have us turn it into a fortress and gave us the tools to finish the job – picks, shovels and axes, and the landscape suffered.

At the Windmill Theatre in Soho, even during the worst of the blitz, the show ran day and night. The jokers joked, the naked beauties displayed their charms and the audiences applauded as the bombs rained down. In the cinemas, a slide might momentarily obscure the film to announce, "An air raid is in progress. Those who wish to go to the shelter are asked to go quietly so as not to disturb the audience."

DRAGONS' TEETH

Then there were the "dragons' teeth." These huge concrete blocks went up all over England in the early summer of 1940 at crossroads and road junctions and other vital points as anti-tank obstacles, covered by concrete pillboxes designed to house machine-guns when necessary. Then somebody realized that they would also restrict British armour in the counter-attack role against the invaders. So, within weeks of construction, pneumatic drills were busy grinding these barriers into dust. Before this happened I remember a cinema in a small Hampshire town with a row of these outside its parking lot with a sign which read, "For the protection of our patrons we have erected these barriers against enemy tanks." It is difficult to imagine cinema-goers calmly watching a movie with German panzers roaring around outside! But such was the Britain of 1940 and 1941.

REPRINTED FROM:
Esprit de Corps, *Volume 6 Issue 11*
AUTHOR: *Strome Galloway*

THE FALL OF HONG KONG

Untrained Canadians are rushed to the Pacific to defend Hong-Kong, an island already declared indefensible by the British.

ABOVE: *The Canadian disembarkation at Victoria on 16 November 1941 brought hope to the tiny Crown colony of Hong Kong. But without naval support or air cover, its defence was a futile exercise.* (IMPERIAL WAR MUSEUM)

EIGHT MONTHS BEFORE THE infamous debacle at Dieppe, a tragedy of equal proportion befell the Winnipeg Grenadiers and Royal Rifles of Canada. Their numbers were not as large as those of the attacking force on that coast line a world away, but in some ways their tragedy was greater. When British command sent 3900 Canadians up the shingled beaches of that French resort town, it actually expected them to succeed. When they sent the two battalions – later known as C force – to Hong Kong, they expected them to die. Half a century later, a shrinking number of Canadians are still paying the price for higher incompetence.

Up to the advent of war with Japan in 1941, the British did not believe that their colony of Hong Kong could, or even should, be held except for a symbolic period and then abandoned. Strategically, it was merely an outpost and no-one felt that it was defensible. None except Canadian-born Major General A.E. Grasett. When Grasett assumed the post of General Officer Commanding, China, he immediately questioned the philosophy of making Hong Kong expendable. He would spend three years convincing his superiors that he was right, until the Japanese Imperial Army came along to prove him wrong.

DISTORTED VIEWS

British planning had for years rejected putting any effort into the defence of Hong Kong, but in 1941, the growing world crisis and Canada's restrained participation in it, combined to cloud men's judgements. Grasett found himself in Ottawa in July of 1941 and while there met with his Royal Military College (Kingston) classmate, Chief of Canadian General Staff, Major General H.D.G. Crerar. Whether accurately or not, Grasett came away with the belief that his tactical theories had Canadian support. When he reported this to his superiors, his view was magnified, distorted and finally taken as a Canadian duty without another consideration of its suicidal nature. The politicians saw the political advantages. Canadian troops in action would send Japan a message and bolster Chinese morale, but the generals failed to make clear the military disadvantages.

The selection process also broke down. The first plan called for highly trained battalions, but this would have disrupted the activities of the 4th Division, just then forming for overseas duty. In the end, the Winnipeg Grenadiers and Royal Rifles of Canada were chosen because they both had some garrison duty. It was felt that manning a fortress was about all these troops would be doing.

FINE LINEAGE

The Grenadiers had spent 16 months in Jamaica, where illness and lack of tactical training left the unit below par. They were led to Hong Kong by Lieutenant Colonel J.L.R. Sutcliffe. The Royal Rifles were possessed of a fine lineage dating back to 1862, but in this war their guard duties had not allowed a great deal of time for large formation tactical training. Their Commanding Officer (CO) was Lieutenant Colonel William J. Home, MC. Both officers were considered competent. Given more time and adequate equipment these units might have served well in another theatre.

With a bit of a push from the British War Office, the Canadians got ready to sail aboard the *Awatea* at the end of October. Last minute additions (many with less than the required 16 weeks of basic training) fleshed out the Grenadiers, but motorized transport never did arrive. It was placed aboard a second ship which got no further than the doomed Philippines.

Grasett's replacement did not seem particularly thrilled to see the Canadians at all. Major General C.M. Maltby, an Indian Army Officer, already held a low opinion of the 2nd Royal Scots, and the apparent lack of training for his latest charges should have given him pause. Maltby, however, thought little of his Japanese opponents and set up his defence at the 'Gin Drinkers Line.'

ARTILLERY OBSOLETE

This first line of defence on the mainland was to be held by the Royal Scots for at least one week. The 2/14 Punjabs and 5/7 Rajputs were to assist them, with demolition teams destroying targets in front. Not only was the line still incomplete but it

would have needed at least four battalions to fight the intended delaying action and seven to hold the eleven miles for any appreciable length of time. The 1st Middlesex and two Canadian battalions were held on the island along with the collective air cover: three Vickers *Wildebeestes* and a pair of *Walrus* amphibians. The artillery was mostly obsolete, with the coastal guns firing armour piercing shells of little use against infantry. Until 8 December none of this really mattered.

Maltby issued a warning and ordered his men to war stations well before the actual attack. When the 'hammer' fell there was little that the tiny force could do. The US Navy was settling into the mud of their Hawaiian base as the Japanese Army was preparing to conquer the British Crown colony.

Expecting stiffer resistance, the Japanese took their time approaching the 'Gin Drinkers Line' and would have settled in for a protracted battle but for the initiative of Colonel Doi of the 228th Regiment. Reconnaissance showed that the Shing Mun Redoubt was lightly held and a quick rush on the night of 9 December delivered the key to the entire line into Japanese hands. Golden and Black Hills followed as the Royal Scots tumbled back toward the island of Hong Kong. By 13 December, the two Indian battalions were evacuated to the Island from their now untenable positions, and the Japanese once again halted to assess the ease with which their attack had succeeded. Though they had lost 400 casualties, they surely must have expected many more. In any case they were well ahead of schedule.

CANADIANS BAFFLED

The Canadians were equally baffled as to why the mainland positions could so easily have been given up. Things were obviously not going according to plan, but they could do nothing but prepare for the next phase.

The Mainland/Island split in the forces was now reorganized as East and West brigades. The Royal Rifles and Rajputs were in the East Brigade under Brigadier Cedric Wallis. The Grenadiers, Punjabs and Royal Scots under Brigadier Lawson were in the western half of the island with the Middlesex manning 72 coastal pillboxes.

After a peace mission was rejected, the Japanese began a systematic shelling of Hong Kong. Heavy bombers joined in and strains began to show among the troops, especially the Hong Kong Volunteer Force among whom there was some variation in dedication.

A week of shelling and bombardment followed the British eviction from the mainland and made life very difficult for the defenders. The Rajputs on the northeastern shoreline seemed to get the worst of it and it was obvious any landing would come here. Maltby ignored the topography and lack of transport and left his forces fairly scattered over the entire island. The Grenadiers were positioned in the west at Little Hong Kong, Aberdeen, and Pok Fu Lam. Reserve and Headquarters were in Wong Nei Chong Gap and Wan Chai Gap respectively. In the east, the Royal Rifles would attempt to hold a perimeter of 15 miles.

UNIT DISINTEGRATED

The Japanese landed three regiments on the Rajputs' front on 18 December. Having endured five days of bombardment, this unit disintegrated and streamed back through the Canadian positions. Their officers and NCO's had died to the last man, and the smoke, dark and rain proved too much for the half-trained recruits. The enemy was now ashore in force and their next opponent would be "C" Company of the Royal Rifles.

Upon being informed of that Fort Sai Wan was occupied by enemy forces, Major W.A. Bishop requested reinforcements from Brigade Headquarters to mount a counterattack. He was informed that there were only friendly forces there and no reinforce-

OPPOSITE PAGE, LEFT:
"General Attack on Hong Kong," by Japanese artist Hoshun Yamaguchi. Viewed from high ground in Kowloon, the modern buildings of Victoria burn across the bay. (CAPTURED JAPANESE ART, U.S. ARMY CENTER OF MILITARY HISTORY)
OPPOSITE PAGE, RIGHT:
On 19 December 1941, CSM John Osborn led his Winnipeg Grenadiers in the capture of Mount Butler from the Japanese at bayonet point. Forced to withdraw and completely surrounded, Osborn returned the grenades the Japanese threw at their position. Unable to reach one of them, he shouted a warning as he fell on the grenade. Taking the full impact of the explosion, he was killed instantly. He was the first Canadian to win a Victoria Cross in WWII. (NAC/PA 37403)

ABOVE:
Positioned atop Jardine's Lookout, the Japanese artillery continues its assault. (IMPERIAL WAR MUSEUM)

ments would be forthcoming. Relations with Brigade did not improve thereafter and only Bishop's handling of "C" Coy prevented a disaster. By skillfully maneouvring and personally inspiring his men, Bishop was able to slow the Japanese advance toward HQ at Tai Tam Gap.

CORNERED

The enemy was deflected from an easy victory by the stalwart efforts of the Royal Rifles, but the fate of the garrison was inevitable. The Eastern Brigade found itself, at the end of the day, cornered, demoralized, and without artillery.

The Western Brigade fared no better. Platoons were being sent to oppose battalions, and scattered battalions were later blamed for being unable to contain concentrated regiments. British officers tried to blame Canadian troops for the growing disaster, but Canadians were bearing the brunt of the Japanese offensive. The Rajputs were decimated in the initial landings. The Royal Scots were destroyed in the first day of battle, and the Middlesex remained in a static defensive role. It was up to the Canadians to hold or attack throughout the final week.

Mount Butler was the scene of the battle's only Victoria Cross. CSM John Osborn led part of his company to the peak and captured it at bayonet point. Japanese numbers pushed them from this position and Osborn covered the withdrawal under heavy fire. Surrounded, the company fought from a low depression where Osborn threw back Japanese grenades. His luck ran out when he threw himself on an inaccessible one, which killed him instantly.

HEROIC DEFENCE

The defence of the Wong Nei Chong Gap lasted until 22 December. Companies of the Royal Rifles had attempted to restore contact to the Western Brigade, but despite some success at Gauge Basin, their numbers were just too small to continue any offensive. The defence of Wong Nei Chong, mostly by "D" Coy of the Grenadiers, was nothing less than heroic. The fall of Mount Cameron, however, opened the road to Victoria, and when "A" Coy of the Rifles was overrun at Repulse Bay in the south, time was obviously running out.

On Christmas Day 1941, the defenders rejected another Japanese offer of surrender in the morning, but by 15:00 hours resistance had already been replaced with exhaustion. In the shrinking southern perimeter, "D" Coy of the RRC made one last desperate rush to restore the line at Stanley. Through a shower of artillery, the Canadians succeeded in coming to grips with their enemy but it was too little, too late. British artillery failed to support and the Canadians fell back again with 70 per cent casualties. At 00:45 hours, 26 December, a formal surrender was agreed upon and resistance everywhere ceased.

JAPANESE NEGLECT AND CRUELTY

Of the 1975 Canadians who were sent to Hong Kong as "C Force," 227 died in the subsequent, futile defence of that island. But the ordeal did not end with surrender; for many, it is where it began. The Japanese showed no compunction for killing prisoners outright, though only 13 died as a direct result of capture. The real tragedy was the neglect and cruelty that followed. Two hundred and sixty-seven Canadians died of malnutrition or mistreatment during four years of captivity. For years afterward our own government refused to recognize the extraordinary circumstances these men had to endure. No apology has ever come from the Japanese and only miserly pensions and "guilt" money has come from Ottawa.

REPRINTED FROM:
Esprit de Corps, *Volume 1 Issue 7*
AUTHOR: *James G. Scott*

RIGHT: *On 7 December 1941, Japanese aircraft attacked the U.S. Pacific fleet at Pearl Harbour. The surprise, early morning attack, resulted in 18 warships sunk or damaged, 188 aircraft destroyed and 3581 servicemen killed or wounded. With unanimous support, President Franklin Delano Roosevelt declared war on Japan and dispatched his forces.*

Unaware Britain planned to abandon Hong Kong, the Canadian government sent two battalions to the island in 1941. Taken prisoner when Japan invaded, Canadian POWs were tortured and enslaved until 1945.

HEROISM AND HYPOCRISY

THE HEROISM LASTED FOR 17 days of battle, and almost four years of anguish as slaves, but the hypocrisy started before Canadians were committed to defend the indefensible island of Hong Kong and continues to this day.

The most recent outburst of the latter was during a photo opportunity in Tokyo. Canadian Prime Minister Brian Mulroney beamed as a Japanese official muttered some kind of an apology for the harsh treatment of Canadian prisoners. Predictably, they never got around to discussing restitution.

Now there is strong evidence that Canadians at Hong Kong were among the victims of Winston Churchill's determination to bring the United States into the war. After a series of reverses, Britain was in desperate need of an ally in 1941. Strong isolationist sentiment in the United States made the prospect of America entering the war somewhat remote, and Churchill was dedicated to luring the United States in as early as May 1940.

Later that summer the Chiefs-of-Staff concluded that Malaya, Singapore and Hong Kong were indefensible and this was reflected in a highly sensitive report which was intercepted by the Germans before they sank the HMS *Automendon.* The document was turned over to the Japanese who then had intimate knowledge of British intentions.

NO CHANCE

Early in 1941, Churchill wrote to General Ismay: "If Japan goes to war with us there is not the slightest chance of holding Hong Kong or relieving it. It is most unwise to increase the loss we shall suffer there..."

Yet for propaganda purposes, forces were strengthened in Malaya and a small build up took place at Hong Kong. According to the Chiefs-of-Staff, the small increase in the Hong Kong garrison, "would show Chaing Kai-shek that we really intend to fight it out at Hong Kong." The same kind of deception was being practised against Roosevelt, and the Canadians became an expendable element in Churchill's strategy.

However, to appreciate the intensity of Churchill's desire to lure Roosevelt into war, one must explore the murky world of code-breaking. In 1939 the British broke a Japanese naval code known as JN-25 and later got equipment from the Americans which enabled them to break the Japanese diplomatic code. At this point the British gave the Americans nothing in return.

Before the fall of France, the British acquired a machine known as "Enigma," and a code which the Germans used for top priority radio messages. This intelligence, code-named *Ultra,* helped Air Chief Marshal 'Stuffy' Dowding husband his dwindling supply of aircraft during the Battle of Britain and enabled Churchill to read Hitler's mind.

Churchill knew of a planned attack on Coventry, England but rather than indicate he had *Ultra,* refused to make available any of 410 anti-aircraft guns. The first hint the defenders of Coventry had of the raid was when the sirens announced the arrival of over 500 Heinkels which pounded the city for ten hours. Some 500 people were killed, 4000 wounded, and 51,000 houses destroyed, but the secret of *Ultra* was intact.

MESS OF INTRIGUE

Churchill apparently made a similar decision in December 1941, when he withheld information from Roosevelt. The American President wallowed in a mess of intrigue and competition between his army and navy who fed him what they thought he should know. As sometimes also happens in peacetime politics, the operation was like a multi-limbed animal without a brain.

For instance, the Americans intercepted a Tokyo request to the Consul in Honolulu for identification and location of all ships in

LEFT:
With bayonets fixed, Japanese soldiers advance through the streets of Kowloon under heavy fire.
(IMPERIAL WAR MUSEUM)

NEXT PAGE:
This Japanese propaganda leaflet was dropped on Hong Kong during the battle for the British colony. It was a fairly accurate impression of the situation.
(DND)

Pearl Harbour. The air intercept went surface mail to Washington where it was translated. The request was for a bomb plot of Pearl, but a copy of the message was never sent back to Hawaii.

About this time the Canadian Government was asked to send two battalions to Hong Kong. Having no knowledge of previous British plans to abandon the island, Canada agreed. Nobody in Ottawa was apprised of the military situation, but nobody asked. In recommending the Winnipeg Grenadiers and the Royal Rifles of Canada, General Crerar figured "the experience they have will be of no small value to them in their new role."

FORCE INSUFFICIENTLY TRAINED

Two weeks later officers in the real world said the force was "insufficiently trained and not recommended for operations." Depots were drained of recruits to make up the required numbers. Some boys were 16, others had less than five weeks service. Bob Jessop, who had done garrison duty in Newfoundland with the Rifles, was among the veterans. Jessop remembers one recruit asking him how to load a rifle and there were reports of others who threw grenades at the enemy without removing the pin.

British and American opinion swung away from the idea that war was imminent. Americans saw an attack on Pearl Harbour having one chance in a million, while the British saw a weakening in the attitude of Japan towards the United States and Britain. But a week after the Canadians arrived in Hong Kong, Churchill got word that a Japanese task force had left the Kuriles.

MESSAGE INTERCEPTED

On 2 December the British intercepted Yamamoto's message to "Climb Niitakayama 1208." This was interpreted to mean attack on the eighth day of the 12th month, Tokyo time. Then on 4 December the final "execute" message told Churchill that the attack was in progress.

Churchill apparently withheld these messages from Roosevelt. The attack might pull America into the war, but if he tried to warn Roosevelt, the latter's signal to his Pacific commanders would be intercepted by the Japanese, who would not only break off the attack but change the code. Eight American boards of enquiry have failed to precisely establish how much warning the Americans had of the attack because key documents have been expunged from records. It's impossible to determine the full impact of Churchill's decision not to communicate with Roosevelt. One thing is certain: the U.S. declared war on Japan on 7 December.

The Canadians were billeted on Kowloon peninsula and gradually took up defensive positions on Hong Kong island, half a mile away. There was apparently no sense of urgency because the Rifles got two weeks disembarkation leave. A defence network, which had been abandoned three years earlier, was undergoing repair. Consisting of trenches and pillboxes, the 'Gin Drinkers Line' stretched for 10 miles across the peninsula. Beyond 30 miles of hills and jungle the Japanese waited for orders to attack.

The first attack hit Hong Kong about six hours after the one on Pearl Harbour. Jessop remembers the sirens as 48 Japanese aircraft bombed and strafed just about breakfast time. Chinese dead were soon piled up in the street and six ancient RAF machines were wiped out at Kai Tak airdrome. For a few days the Canadians commuted to their defensive positions on the island while the advance defenders met the enemy further up the peninsula.

GIN DRINKERS LINE

They soon fell back to the 'Gin Drinkers Line.' On the night of 9-10 December a Japanese force on reconnaissance took a vital redoubt on the line and the British withdrew. This engagement established the pattern for the next 15 days. The waterfront was a scene from hell as civilians fought for places on junks, ferries or anything that floated as they were bombed and strafed. Some delayed departure long enough to loot warehouses. By the 13th all British troops were withdrawn from the mainland.

The Royal Rifles were assigned to the east section of the island while the Winnipeg Grenadiers manned defence posts on the west. Both were integrated with other troops. Small groups were continuously criss-crossing the island as the Japanese tide swept down from the north. The fighting became a montage of small, savage encounters. Roger Cyr remembers cold steel and small groups in hand-to-hand combat in the dark, but there were also attacks in company strength as at Tai Wan Fort. By 25 December the perimeter had shrunk, communications had broken down and units were isolated and exhausted. Many of the Royals had not slept for five days and the defence of the island became a series of fire fights in the hills.

A grenadier force under CSM John Osborn took a peak on the east side of the island by bayonet. Three hours later they were surrounded by a grenade tossing Japanese force. Osborn threw several back at the enemy but one fell out of reach. He shouted a warning and threw himself on the grenade which exploded and killed him. Osborn was later awarded a posthumous Victoria Cross.

Bob Jessop's group was fighting for a reservoir when orders came through to withdraw. Although about 600 of the enemy had been killed in two days, the pressure all across the island was now relentless. On Christmas Day, Jessop and his brother Albert made their way back to Stanley Barracks where a strange calm descended. The men ate and slept aware that some kind of negotiations were going on.

WE WON!

Roger Cyr was leading a small group across country on Christmas Day. Communications didn't exist and when they saw an old civilian they stopped an asked him what

was happening. The old man shrugged and said the war was over. Then he walked down the trail. Although exhausted, Cyr and his men broke into a joyous trot. "We won! We won!" they shouted. A few hundred yards down the trail they ran into a strong Japanese patrol and the war took a different twist. Up to 200 Japanese broke into an emergency hospital where they stabbed 56 patients, mutilated three British nurses and repeatedly raped four Chinese nurses.

While Jessop remembers two days of sleep and rest in Stanley Barracks, Cyr's group were imprisoned in a tennis court. Days were bad, but at night guards invaded the enclosure. Curious about the size of the Canadians, they stripped prisoners and abused their organs.

BURNING BODIES

With the formal surrender, prisoners were put to work burning bodies and cleaning up the shambles on the docks. Later they were pressed into service as slaves repairing Kai Tak. This involved gathering sand and gravel by hand, putting it into baskets which they carried on their heads to repair a runway almost a mile long.

Food, averaging three cups of rice a day, was allocated on the basis of the number who turned up on work parade. Many worked to exhaustion and if they couldn't work, became a liability to the group. This created a collective pressure to go on but malnutrition, diphtheria, dysentery, malaria, skin ulcers and stomach disorders became common physical disabilities. The depths of psychological damage can never be measured. Later in the war prisoners were sent to mines and shipyards in Japan where they worked as slaves and suffered barbarous treatment.

RESTITUTION REFUSED

Japan has refused restitution on the basis that the treaty it signed in 1952 precludes any such arrangements. But the treaty was signed without consulting the Hong Kong veterans. The matter went to the UN where no action was taken. Based on a clause in Human Rights legislation which says a country can't sign away the rights of its citizens, the matter went back to the Canadian government where nothing happened. As of --- it was once again Geneva-bound through the War Amps. But considering the countries who are self-appointed custodians of human rights, the hypocrisy surrounding Hong Kong will probably outlive the people who fought there.

REPRINTED FROM:
Esprit de Corps, *Volume 3 Issue 8*
AUTHOR: *Norman Shannon*

1942 - THE RISING AXIS TIDE

With the onset of the spring thaw, German troops regained the strategic initiative in Russia. Meanwhile, Japan had rapidly expanded their "co-prosperity sphere" across Indo-China and the Pacific, inflicting a number of humiliating defeats on Allied outposts. The Japanese fleet suffered its first major setback at the Battle of Midway. In August, Canadian troops participated in the bloody failure to establish a beachhead at Dieppe and the Afrika Korps was threatening to overrun Egypt. However by year's end, Rommel had been beaten at El Alamein, the United States Marines were launching a counter assault on Guadalcanal and the German Sixth Army had entered a sausage-machine called Stalingrad.

2 JANUARY Japanese troops enter Manila while remaining United States forces withdraw to the Bataan peninsula.

15 FEBRUARY Singapore surrenders to Japanese. Over 130,000 Allied troops are captured in a humiliating defeat.

5 MARCH Russian winter counter-offensive dwindles out after inflicting heavy losses on the Germans.

9 APRIL United States troops on Bataan surrender to Japanese.

18 APRIL General Jimmy Doolittle leads a long range bombing raid on Tokyo to raise American morale.

28 MAY Germans complete successful campaign in southern Russia – 214,000 Russians are captured.

30 MAY Allies mount the first 1000-plane bombing raid against Germany.

4-6 JUNE Battle of Midway. Japanese lose four aircraft carriers in their first major defeat.

7 JUNE Japanese troops land unopposed in the Aleutian Islands.

30 JUNE Rommel reaches El Alamein after a string of victories in North Africa.

JULY-AUGUST German U-boats wreak havoc on shipping in the Gulf of St. Lawrence.

7 AUGUST United States marines land on Guadalcanal.

19 AUGUST Canadian-British raid at Dieppe is repulsed with heavy losses.

24 AUGUST German Sixth Army enters the suburbs of Stalingrad.

23 OCTOBER Battle of El Alamein begins.

4 NOVEMBER Rommel begins to retreat.

20 NOVEMBER Soviets launch counter-offensive at Stalingrad – encircling the German Sixth Army. Hitler orders his troops to stand fast.

28 DECEMBER German relief column is forced back from Stalingrad. The entire Sixth Army is completely cut off.

RIGHT:
On 4 June 1942, Vice Admiral Chuichi Nagumo launched the first strike of 108 aircraft on Midway and the approaching American fleet. Japanese torpedo bombers launch their weapons against USS Yorktown.

RIGHT: *More than 21,000 would serve in the Canadian Women's Army Corps during WWII. But only some 6700 would serve as Wrens with the Women's Royal Canadian Naval Service as this was the last service to recruit and it grew more slowly.*
(NATIONAL ARCHIVES OF CANADA)

Like Kipling's Tommy Atkins, women are recruited for key services when the guns begin to shoot. But after the crisis, they are dismissed and forgotten.

TOMMY ATKINS IN SKIRTS

KIPLING DESCRIBED TOMMY Atkins as a handy chap to have around when the guns began to shoot but a bit of a pest in peacetime. Somehow that description fits the attitude of the Canadian military to women in two world wars.

The work of Canadian women in WWI moved the Militia Council to set up a subcommittee late in the war. Two months before the Armistice, they recommended that a Canadian Women's Corps be formed. The recommendation went into File 13 and even the outbreak of WWII failed to arouse official interest.

Fourteen women's service corps were formed by volunteers in British Columbia just prior to that war. Each member chipped in two bucks to send a delegate to Ottawa to lobby for corps recognition, but once again the idea of a woman's corps gyrated to File 13.

BATTLE OF SEXES

The battle of sexes lasted almost two years as wave after wave of recommendations by women's groups washed over Ottawa. For instance, Air Vice Marshal Billy Bishop politely declined an offer by Lady Rachel Stuart to assist in forming a Women's Auxiliary Air Force, yet by 1941 facing a dearth of air crew, the RCAF called upon six WAAF's to set up what became the Woman's Division.

Within a year, all three services had women's divisions which actively contributed to victory, yet never received the recognition they deserved. Furthermore, the passage of time has brought an end to annual reunions and the brief public reminders of their achievements. This raises the question of what happens to the fine heritage of service established by women in previous wars. In spite of current advances made by women in the forces, there is no definitive work at the Department of National Defence on women's role in war – not on the scale of its outstanding works on Canadian airmen in WWI and coverage of army operations.

NURSE L. MILLER

Yet it's a role which dates back over 100 years when nurse L. Miller arrived in Saskatoon after the battle of Batoche. She was the first of 12 women to serve in the Riel Uprising. Later, some 16 Canadian nurses served with distinction in South Africa and while the nursing service had a structure and a purpose at the outbreak of WWI, most Canadian women started contributing by knitting socks. One Montreal lady knit a pair a day until Thursday. During the rest of the week she would buy yarn and do Red Cross work. While Canadian women didn't necessarily abandon knitting socks, the desire to help in a more positive manner drew thousands to associations like the Red Cross and the Independent Order of the Daughters of the Empire (IODE). Some, such as Katherine Wallis, took bold independent action. She was working in a Canadian-funded hospital in France within four months of the outbreak of war.

Time seems to have eroded from memory the magnificent contribution of the IODE, the Red Cross and the impact of women on industry.

NURSES EARN RESPECT

Nursing sisters followed the troops to England and the Western front. They also served in Salonika, Gallipoli and theatres where Canadian troops had no presence. Throughout the war, many were subject to enemy artillery fire and in 1918 hospitals became targets for German bombers. At Etaples they hit No. 1 General Hospital several times, killing three nurses. At Doullens the bombing of another hospital killed three more nurses and several patients, but the heroism shown by survivors in caring for patients under fire led to a number of military citations. Nursing sisters had definitely become respected members of the club.

The hospital ship *Llandovery Castle* was sunk by a German submarine 116 miles off the Irish coast in 1918. The U-boat fired on survivors for some time in an attempt to destroy evidence. As the ship went down, 14 nursing sisters trapped in an oarless lifeboat

RIGHT:
Members of the Women's Auxiliary Air Force (WAAF) at work in the operations room of RAF Fighter Command. The Air Force was the first service to set up a division for women, and, by 1945, 17,000 would have enlisted in the RAF. (IMPERIAL WAR MUSEUM)

stood as if on parade as they were sucked into the undertow. There were no survivors. Of the 2500 nurses who served overseas in WWI, 46 died.

ANOTHER NURSING GENERATION

In WWII Dieppe casualties flowing into Canadian hospitals in southern England brought another generation of Canadian nurses up to speed. Then, as the war spread, they were sent to the Mediterranean, North Africa, Sicily, Italy. They landed in Normandy and served throughout the North West Europe campaign and a few were part of the Hong Kong disaster.

Medical treatment of wounds was only part of the healing process. One nurse comforted an armless boy who cried at night because his brother had been taken prisoner at Dieppe. The best she could do for him was hold a cigarette between his lips.

The experience of Mrs. Ashton-Kerr brings into sharp focus the often unspoken relationship between nurse and patient. She served in a resuscitation ward in Belgium where all the patients were severely wounded. Penicillin was in short supply so a Canadian, Corporal Vermette, urged that she give his penicillin to a neighbour. The boy in the other bed was a German paratrooper. "I think I must have cheated a bit," she recalled. "I gave them both penicillin but unfortunately it didn't help Corporal Vermette who died shortly afterwards."

Before he died, Vermette asked his nurse to write the following letter home: "Tell them," he instructed, "not to feel bitter about all of this. I was very fortunate to at least come to a hospital and have you write my letter."

UNLADYLIKE AND IMMORAL

When Florence Nightingale cleaned up the medical chamber of horrors in the Crimean War, nursing was considered unladylike and immoral. Although Queen Victoria was soon wishing she had a Nightingale at the War Office, the stigma of women in the service died hard and by 1943 when auxiliaries of the three services were operating in Canada and overseas, about 50 per cent of Canadians surveyed took a dim view of women in uniform.

HOSPITAL SHIP *LLANDOVERY CASTLE* WAS SUNK BY A GERMAN SUBMARINE OFF THE IRISH COAST IN 1918. THE U-BOAT FIRED ON SURVIVORS FOR SOME TIME IN AN ATTEMPT TO DESTROY EVIDENCE.

The image of camp followers persisted; parents did not want their daughters to join for moral reasons while wives of men serving in the forces saw a threat in women in uniform. The new recruits soon realized that they had to go not one but two extra miles; they had to measure up on the job and they had to convince the folks at home that they were not wanton females on the make.

The women of the armed forces covered the first mile with distinction. As the number of trades increased from less than ten to more than 60, women were engaged in flying duties as photographers or wireless instructors. They manned anti-aircraft guns, packed parachutes, plotted the course of ships at sea, and worked in air force operations rooms. At one point in the war, women were considered for pilot training but authorities never came to grips with the possibilities.

FEMALE FERRY BRIGADE

Some Canadian women joined the British Air Transport Auxiliary where a group of women pilots began ferrying aircraft in 1940. They started ferrying Tiger Moths and by 1943 were flying four-engined bombers around fog-bound England, an experience which drew on skill and courage because of a network of barrage balloons and the fact that normal radio communication was denied for security reasons. Although 15 of 100 women pilots were killed, this figure did not exceed the male average for the same number of flying hours in adverse conditions. The experiment with women pilots was originally met with derision by the RAF but when Commander Pauline Gower compiled irrefutable statistics that women pilots were as competent as men, some RAF messes served crow.

In spite of hidebound traditions and prejudice at home, Canadian men and women had a good relationship at the operational level. Perhaps nowhere in the service was there a closer bond between Canadian men and women than on RCAF squad-

***ABOVE:** Women served on several fronts during the war, including in Hong Kong. When the colony fell to the Japanese in December 1941, Army Nurses Kay Christie (pictured) and May Walters became prisoners. To date, they are the only Canadian women with the dubious distinction of being prisoners of war*

rons overseas. Here they shared the tension of the wartime experience.

COVERING THE SECOND MILE

Mabel Gray was in the ops room when she heard her brother's bomber went down in the channel. She went about her duties for 48 traumatic hours before word came in that he had been picked up. To folks in Canada the presence of WD's or any woman's auxiliary brought the war closer to home. But to the combat serviceman it also brought home closer to the war. By 1945, Canada's women in uniform had covered the second mile.

Much has been written about the rehabilitation of male veterans, but we know relatively little about the problems of women whose period of service went from knitting socks to flying aircraft. They were reluctantly recruited then casually dismissed and officially forgotten. Sociologists and military historians have failed to grasp or convey the significance of their service on the social fabric of Canada.

REPRINTED FROM:
Esprit de Corps, *Volume 2 Issue 5*
AUTHOR: *Norman Shannon*

THE SAVIOUR OF CEYLON

Squadron Leader Len Birchall's heroic action in spotting and reporting the approach of a Japanese fleet didn't actually "save" Ceylon – but it enabled a British fleet to escape to the Indian Ocean.

RETIRED AIR COMMODORE Leonard Birchall became the first person to receive the fifth clasp to his Canadian Forces Decoration for his devotion to duty. Birchall had 62 years of distinguished service, but the one aspect of his career which sent reporters scurrying to old world Atlases had to do with an island in the Indian Ocean off the southeast coast of Africa and the dark days of 1942 when Sri Lanka was Ceylon.

The RCAF No. 413 Squadron was formed at Stranraer, Scotland in 1941, and the first year of its life was relatively unhappy and undistinguished. It flew Coastal Command patrols out of the Shetlands in deplorable weather.

Although technically Canadian, less than half the crews were Canadian and the RAF dominated key decisions. When it was ordered to Ceylon in March 1942, four Catalinas flew out and two were rendered unserviceable when the alarm went up a week later, and groundcrew were en route by boat.

PRESENCE IN CEYLON

Three months into their war, the Japanese had taken Hong Kong, Singapore and Malaya. They had invaded the Philippines, Burma, Java, Borneo and Sumatra and two large naval task forces were invading the Indian Ocean. The British, under Admiral Sir James Sommerville, had tried to establish a presence in Ceylon. It consisted of five WWI battleships and 23 other ships, and the most promising feature were aircraft carriers *Indomitable, Formidable* and the light carrier *Hermes.* But all they had to launch were 57 obsolete strike planes and 36 fighters from another age.

The British intercepted a message that Japanese Admiral Nagumo's task force was heading for Ceylon while a second force was heading for the Bay of Bengal. On 4 April, Birchall's Catalina was one of two which took off from Koggala. By daybreak, he was 250 miles southeast of Ceylon and his crew spent the next 12 hours droning at 90 miles an hour in a monotonous search.

They moved further south and extended the search. The Catalina could fly for 32 hours so they had lots of time as P/O Bart Onyette watched the rising moon while waiting to get an astro fix. It put the lone Catalina some 350 miles south of Ceylon and Birchall was about to call it a day when a dot appeared on the horizon.

They flew closer and the dots multiplied.

OPPOSITE PAGE:
"Saviour of Ceylon" Leonard Birchall.
(ROYAL CANADIAN LEGION)

LEFT:
The Catalinas had great endurance as they could fly for 24 hours and had a range of over 3000 miles. Spending most of 4 April 1942 at the controls of his Cat looking and finally finding the Japanese fleet, Birchall and his crew successfully transmitted the information before being shot down in the Indian Ocean. Taken aboard a Japanese destroyer, Birchall would spend the rest of the war in a prison camp. After the war he remained in the forces and held many senior appointments, including that of Commandant of Kingston's Royal Military College.
(NAC)

"As we got close enough to identify the lead ships, we knew at once what we were into," Birchall later wrote, "but the closer we got, the more ships appeared and so it was necessary to keep going until we could count and identify them all."

What they identified was a force of five aircraft carriers containing 360 aircraft, four battleships, three cruisers, 11 destroyers and seven submarines. Carrier-based fighters attacked as Sergeant F.G. Phillips transmitted a message and, on the third transmission, cannon fire smashed the wireless and Phillips was seriously injured. Internal tanks burst into flame and, by the time the crew got the fire out, a second one had broken out and the machine began to break up. They were too low to jump but Birchall got the flying boat down before the tail fell off.

DEADLY LIFE-PRESERVERS

Eight of the nine-man crew managed to get out of the aircraft which was still under intense fire. One air gunner whose leg had been severed went down with the plane. Two were unconscious and were pulled through burning gasoline by other crew members. The injured men wore life jackets and, as enemy fighters continued to strafe, the others were able to dive under water but the men with life jackets were killed. The six survivors were wounded, three seriously, by the time they were picked up by a boat from a Japanese destroyer.

On board the destroyer they were beaten and interrogated but insisted they had not sent out a message. Things did not improve when the Japanese intercepted a message from Koggala asking Phillips to repeat his last message.

Birchall's message had a somewhat strange effect on Ceylon. Merchantmen from Colombo harbour fled to sea hoping to escape detection. Sommerville's task force meanwhile took the somewhat un-Nelsonian route to Addu Atoll where it refuelled and hid some 600 miles southwest of Ceylon.

FACILITIES DAMAGED

Nagumo sent 91 bombers and 36 fighters against Colombo on 5 April and the force was met by 42 land-based Hurricanes, of which 19 were lost to the enemy's seven. One destroyer and one armed merchant cruiser were sunk and shore facilities damaged. Then 50 aircraft later found British heavy cruisers *Dorcetshire* and *Cornwall* which they immediately sank.

Four days later, a second attacking force was spotted by Flight Lieutenant R. Thomas in 413 Squadron's last operational Catalina. He reported the Japanese fleet 200 miles off the port of Trincomalee then went missing.

Shipping was again dispersed and the RAF put up 22 fighters and nine Blenheim bombers of which five were shot down. The port was damaged with one merchant vessel sunk, and the second wave of Nagumo's pilots found the first of Sommerville's ships. They sank the *Hermes* with all aircraft, a destroyer, a corvette and two tankers.

The British then withdrew to East Africa, leaving the Japanese to dominate 8,000 miles of ocean. The attack on Ceylon was a raid rather than an invasion and Birchall's warning, for which he was awarded the Distinguished Flying Cross (DFC), saved lives and resources. The Canadian Press dubbed him "the Saviour of Ceylon" and this has led to some misinterpretation. Although elements of the British forces remained in Ceylon, including No. 413 Squadron, one may be inclined to question what was saved when the British Eastern Fleet withdrew to Africa.

NIGHTLY BEATINGS

Birchall's crew endured three days on the destroyer and then were transferred to the aircraft carrier *Akagi*. The three most seriously injured were sent to sick bay but the other three became subject to nightly beatings en route to Yokohama.

Beatings, starvation, disease and cruelty became part of the lives of all Japanese POW's. Birchall found himself with yet another task in several prison camps. He became the senior officer and, as such, for three and a half years was a key figure in helping others survive.

On one occasion, the work force in a bar-

WHEN FINALLY RELEASED AFTER THE WAR, LEONARD BIRCHALL WAS AWARDED THE ORDER OF THE BRITISH EMPIRE IN RECOGNITION OF HIS SERVICE TO FELLOW PRISONERS. HIS DIARY WAS LATER USED AS EVIDENCE IN WAR CRIME TRIALS.

racks was depleted by jaundice, beri-beri, dysentery, starvation and massive boils. The sergeant of the guard ordered all sick out of bed and began to beat their massive boils. Birchall lost his cool and started swinging; "I took off. A few belts and he was down."

Thrown into solitary, he was beaten and hung up by his thumbs. A Kangaroo court in Tokyo ordered that he be shot. Birchall was taken out and endured the charade of the firing squad loading rifles. The execution was delayed because only honourable people deserved to be shot. The Japs later explained that he would be beheaded. This time he was taken out where he knelt as a sword swished past his head. Then he was thrown into solitary for two weeks.

ORDER OF THE BRITISH EMPIRE

When finally released after the war, Len Birchall was awarded the Order of the British Empire in recognition of his service to fellow prisoners. His diary, consisting of 22 volumes, was used as evidence in war crime trials after the war. But the Canadian government's failure to support Canadians who suffered in Japanese POW camps injects a bitter note which makes a mockery of "devotion to duty." The clasp presented to Air Commodore Birchall in February might have meant much more if it had been accompanied by a declaration that Canada was finally going to support the claim of former POW's for restitution.

REPRINTED FROM:
Esprit de Corps, *Volume 5 Issue 10*
AUTHOR:
Norman Shannon

THE SEA SHALL HAVE THEM

German submarines wreaked havoc on Allied convoys. In June 1942, PQ-17 left Iceland with a strength of 36 merchant ships. Only 12 completed the journey.

ABOVE: *With intelligence reports warning of a planned attack, the Allied ships kept a watch for German ships. But in the midnight sun of the northern latitudes the ships of convoy PQ17 were easy targets in a calm ocean.* *(IMPERIAL WAR MUSEUM)*

BY 1942 GERMAN SUBMARINES were sinking a ship every four hours, and while the number of replacement ships was increasing, so was the number of submarines. Early that year, Canadian Steamships lost the *Lady Hawkins* which went down 130 miles off Cape Hatteras with 250 people onboard. Seventy survivors were dragged out of the oily water into a lifeboat but, when absolutely no more could be taken aboard, Chief Petty Officer Percy Kelly gave orders to pull away. "The cries of the people in the water rang in my ears for years," he later wrote.

Kelly took command of the situation and rationed two kegs of water, hardtack, canned milk, medicinal brandy and rum. They lost the rudder in heavy seas and managed to sail on storm gib for five days before they were picked up. For surviving passengers it was the end of an adventure in terror, but for merchant seamen like Kelly it was just one more episode in a reign of terror. Kelly soon went back to sea and was again torpedoed. This time he spent only three days in a lifeboat before being picked up.

YOUNG SEA DOGS

Not all merchant seamen were *old* sea dogs. George Evans was 15 when the ancient *SS Einvik* fell behind the convoy. They lost two days repairing a broken engine and as the ship bounced through the Arctic darkness a torpedo slammed into its side. Evans grabbed his life jacket and was running to the lifeboat when a second explosion hit him in the back. Stunned, he was helped to a lifeboat, and later got hell for being in the wrong boat.

After nine days of sailing and rowing they touched land. Evans contracted acute bronchitis and a severe cold, along with a

RIGHT:
A ship carrying ammunition and lend-lease supplies to Russia suffers a direct hit.
(IMPERIAL WAR MUSEUM)

BELOW:
Another merchant ship goes down after being torpedoed. In frigid northern waters, survival time was measured in minutes.
(IMPERIAL WAR MUSEUM)

FOR SIX DAYS THE CONVOY FELL UNDER CONSTANT AIR ATTACKS AND SUBMARINES INFILTRATED THE RANKS OF THE SHIPS.

Glasgow hotel bill which he had to pay himself.

When money ran low, Evans signed on as fireman. For a year and a half, Evans worked on ships, hoping to get back home to Sydney. On one occasion, his ship stopped at Sydney for coal, but there was no way he could be relieved.

A DRESS REHEARSAL

In May 1942, Evans was a member of the *Pieter van Hoogh*, one of the 35 ships in a convoy leaving Scotland for Murmansk. For six days the convoy fell under constant air attacks and submarines infiltrated the ranks of the ships. When the exhausted crews arrived in Murmansk, five ships had been lost and three severely damaged. But this was just a dress rehearsal for what was to happen to PQ-17, which sailed out of Iceland late in June.

It was tracked by the enemy from the moment it left and steamed closer to German bases in Norway. The Germans made their move on day seven as ten submarines converged on allied ships. German pocket battleships *Admiral Scheer* and *Lützow* and six destroyers moved north from Narvik to Alafjord. *Lützow* and three destroyers ran aground but the other ships had merely changed ports. However, their movement caused sheer panic where First Sea Lord Sir Dudley Pound ordered naval escorts to withdraw and the convoy to scatter.

Men on the naval escort ships felt anger and frustration at the order. Commander Jack Broome later wrote that the convoy was going like a train when "suddenly, out of an ice-blue sky, PQ-17 was murdered by a single word."

CONVOY SLAUGHTERED

The Germans attacked and slaughtered the convoy. Resentfully Broome retreated amid burning ships. "I am not likely to forget when the first pitiable cry for help came limping from the merchantman who was being attacked by U-boat and plane. Something had gone hopelessly wrong. A trust we believed in implicitly had let us down flat."

In the bright Arctic night, PQ-17 was destroyed, as 24 of 36 merchant ships went to the bottom. Pound had a penchant for protecting the home fleet. Earlier that year, he had kept his ships at Scapa Flow while the *Scharnhorst, Gneisenau* and *Prinz Eugen* made a successful dash from Brest to northern ports. The question Churchill asked then could well have been asked again. "Why?"

Merchant ships would continue to provide a lifeline for Britain and assistance to Russia. Some 210 such ships sailed under the Canadian Red Ensign and 30 of these were lost, at a cost of 1064 men.

REPRINTED FROM:
Esprit de Corps, *Volume 8 Issue 2*
AUTHOR:
Norman Shannon

WAR ON OUR DOORSTEP

***ABOVE:** The lighthouse on Estevan Point was shelled on 20 June 1940 by a Japanese sub. It was the first attack on Canadian soil and resulted in Mackenzie King's decision to intern people of Japanese descent in camps far from the coast.* (NATIONAL ARCHIVES OF CANADA)

When a Japanese sub shells Estevan Point on Vancouver Island, the damage is insignificant but it arouses Canadians to the poor state of our west coast defences.

THE 1942 SHELLING OF the Estevan Point lighthouse on Vancouver Island by a Japanese submarine jolted the Canadian government into realizing that the war was now on its doorstep.

"It was the first attack on Canadian soil that has been made since Confederation," stated Prime Minister Mackenzie King in the House of Commons during debates in 1942.

The 20 June shelling also resulted in the government making two important decisions. The first was to forcibly remove all Japanese residents of British Columbia from their homes and businesses and intern them in camps in central Canada.

The second decision, almost a year later, was to provide troops for a joint U.S.-Canada assault on the Aleutians, a mountainous chain of wind-swept islands of volcanic rock. These islands, which stretched out from Alaska into the north Pacific, belonged to the United States and had been seized and occupied by the Japanese as they expanded their conquests in both the north and south Pacific.

By 1 June 1942, the Japanese had reached the pinnacle of their wartime power. In less than six months since their sneak attack on Pearl Harbour, on 7 December the previous year, their armies had swept victoriously down the coast of the Asian land mass capturing Hong Kong, Burma and the Malayan peninsula, Singapore, Borneo, Java, the Philippines and many other islands in the waters north, east and south so as to dominate the entire Pacific theatre of war. Their prime targets were Midway Island, an outpost of the Hawaiian Islands, and the Hawaiian Islands themselves.

Part of the Japanese plan was to try to lure the U.S. battle fleet away from its Hawaiian base at Pearl Harbour. To do this they occupied the Aleutians in June 1942 as a preliminary to a grand assault on their main targets. Fortunately, the Americans did not fall for their scheme.

MIDWAY ISLAND

American intelligence quickly became aware of these plans. The navy, already widely dispersed in the Pacific did not send any ships to the Alaskan area, but concentrated all its naval power in the vicinity of Midway Island. By the first week in June the Americans had located the Japanese battle fleet on its way to Midway. Using carrier-based aircraft, in a two-day battle the Americans so crippled their opponents that the Japanese fleet was no longer an important factor in the Pacific war. In fact, the Battle of Midway was a turning point of the war in favour of the United States. It was also a triumph of seaborne airpower over seapower alone.

The submarine attack on British Columbia's coast took place two weeks after the destruction of the Japanese fleet. Two of these vessels had been part of the Midway operation, providing flank reconnaissance along the North American coast as their main attack force moved toward its objectives. Hearing of the US victory, they were making their way back to home waters and the shells that fell on Canadian soil were little more than a spiteful farewell.

ESTEVAN POINT SHELLED

The first Japanese shell landed at 22:14 hrs

near the lighthouse on Estevan Point. The lighthouse keeper quickly extinguished the light and the next shot fell just in front of the lighthouse. From then on shells landed thick and fast around the now darkened lighthouse and in the forest immediately behind. Local residents retreated deep into the woods to escape the bombardment. Further up the coast, at Mesquiat (an Indian community), *HMCS Moolock* was patrolling in the area and found some of these natives, who, on being told of the shelling by telephone, had taken to their boats. *Moolock* boarded these people and took them to Vancouver.

Rumours were rife. Reports of an enemy light cruiser turned out to be an American fishing boat. Aircraft were reported, but no aircraft, Japanese or Canadian, were in the area. The incident caused considerable alarm, which was probably all it was meant to do. It was no more than a storm in a teacup.

UNFAIR TREATMENT

In recent years the removal of the Japanese to internment camps has been looked upon by some Canadians as a racist injustice, and those internees still living have received compensation from the Canadian government. This compensation has been displeasing to many other Canadians, particularly those who suffered cruel treatment while undergoing a three-year period as prisoners of war in Japan. Having worked under slave-like conditions on an almost starvation diet, these Canadians who were captured at Hong Kong feel that Japan should now compensate them for their suffering.

Since the shelling of Canada's coast by enemy submarine might have been the prelude to further enemy operations, such as seaborne or airborne raids, the Canadian government cannot be faulted for taking the action it did in the case of the Japanese removals. The loyalty of the Japanese in British Columbia, even the Canadian-born, was considered questionable, unfair though that may seem now. But it was deemed quite possible that if Japanese troops landed anywhere along the British Columbia coast they might well coerce their North American cousins to return their allegiance to the Land of the Rising Sun. After all, at this stage of the war the Japanese, except for their fleet's defeat at Midway two weeks before, had been victorious on all fronts. Blood is thicker than water and the power of the victor over people under its influence can change individual and mass loyalties very quickly. The Canadian government would certainly have been open to criticism if Japanese-Canadian communities had joined up with their former countrymen.

LEFT: *In August 1943, a Canadian brigade joined in the American-led assault on the Aleutian island of Kiska. Believing it to be occupied by a large Japanese force, they were surprised to learn that the Japanese had evacuated the island some two weeks previous.* *("KISKA PATROL" BY EDWARD JOHN HUGHES, CANADIAN WAR MUSEUM)*

THE JOINT UNITED STATES-CANADIAN FORCE ASSAULTED KISKA ON 15 AUGUST 1943.

SEABORNE ASSAULT

Once the Midway battle had been won, the Americans turned their minds to pushing the Japanese off the Aleutians. Several months of bombing blockade failed to evict the Japs from either Kiska or Attu, the two main islands of the Aleutian chain. Consequently, they decided to recover the islands by seaborne assault. On 12 May 1943, the Americans landed on Attu and after a fierce battle captured the island, annihilating the enemy in the process. Only 11 Japanese were taken prisoner. More than 2500 of them died, either killed by the Americans or by mass suicide. With Attu in their hands the Americans began planning for the seizure of the much larger island of Kiska, believed to be garrisoned by 5400 Japanese troops. A Canadian brigade took part in this operation which, it was believed, might be a bloody enterprise indeed. The joint U.S.-Canada force assaulted Kiska on 15 August 1943 (following on the heels of the successful invasion of Sicily by Anglo-American-Canadian forces) only to discover that the Japanese had evacuated the island and returned to Japan some two weeks before. Japanese power in the Pacific was now in decline and fear of further enemy action on Canada's west coast soon disappeared.

Meantime, on the east coast and in the St. Lawrence River things were, for a time, less reassuring. Between June and October 1942, the "Battle of the St. Lawrence" saw U-boats sink 23 ships and kill 700 people, more than the Canadian army would lose in Sicily a year later. The final German triumph in this battle was the sinking of the passenger ferry *Caribou* on 14 October 1942 as it travelled from Nova Scotia to Newfoundland. After that, the penetration of Canadian inland waters by German submarines ended, with very few Canadians ever knowing that it had ever taken place.

REPRINTED FROM:

Esprit de Corps, *Volume 2 Issue 1*

AUTHOR: *Col (ret'd) Strome Galloway*

ABOVE:
The Sikanni Chief Bridge at Nite Post 117 on the Alaska Highway, the first bridge reconstructed in 1943.
(U.S. ARMY PHOTO)

Security of North America's west coast became a priority only after the Japanese occupation of the Aleutian Islands. The result was a tremendous feat of road construction.

NORTH TO ALASKA

THE MILITARY POLICY OF both the United States and Canada in reference to Alaska and the Pacific northwest prior to 1940, can be summed up in one word: neglect.

When Canada declared war on Germany in September 1939, it directed its attention to the Atlantic and Europe, giving little thought to its western defences. Nevertheless, the construction of airfields was authorized and work began at Grande Prairie, Alberta, Fort St. John and Fort Nelson, British Columbia, and Whitehorse in the Yukon. The municipal airport at Edmonton was also expanded.

Neglect gave way to grave concern when the Japanese bombed Dutch Harbour, in June 1942, and landed in the Aleutians. By May 1943, there were more than 2500 Japanese troops on Attu and about 5400 on Kiska.

Even though the islands are nearly 3000 miles north of Vancouver, the Japanese incursion into North America was a source of grave anxiety to Canada as well as the United States. The Americans immediately took countermeasures, launching air attacks against the Japanese garrisons with the assistance of RCAF fighter squadrons flying P-40 Kittyhawks with American markings out of Anchorage and Annette Island. But the Japanese were not the Canadians' only concern; herds of caribou even kept the Kittyhawks grounded as they swarmed over the runways.

In August 1942, the Americans occupied Adak and Amchitka, but it was obvious that additional men and material would be required to dislodge the Japanese from Attu and Kiska, and these could only be brought in by road, a road that did not yet exist.

THE ALASKA HIGHWAY

An overland route to Alaska had been dreamed of long before World War II, but it remained a dream until the Japanese bombed Pearl Harbour and moved into the Aleutians. Now, it was deemed essential as the west coast of Canada and the United States and all of Alaska lay open to a possible Japanese invasion.

The plan was to start a road from the end of the railroad at Dawson Creek and terminate it at Fairbanks, Alaska. It was to be built as quickly as possible to carry military traffic. Later, it was to become a year-round road with wider road beds and permanent bridges built by the U.S. Public Roads Administration.

Canadian cooperation was needed because most of the road would be built through British Columbia and the Yukon Territory. Canada agreed to furnish the right of way, to waive import duties, sales and income taxes and immigration regulations, and to permit the taking of timber and gravel along the way. The Americans agreed to pay construction costs and to turn the Canadian portion of the road over to the Canadian government six months after the war ended. Work began in February 1942.

The construction of the Alaska Highway hit Dawson Creek with the impact of a second gold rush. Quonset huts and supply dumps sprang up and American troops were soon joined by thousands of Canadian civilian workers spreading out to Fort St. John and Fort Nelson. At the other end of the road, workers moved out from Fairbanks and Whitehorse. No time was wasted on engineering niceties. The road looped over hills and cut through forests, a bulldozer leading the way with others following to clear debris. Strung out 30 to 50 miles behind the bulldozers were men felling trees and building culverts and bridges. Overhead, reconnaissance aircraft photographed the next stretch of muskeg and forest to be attacked.

Plagued by mosquitoes and blackflies,

ABOVE:
The 13th Infantry Brigade and the "Devil's Brigade" land on Red Beach on the northern tip of Kiska, 15 August 1943.
(U.S. ARMY PHOTO)

work went on seven days a week, day and night, in temperatures ranging from the sub-tropical to 50° below zero. At the same time, workers on the Canoil Project were pushing a pipeline through the wilderness from the oil fields at Norman Wells on the east bank of the Mackenzie River to Whitehorse, a distance of nearly 500 miles.

On 20 November 1942, the Alaska Highway was officially opened at Soldiers' Summit overlooking Kluane Lake as military bands struck up "God Save the Queen" and "The Star-Spangled Banner." Then the first convoy of trucks pushed on to Fairbanks. In one of the great engineering feats of the century, 10,000 soldiers and 6000 civilian workers carved out a 24-foot roadway, 1400 miles long at an average speed of ten miles a day, completing in eight months a task that would normally have taken years.

OPERATION COTTAGE: KISKA

Japan never had any intention of invading North America. Her strategic aim was to conquer Southeast Asia, form a defensive ring around it, exploit the area's resources, and hope that the Allies would finally accept her control. Her real purpose in the Aleutians was to create a diversion for a far more important attack, the assault on Midway Island in the Pacific.

In the spring of 1942, as an armoured train patrolled the CNR line between Prince Rupert and Terrace, British Columbia, and additional airfields were built for home defence and to ferry aircraft to Russia under the Lend-Lease program, it was decided for political as well as military reasons to evict the Japanese from Attu and Kiska. The U.S. 7th Division staged a vicious assault on Attu on 11 May 1942, annihilating all but 11 of the 2250-man garrison.

For the assault on Kiska, it was decided that a Canadian force should join the Americans. Four infantry battalions – the Canadian Fusiliers, the Winnipeg Grenadiers (reformed after the destruction of the active battalion at Hong Kong), the Rocky Mountain Rangers, and Le Régiment de Hull – were outfitted with American equipment and formed into the 13th Infantry Brigade under the command of Brigadier H.W. Foster. They sailed from Vancouver, 5300 strong, on 2 July for the Aleutian island of Adak to undergo assault training. Many of the men were conscripts, the hated "Zombies" who had not volunteered for overseas service, a problem the government solved by widening the term "home defence."

On 13 August, a combined assault force of 34,000 men set sail for Kiska supported by three battleships, two cruisers and 19 destroyers. Accompanying the Canadians were 2450 men of the Special Service Force, The Devil's Brigade. Storming ashore, they found the island deserted, the Japanese having evacuated Kiska under cover of fog two weeks before. All they found were a few stray dogs, a massive underground defence system, and military and personal gear of every description, including a British naval gun captured at Singapore. Although there were no enemy troops on the island, 24 men were killed by their comrades in the darkness and four died from booby traps left by the Japanese. Fifty others were wounded.

In most combat theatres of the Second World War, the combatants had only to contend with each other. In Alaska and northwestern Canada, however, they also had to do battle with the weather and the wilderness. It was the war's least known combat zone. Most of those who served there had never seen anything like it before, nor would they ever want to see it again.

AUTHOR: *Bill Twatio*

RIGHT: *Canadian corvettes gamely answered the U-boat challenge in their home water. HMCS* Charlottetown *(pictured) lost to U-517 on 11 September 1942 when she was torpedoed in the St. Lawrence near Cap Chat, Quebec, losing nine of her crew.* (PAC)

You could have sold tickets each evening along the St Lawrence as German subs opened the killing season on allied shipping during the summer of 1942.

CANADA'S DARK SUMMER OF 1942

WHEN KORVETTENKAPITAN Karl Thurmann eased the U-553 through the strait of Belisle early in May of 1942, he set in motion a period of panic which historians refer to as the Battle of the St. Lawrence. Were it not for the loss of life and shipping, the summer could have been the time frame for a Norman Jewison film: "the Germans are Coming, the Germans are Coming." Only in retrospect, however, was there irony or pathos in the events of that summer which brought the war to Canada's shores.

REPORTS SLOW

Thinly-scattered RCAF units along the coast were solely dependent on Ma Bell's commercial lines for communications: Co-ordination between the RCN and the RCAF was virtually non-existent. In one case a submarine attack on naval escorts was not reported to the RCAF for six hours. Students in Ansons flew out from Charlottetown to sweep the seas of enemy submarines, and when the occasional Digby patrol aircraft got close enough to drop a depth charge, they didn't detonate properly. When Thurmann started sinking ships in the Gulf, Quebec politicians such as Independent J.S. Roy responded in typically Canadian fashion: he blamed the attacks on a lack of economic grants to the Gaspé region. Then, in the midst of the panic and squabbling over the conscription referendum, Canada was also faced with the staggering casualties from Dieppe.

The inland sea in which Thurmann found himself was 250 miles wide in places with ample opportunity to hide, yet all the traffic funnelled in a predictable stream between Anticosti and Magdelan islands out through Belle Isle. Two days into the Gulf, Thurmann was attacked by an American B-17 out of Gander. Like all air attacks that summer, it was unsuccessful and the American USAF commander at Gander didn't bother informing the RCAF in Halifax.

The news seeped through the next day and at twilight Thurmann sank two steamers off the Gaspé coast.

The RCAF sent a Canso, five Hudsons and 24 Ansons out to search the area, establishing a pattern which was to persist for most of the summer: aircrew looking at empty sea after an attack. As he announced the sinkings to his caucus, Mackenzie King tried to repair some of the damage caused by the referendum three weeks earlier. King stressed the negative in trying to bring the war closer to his French-Canadian colleagues, but it didn't work with members like J.S. Roy, who used the occasion as a platform for more handouts. The Tories blamed the Liberals without offering anything more substantial than rhetoric.

DURING THE SUMMER, U-BOATS AND RUMOURS CONTINUED TO PROWL THE ST. LAWRENCE. IN AUGUST, SINKINGS INTENSIFIED. AN AMERICAN CONVOY BOUND FOR GREENLAND, AND A CANADIAN ONE HEADING FOR GOOSE BAY, LABRADOR, FELL PREY TO HARTWIG'S U-517.

Karl Dönitz, head of the German U-boat campaign, wanted to divert escort ships from the main overseas route from Halifax and American ports. Consequently, he continued to send a few of his raiders into the strait of Belisle, although at no time was there more than three or four undersea ships in the Gulf. For most of the summer, pairs of German subs raised havoc.

LACK OF CO-ORDINATION

On the night of 28 June, U-132 cleared the strait of Belisle and headed up river. A week later it was at Cap Chat, 90 miles upstream of where Thurmann sank the steamers in May. A convoy set off suddenly from Bic Island. One of two Cansos available at Gaspé had just finished a long patrol in support of another convoy, and the second

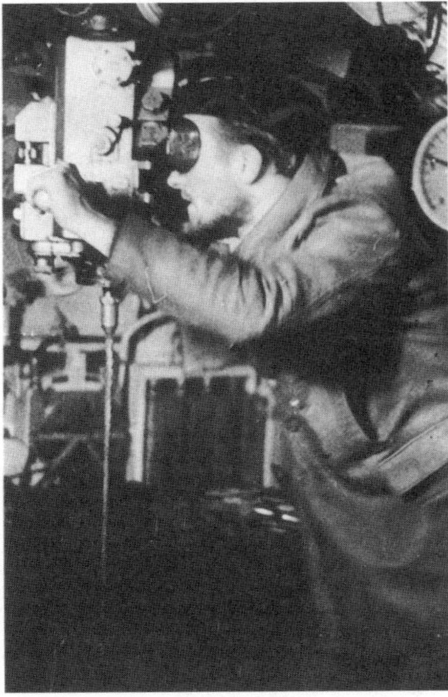

RIGHT:
With eyes glued to his periscope, the captain of a submerged U-boat searches the surface for a target.
(IMPERIAL WAR MUSEUM)

Canso was unserviceable. The RCAF was unable to offer support. The U-132 attacked on a summer evening, sinking two ships at the outset of the duel, and another two a few hours later. The incident showed a complete lack of co-ordination between escort vessels and the RCAF, and also a lack of communication: it was six hours before news of the first torpedo attack reached officials on shore.

During the summer, U-boats and rumours continued to prowl the St. Lawrence. Tight censorship fed the rumours. There were stories of German crews coming ashore for an evening of rest and relaxation and a Black Horse at Mont Joli, or crewmen captured in other locations with ticket stubs from the Bijou theatre in their pockets. In August, sinkings intensified. An American convoy bound for Greenland, and a Canadian one heading for Goose Bay, Labrador, fell prey to Paul Hartwig's U-517. He sank the American transport *Chatham* while later that night a second sub sank two merchant vessels. Six days later, he sank the *Donald Stewart*. The next day an RCAF Digby made the first attack on a submarine in that theatre. It was a qualified success because the premature explosion of the depth charge did more damage to the aircraft than to the U-517, which in two days had shared in the sinking of four ships and an armed yacht.

MISGUIDED AND SLOW

People lined the shore at Cap Chat on 11 September as Hartwig surfaced and sank the corvette *Charlottetown*. Four days later, his sub was spotted by an observer whose report took an hour and a half to reach army channels. Why it was sent to the army is not clear. But by the time it reached anybody who might do anything about it, Hartwig had sunk another ship and fought an engagement with its naval escort. That night, a sister sub sank two more ships and damaged a third. In one two-week sweep of the Gulf, Hartwig and fellow skipper Eberhard Hoffman sank 11 ships.

When Britain asked for ships to be used in Operation Torch in North Africa, the Canadian government complied, but it meant shutting down the Gulf to trans-ocean traffic. Naval escorts had not come to grips with submarines in the Gulf and senior officers welcomed the idea of using them elsewhere. Hartwig immediately noticed a reduction of traffic and an increase in air patrols. But sinkings continued. The *SS Watertown* was sunk on 10 October and three days later the ferry from Sydney, Nova Scotia to Port Aux Basques, Newfoundland, was sunk with a loss of 136 lives.

The RCAF had intensified its patrols, including the use of training Ansons from Charlottetown. The submarines had thus far sunk 21 ships without a loss, but by the end of October, the decline of targets in the Gulf, and the air patrols overhead induced them to go elsewhere. While Hudsons, Digbys and Catalinas were part of the air cover, perhaps it was the Ansons with training crews which struck fear into Hitler's undersea captains, the summer the Germans brought the war to Canada.

REPRINTED FROM:
Esprit de Corps, *Volume 2 Issue 2*
AUTHOR: *Norman Shannon*

THE ENIGMA OF GEORGE BEURLING

Screwball Beurling earned his name at Malta in many ways but in a Spitfire over the embattled island he was supreme.

IN THE DARKEST DAYS of the Second World War, when it seemed that the British Empire would finally see the sun set upon it, the beleaguered citizenry were eager to look to any shining light for salvation. As in the Great War, the casual, romantic heroism of the fighter pilot stirred the imagination and gave rise to legends and tales of morale-boosting exploits. In wartime Canada, we were no less susceptible to hero-worship, and no less endowed with heroes than any other country. Unfortunately, we

ABOVE: *With 31 kills to his record, most of those won over Malta, George "Buzz" Beurling is Canada's highest scoring fighter ace of WWII. After the war he was hired to ferry war surplus aircraft to embattled Israel. But on 20 May 1948, while taking off from Rome with his next delivery of a Norseman, he crashed and was killed.* (PL 14940)

ABOVE LEFT:
The battle for control of this Mediterranean island heated up in 1942 as Malta was strategically invaluable to both the Allies and the Axis forces.

ABOVE RIGHT: *With 30 kills under his belt at the time this photo was taken, "Buzz" Beurling stands proudly with his Spitfire.*
(NATIONAL AVIATION MUSEUM)

have been as quick to let our heroes slip away as we have been to embrace them.

George Beurling was born on 6 December 1921 in the modest town of Verdun, Quebec. His father, Frederick, had recently turned from Presbyterianism to an ultra-conservative sect known as the Exclusive Brethren. Whether the resulting puritanical lifestyle was beneficial or detrimental to George's obsession with flying will always be conjectural, but the lanky, blue-eyed ace from Verdun would spend his short life aloof from his mates and abstinent from alcohol and tobacco. In place of these mind-numbing vices, Beurling studied the art of air warfare, and raised it to a science.

ROADBLOCKS

Throughout the thirties, Beurling did anything to try to get up and fly, but no one else respected his single-minded purpose. One roadblock after another came up: lack of funds, lack of parental permission, lack of education. Not until May 1940 did someone feel confident enough to sign on the future ace; the pilot-starved Royal Air Force (RAF). Beurling jumped on a ship to report (and back and forth again after discovering he had forgotten his birth certificate), but nothing would now stop him from flying.

Not that his fellow enlistees did not think twice about it on occasion. Beurling's obsession led him more than once into conflict with authority. He punched out a sergeant with whom he disagreed over a matter of drill and, not for the last time, buzzed a control tower. After spending time with an Operational Training Unit (OTU), Beurling was assigned to 403 Squadron where he flew only a few uneventful missions. This Squadron became an all-Canadian unit, but because George was RAF he went to 41 Squadron. There, he felt he was being unnecessarily picked on, being assigned to the number 4, or "tail-end Charlie" position in the flight. It was from here that "Buzz" scored his first kill. Bounced by five *Focke-Wulfs*, Beurling's Spitfire was damaged, but he managed to out-manoeuvre and destroy his opponent despite being damaged. Back at base, he received not the expected praise, but angry admonition for breaking formation. This style of warfare did not suit Beurling's lone-wolf style at all, and when he heard about an overseas posting, he jumped at the chance. Within days, he was on his way to Malta.

STRATEGIC ISLAND

This strategic island has known many invaders over the centuries, but probably no greater misery than that period during which she became Britain's isolated "aircraft carrier" in the Mediterranean. Rommel's *Afrika Korps* was tearing up North Africa in early 1942 and he needed Italian supplies to feed his advances. Just as desperately, the British needed to choke off the supply route to save the Suez Canal from capture. Strategically, whoever controlled Malta controlled the "Med" and the world beyond.

Beurling was not the only Canadian at Malta in 1942. Pilot officer R.W. "Buck" McNair shot down nine planes while there, and "Wally" McLeod claimed a dozen more (he would end up with 21 victories overall, but not survive the war). Lieutenant Vernon Woodward flew the Gloster Gladiator biplane and Hurricane in the Western Desert and counted 22 kills, second among Canadians.

LEGENDARY SCORE

The operation that sent the desperately needed "Spits" to Malta was a dangerous one. Stripped of their machine guns and given extra fuel, the planes were launched from the aircraft carries *HMS Eagle* and *USS Wasp,* while at their extreme limit. The Royal Navy dared come no closer. Not every plane made it and those that did often found

RIGHT TOP: *The Supermarine Spitfire has been called one of the best all-round aircraft of the Second World War. (PAINTING BY R.W. BRADFORD, NATIONAL AVIATION MUSEUM)*
RIGHT MIDDLE: *After his Focke-Wulf 190 is hit from behind by a Spitfire, the pilot makes a daring jump from his doomed aircraft. Rarely was such action caught on film.*

BY OCTOBER, BEURLING HAD TWO DOZEN KILLS, A CHEST FULL OF MEDALS, AND A WASTED BODY AND MIND THAT COULD STILL LASH OUT TO DESTROY OPPOSING PLANES, BUT COULD ALSO MAKE MISTAKES.

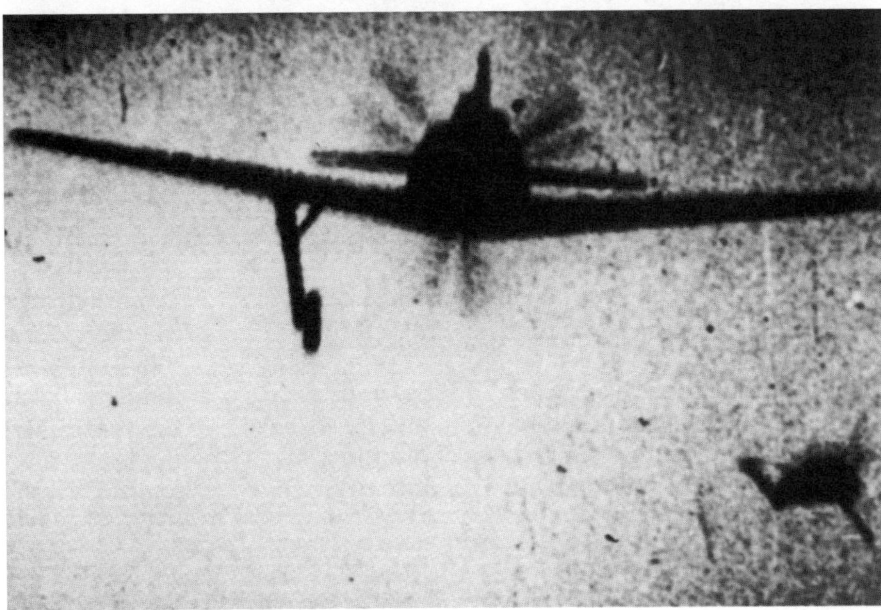

themselves turned around and back in the air within hours. Beurling's first problem after landing was to live down his reputation as a dangerous loner. Only after a showdown, however, with Flight Commander P.B. "Laddie" Lucas, did George start to play the game by the rules. Within a month, his score was mounting to legendary levels.

Beurling developed three methods for improving his skills: he exercised his eyes to focus at changing distances, he recorded all his combat experiences in a black book and memorized the required mathematics, and he shot lizards. Shooting lizards with a .38 Smith and Wesson as they skittered through the baking dust of Takali air field enabled him to play out an attack on moving targets. Coupled with an obsessive attention to detail about the aircraft he was using that day, Beurling compiled a list of eccentricities as long as his victories.

END OF GLORY DAYS

July 1942 was George's best single month. On the 6th, he shot down a Messerschmitt and two Italian fighters while damaging a bomber. (For his efforts, he received a Distinguished Flying Medal.) Endless waves of Italian bombers came to pound Malta with their fighter escorts, and numerous smoking hulks were left in evidence of George Beurling's incredible skill. Taking every opportunity to fly, Beurling would take on two or three missions a day. Unfortunately, combined with the poor quality of food available, his health was deteriorating rapidly. Gastrointestinal difficulties and skin problems often laid him out for days, and the mental strain threatened to crack him as it had done so many pilots before.

By October, Beurling had two dozen kills, a chest full of medals, and a wasted body and mind that could still lash out to destroy opposing planes, but could also make mistakes. On the 14th, Beurling spotted a JU-88 and two ME-109s, but he forgot to beware the "Hun in the Sun." His Spit was ripped by cannon fire as suddenly as he had delivered it to so many others. The plane fell 16,000 feet before Beurling, hit in the chest and left leg, could get himself out. He managed to survive this downing, but his glory days as a Knight of Malta were over.

Only 21 years old, the young ace would now be called upon to tour Canada as a living symbol of selflessness and devotion to duty, two things that George Beurling never much cared about. With the grinning William Lyon Mackenzie King using the battered pilot as a poster boy, George's future would not be so appealing as his past.

REPRINTED FROM:
Esprit de Corps, *Volume 1 Issue 8*
AUTHOR: *James G. Scott*

DIEPPE - TRAGEDY TO TRIUMPH

The story of Dieppe is widely known in Canada, and frequently analyzed. The fact that a force composed primarily of Canadians was annihilated on that French beach 50 years ago is not in dispute. Why they were annihilated, and by whose orders, has long been a matter of contention. In their book, *Dieppe: Tragedy to Triumph*, Brigadier General (retired) Denis Whitaker and his wife Shelagh, explore the political and strategic side to this battle as well as the tactical. (As a captain in the Royal Hamilton Light Infantry, Whitaker was in the first rush up that murderous beach, and one of the lucky few to escape alive.) They conclude the sacrifice was not in vain.

POINT OF NO RETURN

Operation Jubilee – the raid on Dieppe – began at 01:24 hrs on 19 August 1942, in a small room in the top story of a remote house on the Sussex coast.

The radar officer on the graveyard shift at Beachy Head picked up echoes of an enemy convoy heading from Boulogne to Dieppe - dead in the path of the Anglo-Canadian assault force of 6000 men. He alerted the Commander-in-Chief Portsmouth, Admiral Sir William James. Three minutes later, James relayed the warning to Operation Jubilee's naval force commander, Captain John Hughes-Hallett, on the command ship, the destroyer HMS *Calpe*. The warning went unheeded. *Was it not received?*

AT 0244 HOURS, TWO SOUTH-COAST RADAR STATIONS ONCE MORE PICKED UP THE GERMAN CONVOY'S ECHO. BY NOW IT WAS CLEARLY ON A COLLISION COURSE WITH THE DIEPPE RAIDERS. AGAIN, ADMIRAL JAMES URGENTLY SIGNALLED THE COMMAND SHIPS: UNIDENTIFIED VESSELS WERE ON A DIRECT LINE WITH THEM. STILL THE FLOTILLA FORGED AHEAD.

In the wardroom of the *Calpe*, the Canadian in charge of the military operation, Major General Hamilton Roberts – unaware of the threat – peered at his watch. It would soon be 03:00 hrs: officially, the point of no return. In minutes, the landing ships would be at their allotted positions 10 miles off the coast of France, ready to lower their assault landing craft (LCAs) into the Channel waters. Already, the small boats were swinging from davits as troops clambered aboard, clumsy under their 60-pound burdens of weapons, grenades and ammunition.

The tank landing craft (LCTs) and small wooden R boats (unarmed landing craft personnel) had made the uncomfortable crossing and were now bobbing here and

OPPOSITE PAGE: *The invasion fleet departs for the ill-fated raid on the beaches of Dieppe. A German convoy spotted the flotilla and alerted their comrades of the impending attack.* (*NAC PA171080*)
ABOVE: *Casualties and dead line the main beach of Dieppe. A German soldier walks amid the wreckage.* (*NAC*)

there, waiting for the final run-in to begin.

Unaware of the impending disaster, the assault force of 4961 officers and men of the Second Canadian Infantry Division, and 1057 British commandos and 50 US Rangers, sailed serenely south through the calm Channel waters. It was a warm night, moonless. In 13 separate groups, the 237-ship flotilla had steamed without incident through the quarter-mile-wide paths being cleared by the mine-sweepers, and assembled off the French coast to make their final approaches. All was in darkness, silent except for the hum of the engines, the gentle slap of water on the hulls, and the murmur of men bemused by the battle ahead of them.

For Hughes-Hallett, it was a heady experience to go into action – his first action as a captain – in the greatest amphibious operation since Gallipoli. The sight of hundreds of ships and craft filling the horizon had a "certain dream-like quality" after so many months of planning. The flotilla was manned by 3000 British sailors. There were eight destroyers as well as a variety of crafts such as gunboats, flak ships, converted Channel ferries put to use as troop carriers, and a vast number of landing craft for personnel and armour.

At 02:44 hrs, two south-coast radar stations once more picked up the German convoy's echo. By now it was clearly on a collision course with the Dieppe raiders. Again, Admiral James urgently signalled the command ships: unidentified vessels were on a direct line with them.

Still the flotilla forged ahead.

Several other of the destroyers in the flotilla also intercepted the warning. They had not sighted enemy vessels on their radar screens and were perplexed. But they maintained an uneasy silence, believing that the *Calpe* would take charge.

Strangely, the man to whom this vital intelligence was sent, Captain Hughes-Hallett, did nothing. Had he not received the signals? Why was he not acting upon them?

There would be no sleep for Major General Ham Roberts that night. Although he turned in for a brief rest, it was only to lie awake, tossing on the narrow berth and – for the hundredth time – mentally reviewing the plan of Lieutenant General Bernard Montgomery, and that it had received strong votes of approval by Canada's senior officers, Generals Andrew McNaughton and Harry Crerar.

In a few hours, ten separate units would force landings on eight different assault points. But if any one of them failed, he reflected, the entire operation was in jeopardy.

A VERY POLITICAL WAR

The myth that Canadian corps soldiers were howling for a fight has gone on for 50 years. Well-regarded military histories have perpetuated it: "the morale of the forces was suffering because of lack of opportunity for

fighting." Another: there was "forlorn and increasingly vocal resentment" as Canadians "languished at garrison duties in England." And still another: it was "common knowledge that the troops were browned off."

As a platoon commander and later as a commanding officer, I can attest that we weren't "browned off." I don't believe the morale in the Rileys was suffering, nor was it in any other units I saw or heard about in England. Many veterans will corroborate this: for example, Major General Dan Spry, who commanded the Third Canadian Division, and Lieutenant Tom Taylor of the Royal Regiment who, as a Dieppe POW, surely qualifies as a specialist in troop morale.

REMARKABLE TRANSFORMATION

The men were keen. They may not have liked the 25-mile marches, but who does? There was a very positive side to the experience of being in Britain. There can be few veterans today who would not agree that living in England was a rewarding experience. Colonel Stacey, who researched the subject in depth, called the transformation of the Canadian soldier's relationship with the British people "remarkable" for its warm goodwill.

We certainly didn't feel we were "languishing." We believed we were fulfilling a role. Our job was to defend England from enemy invasion. There was always that possibility of a German paratroop attack.

MAJOR PAUL SAVOY TOOK COMMUNION IN A SUSSEX SCHOOLHOUSE AND THEN CLIMBED ABOARD HIS BATTALION'S SHIP. HE WOULD DIE MOMENTS AFTER HE TOUCHED DOWN ON THE SHORES OF DIEPPE'S MAIN BEACH.

I can't remember a lot of crime. Sure, there were a few guys who didn't get back from leave on schedule, but there weren't a lot of criminal offenses.

Another popular myth has to do with the fact that Canadian troops at Aldershot booed the prime minster when he addressed them in August 1941. Yes, they did boo him, and this has since been attributed to the restlessness and belligerence of the men who were there - and to the "morale problems," reports of which were so greatly exaggerated.

I was present that day. It was a very cold, wet afternoon. Many of us had travelled 50 miles or more to reach Aldershot on time, and we were assembled at the sports stadium, fortunately under cover of the grandstand. However, a special colour guard had been assembled, and was formed up in the open awaiting King's arrival. The prime minister was delayed by several hours and evidently did not bother to send word ahead. The guard and bands were kept standing in the belting rain all that time, soaked and cold. This cavalier treatment was what made the men so furious. When King finally arrived, they booed.

MOMENTARY ANGER

It was not from sagging morale, not from any fever-pitch for battle - it was just momentary anger at thoughtless treatment of soldiers.

It quickly passed.

"I bring you greetings from your wives and loved ones," King began.

"But did you bring us any cigarettes" a bold voice shouted from the back.

"I'll see that you get lots of cigarettes!" King, ever the politician, promptly retorted.

Whereupon he was cheered.

When we were posted to England - voluntarily giving up our homes, families, and employment - we thought we were serving our country. We never dreamed our sacrifice might actually be viewed by Canadian politicians as a period of idleness or dissipation.

If we'd been ordered to battle, anywhere, we would have gone, with determination and enthusiasm - as we did, to Dieppe. After all, we had volunteered to fight and we respected that commitment. But we certainly weren't agitating for it. It's all right for the press to criticize the fact that we hadn't seen much action - their lives weren't on the line. I sure wasn't pushing my neck out and saying I wanted to get shot at.

I was overseas for almost six years, and I think morale was pretty good – except perhaps when we were fighting in the fall of '44 with untrained reinforcements. Then we again realized that the government didn't give a damn about us.

Morale would not have been as good if we had known then what we now know – that we were pawns being moved by political whim. We were there to help win a

LEFT:
In the disastrous raid on Dieppe, Canadians who survived the landing were taken prisoner and marched through city streets to holding areas in the rear. Of the 1874 Canadian POWs, 568 were wounded and 72 would die before being released.
(DND)

RIGHT:
A German NCO leads his infantry troops as they rush to man new defensive positions on the Dieppe headlands.
(BUNDESARCHIV, KOBLENZ)

war – not to be vote-getters for Mackenzie King [or help Churchill offset the recent British loss at Tobruk].

THE RESTIVE WOLFHOUND

Several platoons from the Essex Scottish, believing they were on yet another exercise, left some of their weapons and ammunition behind. They were forced to borrow 20 Tommy guns and ammunition from the ship's stock after their craft – the converted ferryboats *Prince Charles* and *Prince Leopold* – sailed. The machine-gunners of the Toronto Scottish discovered too late, while setting up their weapons in the bows of their assault craft, that they had no tracer bullets. These were essential in helping them zero in on their targets. The Camerons found their equipment dumped in a pile, the explosives unlabelled, the Stens still thick in grease. Because only the C., Lieutenant Colonel Gostling, and a few of his officers had any experience with Stens, the soldiers spent most of the crossing attempting to clean and to familiarize themselves with the weapon – all in the dark.

Aboard the *Prince Albert*, the officers of Lovat's No. 4 Commando had a pre-dawn breakfast of stew, for which they were charged an outrageous 13 shillings and fourpence. "The stew needed more salt but no one reached for it and we ate in preoccupied silence," Major Derek Mills-Roberts recalled. Lieutenant Colonel Torchy Durnford-Slater No. 3 Commando was to have hardtack, free, while contorted into one of the 32 wooden 20-man R boats. The U.S. Rangers aboard squirmed uncomfortably on the hard benches, confined even more by their bulky life jackets.

The Royal Regiment of Canada embarked two of its companies aboard the *Queen Emma,* the remaining two on the *Princess Astrid*. Edward Force – comprising three platoons of the Black Watch (Royal Highland Regiment of Canada) and some artillery personnel under command of Captain Ray Hicks – sailed on the *Duke of Wellington*. The Black Watch, whose assignment was to protect the Royal's left flank, had not had any Isle of Wight training either. While the ship was still in port, one young Jock began priming grenades with more enthusiasm than skill. One of these exploded, killing the soldier and wounding 18 others. The corporal in charge of moving the casualties ashore returned too late; his ship had sailed without him.

There were grim coincidences everywhere. A trooper in the Calgary Tanks named Charlie Rodgers had been trained for the assault as a gunner in Lieutenant Bennett's tank. He was replaced at the last moment when the original gunner came back from hospital unexpectedly. Bennett's tank would suffer direct hits. Both he and his gunner would be taken prisoner.

Royal Hamilton Light Infantry (RHLI) company commander, Major Norry Waldron, returned to camp from a course just in time to take command of his company for the raid. He would be killed leading the survivors of his company through a gap blown in the wire barricade on the beach.

There had been no intention of permitting the battalion's padre, honorary Captain John Foote, to accompany the raiders. "I know what's in the wind, Bob. I want to go," he insisted to his reluctant CO, Bob Labatt. After the battle, Foote, just as stubbornly, would refuse to be evacuated from Dieppe; instead he would stay with "his boys" in POW camp.

The CO of Les Fusiliers Mont-Royal, Lieutenant Colonel Dollard Ménard, had told one of his officers, Major Paul Savoy, that he was too old for the raid. Under pressure, Ménard relented. With the rest of his battalion, Savoy took communion in a Sussex schoolhouse and then climbed aboard his battalion's ship. He would die moments after he touched down on the shores of Dieppe's main beach. Ménard, for his part, was the only CO of the seven major Canadian units engaged, who would return from the raid, albeit several wounded.

The Queen's Own Cameron Highlanders of Winnipeg, complete with the battalion piper, Lance Corporal Alec Graham, crossed in R boats. Graham was to pipe his unit ashore. He would still be clutching his bagpipes when he was captured some hours later.

The South Saskatchewans, who would precede the Camerons onto the Pourville beaches, were luckier: they crossed in destroyers, only climbing aboard the LCAs 10 miles or so offshore.

Across Sussex, the Second Canadian Infantry Division battalion areas were by now almost abandoned. The few light-duty personnel remaining at them had been told that the men were off on a two-day exercise.

At the Riley headquarters, the officer left behind was my close friend, Captain Jervis O'Donohoe, the assistant adjutant. Jervis stood at the gates to see us off.

The next time I saw him, 32 hours later, he was standing rooted at the same place, tears streaming down his face, as the small straggle of weary and begrimed infantrymen who had survived Dieppe filed silently in. The one officer in the battalion who had come through the battle without being wounded, killed, or captured, hugged him, weeping freely. That officer was myself.

In total, 65 per cent of the Canadians in the six assault battalions were casualties. The 2nd Infantry Division was destroyed at Dieppe.

ABOVE:
After the disastrous Dieppe raid, those who managed to retreat to landing craft were evacuated to destroyers.
(NAC/PA 116298)

"HAD DIEPPE TURNED OUT TO BE A CHEAP SUCCESS, THERE WOULD HAVE RESULTED A FALSE AND QUITE INADEQUATE APPRECIATION OF THE PROBLEM OF INVASION. THE 'SOBERING EFFECTS' OF THE DIEPPE OPERATION, HAVE HAD AN IMPORTANT EFFECT ON ALLIED POLICIES, STRATEGY AND OF COURSE, COMBINED SERVICE TACTICS."

DIEPPE TO D-DAY

Was Dieppe a Failure or a Success?

General Crerar believed that "had Dieppe turned out to be a cheap success, there would have resulted a false and quite inadequate appreciation of the problem of invasion. The 'sobering effects' of the Dieppe operation, in my opinion, have had an important effect on Allied policies, strategy and of course, Combined Service tactics."

Philip Ziegler, Mountbatten's official biographer, concluded, "If there had been no Dieppe and the invasion proper had been conducted with similar insouciance, the bloodshed would have been on a scale many times greater, the course of the war might have been turned."

Historian Eric Maguire went one step further; stating that without the experiences of Dieppe, it is unlikely that Overlord would have taken place; and that had it been attempted, it would surely have failed.

From the beaches of Normandy, General Eisenhower signalled Mountbatten: "Except for Dieppe and the work of your organization we would have been lacking much of the special equipment and much of the knowledge needed for the invasion."

On June 10, 1944, six men composed a letter to the former commander of Combined Operations at the time of the Dieppe raid: Lord Louis Mountbatten:

Today we visited British and American armies on the soil of France. We sailed through vast fleets of ships with landing craft of many types pouring men, vehicles and stores ashore. We saw clearly the manoeuvre in progress and in progress of rapid development.

We shared our secrets and helped each other all we could. We wish to tell you of this remarkable technique and therefore the success of the venture has it origin in developments affected by you and your staff of Combined Operations.

The letter was signed by Winston Churchill, Field Marshal Lord Alanbrooke, Field Marshal Smuts, General George Marshall, Admiral Ernest King, and General Hap Arnold.

I am appalled when people with little or no operational experience attempt to dismiss the lessons learned at Dieppe as inconsequential. These lessons, both strategic and tactical, saved countless lives as a result of their far-reaching influence on the success of future operations.

The courage and sacrifice of our men of Dieppe was clearly not in vain. The men of D-Day landed with a strong umbrella of air and artillery support. Their assault equipment – landing craft, armour and weapons – were superb. Their intelligence was accurate.

These assault skills and technical innovations were "bought and paid for" by Second Canadian Infantry Division at Dieppe.

REPRINTED FROM:
Esprit de Corps, *Volume 2 Issue 3*
AUTHOR: *Denis and Shelagh Whitaker*

THE SPOOKS TEN GODFATHERS

British radar expert, Jack Nissen, had too much top-secret technology in his head when he went to Dieppe. So they gave him ten Canadians to protect him… or to execute him if captured.

OF THE 6086 MEN in the Dieppe raid, Jack Nissen had the best chance of not being captured; he also had a better than average chance of being killed because Canadian guns were trained on him throughout most of his seven hours at Pourville. An RAF radar expert, Nissen's task was to study the operation of German radar at Caude-Cote, two miles west of Dieppe. The order covering his assignment added that the South Saskatchewan regiment would provide "adequate protection as the RDF expert must under no circumstances fall into enemy hands."

Circumstances, seemingly unrelated, linked Flight Sergeant Nissen to this strange moment in history. Earlier that year, a British commando raid on Bruneval, about 12 miles north of Le Havre, enabled an RAF radar technician to dismantle a German *Wurtzburg* radar installation and haul pieces back to England for examination. The attack had come as a complete surprise to the Germans and Air Commodore Victor Tait, head of RAF radar, sent a message to British sites. It was a simple warning not to let the same thing happen to them.

Jack Nissen responded by staging successful attacks on his station. The exercises simulated a seaborne attack and Nissen's initiative caught the attention of Tait. Lord Louis Mountbatten had just been appointed head of combined operations which was selecting other targets on the French coast. Among other things they needed information on the enemy's *Freya* radar but the man who had been at Bruneval said no thanks to a return engagement. In an interview with Tait and Mountbatten, Nissen agreed to investigate *Freya* 28 near Dieppe. Both Tait and Mountbatten pointed out the danger of the situation because Nissen had technical knowledge which must not fall into enemy hands.

WOUNDED WILL BE SHOT

Nissen was then handed over to a pompous Intelligence Officer who stressed the secrecy of the mission and read four pages of the Defence of the Realm Act, during which Nissen fell asleep. However, he was fully awake when the Wing Commander pointed out that under no circumstances would he be taken prisoner. "Ten men will be assigned to help you, but if you are wounded and cannot make it back you will be shot," Nissen was told. His medical kit would also contain a pill whose effects would be immediately lethal.

Nissen's recollection of those days is that a tug-of-war was developing between Mountbatten and Field Marshal Montgomery over the nature of the raid. Mountbatten favoured a swift strike by small forces such as the raid on St. Nazaire. Montgomery broadened the objectives and called for a larger force which the army could provide from amongst impatient Canadians. The frontal attack at Dieppe was not in Mountbatten's original plan because it was not considered suitable tank terrain. His plan had tanks landing at Quibberville some six miles to the West, but the final version of the plan called for a complex frontal attack and a wish list of objectives, although Montgomery was no longer personally involved.

In late June, Lieuteant Colonel Cecil Merritt called Captain Murray Osten to his office on the Isle of Wight. Merritt explained that an Radar Direction Finding (RDF) expert was joining "A" company and Osten would have to detail men to cover him as they fought up to Freya 28 at Pourville. Osten saw no problem. Merritt explained that if the RDF man was wounded or couldn't make it out, Osten would have to deal with it.

ABOVE: *The Freya radar tower at Dieppe was little more than a side show for the main raiding force, but for Jack "Spook" Nissen and his ten "bodyguards," it was the main event. (NATIONAL ARCHIVES OF CANADA)*

THE GODFATHERS

When Nissen reported to Norris Castle, he was turned over to Sergeant James Blackwell, a WWI retread and signals man. Corporal Graham Mavor and Les Trusell, two to the best shots in the regiment, were assigned to lead two squads of four men each. A special parade was held and Jack Nissen, in an ill-fitting army uniform without insignia, was invited to select his eight bodyguards, Godfathers. Sergeant Major Ed Dunkerly was about to introduce Jack to the group when the RDF man indicated he didn't want to know any more names. He already knew of Mavor, Trussell and Charlie Sawden and felt the less anybody knew about anybody else the better. "No names, no pack drill," Nissen concluded. So the strange relationship between a Cockney lad and ten tough citizens from Saskatchewan was born.

The Canadians suspiciously surrounded Nissen who spoke with caution fearing that his RAF jargon might give the game away. Today he laughs about it, but late in June of 1942 it was a major concern. "I don't want to know any of you," Jack reminded them, "but I've got to call you something. My name's Jack."

"I'll call you Spook."

CULTURE SHOCK

This came from a man who looked like an Indian and sucked a cigarette through yellow stained fingers. A man originally from Quebec (but who got drunk in Regina and ended up sober but in the army) was called "Frenchie." Then there was Red and Silver because of their hair, and Bud, a lumberjack who fondly remembered his buddies in the Saskatchewan woods. The last man's grin reminded Jack of Sunny Jim, the breakfast food character. It was a session heavy with cultural shock for Jack Nissen, a gentle youth born within the sound of Beau Bells. He got to know these men without knowing their identity in the training which followed.

Shortly before 05:00 hrs on the morning of 19 August, the engines of the landing craft screamed into reverse. Two hundred foot cliffs loomed in the darkness. The RDF station was at the top of the cliff but they'd come too far east. The LCA rocked broadside into the incoming tide and clawed its way westward.

The second mistake was going too far west and having to cross the river Scie to get back to the radar site. As they completed their run in they came under light artillery fire and a sergeant from "A" company thrust a bayonet towards Jack's throat while Jack jabbed him in the gut with a revolver. It was the result of an argument over equipment and also resentment which had been festering for weeks because Jack had drawn too many men from the sergeant's platoon. Jack and the sergeant established a standoff and Frenchie took a final swig of rum from his water bottle as the ramp dropped.

EIGHT FOOT SEAWALL

They hit the beach running uphill on marbles towards an eight foot seawall. Red and green lights danced lazily out from the cliffs and these were transformed into a hail of tracer bullets which swept the next craft to land. The seawall wore a crown of barbed wire with a gap in it. John McLeod found a nearby ladder and mounted the wall. The promenade was under distant fire when Nissen climbed the wall and huddled against a house. An alarm clock went off

just above his head and a woman peered briefly into the darkness. She muttered something and slammed the shutters.

While waiting for his group to assemble, Nissen noticed a post containing communication lines to the west. He climbed the post and cut the lines which led to gun emplacements. British commandos had gone in on Orange Beach where Ken Dearson, Mountbatten's communications specialist was about to neutralize a lighthouse which was the communications centre for the German army, navy and air force.

INHUMAN BRAVERY

Nissen's escort assembled and dashed from house to house towards the bridge. The road beyond was the floor of a valley between a cliff and a high place, the 200-foot cliff on the left housed *Freya* 28 and was dotted with gun positions. Murderous fire from a nearby pillbox stopped traffic on the bridge. Charlie Sawden waited until the enemy gunners were reloading then trotted to the emplacement and dropped in two grenades. Colonel Merritt, meanwhile, arrived on the bridge which was under heavy fire and very deliberately began directing traffic. The sight of the tall officer on the bridge waving his helmet and urging the men onward galvanized the regiment. Merritt made several trips across the narrow bridge and was later awarded the Victoria Cross for almost inhuman valour. Captain Murray Osten led "A" company across but he was hit and blown into the water. He emerged, wounded, dripping seaweed but still very much in command. Then, just beyond the bridge, Jack looked down at the dead face of the sergeant who had argued with him moments earlier. Spook understood the man's resentment at losing some of his best men to the radarman and bodyguard.

Murray Osten led the group inland to where a road curved up behind the radar installation. Mavor and Charlie were killed on the way in. Crawling through a ditch, Nissen was pounded by a sudden explosion. It was the man 20 feet in front of him, who had been carrying mortar shells. They wormed their way up the hill and by the time they reached the shelter of a road below the *Freya* station about 24 of "A" company's 100 men remained. Nissen crouched with Osten looking uphill to the formidable radar installation.

PUNY FORCES

Anchored in concrete, with a thick skirt of gravel, dirt and barbed wire, *Freya* defied their puny forces which had no radio communication and few mortars. Nissen and Les Thrussel went back down to Pourville for help; more mortars and an attempt to range naval guns on *Freya* 28. The bridge was now littered two deep with dead and Pourville was in ruins. Radio communications were a shambles and there was no way of raising the command ship.

Jack recruited some Camerons with mortars and went back up the hill. The barbed wire, the machine gun nests and pill boxes on two sides of *Freya* still doomed the prospects of attack. Nissen went back to Pourville where he found Merritt, who seemed to have aged considerably in the five hours of battle. Merritt was able to assign a few more Camerons but by the time they got to the top of the hill casualties had reduced their limited number. They still didn't have sufficient strength to attack.

Nissen crouched on the down side of the road and a machine gun burst raked the

MURDEROUS FIRE FROM A NEARBY PILLBOX STOPPED TRAFFIC ON THE BRIDGE. COLONEL MERRITT ARRIVED ON THE BRIDGE AND VERY DELIBERATELY BEGAN DIRECTING TRAFFIC. THE SIGHT OF THE TALL OFFICER ON THE BRIDGE WAVING HIS HELMET AND URGING THE MEN ONWARD GALVANIZED THE REGIMENT.

ABOVE:
With tanks and vehicles churning up the gravel, men run up the beaches of Dieppe under intense machine-gun fire and shelling. Canada's first serious encounter with a formidable enemy proved a tactical failure, suffering over 200 wounded and nearly 1000 dead.
("DIEPPE RAID" BY CHARLES COMFORT, CANADIAN WAR MUSEUM)

OPPOSITE PAGE:
Colonel Cecil Merritt, VC. Landing near Pourville, the South Saskatchewan Regiment was to cross the Scie River as part of their objective. After the first group was mowed down by machine-gun fire, Colonel Merritt, with his helmet hanging from his wrist, repeatedly led his men over the bridge. Destroying pillboxes as they moved inland, Merritt was wounded twice as he organized his men in their withdrawal and gave them cover fire. He would be captured and spend the rest of the war a prisoner at Camp Eichstatt in Bavaria.
(NATIONAL ARCHIVES OF CANADA)

ground. Broken twigs or bits of rock slashed his face. Osten turned in alarm as blood streamed down Nissen's face. Had the dreaded moment arrived? Not quite. Nissen decided to crawl up to *Freya* and cut the telephone lines. At one point in his 40-yard crawl, he felt the earth vibrate. He had crawled next to a buried machine gun post which was firing below. Nissen edged forward, climbing a 15-foot pole where he snipped seven wires and dropped to the ground. Then he cautiously slithered back to Osten and decided to intercept one of the allied tanks which would be coming through to help with the withdrawal.

HOSTILE GEESE

Nissen went inland to a crossroads and waited, his escort somewhat diminished. The approaching tanks were German. Frenchie was hit and Jack shoved a rosary in his hands while murmuring a brief Yiddish prayer. With German infantry closing in on them, they ran through farm yards fighting hostile geese. Silver, the sixth escort, died of a stomach wound. They fought their way down to Pourville – now under siege – and Lofty was killed as they reached shelter in the promenade.

Nissen recovered an abandoned anti-tank gun and Bob Kohaly helped him load it. Two shots at a building on the cliff produced a brief lull, followed by a dash for the beach. Kohaly was hit shortly afterwards, but both made it to landing craft. Merritt fought a rear-guard action until his men were out of ammunition. Then the proud survivors marched into captivity.

When Nissen cut the landwires at *Freya* 28, it helped confirm what Tait wanted to know about how one radar station fed into another. Jack's observation that *Freya* could interrupt a sweep to lock onto an aircraft strengthened Tait's suspicion that *Freya* was a precision radar. The subsequent development of a Mandrel jamming device saved thousands of lives on D-Day.

TEN GALLANT MEN REMEMBERED

Nissen has maintained a warm friendship with the survivors but regrets the name game he had to play with his Godfathers. It still leads to confusion in his mind. But he clearly remembers ten gallant men. "I see their young, strong faces every day."

Colonel Cecil C.I. Merritt, VC, the man who wrote a brilliant page in Canadian military history 50 years ago, now wants to close the book on Dieppe. He sees no reason why the anniversary has to be observed with such dedication and a spate of books. Perhaps the answer lies in our British heritage which has a penchant for celebrating failures such as Balaklava, Gallipoli, the Somme and Dunkirk. Merritt suggests that remembrance of the sacrifices at Dieppe could now be covered by an epic poem like *The Charge of the Light Brigade*.

REPRINTED FROM:
Esprit de Corps, *Volume 2 Issue 3*
AUTHOR:
Norman Shannon

ATTRITION OVER DIEPPE

Two years after the Battle of Britain, the new head of RAF Fighter Command was thirsting for an air battle.

In the early morning hours of 19 August 1942, a squadron of Spitfires makes their way to Dieppe in support of landing forces. (PAINTING BY WALTER WRIGHT)

WHILE SOME WRITERS INSIST that the lessons learned at Dieppe were a tough necessity, two ghosts from WWI haunt the operation and raise the questions: how many men have to die before planners learn a lesson, and must such lessons be relearned with each generation?

At Gallipoli in 1915 the operation failed because of inadequate covering fire, hostile cliffs, and failure to use sufficient capital ships in the narrow Dardanelles strait. The same elements of failure were present in the Dieppe planning which also borrowed heavily from a ghost from the Western front. The ghost of Hugh Montague Trenchard must have smiled as the air plan for Dieppe evolved. Major General Trenchard was the hard-nosed commander of the RFC in France in WWI and his aggressive policy of dominating enemy sky made him the architect of aerial attrition on the Somme, and later during Bloody April when he lost 316 aircrew. Trenchard insisted on Distant Offensive Patrols; sending his fighters into 'Hunland' on wasteful excursions while enemy fighters pounced on unarmed or cumbersome machines at the front.

Trenchard had many virtues as a leader but his inflexible policy of claiming enemy sky put the RFC on the long end of a 4:1 loss ratio during that month in 1917. His critics could see no advantage in staging combats simply for the sake of following a blind policy of aggression, while vulnerable allied machines fell along the front.

The air action at Dieppe was hailed as a success on the night of 19 August when the full dimension of tragedy began to trickle in. Claims were distorted, just as they were during the Battle of Britain when the RAF claimed 175 German aircraft were shot down. The air action over Dieppe has somehow survived as a victory although RAF losses were twice those of the enemy, and the day was more like a demolition derby than a planned air battle.

FINAL AIR PLAN

The final air plan for Dieppe was a page from Trenchard's book: its purpose was to provide support for the landings and to provoke the Luftwaffe into the greatest air battle of the War. The strange array of aircraft assembled for the job suggests that the priority lay with the latter objective. Of 70 squadrons, 61 were fighters, two fighter-bombers and two medium bombers. There was an assortment of smoke-producing aircraft. Presumably the Gallipoli experience was recognized, as the original Dieppe plan called for 300 bombers to support the landings. It was approved by the chiefs-of-staff, but "Bomber" Harris, who had started his thousand-bomber, career-enhancement raids, was ill-disposed towards diversion from his personal agenda. Furthermore, Harris maintained that his bombers could not provide the precision required to bomb the waterfront and not create chaos in Dieppe.

Bomber Command was capable of dropping bombs on enemy airfields. An attack synchronized with the landings could have immobilized the enemy's air force, at least temporarily. But Harris dismissed providing air support, just as the navy resisted providing fire power. Lessons of Gallipoli notwithstanding, the channel is little more than 20 miles wide between Dieppe and Newhaven, and the navy refused to send capital ships in to provide covering fire.

Combined Operations was a new concept and Lord Mountbatten new to the job. His plan for a commando-style raid on either flank of Dieppe may have worked as previous ones had done at St. Nazaire. General Montgomery could not resist a frontal attack. Montgomery left for North Africa, disenchanted with the entire scenario, but the army mustered enough strength around the planning table to keep the idea of a tank landing at Dieppe alive. As indicated, there was original recognition of the need for bomber support, but bit by bit the once feasible plan became a smorgasbord where commanders picked up choice bits and rejected anything which interfered with their personal agendas. With Bomber Command and the navy refusing to participate with covering fire, and calling for a frontal attack, the smorgasbord became a dog's breakfast.

MAGNIFICENT RAID

At 04:45 hrs on the morning of 19 August, Spitfires began shooting up Ailly lighthouse, a communications centre on the western flank where Lord Lovat's 4th Commando came ashore to silence the guns at Varangeville and cut communications at Quiberville. The air support was an asset and Lovat's men carried off a magnificent raid with objectives accomplished. No other unit would report success that day. The point at issue here is how much did Spitfires really help the ground forces? Lovat's men worked with professional preci-

RIGHT: *A Boston medium bomber flies over the smoke screen laid by the ships below off the beaches of Dieppe. Seconds later, it would drop its load of bombs on the French port.* (NATIONAL ARCHIVES OF CANADA)

sion and silenced the guns without enemy air opposition. So what were the Spitfires doing other than drawing flak and waiting for enemy fighters?

Other landings took place without enemy air opposition; eight navy destroyers provided covering fire, along with Hurricanes armed with 20mm cannon. Air Vice-Marshal Leigh-Mallory worried that the *Luftwaffe* might not come out and fight because it was two hours before the *Focke-Wulf* 190's appeared. By then, provoking the enemy became his major concern.

Four of six Hurricanes went down in an attack on the headquarters of the 110 Infantry Division at Arques-la-Bataille and two failed to find the target. The failure was of little consequence, but reflected badly on Combined Operations Intelligence. The 110 Division had been serving on the eastern front for some time.

The American 8th Air Force bombed a German fighter drome at Abbeville and put it out of action for two hours. Although the B-17's had only recently started to operate against Germany, the Abbeville strike was effective and leads one to wonder what conditions on the beach would have been like if Harris had been induced to throw the weight of bomber command on fighter bases.

The allies put up 730 Spitfires, Hurricanes, Mustangs and Typhoons. The Typhoons of that time were not the efficient army support weapons they became following D-Day, but they and the Hurricanes were the only effective ground support aircraft. As the day moved on, the sky rained spent cartridges with aircraft clashing in over 3500 sorties. Leigh-Mallory got his wish but it was a day of pure attrition. Pilots were expendable, and all were victims of the commander's hallucinations of destroying the Luftwaffe in one battle. German bombers sank the destroyer HMS *Berkeley* but at the end of the day the RAF claimed a victory (96 planes shot down and 39 probables shrank to 49 destroyed under post-war scrutiny). RAF losses were 106 of which 13 were RCAF. The day was a sad affair illuminated only by the gallantry of the crews who were thrown into battle to destroy the Hun in the air.

The one startling aspect of Dieppe planning is the apparent lack of direction. It was a war plan established by a changing committee which failed to establish a strong consensus. Since Gallipoli the British army and navy were not noted for joint ventures. Combined Operations was the first major step towards such activities but Lord Mountbatten was obviously outflanked by the politics of war which permitted Air Marshal Harris to decline to participate. Perhaps the greatest lesson of Dieppe was that Dwight Eisenhower was shortly to be assigned to bring entrenched interests of a few into line with national and Allied interests.

REPRINTED FROM:
Esprit de Corps, *Volume 2 Issue 3*
AUTHOR: *Norm Shannon*

CANADA'S SECRET ETHNIC WARRIORS

The British used Canadians of various ethnic origins as underground agents.

ONE OF THE STRANGEST features of WWII was the secret war fought behind enemy lines in which Britain looked to a multicultural Canada for recruits. Many of the 28 Canadians who were dropped into France as agents were French Canadian and as the war spread Canadians of Yugoslavic, Italian and Chinese extraction joined the secret army. Of course the unit also drew a variety of off-beat Anglos who had language skills and knowledge of a particular country, (such as the expert on Yugoslavia who was 49 and had one eye, yet was determined to become an RAF fighter pilot).

At first glance purists would dispute the assumption that the boy from Trois Rivieres could pass as French, particularly in Paris. Fortunately, during the war France was chock-a-block with transients and Canadian accents were never the cause of apprehension. However, in times of stress agents had to discipline themselves against uttering even an occasional blasphemous "Tabarnac!"

Gustave Bieler was the first Canadian to drop into France, jumping from a Whitley bomber south-west of Paris on 18 November 1942. The Montrealer landed on rocks and severely injured his spine. His radio operator got him to a safe house in Paris where he was hospitalized for six weeks under an assumed name.

SPECIAL OPERATION EXECUTIVE

Bieler belonged to the clandestine British organization known as Special Operation Executive whose purpose was to recruit, train and direct saboteurs in France. Such groups organized into cells, harassed the enemy, and were dedicated to inflicting damage. The work of SOE was not appreciated by other British clandestine units such as MI6 which quietly went about the job of gathering intelligence. SOE operations made noise, filled a sector with increased German patrols and brought reprisals.

Five months later, still hobbling, Bieler was interviewing candidates for sabotage in a village near St. Quentin. He trained the successful ones and soon 23 teams were operating in the Lille-St. Quentin region. Within six months the RAF made 16 drops of money, arms and explosives. When RAF bombs failed to damage locks at St. Quentin, Bieler put them out of action by placing time bombs below the gate. His men then used the rest of the bombs to destroy 40 loaded barges. Bieler's network expanded and developed sophisticated methods of sabotaging trains, planes, vehicles and communication lines.

A LONELY WAR

As Bieler's group waged a successful campaign in a lonely war, other Canadians were parachuted into France. Charles Duchalard was dropped in south-west France to establish a beacon transmitter which would guide RAF aircraft to surreptitious landings. He was then to join an underground group as radar operator, but the Germans rounded up the group the day after Duchalard made contact. He then joined an escape line, helping allied airmen.

Within six months, London was asked by the underground to recall Duchalard claiming he had a tendency to speak English, drink heavily and smoke American cigarettes. He was considered a menace to security and the resistance decide to boot him. The British got him out before this happened, but SOE found no more useful employment for Duchalard.

Not all assignments followed the success of Bieler's. Apart from the skill of the agent, chance and German counter-measures were big factors in the secret war. Joseph Chartrand, an insurance salesman from Montreal, was a friend of Bieler's who worked as a statistics clerk at army headquarters in London. They met and Bieler

CARTE D'IDENTITE
Nom DesJardin
Prénoms Marcel Jean
Nationalité
Profession
Né le
Domicile
SIGNALEMENT
Taille
Cheveux
Moustache
Dos
Visage
Yeux
Teint
Signes Particuliers
Témoins :

made an offer Chartrand couldn't refuse; he would try to get him into the SOE. On 14 April 1943, the former statistics clerk was dumped on a meadow in the Loire. After an all-night journey, the small party was catching its breath at a girl's school in Tours when Germans arrived to examine textbooks.

TICKING BOMB

Chartrand and his companion were hidden, but things didn't improve much. In Rouen he was picked up for violating curfew and the details were handed over to the Germans. His credentials were that of an insurance agent and the Germans were highly suspicious of such a cover because it provided easy access to any part of the country. Furthermore, Chartrand was one of the few Canadians who used his real name. His chief wisely decided that Chartrand's presence in Rouen was a bomb waiting to explode. He arranged for a man called Claude Carton to join an underground circuit near Tours, close to where Chartrand started his mission.

From June to September, Chartrand helped organize air drops and gave weapons training to the Butlar circuit. Then in September the head of the circuit was arrested in Paris and the German vice squeezed tighter. Chartrand adopted another identity and went into hiding, but was arrested by two Gestapo agents. As they entered the village, one agent went down a side street. Chartrand and the other rode their bicycles towards Gestapo headquarters. With 300 yards to go, Chartrand threw his bicycle at the German and escaped. With no identity and little money, he made his way to Paris where he happened to meet his former circuit chief. He was shuffled around Paris until late autumn when a British motor gunboat picked him up off the Normandy coast.

PROSPER CIRCUIT DOOMED

Frank Pickersgill, brother of Parliamentarian Jack, was doing post graduate work in Europe during the 30's and was living in Paris when war was declared. He dallied a bit too long as the Germans overran France the following spring. Attempting to work his way out of the country, he was arrested and packed off to labour camps for two years. In March 1942, he escaped with another prisoner and got to England via Lisbon. Pickersgill joined the SOE and in June 1943, he and radio operator John Macalister of Guelph jumped into France to help organize a sub-circuit of a larger group. The Prosper circuit had been penetrated and was doomed. The Canadians delivered three new radios and coded messages for agents, but when these fell into German hands, the enemy closed in and arrested several hundred, including Pickersgill and Macalister.

SECURE FARCE

The Germans then began sending messages to London on Macalister's set, arranging for drops of supplies and money. This continued throughout the winter of '43-'44, resulting in the loss of a number of SOE agents. Seven of ten transmitters reporting to London were in German hands. Either the British were responding without demanding security checks or the Germans knew the checks. Neither scenario reflected well on the SOE which kept sending agents out to die. Nine months after Pickersgill's imprisonment, in a drop supposedly ordered by him, Francois Deniset and Robert Byerly were dropped into the hands of the Gestapo. Six more followed, including Romeo

OPPOSITE PAGE: Secret Agent Ray LaBrosse's forged identity card helped him to move about France undetected as Marcel Desjardins. (COURTESY RAY LABROSSE, VAC)

MAIN: This German munitions train was one of the underground targets as D-Day approached. Bieler's cell derailed 20 trains, damaged 31 locomotives and cut the Paris-Cologne line 13 times. (NAC PA 115860)

Sabourin of Montreal.

Alcide Beauregard, of the Eastern Townships, was landed on 8 February near Tours, and joined a circuit at Lyon as a radio operator. He set up operations in a school and in spite of warnings from London, continued to transmit from one spot. He was caught on 15 July and shot with 120 resistance members a month later. After the shooting, the Germans tossed hand grenades onto the bodies.

10,000 FRANCS PER PERSON

A serious breakdown developed in underground operations in northern France on the eve of D-Day when they would be needed most. Collaborators like Lucien Pierei were responsible for the Gestapo's penetration of circuits: he sold people at 10,000 francs apiece, and did so well at it that several hundred resistance fighters were awaiting execution in a prison in Amiens. RAF Mosquitos, in a daring raid, blew out one wall of the prison to liberate the secret army.

Bieler had become one of the most successful and respected circuit leaders, yet in mid-January 1944, the Germans swept into the café and arrested him and his radio operator. They later rounded up 40 members of the network. He was beaten, his kneecap broken, his back dislocated and after three months of brutal interrogation, he was thrown into solitary confinement. Then in September he limped out to a courtyard and was shot. The shooting was a tribute to Bieler's guts and professionalism. The Germans usually hanged agents as terrorists or spies.

CREMATORIUM THE ONLY ESCAPE

Meanwhile, Pickersgill and Macallister had been sent to Buchenwald where the only escape route was the crematorium. Romeo Sabourin, who dropped into the arms of the Gestapo, was also there. Three weeks after their arrival, the loudspeaker called for 15 of the prisoners who were marched out. They never returned. September 9th, the day Bieler was shot, another 16 were called including the three Canadians. Pickersgill's broken body led the forlorn group out into the courtyard where they were thrashed and thrown into a bunker. The next night most of the group were taken to the crematorium. Sabourin, Pickersgill and Macallister were hanged from meathooks in a wall, slowly choked to death by piano wire.

That same month Francois Deniset and Robert Byerly were executed in a concentration camp in Poland. The six Canadians were part of an imperfect organization which at times played an amateur's game. But it helped create a stronger resistance which would save numerous lives after D-Day.

REPRINTED FROM:
Esprit de Corps, *Volume 2 Issue 7*
AUTHOR: *Norm Shannon*

CANADIANS GO TO NORTH AFRICA

For the Canadian army, some 348 officers and men became combat's leading edge as they headed to North Africa.

ON 8 NOVEMBER 1942 the world awoke to the news that Anglo-American forces had opened a Second Front. It was not the long-awaited cross-Channel invasion of France as expected. Actually, it was the result of the triumph of British strategy over that of Americans. The invasion of the French colonial empire along the North African coast, from Morocco to Tunisia, was a substitute for the "real" Second Front as visualized by the press and public of the globe, and as desired by the American President and his Chiefs of Staff.

NECESSARY LESSONS

The Dieppe Raid of the previous August had proven that the Allies were in no position to mount a successful invasion of the heavily fortified French coast for many months to come. It had been a disaster. It had, however, vindicated the British view and silenced the American clamour for a mad dash against the West Wall with half-trained troops and inadequate weapons and equipment. The raid taught many needed lessons as to the weakness in current tactics, the lack of knowledge of the specialized type of equipment, and the degree of fire power required, to obtain a lodgement by penetrating the West Wall.

Nevertheless, the hard-pressed Soviet Union continued to urge the Allies to do something, and even made it quite clear that if the Allies did not do something in a pretty big way the Soviets might have to throw in the sponge and thus free several million German troops to oppose any Allied invasion of Western Europe.

ABOVE LEFT:
Strome Galloway was one of the few Canadians to join the British 1st Army on the Tunisian front as part of "Q" list. The first hand combat experience gained by these specially selected junior leaders proved invaluable when they returned to their regular units.
(COURTESY STROME GALLOWAY)

ABOVE RIGHT:
Field Marshal Erwin Rommel briefs his senior commanders from a half-track vehicle in the North African desert. On 2 November 1942, while facing assaults from numerous fronts and, with gas and supplies dwindling, the "Desert Fox" was told to "stand and die" by Hitler. Instead, he broke and retreated.

IMMATURE OPINIONS

After much persuasion and a final blow to their immature opinions – the Dieppe failure – the American planners fell in with the British and agreed to the North African invasion, code-named Operation Torch. The North African strategy had two aims: To liberate the French colonies of Morocco, Algeria, and Tunisia from the grasp of the Vichy Regime, and to meet up with Montgomery's victorious 8th Army advancing from Egypt through the Italian colony of Libya, thus crushing Rommel's famed *Afrikakorps* and its Italian allies in between. The plan worked, but it took six months to carry it out. Even so, it was the first complete Allied victory of the war, and it destroyed in their entirety, the Italo-German armies in North Africa In the last week of the campaign alone the prisoners of war taken by the Allies totalled a quarter of a million, of which 125,000 were Germans. Although Rommel himself escaped to Germany, leaving his beaten troops to be surrendered by Colonel General Hans-Jürgen von Arnim, the defeat was a bitter blow to Germany and a great morale booster for the British and Americans. It also encouraged the French Resistance in Metropolitan France to increase their endeavours and freed the Mediterranean Sea from any meaningful opposition. It also paved the way for the invasion of Sicily and Italy, which took place within eight weeks of the Tunisian victory.

FIRST CANADIAN OPPORTUNITY

Canadians played a very small part in this first Allied victory of the war, although the Royal Navy and RCAF operated along the coast and in the air over the battlefields. But, apart from the nine hour ordeal of Dieppe, it was the first opportunity Canadian soldiers were given to learn the game of war on its actual playing field.

When news of the invasion of North Africa came over the radio that November day it not only surprised the world, but it dampened the spirits of the Canadian Army in England like a wet blanket. Thousands of Canadians had been training in England for three years; others from 18 months to two years. They began to wonder if they would ever fight in a real campaign.

Once more British troops were being sent into battle – this time alongside Americans who had only staged in the United Kingdom for less than six months. Furthermore, many of these Britons and Americans had been civilians long after the 1st and 2nd Canadian Divisions had arrived in England; before the U.S. had even entered the war, or before Britain's conscription call-ups had put thousands of its young men into battledress. The Canadians were getting fed up with jibes about being a sort of "home guard," – the threat of German invasion was obviously over and the husbands, fathers and sons of their British hosts were fighting, and had been fighting, in Greece, Crete, Abyssinia, Libya, Egypt, Burma, Singapore and now in Algeria and Tunisia. The only all-volunteer army in the war, with only the overnight fiasco of Dieppe to prove they were meant to fight, morale hit a new low.

For a few of their number – 201 officers and 147 senior NCO's – the new front was to prove a chance for action, a learning experience which would give them the feel of battle and the role of first-hand informants to their own comrades on their return to Britain. Moreover, this small entry into a large-scale campaign indicated that eventually the Canadian Army Overseas was to get into action.

THE "Q" LIST

Known as "Q" List, the selected Canadians left in monthly drafts to join British 1st Army

on the Tunisian Front, the first leaving in December. (The posting to the British forces was for three months.) The final draft arrived too late to see any fighting, as the German surrender took place on 12 May 1943. The others saw plenty of fighting, suffering about ten per cent casualties. This was not large, but it must be understood that a proportion of each Canadian draft was from the services where casualties are less heavy than in the infantry, armour and engineers. Several Canadians were decorated. Others received promotions in the field and the casualties included all three categories, killed, wounded and prisoners of war.

On arrival at their British units the Canadians, officially described as "observers," were fitted into established vacancies like any other reinforcements, depending on their ranks in the Canadian Army. At one time the 2nd London Irish Rifles had a 2IC, three company commanders, a platoon commander and a Company-Sergeant Major, all Canadians, as they had been badly hit in a bitter battle just before one of the Canadian groups arrived. Most units were sent one Canadian officer and one Canadian senior NCO.

Where possible the Canadians were sent to those British regiments with which their regiments were historically affiliated. For example, Captain Eddie Dunlop of Toronto's Queen's Own Rifles went to the Buff and Lieutenant Paul LaPrairie of the Irish Regiment of Canada went to the London Irish Rifles. Major Frank White of Lord Strathcona's Horse became 2IC of the famous 17th/21st Lancers of Charge of the Light Brigade and Omdurman legend. Sergeant G.A. Hickson, who had won the DCM at Dieppe with the RCE, gained an MM for his bravery while with his British counterparts. The Canadian record was a good one, though minuscule.

INVALUABLE EXPERIENCE

The experience gained by these specially selected junior leaders was of invaluable benefit when they returned to their own units in Britain. They were listened to and believed in a way that no text book or unblooded instructor could be. The battlefield's atmosphere, men's reaction to its dangers and hardships, were conveyed with authority. The North African veterans who had actually been machine-gunned, mortared, gone on patrol, been attacked by enemy infantry and armour, or had been Stuka dive-bombed, were able to prepare their comrades far better than months of sterile training could. When the 1st Canadian Division invaded Sicily two months later, accompanied by their own veteran officers and NCOs, though few in numbers, they had more confidence than had they not heard advice from mouths which knew what to expect. Doubtless, the same benefits were seen in the other divisions as they waited in England for their time to come.

The idea that at least some Canadians could gain advanced battle experience and, if they lived, could bring it back to their comrades in England, was a good one.

ABOVE LEFT:
As 1942 came to a close in North Africa, Rommel was on the run and British medium Crusader tanks were in hot pursuit of the retreating Panzers. By 23 January 1943, Rommel had entered Tunisia and the battle for the Western Desert was over. Erwin Rommel's reinforcements arrived from Germany too late, and Montgomery's victory at El Alamein marked the turning point for Britain.
(IMPERIAL WAR MUSEUM)

ABOVE RIGHT:
Taking command of the Eighth Army in the Western Desert in August 1942, General Sir Bernard Montgomery launched a counter-offensive against Rommel at El Alamein on 23 October. After 12 days of heavy fighting and at the cost of 13,000 casualties, Britain succeeded in pushing the Germans back and marked the first major Allied victory of the war.
(IMPERIAL WAR MUSEUM)

REPRINTED FROM:
Esprit de Corps, *Volume 2 Issue 6*
AUTHOR:
Colonel (ret'd) Strome Galloway

(Colonel Strome Galloway served as one of the Canadian company commanders in the 2nd London Irish Rifles.)

By late November 1942, the casualty rate of RAF bombers was almost five per cent. On 2 December 1942, a crew of Canadians risked their lives, gaining information which helped develop future radar jamming devices.

CLOSING THE RADAR GAP

ABOVE:
A Junker JU88 night-fighter fitted with airborne interception radar.

THE RAF FLEW OVER 307,000 night sorties against Hitler during WWII and their encounters with the enemy in the hostile skies of Europe have become legend. While almost 8,000 crews were lost, most flew with a determination to avoid enemy fighters. But then there were a few crews like that of Ted Paulton of Windsor, Ontario, who flew out bombless each night trying to bait enemy night-fighters to attack their wayward Wellingtons.

Navigator Bill Barry remembers that enthusiasm ran high when the crew finished at an Operational Training Unit and the prospect of going on operations in a four-engined Halifax, Stirling or the new Lancaster loomed.

SHATTERED HOPES

"Our hopes were shattered when we arrived at 1474 Flight, Gransden Lodge, Bedfordshire, to find only five Wellingtons," Barry said recently. The unit had six Wellingtons but one had been lost on operations a week earlier. "Another disconcerting bit of data gleaned from our observations was that there was no bomb dump," he added.

An interview with the Commanding Officer didn't help. They flew navigation and gunnery exercises but didn't have a clue as to the nature of their operations. When they asked other crews what it was all about, they got a shrug: "You'll know soon enough!"

Two weeks later, Paulton's crew were told they were going to Karlsruhe as part of a regular bombing operation. But instead of bombs, they carried a specially trained radar and radio technician who sat behind a lot of strange-looking telecommunications equipment which was installed on their Wellington. They were routed to Karlsruhe with the main bomber stream.

UNENLIGHTENED

"It became clear that our task was the investigation of enemy radar and radio emissions over the target area," Barry said. "But the Special Operator did not enlighten us regarding what we hoped to receive or what we had received."

They did ten more ops with 1474 Flight – then the only airborne unit doing radar and radio intelligence. Their flights took them to Bomber Command and Coastal Command targets as heavy secrecy hung over Gransden Lodge.

ELECTRONIC CHESS GAME

The war became an electronic chess game. According to Winston Churchill, by the end of 1942 the British knew how the German defence system worked and how to cope with it – but a major gap existed in British knowledge of the Lichtenstein system used on night-fighters.

The RAF euphoria over the 1,000 aircraft raid on Cologne in May 1942, turned to bitterness and lowered morale as the enemy expanded its defence network and launched a new tactic. Freya radar stations picked up the bomber stream and then two Wurzburg stations came into play: one tracked a bomber — usually a straggler — while the other beamed a night-fighter onto it. The bombers were particularly vulnerable because the attacks, coming from below in cloud or darkness, were extremely difficult to spot. By late November 1942, the casualty rate was almost five per cent.

On one occasion, Ted Paulton's brother, a pilot with Coastal Command, visited Ted's station at Gransden Lodge and showed a curiosity in the five mysterious Wellingtons of the Radar Investigation Flight. When Al asked to visit his brother's aircraft,Ted waved him off, warning that: "If you're caught around that kite they'll probably shoot you!"

SPECIAL OPERATOR

The Canadian crew included navigator Bill

Barry of Delta, British Columbia; Wireless Air Gunner Bill Bigoray of Edmonton and gunners Ev Vachon of Quebec City and Fred Grant of Brockville, Ontario. After ten ops, Petty Officer Harold Jorden was assigned as special operator and, on 2 December 1942, they were briefed for a raid on Frankfurt.

As if the ancient Wellington were not slow enough, Paulton's route was deliberately designed to make them fall behind the bomber stream. "This was to increase the likelihood of being attacked as soon as we left the main stream," Bill Barry explained. It worked!

ABOVE:
The Vickers Wellington long-range bombers were used extensively by Bomber Command on night missions. In May 1942, these aircraft carried out the first 1000-bomber raid on Cologne. (IMPERIAL WAR MUSEUM)

RIGHT:
The airborne interception (AI) radar on a German ME-110 night fighter checked by a technician. The development of such devices increased the success rate of night fighting, and forced the Allies to develop jamming equipment with which to protect themselves. (IMPERIAL WAR MUSEUM)

FOLLOWED…

Shortly after they left the bomber stream, Jordan monitored an enemy aircraft following them. The intercepted signals from the night-fighter told him it was transmitting on 492 megacycles and Bill Bigoray got the first message off to base.

"The Ju-88 closed in and opened his attack; Paulton threw the Wellington into violent evasive action. We lost the attacker momentarily but he was soon back with his cannon fire," Barry added.

As the aircraft plunged, Jordan yelled on the intercom for Bigoray to get off a second message. The special operator was hit in the left arm but continued to monitor the fighter whose second attack ripped the rear turret.

Ev Vachon was hit by shrapnel and the hydraulics which powered the turret were shot away. "I rotated the turret by hand and tried to keep the Ju-88 in sight. It was dive starboard go as we started down from 12,000 feet."

WIMPY SHREDDED

The Ju-88 shredded the Wimpy with another burst and this time Jordan was hit in the jaw. Bigoray continued to try to raise base until still another attack smashed the front turret. Grant was hit in the leg and trapped in a turret which wouldn't rotate. Bigoray started forward to help Grant. Jordan saw another attack coming from below on his screen and yelled for Paulton to dive. Part of the next burst hit Bigoray in the legs and, in the next attack, Jordan was hit in the eye.

Bill Barry pulled Grant from the useless turret while Vachon moved from the unserviceable rear turret to the astrodome where he opened a running commentary but was soon hit a second time. The attacks continued until the Wellington was down to 500 feet. Paulton managed to elude the Ju-88 by briefly turning back towards the target, but when Barry later gave him a course for home he knew he was flying a very fragile bird.

The pilot had no control over the engines

RIGHT:
Ted Paulton, Everett Vachon, Fred Grant, William Bigoray and William Barry were sent out in a Wellington on the night of 3 December 1942 as bait to identify the Germans airborne interception radar device.

because both throttles were either jammed or shot up. A hydraulic leak made turrets, flaps, brakes and undercarriage useless. Jordon had lost his right eye, Bigoray lost the use of both legs when a cannon shell exploded under his table,Vachon now had lost considerable blood from extensive shrapnel wounds and Grant had part of a cannon shell lodged in his leg.

"WE HAVE TO DITCH!"

By the time they reached the English coast, they had decided to ditch. But Bigoray didn't think he'd be able to abandon the ditched aircraft before it went under because he couldn't walk. He was pushed out over the water and his chute delivered him to Ramsgate.

At about 0800 hours on 3 December, Frank Arnold and Roland Raines were paying out sprat nets off Kingsdown, England. About half a mile away a bomber crashed into the sea. The fishermen cast off the nets and raced towards the sinking bomber, not knowing whether it was British or German. Three of the crew were badly wounded and by the time they were all loaded into the

THE CREW SURVIVED THE MISSION ALTHOUGH JORDAN LOST AN EYE AND BIGORAY WAS LATER KILLED.

little sprat boat it was floating at the gunwales.

In the hospital at Deal, Jordan asked Bill Barry to repeat the radar frequency and other characteristics of the night-fighter transmission three times.

"Then he lost consciousness suddenly, as though it had been rehearsed," Barry today remembers.

The crew survived the mission although Jordan lost an eye and Bigoray was later killed. Jordan was awarded a DSO, Paulton and Barry were commissioned and given DFC's, Vachon and Bigoray were awarded the DFM, and Fred Grant was mentioned in dispatches.

Today, Bill Barry and Ev Vachon are the only survivors. It might be presumptuous to suggest that the information they brought back led to all future jamming devices, but it was a key element in broadening the information base. It was so important that the Prime Minister mentioned the operation in *The Hinge of Fate*, Vol. IV of *The Second World War*.

HISTORY SAYS…

Churchill wrote, "On the night of 2 December 1942, an aircraft of 192 Squadron was presented as a decoy. It was attacked many times by an enemy night-fighter radiating the Lichtenstein transmissions. Nearly all the crew were hit. The special operator listening to the radiations was severely wounded in the head but continued to observe with accuracy. The wireless operator, though badly injured, was parachuted out of the aircraft over Ramsgate and survived with the precious observations. The rest of the crew flew the plane out to sea and alighted on the water because the machine was too badly damaged to land on an airfield. They were rescued by a boat from Deal. The gap in our knowledge of the German night defences was closed."

REPRINTED FROM:
Esprit de Corps, *Volume 7 Issue 7*
AUTHOR: *Norm Shannon*

1943 - REVERSAL OF FORTUNES

As the Industrial and military might of the United States was brought to bear, the over-extended Axis forces were forced onto the defensive. Improvements in technology and tactics were steadily winning the war against U-boats and massive Allied air raids were draining the Luftwaffe's resources. The tremendous losses suffered by Germany at Stalingrad and Kursk meant the once invincible Wehrmacht would no longer be capable of sustaining an offensive. By year's end Allied forces had captured North Africa and Sicily and gained a toehold in Italy. In the Pacific, Japan had been forced from Guadalcanal, the Aleutians and Tarawa.

2 FEBRUARY The German Sixth Army surrenders at Stalingrad. Of the original 220,000 soldiers, only 90,000 were left alive to become prisoners of war.

14-22 FEBRUARY American troops in battle for the first time suffer a humiliating defeat at Kasserine Pass in Tunisia.

11 APRIL American and Canadian troops recapture Attu Island in the Aleutians.

22 APRIL The last German troops are evacuated from North Africa.

16 MAY The RAF "Dambusters" launch a successful attack against the Ruhr dams in Germany.

4 JULY Germans launch massive offensive (Citadel) at Kursk.

9-10 JULY Operation HUSKY: British, American and Canadian troops land in Sicily.

12 JULY German attack fails at Kursk and Soviets launch counterthrust.

12 AUGUST Germans evacuate Sicily.

3 SEPTEMBER Allies land in Italy and begin fighting up "the boot."

29 SEPTEMBER Italy signs Armistice with Allies.

13 OCTOBER Italy declares war on Germany.

23 NOVEMBER In the Pacific, American marines complete the conquest of Tarawa Atoll.

21 DECEMBER Canadian troops enter Ortona. The heavy street fighting and high casualties earn this Italian town the nickname, Little Stalingrad.

RIGHT: *The Church of Santa Maria served as background for brigade headquarters' Christmas dinner in Ortona, December 1943.* (DND)

RIGHT: *A flight of Boeing B-17 Fortress bombers is accompanied by a squadron of distinctive twin-boomed Lockheed P-38s. the bombings raid on Berlin in 1943 caused extensive damage on the third largest city of the world, strategically and negatively affecting German morale.* (PAINTING BY JOHN LAVALLE, U.S. AIR FORCE ART COLLECTION)

FROM TINY TO TITANIC

The Canadian navy got off to a slow, faltering start, but by 1943 a Canadian commander was in charge of convoys out of Halifax as the tide of battle changed.

ABOVE: *The modernization of the Royal Canadian Navy included the addition of four powerful Tribal class destroyers –* Athabaskan, Haida, Huron *and* Iroquois *– in 1942-43. During their service, they fought numerous intense night actions, including this one against German warships in the English Channel.* (PAINTING BY TONY LAW, CWM 10248)

CANADA'S ROLE IN THE Battle of the Atlantic has been largely downplayed by American and British historians, while it has been generally regarded as a hard fought, but victorious ordeal by Canadians. As late as the spring of 1943 both points of view held their elements of accuracy: our Allies were not entirely impressed with our efforts, and the agonies of the overstretched Royal Canadian Navy and merchant mariners were real. The perceptions diverge at the political level. Did Canada do everything possible to fight this crucial battle, or did years of neglect from Ottawa leave the Navy years behind its allies, almost unable to catch up before the war's end?

The record of the Allied navies against the U-boat menace swung back and forth from temporary mastery to heartbreaking failure. Only weather, a change in the strategic focus, or application of technology could give the North Atlantic escort forces respite from the attentions of German Admiral Karl Dönitz's submarines. The battle began slowly because U-boat numbers were not great and German resources were being spread thinly. The attack on Norway diverted submarines north in spring 1940, but the subsequent fall of France moved their bases closer to the convoy routes. The convoy system was improved with experience, but Dönitz was able to apply his wolf-pack tactics with greater success. By 1942, monthly tonnages lost to U-boats were rising over the half-a-million mark.

SUBMARINE EFFECTIVENESS

After the Americans entered the war in December 1941, the number of ships lost to submarine action actually increased. Along the eastern seaboard of the US, vacationers watched in awe as tankers and freighters exploded from torpedo hits. Behind the dumbstruck tourists the lights of Miami and Atlantic City blazed brightly, outlining ships for the gleeful U-boat captains. Only after the organization of coastal convoys (with RCN assistance), and the realization of the American public that there was a war on, were losses reduced.

If the Americans were slow to learn the lessons Britain had so painfully acquired, they at least showed little hesitation when it came to applying their industrial expertise. Prefabrication of ship sections allowed ugly, but functional Liberty ships to slip down the ways at an astonishing rate. (Albert Speer later applied this technique to German submarines, but it was too late to turn the tide. It is often overlooked that Germany did not convert her economy to "total war" until well into 1942.) The Americans occupied Iceland in the summer of 1941 and from there Very Long Range (VLR) Liberators flew out over the ocean to strafe and depth charge unwary U-boats. In March 1943 the USS *Bogue* became the first purpose-built escort carrier to assist the RCN in the North Atlantic, and bring air cover along with the convoy.

TECHNICAL BOOSTS

Detection and attack received technical boosts throughout the war, but only in the spring of 1943 did they begin to establish mastery for one side. Fortunately, it was for the Allies. The British had developed asdic at the end of the Great War, and erroneously felt that this alone would nullify submarine threats. As the RCN was virtually a subordinate branch of the Royal Navy, naval philosophy in Canada followed dutifully behind. Unfortunately, with only six modern ships and shore facilities to match, the RCN was in no position to take its place beside the world's great navies. That it did so by 1945 is no credit to Mackenzie King's leadership, but to the men who were forced to learn, build, fight and too often die in the very crucible of war they were being asked to manage.

It is apparently a fact of our Canadian culture that we refuse to perceive ourselves as a military people. Despite early wars on our soil between natives and colonists, despite periodic rebellions and invasions, and despite being compelled by politics to join in most of the twentieth century's wars as combatants, we hold our apathy very dear

when it comes to Armed Forces. No sooner does one war end than we revert to pacifism and demand that our forces make themselves 'relevant'. By 1939 the airforce, army and navy had all fought their battles to stay relevant while stripping them of materiel, but were reduced to skeleton infrastructures lacking modern equipment. The first part of the war would be spent doing training and organizing that should go on in peacetime.

WHY GO TO WAR?

The question was asked: why go to war over Europe? Would it not be prudent to supply foodstuffs and materials at inflated prices rather than actually fight? The question crossed the mind of Mackenzie King when he agreed to set up the British Commonwealth Air Training Plan, but the answer came crashing home in the summer of 1942. That year *Kapitan-leutenant* Paul Hartwig in U-517 and others sank nearly two dozen ships in the Gulf of St. Lawrence. If Canada had remained a neutral it is unlikely she would have escaped the tragedy of those submarine attacks. If vital supplies were threatened with interruption, or if adjoining territory to the U.S. was in danger, action would have been taken. As the saying goes: "You're always going to have an army (or navy) in your country; yours or someone else's."

The overriding problem of the RCN through the first three years of the war, was the fact that so much was asked by so many of so few. The peacetime naval command was under Vice Admiral Percy Nelles and when war come he and his small staff were swamped. Any navy is composed of more than just the number of hulls it can claim. Training of individuals and ships, logistics support and refit capabilities are all necessary to make the ships effective. The RCN didn't have time for training, room for refits, or the number of experienced personnel to overcome these shortfalls, While RN ships were being fitted with the latest radars and sonars, Canadian ships were being fuelled up and sent back out for another run. Men were exhausted; learning on the job or dying on it, and falling farther behind in the technological race. The Canadian-built Type 286 Radar was unreliable and the only RCN ship with High Frequency/Direction Finding (HF/DF), which could home in on U-boat transmissions, was HMCS *Restigouche.* She "procured" it from an American depot in Londonderry.

UNWAVERING COURAGE

Still, there were successes and these were a result of expert seamanship and unwavering courage. In August 1942 Lieutenant

***TOP**: In one of the longest battles in the sea war, U-744 finally surfaced on 5 March 1944 after 32 hours of continuous action by* HMCS Fennel *(left),* HMCS Chaudiere *and five other escorts. Some 275 depth charges were needed to force the severely damaged German sub to the surface. (NAC)*
***ABOVE:** Out of the fog came U-210. After a wild chase with deck guns blazing, HMCS* Assiniboine *rammed and sank the U-boat on 6 May 1942. Sustaining severe damage, she returned to Halifax for repairs with the survivors of the German sub. (NAC)*

sky and asdic sets 'pinged' tantalizingly but without solid contact. Eight ships were destroyed, including an ammunition ship whose blast may well have sunk its assailant, U-132. The convoy was crawling across the Black Pit desperately trying to regain the air cover available toward Iceland. Though a Royal Navy destroyer joined from another convoy, nightfall brought the same brutal result. HMCS *Amherst,* investigating a torpedoed ship, got a solid asdic contact. Survivors floundered in the chilling seas as Lieutenant Louis Audette made the harsh decision to fire a depth charge pattern. The explosion would crush the men, but might save others from a similar fate. At the last moment, power to the asdic failed and Audette cancelled the attack; surely one of the few times this was met with a sense of relief.

TOP: *Commonly known as "Huff-Duff", High Frequency/Direction Finding (or HF/DF) played a vital role in the war at sea, especially defending against U-boats hunting in wolf packs. The HF/DF found a bearing intersection between two or more high frequency transmissions to pinpoint U-boat locations. With a range of 50 miles compared to the Asdic's limit of a mile or so, the Huff-Duff is located above the bridge and looks like two intertwined rings. On the ice-covered corvette HMCS* Shawinigan, *it is left of the sailor. (DND)*

ABOVE:
Submariners who succeeded in escaping their sinking U-boat in the frigid waters of the North Atlantic are rescued by their enemy. (DND)

Commander John Stubbs, in command of HMCS *Assiniboine,* was suddenly confronted with U-210 in a fog bank. A wild chase ensued during which both vessels blasted each other at close range with their deck guns. In flames, *Assiniboine* rammed the submarine and sent it to the bottom. Her Type 286 radar had been useless throughout the engagement.

Canadians got more than their share of slow convoys and these were most vulnerable to wolf-pack tactics. The lack of modern equipment and trained personnel was inviting criticism from Allied officers even as they expected more from the painfully expanding RCN. The enemy asked nothing but a weak escort and a big fat convoy. In late 1942 they got their wish.

SC 107 was under the protection of escort group C4: HMCS *Restigouche* and four corvettes. Across her route was Group *Veilchen,* waiting in the cold, black ocean for the approaching victims. *Restigouche,* and the rescue ship *Stockland* each had HF/DF and they could plot the U-boat positions from the messages between them. However, *Restigouche* was the only destroyer and could only do so much. HMS *Celandine* chose this fateful moment to lose her radar.

The wolf pack attacked at night and promptly swamped the escort. Flares lit the

AN EASIER JOB?

Over five days 17 U-boats had savaged SC-107 claiming 15 of the 42 ships. Escort vessels had been stripped from the North Atlantic to cover the convoy en route to North Africa and Operation Torch, but no excuses could be entertained. England needed her oceanic lifeline even more because of the diversion. Churchill was worried as much about this as the breakdown in morale among the merchant seamen. If they perceived that they were expendable, how could they be convinced to continue this fateful effort? The answer seemed to be to give the Canadians an easier job; the UK-Gibraltar route.

The order was a slap in the face to the RCN who could admit that their expansion represented problems, but being pulled from the North Atlantic was like being sent from your own front yard. Unfortunately, the Christmas convoy ONS154 ('outbound' from the UK) suffered a similar fate to SC-107 and for similar reasons: the escort was weak and poorly co-ordinated. Five corvettes got the Type 271 radar and lead ship HMCS *St. Laurent* got HF/DF, but the equipment was untried. The nights were a hell of crisscrossing tracer and exploding ships. By day the subs could lurk on the horizon; visible but unreachable. HMCS

ABOVE:
Few knew that the Germans had established a weather station on the shore near Martin Bay, Labrador. German submarine U-537, at anchor in the bay in October 1943, was photographed from the station.
(DND PMR 81-329)

Battleford fought off four U-boats but lost the convoy when it made an unannounced course change. Lieutenant Commande Guy Windeyer was losing control of his command and he finally broke down. First Lieutenant Fred Frewer took over, but the battle played out. Fourteen ships were lost along with hundreds of men, and the RCN had to admit it needed some help.

CANADIANS TAKE CHARGE

What it needed was re-organization, and as happens with great countries in times of crisis, great men come to the fore. The fighting officers knew what was wrong and began to win back control of the war. Rear Admiral Victor Brodeur, on the Canada-United States Permanent Joint Board on Defence, began to demand that the Americans recognize Canadian contributions and to pay due respect.

Through Nelles, Acting Captain Horatio Nelson Lay (Director of Operations, Ottawa) asked for, and got, a three way conference on convoys. On 1 March 1943, Brodeur opened the conference by declaring the sovereignty of all Canadian Armed Forces under their national government.

The Atlantic Convoy Conference decided to dedicate US escort carriers to the battle, to strengthen the Liberator force, and to divide the North Atlantic between the British Admiralty (under Commander-in-Chief Western Approaches) and a new C in C Canadian North Atlantic. This gave its commander, Rear Admiral Leonard Murray, control of all anti-submarine and airforces west of 47 degrees longitude. Murray became the only Canadian to command a theatre in the war.

March of 1943 was one of the costliest months in terms of shipping losses, but improved organizations, equipment and an influx of escort vessels turned the tide. In April the losses fell by half, and May decreased again. Of greater importance was a corresponding and dramatic rise in U-boat losses. The Allies had far to go, the RCN farthest of all, but the corner was turned.

REPRINTED FROM:
Esprit de Corps, *Volume 2 Issue 9*
AUTHOR:
James G. Scott

THE NIGHT THE DAMS FELL

Guy Gibson recruited the best of the best for the most difficult bombing attack of the war and several Canadians were among the elite crews in action.

BARNES WALLIS WAS A tweedy English aircraft designer with high credentials at Vickers-Armstrong. He developed a fixation with building better bombs. His specific area of interest by 1939 became a string of Ruhr dams and the bombs which would destroy them.

Water did not compress, so Wallis worked on a way to bring the latent power of water under pressure, into play. He peddled versions of his theory around London for three-and-a-half years, but the wall of official indifference was as difficult to breach as the Moehne dam in the Ruhr.

Finally, in February 1943, the concept of the radical bomb dropped from a low level was approved. It immediately became a matter of extreme urgency; water levels in German dams would be receding within about 90 days. At this point all that existed was paper. The seven foot bombs, designed like oil drums, had to be built; aircraft had to be assembled and modified because the bombs were carried laterally, and finally crews had to be assembled and trained for exacting work.

Air Vice-Marshal Ralph Cochrane was handed the prickly problem of pulling together "the details" of a mysterious raid. The night the project was dumped on Cochrane's desk, Wing Commander Guy Gibson was flying his 173rd operation. He developed engine trouble on the way to Stuttgart and had difficulty maintaining height. Over the target, he managed to labour up to height and drop his 8000-pound blockbuster. Then the 25-year old pilot went diving into the darkness, racing for home and leave, having completed his third tour.

LEFT AND BELOW: *A bouncing bomb is dropped from a specially modified Mosquito bomber in preparation for the dambuster raid on the Möhne Dam along the Ruhr River on 16 May 1943. Nineteen bombers would be used in an attempt to paralyse the industries along the Ruhr by emptying the water reservoirs that supplied them.*

But next morning, instead of being on leave he was in Cochrane's office at 5 Group, trying to make sense of what little Cochrane would say about doing one more trip.

SOMETHING BIG

About ten days later, Gibson arrived at Scampton to take command of Squadron X. While the Air Ministry was still trying to come up with a number, Gibson and Cochrane had personally selected 147 men in 21 crews. Gibson's crew were among the 30 Canadians in the finely balanced Commonwealth squadron. Every man in the group had flown one tour, some two. As the crews gathered, it was obvious from the talent in the much-decorated group that something big was up.

That first night in the mess Gibson circulated, meeting a number of acquaintances he had personally selected. Danny Walker and Joe McCarthy were among the friends invited to join the elite force. Others were selected on the basis of a strong operational performance. As Gibson made the rounds, his black Labrador followed, slurping beer at each stop. Gibson was unable to answer repeated questions about their mission and when he left the mess, the dog followed having now developed a fuel leak which traced his path to the door.

Flying at treetop height in Lancasters, the crews were actually encouraged to get down on the deck. Aircraft windows were fitted with amber screens and crews wore blue glasses to simulate night conditions. Then, as training progressed, they selected lakes where a height of 60 feet and a speed of 240 mph became magic numbers. Wallis had figured that the bomb had to be dropped 245 yards from the dam and this also had to be worked into the equation.

Boffins came up with a simple idea of putting two spotlights under the fuselage and adjusting them so they converged at 60 feet. There is little to substantiate the legend that one navigator got the idea while watching spotlights converge on a performer's breasts during a strip-tease.

ELEMENTARY TRIG

A device even more simple was used to solve the problem of distance using elementary trigonometry. It consisted of a plywood triangle with a nail at each end of the base while a peephole ran through the apex. Each target dam had towers 600 feet apart. When the nails were lined up with the towers, Gibson was assured the aircraft were at precisely the right distance to release the bombs. Crews tried the piece of plywood on an English dam with dummy towers and it worked, but it was late April before a test bomb fell cleanly and did what it was supposed to do.

It was May before the first of the modified Lancasters arrived, looking somehow grotesque without a bomb bay. More practice flights brought better results and when the actual bombs arrived at Scamp-ton they were still warm to the touch, having just been filled with explosives. When one of the bombs was winched to the belly of "P" Popsie, the release circuit failed and five tons of bomb crashed to the ground. There was a fast exodus followed by considerable debate on whether it would or would not explode. Fortunately, the nays had it.

PLANS LAID

A briefing on the afternoon of 16 May ended weeks of speculation for 617 Squadron. Nine aircraft in waves of three would attack the Moehne dam, and when it was breached, those with bombs would go on to the Eder. The second group of five Lancs was to hit the Sorpe, and five machines in the third group were to take off later as reserve. The Moehne ran 850 yards at a height of 150 feet and a depth of 140 feet at its base. It imprisoned 134 million tons of water. The Eder dam to the east was even larger and both were of solid concrete while the Sorpe dam, although smaller and largely earthen, controlled a vital water supply to the highly industrialized Ruhr.

At 21:25 hrs that evening, Gibson's "G" George barked to life. In addition to the tension brought on by waiting, Gibson's dog

CANADIAN DAM BUSTERS

SURVIVORS
Sgt Stephen Dancia
Sgt Fred Sutherland
Sgt Harry O'Brien
F/Sgt Kenneth Brown
F/Sgt Harvey Weeks
F/Sgt John Thrasher
PO Tony Deering
Sgt Bill Ratcliffe
F/Sgt Don MacLean
F/Lt Joe McCarthy (American)
F/Sgt Grant McDonald
WO2 Percy Pigeon
FO Terry Taerum
FO Danny Walker
Sgt Chester Gowrie
FO Dave Rodger

DEAD
FO Robert Urquhart
WO2 Abram Garshowitz
PO Floyd Wile
PO Lewis Burpee
FO Kenneth Earnshaw
F/Sgt James McDowell
PO Vernon Byers
F/Sgt Frank Garbas
WO2 Joseph Brady
WO2 Alden Cottam
WO2 James Arthur
FO Vincent MacCausland
FO Harvey Glinz

POW
PO John Fraser

***ABOVE:** A reconnaissance photo taken the day after the attack shows the gap in the Möhne Dam and the low water level in the reservoir. Although the mission was a success, the damage caused did not affect the industries as significantly as Bomber Command had hoped.*

had been struck by a car and killed. Gibson arranged to have him buried at midnight while they were over Germany.

According to navigator Terry Taerum they crossed the channel at 50 feet and 203.5 mph. Norfolk faded into the sunset and the Dutch coast soon became a black line and then a glow in the moonlight. They got light, scattered flak at the coast and then Martin and Hopwood drew closer to Gibson. They leaped high tension lines and roared towards Eindhoven, a night-fighter nest.

CASUALTIES

The wave going against the Sorpe approached from the north and slanted across the Zuider Zee; a land-locked bay which extends 50 miles into Holland from the North Sea. The water was flat and dark; as Geoff Rice discovered when he slammed into it at full throttle. The impact ripped the belly apart and the bomb was torn from its mount. The Lancaster was still flying however, and Rice decided to call it a night and fly home.

Up ahead, Les Munro caught a burst of flak which knocked out his wireless. Without radio, Munro could not direct the attack on the Sorpe nor follow bombing instructions, so he aborted. Flak got Australian Flight Lieutenant Barlow's machine and it crashed with a blinding flash. Canadian Harvey Glinz was one of the dead. Then Vernon Byers' aircraft was destroyed and fellow Canadian James McDowell died with him. Joe McCarthy – delayed on take-off – was the only member of the Sorpe flying towards the target but he was some miles behind.

SECOND WAVE

Dinghy Young led the second wave of the southerly group across enemy coast at Rosendaal, just east of Dunkirk. Bill Astell fell behind and the night swallowed him up. Frank Garbas, Abram Garshowitz and Floyd Wile were three Canadians who were lost with him. About an hour later, after a duel with searchlights and anti-aircraft guns, Gibson circled the Moehne Lake and prepared to attack.

The Lancaster screamed out of the dark hills, across the man-made lake. Bomb-aimer Spam Spafford flicked on an engine which began rotating the bomb to give it backspin. Taerum flicked on the belly lights and flak immediately rolled up from the shore. The lights converged and the airspeed nudged 240 as the Lancaster shuddered and the rotating bomb built up speed. Gibson held the machine between the towers while Spafford sighted through the piece of plywood and waited for the nails to line up on the towers. Suddenly there was another shudder as Al Deering opened up on the towers from the front turret and this ended in a lurch as the bomb rolled across the water like a bowling ball. The plane leaped the dam and when Gibson looked back he saw the lake leap back; a wall of water 1000 feet high towered above him.

25 FOOT WATER WALL

A few minutes later, Hopwood attacked, but became a flamer when hit by flak. He continued his attack but the bomb overshot. Then the plane exploded and lost a wing. Mickey Martin flew the third attack through heavy flak and scored a hit, but the dam held. Then Dinghy Young – who had twice come down in the channel – rolled his bomb into the dam as did Maltby who followed. This time the concrete split and 134 million tons of water began to pour out through a 100-foot gap, creating a wall of water 25 feet high. As they left the area and the glow of Hopwood's burning bomber, the crews didn't know that John Fraser had miraculously jumped. He and an Australian air gunner became prisoners of war, while Canadian navigator Ken Earnshaw died with the others.

Gibson ordered four aircraft to follow him to the Eder which lay deep in a ravine. It was a difficult approach in daylight, almost suicidal at night. Dave Shannon made six attempts to get into position and withdrew to study the terrain. Henry Maudslay tried and hit the parapet, but blew himself up. Alden Cottam and Robert Urquhart were two more Canadians added to the night's casualties.

SORPE HOLDS

Shannon hit the dam and Knight finally scored with the last bomb. This time 200 million tons of water crashed through the breach. Meanwhile, Joe McCarthy, the only survivor of the northern formation, found and bombed the Sorpe dam. Aircraft from the reserve flight were diverted. Lewis Burpee and two Canadian crewmen James Arthur and Joseph Brady were lost. Kenneth Brown reached the Sorpe and after several attempts, his bomb-aimer Stephen Dancia found the target. Although damaged, the dam held.

The aircraft flew back at 50 feet to dodge flak. But it didn't work for Dinghy Young who was hit over Holland and later ditched. The crew, including Vincent MacCausland, was lost. Ten of the 19 aircraft which left Scrampton returned and a party broke out, but Gibson left to write 56 telegrams to next-of-kin, of the total missing, only three were alive.

BEAT IT HOME

Later 33 men were decorated, including a Victoria Cross for Gibson whose conduct in directing aircraft over the dams introduced the master-of-ceremonies technique used four months later at Peenemunde. Gibson was taken off flying for some time, but in September 1944, the RAF had one more job for the superb air commander. Having dropped target indicators on a pathfinder mission, he stayed around to observe the bombing. "Nice work chaps, now beat it home!" he called. This time luck ran out for Guy Gibson. He didn't make it home.

REPRINTED FROM:
Esprit de Corps, *Volume 3 Issue 5*
AUTHOR: *Norman Shannon*

RUN-UP TO HUSKY

ABOVE: *Motor Torpedo Boats (MTBs) were used in many theatres and on many operations throughout the war.* *(PUBLIC ARCHIVES OF CANADA)*

A time when Canadian skippers from the prairies learned the lessons of sea war such as; when you drop 11 depth charges, have the engines on full forward.

THE FIRST OF THE Canadians at sea began to drift to the Mediterranean in late 1940 as Canadian captains appeared on motor torpedo boats (MTBs), gunboats or Fairmiles based at Alexandria, Malta or Gibraltar. They were the dispossessed, the first of some 4,000 who served in the Royal Navy on ships of all sizes and in all theatres. At one time more than half of all radar officers in the Royal Navy were Canadians.

When Flotilla 10 lost five of its nine MTB's under bombing in Crete, Alex Joy was one of the four commanders who started to operate out of Mersa Matruh, where the British lines were then anchored. For several uneventful nights, they patrolled the coast of Egypt on seek and destroy missions, and a year later helped evacuate part of the besieged garrison at Tobruk from under German guns.

MTB's from Malta cleared acoustic mines from the approaches to the island, intercepted enemy convoys, and shot up whatever they could find. All Flotillas became adept at diversions such as the attack behind Field Marshal Erwin Rommel's lines as he awaited Montgomery's drive. The intrusion led Rommel to divert 10,000 men to the location.

In May 1943, four colourful commanders moved from the Atlantic force where they had been extremely active, to the Mediterranean, where they became even more active. The activity started en route, in a gale on the Bay of Biscay, as the convoy was spotted by a German *Focke-Wulf* Condor. The pilot circled and signalled something but made no attempt to attack.

FLAMES WASHED ALONG DECK

Cornelius Burke, Tommy Fuller, Tommy Ladner and Doug Maitland bobbed through 30 foot waves as darkness made keeping station almost impossible. Around midnight Maitland's boat was riddled with machine gun fire from a submarine. An auxiliary gasoline tank was punctured and flames washed along the deck. Maitland rammed the throttles forward and attacked the mountainous sea in the frail craft which shuddered under the impact, but the waves swept the deck clean of burning fuel.

In a nearby boat, Tommy Fuller was mystified by the sight of the burning boat which suddenly vanished. It was like tales

ABOVE LEFT: *After a series of depth charges, the German submarine U-224 surfaced in the path of* HMCS Ville de Quebec *on 13 January 1943. The Canadian corvette then rammed the U-boat, throwing one of her gun crew, who was rushing to man the deck gun, overboard. She disappeared from sight in about four minutes.*
(BY H. BEAUMENT, CANADIAN WAR MUSEUM)
ABOVE RIGHT: *These Canadian corvettes are en route across the Bay of Biscay as part of Operation TORCH in the summer of 1942. note the ammunition for the MK.IX gun is placed for ready access.*
(BRITISH MINISTRY OF DEFENCE)

of the mystery ship on Chaleur Bay but Fuller had no time for folklore. As the enemy sub shot up Maitland's boat, a second U-boat surfaced and collided with the first. Fuller and another MTB captain spent some time picking up survivors. Fuller picked up a cook whom he assigned to his galley as Jock MacPherson, personal chef.

The exploits of Fuller in the Adriatic, and all of the captains later in the war, in both the Mediterranean and in Normandy, is like a page from an old Errol Flynn script. But the more conventional forces began to arrive in England early in 1942.

NOT A HAPPY SHIP

HMCS *Iroquois* spent six months of shakedown cruises and shape-up modifications and by summer was still not a happy ship. Part of a destroyer force working out of Plymouth, she was two days out on 9 July, escorting a convoy of troops to Gibraltar. Towards evening they were spotted by three *Focke-Wulf* Condors which bombed two of the three troopships and set them ablaze. They attacked the *Iroquois* but withdrew under fire and the escort ships collected all but 57 of the survivors. Then, turning back to Plymouth, the *Iroquois* later picked up the survivor of an enemy submarine which had been sunk the previous day.

The survivor happened to be the captain, who sent his uniform out to have it cleaned upon arriving in Plymouth. When it was returned, a badge was missing. The U-boat captain complained vigorously to the ship's captain who, in turn, cancelled all leave. This had a somewhat demoralizing effect on the crew which had behaved well in battle and when they were ordered out to sea again many opted to decline duty. Not since Fletcher Christian stared down Captain Bligh had Plymouth seen such an explosive situation. Fortunately it was resolved when the irate captain collapsed with a heart attack and was removed from command.

STRANGE BATTLEGROUND

Although *Iroquois* went to Scapa to join the home fleet, other Canadian ships were then operating out of Plymouth. HMCS *Athabaskan* was joined by corvettes *Edmundston*, *Calgary* and *Snowberry* and all spent much of the summer on sweeps of the Bay of Biscay, a strange battleground where German ships and aircraft threatened convoys to beleaguered Malta, while allied formations threatened German shipping.

In preparation for Operation Torch in the summer of 1942, Canadian ships and crews were quietly co-opted for the Mediterranean, straining still further the Royal Canadian Navy's limited resources. Presumably, preparations were conducted on a need-to-know basis and the Admiralty concluded that the Canadians didn't need to know much. One of 17 corvettes assigned to the mystery operation was HMCS *Algoma*, and when she left Halifax the crew was convinced their destination was Murmansk so they loaded up with winter gear.

One new officer wrote home for his sheepskin coat, yet on Christmas Day he lounged in his bathing suit at anchor in Gibraltar. Warmed by the glow of a letter from home, he read that the mercury in rural Manitoba had dropped through the bottom of the thermometer at -60° Celsius. But there was a down side to the day – when the crew went ashore there wasn't a white uniform in the lot.

TRAINING LEVEL UNINSPIRING

When the reinforcements left Halifax, the level of training was not inspiring. Some officers had six months in the navy, four of which were spent watching the universe unfold at Kings. The highlight of the seamanship course was a trip on a yacht from

***German Dornier Do.17 bombers fly in formation. Spotting ships in the Bay of Biscay, they released gliding bombs and succeeded in sinking a British sloop and damaging* HMCS Athabaskan.**

Halifax harbour to the Northwest Arm, during which they learned to tie knots. Many felt a sea breeze for the first time when the convoy cleared harbour, and then they dropped off the edge of the world.

One such graduate of Kings was an asdic officer on a corvette which shall remain nameless. The mid-Atlantic was crawling with wolf packs which ultimately sank 16 ships. When he got a hard contact, it was just like the classroom and with the hair on the back of his neck standing up, he ran through the procedure. They closed on the submarine and he executed the order to fire a pattern of ten depth charges. Mysteriously, he only heard one explosion.

An impromtu investigation by an irate skipper revealed that few of the deckhands knew anything about depth charges. One was surprised to learn that a charge didn't have a primer at both ends. The officer was given 24 hours to shape up the crew, but the submarine packs renewed their attacks at dusk the same day. With merchant ships going up in flames and star shells bursting overhead, the asdic picked up another hard contact dead ahead at 500 yards.

The crew was at action stations, determined to carry out the procedures drummed into them. With the order to fire, they managed to release 11, not ten, depth charges, but the "full ahead" order never reached the engine room. The corvette barely cleared the pattern when blue flame, smoke, dust, and noise ripped through the engine room. Convinced they had been torpedoed, the crew switched off the engine and headed for lifeboats.

With the corvette dead still in the water, a 10,000 ton merchant ship bore down on it. The engine crew was coaxed out of the lifeboats and persuaded to start the engine in time to avoid disaster.

Three of the earlier corvettes to arrive in the UK that summer were spotted in the Bay of Biscay by 21 enemy aircraft. The German Dorniers made a strange attack, flying parallel to the ships and then turning at right angles. At this point some launched gliding bombs which were controlled inexpertly from the aircraft because none hit the ships. But the performance soon improved.

Two days later, another swarm of Dorniers had more luck. One gliding bomb sank a British sloop while a second went through the *Athabaskan* which, after a tense four-day trip, managed to get back to Plymouth. Despite threats from above and below, Allied ships finally won an edge by late 1943, which meant reasonable passage of supplies to North Africa and Gibraltar. They became aggressors, putting a squeeze on German shipping.

Canada contributed 17 corvettes and six flotillas of landing craft to Operation TORCH landings in North Africa. Although the landings went well, the ground war turned bitter during the winter creating

***ABOVE:** Glide bombs such as the German V Fritz X damaged many Allied ships as the Germans increased their proficiency.*

heavy demands on the supply line from the U.K. to Gibraltar to Bonne. Ships from the trans-Atlantic run were used to fill in.

Although one corvette tried to ram a torpedo thinking it was a submarine, that fall and winter was a time of grim learning for crews. *HMCS Ville de Quebec* successfully rammed and sank a submarine and the *Port Arthur* sank an Italian U-boat. *HMCS Regina* captured another.

But the victories were not without cost: *Weyburn* struck a mine and later sank and the *Louisbourg* sank after being hit by an aerial torpedo. By spring large convoys were getting through and 2755 vessels were assembled in Suez for the invasion of Sicily. On 10 July, Operation HUSKY ended three years and one month of defensive warfare.

REPRINTED FROM:
Esprit de Corps, *Volume 2 Issue 10*
AUTHOR: *Norman Shannon*

ABOVE:
British soldiers descend from their infantry landing craft (LCI) and make their way to the beaches of Sicily on 10 July 1943. The first large-scale European invasion since Dieppe, Operation HUSKY included 140,000 troops carried in 3000 ships and landing craft.
(IMPERIAL WAR MUSEUM)

A month after landing in Sicily in 1943, Canadians would have an answer.

"YOU CALL *THIS* A WAR?"

LESTER PEARSON CONSIDERED IT a good night's work. At 21:40 hours on 9 July 1943, the Canadian chargé d'affaires had hurried to the White House on a matter of grave national importance. Moments later he was ushered into the Oval Office for a hastily arranged meeting with President Roosevelt. In his briefcase he carried a communiqué from Allied Headquarters in Algiers announcing Operation HUSKY, the invasion of Sicily by Anglo-American forces. His government, he told the president, was most concerned that the announcement of the invasion, now just hours away, made no mention of the participation of Canadian troops. The president assured him that he would take steps to see that this was done.

Pearson hurried back to his embassy and sent a cable to Ottawa, still in doubt if the changes could be made in time. At midnight, he started for home. As he was driving down Connecticut Avenue listening to dance music on the car radio, he was startled to hear a voice break in: "We interrupt this program for a news bulletin. British, American and Canadian troops, under the command of General Eisenhower, have commenced landing operations in Sicily." He breathed a sigh of relief.

PLEDGING THE NATION

Prime Minister Mackenzie King was relieved too. It was "excessively warm, the hottest day, I think, thus far this year," he noted in his diary. He had spent the day finishing a speech on the theme "Canada will not fail her fighting men," which he thought "should attract the headlines and be a pledge of the nation at this time." It was a speech that, until Pearson's cable arrived, he was not sure he would be able to deliver.

Inactivity and deterioration of morale among the troops overseas – some had been training for more than three years – had softened his insistence that the army remain a single unit under Canadian command. He had taken the initiative in pressing for Canadian involvement in the landings in Sicily, and the First Division, the famous "Old Red Patch" under the command of General Guy Simonds, had sailed from Scottish ports on 12 June to serve with Montgomery's 8th Army. Except for a few bloody hours on the beach at Dieppe the year before and the ill-fated Hong Kong expedition, it would be the first time that Canadian soldiers would be involved in combat since the start of the war. King fervently hoped that casualties would be light.

With the official announcement of the invasion, the Prime Minister felt free to issue his own statement lauding Canadian troops as being "in the forefront of an attack which has as its ultimate objective the unconditional surrender of Italy and Germany." After a sandwich and some gingerale with little Pat, his beloved terrier, he went to bed at one o'clock in the morning. Seven hours later, he addressed the nation on radio.

ON THE BEACH

Farley Mowat, a beardless 22-year-old lieutenant with the "Hasty Pees," (the Hastings and Prince Edward Regiment), knew next to nothing about Sicily. He vaguely remem-

LEFT:
As the day progressed, the number of ships delivering transport and mechanized equipment increased. Bulldozers assist in pulling the equipment through the loose Sicilian sand. (DND)

ABOVE:
As a 22-year-old, Farley Mowat first saw action when he came ashore on Sicily's beaches with the Hastings and Prince Edward Regiment.

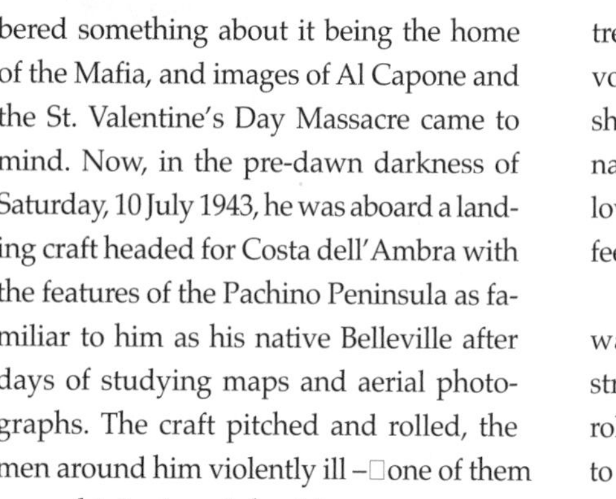

bered something about it being the home of the Mafia, and images of Al Capone and the St. Valentine's Day Massacre came to mind. Now, in the pre-dawn darkness of Saturday, 10 July 1943, he was aboard a landing craft headed for Costa dell'Ambra with the features of the Pachino Peninsula as familiar to him as his native Belleville after days of studying maps and aerial photographs. The craft pitched and rolled, the men around him violently ill – one of them across his back and shoulders.

At 14:45 hours, the Royal Navy monitor *Roberts* opened fire with its 15-inch guns and the whole arc of the horizon lit up. Shells screamed overhead and the coastline seemed to rise up before being swallowed in smoke and flame. Fighter-bombers from the RCAF's 417 City of Windsor squadron strafed the beaches at first light. Streams of tracer-fire soared toward the landing craft from bunkers and buildings inland. With a muted thump, "a vast, yeasty waterspout smelling of brimstone" rose alongside, drenching the men. Mowat was desperately searching for a landmark when the craft touched down on a sandbar a hundred metres offshore. The ramp dropped and, revolver in hand, Tommy-gun slung over his shoulder, and webbing bulging with grenades and ammunition, he shouted, "Follow me, men!" and stepped off into eight feet of water.

Mowat made no attempt to thrash his way to the surface, but simply walked straight ahead until his head emerged. A roller picked him up and dropped him on to the beach. "I rolled over and looked seaward," he recalled, "and saw a hundred men wallowing comically out of the depths, like a herd of seals hurrying to land upon a mating beach." They were soon moving inland in withering heat, kicking up clouds of choking, white dust. The temperature would reach 45° Celsius (114°F) during the day. The CBC's Peter Stursberg, lugging heavy recording equipment, complained that the "scorchingly hot sun was frying the skin on my face."

FORRYET EYELANDERS

Along 160 kilometres (100 miles) of coast, thousands of other men were struggling ashore. To Mowat's right, on Sugar Beach, the Seaforths, Loyal Edmontons and Toronto's 48th Highlanders landed with a skirl of bagpipes to be greeted by an ancient Sicilian waving his arms and shouting, "Forryet Eyelanders, Forryet Eyelanders!" The old man, it was discovered, had once owned a fruit store on Elizabeth St., behind the University Avenue Armouries where the 48th drilled in peacetime. Opposition was surprisingly light, with the Canadians suffering few casualties. One relieved soldier spoke for most when he remarked: "Call this a war? …I wonder if it's all like this?"

He would have an answer less than a month later when the Canadians were pulled out of the line into reserve after losing 2310 officers and men, including 502 dead. So, too, would Mackenzie King.

REPRINTED FROM:
Esprit de Corps, *Volume 8 Issue 3*
AUTHOR: *Bill Twatio*

RIGHT: *In single file The RCRs march into the Sicilian hills. They would endure five days of grueling marches in the blazing sun before coming face-to-face with the Hermann Göring Division.* (NAC/PA 23123-N)

ARRIVAL IN SICILY

Aside from the Dieppe encounter, most Canadians spent two and a half years in England waiting for action.

DURING THE NIGHT OF 9 July 1943 "the greatest combined operation in history" was being marshalled on the waters between Malta and Sicily. It was code-named Operation HUSKY and there were three reasons why it was taking place.

First, following the defeat of the Axis forces in North Africa the previous May it was considered necessary to continue to take the strain off Russia. It was utterly impossible to mount an attack on France from England until another year of preparation had taken place, and it was logical that with a large number of troops available in North Africa with ample shipping, such strength should be used and not allowed to stand idle.

Second, both sides of the Mediterranean had to be cleared of the enemy to make it a safe route for Allied shipping to the Far East and Pacific War with troops and material to fight against Japan, since the route around the Cape of Good Hope took weeks longer and used up valuable shipping due to the much longer turn-around.

Third, Italy was now weak and faltering and could probably be knocked out of the war if its home territory was invaded without delay. Before midnight, British glider troops and American paratroopers had come down from the sky onto Sicilian soil. Most gliders crashed or were shot down in error by Allied ships at sea. The parachutists were scattered far and wide. The airborne assault was far less successful than had been hoped for. Under cover of darkness 160,000 British, American and Canadian troops on the nearly 3000 ships and landing craft prepared to land on Sicily's shores. These were the British 8th Army of North Africa fame led by General Bernard Montgomery and the newly-formed United States 7th Army, the latter having been built around the U.S. II Corps, also with North African experience, under General George S. Patton. Commanding both armies was British Field Marshal Sir Harold Alexander as commander of 15th Army Group, while American General Dwight D. Eisenhower was the overall politico-strategist.

UNTRIED DIVISIONS

Both armies had been augmented by untried divisions, the 45th (Thunderbird) Division had sailed from Norfolk, Virginia, and met up with 7th Army in the Mediterranean. The 1st Canadian Division had sailed from the Clyde in Scotland joining 8th Army in Maltese waters.

It is noteworthy that the first communiqué from Algiers announcing the Sicilian invasion used only the term "Allied Forces," but a supplementary communiqué from Washington also dated 10 July 1943 spoke of "Anglo-American-Canadian armed forces." Prime Minister Mackenzie King in a broadcast that same morning, also stressed the presence of Canadian soldiers in the operation.

Waiting for the invaders were 200,000 Italian soldiers and 62,000 Germans. The Allies landed more troops and vehicles than they were to land in Normandy on D-Day 1944. The Canadians numbered a mere 20,000, but when the campaign ended 38 days later they had marched farther and fought harder battles than most of the rest of the 8th Army. To begin with the Canadians were lucky, suffering only 75 battle casualties the first day. Their opponents, the Italian 206th Coastal Division, did not put up much of a fight. Token resistance followed by wholesale surrenders made the landings almost a walk over. Then followed five days of gruelling marches in blazing sunshine and clouds of white dust. On 15 July the leading Canadian troops bumped into the German Hermann Göring Division and began three weeks of almost continuous fighting from set-piece battles to light sub-unit skirmishes.

A lone infantryman probes enemy lines.

***ABOVE:** Author Major Strome Galloway was a Royal Canadian Regiment company commander in Sicily. He would later serve as second-in-command and, occasionally, as acting-commander of the RCR in Italy.* (COURTESY STROME GALLOWAY)

Meantime, Patton's 7th Army had fought off German counterattacks on their beachhead and were making sweeping, wheeled advances through their designated western half of the island. The 8th Army, less the Canadian Division, was stalled before Catania on the east coast. The Canadians, in the middle, were learning that war could be deadly. In one unit, The Royal Canadian Regiment, both the Commanding Officer and the 2nd-in-Command were killed in hand-to-hand combat with the enemy.

Total Canadian battle casualties for the campaign were 490 killed and 1949 wounded, sufficient for less than 30 days of battle to indicate that Sicily was no picnic.

It is also safe to say there was a general feeling of pride at home and at the front, given that Canadians had acquitted themselves very well in their first sustained action.

The most spectacular Canadian action was the capture of the forbidding Assoro heights by the Hastings and Prince Edward Regiment, whose skill in fieldcraft was praised in German battle reports.

Following the campaign General Montgomery visited the Canadians and praised them for their services, saying, "I regard you now as one of the veteran divisions of my Army, just as good as any if not better." This statement was taken with a grain of salt, for the troops knew of their failures as well as their successes. One brigade commander and two battalion commanders had been relieved of their commands and sent home. On the other hand Lieutenant Colonel Bert M. Hoffmeister and his Seaforth Highlanders of Canada, had performed so well that he went on to become a brigadier and then a major-general commanding the 5th Armoured Division and, two years later, was selected to command the proposed Canadian contribution to the war against Japan. Four other battalion commanders were promoted to the command of brigades. Sicily was indeed a testing ground for many battles to come, both in Italy and northwestern Europe. According to Montgomery, the Divisional Commander, General Guy Simonds, emerged from the war as Canada's best general. Apparently Simonds learned from the mistakes he made in Sicily. And so did we.

CAMPAIGN WON

Although the Allies won the campaign in Sicily, it was in several ways a hollow victory. Montgomery and Patton did not coordinate their tactics as they should have. Instead of destroying or capturing the enemy forces, as was done in Tunisia three months before, they first allowed approximately 60,000 Germans to cross into Sicily from the Italian mainland with more than 13,000 vehicles, then allowed them to evacuate some 50,000 to the mainland, plus about 90,000 Italians. Much of the blame for this can be laid on the Royal Navy who hesitated to approach the Messina Straits for fear of mines, and the RAF who were dissuaded from attacking the reinforcements and evacuation convoys across the straight because of the heavy German flak.

Despite such a large scale getaway by the enemy, the 8th Army captured more than 3000 Germans, and together the two Allied armies killed 12,000 Germans and 2000 Italians. They also wounded 5000 Italians and captured 117,000 others. About 16,000 Germans were wounded. All these figures are open to question, as most books and documents vary by several thousand in each case.

The Americans had 2800 killed, the British (including the Canadians) 2400. American wounded were 6300, British (including

Capturing key strategic targets such as railway stations was a means to cutting off vital transportation and supply lines from the enemy.
LEFT: American mortars provide cover fire as the troops make their way into the Sicilian hills.

Canadians) 6400. One strange set of figures is that the Americans had no missing-in-action, whereas the British had 2644. And although the Americans had 598 captured by the enemy, the British had just four. The arithmetic of battle is always difficult to reconcile and all such figures should be read with caution.

DON'T BELIEVE EVERYTHING

The writer took part in the entire campaign as an infantry company commander, recalling 10 July as the day he decided not to believe everything he was told. First, he was told that the landing would take place under cover of darkness. However, because of delays caused by naval lack of expertise, the troops landed under the mid-day sun. The landing was to be dry-shod, that is, when the assault craft doors were dropped the troops would step out onto the sandy beach. Actually, when we stepped out we went up to our armpits in icy Mediterranean water, not good when loaded with 60 pounds of ammunition, weapons and equipment! Then, having crossed the beach, the troops would have cover from view as they moved through vineyards six feet high. Apparently, no one told our intelligence people that the vines would be cut down to within less than a foot at that time of year. The next piece of information was that my company would be able to reach its objective, a coastal battery, shielded from hostile fire, as the aerial photo showed a sunken road leading directly to it. Unfortunately, the photo had been misinterpreted; it was not a sunken road but a ridge with a road running along the top of it, fully exposed to enemy view and fire. The final bit of "intelligence" was that, although the Italians had not fought very well in Africa, here on their home soil they would put up a bitter fight. Fortunately, on our battalion front, they did not. After a few token bursts of fire which killed three of our men and wounded one officer and four or five men, they surrendered in hordes.

Upon reaching the battery that was my company's objective, one of my sergeants came upon a dugout door. He heard voices. Firing one shot, which wounded one Italian, he succeeded in getting a captain and 37 artillerymen to come out with their hands up, shouting, "Guerro finito." For them it was. Over on my right another company had a brief fire fight until two of its privates did a battle drill movement, got behind the bothersome machine gun post and, after throwing a couple of grenades, rushed in and bayonetted the gunners. This allowed the whole company to move forward, which in turn brought about 200 Italians out of their positions with their hands up. Privates Joseph Grigas and Jack Gardner got a DCM and an MM respectively, for this act.

BIZARRE BAPTISM

There is no doubt the Italians were fed up with the war, hated the Germans and looked upon the British and Americans as their friends. Many brave battles were fought by Italians in picked units during both World Wars, but the over- and underaged members of the 206th Coastal Division were only too glad to call it quits. With this rather bizarre baptism of fire we prepared for the bloody part of the campaign. The three British divisions on our right fared almost as well. The Americans did their heaviest fighting the first two or three days and then had things somewhat easier. As for me, I tripped over the barbed wire around the battery position, gashed my bare inner thigh on a two-inch barb and bled almost like I had a real wound.

REPRINTED FROM:
Esprit de Corps, *Volume 3 Issue 2*
AUTHOR:
Colonel (ret'd) Strome Galloway

ANDY'S AGONY

After years of insisting that Canadian units not be split up and assigned to the British, the politics of war close around General Andy McNaughton like a vice.

THE FIRING OF A GENERAL

ABOVE: *General McNaughton with Canadian Minister of National Defence J.L. Ralston in 1942. By 1943, as the Army was being reorganized by the British, McNaughton resigned in frustration – to the relief of Ralston and General Ken Stuart.* (PUBLIC ARCHIVES OF CANADA)

A FUNNY THING HAPPENED to General Andrew McNaughton on his way to the war: he lost his army. When the man who commanded the Canadians for four dreary years in England visited his troops in Sicily in 1943, he was not allowed to see them. Imperious Field Marshal Montgomery offered various excuses, but McNaughton's humiliation in Sicily was just one more skirmish in a struggle which had been going on since Vimy Ridge during WWI.

In almost four years as commander of the Canadians in England, McNaughton fought both the Brits and later Canadian politicians to maintain the autonomous nature of Canadian troops in the UK. His quest for a distinctly Canadian army went back to Vimy, and that was where he also picked up his first enemy in khaki.

SITING ADVANCE

Before the 1917 battle, then Lieutenant Colonel McNaughton was asked for advice from Major General Currie about the siting of two brigades of guns. He advised moving the guns 1000 yards back down a slope, to sharpen the trajectory on the far side of the ridge. The man who originally sited the guns was Major Alan Brooke, a Britisher with a long memory and a penchant for revenge. When McNaughton brought the Canadians to England in 1939, General Sir Alan Brooke was two appointments away from being Chief of the Imperial General Staff.

Between the wars McNaughton's brilliance as a lecturer, and his outspoken views on autonomy of Canadian forces, continued to fan the antagonism between the two men. Essentially, McNaughton insisted that Canada's army be under Canadian control and not be parcelled out to British units. When Brooke became CIGS animosity flared into warfare.

With the War Department and Churchill at odds over whether to defend Calais or Dunkirk, in 1940 Brooke planned to feed Canadians into a defensive line piecemeal. Although the action failed to materialize, it rankled McNaughton and when Brooke was made commander-in-chief of Home Forces a few weeks later, the two men arrived at an understanding: 'You'll obey my orders,' Brooke insisted. 'Only if they're proper ones,' Andy replied. McNaughton's relationship with the War Office had been reasonable in spite of his insistence on Canadian autonomy, but when Brooke became Chief of the Imperial General Staff months later, McNaughton had a devout enemy in the highest of places.

RALSTON BLASTS MCNAUGHTON

As if that were not enough, he established a foe on the home front in 1941. He had agreed to send 800 Canadians to raid the port of Trondheim, Norway. Although J.L. Ralston was Canada's finance minister at the time, he took it upon himself to blast McNaughton for acting without the consent of DND, and presumably the government. The issue concerned the commander's right to take urgent military action outside the UK and McNaughton said: "This broke what little trust I had in Ralston... and I never regained it."

When Ralston became Defence Minister in 1941, it opened an era of wrangling over policy which did little to enhance the Canadian war effort. Publicity following the Dieppe raid, much of it ill-informed, cast a shadow over McNaughton's reputation because he refused to be drawn into the controversy over whether or not Canadians insisted on a frontal attack. Canadians had no part in drawing up the original plan, but had agreed to it.

FIT TO COMMAND?

A year later, the vise closed around McNaughton during an Anglo-Canadian army exercise in England. General Sansom's 2nd Corps, new and untrained, did not perform well in Exercise Spartan. The Head of Home Forces, General Sir Bernard Paget, urged McNaughton to dismiss Sansom. When he refused, Brooke was only too

LEFT: General Sir Alan Brooke and McNaughton held a mutual animosity for one another, dating back to a shared action in the First World War. Brooke is seen here with General Bernard Montgomery seated on his right. (*IMPERIAL WAR MUSEUM*)

pleased to take the matter up with the Canadian Chief of Staff General Ken Stuart. Ralston raised the refusal as an indication of McNaughton's fitness to command. Brooke also took the opportunity to bad-mouth his old rival at a high level conference in Washington, while Mackenzie King considered the impact of McNaughton's dismissal on the Liberal government and the looming conscription issue.

A MAJOR ISSUE - AGAIN

In spite of heavy casualties at Dieppe, the politics of having Canadians in action was again a major issue in Canada less than a year later. The Canadian army was the only force whose birth rate exceeded its death rate and the fear that the war might somehow end without participation in combat nagged Canadians – especially politicians and journalists.

McNaughton had agreed to the participation of some Canadian troops in Sicily but maintained the conviction that the Canadian army should be an entity. He was adamant that upon completion of their task in Sicily, forces assigned there would rejoin the Canadian army for operations as a unit.

NOWHERE TO TURN

During the summer and fall of 1943, McNaughton was ground between millstones in London and Ottawa. On the one hand his old enemy Brooke wanted him out of the way because he was about to appoint Montgomery to command the 21st Army Group, and he knew McNaughton could never work under him. The original dispute over Exercise Spartan was now somehow interpreted as McNaughton's lack of fitness to command. Part of McNaughton's trouble at home derived from the fact that he considered the invasion of Italy a waste of time (with some justification as it took twice as many troops to invade as defend). Ralston and Stuart offered Canadians for Sicily, the Mediterranean and then Italy with no strings attached. For political reasons they were dispersing the Canadian army which McNaughton had built up since 1939.

The intrigue between London and Ottawa reached such a pitch that McNaughton resigned, giving as a reason his loss of confidence in Ralston. His health became a public issue instead of fitness to command, a position filled by General Harry Crerar. In Ottawa, the living embodiment of the spirit of Vimy Ridge caused nervous shock waves when the press asked about his health. As far as he knew, his health was fine, but if the press wanted the official version, they'd have to go to the bureaucrat who issued the original story of his failing health.

REPRINTED FROM:
Esprit de Corps, *Volume 3 Issue 4*
AUTHOR:
Norman Shannon

Murphy's Law usually prevails and text book battle scenarios usually go awry. At Motta in Italy it was different.

THE POINT OF THE ARROW, ITALY 1943

ONLY ONCE IN 23 1/2 MONTHS of fighting the Germans as an infantry officer in Tunisia, Sicily, Italy and Holland, did I experience a tactical plan made, carried out and brought to a successful conclusion as laid down in the textbook. Usually, the enemy, our higher authority, the ground, the weather, or some other friction of war caused changes to our battle plans.

The operation I have in mind took place on 1 October 1943 when my company of The Royal Canadian Regiment acted as vanguard infantry for the British Eighth Army drive across the Foggia Plain to regain contact with the enemy. The textbook calls this type of operation The Advance to Contact. It lays down a sequence of tactical moves, any one of which can be put off track by unexpected battlefield events.

ADVANCE TO CONTACT

In modern warfare, The Advance to Contact is carried out by a specially organized force of all arms, the leading element of which is called the Vanguard. This consists of a lightly armed, fast moving reconnaissance unit which drives off into the unknown, hoping to locate the enemy by drawing his fire. Having pinpointed the foe it then disengages and more heavily armed tanks are called forward to blast through the enemy position. The tanks must be closely followed by infantry, for, although they are able to take a position, they can neither flush out the enemy's infantry, nor hold the position without the skills of foot soldiers. They become "sitting ducks" when static, particularly in built-up areas. If opposition is still too strong then the Advance Guard (the remaining infantry companies and supporting arms such as field artillery, anti-tank guns, engineers and other odds and sods), deploys and the battle develops, probably involving the Main Body in due course.

On the evening of 30 September my Commanding Officer, Lieutenant Colonel Dan Spry, told me that my company was to be detached from our Regiment and that I was to report to the commander of the British Eighth Army's vanguard for my orders.

POINT OF THE ARROW

"Strome," he said, "you've seen those maps in the *Daily Telegraph* with a big black arrow showing where our forward troops have reached. Well, on tomorrow's map you are going to be the point of the arrow." He explained that the remaining companies of our Regiment were to be in the Advance Guard. We were leading Eighth Army's thrust into central Italy to seek out the rear of German Field Marshal A. Kesselring's Tenth Army, which was engaged against the Anglo-American Fifth Army struggling to break out of the Salerno bridgehead. Supposedly, we were rushing to the aid of a less successful General Mark Clark!

My company was to be loaded into three-ton trucks as the infantry element of the Vanguard, which would precede the Advance Guard by several miles. Further back would be the Main Body, the forward higher formations detailed by Eighth Army for the accomplishment of Montgomery's strategy. When this great column of men and material bumped the enemy, my men and I would be first to actually grapple with the enemy. On reporting to the Vanguard commander, Lieutenant Colonel Adams, of Princess Louise Dragoon Guards, as the reconnaissance regiment was named, I was told that the Vanguard would consist of:

- an armoured car squadron of the PLDG for reconnaissance;
- a tank squadron of the Calgary Regiment to gun down the enemy posts;
- my infantry company, to assault and clear the enemy away with bullet and bomb, and bayonet if necessary;
- a battery of the 2nd Field Regiment, Royal Canadian Artillery and 2 $^{1}/_{2}$ sections of Engineers in my direct support for the assault.

Mortars and artillery fire from the Royal Canadian Artillery provided support to then-Major Strome Galloway and his RCRs as they entered the village of Motta. (NAC/PA 136303)

DEBUSSING

The Vanguard moved off at 05:00 hours according to plan. Briefly, the armoured cars were to keep moving ahead until fired upon, then return the fire but move to the flanks and let the tanks move up to blast the enemy position. The infantry would then be "debussing" and moving into position for the assault. That is how the drill book said it was to be done. And that is how we did it.

By 20:00 hrs we had moved with considerable speed across the Foggia Plain and were approaching the Daunia Mountains, foothills of the towering Appenines. Two of the PLDG troops began driving up the twisting hillside road which led to the village of Motta. Suddenly they were fired on. They had located the enemy. Their lightly armed vehicles withdrew to the flanks, thus allowing the Calgary tanks to come forward to blast the enemy position. But, as the leading tank entered the narrow village entrance it was hit by an anti-tank shell and immediately brewed-up, blocking the road. No other tanks could enter the winding roadway with three-storey buildings along each side.

I had been riding in a Bren gun carrier which Adams had put at my disposal. I hustled up to the PLDG squadron HQ to "get myself in the picture." Having done this, I raced back to my company, halted along the road and led the three trucks up to my selected "debussing" point. As the platoon sergeants began leading their men to the forming-up place, which I pointed out to them, Adams arrived and detached one of my platoons to support a subsidiary mobile column moving along our right flank three or four miles away. This left me with just 60-odd men.

When supporting artillery battery commander, Major Bob Kingstone, arrived from the rear to give covering fire for my assault, I issued my attack orders and sent the two platoon commanders off to join their platoons. As I was giving out my orders I was amazed to notice a Photo Unit NCO taking movies of us. This was the first and only time I ever saw an army photographer in a battle area.

Major Kingstone's 25-pounders started to shell the village and my two platoons began their assault. Immediately a hail of small arms fire drove one platoon to ground, killing the platoon commander and wounding several men. The other platoon was caught between heavy machine-gun and mortar fire from both flanks. Watching this I decided that Motta was too hard a nut to crack

ABOVE:
British infantry make their way into the hills of Sicily. In June 1943, Sherman tanks waited to move forward toward Messina.

with my small force. The tanks were useless, as the blazing tank still blocked the one narrow entrance to the village. Only infantry could get into the narrow, winding street, or through the buildings which seemed to grow out of the steep hillside on which the village was built.

CODE "SUCCESS"

I got in touch with the Advance Guard and Lieutenant Colonel Spry put another company under my command. When its three platoons arrived it was dark and rain began to fall. With our movements thus obscured and with bold leadership, particularly at the section commanders' level, the village was seized before dawn. A few prisoners were taken, what had apparently been the German first aid post had plenty of blood on its tiled floor, and as the leading platoon reached the far end of the S-shaped village street they saw ten enemy vehicles in full flight making for the high ground some two miles beyond. I sent back the agreed coded word for "Success." My little fight had cost me one officer and six men killed and about an equal number wounded.

Shortly afterwards, Spry arrived on foot trailed by his command group of orderlies and signallers and the remainder of his battalion strung out along the hillside road behind him.

"The Mayor of Motta, I presume?" he quipped.

I came to attention, putting my walking stick under my left armpit, touching the peak of my cap in the approved Royal Canadian Regiment salute and replied: "Sir, Motta is yours."

Soon we were pressing forward to regain contact with the enemy who had begun shelling us from his new position. The Vanguard reverted to part of the Advance Guard and behind us the Main Body was deploying for an attack on a broad front. It had taken almost 24 hours from departure to cross the Foggia Plain, feel out, assault and drive off the enemy's outposts. Now the real battle could begin. For once, the textbook sequence had gone without a hitch and produced the most perfect tactical scenario I was ever privileged to experience.

REPRINTED FROM:
Esprit de Corps, Volume 4 Issue 10
AUTHOR:
Colonel (ret'd) Strome Galloway

ECHOES FROM PEENEMÜNDE

The RAF raid on rocket development at Peenemünde was a success but the question that haunts history is why they didn't return before the enemy decentralized the operation.

THE GERMAN AEROSPACE industry sort of cancelled plans to observe the 50th anniversary of the day Werner von Braun first got his V-2 rocket to soar in 1942. The planned 1992 observance, to be held on the sad little island of Peenemünde in the Baltic, was officially scrapped when the British protested. But unofficially, the folks who brought the world guided missiles met anyway. Winston Churchill, grandson of the wartime Prime Minister, fired a salvo which insisted that "civilized nations do not celebrate weapons systems." Churchill failed to explain how the unveiling of a statue of 'Bomber' Harris by the Queen had nothing to do with celebrating weapons systems.

For some, the controversy over Peenemünde will evoke bitter memories while Bomber Command veterans will remember a well-executed raid and some 280 missing comrades. For others, the ghost of Peenemünde will bring back echoes of questions about the affair which cost some 9000 lives.

An interest in rocketry was not suddenly thrust upon the world that day in 1942 when Werner von Braun got a rocket to fly 119 miles down range at Peenemünde. Robert Goddard started rocket experiments during WWI, but his native United States showed little interest in the fad. German research, however, took up the challenge between the wars and by the early 30's had achieved a number of successful, if brief, flights.

RAPID PROGRESS

General Walter Dornberger was the first to try to bring organization to the work at an army test base. With a limited budget, he hired top scientists such as von Braun and by 1937, a team of 300 moved into Peenemünde. Soon a large, operational rocket was undergoing test flights. The *Luftwaffe* farmed out projects to industry, and shortly an estimated one-third of all scientists were working on some aspect of rocket research. On the brink of war, the German War Ministry called for a rocket which could drop a ton of explosives on London and had a range of over 150 miles.

All the above took place before the war and raises the question of British intelligence and counter-action. Intelligence appears to have been reasonably good, but counter-action when war was declared was non-existent. In October 1942, a German 46-foot rocket was blasted 50 miles up and 119 miles down range resulting in substantial funding for Dornberger's program. Staff and activity increased and the rocket was soon refined to the point where it had a range of 260 miles and speed of 3000 mph.

LEFT: *The long-range V1 flying bomb dives upon London, June 1943. Flying at a speed of 375 mph, she would be launched on a direct line to a large target area where, out of fuel, it would fall to the ground in a slanting crash dive.* (U.S. AIR FORCE)

VENGEANCE MACHINES

British intelligence, rumours and aerial photographs monitored the activities at Peenemünde, and although Hitler was originally not enthusiastic about rockets, he became a convert after the destruction of Hamburg in July 1943. The missiles became the *Vergelung* or vengeance machines. Hence the names V-1 and V-2.

The Polish underground provided the British with details of German research and even managed to have slave labourers transferred to Peenemünde where rumours were soon confirmed. Aerial reconnaissance added to the evidence. Although the first successful rocket launch came in October 1942, and the first V-1 flew in December, Bomber Command allowed another eight months to elapse before it struck at the island. By then it was an intricate complex of workshops, housing, laboratories and test sites for V-1 and V-2 rockets.

ORDER RESTORED

The Allied raid on the night of 17 August sent almost 600 aircraft against the site where a number of small buildings were widely dispersed over three areas. The plan was to hit housing, production works and experimental works in three successive waves, spaced approximately 15 minutes apart. The force of Lancasters, Halifaxes and Stirlings needed a clear moonlit night in order to identify targets.

Target indicators dropped for the first wave landed in an area occupied by Polish prisoners instead of the housing estate, residence of scientists and technicians. Before this tragic situation could be corrected, a number of Polish workers were killed. The enemy set up a smoke screen which obscured the target area, but Group Captain J.H. Searby calmly circled the area diverting crews to other markers and restoring order. Johnny Fauquier of the Canadian Six Group acted as his deputy, flying over the target, but below the stream, for 45 minutes exhorting crews to drop bombs with care. Bombing heights were from 4000 to 10,000 feet although some crews bombed at 15,000. Miraculously, nobody was hit by friendly bombs.

SUCCESSFUL RAID

The first wave had a relatively easy time of it because flak was light and there was no enemy fighter action. Mosquitos sent against Berlin drew off enemy fighters, but not for long. Me-110's with twin upward firing cannon hit the final waves of the main force and 40 aircraft were shot down and 32 damaged. RAF dead was 245, including 60 of the Canadians who lost 12 aircraft. The cost was high but the raid was considered a success.

Considerable damage was inflicted on the site and some 735 people were killed. Some were scientists, but unfortunately, most were slave labourers, probably those who provided information on the target. General Dornberger estimated that the raid put the development of a rocket back four to six weeks. There's little doubt that the raid delayed the development of both programs, but the airfield where V-1 tests were flown was untouched as was the V-2 test stand and a liquid oxygen plant. Furthermore, the brains of the program were still intact. Bomber Command's failure to deliver a turnaround knock-out raid mocked the valour and skill of the crews who hit Peenemünde. It gave the enemy a chance to move equipment and personnel into Poland, beyond the reach of the RAF. The V-1 development program went ahead until production was farmed out to German firms. The rocket team survived. The Americans offered to do a daylight raid on Peenemünde but the RAF felt it unnecessary; presumably a return trip would be interpreted as a failure of the first raid.

OBSESSED WITH BERLIN

Tactically, the raid was a success but the strategy of not going back to clean up critical loose ends raises serious questions. Bomber Harris was obsessed with destroying Berlin and a week after the Peenemünde raid sent 727 aircraft against the German capital. Within three months, he was predicting to Churchill that the destruction of Berlin would bring about the collapse of Germany. Yet two months after the bombing of Peenemünde, the British had photos of V-1's on a ramp at Peenemünde and took

The V-1 missile carried a 1870-lb explosive warhead and was developed at Peenemünde's research station. The missile weighed 4858 pounds, had a wing span of 17'6", a length of 25'4.5" and carried 150 gallons of fuel.

no action.

By the spring of 1944, instead of collapsing, Germany had plans to launch 6000 flying bombs on England. The RAF and the American Air Corps frantically destroyed 90 launching sites on the Pas de Calais and Cherbourg peninsula by the end of April but this failed to halt the arrival of the V-1.

TERRIFYING SILENCE

The first V-1 struck England on the night of 12 June 1944 near Gravesend. A small aircraft with a 17-foot wingspan, it cruised at 400 mph and packed a ton of explosives. When the jet engine clicked off, there were terrifying seconds of silence and then an explosion. Four fell that night, and two nights later 144 crossed the coast and 73 exploded on London.

Stripped-down Tempests, Spitfires and Mustangs gave the pilots virtually no speed edge over the new weapons. The twin-engined Mosquitos were also extensively used. Air defences were shifted so that balloons and anti-aircraft guns formed a belt on the south coast. The fighters roamed seaward and inland of the belt. By the end of August, of the 97 bombs sent against England in one day, 90 were destroyed. The enemy countered by launching bombs from Heinkel aircraft and these approached England from a different direction. By the end of September, 7503 V-1's were launched against England and over 2400 fell on greater London, killing 3000 and seriously injuring 10,000 people. With an average of 100 bombs a day, fighters accounted for about 30 per cent destroyed while anti-aircraft fire was also effective.

MOBILE LAUNCHES

Although some defence was devised against the V-1, there was no defence against the V-2 which began its terror campaign on 6 September 1944 against Paris, France, then England, the city of Antwerp, Holland, and, finally, the Ludendorff bridge at Remagen, Germany. They struck from a height of 70 miles at 3000 mph, with chilling efficiency. During the first ten days of the V-2 campaign, two a day fell on London and officials explained that the city was having problems with gas mains. V-2 launching sites were mobile and difficult to locate and, although bombed, continued to pose a threat to London until they were either overrun by Allied troops or forced to move eastward.

Flying bombs and V-2's killed some 9000 people in England and Antwerp and inflicted heavy damage. While it may be argued that it was too late for the V weapons to change the course of the war, had the V-2's appeared three months earlier they certainly would have changed the history of the invasion. Was the heavy loss of life necessary or could it have been avoided by a quick Bomber Command turnaround at Peenemünde? The answer seems to lie with Harris' impatience with intrusions on his march to glory. His version of strategic bombing failed, but he did get that statue.

REPRINTED FROM:
Esprit de Corps, *Volume 3 Issue 3*
AUTHOR:
Norman Shannon

INTREPID

Vital to the war effort was the underhanded world of spies and espionage. A "quiet Canadian" was to prove himself the master of the intelligence front.

IN NEW YORK'S ROCKEFELLER Center William Stevenson, "the quiet Canadian," directed one of the world's great secret service networks.

When Grace Garner, a former Toronto magazine editor answered an advertisement in a New York newspaper, she did not discover for some time that she had joined the secret service. Directed to the 36th floor at 630 Fifth Avenue in the Rockefeller Center, she past an armed guard into the office of British Security Coordination (BSC), signed a copy of Britain's Official Secrets Act, then went to work in what was ostensibly a branch of the British Purchasing Commission. She found so much emphasis on security that "for a long time I was like someone on an assembly line who puts on a few nuts and bolts and doesn't know what the end product is." When she did learn the director's name, it meant nothing to her. In time, as his personal secretary, she would learn that William Stephenson was a master of espionage.

He was a 45-year-old native of Winnipeg, a WWI fighter pilot who had shot down 20 enemy planes in six weeks, and was the inventor of a machine to transmit photographs by radio. He was a millionaire before he was 30. Between the wars he travelled widely, cultivated people in high places, and listened. What he learned about German preparations for war, he passed on to Winston Churchill, who became a close personal friend. "That," he said, "was my only training in espionage." Eventually, he would direct an organization that turned enemy spies, penetrated foreign embassies to secure diplomatic codes and ciphers, and trained agents for intelligence and subversion in enemy-occupied territories.

ULTRA

A week before Hitler overran Poland, Polish cryptologists provided the British with a purloined German Enigma machine. Although not technically a weapon of war, it would become one of the most important items in the Allied arsenals. The Ultra reports which flowed from deciphered codes from Bletchley Park north of London, would provide military and political leaders with detailed information about the enemy's plans for the rest of the war. Stephenson's friendship with Churchill now took on a new significance. Days after he became Prime Minister in 1940, he dispatched Stephenson to Washington as "Intrepid" to convince President Roosevelt that Britain would not be beaten and that she had secrets to share.

Stephenson obtained approval from the President for British counter-intelligence agents to operate in the United States and, working closely with an influential New York lawyer, William J. "Wild Bill" Donovan, established close ties between British and American intelligence services. Stephenson and Donovan, the future head of the Office of Strategic Services (OSS), became the go-betweens who processed top-secret intelligence for Roosevelt and Churchill

BRITISH SECURITY

Working out of the Rockefeller Centre, Stephenson's organization, which directed British intelligence operations throughout the western hemisphere, was mostly staffed by Canadians – senior business executives on loan and some 800 women. Its primary task in the early years of the war was to provide factual information to offset isolationist and anti-British sentiment and to maintain the flow of war materials to Britain. Stephenson played a leading role in the negotiations that led to the transfer of 50 U.S. destroyers to Britain in 1940, and he and Donovan were largely instrumental in obtaining 100 B-17 Flying Fortresses for the RAF and over a million rifles for the British Home Guard. "My task," he later said, "was to convince the Americans that material assistance would not be improvident charity but a sound investment."

ABOVE: *In 1922 William Stephenson invented a method of sending photos instantly by wireless transmitter. A millionaire with many interests, he shared ownership of Shepparton Studios with film director Alexander Korda.* (H. MONTGOMERY HYDE)

One of the hundreds of Canadians in BSC was its communications expert, Benjamin de Forest "Pat" Bayly, a University of Toronto electrical engineering professor who was able to adapt ciphering machines to carry the immense amount of secret traffic that passed daily between New York and the various organizations in London that Stephenson represented. Another Canadian, T.G. "Tommy" Drew-Brook, operated Station M, an organization in Toronto specializing in the fabrication of letters and documents. Drew-Brook was also responsible for setting up a secret training establishment in Ontario.

CAMP X

Stephenson wanted to be sure that facilities for training American spies and saboteurs would be available when the United States entered the war. Accordingly, Drew-Brook was instructed to purchase a 200-acre farm fronting Lake Ontario between Oshawa and Whitby. Army engineers erected barracks and dug underground rifle ranges. Sealed off with barbed wire and patrolled by armed guards, the camp went into operation in August 1941.

Trainees wore Canadian Army uniforms and received Canadian pay and allowances. "We were taught to use every type of weapon," a trainee recalled. "We had to go into a dark room, find a bag full of revolver parts, put them together and come out shooting. The same with automatic weapons." They also learned about radio, explosives, invisible ink and forgery.

Most of the school's 500 graduates, including Ian Fleming, future author of the James Bond novels, were absorbed into British units, but some were RCMP and FBI officers learning how enemy agents might work in Canada and the United States. After the U.S. entered the war, American agents were trained at Camp X and would form the nucleus of Donovan's OSS.

Grace Gardner never regretted her decision to join BSC. She described Stephenson as "a brilliant man with a mind like a steel trap." Overworked, she said that "if he had asked us to start a 24-shift, we'd have accepted it without a whimper. We'd have given our lives for him." She was convinced that he was among "the small group of men without whom the Allies would not have won the war."

AUTHOR: *Bill Twatio*

Bomber Harris promised to end the war by destroying Berlin. He reduced the city, and much of Germany, to rubble but the enemy fought on.

THE BATTLE OF BERLIN

NEXT PAGE: *Between August 1943 and March 1944, Berlin and other German industrial cities were the targets of Bomber Command. Over 30,000 tons of bombs were dropped on Berlin alone during that period. Lancaster, Halifax and Stirling heavy bombers were primarily used to conduct these missions.* (DND/PL 144274)

LEFT: *Going through final preparations before taking off on a nighttime bombing mission, the crew of this bomber hoped that, once their fighter escort left them, they would return home safely from their sortie.* (PAINTING BY DAME LAURA KNIGHT, IMPERIAL WAR MUSEUM)

THEY LAY SMOKING IN the grass beneath the wings of their aircraft in the gathering darkness, quietly chatting with the ground crews until the time came to swing themselves up into the fuselage. Pilots and engineers fired up engines and tested throttles and switches, wireless operators sent test signals, gunners checked their guns and ammunition and bomb-aimers adjusted their sights. With a thumbs up, windows were slid shut as battery carts and wheel chocks were pulled away and they lumbered to the end of the runway. A green light flashed from the control tower, engines roared in great clouds of flame and smoke and one by one they rushed into the night.

LONGEST BOMBING OFFENSIVE

From neighbouring airfields in Yorkshire and down the east coast of England, hundreds of heavily-laden Lancasters, Halifaxes and Stirlings struggled into the air and formed up into a great stream over the North Sea. Some flew straight and level, some weaved, changed course constantly or "jinked," pulling up, rolling and falling back. Gunners fired test bursts and the crews settled down to the drone of engines, the cold, the hiss of oxygen masks and the reek of aviation fuel; spectral shapes moving about in the dark. Four hours later they would be over Berlin.

The Battle of Berlin was the longest and most sustained bombing offensive against a single target in WWII. Between August 1943 and March 1944, Bomber Command flew more than 10,000 sorties and dropped over 30,000 tons of bombs on the city. It was the supreme effort to end the war by aerial bombing. "We can wreck Berlin from end to end," Air Chief Marshal Arthur Harris told Churchill in November 1943. "It will cost us between 400 and 500 aircraft. It will cost Germany the war."

Known to aircrew as "The Big City," Berlin was the third largest city in the world with a pre-war population of four million spread over 900 square miles. It was the administrative centre of Germany and its new empire, a major communications centre and the home of much war industry including the Alkett factory at Spandau that produced self-propelled guns and half the Wehrmacht's field artillery, the Boriswereke locomotive factory, the D.W.M. and D.W.I. combines that produced small arms, mortars and ammunition, and Zeiss, Daimler-Benz and Siemens, the giant electrical firm. There was no doubt about the importance of Berlin as a target. But there was equally little doubt about the difficulty in attacking it.

Bad weather and distance would take a toll – Berlin was 650 miles from British bases. So too would the Luftwaffe's night-fighters guided by a great arc of radar stations from Denmark to the Swiss frontier, skilled now in their new "Wild Sow" tactics. Some, armed with Shrage Musik (upward firing cannons), would slip into the bomber stream unseen, picking up exhaust flames. A belt of searchlights some 30 miles from the centre of the city and another of anti-aircraft guns ten miles further in ringed the city. The guns, with a range of up to 45,000 feet, would provide formidable high fire until the fighters arrived. Sergeant Ferris Newton, a Canadian pilot flying a Lancaster with 76 Squadron, recalls:

> *The first thing we have to do is fly through a wall of searchlights; they are in the hundreds – in cones and in clusters. It's a wall of light, with very few breaks, and behind that wall is an even fiercer light, glowing red and green and blue. It is pretty obvious as we come in through the searchlight cones that it is going to be hell over the target ... There is one comfort, and it has been a comfort to me all the time we have been going over, and that is that it's quite soundless; the roar of our engines drowns out everything else. It is like running straight into the most gigantic display of soundless fireworks in the world.*

DESTRUCTION

The first raids destroyed several factories, Albert Speer's private office in the War Industry Ministry, the Naval Construction Headquarters, embassies along the Unter den Linden, the Kaiser Wilhelm Memorial Church at the end of the Kurfurstendamn, the Ka De We department store, the Harrod's of Berlin, and the famous Romanisches Cafe.

The zoo was hit as well, giving rise to terrible rumours of lions roaming the streets, as were two hospitals, theatres, museums and Hitler's private train. Unfortunately, the Führer was in East Prussia at the time. Over 2000 civilians died, including 500 killed in a single shelter that took a direct hit. "I just can't understand how the English are able to do so much damage to the Reich capital in one air raid," Propaganda Minister Josef Goebbels wrote in his diary. "The picture that greeted my eye in the Wilhelmplatz was one of utter desolation...Blazing fires everywhere... Hell itself seems to have broken loose over us. We have lived through an indescribable experience and survived what seems like the end of the world."

But within 48 hours he would also note: "The Wilhemplatz has already undergone quite a change. The fires are out, the atmosphere is clear, smoke has disappeared. There is no blaze left to extinguish. In short, although one sees the bare ruins of buildings ... the most serious catastrophe has already been overcome. It is remarkable how fast everything goes. I thought it would take weeks; in reality only two days were needed to get back to some semblance of order."

Operations ebbed and flowed with the lunar cycle, the crews braving cloud, fog, icing and intense cold. "Crews were weary and angry, strained and more fearful of their next trip than usual," Pilot Officer Joe Sheriff remembers. "We cursed 'Butch' Harris for his unrelenting demands and his apparently uncaring attitude towards his own men." But they pressed on. In 19 major attacks, Canada's 6 Group lost 91 aircraft and 664 aircrew. Bomber Command lost the equivalent of its entire front line strength. The British Official History states: "The Battle of Berlin was more than a failure. It was a defeat."

BOMBER COMMAND CRITICIZED

Bomber Command has come under fire from a whole generation of revisionist his-

torians since the 1960s, claiming that the bombing offensive against Germany was immoral, wasteful and ineffective. The Battle of Berlin was part of a great battle fought virtually every night for five-and-a-half years. The last word on the outcome of that battle must be that of Hitler's head of Arms Production, Albert Speer, who wrote:

> *The real importance of the air war consisted in the fact that it opened a second front long before the invasion of Europe. That front was the skies over Germany. The fleets of bombers might appear at any time over any large German city. The unpredictability of the attacks made this front gigantic; every square meter of the territory we controlled was a kind of front line. Defence against air attacks required the production of thousands of anti-aircraft guns, the stockpiling of tremendous quantities of ammunition and holding in readiness, totally inactive for months at a time, hundreds of thousands of soldiers. As far as I can judge from the accounts I have read, no one has yet seen, that for Germany, this was the greatest lost battle of all.*

REPRINTED FROM:
Esprit de Corps, *Volume 6 Issue 2*
AUTHOR:
Bill Twatio

STRONG DELIVERERS

Contrary to popular belief in female frailty, women ferry pilots delivered 300,000 aircraft to the RAF.

PERHAPS NOTHING REFLECTED the tide of public ignorance about women pilots better than a statement which appeared in *The Aeroplane* magazine at the start of WWII. Editor C.G. Grey pontificated that "the menace is the woman who thinks she ought to be flying a high-speed bomber when she really has not the intelligence to scrub the floor of a hospital."

Grey had been dispensing such garbage since the previous war when he complained about the lowered tone in RFC messes, ostensibly because it was filling up with colonials and "the brats of shopkeepers" instead of gentlemen aviators. Somehow Grey was able to influence public opinion in England for over a quarter of a century, and, as a result, women pilots like Britain's Pauline Gower faced a major struggle in 1939 that had nothing to do with Hitler.

When war began Gower was a commissioner in the Civil Air Guard and an active pilot who owned an air taxi. As the CAG was absorbed into the Air Transport Auxiliary, Gower used her connections to pressure the Ministry of Aircraft Production and the Air Ministry to form a women's section in the ATA. She started with eight pilots who each had over 600 hours. Based in Herfordshire, they had to pay for their own lodgings and, although they got to wear a uniform, it had about as much impact on the military as that of a London bus driver.

DANGEROUS WINTER

During the miserable and dangerous winter of 1939, they ferried Tiger Moths to remote fields in England and Scotland. The trip north in an open cockpit sometimes took up to two weeks. Pilots weaved through a network of balloon barrages in

LEFT:
With the manpower crunch affecting front line forces, women pilots were used to ferry planes wherever possible. As part of the Air Transport Auxiliary (ATA) the women flew Tiger Moths, Spitfires,Hurricanes, Hudsons and Wellingtons from one Royal Air Force airstrip to another in England. Some would pilot as many as 67 different types of aircraft.

low, hanging, dark clouds while trying to skirt anti-aircraft corridors. The only navigational aid was a map on their knee as they were denied normal radio contact. Busy Royal Air Force training circuits, anti-aircraft batteries and enemy intruders were also constant concerns.

Having landed at an RAF field, women pilots had to hitch a ride or walk to the nearest village looking for a bed. For some reason, providing accommodations was beyond the intellectual capacity of the RAF. Upon landing at one field, a woman ferry pilot asked a mechanic directions to the nearest lavatory. She was directed down a line of aircraft, a turn to the left and under the wing of a bomber.

WOMEN MEET THE DEMAND

The fall of France and the Battle of Britain increased the demand for delivery of aircraft from factories, and this forced the ATA to permit women to fly more types of aircraft, including operational machines. The list was gradually extended to Spitfires, Hurricanes and four-engined bombers. Women were permitted to fly in dirty weather around the United Kingdom but were never allowed in the big league of trans-Atlantic flights. Flamboyant Jackie Cochrane, an American with an impressive number of hours and a flair for publicity, worked out a deal with the USAF's Hap Arnold whereby she would fly the Atlantic. She handled the crossing but had to relinquish controls on take-off and landing to a male pilot.

PROVIDING ACCOMMODATIONS [FOR WOMEN PILOTS] WAS BEYOND THE INTELLECTUAL CAPACITY OF THE RAF.

The significance of Cochrane's flight is obscure but her association with Pauline Gower is not. When Gower explained what the women's section was doing and Cochrane's politicking in Washington was completed, it resulted in American volunteers for Gower's unit. About 40 were recruited and over 25 found their way into the British ATA.

UNWANTED IN CANADA

When war came to Canada some 90 women had pilot's licenses, five of which were commercial, yet not one woman was gainfully employed as a pilot. Hope flickered when the British Commonwealth Air Training Plan was announced but soon spluttered out in recruiting offices across the country. Women pilots were told that the RCAF was simply not hiring women. In fact, it would be almost two years before women were accepted for ground duty.

Although the ATA did no formal advertising, word soon got around and one of the first Canadian women to get it was Helen Harrison. She probably holds the all-time record for rejections. First the RAF turned her down although she had 2600 hours at the time, and was rejected as a civilian instructor for the military because she was a woman. The RCAF turned her down because she wore a skirt. Finally, she went to Washington where she showed her log book to Jackie Cochrane. It showed 2600 hours, an instructor's rating, multi-engine time, and instrument endorsements. Harrison held a commercial license in four countries. Cochrane quickly sent her to Dorval for a check out on a Harvard and, within a few months, Helen Harrison became the first of five Canadians to fly with the ATA.

ROCKY MOMENTS

Harrison's career with ATA was not all high flight. Her first assignment ended in a farmer's field, but she got a commendation instead of a reprimand. She 'greased' a Hurricane on landing because of flap trouble, landed on the wrong runway and pointed the Hurrie's tail at the stars. However, in two years she logged 500 hours in 34 different types of aircraft.

Marion Orr was the next Canadian to join the ATA, logging 700 hours on 67 types of aircraft. A third volunteer, Elspeth Russel Burnett, compensated for a height of five feet two inches by stuffing cushions behind her when flying Hudsons and Wellingtons. Vi Milestead, who was somewhat shorter, also used a black handbag to help conquer leg reach on twin-engined aircraft. Vera Stodl was one of the women who graduated to four-engine bombers and logged over 1000 hours on 65 different types of aircraft.

The facility with which ATA women pilots transferred from one type of aircraft to another was a matter of concern and mystification to RAF pilots. They were shocked at the common sight of a female pilot climbing out of one aircraft and then getting into a completely different type and taking off. What they did not know was that the ladies borrowed from the book of the German officer who later appeared in the movie *Those Magnificent Men in their Flying Machines*. He was the one who flew while reading a book and muttering:, "A German officer can do anything!"

ATA pilots were convinced that one aircraft was essentially the same as the other, and all they needed to know about differences was contained in a dandy little blue book which they carried on their laps. It worked on the basis of, "What the Hell! All airplanes have wings and engines and stuff!" The key was in relationships between lift, drag and thrust and somehow the blue book had these worked down to simple numbers. Or maybe it was magic! Whatever, the blue book worked because the safety record of women pilots was better than men's.

OPERATION PEAK

At the peak of operations there were 166 women in the ATA, and ferry pilots were delivering 6000 planes a month. With the invasion, delivery routes were extended to France and Belgium and some ATA pilots flew supplies and VIP's to Italy and the Middle East. Of the 1318 pilots in the ATA, 154 were killed in the course of ferrying more than 309,000 machines.

When the United States entered the war, many of the pilots Jackie Cochrane had recruited served out their 18-month contract and then returned to the U.S. Cochrane did so in the fall of 1942 and was surprised and peeved at some of the changes that had taken place. Women flyers were being recruited for a Women's Auxiliary Ferry Service (WAFS) and the operation was being directed by Nancy Love, a competent pilot with 1200 hours, but a rival as she and Cochrane did not see eye to eye on the nature of the organization. More importantly, Cochrane thought she should be directing it.

Sergeant K.W. Horsman was just one of the women who flew with Air Transport Auxiliary as a pilot ferrying planes for the RAF. *(DND/PL 11312)*

ATA PILOTS WERE CONVINCED THAT ONE AIRCRAFT WAS ESSENTIALLY THE SAME AS ANOTHER.

Finally, Cochrane got Washington to agree to a related training program for potential WAFS pilots with herself as head. Later, she applied pressure to have the two organizations amalgamated into the Women's Airforce Service Pilots (WASP) with herself as director of pilots and Love as the WASP executive at Air Transport Command.

YOU'RE ON YOUR OWN

Lee Warren was the only known Canadian to join the WASPs which grew to almost 1100 pilots. They delivered 12,650 aircraft while flying 60 million miles. Thirty-eight lost their lives and parents had to pay to recover the bodies and bring them home for burial. Officially, the coffin did not even get a flag.

As the Allies gained ground in Europe, the surplus of male pilots in the U.S. brought an abrupt end to the WASP program. In England women ATA pilots were in greater demand as delivery routes were extended. Then, one by one, they were unceremoniously dismissed. The performance of both ATA and WASP pilots matched and sometimes exceeded that of men, but women received little recognition. Presumably ATA women killed or injured while flying for their country were eligible for civilian war pensions or allowances. But dependants of WASP pilots received no recognition from their country, although dependants of servicemen killed in the same crash were eligible for pension. It would not be until 1975 that WASP personnel were finally recognized. The Victorian views and chauvinistic attitude of C.G. Grey cast a long shadow into the 20th century.

REPRINTED FROM:
Esprit de Corps, *Volume 2 Issue 10*
AUTHOR:
Norm Shannon

RIGHT:
Mule trains proved invaluable in transporting weapons, ammunition and supplies across the rugged, mountainous Sicilian countryside. Even though supplies were mostly transported to men in front line positions at night, mules and their handlers at times came under fire causing fatalities or injuries to the muleteers.
(NAC/PA 23913)

WHEN FLANDERS FIELDS CAME TO ITALY

When rain, sleet and snow hit the mountains of Italy, it turned the war into a trip back in time.

BY THE END OF December 1943, the British Eighth Army's drive up the Adriatic coast with a view to outflanking the Germans' line at Monte Cassino and capturing Rome by Christmas had come to a bloody, muddy halt. The 1st Canadian Division and the 1st Canadian Armoured Brigade were both in the forefront of the operation. They had crossed the Moro River, had cleared the seaport town of Ortona, and in a state of exhaustion faced the German winter line, called the Gothic Line, along the Arielli River.

Canadian casualties had been heavy. Between 5 December, when the Division entered the fray, and 27 December, when the enemy broke contact and withdrew behind the Arielli, our casualties were 695 killed, 1738 wounded and 1773 sick, for a staggering total of 4206, virtually a third of the Division and Brigade's fighting strength. The previous five months in Sicily and southern Italy had, of course, seen a mounting casualty list. In the writer's own battalion, of the 41 officers and 715 men who landed in Sicily on 10 July, less than 200 were with the battalion on New Year's Day 1944. Of the 41 officers, only nine remained, and of the nine, six including the writer, had been wounded. The face of the battalion, as that of the 1st Canadian Division, had changed.

POSITION WARFARE

So had the battlefield. We no longer fought in sun-drenched hill country, through peaceful orchards or vineyards heavy with grapes, or along dried-up river beds, or rutted roads inches deep in white dust. Our battleground now was the low-lying, muddy no-man's-land separating our barbed wire-encircled strong points, our scattering of water-logged slit trenches and our sandbagged, ruined peasant cottages, most of which were partially or even wholly roofless. It was position warfare. Our eyes stared across the landscape of mud, shattered trees, and shell-riven farmsteads at an unseen enemy who was occupying his time the same way. Every once in a while his mortars and guns gave us a blast. Then we would answer his impudence with the same treatment. Occasionally, indirect machine-gun fire would knock the branches off the remaining, leafless trees, or spatter against the stone walls of our fortified farm dwellings. Frequently, the plaintive cry "stretcher-bearers – at the double" could be heard as some unfortunate received a bullet or a shell fragment with his number on it.

Rain fell. Sometimes an icy gale blew in from the coast. The odd snow flurry added to the misery, and every night some poor souls were detailed to crawl out of their slits and make their way toward the enemy lines, either as listening patrols to try to discover what the Germans were doing, or to attempt as a fighting patrol to grab an unsuspecting enemy for questioning by our intelligence people, hungry for information as they waited in the relative comfort of their lighted and heated caravans at Brigade or Divisional Headquarters. These patrols cost us human lives and were singularly unpopular as nocturnal employment. The information they got, if any, was negligible. Once a subaltern from another regiment actually killed a German and was rewarded by the Divisional commander with a bottle of whiskey.

It was as if Flanders Fields had come to Italy, as if Ortona were another Ypres and it was 1915 instead of 1944. True, our defences differed to some extent: instead of long parallels of six-foot deep trenches behind apron after apron of continuous barbed wire entanglements, our positions were sited in small groups of fire-supporting two-man slits no deeper than breast height.

They were good protection except for a direct hit. Our wiring was used as a warning device only. It was hung with stones in tin cans; these would sound the alarm if an intrusion were taking place. In mid-century warfare with tanks in the field, the old-style

RIGHT:
After heavy fighting, the streets of Ortona were littered with rubble and burning vehicles. German mortars damaged a truck, jeep and a Canadian Bren gun carrier. (DND)

OPPOSITE PAGE, LEFT:
Addressing the men of the Royal Canadian Regiment, General Andy McNaughton was adamant that the Canadian army should be assigned for operations as a unit. (NAC/PA 23626)

OPPOSITE PAGE, RIGHT:
A universal Bren gun carrier passes through British positions in Italy. A full-tracked vehicle with a top speed of 32 miles per hour, the Bren gun carrier had an open top and carried just five soldiers. Having a limited effectiveness as an armoured personnel carrier (APC) because of its size, they were mostly used for reconnaissance and fire support missions. (IMPERIAL WAR MUSEUM)

defensive wire that hung up attacking infantry in World War One was useless and easily torn up by tank tracks.

MIGHTY MAROON MACHINE

This was the scenario when General Harry Crerar came out to Italy bringing with him a Corps Headquarters and his Mighty Maroon Machine. The 5th Canadian Armoured Division was so called from the patch of maroon cloth sewn on their sleeves as their Divisional insignia.

The author well remembers Crerar's first visit to the Ortona front. He stood in the frozen mud, behind him the shattered farmhouse that served as our Battalion Headquarters. He leaned on his walking stick, slowly shifting his gaze from right to left and back again.

"Why it's just like Passchendaele," he murmured. "Just like Passchendaele." Since none of us had been at Passchendaele, and since some of us had not even been born then, we nodded in agreement and heard even more about the mud of Flanders, the rainfall in the Ypres Salient, the misery of trench warfare. Then the general returned to his comfy caravan ten miles behind the line and left us to the mud of Italy, the rainfall in the Ortona Salient and the misery of modern position warfare.

THE MUD DEFIED OUR JEEPS, BUT THERE WAS AN ADDED DANGER: IF ATTEMPTS WERE MADE TO PROVISION THE FRONT LINE BY JEEP, THE NOISE OF THEIR MOTORS, ESPECIALLY IF STRUGGLING TO GET FREE OF MUDDY RUTS, SOON BROUGHT DOWN ENEMY MORTAR FIRE.

The first three months of 1944 were indeed the winter of our discontent. With slight variations it was 1915 all over again. You kept your head down by day and you administered yourself by night. Mule trains trudged over the muddy fields after dark, bringing the next day's rations and the nightly issue of rum. The mud defied our jeeps, but there was an added danger; if attempts were made to provision the front line by jeep, the noise of their motors, especially if struggling to get free of muddy ruts, soon brought down enemy mortar fire.

MULES AND SHEPHERDS

Even our mule trains sometimes came under fire causing fatalities among our faithful muleteers and the quartermaster blokes who shepherded the reluctant beasts of burden through the night. Obviously, the enemy knew we must keep our line furnished with food, ammunition and repaired equipment. They also knew that there would be nightly traffic of lightly wounded, leave personnel or special duty personnel moving between the front line and our administrative and command echelons a mile or more in the rear. So, naturally, they laid down periodic "hates" of mortar, or artillery, or even indirect machine-gun fire. They just had to score some hits. And so our casualty list continued to lengthen both night and day during the three winter months.

Three incidents come to the writer's mind from that miserable, boring, stagnant time. The first was an abortive daylight attack put on by that very gallant and battlewise unit, the Hastings and Prince Edward Regiment, coming from the eastern Ontario counties so named, but called by most of us "The Hasty Pees."

This attack apparently had two aims: First, to show the enemy that the Canadians were still "offensively minded" thus keeping them from thinning out their Ortona front to provide troops to counterattack the precarious Allied beachhead at Anzio. The second reason, so it was said, was to keep our troops from getting bored!

The fact that the troops would rather get bored than get killed never seemed to enter the planners' heads.

NEAR DISASTER

The Hasty Pees met with near disaster, but, despite this, were ordered to renew the attack next day, which they did. More than one third of the battalion's assault strength was lost in these two efforts. Nothing was gained except the troops could, if they wished, take renewed pride in their courage. I remember seeing a good friend, Major Stan Ketcheson, of Trenton, Ontario, who commanded the action, coming back in a jeep ambulance with a grey face, wrapped in a grey blanket with a grey winter sky above him.

The next memory was of the endless, and, to most of us, meaningless, patrol activity that was carried out every night. In these three months my own unit, the Royal Canadian Regiment, carried out 64 of these patrols. The damage done to the enemy, or the information gained by them, was not worth the effort. But we were told that we must "dominate no-man's-land." Apparently we did that, as the Germans proved good watchers. They very rarely patrolled forward of their lines, other than to establish ambush patrols on our likely approaches to their positions. What this did to our patrols can be easily imagined. Our troops were brave enough, but it all seemed so pointless.

My third memory has to do with the Canadian Volunteer Service Medal, or the "Everybody Gets One" as we called it. Rolls of the ribbon were delivered from the base, plus envelopes full of little silver maple leaves to be attached to the ribbons of those with overseas service. Since all of us were overseas, we were all entitled to the maple leaf, but dozens did not have the 18 months voluntary service required to qualify for the medal itself. So they could not get the ribbon to put the maple leaf on! Because of the fall off in recruiting we were getting reinforcements at that time with less than six months training.

SAWDUST-PACKED RUM JARS

At that particular moment I was working out of Battalion Headquarters. In allocating the nightly issue of sawdust-packed rum jars for the forward companies, I had put a great big roll of medal ribbon in each box. Naturally, when the boxes were opened, the troops, who had never heard of the award, wondered who was to get these colourful bits of silk. The more cynical didn't ask "who?" they asked "why?"

ABOVE: *Standing in his slit trench, a soldier of the West Nova Scotia Regiment mans his PIAT rocket launcher. The development of the hollow-charge (also called shrapnel-charge) explosive ordnance permitted the foot soldier to fire a hand-held weapon capable of stopping a tank.* (NAC/PA 1531981)

Such were those months in 1944 when it seemed as though Flanders Fields had come to Italy, bringing the same old mud, the same old boredom, the same old death by day and death by night, the same old rum ration, and an elderly general whose mind went back to Passchendaele.

REPRINTED FROM:

Esprit de Corps, *Volume 3 Issue 9*

AUTHOR:

Colonel (ret'd) Strome Galloway

For two hours on Christmas Day 1943 weary Canadians came in from the war in Ortona where they ate and thought of home.

THE MEN WHO CAME TO DINNER

LEFT: Men of the Seaforth Highlanders celebrate Christmas at the front. Drinking local wine, the men enjoy a brief respite from the daily fighting. (NAC/PA 163936)

ON CHRISTMAS EVE 1943, between the burp of *Schmeissers*, the Canadians could hear voices in the enemy trenches. Voices singing *"Stille Nacht …heilige nacht"* made Christmas at Ortona even more bizarre and the next day the Seaforth Highlanders went to the church of Santa Maria di Constantinipoli not to pray but to eat. There had been ample praying on the 450-mile drive up the Apennine spine and on Christmas morning the padre was wise enough to let religion find its own level as the men came in from the killing ground for two hours of Christmas.

Pork sizzled in cookers behind the altar and the first sip of beer eased some of the tension which almost four months of combat etched on weary faces. Conversations started haltingly and then grew almost hysterically as men re-discovered the simple art of talk. When the memorable meal was finished, empty plates were stacked on the altar as the reality of war blended with the Christmas story and thoughts of home. Then it was time to go back.

Uptown, in another church, legend had it that whoever looked upon the tomb of St. Thomas would get safely to Rome. The Canadians were tasked to get through Ortona to link up with a road which led to Rome, but every time a man stepped outside he ran an exceedingly good chance of becoming dead. Casualties since September's invasion of Italy ran to about 4000 all causes, and they were still mounting. Small wonder that few Canadians were impressed by the legend of St. Thomas.

AT BEST THE ITALIAN CAMPAIGN WAS A MARRIAGE OF RELUCTANT PARTNERS.... WHEN CANADIANS INVADED THE "SOFT UNDERBELLY OF EUROPE" ON 3 SEPTEMBER 1943, THEY WERE PAWNS IN A CONFUSED MILITARY CAMPAIGN

At best the Italian campaign was a marriage of reluctant partners. For two years the Americans had been thirsting for an invasion in North-West Europe, although terribly unprepared, and saw no point in committing forces to Italy. The British, on the other hand, wanted to reduce the enemy's strength, tie up his forces and establish a line of communication through the Mediterranean. The reason for the latter is not obvious since the war in North Africa was over. As for tying up troops, the advantage was definitely with the superbly entrenched enemy. When Canadians invaded the "soft underbelly of Europe" on 3 September 1943, they were pawns in a confused military campaign and Canadian politics, which ultimately cost General Andy McNaughton his job.

Canadian losses at Dieppe notwithstanding, Mackenzie King had long been seized with the idea of having Canadians more actively involved in the war. During the North African campaign he continuously pestered Churchill to get the Canadians in action. As a result, the 1st Canadian Division and the Three Rivers Tank regiment were part of the invasion of Sicily. McNaughton stipulated that the army not be split up and that troops sent to Sicily be returned to England in time for the invasion of NW Europe. But when landings in Sicily led to the invasion of Italy, the Canadian government decided not only to leave the 1st Division in Italy, but to add to it to form an army corps, much against the wishes of the British.

Although it reached a conclusion in January 1944, this muddled scenario was being played out, unknown to field commanders, when the 1st Canadian Division and the 1st Canadian Tank Brigade crossed the straits of Messina on 3 September 1943. It was a pleasant 10-mile cruise which ended in a long walk in the sun; the operation was a feint for a larger landing by the Americans which would come at Salerno in six days. Canadian columns marching north over parched mountains met exuberant Italians coming south, rushing like lemmings not to the sea, but to give themselves up.

LEFT:
The action at the Moro River on 5 December 1943 marked the beginning of the bloodiest month of fighting the Canadians would encounter in the entire Italian campaign. Men of the Hastings and Prince Edward Regiment, as seen through the turret ring of a wrecked German tank, move forward.
(NAC/PA 136215)

VANISHING ENEMY

North of Reggio di Calabria, the Canadians were soon in the mountains where mules became man's best friend. The Apennine mountains run down the spine of Italy and are serated by rivers. In the summer of 1943 they were also serated by German defence positions and as the Canadians moved north, the war became a series of brief engagements and a vanishing enemy who fought well and then withdrew.

Within 17 days of the landing, the Canadians took Potenza, a communications centre, just south of the major airport at Foggia. An entry in a German war diary suggests that the Canadians had already established a reputation: "Opposite the 26th Panzer Division, the 1st Canadian Infantry has appeared again which explains the rapid advance of the enemy."

CAPTURE AND ESCAPE

After Foggia, the Canadians moved northwest clearing several Apennine locations. By 13 October The Royal Canadian Regiment and 48th Highlanders moved to the outskirts of Campobasso with the Hastings and Prince Edwards in reserve. After a night skirmish, the Canadians walked into Campobasso next morning. However, Major Bert Kennedy and two privates of the Hasty Pees were captured when they tried to link up with the RCR's, and four days later Kennedy was on a truck bound for Rome and a prison camp. As it slowed to round a sharp turn, he jumped, and ended up in a brook below. It was raining and the guards seemed to have more important business elsewhere. They fired a few shots in Kennedy's direction and moved on. Kennedy lived on the land and with Italian peasants for 25 days. He finally contacted an American patrol and returned to duty although he lost 15 pounds in the adventure.

MILTON MCNAUGHTON WAITED TWO HOURS FOR THE ENEMY SHELLING AND SNIPER FIRE TO ABATE.

The enemy counted heavily on the snows and rain of November to bring the fighting to a close for the winter. Meanwhile they waited in winter defensive positions on the north bank of the Sangro River. Late in November, the British 78th Division broke through the German Hitler line in a five-day battle, then the 1st Canadian Division moved through to take up the pursuit.

BRIDGES BLOWN

The Canadians made their way up a coastal plain about two miles wide with mountains on the west and the Adriatic on the east. Every mile a gully and rushing torrents impeded movement. The Germans had methodically blown up all bridges and followed the progress from the high ground, shelling at will. By early December, the Canadians faced yet another river.

As the Canadians prepared to cross, enemy shelling increased. Milton McNaughton waited two hours for the enemy shelling and sniper fire to abate. His job was to drive a bulldozer into the Moro River to gouge out a diversion, enabling them to bring equipment across. While waiting, he went out and got himself two German prisoners. Then he said 'the hell with waiting' and drove out where he worked under fire for five hours. Two hours later the tanks rolled across and San Leonardo was taken.

RAIN, MUD AND BODIES

The 1st Division then moved towards the Ortona-Orsogna road but a ravine stood between the Canadians and the road. Here the Germans were strongly entrenched in the slopes, protected from artillery. When firing stopped, they came out and fought savagely and held. Heavy rains churned the floor of the gully to a thick mud worthy of Passchendaele; and the dead built up in repeated attacks and counterattacks. Finally, after five days the Seaforths and the West Nova Scotias each breached the defences with Ontario Regiment tanks as back up and established a bridgehead beyond the Gully.

Next morning the Royal 22nd Regiment was ordered to take a cluster of farm buildings known as *Casa Berardi* and a critical crossroads beyond on the road to Ortona. With Captain Paul Triquet were 81 men and

RIGHT:
From his vantage point inside an artillery-damaged building, a German paratrooper keeps a watchful eye for any sign of movement. Their strong defensive positions led to a month of intense fighting before they were pushed back.

seven Ontario Regiment tanks. While intelligence reports suggested that the Panzer unit holding the area had been badly mauled, they didn't mention that it had been relieved by a fresh parachute battalion armed with tanks, one of the best in Italy.

HEAVY LOSSES

After a one-hour barrage, the Canadians advanced across the ravine with infantry leading the tanks. They took one outpost where an officer was suffering from shellshock but a few hundred yards further on the slap of 88's (German tanks), destroyed one of the Canadian tanks. Countering fire knocked out one of four attacking tanks. There was a brief pause as a woman led two children away from the area, and then the Canadians destroyed a second enemy tank. Triquet lost 30 men and his radio was smashed in the heavy fighting.

They pushed on towards the houses a mile and a half away, every foot costing casualties. By late morning, Triquet's losses stood at 50 men and they were surrounded by the enemy. Triquet decided the safest course was to take their objective. The 14 survivors reached Casa Berardi seven hours after they started and then the job of cleaning out the houses began. Although they drove the enemy out, many returned during the night. Ammunition was exhausted and Major Smith's lead tank was knocked out. The others formed a circle with two infantrymen in slit trenches guarding them throughout the night.

Next day brought heavy shelling which wiped out half a relief company. The last member of Triquet's headquarters company was killed while urging him to eat, and Triquet spent the rest of the day under fire hopping from trench to trench, encouraging his men. After midnight on the second day, a squadron of tanks arrived with reinforcements for the Ontario Regiment. Four days after the attack went in, the Royal Canadian Regiment made contact but came under heavy attack with many casualties.

MOUSE-HOLING

Promoted to major, Triquet was awarded the Victoria Cross. He later wrote: "The RCR dead were buried not far from our dead – French Canadians and English Canadians sleeping their last sleep side by side." The RCR and the 48th Highlanders took the vital crossroads on 19 December and two days later the Loyal Edmontons and the Seaforths were fighting in the streets of Ortona which had now become a prestige battle the Germans did not intend to abandon. The 1st Parachute Division toppled houses to block passage and force the Canadians along routes lined with mortars, anti-tank guns and machine guns. They also mined buildings. Twenty-four men of the Edmontons were buried alive when the enemy blew up a building as they entered. One was recovered three days later. In response, the Edmontons later lured two dozen Germans into a block house and blew it up. Three Rivers tanks became adept at blasting paratroopers from the upper floors of buildings and the infantry developed the technique of mouse-holing. The idea was to blow a hole from the wall of one building to another, usually on an upper story, then grenades and submachine-gun fire cleared the adjacent room and house. Canadians became superior mouse-holers and could clear a block in the 10,000 population seaport without touching the ground floor.

CHRISTMAS FIGHTING

When some of the troops came to dinner on Christmas Day, the fighting was still going on. About the time of the first sitting, Major Alex Campbell of the Hastings and Prince Edwards was leading a company attack on a strong point west of the city when he was killed. He had recently written a poem evoking God's help in his command, and the last two stanzas of the poem first published in the *Maple Leaf* say it all:

Make me more willing to obey,
Help me to merit my command,
And if this be my fatal day
Reach out O God, they helping hand
And lead me down that deep dark vale.
These men of mine must never know
How much afraid I really am
Help me to lead them in the fight
So they will say - "He was a man."

REPRINTED FROM:
Esprit de Corps, *Volume 3 Issue 6*
AUTHOR:
Norman Shannon

1944 - BEGINNING OF THE END

Winter offensives by the Soviets inflict staggering losses on Germany as the Allies wrest strategic control of the Atlantic sealanes. In the Pacific, the United States navy rules the waves and one-by-one the Japanese island fortresses are being overwhelmed. In June, the long-awaited Second Front is opened in Normandy and the war's outcome is no longer in doubt. However, the Axis powers remain full of determined fight and the Allies suffer a number of unexpected reversals.

***BELOW**: A German gun crew prepares their light anti-aircraft gun for the next Allied bombing raid.*

***BOTTOM**: A squadron of Bristol Beaufighters from Coastal Command attack enemy shipping in the North Sea. Armed with rockets and possibly a torpedo, they were used with Wellingtons and Hampden bombers in anti-shipping strikes. (DND)*

22 JANUARY Allies attempt to outflank Germans in Italy with landings at Anzio.

4 FEBRUARY Japanese launch the Arakan offensive in Burma.

4 MARCH United States air force launch the first bombing attack against Berlin.

15 MARCH Battle for Monte Cassino begins.

11 MAY Germans give up Cassino and retreat to the Gustav Line in Italy.

6 JUNE D-Day landings. Over 176,000 Allied troops successfully storm four Normandy beaches.

19-21 JUNE At the Battle of the Phillipine Sea, the Japanese lose two aircraft carriers and 300 aircraft in a decisive defeat.

20 AUGUST Canadians seal off the Falaise Pocket, culminating with the Allies' successful breakout from the Normandy beachhead.

17 SEPTEMBER American and British paratroops launch ill-fated 'Market Garden' operation at Arnhem. German resistance stiffens.

26 NOVEMBER Soviet army advances into Budapest.

16 DECEMBER Germans unexpectedly counter-attack in the Ardennes, forcing Allies onto the defensive in what is known as the Battle of the Bulge.

***BELOW RIGHT**: Although the RCAF's bombing squadrons had many successes, they often came with a heavy price. With no sign of the crew bailing from the aircraft, this Halifax bomber goes down with the fuel tanks in both wings ruptured. (NAC/PL 144284)*

RIGHT:
German prisoner of war camps were designed under this typical layout, and offered a relative degree of comfort when compared to others such as those operated by the Japanese. There were some 30 prison camps in Germany, ranging from fortified medieval castles like Colditz Castle, where repeat escapees were sent, to compounds of simple, wooden huts. Officers' camps were known as Oflags while those for other ranks were Stalags, and the treatment received depended very much on rank.

BEHIND THE WIRE

The toughest part of being a POW was maintaining a sense of mission. So tunnel digging became a passion, though few Kriegies ever hit a home run.

"ABANDON AIRCRAFT! Jump! Jump!"

These were the last words some 2500 Canadian airmen heard or uttered in doomed aircraft over Hitler's Europe. Some, pilots of single engine aircraft, just jumped. The lucky ones ended up as prisoners of war or *Kriegsgefanger* or, as they defiantly and proudly called themselves, just plain Kriegies.

Tony Little heard the words from his pilot as fire ate away at the wing of his Halifax bomber one night in January 1945. He jumped, landed hard, and spent hours drifting in and out of consciousness with a concussion. He remembers a pig pen, a house and a jail with a helmeted guard 12 feet tall. The second time he saw the guard, Little had recovered somewhat and the guard had shrunk to human proportions. It was the first day of his life as a Kriegie.

Pilot Sergeant Gilles Lamontagne screamed the words the night his aircraft was attacked by a night-fighter after crossing the Dutch coast. The cockpit was burning and the third attack set the entire Halifax ablaze. He would go on to become mayor of Quebec City for 12 years, Minister of National Defence and Lieutenant Governor of Quebec.

A former minister of Veterans Affairs, Roger Telliet was also a Kriegie as was Bruce Britain, a former deputy minister. They all fell from the sky and went on to the life of a Kriegie and to be members of one of the most exclusive clubs in Canada: the RCAF POW Association.

FROM HUNTER TO HUNTED

The Kriegies still remember those incredible seconds as they passed over from the hunter to the hunted; from combat airman to Kriegie. For most bomber crewmen there was a terrible sameness about it: night; cold; cramped quarters; noise; an explosion; cordite; a leap into darkness; and the terror of being alone in a hostile country. Many are not quite sure whether they were victims of flak or night-fighters, but in a matter of seconds – minutes at most – they were transported from the familiar surroundings of their bomber to the loneliness and terror of being a hunted animal in enemy territory.

Stuart Leslie was a pilot of a Halifax that was attacked by a night-fighter while bombing a marshalling yard at St. Elaine. The bomber began to burn and the enemy was raking them on another pass from below. Leslie gave orders to abandon aircraft and had just released the hatch over his head when the Halifax exploded. He was blown clear, the only crewmember to survive.

DON'T STAND THERE LOOKING STUPID!

Ed Rae's pilot gave orders to abandon aircraft and Rae moved back from the rear turret to the escape hatch. The aircraft was filled with flame, smoke, and explosions. A burning city moved across the open escape hatch and Rae paused. He decided to wait until the bomber landed. Then he'd simply walk away. He saw his mother through the smoke who said approximately, "Eddie are you just going to stand there looking stupid?" He leaped through the hatch.

Jim Finnie moved from the rear turret of his doomed Halifax to find the mid-upper gunner struggling with a popped parachute. Finnie told him to grab silk and they went through the hatch together. Miraculously the mid-upper chute was not tangled and they floated down to captivity with a strange sense of relief. Floating down was a nice interlude, according to one Kriegie. Stuart Hunt's Halifax fell to an Me 110. Hunt jumped and, as he drifted down, clutched the parachute ring because he had heard it was worth 20 quid.

LEFT LEG LEFT

The experience of fighter pilots was slightly different. They usually went down in daylight and often from low levels. Don Morrison flew fighter cover for the American B-17s that hit the Luftwaffe airfield at Abbeville on the day of the Dieppe raid. On the way home his section of Spitfires peeled off towards Dieppe. Morrison shot down a FW 190 which exploded, its debris knocking out his Spitfire. He jumped and was rescued. The day's action brought his score to six enemy aircraft destroyed and five probables. Less than three months later he was shot down over St. Omer. With his left leg was blown off when he jumped. He was unconscious for ten days.

Ivor Harris was hit at 100 feet while on a fighter sweep. Smoke and flame filled his Spit. He pulled back on the stick, got stuck in the hatch and kicked his way clear. In less than 30 seconds he was on the ground, somewhere in a heavily fortified area of the coast. As he edged around a minefield, a small German with a large gun appeared from around a sand dune.

PHASE TWO

Phase two of the Kriegies' trauma came when they touched ground or water. Stan Croft did not get to use his parachute. When something hit the starboard engine, it flipped the bomber over on its back and plunged it into the water. Croft was knocked unconscious but came to in the water. He and his pilot were picked up by a Dutch fisherman who took them into port where Germans were waiting.

Ed Rae lay on his back for some time feeling very alone. His crew was scattered and he had no idea where he was. He spent the night in a haystack. The next day, Rae pinched a bike which he rode until he had a flat tire forcing him to abandon it in a small village. He then heard footsteps behind him and a guttural voice ordered "Come!"

LEFT:
This tunneller at Stalag VIIIB was photographed by Kenneth Hyde with his contraband camera. His photographs provided valuable documentation of life as a German prisoner of war.

ED RAE LAY ON HIS BACK FOR SOME TIME FEELING VERY ALONE. HIS CREW WAS SCATTERED AND HE HAD NO IDEA WHERE HE WAS.

Gib McElroy evaded capture for three days after jumping. At this stage of the war, just before D-Day, they had been told not to contact the underground; the underground would contact them. On the third day at dusk, lonely and a little afraid, the boy of 19 decided to try the clergy for help. As he walked towards the church, he heard someone behind him who asked "English?"

"Canadian!" McElroy replied as he turned around and faced the gun of a collaborator.

Jim Umshied was suspended 25 feet up when his chute fouled in a tree in Denmark. Come morning, he blew a whistle which attracted farmers and kids. The farmers hid him but then the police arrived and explained about having to turn him in "because who knew how kids talk? Then it would be bad for all of us." Jim shrugged. Why spoil a Quisling's day?

Stuart Leslie became an evader. The Belgian underground worked him into their system and he was moved from place to place for weeks. They provided him with civilian clothing and identification. But a mole was at work. One night, as he was sent to a safe house, the escape line was decimated. Leslie remained there unattended as that particular cell in the line collapsed, but three days later he re-established contact with the escape line and was sent to Namur in the Ardennes, hoping to join the Maquis. He was apprehended in a small village and became prisoner first of the Luftwaffe, and then the of Gestapo – the two organizations which waged war for souls, minds and bodies of Allied airmen. Leslie was taken to Gestapo headquarters at St. Giles prison in Brussels where he was grilled repeatedly for weeks. As the British closed on Brussels, the Gestapo became preoccupied with escape. Prisoners were loaded onto a train which, thanks to Belgian crews, suffered numerous delays in getting out of the station. Leslie escaped at the outskirts of Brussels and was one of the first POWs to enjoy the sight of the mighty Gestapo running for the border and their Fatherland.

CREATIVE INTERROGATION

Most Kriegies went through a sieve. They landed in a farmer's field and, if not apprehended by the military, they ended up at the local police station which turned them over to the military. A few lucky ones chanced upon the underground and their route was different, but most were pushed through the system. Sometimes Luftwaffe interrogation was a piece of cake. They were

RIGHT: *Of the men involved in The Great Escape from Stalag Luft III on 24 March 1944, 73 of the 200 prisoners made their escape – but only three men made it to safety. Some of the Canadians who worked on the 240-foot tunnel included Ted Sangster and John "Scruffy" Weir (standing), Wally "the tunnel king" Floody, and Henry Birkland. Of the 50 escapees captured and killed by the Gestapo, six were Canadian, including Birkland.*
(PAUL BRICKHILL, FABER AND FABER LIMITED)

creative and relied on the bond between airmen, so the enemy would try to engage prisoners in shop talk. One Kriegie ended his session with the information that the Germans had a flying bomb.

However, there were some notable exceptions. Geoffrey Ruff came down hard and broke his leg. He was picked up but received no medical help. He fainted when he set his own leg in his cell. Later a German officer with a riding crop came into the cell and, when Ruff refused to talk, the German tapped Ruff's broken leg several times with his riding crop. "Tell us what we want to know!" When the pain subsided, Ruff saw a man, an unhappy man, who said: "You are the dumbest officer I have ever seen. If the rest of the RCAF is like you, we will surely win the war."

Larry McCosham remembers being thrown into a small windowless cell. After each interrogation, the heat would be turned up in his cell because he had not told them what they wanted to know. According to McCosham, he passed out the night it reached 150 degrees. After interrogation the Kriegies went to a Dulag, a holding area for the Stalags to which Canadians were sent.

BY JANUARY 1945, THE RUSSIANS STARTED A DRIVE ON A HUNDRED MILE FRONT... IT BECAME A DEATH MARCH FOR CAPTIVE AND CAPTOR ALIKE

Here the struggle for survival took on a different tone.

STRUGGLE FOR SURVIVAL

Some 6500 British and Commonwealth airmen were prisoners of war, but only a few ever made it to freedom. Three of these were Canadians. While escape was the motivating force, it would be wrong to suggest that every POW was filled with an inordinate drive to escape. First, the chances diminished dramatically once a prisoner reached a Stalag. But the concept of escape became a way of twigging the Hun's nose and keeping him occupied. For instance at Barth, a camp on the Baltic, in less than two years 53 tunnels were dug; only four men escaped and only one reached England. But tunnel digging remained the Kriegies' number one sport. Each camp had an escape committee that coordinated tunnel jobs and brought the amazing resources of the POW community to bear on a project. The best known escape attempt occurred at Stalag Luft 3 at Sagan where 6090 Kriegies were gainfully employed for months.

ROLE OF SCROUNGER

At least two Canadians were key members of the well-organized committee. Although the movie *The Great Escape* was disturbingly accurate in most respects, it seemed to have an identity crisis when it portrayed the work done by Barry Davidson. He was shot down early in the war and had spent almost three years behind the wire when the Sagan escape was planned in 1943. In the film, James Garner filled the role of the Yank called Scrounger, which was Davidson's primary duty. Davidson had cultivated German ferrets and was able to have ink, maps and other items smuggled in, while Keith Ogilvy acquired a ferret's wallet giving the committee access to identity documents. Garner was obviously a composite character who just happened to be a Yank. A tailor shop was set up, false identity cards were run off and photographs taken. While these preparations were underway, Wally Floody, the tunnel king, took charge of tunnelling 240 feet to beyond the wire. Seventy-six escaped though 73 were recaptured and 50 were shot, including Canadians James Wernham, George Wiley, Patrick Langford, George McGill, Henry Birkland, and Gordon Kidder.

TOUGHEST BATTLE

The toughest battle Kriegies had to fight was with themselves and putting time to good use. Barry Davidson helped organize hockey games on rinks flooded with buckets. Then there was the theatre, and Art Crichton who fronted the sweetest band west of the Elbe. Ken Hyde embarked on a career as photographer, a strange choice considering the restriction of cameras. Yet he compiled a remarkable array of photographs and each one was a personal victory. Books took on a new meaning for active young men and Canadian Legion Educational Services sent over 60,000 textbooks and 1900 university courses through the Red Cross. One Kriegie decided on theology. When the textbook finally arrived, he leafed through it with a frown. Then he muttered, "This damn thing's nothing but religion!"

The Red Cross was a major source of support as it gave many the will to go on. In the final months of the war, with transportation disrupted and the POW population at its peak, supplies or the delivery diminished. In at least one camp, stores of Red Cross supplies fell into Russian hands as they moved closer to Berlin.

DEATH MARCH

By January 1945, the Russians had started a drive on a hundred-mile front, and 10,000 POWs and thousands of civilians began to withdraw in -20° Fahrenheit. It became a death march for captive and captor alike. Although camps like Stalag 3 had a store of Red Cross parcels, the men were forced to leave with what they could carry on their backs or homemade sleds. Soon exposure took its toll and the rigours of the march hit the guards hardest because they were older. The weakest rode in Kriegie sleds. Some even gave their weapons to Kriegies to carry in a strange juxtaposition of roles.

Several camps were involved and the grim episode has never been adequately documented because of the confusion. Some Kriegies were loaded onto boxcars and, at 65 to a car, it became a tangle of arms and legs. There was no food or sanitation; dysentry was common. On at least one occasion the doors remained locked for three days. This was the point when the last reserves of courage began to slip away. One man remembered eating a handful of oats like a horse and then sobbing on a comrade's shoulder. Some fell into Russian hands and were not released until three months after VE-Day, but there is evidence that some were never released.

REPRINTED FROM:
Esprit de Corps, *Volume 2 Issue 5*
AUTHOR:
Norman Shannon

LEFT:
When Germany learned that their soldiers who were captured at Dieppe were handcuffed, they retaliated by doing the same to some Canadians.
(PHOTO BY POW KENNETH HYDE)

STALAG BOWMANVILLE'S GREAT ESCAPE

German prisoners in Canada were also dedicated to digging tunnels and on one occasion it worked... sort of.

OF THE THOUSANDS OF GERMANS IMPRISONED IN CANADA, ONLY ONE MADE IT BACK TO GERMANY.

THE ROLE OF THE POW in WWII transcended nationalism and, while theorists in London and Berlin insisted it was the duty of prisoners to escape, it was a theory much in need of a reality check. Chances of a successful escape were exceedingly low. Of the 6500 RAF POWs in German hands and the hundreds of tunnels dug, less than three dozen men actually hit a home run. Of the thousands of Germans imprisoned in Canada, only one made it back to Germany. However, there was a remarkable similarity in how prisoners on both sides played the escape game even though escape itself was not a probability.

When some 640 Luftwaffe officers and submariners checked into Bowmanville, Québec, they were stunned at the lavish surroundings. It had been a posh correction facility for wayward boys, sporting a theatre, indoor swimming pool, gymnasium and later, tennis courts. Both groups luxuriated in their version of a Club Med on the St. Lawrence, but the first trace of conflict came as a result of something which was happening in Europe.

In 1942, the British clumsily committed to paper an order that prisoners would be bound so that they could not destroy documents. Unfortunately, someone took the order in a briefcase to Dieppe where it was recovered by the enemy. Two months after the Dieppe raid, four German prisoners were found shot with hands tied behind their back following a commando raid on the Isle of Sark. In response, the Germans shackled 1376 Dieppe prisoners and the issue escalated.

WAR IN PRISON

The British War Office then decreed that German prisoners be shackled. Although a growing number of prisoners were now being kept in this country, Canada was not

RIGHT: *German POWs enjoy their stay at Stalag Bowmanville by playing a game of pick-up hockey. Some 30,000 German and Italian prisoners of war were held captive on Canadian soil.* (NATIONAL ARCHIVES OF CANADA)

consulted on what were technically British prisoners. Eventually, 30 prisoners were to be symbolically handcuffed. When the Germans were asked to provide volunteers, they refused and armed themselves with baseball bats and hockey sticks.

In October 1942, the clash of wills led to a clash of forces as troops tried to isolate prisoners. A security guard was held hostage but escaped under friendly fire in which one prisoner was slightly wounded and two suffered bayonet wounds.

Although *Time* magazine distorted the events, the adversaries knew the facts. The POWs had resisted a legal but ill-advised order. After the original conflict, they conceded game, set but not match to their captors. The escape game then went into high gear.

POW INGENUITY

The ingenuity of POWs at plotting escapes is legendary. One of the briefest on record was at Stalag Luft 3 when an RAF prisoner walked through the gate disguised as a nurse. He was through the gate when the guards noticed he still wore a handlebar moustache.

At Bowmanville, two prisoners painted their way out. Dressed in coveralls and carrying two ladders, they approached a post which they painted bright yellow. Then they mounted the first ladder and slung the second over the fence. They dismounted on the far side and finished the paint job. Then they went on to the second fence and repeated the process. At this point they paused for a fag and then sauntered into the woods.

A second team appeared with a variation of the same routine, but instead of painting they pounded nails into the posts. Both groups gained the outer fence but were later recaptured. Their performance echoed the performance of two American airmen at Stalag Luft 3. They decided that a number of fence posts in the curved wire enclosure blocked the view of guards at either end. As other inmates played baseball, staged fights and otherwise kept the inner compound alive, the two airmen went out and cut the first wire. In broad daylight they casually walked to the second wire and did the same thing. They walked and ran towards the woods where they enjoyed a five-day cruise before being recaptured.

COMPETITION

A competition developed between German airmen and submariners at Bowmanville, as both groups were each now working on escape tunnels. The plan brought out artists with an uncanny knack for forgery and word of the intent reached Germany through a personal letter and a code known as Ireland. The German navy supplied money, maps and other documents all incorporated into the covers of Red Cross books.

Prisoners would be picked up by submarine near Caraquet, New Brunswick, as this was the summer and the subs owned the St. Lawrence. Work on the tunnels went ahead rapidly until inmates miscalculated how much sand a ceiling would hold. The ceiling in one room collapsed and somehow the prisoners were able to keep the evidence from the guards. The tunnel was later abandoned because of water.

The airmen's tunnel in the next building was later discovered and the great escape was over. But not quite. Lieutenant Commander Heyda reasoned that if a submarine would be waiting at Caraquet someone should meet it. He rigged a bosun's chair on a pulley which he slung over a wire which ran over hydro lines and flew off into the night like Peter Pan. With forged documents and a Canadian army uniform, he made his way to Bathurst and then east to Caraquet. Posing as a discharged soldier, he

RIGHT:
Some 30,000 German and Italian prisoners of war were held captive on Canadian soil. Of these, only one POW held captive in Canada successffully made his escape to the Fatherland. Luftwaffe Oberleutnant Franz von Werra escaped from a train near Prescott, Ontario on the night of 23 January 1941, crossing into the United States before returning to Germany.

PRISONERS, IN COVERALLS AND CARRYING LADDERS, APPROACHED A POST WHICH THEY PAINTED BRIGHT YELLOW. THEN THEY SLUNG ONE LADDER OVER THE FENCE, DISMOUNTING ON THE FAR SIDE AND FINISHING THE PAINT JOB.

walked through an army picket with a cover story of doing a geological survey on Maisonette Point.

AMBUSH

Rolf Schauenburg had been waiting in U-536 for two days and, at the appointed hour, he nosed the submarine within 600 yards of the New Brunswick shore and waited for a Morse signal while two men stood by with a dinghy to pick up escapees. The first hint of trouble came when he got a signal on an unassigned frequency which had nothing to do with the predetermined code. A light blinked an even stranger signal on shore: "Komme! Komme!"

Heyda moved out onto the curving beach and, just as he was to signal the dinghy, he was nudged by rifles of Canadian soldiers who took him to the nearby lighthouse.

Schauenburg heard the sound of ships as a destroyer, three corvettes and five minesweepers swept into the bay and blocked its entrance. Then the depth charges drove U-536 to the muddy bottom of Miscou Flats.

SUB STALKING

When Heyda was taken to Lieutenant Commander Desmond Piers in the lighthouse, it concluded a game which had been going on for weeks. The Royal Canadian Mounted Police had spotted the tunnels during the digging and the games began. Naval Intelligence had cracked the Ireland code so the Canadian captors had been playing cat-and-mouse with the prisoners for months. Several scenarios were developed. One consisted of picking up the escapees once out of the tunnel but simply reporting a mass escape. Subsequent news releases would account for all but seven of the escapees, who would be used as bait for the submarine.

The Canadian ships stalked the submarine for two days, dropping depth charges. Schauenburg virtually bumped bottom as he hugged shore and worked towards the entrance of the bay. The sub fouled the nets of a fishing trawler which threatened to hold it captive. The crew could hear the scream of the trawler's winch as the submarine eventually broke free, its rails festooned with fish netting. Schauenburg eluded the flotilla and about a week later, some 180 miles south of Newfoundland, he sent a radio message: "Operation MAGPIE blown."

REPRINTED FROM:
Esprit de Corps, *Volume 5 Issue 10*
AUTHOR: *Norman Shannon*

WHEN FEW ROADS LED TO ROME

As German resistance stiffened, the Allied advance up the boot of Italy slowed to a crawl.

WHAT STARTED AS mutual disharmony between the Yanks and the British in Italy might have ended in bloodshed as American General Mark Clark threatened to turn his guns on the Brits if they moved towards Rome to spoil his parade.

The earlier invasion of Sicily had come almost as an afterthought to the victory in North Africa. Churchill was obsessed with the idea of "invading the soft underbelly" of Europe, but the Yanks later cynically observed that the soft underbelly had become a tough old gut.

Both forces went their different ways in Sicily and had been there six days before the Combined Chiefs of Staff decided that Italy should be invaded next. While the Allies debated where to invade, Mussolini was dismissed in favour of General Pietro Badoglio. Hitler threatened to seize Rome and take King Victor Emmanuel III prisoner while moving strong forces into northern Italy.

As the Canadian 1st Division fought its way up through the mountains of Sicily, General Andrew McNaughton was forbidden to visit his troops. According to General Bernard Montgomery, if McNaughton showed up without per-mission, he would be arrested.

REARGUARD ACTION

The Axis fought a rearguard action for 39 days and, when they withdrew to Italy, took 125,000 men and 10,000 vehicles. The withdrawal of German Commander Albert Kesselring's troops set the pattern for what was to follow in the long fight for Rome.

The British and Canadians crossed the Messina Straits on 3 September. On one

RIGHT:
The terrain in Italy lent itself to fighting a defensive position. Here, men of the 48th Highlanders keep a close eye on the rubble-filled streets in the Ortona sector. By the time the Gustav and Hitler Lines were breached, and Rome attained, the Allied soldiers were exhausted. (NAC/PA 163411)

OPPOSITE PAGE:
As they made their way toward Rome, resistance was met every step of the way. In the mountain village of Campochiars, men of the Carleton and York Regiment carefully make their way through deserted streets, while keeping a watchful eye for the sniper who killed the villager (photo centre). (NAC/PA 114482)

landing craft, the captain fed his monkey lemonade and added gin for his officer guests. Five days after the landing, Italy surrendered and Hitler seized Rome and quickly reinforced positions in southern Italy.

The Americans landed up the west coast near Naples, while Field Marshal Kesselring rushed a division to Salerno in anticipation of the action. His strong counterattacks almost drove the Americans back into the sea, but they managed to retain the beachhead about 30 miles south of Naples. Field Marshal Montgomery's forces covered 200 miles to briefly link up with the Americans, but then both armies again went their separate ways: the Americans covered the west coast while the British and Canadians fought their way up the spine of the Apennines to the Adriatic Sea.

BARRICADES

Kesselring established a series of strongpoints in the mountains and the Canadians worked their way up the Apennines Mountains, seizing roads at Campobasso and Vinchiaturo. In addition to natural barriers, they faced barricades of wire, concrete, log breastworks, caves, dugouts and gun emplacements.

In one relatively small area, Kesselring's engineers had set 75,000 mines, and blown up seven miles of bridges and 400 miles of railway track. As the Canadians fought their way towards the Sangro River, donkeys became their staunchest if stinkiest ally.

By early December, they fought their way across the Moro River and engaged a heavily defended cliff known as The Gully.

SPECTACULAR ASSAULT

On the approach to Ortona, Captain Paul Triquet won the Victoria Cross for a spectacular assault on a strongpoint at Casa Berardi.

The Canadian Corps was part of an Eighth Army thrust to Pescara, which lay 25 miles north of Ortona and had a road link with Rome.

They fought their way into Ortona where almost every house bristled with machine guns and mortars while tanks lurked in every pile of debris. The Canadians developed a technique of "mouseholing" where the only way to get down a street was to blow a hole from one building to the next and then rush through with grenades or sub-machine guns.

VAMPIRES

Three days after Christmas, forward parties of Canadians suddenly failed to find any Germans. The enemy had withdrawn like vampires at the approach of dawn, but the Eighth Army was too exhausted to pursue.

The Ortona sector, which anchored the Gustav Line in the east, became somewhat stagnant. Kesselring now had four divisions defending the Adriatic sector and two against the Yanks who had entered Naples in late October and had moved up to a position south of Gaeta.

On 22 January, the United States 6th Corps—plus British troops—landed at Anzio some 50 miles behind the lines and caught Kesselring completely off guard. By the end of the day, 36,000 men were ashore, but Major General John Lucas failed to exploit the element of surprise. His long delay enabled Kesselring to rush in reinforcements and surround the beachhead, a situation which led Churchill to lament that "instead of hurling a wildcat ashore, all we got

was a stranded whale."

After eight days, Lucas sent two battalions of Rangers out on reconnaissance: one was completely wiped out and the other had six survivors. The plan to reach Rome through Anzio not only failed but threatened to become another Dunkirk. General Mark Clark now turned to a third road to Rome. It was Highway No. 6 which was dominated by the heavily defended Monte Cassino. The mountain also dominated the Liri and Rapido valleys and was topped by an ancient monastery.

The Germans had some 100,000 men in the area and had been preparing defences for three months. Clark had troops from some 25 nations under his command at different times. He would later complain of the diversity in equipment, food, communications and cultural differences. As some refused to kill on certain days, it was difficult to organize assaults on enemy positions.

BREAKTHROUGH

For four months, several major assaults failed to take Monte Cassino. By 12 May the British 13th Corps reached route No. 6 and the Canadians broke through the Hitler Line. After being repulsed in one assault on Monastery Hill, the Poles tried again the next day and found it deserted. Once again the enemy had withdrawn like ghosts in the night. In four intense battles, Monte Cassino cost the allies 115,000 casualties.

On 23 May, the Americans launched a drive from Anzio where the Allies had lost an additional 40,000 men. Soon Kesselring's forces were in full retreat. But instead of vigorously pursuing, Clark spent a few days on photo ops in front of roadsigns that led to the open city of Rome. It was at this point that Clark was reported to have said that, if the British turned in their pursuit of Kesselring, he would have his troops fire on the Eighth Army.

Three days before D-Day, Clark had his parade into Rome, but Italy soon became the forgotten war. Meanwhile, Kesselring had moved his strong forces northward and the bitter war which followed gobbled resources and drove up casualties for almost another year.

REPRINTED FROM:
Esprit de Corps, *Volume 6 Issue 2*
AUTHOR: Norman Shannon

TARGET FOR TONIGHT

Considering the weather and the route through concentrations of enemy night-fighters, RAF senior officers could not believe it when Nuremburg remained a target.

THE TELETYPES AT HIGH Wycombe started rattling out the news about 10:00 hours on the morning of 30 March 1944: Ops were on but the target was not given. News filtered down to eight bomber groups and 77 squadrons at 54 operational stations. Although target details were not given, experienced hands read bad news when groundcrews began topping up gasoline while cutting back the bomb load on machines readied for an operation that had been scrubbed the previous night.

At Bomber Command Headquarters at High Wycombe, there was silence as Air Marshal Sir Arthur Harris pondered the target. Three months earlier when he sought more Lancasters, he had promised the Air Ministry that by 1 April his campaign of area bombing would produce "a state of devastation in which surrender is inevitable." He had two days left and there was no sign of a break in German morale or substantial loss of war production.

POOR BOMBING RESULTS

During the past month, there had been poor bombing results in strikes on Stuttgart, Berlin and Frankfurt. Eleven nights ago he lost 78 bombers and 546 men over Liepzig. This was followed by a raid on Berlin where unpredicted winds scattered the bomber stream and bombs fell on 126 centres other than Berlin. Losses that night were 511 aircrew, and, although it occurred less than a week earlier, Harris shoved the figures to the back of his mind and selected Nuremburg, meaning his bombers would be flying some 900 miles through enemy sky in moonlight, possibly without cloud cover.

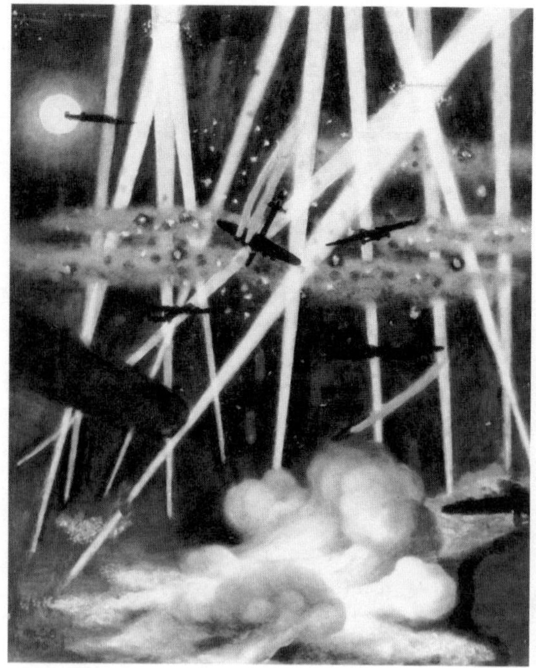

There was a murmur of disbelief as Harris selected the target and left the operations room for the planners to work out the details of the route.

During that afternoon, weather flights by Mosquitos brought bad news. The planners had come up with a route which consisted of a 265-mile leg which led arrow-straight from Aachen at the German border, to south of Bonn and deep into Germany. Then it turned south for some 80 miles to Nuremburg. Mosquito reports disabused the planners of the hope that cloud would cover the route. The bombers would be flying in moonlight so bright crews could read lettering on adjacent aircraft.

In addition the 68-mile bomber stream had been routed close to two beacons which were used to assemble German night-fighters. Mosquito pilots, who knew the area, protested that the bombers would be running into a nest of night-fighters, but when Harris returned to the Ops room that afternoon, to the surprise of most present, he refused to cancel the operation or change the route.

FIRST LEG

The first leg of the route took the bombers from their bases to a point southwest of Liege. Of the 77 bomber squadrons, the 13 from No. 6 (RCAF) Group, located to the north of England, faced an eight-hour trip of some 1600 miles.

CREWS ON THE BATTLE ORDER FADED INTO A TWILIGHT ZONE WHERE THEY LITERALLY COUNTED OFF THE HOURS OF THEIR LIFE.

Lord Hugh "Boom" Trenchard, who had commanded the Royal Flying Corps in France during WWI, habitually visited squadrons before a major battle to jolly up the airmen. A typical comment in 1917 was that it was more important for pilots to shoot down a given balloon than to come back.

On the afternoon of 30 March 1944, Trenchard was up to his old tricks. He visited No. 103 Squadron at Elsham Wolds and stunned crews when he told them their life expectancy was to be greatly reduced because of the maximum effort.

COUNTING OFF THE HOURS

Throughout all eight bomber groups, pilots, navigators, and bomb-aimers met in the afternoon chill to work out primary details of the flight plan. Then, as they waited, crews on the battle order faded into a twilight zone where they literally counted off the hours of their life. Bets at poker and Seven-toed Pete became extravagantly reckless. A week ago over 500 men went for the chop over Berlin, and Nuremburg promised to be worse. One pilot asked a WAAF friend to think of him at one o'clock the next morning. She did, but at 01:38 hrs he was blown out of the sky.

Finally, the briefing officer formally announced what everybody on 77 squadrons probably had known for hours: "The target for tonight is Nuremburg." By midnight most of No. 6 Group's machines were airborne, part of the 782 aircraft that were making their way to their rendezvous.

While the bombers flew towards a rendezvous point in the North Sea, two other operations by Mosquitos were timed to draw enemy fighters northward, but enemy night-fighters refused to be deked. A mine-dropping operation near Heligoland by the Moose Squadron sowed 112 mines but did not divert the main fighter force.

COLD CONTRAILS

So when the Nuremburg force crossed the Belgian coast it did so in moonlight, and the cold air at 20,000 feet left behind clouds of contrails which marked the path of the bombers for 420 miles.

By 1944, the air war was well into the realm of electronics and, for the Germans, it had come full circle. The British had first

LEFT:
The Avro Lancaster, introduced in 1941, proved an excellent and easy-to-fly aircraft, capable of carrying large loads of conventional bombs and, with some adjustment, could carry special stores as the -16 Dambuster bombs, 12,000 lb 'Tallboys' and 22,000 lb 'Grand Slams.'
(IMPERIAL WAR MUSEUM)

OPPOSITE PAGE, LEFT:
The heavy concentration of German searchlights and flak made Allied target runs a horrifying experience.
(NIGHT TARGET, GERMANY, *BY MILLER BRITTAIN, CWM 10889*)

OPPOSITE PAGE, RIGHT:
Air Marshal Sir Arthur Harris inspects reconnaissance photos as he plans for the next raid by Bomber Command.
(IMPERIAL WAR MUSEUM)

successfully dropped *window* or tinfoil in the raid on Hamburg in July 1943. The impulses, picked up by radar, befuddled the enemy for some time until Major Hajo Herrmann convinced his superiors that part of the answer was to forget electronics and use eyesight and height to spot the bomber stream. A system was developed whereby FW 190s and Me 109s would fly above the bomber stream and above anti-aircraft fire. These Wild Boar pilots were effectively able to pick up RAF bombers against the glare of searchlights and flares.

TAME BOARS

A second system, known as Tame Boars, depended on electronics. Me 110s were directed in the vicinity of the bomber stream by ground control, then pilots took over by airborne radar and infiltrated the bomber stream.

On the night of the Nuremburg raid, the first German move was to launch 246 night-fighters. Tame Boars from the 3rd Fighter Division were directed to beacon Ida which lay directly in the path of oncoming bombers. Most of the Me 110s were equipped with twin cannons mounted to fire upwards. Contrails chalked the course of each bomber as it rode a tail wind of up to 80 mph and the *Luftwaffe* fighters closed in for their greatest air battle of the war.

FLIGHT OFFICER J.D. LAIDLAW'S HALIFAX TOOK A MORTAL BURST FROM A NIGHT FIGHTER

Helmut Schulte crept under four bombers and destroyed all with only 56 rounds. Martin Becker did not have the upward mounted cannon or *Schrage Musik* and had to manoeuvre in the usual manner. He destroyed six bombers in 30 minutes. Then, after landing and refuelling, he shot down a seventh which was on its return flight. Soon after the engagement, bombers were falling from the sky at the rate of one a minute. One pilot counted 40 burning aircraft and several aircrew stopped counting.

FLAK COMING...AND GOING

Flight Sergeant Tom Hall's crew was on its second operation, the first having been a shaky-do to Berlin a week earlier when strong tail winds had pushed them over the target early. Hall orbited through flak and fighters in order to bomb on time, but winds pushed them over the Ruhr where they were hit by flak on the return flight. Hall nursed the Lancaster with two burning engines back to England where it was written off.

On the second deadly leg to Nuremburg they were hit again. Hall gave orders to bail out but the machine was soon diving into a spin. It blew up and only two members of the crew survived, their operational career having lasted five days. Flight Officer J.D. Laidlaw's Halifax took a mortal burst from a night-fighter and, before he died, Laidlaw ordered his crew to jump. The flight engineer was dead and a seriously wounded navigator blocked the front exit. Three men escaped through the rear hatch, but Flight Officer Martin Corcoran refused to leave his navigator.

HEROISM OF HUNDREDS

The heroism of hundreds like Corcoran was only surpassed by the cynicism of the man who refused to cancel the operation.

At the second turning point, fighter activity slackened as the enemy seemed to suspect the target was further east. But the short leg to Nuremburg soon became cluttered with confusion, drift, poor navigation and poor bombing. One group of aircraft, fed wrong winds by wind-seeking broadcasts, turned early and bombed Schweinfurt instead of Nuremburg while others bombed adjacent centres. Consequently, the concentration of bombs on Nuremburg half destroyed one factory and did minor damage to a second.

ALMOST HOME FREE

On the homeward leg, Flight Officer Jim Moffat heard his pilot, Squadron Leader Turkey Laird, yell, "What in hell was that!?" As he spoke, a Lancaster ripped off the top turret of their Halifax and sliced through the fuselage and port rudder a few feet from Moffat's rear turret. Moffat left the turret but the rear hatch was jammed and he was literally sucked through a gash in the fuselage of the doomed bomber. Moffat fell clear, but 13 men in the two crews perished as the two bombers fell into Belgium. Moffat became one of 15 veterans of the Nuremburg raid who lived out the war as an evader, while 152 became prisoners of war and 545 were killed. Of these, 109 were Canadians. The RAF was fond of counting aircraft instead of men and put the loss at 108 aircraft.

LAST TARGET

Nuremburg was the last target in the four-month battle of Berlin during which Harris lost 3750 aircrew, 1300 from No. 6 Group, but failed to do anything but stiffen German morale and create rubble. Defiant, petulant and stubborn, Harris had defied his chief Air Marshal Portal in selection of targets, but firmer hands at Supreme Headquarters of the Allied Expeditionary Force were about to take over and divert Harris from his private war. It had to do with something called D-Day.

REPRINTED FROM:

Esprit de Corps, *Volume 5 Issue 7*

AUTHOR: *Norman Shannon*

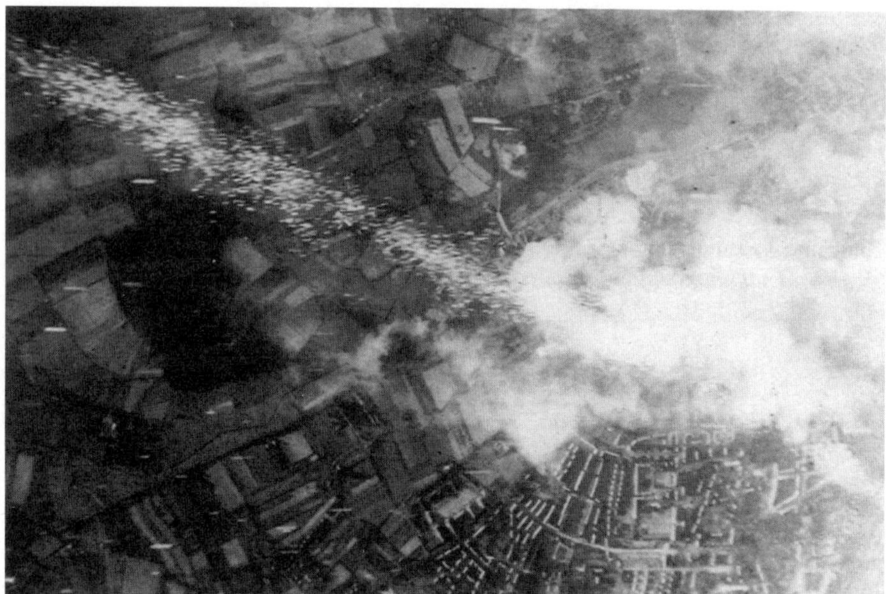

ABOVE LEFT:
Commander of No. 6 Group, Air Vice Marshal "Black Mike" McEwen, inspects the bomb load of a Lancaster that includes a 4000 lb Cooke and 1000 lb bombs.
(DND/PL 43699)

ABOVE RIGHT:
With Germany's development of radar, British scientists were forced to develop counter-measures to protect their aircraft, including the use of "window" or "chaff" – strips of aluminum foil dropped by aircraft to reflect radar signals back as false blips on radar screens by altering transmission frequencies.

LEFT:
A window of aluminum foil falls like a shower over Munster, Germany, in September 1944 in an attempt to confuse flak-control radar.
(NAC/PL 144263)

RIGHT: The French Renault light tank, called the Mosquito, was used during the First World War. But, in the fall of 1940, General Frank Worthington bought 265 of those kept in American storage and used them as training vehicles for the newly-created Armoured Corps. (U.S. SIGNAL CORPS)

To the press, he was 'Fighting Frank.' To everyone else, the father of the Canadian Armoured Corps was simply 'Worthy.'

MAJOR GENERAL FREDERICK FRANKLIN WORTHINGTON

AS THE GENERAL LAY dying in an Ottawa hospital in the final days of 1967, his family insisted that horses not be present at his funeral. "Hell," his son said, "if he felt a horse would have the last laugh, he wouldn't go." They had been the bane of the old soldier's life as he fought to introduce tanks into the Army and accordingly, when he died, he was carried to Christ Church cathedral aboard an armoured scout car. A few days later, his body was flown to Camp Borden and buried on a hill in a park across from the base museum surrounded by vintage tanks. It is a fitting resting place for Major General Frederick Franklin Worthington, the father of the Canadian Armoured Corps.

Rest had played little part in his life. He was a fiery bantam of a man, 5'7" in maturity, with a quick temper and a quicker sense of humour. Above all, he was a driven man and a visionary in his views on the use of tanks and armour in modern warfare. To the Press, he was "Fighting Frank;" to everyone else, simply "Worthy."

He was born in Los Angeles in 1890, the son of a successful surgeon of Scottish descent originally from Cooperstown, New York. Among his ancestors he counted James Fenimore Cooper, author of *The Deerslayer* and *The Last of the Mohicans*. His life would be an adventure far beyond those literary efforts.

BACKGROUND

Orphaned at 11, Frederick made his way to Nacozaro, Mexico with an older half-brother who was employed as an engineer at a gold mine. Soon known to the Mexican miners as "Frederico," he became a water-boy working 12 hour days, seven days a week, for 25 cents a day. He later worked as a skip-boy in the smelter and as a swamper, dumping 300 gallon tubs of slag.

In 1902, little more than a year after his arrival, the mine was raided by Pancho Villa whose men shot and killed the entire office staff including his engineer brother. He was taken in by an alcoholic English remittance man named Grindell. Grindell, often called "The Schoolmaster" because he had been to Oxford, shared an adobe hut with the boy on the edge of town. In his sober moments he tutored him and gave him the run of his bookshelves stimulating a lifelong passion for reading. He also taught the boy how to handle a gun and they spent much time together hunting. Two years later, Grindell disappeared while on a prospecting expedition. The 14-year old Frederico stayed on at the mine for a time, but was forced to flee when he accidentally killed a man while driving an ore train down a steep slope. He made his way to the coast at Guaymas where he signed on as a cabinboy aboard a barquentine headed for the South Pacific. Frederico was renamed "Worthy" by his shipmates.

A LIFE AT SEA

For the next several years he sailed aboard a number of ships, making port at Hawaii, Samoa, Kobi, Vladivostok, and Hong Kong. In the spring of 1906, he briefly set foot in Canada for the first time at Vancouver before moving on to San Francisco. Shore leave in that port unfortunately coincided with the Great San Francisco Earthquake. Unhurt, he helped with rescue efforts in the burning city before shipping out again on a tramp steamer bound for Guatemala. Disgusted with conditions on board, he jumped ship at Corinto, Nicaragua, and soon had his first taste of war.

One morning while walking along the harbour, he spotted a gunboat crew trying to fix a Gatling gun. Endowed with an intuitive understanding of weapons and an ability to repair them, he quickly had it working. The startled captain immediately

***RIGHT:** A Canadian-built Ram tank is unloaded from a freighter in England in March 1942. Combining the best features of U.S. and British tank design in 1940, it would be superceded by the Sherman tank as the most successful Allied tank of the war.*

recruited him and placed him in charge of a gun crew of 15 Nicaraguans. He was involved in a war between Honduras, El Salvador, and Nicaragua and saw fierce fighting in the Gulf of Honduras. He was caught up on the losing side in a subsequent civil war and was forced to seek sanctuary aboard a British ship whose skipper unceremoniously dumped him in Panama.

Unperturbed, he took up prospecting in Mexico where he was captured and held for ransom by Yaqui Indians. He bought his freedom by showing them how to use an automatic rifle. He then took up gunrunning in Cuba with a view to financing a trip to this ancestral home in Scotland, but the trip had to be postponed when he landed in a Cuban jail. Upon his release he went to sea again as a junior engineering officer aboard the *Ponce de Leon.* He had to quit in Puerto Rico after using a wrench to crush the skull of a man who attacked him with a knife. He made his way around Cape Horn to San Francisco, and celebrated his 21st birthday in 1911 by riding off to join Madero's forces in the Mexican Civil War. Ironically, he fought alongside Pancho Villa who had killed his half-brother.

The outbreak of World War I found him alone and broke in New Orleans hoping to make his way to Scotland to join a Highland Regiment. He got as far as Montreal. He was in the city for less than an hour when he spotted a soldier on Peel Street in a Black Watch kilt who directed him to a recruiting station. To his dismay, he found that he was in the Canadian, not the British Army. At the end of March 1915, he was off to Europe to fight for his adopted country.

BATTLEFIELD EXPERIENCE

After training in England, the Black Watch moved on to France in February 1916, to be introduced to the miseries of trench warfare. Worthy adapted better than most, having known few of the comforts of life his comrades missed. He was promoted to corporal and twice awarded the Military Medal before receiving a battlefield commission. At the Somme in July 1916, and later at Cambrai, he saw tanks in action for the first time and his imagination was fired by their potential. In March 1918, he joined the 18th Machine Gun Company which was later absorbed into the 1st Canadian Motor Machine Gun Brigade.

The Brigade was the brainchild of Major General Raymond Brutinel, a former French Army officer. An engineer living in Canada at the outbreak of war, he conceived the idea of creating a mobile armoured force. His Brigade was to be the first mechanized formation in the Allied armies, and a forerunner of the armoured division. Worthy, by now an ardent champion of mobility and mechanization, served as a captain in the brigade until the end of the war, earning two Military Crosses.

The Brigade returned to Canada in the late spring of 1919 and was forced to dispose of its vehicles and revert to horses to the dismay and disgust of the men. Nonetheless, Worthy decided to remain with the forces and, on 1 January 1920, became a member of Canada's regular army with the rank of Captain in the Machine Gun Corps. A number of brief assignments followed until he was posted to the Princess Patricia's Canadian Light Infantry in Winnipeg.

FAMILY MAN

In 1924, he married Clara Ellen Dignum of Toronto. The youngest of six girls, she was the tomboy of the family and nicknamed "Larry" by her father who described her as "my only son." It was to be a happy and enduring marriage despite an inauspicious beginning; the couple was forced to spend their honeymoon on a training course at the Machine Gun School on the Salisbury Plain. A son, Peter, later a distinguished journalist and publisher who would serve in his father's old regiment in Korea, was born in 1927. Robin, a daughter, was born two years later.

The peacetime Permanent Force was a pale reflection of the Canadian Corps that had fought in the Great War. Fewer than 5000 served in its ranks and every unit was under strength. Pay was poor, promotion slow, and modern equipment woefully lacking. Moreover, a hidebound cavalry mentality prevailed and there was widespread prejudice against mechanization and attitudes did not change with the outbreak of war. In the winter of 1940, for example, the

Director of Engineering Services told the Military Institute in Toronto:

"The ultimate weapon which wins wars is a bayonet on a rifle carried by an infantryman through the mud. No one knows how useful tanks will be. The Polish campaign was no true indication of the power of mechanized armies. The usefulness of the aeroplane, though considerably improved since 1918, also remains to be seen."

Worthy, the tank enthusiast, was a voice crying in the wilderness and considered something of a crackpot for his views. His favourite epithet throughout these lean years was, appropriately, "The man is so stupid he's often mistaken for a cavalry officer." On the eve of war, he was roundly criticized by those same cavalry officers for a speech he gave in which he predicted that the Germans would use armour to go around the Maginot Line. He had kept abreast of developments in armour during the Thirties and, while on course at the Royal Tank School in Dorset, had come under the influence of Major General J.F.C. Fuller and a group of his disciples known as "The Dangerous Young Men." Fuller had written brilliantly on the use of tanks, but was prematurely retired, and his books suppressed when he became overly critical of the War Office. The Germans, however, read and used his works and those of his friend Basil Liddell-Hart as textbooks on which to model their Panzer divisions.

Back home, and against the odds, *Colonel* Worthington was able to form a fledgling armoured school at Camp Borden using Carden Lloyd machine gun carriers. These were the only tracked vehicles in service until 1938. With another war appearing inevitable, the Department of National Defence grudgingly allocated sufficient funds for the expansion of the school which duly became "The Canadian Armoured Fighting Vehicles Training Centre." This lofty sounding organization was equipped with two obsolete Vickers light tanks obtained from Britain, and numbered fewer than 100 personnel.

Six battalions of the Non-Permanent Active Militia, which had been designated as armoured units, began training in the summer of 1938. Despite a lack of equipment, including wireless sets, the school did its best to teach them the basics of gunnery, driving, and maintenance. Model "T" Fords were converted into "tanks," simulators improvised, and "anti-tank guns" built out of sewer pipe mounted on car axles. Training accelerated with the outbreak of war and Borden was transformed into a vast construction site teeming with troops. In August 1940, the Canadian Armoured Corps was formed, its motto, "Through mud and blood to the green fields beyond." The first units were the Ontario and Three Rivers Regiments, the First Hussars, and the Fort Garry Horse. The First Canadian Tank Brigade proceeded overseas in June 1941, where it was issued with British Matilda and Churchill tanks. Canada would eventually field an additional two armoured divisions.

LEFT:
His years as a youth more akin to those of a character in a novel than of a military commander, Frank Worthington had many life adventures before retiring from the Canadian Army as a major general in 1948. Unconventional and plain spoken, Worthy was also the father of the Canadian Armoured Corps, helping it to develop since its inception during the First World War. (DND)

$32,000 WORTH OF "SCRAP IRON"

In the fall of 1940, Worthy got word that there was a number of 1917 Renault tanks in storage at the Rock Island Arsenal in Illinois that were about to be sold for scrap. He hurried south, and, after a hard day's bargaining with an American officer named George S. Patton, bought 265 of them for $120 each along with 45 tons of spare parts included in the deal. The U.S. neutrality laws were circumvented by a manifest listing two train loads as "scrap iron" destined for the "Camp Borden Foundry." They crossed the border without incident and were put to use as training vehicles for the new Armoured Corps.

Tanks were in short supply in 1940, and Britain, bombed and under threat of invasion, was no longer able to supply Canadian needs. Instead, orders were placed in Canada. In early 1940, despite Worthy's objections that they were obsolete, Valentine Light Infantry Support Tanks began to be produced at the Canadian Pacific Angus Shops in Montreal. By 1943, 1420 were built, incorporating Canadian design improvements. Most were shipped to the Soviet Union where they were highly praised. Few entered Canadian service.

As early as 1937, Worthy, with a group of friends at the Royal Canadian Military Institute, had been working on a Canadian tank design. Their concept of a medium, low-silhouette tank, built with American components, was accepted by the Department of National Defence, and production began at the Montreal Locomotive Works in 1941. The tank, the only tank ever completely designed and built in Canada, became known as the "Ram," after an animal honoured on the Worthington family crest. Unfortunately, Worthy could not convince the Department with regard to its armament. The six-pounder, a pea-shooter, had been declared the standard for British medium tanks in 1940. Worthy demanded a heavy weapon and wanted to mount a 3.7 inch anti-aircraft gun. The undergunned Ram, as a result, was rendered obsolete even before it began to roll off the production lines. Nearly 2000 were built by 1943. They never saw battle but were used for training in Canada and Britain. Some had their turrets removed and became the Kangaroo, an armoured personnel carrier. The Ram chassis became the basis for the Sexton, an excellent 25-pound self-propelled gun. The design also influenced that of the American M4 Sherman, which became the mainstay of the Canadian and Allied armoured forces.

On 2 February 1942, following a brief visit to General Andy McNaughton, the Canadian Army Commander in Britain, Worthy was promoted to major general and given the task of converting the 4th Infantry Division to armour. He joined the Division at Debert, Nova Scotia in March. At the end of the month, 165 new Ram tanks arrived by train from Halifax without drivers or instructors. As Worthy and his aide Lieutenant Colonel George Gaisford were the only two with experience in armour, they personally drove them off the flatcars. Training began at 04:00 hours each morning with Worthy and Gaisford giving tank driving lessons to designated instructors. They would practice with them until 08:00 hours, have breakfast, then get down to the business of running a division. Training continued in shifts until midnight. Worthy's drive, efficiency, and humour soon earned him the respect and affection of the officers and men.

After safely crossing the Atlantic, the 4th Division resumed training in England in preparation for the invasion of France. Worthy, however, would never command it in battle. In February 1944, at the age of 54, he was declared too old for an active field command and ordered to return to Canada. It was the disappointment of his life. Perhaps in the pain of handing over his command, he forgot that he had already fought and won a critical battle of the War – the battle for tanks.

Worthy retired from the Army in September 1948, after serving as Commandant at Camp Borden, and as Commander-in-Chief, Pacific Command. The same year, he was named Civil Defence Co-ordinator for Canada and served until 1957 when he went into private business. His retirement years were active and full. As always, he was an avid reader, he hunted and fished, and became an accomplished painter. The Royal Canadian Armoured Corps remained his pride and joy and the Armoured Corps Weekend each August at Borden was the highlight of his year. "Most people hope to go to Heaven when they die," his wife said of him, "but not Worthy. He's going to Camp Borden." On a winter's morning in 1967, his wish was granted.

REPRINTED FROM:
Esprit de Corps, *Volume 2 Issue 4*
AUTHOR: *Bill Twatio*

CARE AND COMFORT

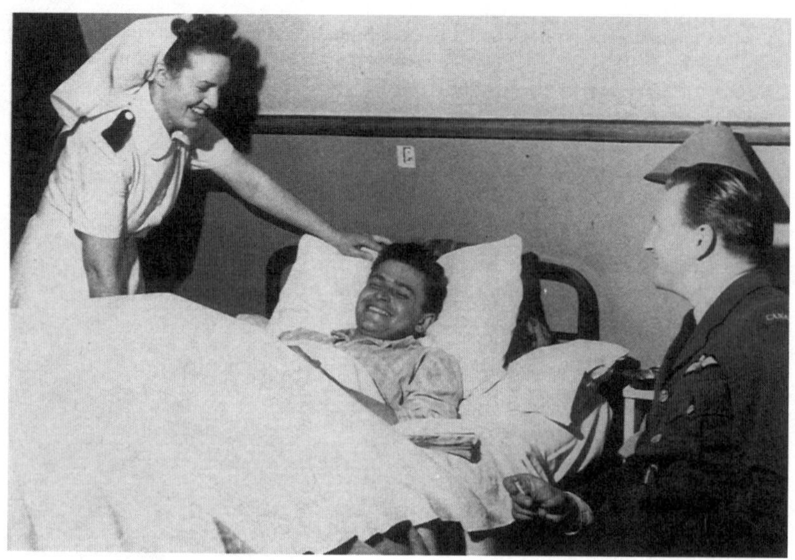

Thousands of Canadian women volunteered to join the RCAMC as nursing sisters. Their efforts and sacrifices were greatly appreciated by the frontline troops, who dubbed them, "Angels of Mercy."

AT THE END OF the First World War, 1094 Canadian nursing sisters had served in England, 792 in France and Belgium, and another 538 at home. Twenty-one had been killed, 18 had succumbed to disease and seven died in Canada. But they had made their mark.

A postwar policy of disarmament led to reorganization and cutbacks, and, by the late 1930s there were only nine nursing sisters in the regular army. Of 1010 reserve positions, only 248 were filled.

When WWII was declared, the Royal Canadian Army Medical Corps (RCAMC) was not at first fully mobilized or recruited up to strength. The first 129 nursing sisters did not go overseas until 8 June 1940.

Once in Britain, the nurses set up in Taplow, so well remembered by WWI veterans. By July, nursing sisters were hard at work treating the broken limbs of apprentice Canadian motorcycle dispatch-riders, however no nurses reached the continent. No. 15 General Hospital was destined for the front, but the fall of France precluded its deployment.

RCAF NURSING SERVICE

Back in Canada, the RCAF Nursing Service came into being in September 1940. Membership rose from an initial 12 nursing sisters (without commissioned status until 1942) to 481 by the end of the war. Eleven months later the Navy followed suit, establishing the Naval Nursing Branch. Three hundred and forty-three served, most in Halifax or Newfoundland. One was killed when the ferry carrying her back from leave was sunk by a U-boat.

For Canadians in Britain, 1941 was a tedious year. More hospitals arrived, setting up in Aldershot and Marston Green. Nursing air-raid victims provided some action, but for most, life consisted of training, exercises and practice alerts. On the other side of the world, however, two nursing sisters reached Hong Kong on 16 November 1941 and, three weeks later, became the first Canadian nurses into combat during WWII. After surrendering to the Japanese on Christmas Day, they endured 21 months of captivity before being exchanged in September 1943.

The nurses remained untested through much of 1942, although the Dieppe raid in August brought 600 casualties into Canadian facilities in a matter of days. One hospital alone reported 95 operations in 15 hours.

CLOSER TO THE FRONT LINES

In July 1943, a number of nursing sisters relocated to Sicily and North Africa. After the Italian invasion, No. 14 General Hospital sailed for Caserta, but the ship was sunk by German planes, but no nurses were harmed in the incident. By 1944, women were being employed for the first time in field units virtually on the front lines.

A perpetual irritant was the policy which prevented married nurses from serving near the front. One woman who married in North Africa was transferred back to Britain, then permitted to return when her husband was killed!

The first nursing sisters landed in France on 9 July 1944, setting up six miles from Caen. Others followed in the months to come. During the fighting through France, No. 1 General Hospital was temporarily established in a monastery, complete with cherubs and angels painted on the ceilings. After surgery, patients sometimes awoke to look upwards…and wonder! By spring of 1945, nurses had been subjected to V-2 attacks, artillery bombardments and partisan raids, all the while continuing their life-saving duties. With the German surrender in May many volunteered for the Far East, but none arrived before hostilities ended.

NUMBERS SLASHED

By VJ-Day, the RCAMC had some 3656 nursing sisters on strength, two-thirds of them serving overseas. They had staffed 100 major hospital units, treated over 60,000 patients and won 386 awards.

OPPOSITE PAGE: *After crew members were rescued from their dinghy after bailing out of their Halifax bomber, they received care from nurses in hospital. (DND/PL 31799)* ***ABOVE:*** *Nurses of No. 10 Canadian General Hospital of the Royal Canadian Army Medical Corps arrive at Arromanches, France, on 23 July 1944. (NAC/PA 108174)* ***BELOW:*** The Lady Nelson *in port in Naples in January 1944. Clearly identified as a hospital ship with her red stripe and cross, she was painted all in white and travelled with all her lights on. She was never stopped or boarded by Germans, although they would be in their rights to do so perhaps because she sometimes carried German POWs. She made 37 trans-Atlantic voyages. (NAC/PA 112259)*

ABOVE: In addition to serving as nursing sisters during the Second World War, women also drive ambulances, going close to the front lines in France to transport wounded to hospital. (CWM)

With the advent of peace, nursing services were slashed from the ranks. By 1947, there were only 30 Army, 30 Air Force and 20 Navy nurses left in the Regular Force.

Sixteen Canadian nurses served in Japan or Korea during the Korean War, although there was no Commonwealth Hospital in Korea itself until 1952. Eight remained after peace was declared in 1953 to help handle repatriated POWs. At home, the first four RCAF nursing sisters became para-rescue specialists in October 1951. Many more followed them.

In 1959, the nursing and medical services of all three armed services were integrated. Nurses participated in several UN operations after Korea, including Cyprus and the Middle East. By 1975, there were 372 nursing sisters in the CAF, 19 of them serving overseas with NATO or the UN. At the end of the 20th century 400 nurses graced the rolls.

UNDER INDESCRIBABLE CONDITIONS, NURSING SISTERS TREATED EVERYTHING FROM BATTLE WOUNDS TO AMOEBIC DYSENTERY AND ENTERIC FEVER.

ANGEL OF MERCY

In Canada's Parliament Buildings a mural hangs in the Hall of Fame which depicts the draped figure of Humanity, flanked by a nun nursing a child and a pair of uniformed nursing sisters tending a wounded soldier. It hangs in memory of the thousands of Canadian women who succoured the sick, wounded and dying of this nation's conflicts.

However, perhaps the best memorial comes from one unknown private fresh from the battlefields of Italy. Awakening after surgery to the kind smile of the duty nursing sister, he was heard to exclaim, "Gawd, it's an angel of mercy!" He speaks for all.

REPRINTED FROM:
Esprit de Corps, *Volume 2 Issue 8*
AUTHOR: *Andrew Moxley*

BLACK MIKE

As Air Officer Commanding, No. 6 (RCAF) Bomber Group, "Black Mike" McEwen's credo was leadership by example.

NEARLY FORGOTTEN TODAY, ONE of our country's foremost and distinguished World War II commanders was an air war hero of an earlier time who, after the Second World War, was once described by Marshal of the Royal Air Force Sir Arthur "Bomber" Harris, as one of his best "bomber barons."

He was Air Vice-Marshal Clifford MacKay "Black Mike" McEwen, CB, MC, DFC and Bar, Commander of the Bath (CB) of the United Kingdom, Commander of the Legion of Honour of France, Commander of the Legion of Merit of the United States, and holder of Italy's Medal Valoria and the Croce de Guerra.

In the First World War he was a contemporary of Billy Bishop and Raymond Collishaw, and, in Italy, was a wingmate of ace Billy Barker. At the age of 22 he had over 24 confirmed victories, and had earned three British decorations and two from our then-ally. At age 48, during the second of this century's Great Wars, McEwen was Air Officer Commanding of No. 6 (RCAF) Bomber Group. Under his leadership, 6 Group was forged into one of the finest offensive forces in Europe, contributing substantially to the defeat of Nazi tyranny.

LEFT:
The damage inflicted on German cities like Bremen by the bombing raids in 1943-44 was extensive, and most city centres were reduced to empty shells. The firestorms created raging fires that were so hot the "temperature reached the ignition point for all combustibles, and the entire area was ablaze," wrote an eyewitness to the Hamburg raids of 1943. "In such fires complete burn-out occurred... and only after two days were the areas cool enough to approach." In just one week, some 50,000 were dead and nine square miles in Hamburg were gutted by fires. (DND)

OPPOSITE PAGE:
As one of Canada's aces in the First World War, with 34 victories, Air Vice-Marshal Clifford M. "Black Mike" McEwen took over command of No. 6 Group just when it would begin preliminary attacks in the build-up towards D-Day. (CWM)

IN 1945, BLACK MIKE BECAME AOC OF EASTERN AIR COMMAND IN HALIFAX. HE RETIRED FROM THE RCAF THE FOLLOWING YEAR AND SETTLED IN MONTREAL UNTIL HIS DEATH IN 1967.

CHANGE IN CAREER

Clifford McEwen, later known as "Black Mike" due to his dark complexion, was born in Griswold, Manitoba, in 1896. He originally wanted to be a clergyman, but the intervention of World War I set him on course for a lifetime air force career.

Leaving the University of Saskatchewan in March 1916, he enlisted as a private in the 196th (Western Universities) Battalion, Canadian Expeditionary Force, proceeding overseas shortly thereafter. Now a corporal, Black Mike was commissioned in June 1917 as a lieutenant and was seconded to the RFC, now folded into the fledgling Royal Air Force, for pilot training on Camel fighters at Reading in England. He soon proved himself to be a superb pilot, and a natural leader, when he joined 28 Squadron in France.

NINE-MONTH CAREER

McEwen's combat career, spanning as it did but nine months, did not really begin until his squadron was rushed to Italy to shore up that ally's fortunes after the many disasters of October 1917. He flew on his first offensive sortie on 29 November, shared in the destruction of an Austrian balloon the next day, and made his first confirmed kill a month later, on 30 December 1917 of a German Albatross. His last would be a German D-111 on 4 October 1918.

CITATION EXTRACTS

Impressive indeed are the following extracts from the official citations for Black Mike's three World War I British decorations, as were published in the London Gazette:

An acting captain at the end of the war, he reverted to lieutenant and for a time worked with Bishop and then Barker in organizing our first Canadian Air Force, in England. He returned to Canada to be demobilized in 1919, joining second air force, the Air Board. When the Royal Canadian Air Force came into being on 1 April 1924 he was one of the "originals," being commissioned as a flight lieutenant.

Married in 1927, Black Mike was promoted to squadron leader in 1929, wing commander in 1937 and group captain in early 1939.

During the interwar years he attended numerous staff college and other courses and served in many capacities. He also flew practically all types of aircraft on strength in the RCAF and RAF, and qualified as a parachutist.

In 1941, Group Captain McEwen was promoted to the rank of Air Commodore to head up a group under the British Commonwealth Air Training Plan. He was posted overseas in late 1943 to command 62 Base, 6 (RCAF) Bomber Group, Linton-on-Ouse, Yorkshire. It was on Leap Year Day of 1944 that McEwen was promoted to Air Vice-Marshal, and named Air Officer Commanding, 6 Group.

He held this position until after the unconditional surrender of Nazi Germany at Rheims, France, on 8 May 1945. As AOC, Black Mike's credo was leadership by example, albeit in his case illegal, because when he flew on operations as a second pilot, he was usually dressed in the uniform of a sergeant. Despite an almost total ban by the highest of authorities, Bomber Harris winked at McEwen's actions, wanting him to continue ruling the Canadian bomber barony. However, what he was doing was soon known throughout 6 Group and then throughout all of Bomber Command, clearly inspiring many Canadians and others to greater things.

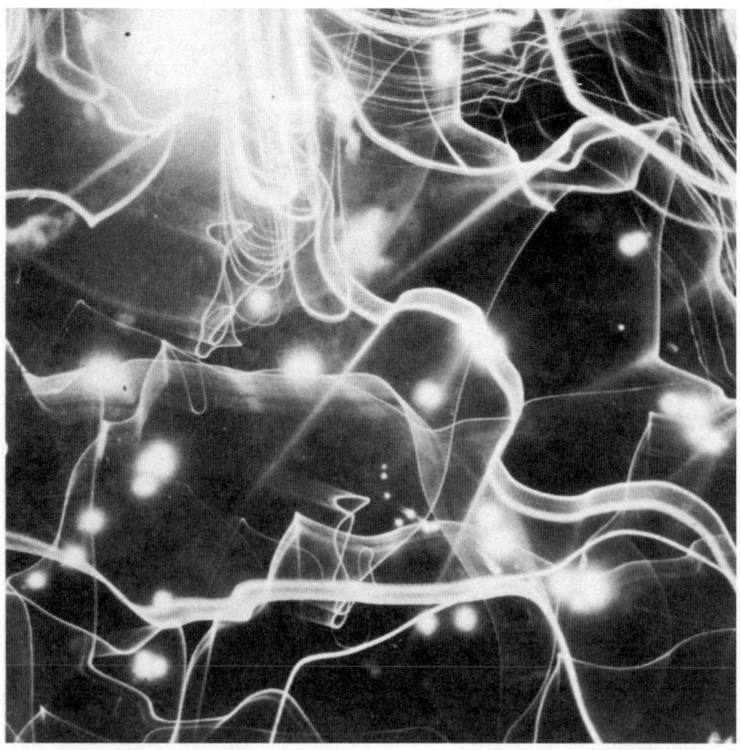

LEFT: *During nighttime raids, a bomb-aimer's view was reduced to the study of intricate patterns of light that were created by searchlight beams, flak, skymarkers, exploding bombs and the glow of ground fires.* (NAC)

ON THE GROUND AS WELL AS IN THE AIR, HE WAS A STICKLER FOR DISCIPLINE, STANDARDS AND TRAINING.

FLYING RAGGEDLY

Group Captain Bill Swetman, DSO, DFC, CD, a wartime commanding officer of 426 (Thunderbird) Squadron, vividly recalled the last trip. At the last possible moment, Sergeant-Pilot McEwen was driven up to Swetman's Lancaster Mark II on the Linton-on-Ouse tarmac and the AOC climbed aboard. This trip was particularly interesting, as the bomber streams were flying raggedly, many with aircraft lights on. Black Mike soon put a stop to this practice throughout all of Bomber Command by threatening to send up Mustang fighters under his control to shoot offenders down.

On the ground as well as in the air, he was a stickler for discipline, standards and training. Still, he was fully aware of the stress endured by his air and ground crews. Within reason, his office door at Allerton Hall, 6 Group's headquarters, was open to any of the group's men and women who wanted to see him.

SLEEPLESS DURING OPERATIONS

Black Mike never slept when his group was operational. He attended as many debriefings, then known as interrogations, as he could, informally chatting with the returning, tired crews.

He was later appointed AOC (Designate) of Tiger Force, Canada's intended contribution to the continuing bomber offensive against the Japanese Empire. But when Tiger Force was disbanded after Japan's unconditional surrender to General Douglas MacArthur aboard the *USS Missouri* in August 1945, Black Mike became AOC of Eastern Air Command in Halifax. He retired from the Royal Canadian Air Force in the autumn of 1946, taking up residence in Montreal.

He became an internationally-known and respected aviation consultant, a director of Trans-Canada Air Lines (now Air Canada) and a long-time president of the Last Post Fund. He passed away in 1967, leaving his wife of 40 years and three daughters. Black Mike is buried in the Fund's Field of Honour Cemetery in Pointe Claire, Quebec.

REPRINTED FROM:
Esprit de Corps, *Volume 7 Issue 4*
AUTHOR: *Howard B. Ripstein*

THE HOME FRONT

Oceans away from the battle fronts, it was a very good war indeed.

THE WAR WAS A bonanza for Canada. Shipyards on both coasts, along the St. Lawrence and Great Lakes could barely meet the demand for corvettes, frigates, freighters and minesweepers. Car plants retooled to build jeeps, trucks and armoured cars. The near-moribund aircraft industry was revived and turned out Anson trainers, Harvards, Bolingbrokes, Cansos, Hurricanes, Mosquitos and Lancaster bombers. Life quickened and the entire country seemed to be on the move.

Airfields were laid out near quiet Prairie towns. Halifax was swamped with sailors. Vancouver was overrun by itinerant workers. Tens of thousands migrated to Montreal to find work in war industries, accelerating Quebec's transformation into an urban and industrial society. Between 1941 and 1945, 5500 tanks, armoured personnel carriers and self-propelled guns rolled off the production lines at the CPR Angus Shops and at Montreal Locomotive Works – more than were built by Italy and Japan combined.

ABOVE:
With mounting pressure from British Columbia media, and support from politicians, the federal government capitulated and, in February 1942, ordered that all enemy aliens – including German, Italian and Japanese – be relocated to internment camps, their property sold without compensation. In 1988, the federal government formally apologized for the treatment received by the Japanese community during the Second World War.
(NAC/C 46356)

OPPOSITE PAGE:
With substances like tea, coffee, butter and meat subject to rationing, food coupons became part of Canadians' daily lives. The purchasing of gas and liquor was also controlled by the government.
(NAC/PA 108300)

In Toronto, Massey-Harris switched from producing farm machinery to aircraft parts. The John Inglis Company expanded to 17,000 workers, building Bren guns as well as engine components. Research Enterprises manufactured radar sets, range finders, prismatic gunsights and other precision optical equipment. TipTop Tailors turned out uniforms, converting the company's cafeteria and auditorium into factory space. It was soon producing 25,000 a week, faster than the government could enlist men. And many a worker slipped a "God bless you" note into a pocket. At Casa Loma, technicians worked under heavy security to produce highly secret anti-submarine devices.

The city, however, unlike rollicking, wide-open Montreal, maintained its reputation as a cold and forbidding place for newcomers – the Belfast of the North, possessed of a stern Presbyterian soul. "We All Hate Toronto," Lister Sinclair sang in a CBC broadcast:

"In Toronto the Good,
it's quite understood,
that sin is a thing to bewario,
If you are bad be sure to be sad,
for nothing is fun in Ontario.
The people are pure and vengeance sure descends on a budding Lothario.
The same is true of anyone who, prefers not to drink in a dairyo.
They let him drink beer, but make it quite clear, it's really a crime in Ontario.
In short you might say, if life is a play, Toronto's the censored scenario. "

AFTER MUCH DEBATE, A NEW UNEMPLOYMENT INSURANCE PLAN CAME INTO EFFECT IN 1940 JUST AS THE COUNTRY WAS MOVING TOWARDS FULL EMPLOYMENT WITH THE ARMED FORCES AND INDUSTRY WAS COMPETING FOR MANPOWER.

The Gross National Product doubled in the first three years of war – the greatest period of growth in the country's history – and there were jobs for everyone. Even nature cooperated, with farmers bringing in bumper crops to meet an insatiable demand.

After much debate, a new Unemployment Insurance Plan came into effect in 1940 just as the country was moving towards full employment with the Armed Forces and industry competing for manpower. The following year, several Unemployment Insurance Commission offices reported that not a single claim had been filed – a far cry from March 1940, when 612,000 Canadians were still subsisting on public relief. A National Selective Service Agency was set up to coordinate the nation's manpower resources, controlling the hiring, firing and general movement of employees. J.L. Ralston, the Minister of Defence, and C.D. Howe, Minister of Munitions and Supply, were locked in a struggle for bodies, with Howe informing his cabinet colleagues that war production could not stand the constant

***LEFT**: Canadian Car and Foundry produced more than 1400 Hawker Hurricane fighters in their Fort William, Ontario, plant. Most Hurricanes would be ferried to Britain.* (SOUTHAM ARCHIVES)

***OPPOSITE PAGE:** In September 1940, the federal government created a "Special Committee on Orientals in British Columbia" and, although they reported that the Japanese had not done a single subversive act, Japanese Canadians had to register with the RCMP and provide photos and fingerprints. On 7 December 1941, Japanese fishing vessels in British Columbia were impounded.* (PUBLIC ARCHIVES OF CANADA)

leaching away of essential workers. In 1942, he told the House that "our whole war effort is being distorted at the present time by the undue emphasis now being placed on men for the army overseas. "

"It's a mess," Humph Mitchell, the Minister of Labour, complained. "We have overextended ourselves in every direction. We have taken on more army than we can support, more war industry than we can operate, more food production than we can handle."

THE GROSS NATIONAL PRODUCT DOUBLED IN THE FIRST THREE YEARS OF THE WAR, THE GREATEST PERIOD OF GROWTH IN THE COUNTRY'S HISTORY AND THERE WERE JOBS FOR EVERYONE. EVEN NATURE CO-OPERATED, WITH FARMERS BRINGING IN BUMPER CROPS TO MEET AN INSATIABLE DEMAND.

YOU'RE IN THE ARMY NOW

The National Resources Mobilization Act of June 1940, requiring compulsory military training for single men under the age of 45, effectively dried up the labour pool. Registration of every Canadian over the age of 16 began on 19 August, and 802,458 single men and childless widowers became liable for military service, leading to a rush for the altar as only those married before 15 July would be considered married under the Act. Thirty thousand conscripts reported for a month's training in October and were issued bits and pieces of uniforms and ancient American rifles, which were imported to replace the stock of equally ancient Ross rifles that had been shipped overseas for the defence of Britain. Target practice was strictly limited due to a lack of ammunition. The fledgling Armoured Corps trained with Model T Fords converted into tanks, and antitank guns were fashioned out of sewer pipe. Accommodation for the draftees was sorely lacking, with public buildings and exhibition grounds pressed into service. Some continued to live at home for weeks to come, only reporting for parades.

The term of service was extended to four months in February 1941, and for the duration of the war in April. Although the Prime Minister clearly stated that he would not introduce conscription for overseas service – "Let me emphasize the fact that this registration will have nothing whatsoever to do with the recruitment of men for overseas service," he said in the House of Commons – the Act would cause problems in the future, for Canada now had two armies, one for active service and one for home defence. The latter were the hated Zombies – the living dead of wartime, neither civilians nor full-fledged fighting men.

WE'RE IN THE MONEY

The Federal Government, which had not played a large part in Canadian life, now became very intrusive. A bewildering array of government directives, rules and regulations, coupons and ration books became part of daily life. In 1942, Ottawa took over corporate and personal income taxation from the provinces and introduced an income tax on those who earned over $660 a year. In return, it assumed responsibility for provincial debts, relief for the unemployed and paid a national adjustment grant based on fiscal need. The provinces were not pleased. Premier Mitch Hepburn of Ontario arrived at a federal-provincial conference in Ottawa to discuss the changes "with blood in my eye and dandruff in my moustache." Premier T.D. Pattullo of British Columbia, "a compound of inordinate vanity and thickheadedness," according to Mines Minister T.A. Crerar, described the conference

as "the god damndest exhibition and circus you can imagine."

But the government was determined, as far as possible, to pay for the war through taxation. Corporations were hit with an 18 per cent tax on profits and an excess-profit tax of up to 100 per cent. A compulsory savings plan also came into effect amounting to eight per cent of taxable income for singles and ten per cent for couples, repayable after the war. Still, Canadians had more money than ever to spend. Wages more than doubled and a blanket price freeze, administered by former CPR President Donald "The Price Czar" Gordon, and his Wartime Prices and Trade Board, kept inflation in check.

After a sharp rise in the early months of the war, the cost of living settled down and increased by only 2.8 per cent from October 1941 to May 1945, with the cost of fuel and electricity actually falling. Room and board could be had for around ten dollars a week. Men's broadcloth shirts cost 89 cents or three for $2.50 at Eaton's which also provided reasonably-priced, made-to-measure officers' uniforms. Tip Top Tailors offered men's suits for $27.50 and winter coats for women for $22.95. Boneless rib roast sold for 31 cents a pound, pot roast for 16 cents, leg of veal for 17 cents and lamb

VESTS, PLEATS, PATCH-POCKETS, DRESSES WITH MORE THAN NINE BUTTONS AND HEMS OF MORE THAN TWO INCHES, TWO-PANT SUITS AND CUFFS ON MEN'S TROUSERS BECAME THINGS OF THE PAST. BUREAUCRATS IN OTTAWA POINTED OUT THAT 54 SAVED CUFFS WOULD MAKE ONE SOLDIER'S BATTLEDRESS.

for 24 cents a pound. Coffee was a nickel and most lunch counters would throw in a hamburger for a quarter. A Ford four-door with a heater, defroster and radio went for $925. All civilian car production came to a halt in Canada and the United States on 15 January 1942, with new cars on hand parcelled out to doctors and police. "In the dealers' holiday-decorated showrooms," *Time* reported, "the stillness of death prevailed as auto dealers and their employees were laid off." They were quickly absorbed into war industries. Production was booming and many plants had reached the limits of their capacity by the end of 1942. Work was then subcontracted out to whoever had a spare machine. Production peaked in 1944, giving credence to Churchill's observation that gearing up for war is a four-year process: "The first year produces nothing, the second very little, the third a lot, and the fourth, a flood."

Crown corporations, a uniquely Canadian blend of public and private enterprise, were set up as purchasing agents for vital war supplies while an Industries Control Board, a who's who of corporate Canada, regulated the most essential sectors of the economy. Each controller was armed with an Order-in-Council passed under the War Measures Act establishing broad powers for action and, if need be, coercion. Oil Control was the most unpopular. Its maxim "NOT ONE DROP OF GAS WITHOUT A RATION COUPON" was enforced by inspectors supported by a network of snitches.

More Canadians than ever joined unions and, despite the wartime demands of duty, steadfastness, and self-sacrifice, struck with alarming frequency. Strikes for higher wages and union recognition were commonplace in almost every vital industry – at the National Street Car Company in Malton, Canadian General Electric in Toronto, Canadian Cotton in Hamilton, at coal mines in Cape Breton and gold mines in Kirkland Lake, at shipyards in Lauzon, Quebec, and in Midland and Kingston, On-

LEFT: *In 1943, Quebec City was the site of an Allied conference to determine a collective strategy. Prime Minister Mackenzie King (seated left) took his place alongside American President Roosevelt and British Prime Minister Winston Churchill.* (PHOTO BY DAVID CHRISTOPHER)

THE WAR CREATED NEW OPPORTUNITIES FOR WOMEN [TO WORK]. AT THE PEAK OF PRODUCTION 439,000 WERE EMPLOYED IN SERVICE INDUSTRIES AND ANOTHER 373,000 IN MANUFACTURING. IT WAS THE AGE OF ROSIE THE RIVETER AND THE BREN GUN GIRL.

tario. "A civilian," a sailor remarked, "is a nasty thing to contemplate at any time, but a shipbuilding civilian is the nastiest."

Newspaper editorials called for responsible unions and anti-strike legislation. The King government responded in February 1944 with Order-in-Council PC 1003, the so-called Magna Carta of Canadian labour law that guaranteed the right of workers to form and join accredited unions, forbade unfair labour practices and established compulsory collective bargaining.

VICTORY GARDENS, SLOPPY BEER

"MAKE DO. REMAKE, EAT IT UP, WEAR IT OUT," the Consumer Branch of the Wartime Prices and Trade Board exhorted. Although coupon rationing was introduced in 1942 for sugar, tea, coffee, butter and gasoline, it was never particularly onerous as each person with a ration book was still allowed six ounces of butter a week and two-and-a-half pounds of meat depending on cut; and most people in this pre-supermarket age knew a friendly grocer who would slip a little extra into a bag for a regular customer. Restaurants were ordered to observe meatless Tuesdays and Fridays. Tires were next to impossible to come by and drivers were limited to 120 gallons of gasoline a year. "A GALLON A DAY KEEPS HITLER AWAY!" a wartime slogan said. Liquor was rationed at a 12-ounce "Mickey," four bottles of wine and a case of beer a month and you needed a license. Cigarettes were scarce, but were readily available along with everything else on the thriving black market, a market that also contributed to government coffers with 23,416 prosecutions bringing in $1.7 million in fines. Hoarding was illegal, punishable by a $5000 fine and up to two years' imprisonment. Five dollars or five days and a stern lecture from the judge was the usual punishment.

Bootleggers and Blind Pigs thrived, charging outrageous prices for bathtub booze, sometimes laced with deadly additives. In May 1942, de-icer in a bottle of "gin" killed three Winnipeg women and an airman. The teetotalling Prime Minister took to the airwaves to promote temperance, informing his listeners that the consumption of beer, wine, and liquor had increased 37 per cent since the outbreak of war. "Those who indulge themselves too frequently and too freely will break under the strain," he warned and announced that his government was about to prohibit the advertising of "spirituous liquors" for the duration of the war. He confided to his diary that he had considered "reducing somewhat the strength of beer but the argument was that Government would get little thanks from the temperance people for a nominal reduction and no end of grousing from miners and others on the score of the King Government having supplied them with sloppy beer."

For some inexplicable reason – much was inexplicable during the war years – potatoes were scarce while rice was plentiful. Victory Gardens bloomed in backyards and empty lots. The newspapers were full of helpful household hints, new recipes and tips for novice gardeners. The National Salvage Division of the Department of War Services urged housewives to become munition workers in their own kitchens by saving fat, a source of glycerine used in high explosives. "Help smash the axis!" they were told. "Save every drop of fat and every bone!"

Vests, pleats, patch-pockets, dresses with more than nine buttons and hems of more than two inches, two-pant suits and cuffs on men's trousers became things of the past, bureaucrats in Ottawa pointing out that 54 saved cuffs would make a soldier's battledress. Quality was poor. Shoes fell apart in the rain, sweaters unravelled and manufacturers used the cheapest of fabrics to get around the price freeze. Silk stockings disappeared. When nylons came on the market a few months after the war, Eaton's in Toronto sold them at a rate of 2000 pairs

an hour. In the meantime, women resorted to leg paint, "stockings in a bottle." Ladies' hairdressers and beauty shop owners of Canada were challenged to create a hairdo that was simple and practical for those engaged in war work, "but feminine at all times."

A WOMAN'S WORK IS NEVER DONE

The war created new opportunities for women. At the peak of production 439,000 were employed in service industries and another 373,000 in manufacturing. It was the age of Rosie the Riveter, the Bren Gun Girl and the girl of the popular jingle

". . . that makes the thing
That drills the hole, that holds the spring
That drives the rod, that turns the knob
That works the thingummybob.
It's a ticklish sort of job
Making a thing for the thingummybob
Especially when you don't know what it's for.
And it's the girl that makes the thing
That holds the oil that oils the ring
That makes the thingummybob
That's going to win the war . . . "

Thousands more, at 80 per cent the rate of pay of men, would serve as nursing sisters and in every theatre of war in the Canadian Women's Army Corps, the WREN's and RCAF Women's Division.

Long-faced children, visions of model Spitfires and Little Orphan Annie dolls dancing in their heads, were presented with War Savings Stamps and Certificates as Christmas and birthday gifts. But they cheerfully collected bottles, cans, and milkweed for parachutes and joined in scrap drives. Five thousand dish pans, 10,000 coffee percolators, 2000 toasters and 1000 double-boilers would build a bomber, they were told. When the War Exchange Conservation Act forbade the importation of all "nonessential" products including comic-books, they bought the new "Canadian Whites," comics printed in black and white, and thrilled to the adventures of Dixon of the Mounted, Nelvana of the Northern Lights, Canada Jack and Johnny Canuck, "Canada's answer to Nazi oppression."

Stamps, certificates, and War and Victory Loan campaigns brought in an astounding $10. 2 billion for the war effort. That money, when bonds were redeemed in 1945, would fuel a totally unexpected postwar boom.

"This is not only a war of soldiers in uniform," the Director of Public Information breathlessly informed Canadians. "It is a war of the people – of all the people – and it must be fought, not only on the battlefield, but in the cities and in the villages, in the

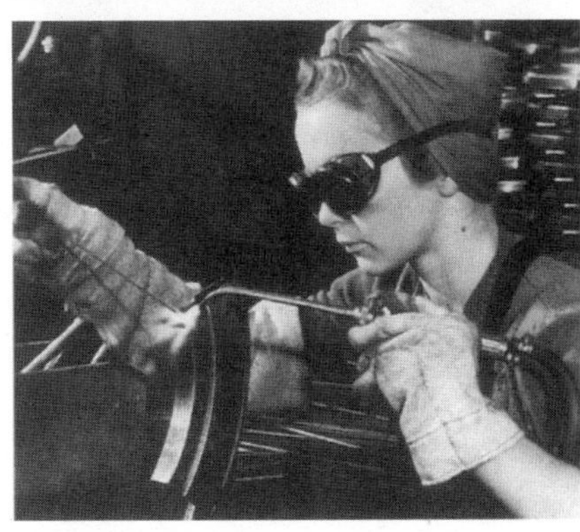

TOP LEFT:
An improvised training tank: Model T Ford with steel plates welded in place. These would be used by the newly-created Armoured Corps because of the limited supply of real tanks. (IMPERIAL WAR MUSEUM)

TOP MIDDLE:
Invigorating Canadian industries with the war effort was Clarence Decatur Howe, the New England-born Minister of Munitions and Supply. Here, C.D. Howe is seated in the 500,000th military vehicle built in Canada. Production of civilian vehicles halted as assembly lines were converted to manufacture trucks, scout cars and Bren gun carriers. Over 800,000 military vehicles were produced during the Second World War. (NAC/C 68669)

TOP RIGHT AND ABOVE:
As men left the workforce to join the war, women gladly filled their vacancies. Performing such non-traditional jobs as welder, and assembly line and factory worker, women would be forced to return to their homes at the end of the war. (IWM; NAC/C 75211)

LEFT: *Minister of Munitions and Supply, C.D. Howe, inspects the first Valentine tank to come off the assembly line at Montreal Locomotive Works on 27 May 1941.* (PAC)

factories and on the farms, in the home and in the heart of every man, woman and child who loves freedom! ...This is the people's war! It is our war!"

THE MINISTER OF EVERYTHING

The omnipresent C.D. Howe, a transplanted New Englander who had made a fortune building grain elevators in the west, was the most powerful man in the country next to the Prime Minister. Returning to Ottawa after his ship was torpedoed en route to England in December 1940, Howe set to work with a vengeance orchestrating the production effort and, where necessary, creating Crown corporations to turn out everything from rifles to synthetic rubber. The task was formidable as Canadian industry had never built a tank, a combat aircraft, sophisticated electronics, or modern rapid-firing guns. His Department of Munitions and Supply, staffed he said, "by men of experience, men who know values, men of absolute integrity," could tell businessmen what to make, where to sell and when to deliver. He was the hardest working man in the Cabinet, *Maclean's* magazine claimed, and the toughes, letting out contracts for staggering figures, building streamlined factories, and looking on a million dollar order as small change. How he stood up under the strain of 14 hours of work a day, his meal hours incidental to conferences, is a mystery.

Called a "virtual dictator" by some and a "fascist, but a nice fascist" by others, Howe had critics in high places, notably Minister of National Defence J.L. Ralston, and Finance Minister J.L. Ilsley. In March 1941, Ralston told colleagues that "he had no confidence whatever in Howe," having great difficulty extracting tanks from his department feeling that Britain was supplied at the expense of the Canadian army. Ilsley, whose work load was so heavy that he told a friend that he woke each day wishing he could die, was concerned about production costs and complained that "Howe is running a government of his own."

Leonard Marsh, a young British-born economist from McGill, was equally busy at the Department of Pensions and National Health, creating a blueprint for the future welfare state. In the Speech from the Throne on 27 January 1944 incorporating many of the recommendations of the Report on Social Security in Canada, the King government presented the most ambitious domestic program in Canadian history: It promised that social security and human welfare would be the cornerstones of its legislation and that there would be useful employment for all who were willing to work. Old age pensions were to be increased, family allowances introduced and veterans retrained at government expense after the war. The next year the King government won a crushing victory at the polls.

Despite Ilsley's concerns about Howe's growing power, William Lyon Mackenzie King, Canada's perpetual Prime Minister, a fussy, demanding bachelor given to seances and spiritualism, whose closest confidants were mediums and his Irish terrier Pat, was still very much in charge. His first battles of the war were political. A challenge from the nationalist Duplessis government in Quebec based on anti-war sentiment was beaten back when Adelard Godbout's Liberals, with help from Ottawa, defeated him in a provincial election. When Ontario's Mitch Hepburn carried a resolution in the Legislature on 1 January 1940, "regretting that the Federal Government has made so little effort to prosecute Canada's duty in the war in the vigorous manner the people of Canada desire to see," he seized the opportunity to call a national election, taking 184 seats, 123 more than the Conservatives and the largest majority since Confederation. Doctor R.J. Manion, the Conservative leader, who had been certain of victory weeks before, issued a terse post-election statement: "Let us get on with the war." On hearing that he was in financial straits after being dumped by the Party in favour of R.B. Hanson, a Fredericton lawyer, King arranged to have him appointed Director of Air Raid Precautions. When George

RIGHT: *In March 1939, an anti-conscription rally was held in Montreal. Mackenzie King promised then, and again on 8 September, that there would be no conscription for service overseas. In October 1939, the Liberals wanted to make that clear as Quebec held a provincial election.* *(NAC/PA 107910)*

McCullagh of the *Globe and Mail* asked him how he liked working for "that little son-of-a-bitch," Manion replied, "Well, I find it not a bad change from the sons-of-bitches I was working with."

A colourless, uninspiring, sleep-inducing public speaker who droned on in a flat, convoluted monotone, he would never win the hearts of the Canadian people.

But he brought to office a wide-ranging intelligence, balance, immense knowledge of government and politics, and dedication to the good of the country; qualities much needed to see Canada through a desperate war. He presided over strong cabinets, readily delegated authority and let his ministers do their jobs. He was a master political manipulator, capable of ruthlessness. "When Willie goes to work it is always a 25-act tragedy with the throat slitting in the second last scene but one and the final curtain falling on him commiserating with the victim's widow if he has one," said King-watcher Grant Dexter of the *Winnipeg Free Press.*

Charles Ritchie, a young diplomat, man-about-town, and private secretary to Vincent Massey, Canada's High Commissioner to Britain, had occasion to observe King at close quarters during the war. A perceptive and elegant diarist – Canada's Pepys – "thrown by chance and temperament into the company of a varied cast of characters in the stepped-up atmosphere of war with its cracking crises," he too well knew that it was folly to underestimate King. In London he felt his "disembodied presence brooding over us. It was not a benevolent influence. In the flesh he was thousands of miles away, but he needed no modern bugging devices to detect the slightest quaver of disloyalty to his person or his policies. Perhaps through his favoured spiritualist mediums he was in touch with sources of information beyond Time and Space."

"Luncheon with Mackenzie King," he wrote in April 1945, while on his way by train to San Francisco for the founding conference of the United Nations. "I was charmed by the fat little conjurer with his flickering, shifty eyes and appliqué smile. He has eyes that can look like grey stones or can shine with amusement or film with sentiment. He chats away incessantly – he seems very pleased with himself, delightfully so, pleased with his own cleverness and with his own survival." The flickering grey eyes missed nothing of note in Ottawa.

Ottawa was bursting at the seams with soldiers, sailors, and airmen, "dollar-a-year" men recruited from private industry, consultants, contract-seekers, technical advisers, hangers-on and 30,000 newly-hired civil servants. Evacuees from English public schools were boarded at Ashbury College in Rockcliffe Park, while Princess Juliana of the Netherlands took up residence. Jimmy Cagney came to town to film *Captains of the Clouds.* Gold, securities and currency reserves from Britain, Belgium and France were secretly stored in the vaults of the Bank of Canada for safekeeping. As well as being the headquarters for all three armed services, the city became the largest flight-training centre in the country and reverberated with the constant roar of aircraft.

Accommodation was at a premium. When Louis St. Laurent, a wealthy corporation lawyer and future Prime Minister, arrived from Quebec City to take up his duties as Minister of Justice in December 1941, he was lucky to rent a two-room apartment, one so small that his wife had to store groceries under the bed. A survivor of wartime Ottawa recalled:

"A basement would be cut up into four suites you could only charitably call cubicles, with one toilet and one washtub for four families or four couples. The tops of old wrecks of houses would be divided in two, and that would bring in $120 a month, $60 each side, which was a lot of money in those days.

"No pets. No parties after 11 P.M. No replacing 40-watt bulbs with 100-watt bulbs. No children in some places. No laws protecting the renter. Rent ceilings all right, but if the tenant didn't pay what was asked, regardless of the ceiling, he just didn't stand a look-in. And other things, on and on. No

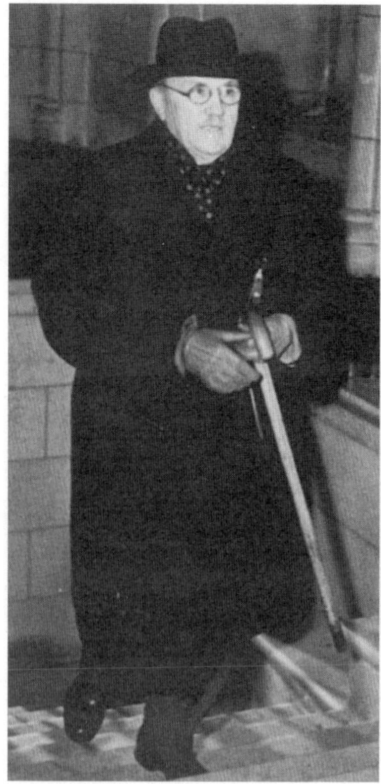

heat until mid-November and after late April. Half a mile to the street car, maybe. And there was never any doubt in some of those landladies' minds that the woman of a couple was a slut just waiting for her husband to go overseas and the husband some kind of whore-master."

Working in hastily-constructed "temporary" buildings – some lasting into the 1980s – the ill-housed mandarinates would help transform Canada into an industrial power. By war's end, Canada would be the fourth largest producer of weapons and munitions in the world and a major supplier of raw materials and foodstuffs, wealthy enough to provide interest-free loans to Britain and make an outright gift of one billion dollars.

ABOVE: *The idea of conscription was as volatile in 1939 Quebec as it had been in 1917. Ernest Lapointe **(left)**, Minister of Justice and longtime leader of the federal Liberal party in Quebec, declared that he and his Quebec colleagues would resign from their positions in Cabinet should conscription be introduced. Maurice Duplessis **(right)**, wanting to exploit anti-conscription sentiment, called for an election in 1939, saying that a vote for his Union Nationale party was a "vote against conscription and participation." Playing hardball paid off for the Liberals as Duplessis and his party were defeated.*
(ABOVE LEFT – NAC/C 26553, ABOVE RIGHT – NAC/C 19526)

WEST COAST CODA

It was a very good war indeed, unless you were a Canadian of Japanese descent. Suspected of espionage and fifth-column activities, vilified by hysterical politicians and press, their property was confiscated and they were evicted from their homes on the West Coast in January 1942, following Japan's attack on the United States Pacific fleet at Pearl Harbour. "It is the government's plan to get these people out of British Columbia as fast as possible," said Ian Mackenzie, Minister of Pensions and National Health and British Columbia's representative in the Cabinet. "Every man, woman and child will be removed from the defence areas of this Province and it is my personal intention, as long as I remain in public life, to see that they never come back here." Herded into pens at the Pacific Exhibition Grounds in Vancouver, some 22,000 were then moved into internment camps in the interior.

It was not Canada's finest hour.

AUTHOR: *Bill Twatio*

THE LIRI VALLEY

Breaking the Hitler Line (in the Liri Valley) in May 1944 was a bloody affair. For a total advance of 11 miles, the Canadian corps suffered 789 men killed, 2463 wounded and 116 captured.

THE LIRI VALLEY OFFENSIVE, the breaking of the Gustav and Hitler Lines, or the advance on Rome. Call it what you will, it was the first battle engaged in by a complete Canadian Corps since the pursuit to Mons 26 years before. The operation began on 11 May 1944 and ended, so far as the 1st Canadian Corps was concerned, on 3 June 1944. The next day, the American Fifth Army entered Rome and, on 6 June, the Allied forces of General Eisenhower assaulted the coast of France.

Italy was no longer the Second Front, it became a secondary, and an almost forgotten, front. Also, the Liri Valley campaign, which saw a stunning German defeat and the capture of the Eternal City, began almost immediately to fade from the memory of man.

There were still nine more months of fighting in Italy for the 1st Canadian Corps before it quit the Mediterranean area and moved up to northwestern Europe to join 2nd Canadian Corps in the Victory campaign of mid-1945.

MASS FIRING

Rome was the prize promised the Allied armies in Italy when, on 11 May at 23:00 hours the 1700 massed guns of the American Fifth and British Eighth Armies opened fire. It was said to be the biggest artillery barrage since World War One.

The first Canadians to enter the fight were two armoured regiments, the Calgaries and the Ontarios, both in support of the 8th Indian Division. Their task was to cross the Gari River along which stretched the Gustav Line – dug-in German positions

RIGHT:
After months of heavy fighting, the 1st Canadian Corps finally breached the Hitler Line in May 1944. With the collapse of the Gustav Line, the advance north of Rome was in full gear.
(PAINTING BY CHARLES COMFORT, CWM 12296)

anchored on Cassino and stretching across the Liri Valley and the coastal mountain range to the Tyrrhenian Sea. The Polish troops and some British formations drove along the mountains on the right flank, the Poles capturing Monte Cassino.

HALF A MILLION ALLIES

Half a million Allied soldiers took part in the month-long campaign. The British Eighth Army, included the 1st Canadian Corps, which consisted of the 1st Canadian Infantry and 5th Canadian Armoured Divisions, advanced down the valley floor. On the left, the French *Corps Expéditionaire* moved along the coastal mountain range, while further up the peninsula and much nearer to Rome, the bogged-down American Fifth Army was to burst out of its four-month old stalemated bridgehead to cut off the expected retreat of the German Gustav and Hitler Line garrisons as they fled to Rome. As it happened, the Germans were driven from their two defensive lines, including the strongpoint of Monte Cassino on which the Gustav Line was hinged, and did flee toward Rome, but the American general, Mark Clark, disobeyed the orders he had received from his superior British commander, General Sir Harold Alexander and changed his direction of attack. Instead of cutting off the retreating Germans, he "beat the British Eighth Army into Rome." He also allowed the Germans to escape up the peninsula to their prepared next line of resistance in Northern Italy, called Gothic Line. There, three to six months later, the British lost 60,000 men and the Americans 20,000 in an attempt to win the war in Italy before the year's end. For a number of reasons they were unable to do so.

GUSTAV LINE BREAKS

The Gustav Line was broken by 16 May and the 1st Canadian Infantry Division passed through the 8th Indian Division into the open country between the Gustav and Hitler Lines. All three of its brigades were engaged in skirmishes with enemy outposts of the Hitler Line. Many prisoners were taken, but casualties were relatively light. By 20 May the Army Commander issued orders for the attack on the Hitler Line proper. The attack was to take place on 23 May with the 1st Canadian Infantry Division charged with piercing the Hitler Line and making a gap through which the 5th Canadian Armoured Division could race through to reach the Melfa River and cross it before the Germans could turn it into another barrier.

A BLOODY AFFAIR

The breaking of the Hitler Line proved a bloody affair. It was a much more heavily fortified line than the Gustav Line. *Panzerturm*, miniature fortresses constructed of steel tank turrets mounted on concrete and housing anti-tank guns, machineguns and rocket projectors, studded the front and were so dug in that they could not be seen by the approaching Canadians until they were almost on them. The 48th Highlanders were chosen to make the initial breach in this formidable line of defence, following a probing attack by the Princess Louise Dragoon Guards, the division's armoured reconnaissance regiment. Both units fought their way into the midst of the Hitler Line, but were unable to pierce it.

THE BATTLE WIDENS

Gradually the battle widened, and the Divisional commander committed his other two brigades. For three days the infantry battle continued. In 2nd Brigade, the PPCLI, the Seaforths and the Edmontons, fought desperately to penetrate the Line's left flank and suffered heavily. No men could have fought with greater bravery, but their casualties were so heavy that their progress was limited to getting into the Hitler Line, but not through it. However, they had so mauled the defenders that when the 3rd Brigade was sent in, the Carleton and Yorks, the West Nova Scotias and the Van Doos managed to get through in what the divisional commander later called the 1st Division's "most outstanding tactical success in any single day of fighting in the war."

Meanwhile, the 48th continued their isolated battle in the centre of the line. Now

RIGHT:
Soldiers dash for cover as they move from one location to another along the Hitler Line.
(NAC/PA 136205)

the brigade commander sent in the Hastings and Prince Edward Regiment with British tanks from the 142nd Royal Tank Regiment. Then, the trapped Canadians and their rescuers captured 300 Germans and killed or wounded a hundred more. On 24 May the RCR occupied Pontecorvo, as the battle-weary 48th drew breath. As dozens of Germans crawled out of the rubble of this pivot on the Hitler Line, Lieutenant Bill Rich, who had led his scout platoon into the battered town, boldly climbed into the church tower and rang the bell to announce the city's capture.

RIGHT:
As the Allies made their way towards home they were greeted by one of the Hitler Lines' primary defences . The Panzerturm – a tank turret emplaced in concrete – was an immovable fortress.
(NAC/PA 114917)

FIRST DIVISIONAL BATTLE

It was now the turn of the Canadian armour to exploit the victory, and this they did. It was their first divisional battle since arriving in the Italian theatre the previous winter. Two strike forces were organized for this effort, comprised of the B.C. Dragoons with an infantry battalion, the Irish Regiment of Canada, and Lord Strathcona's Horse with the motorized Westminster Regiment.

They reached the Melfa River in a matter of hours, fought a desperate tank battle in the bridgehead that was seized by the Westminsters, and succeeded in putting the Germans into headlong flight. At first it seemed that the Germans would smash the bridgehead.

But the valour displayed by the Strathconas and the Westminsters denied the enemy their aim, winning the Victoria Cross for Major Jack Mahony of the latter regiment, and the DSO for Lieutenant Edward Perkins of the former.

PURSUIT BATTLE

The next week saw a pursuit battle with plenty of skirmishes, fairly light casualties and a considerable number of prisoners taken. On 28 May the 1st Division passed through the Armour and continued the pursuit. Rome was almost in sight. But 1st Canadian Corps was not to be its captor. As previously stated, the American Fifth Army did a neat turn in their break-out from the Anzio bridgehead, cutting off the 8th Army, and thus the Canadians, from sharing the prize of Rome.

The Liri Valley campaign cost the 1st Canadian Corps 789 men killed, 2463 wounded and 116 taken prisoner. The Corps advanced 41 miles, captured 1400 Germans and killed and wounded many others. The price of victory is always high.

As 1st Corps rested in the burning sunshine and dust of the Valmontone countryside, 20 miles south of Rome, the 3rd Canadian Division with their British and American comrades stormed the beaches of Normandy. World War Two had begun its final phase.

REPRINTED FROM:
Esprit de Corps, *Volume 3 Issue 12*
AUTHOR:
Colonel (ret'd) Strome Galloway

DOWN TO THE SEA IN SHIPS

Turbulent weather and silent death awaited Canadians as they first ventured out onto an ocean battlefield.

ABOVE:
A squadron of Bristol Beaufighters from Coastal Command attack enemy shipping in the North Sea. Armed with rockets and possibly torpedos, they were used with Wellington and Hampton bombers in anti-shipping strikes.
(DND)

THE ROYAL CANADIAN NAVY of WWII enjoys a justified reputation as a gritty, hard-working fighting force that took on the dirtiest weather, the most skilled opponents, and overcame serious early handicaps. By the war's second-last year, Canadian sailors had better training, better equipment and more autonomy, but that still didn't guarantee success on the cruel sea. War, for all its application of science and technology, is the art of managing uncertain outcomes. War at sea asks the most of man and his technology, and is rarely satisfied with less than cruel tragedy.

Canada's navy had an inauspicious beginning as a skeletal training force of 3700 men and six destroyers when war announced itself in 1939. The process of building up an adequate fighting force took several years and several thousand lives. Politics, as well as science, had to be led kicking and screaming into the North Atlantic, not only to protect the interests of our Allies, but of Canadian lives as well. Leaders would do well to examine the record of 1939-1943 rather than point simply to victory in 1945, and pat our ancestors on the back for their strenuous efforts. Ottawa-bound scientists pooh-poohed HF/DF (High frequency – Direction finding) and 'hedgehog' multiple anti-submarine bomb launchers as unproven, and resisted their introduction on Canadian ships. Canadian-built radars were inferior, and lack of pressure on British sources left Canadian corvette refits at the back of the queue. Until Admiral L.W. Murray took over command of the Northwest (later North) Atlantic theatre, Canadian autonomy was treated as a sick joke: Americans and British both viewed their junior ally as an obnoxious brat who required rescuing more often than rewarding.

THE CRUCIBLE OF WAR EVENTUALLY FORGED A FORMIDABLE WEAPON. ACROSS CANADA INDUSTRY LASHED ITSELF TO THE WAR EFFORT AND PERFORMED PRODIGIOUS FEATS.

CRUCIBLE OF WAR

But the crucible of war eventually forged a formidable weapon. Across Canada industry lashed itself to the war effort and performed prodigious feats. Shipyards were no different, although strategic decisions often interfered with tactical necessities. Unable to contain their desire for a 'big ship' navy, Naval Service Headquarters insisted on building Tribal-class destroyers in Halifax. The drain on manpower and resources slowed corvette upgrades and left too many escorts in port when the need at sea was greatest. Eventually not only were corvettes being refitted with new guns and weapons, larger bridges and forecastles and working radars, but twin-screw frigates and destroyers were also built in Canada. By the end of 1943 the RCN had 306 warships. The six original destroyers were joined by eight from the US, eight handed over from the RN and four other Tribal-class destroyers, British-built for the RCN. (Altogether 28 destroyers flew the Canadian ensign in WWII along with two cruisers, two aircraft carriers, three armed merchant cruisers and innumerable smaller vessels.)

The RCN lost destroyers as well. HMCS *Fraser* was sunk in June 1940 (in a collision with HMS *Calcutta*), the *Margaree* four months later in a convoy mishap. The first *Ottawa* (a second of the name survived the war) was torpedoed in September 1942, and one year later *St. Croix* met the same fate. HMCS *Haida*, on the other hand, had an illustrious and successful career. Under Commander Harry de Wolf, she participated in the destruction of two enemy destroyers, a minesweeper, U-971 off the Breton coast, and 14 other warships. On 30 April 1944 she also witnessed the death of her sister.

A Beaufighter X fired its rockets on the grounded German destroyer (see opposite page), assuring its unserviceability. (DND)

LEFT:
The modernization of the Royal Canadian Navy also included increased sophistication in its electronic systems, including the control equipment in the sonar hut of this corvette. (NAC/PA 13996)

ACTIVITY AT A HIGH PITCH

With the D-Day landings only weeks away, activity along the French coast was at a high pitch. Allied naval forces prepared the English Channel for the up-coming crossing while heavy bombers pounded the Normandy region (and Pas de Calais, for a diversion). On 29 April *Haida*, and HMCS *Athabaskan*, sailed from Plymouth to screen mine laying operations off the Cherbourg peninsula. The night passed quietly, although both crews stood at their stations and stared intently into the darkness.

With only 15 minutes left before turning for home, two sinister shapes frothed across the patrol area. A shout went up, flares burst overhead as *Haida* and *Athabaskan* opened up on a pair of German, Elbing-class destroyers. Tracer fire seared the night and shell bursts lit up the combatants. As the Canadian gunners blazed away, the German ships laid a smokescreen and turned tail. Behind them a fan of torpedoes rippled through the black water leaving a phosphorescent trail.

Anticipating the manoeuvre, the two RCN ships immediately altered course before taking up pursuit, but for *Athabaskan* the uncertain outcome rushed upon her with deadly impact. The enemy torpedo struck her abaft on the starboard quarter. The thunderous explosion blew her two aft gun positions away and crushed her propulsion gear. Fires raged as the stricken destroyer began to settle in the water.

COUP DE GRÂCE

Haida kept up fire on the two assailants, but ten minutes later another deadly missile supplied the coup de grâce. Farther up the tortured starboard side the second torpedo ripped through the crippled *Athabaskan* and sent her listing heavily in the water. 'Abandon Ship' was sounded and battered and wounded men helped each other into the boats. *Haida* had succeeded in driving one of her enemy aground and she returned to assist her sister ship. (The smoking hulk of the German ship would be photographed on the rocks by RAF Spitfires the next day.) At 04:27 hrs HMCS *Athabaskan* exploded and her burning hull saluted the sky before gliding into the depths. Wreckage was everywhere and burned sailors clung to what they could. *Haida*'s crew was still engaged in battle as she attempted to drop life rafts to survivors. Later, nets were lowered over the side and the Canadian sailors found renewed strength trying to save as many fellows as they could. Unfortunately, dawn was creeping into the sky over the enemy-held coast, and to linger would invite the *Luftwaffe* to claim a victim of their own.

130 DIE

Haida began to move forward slowly, preserving every affordable moment for rescue efforts. "Get away *Haida,* get clear," someone shouted, and a sailor later insisted it was young Lieutenant Commander John Stubbs, captain of the *Athabaskan*. Survivors claimed to have seen him, his arms severely burned, encouraging his sailors to sing and keep up their spirits. He, along with 129 officers and men, did not survive the cold, wet night adrift in the Channel. Forty-four were rescued by their mates, while 83 others were picked up by the Germans.

RCN Ships could not linger on the defeats nor allow the heat of revenge to dis-

LEFT: *The German destroyer that was driven ashore on Ile de Bas by HMC Ships* Haida *and* Huron *on 9 June 1944, was finished off by rockets fired by Beaufighters of No. 404 Squadron.* (DND) ***OPPOSITE PAGE, TOP RIGHT:*** *The development of radar during WWII proved one of the most useful weapons, both in air and at sea, and was fully exploited by the Alies. The electronic eye of the radar (or ASDIC) allowed a seaman to determine the distance and bearing of an object at sea.. When used in conjunction with other ships, it was possible to vector in on enemy ships with more precision. The operator is looking into a large disc called a PPI (Plan Position Indicator) scope.*

tract them from the ongoing tasks they had to perform. Retribution, however, was not long in coming. HMC Ships *Ottawa* (the second), *Kootenay* and *Chaudiere*, all destroyers, were operating in the Bay of Biscay in August 1944. Operation Kinetic was being conducted to assist French Maquis resistance fighters ashore. Even as American forces broke out of the bocage country to race to Argentan (south of Falaise), German pockets of resistance remained behind facing the Atlantic Ocean. They were trapped, obviously, but the French were still too weak to take the towns, and the Germans could still be supplied from the sea. Operation Kinetic sought to pry German fingers from the west coast of France, and the blockade succeeded beyond expectations.

AS THE CANADIAN GUNNERS BLAZED AWAY, THE GERMAN SHIPS LAID A SMOKESCREEN AND TURNED TAIL. BEHIND THEM A FAN OF TORPEDOES RIPPLED THROUGH THE BLACK WATER

CANUCKS POUNCE

On 18 August HMCS *Kootenay* first picked up an asdic contact as the trio returned from patrol. That it was a U-boat was uncertain but the three Canadian ships pounced upon it and were rewarded by a diesel oil slick and air bubbles. Depth charges rained down on the suspected submarine for the rest of the day, and HMCS *Chaudière* was left to patrol the spot through the night. She left, but Portsmouth was unsatisfied and sent her right back to try again. After three runs at a contact on 19 August enough wreckage bubbled to the surface to convince the Canadians they had succeeded. All three ships were credited with destroying U-621.

The next day, the scenario was repeated as the three RCN destroyers were preparing to return to Londonderry. An asdic contact was bombed off the screens and further attacks proved inconclusive as night closed in. Only much later was official credit given to the deadly trio for U-984. (After the war, the Allies were able to compare their logs with German records.) RCN: two subs in two days, U-boats: zero.

ALLIES INVITED ASHORE

It was not often that the RCN, who had suffered so much and worked so hard, were able to engage directly in celebrations with liberated Europeans. One little known occasion took place on the Ile d'Yeu off the coast of France on 26 August 1944. The Canadian destroyer, *Iroquois* was in the company of HM Ships *Mauritius* and *Ursa* when they sailed past the French island. A small boat was observed heading out and it was obvious they wished to attract the attention of the three sleek, deadly warships. The German garrison on the island had left the day before, and this small seaborne committee was inviting the Allies to come ashore, gather the abandoned intelligence, and if possible, spare some supplies for the transition to Liberated France. *Iroquois* sent a party of two officers and three ratings ashore while she continued her patrols. The next day they were to be picked up.

ISLANDERS OVERJOYED

The islanders were so overjoyed that their bell-ringing prohibited use of the church tower as a signal point. The five Canadians were carried into the town on the native shoulders and were treated to a warm spontaneous reception. However, there was work to do, and the liberators excused themselves from the celebrations to carry out their tasks. At 13:00 hrs a parade of townspeople, laden with cakes, fruit and wine (including champagne for which a collaborator had no more use) showed up at the Canadian outpost, and a welcome break lasted for some time before duty re-intervened.

Before departing the next day, the head of the local French veterans association requested that the Canadians join in a commemorative ceremony for the Allied flyers whose bodies the islanders had recovered from the sea in the preceding years of war. The departure was accompanied by the same spirited cheers as was the arrival. Eight months later, war, for everyone concerned was a thing of the past. *Iroquois* sailed for Halifax and the uncertain outcomes of a peacetime navy.

REPRINTED FROM:
Esprit de Corps, *Volume 3 Issue 11*
AUTHOR: *James G. Scott*

THE DEVIL'S BRIGADE

CANADA'S FIRST SPECIAL SERVICE FORCE

After a somewhat anti-climatic debut in the Aleutians, the elite Canadian-American unit known as the Devil's Brigade, proved their mettle in the mountains of Italy.

THE AMERICANS CLEARED THE Japanese from Attu in the Aleutian chain in May 1943, and planned to follow-up on Kiska. Prime Minister Mackenzie King wanted to relieve pressure for conscription by giving National Resources Mobilization Act recruits an image of defending the country instead of sitting on their butts enjoying the flora and fauna of Alliford Bay. Although a number of regular force troops were part of the 5300 Canadians in the 13th Brigade formed for the operation, the inclusion of NRMA personnel had strong political overtones.

The 13th Brigade became part of an American force which also added the First Special Service Force to its strength. An untried group of 2400, the FSSF was about one-third Canadian and five of its six battalions were commanded by Canadians. Highly trained in mountain warfare, as ski troops and parachutists, the group was conceived as sabotage units, but at the time of the Kiska operation had reverted to combat duties. Kiska was to be their first action.

The FSSF led the assault and the landing went very well. But the first men on the rocks of fog-bound Kiska heard only the surf and the barking of a hungry dog who was abandoned when the Japanese quit the island 18 days earlier. The unit regurgitated its frustration for four months until General Mark Clark called for its help in Italy.

Clark was mounting an offensive against the western hinge of the Bernhard Line, a series of defence positions dug into mountains and part of a network which blocked allied progress. The FSSF moved into action when the Canadians were fighting towards Ortona at the eastern end of the line.

THIRD TIME LUCKY?

The allies were looking for a road to Rome and the only practical route in the west was through the Mignano gap which was dominated by three strongly defended peaks. Two attempts to take the fortress on Monte La Difensa failed in November, and the next month it became the objective of FSSF.

The trail leading to the south side of La Difensa was ringed with enemy gun emplacements, but the north side was worse. It was topped by a 1000 foot rock wall and crowned by a series of ledges which thrust out like knuckles of a giant fist. Major General Robert Frederick, the brigade commander, decided to take the impossible route, counting on the element of surprise.

Colonel D.D. Williamson, a Canadian, led the attack regiment half way up a steep ravine in darkness and freezing rain. Two other regiments followed at one hour intervals. They waited in a pine scrub as daylight brought the warmth of the sun. They checked equipment and made haste to wait as the day lengthened and fighter-bombers droned overhead. The war seemed to swirl around them until 1630 hours when fire from 245 guns hit the top of the mountain, causing it to erupt like a volcano. It was dark before the spearhead moved up to the base of the rockface and by 2230 hours the first of the climbers had started the ascent.

The battalions climbed the cliff in the dark and by dawn another Canadian, LCol T.C. Mac William led the assault on the summit where they cleared the enemy from pillboxes and caves.

HINGE BROKEN

One battalion held Monte la Definsa and repulsed a counterattack while another moved along a narrow ridge towards a second mountain. Mac William was killed by mortar fire minutes after giving the order to advance, but within five days three critical defensive positions fell to the allies, and the hinge of the Bernhard line was broken. Although the FSSF suffered 400 casualties in its first action, it established itself as a top fighting unit. What the 3rd Division had failed to do in 12 days of attacks and high casualties in November, 300 men of the FSSF did in two hours of combat.

TOUGHEST BUNCH OF CITIZENS

The man who moulded the outfit left a very personal stamp on it, yet in appearance Robert Frederick looked more like a bank teller than John Wayne. Frederick had gathered the toughest bunch of citizens in North American about him. All were unorthodox, loners with a strong independent streak and a pronounced ability to improvise. Their training had been extremely tough, and Frederick had personally led them through most of it. His philosophy was to lead them into go-for-broke situations and let them improvise their way out. During the course of doing this, he was wounded several times.

Churchill called Frederick "the greatest fighting general of all time." However, other generals who where less prone to lead their men called him "that crazy sonofabitch."

STRONG POINTS CLEARED

Although the Bernhard line was penetrated, it was necessary to clear more peaks before the Mignano Gap could be fully exploited. The North Americans, as they were now known, spent about a month clearing strong points and finally cleared Mount Mojo which looked down on Cassino. A third Canadian, Lieutenant Colonel T.P. Gilday led the assault which finally drove the enemy from Mojo.

A landing at Anzio was a resounding success but it didn't go anywhere. Although the area was defended by two tired battalions, Gen John Lucas failed to send spearheads towards Rome some 30 miles to the north. Instead he insisted on building up his force, a tactic which offered the worst of both worlds: he was in no position to inflict damage on the enemy from the beach; the enemy grew stronger by the day and was in a position to inflict damage on him.

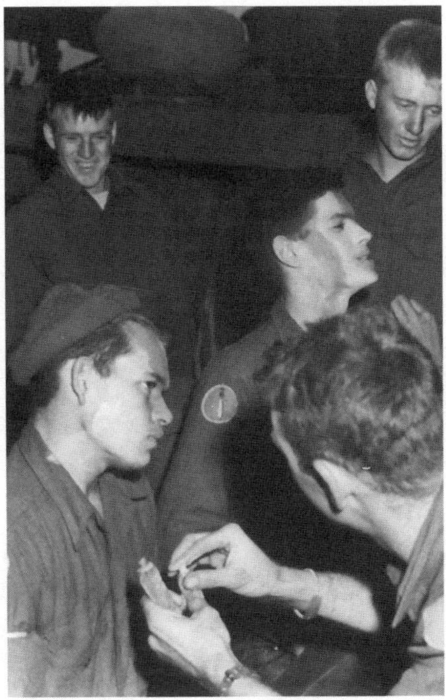

OPPOSITE PAGE:
U.S. and Canadian soldiers land on what they believed to be the Japanese-held island of Kiska. The amphibious operation was unopposed as the Japanese had already withdrawn from the Aleutians.
LEFT:
Men of the Devil's Brigade apply their camouflage paint prior to a patrol.

Although General Alexander expressed his desire to Churchill to see patrols striking inland, neither he nor Lieutenant General Clark were forceful about it. After they visited Lucas, nothing changed and troops said of the generals "they came, they saw and they concurred."

The North Americans were given the job of anchoring the right flank of the defensive line which arched around Anzio. The force was now reduced to half its original strength and it entered another kind of war in the flat country dotted with farms. It was a war of lonely night patrols, silent killing with an occasional attack in force when armour support was available. The men of the force blackened their faces before a patrol and their skill at infiltrating struck terror in German units. So there would be no misunderstanding, they left brigade insignias behind as calling cards. The diary found in the pocket of a dead German officer read: "The Black Devils are all around us every time we come into the line and we never hear them come."

Sergeant Tommy Prince, a native Canadian from Manitoba, was one of the men who excelled at solitary patrols, stealth and the unorthodox. When German tanks were firing at allied lines and moving before gunners could raise answering fire, Prince took a telephone and crawled out 1800 yards to a deserted farmhouse within 200 yards of the enemy. At daylight he spotted two tanks and phoned back their position. Both tanks were destroyed. The following day a shell rattled the house and cut Prince's telephone line. Digging out a hat and black coat, Prince became an instant, excitable Italian farmer. He stomped out to his chicken coop, hurling invective at both sides. Then he slipped around behind the coop and repaired the line. He returned to the house where next day, with the phone working, he bagged two more Tiger tanks.

HEAVY CASUALTIES FOR THE DEVIL'S

But the experienced enemy was no easy mark for the Devil's Brigade and casualties were heavy. When the enemy planted plastic mines on a path used by North Americans, 32 men lost legs in one night. When the allies broke out of Anzio four months after the landing, the Black Devils again headed for the mountains. Fighting off counter-attacks, they were at the point in the allied thrust on Rome and were among the first into the city. The Brigade which started with about 2400 men suffered 2300 casualties in its brief combat career, but its proudest moment was when it marched into Rome on 4 June. But the glory of Rome was short-lived as it was for all participants in the Italian campaign. Two days later the invasion of Normandy grabbed the world's attention and Rome gradually became a place folks visited to see the Pope or throw coins in the fountain.

REPRINTED FROM:
Esprit de Corps, *Volume 3 Issue 9*
AUTHOR: *Norm Shannon*

RIGHT: *With faces painted for camouflage, the men of the British 6th Airborne Division would be among the first to land in preparation for the beach landings on 6 June 1944.* (IMPERIAL WAR MUSEUM)

A curious peek at a top-secret diorama of D-Day nets Finn air miles galore. He is virtually kidnapped by the 6th Airborne and dumped into France minutes into 6 June.

JOHN FINN'S LONGEST NIGHT

IN 1944 A YOUNG Newfoundland officer anxiously straddled a motorcycle on a barge approaching the Normandy coast. His eyes held the gleam of immortality as he revved-up the engine and waited for the ramp to drop. A member of an advanced party of Newfoundland's 59th heavy regiment, he was consumed with a desire to be the first Newfoundlander into Europe. The ramp dropped and he gunned the motor and went shooting off into what he thought was six inches of water. The barge was on a sandbar. So read six feet of water, and a remarkably short trajectory into history.

But the dream died hard. Some weeks later, it seized a diminutive corporal as a barge approached shore. A premature leap dropped *him* into six feet of water. Alas! He was short and no swimmer! His buddies fished him out but his dream of glory went as soggy as his socks. What neither man knew after the D-Day landings was that brother Newfoundlander John Finn had been on the continent for seven weeks, landing there the night before the invasion.

LEGEND GROWS IN THE TELLING

A funny thing happened to John Finn on his way to the invasion, and the years and his buddies in the 59th regiment apparently add to the legend each time the story is told. Some tell you that Finn stumbled across the invasion plans and was detained and stuffed aboard a glider by the British 6th Airborne because he knew too much. As 5300 ships crossed the channel and a parade of bombers pounded the Normandy coast, Finn was dumped at Ranville near Caen. Historian G.W. Nicholson in his excellent book, *More Fighting Newfoundlanders*, confirms that Finn, a jeep driver, "unaccountably found himself . . . in a group of officers and men who were looking at films of the French countryside and being briefed about a highly hush-hush operation – no less than a *coup-de-main* landing by an airborne force behind the enemy's lines to secure vital bridges across the Orne river before the D-Day assault began. From that moment a curtain of rigid security prevented Finn from returning to his unit."

This could be taken to mean that General Windy Gale, the hard-nosed commander of the 6th Airborne, took his usual decisive action. In recent years, Finn suggested that the stories have become fanciful. "They get wilder every time the regiment meets. Makes a man feel like tucking his head under his arm." The briefing story is a bit much, according to him, and he suspects that some of his mates from the regiment may have been having the historian on. Yet Finn's own story is not really different.

THE AIR ATTACK ON THE FORMIDABLE DEFENCES AT MERVILLE HAD FAILED TO DO ITS JOB. IT DOMINATED AN INTRICATE DEFENCE NETWORK.

THE FOO MARKET

In the spring of 1944, Finn and ten other candidates from the regiment went to Salisbury for a forward observation officer (FOO) course. They were into heavy physical training and parachute jumps when the bottom fell out of the FOO market. Most of the other candidates were recalled to the regiment but Finn wasn't.

He languished at Salisbury, underemployed as a driver. Then a job opportunity presented itself from a strange source, according to Finn. The British 6th Airborne were looking for specialists and Finn's experience as a driver-signaller became highly marketable. Considering the fact that this was a few days before D-Day, joining the airborne was like signing on as piano player aboard the *Hindenburg*. A web of tight security did close around Finn, and all his newfound friends, and on the wet, windy night of 5 June they were stowing aboard *Horsa* gliders.

OPERATION CURSED

The plan for the night was bold; the execution chaotic. Parachutists were to be dropped at key locations on the left flank of the invasion beaches. They would secure positions and prepare landing sites for the gliders with troops, mortars, shells and heavy equipment. The operation was cursed by strong winds, heavy rain, strong enemy opposition, miscues, poor navigation and just bad luck. As the gliders were released from six tow aircraft and swooped towards the ribbon of the Orne river and nearby canal, Finn wrestled with a nagging scenario. What if Eisenhower called the whole thing off because of lousy weather?

Some parachutists were dropped miles from targets. Others were trapped in tall trees while many drowned in the marshes of the Dives river, sucked down by heavy equipment. Gliders were released prematurely or miles from the drop zone; a number fell from the sky like meteors while 100 bombers pounded gun installations at Merville, disturbing only fields of cows. Yet the plan worked because there is no defence against absolute confusion.

LUCKY JOHN

Finn's group was lucky. They made a reasonable landing 20 minutes after midnight and secured their first objective, a bridge over the Orne canal about 5 km inland. Men found themselves alone in the darkness, listening in terror for the snap of a twig. The sky was ripped by naval shelling, flak, and explosions from nearby Merville where giant naval guns threatened the beach where men would be coming ashore at dawn.

Lieutenant Colonel Terrance Otway was dumped out of his aircraft miles from target. His force of 600 paratroopers was widely scattered along with lost equipment. Otway assembled some of his men by crawling through the night blowing a hunting horn. Blackened figures in smocks of green and brown and yellow struggled under heavy loads of equipment towards the sound. It was the night Murphy's Law was born. Otway's battalion was to knock out the guns at Merville but he could only assemble about 120 men. The glider train

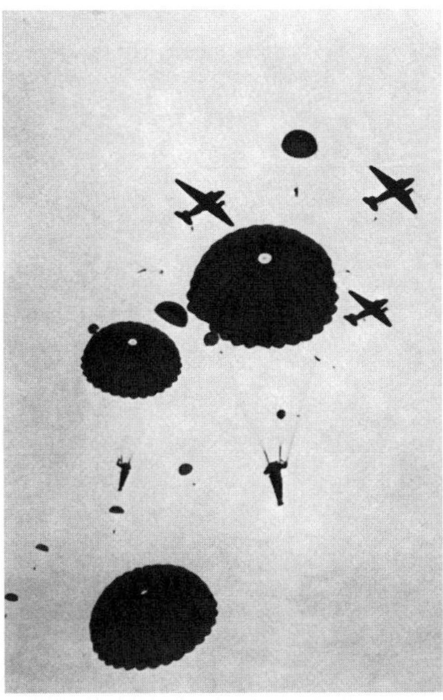

which was to bring jeeps, anti-tank guns, mortars, flame throwers, bangalore torpedos, and other vital supplies was lost. The air attack on the formidable defences at Merville had failed to do its job. It dominated an intricate defence network. First there was the mine wire, more mines and trenches and tunnels loaded with machine guns and manned by 200 men with rifles and *Schmeissers* sub-machine-guns The massive 150 mm guns looked down on Sword beach where the British would be landing in a few hours.

THE UNRAVELLING CONTINUES

Otway's battered group started by cutting through the outer wire. Then the next phase of the plan started to unravel. Two gliders appeared overhead, the third had to return to England. Loaded with Royal Engineers, their job was to land inside the compound at the signal from Otway. But as they circled under heavy fire, Otway watched helplessly because the mortar with which he was to fire a starshell was lost. The gliders finally broke off, one crashing in flames, the other joining Canadian paratroopers at Mesnil.

Ninety minutes before the first landings, Bangalore torpedos blasted holes in the wire and Otway's men went in. Long savage moments of hand-to-hand fighting followed. Just before dawn, Otway found Lt Dowling in one of the tunnels. Grasping his side, he reported, "Battery taken as ordered sir. Guns destroyed."

LEFT:
Training of airborne troops was extensive prior to the Allied invasion of Normandy, and the planning for D-Day was conducted with the utmost secrecy.
(PAC/PA 132785)

Otway went out and fired a yellow flare. Mission accomplished. When he came back in Dowling was dead, one of the 93 casualties in the small force. The guns at Merville were silent when the troops landed minutes later.

ALL-NIGHT PARTY?

The bridge at Ranville was secured. It's now known as Pegasus Bridge in honour of the airborne men who liberated it. Across the canal at Benouville there's another memorial to the night John Finn and some 4200 airborne and paratroopers walked out of the darkness. It's a café which has the distinction of being the first building liberated in Europe. John Finn remembers that night. A French civilian waited for him at the end of the bridge, directing him into the café for a drink. It was George Gondree, the owner, who has since turned his café into a museum to the Airborne. For decades George has been telling visitors about the magnificent party which went on all night as the war raged around them. Finn remembers having one drink and leaving. So do others. Years later one paratrooper remembered it this way. "George was out on the bridge like a traffic cop. All these lost people walked out of the darkness dazed and scared. They'd go in and have a drink and it was almost like taking communion. Then they'd walk down that road in the night looking for their units."

John Finn agrees. "If George remembers an all-night party it's because his guest list was the entire 6th Airborne," he chuckles.

REPRINTED FROM:
Esprit de Corps, *Volume 2 Issue 1*
AUTHOR:
Norman Shannon

RIGHT:
After months of planning, the army, navy and air force began to assemble their crafts for the planned invasion of Normandy. In Southampton, as in numerous ports all over the south of England, camouflaged Landing Craft Tanks (LCTs) were loaded with tanks and trucks, awaiting the signal for Operation OVERLORD to begin.
(IMPERIAL WAR MUSEUM)

Cold and seasick, Canadians hit Juno Beach where they soon establish a beachhead. Some units of the 3rd Division fought their way inland to within sight of Caen. Then things g0t worse.

ASSAULT!

***THE MYSTERY OF D-DAY** is how over 6000 vessels could approach the coast of Normandy, unload some 133,000 men and remain undetected by radar or patrol boats. Part of the answer may lie with the Germans' pre-occupation with the Pas de Calais area to the north and the stormy seas in the channel. While the first of the minesweepers were already at work in the channel, Field Marshal General von Rundstedt completed a report which concluded that, in view of the heavy weather, there was no immediate prospect of an invasion.*

On 5 June Field Marshal General Erwin Rommel went on leave, giving some units permission to stand down. Yet throughout the day the BBC broadcast the lines of a Verlaine couplet 15 times. The words "soothes my heart with monotonous langour" told an army of underground workers that invasion was at hand. The Germans failed to heed the obvious warning.

D-DAY OPENING

The last of the RAF heavies were heading home by 05:00 hrs, having dropped 5300 tons of bombs and American heavies were about to add another 5900 tons. Soon white-ribbed Mitchell and Boston bombers of the 2nd Tactical Air Force would add to the curtain of steel in historic operations which were surprisingly dull for many of the crews. Then fighter-bombers would fly a beat over the 60-mile front. Thousands of Canadians were part of the air assault.

In spite of the night bombardment and the fierce fighting by airborne troops at both ends of the front, some 6000 ships were able to pause or anchor undetected seven miles off shore. Sixteen ships of the 31st Canadian minesweeping flotilla bobbed a scant mile and a half off Omaha beach, having cleared the way for the armada which followed.

IMPRISONED

About 10,000 Canadian sailors manned 110 ships, including transports such as *Prince David* and *Prince Henry* and their destroyer escorts. Dozens of corvettes and frigates escorted landing craft and barges across the violent channel. Lieutenant Colin Graham commanded a troop of four tanks with the Sherbrooke Fusiliers. He remembers 16 men and four Sherman tanks being imprisoned within the narrow confines of the landing craft with white water smashing overhead and the only link with reality being the magic of instant cocoa. It involved some kind of a device which ignited and produced an instant brew-up.

For all troops the misery of D-Day started long before they approached the enemy coast. Rifleman Bob Smellie of the Royal Winnipeg Rifles was imprisoned for three days along with two companies, in a small steamer which had seen much better days and had no provisions for cooking food. Then, at about 0400 hours off Normandy, in an ironic gesture to a shipload of seasick men, the ship's crew made a grill by burning gasoline in oil drums with metal plates on top. Then they served bacon.

CANADIANS HEAD TO JUNO

The Canadian 3rd Infantry Division commanded by Major General R.F.L. Keller consisted of some 15,000 Canadian soldiers from 13 regiments were to be landed in a four mile section of the British Sword Beach known as Juno. It extended from Vaux on the right to St. Aubin on the left and contained four closely linked villages.

Thousands of Canadian airmen had already been involved in the bombing operations and the 1st Canadian Parachute Battalion was already holding positions inland near Ranville. Some 30,000 Canadians were actively involved in the early stages of the invasion. For some the most terrifying mo-

ment of the morning was the trip over the side on the *Prince Robert*, down landing nets, to where landing craft jumped six feet and threatened to smash them against the side of the ship.

ARRIVAL SCHEDULE

The run-in started at 05:30 hrs as the slow Landing Craft Tank with the amphibious squadrons of armoured regiments aboard nosed towards shore. Some LCT's made the trip directly from England and timed their arrival to precede the infantry. Support craft moved inland about an hour after the LCT's. Next came the Landing Craft Assault which were loaded with beach clearing vehicles and the AVRE's (Armoured Vehicles Royal Engineers) which could hurl heavy charges at bunkers and whose flail tanks cleared minefields. Then came the leading companies of the four infantry regiments; the Winnipeg Rifles, the Regina Rifles, the Queen's Own Rifles and the North Shore. Each sent two companies in the first wave, and two in the second about 15 minutes later.

Rocket firing ships took station behind the first companies and sent down a barrage which concentrated on gun emplacements at Vers-sur-Mer and Beny. Then special LST's mounting 96 Priests, 105-mm self-propelled howitzers, followed. Each Priest fired three shells every 200 yards as they approached, saturating the beaches with an estimated 17,000 rounds.

THE REAL ENEMY

The run-in was extremely rough and many craft lacked power to make way against the heavy seas. The LCA(Hedgerows) eventually had to be towed ashore but in the confusion only one of nine reached the correct beach. The approach's real enemy was not the 400 men waiting behind guns on shore, but raging surf. Vessels broke their tows and floundered. Beach clearing vehicles and engineers went astray while amphibious tanks were late in arriving at their destinations.

Most of the infantry who survived the 70-minute run-in were so seasick they were finally eager to jump into churning breakers. The landing craft bounced like corks. With waves breaking over the front and pumps not working, most of the men on Bob Smellie's craft were ordered out onto the deck over the engine. Soaking and sick, Smellie felt himself falling overboard. The hand of a sergeant grabbed him and a voice yelled, "We can get along without you, but we can't get along without your Bren."

ABOVE: *Taken by a U.S. P-38, this reconnaissance photo of the Normandy beach defences at low tide provided invaluable information to the strategic planners of Operation OVERLORD. (U.S. AIR FORCE)*

When Larry MacDonald fell into his craft, the first thing he heard and smelled was bilge water and it wasn't a pretty image. A signaler with the Royal Canadian Corps of Signals, MacDonald was not in one of the early waves and this was part of his problem on the run-in.

DRY-HEAVE STAGE

A number of infantrymen had been in the LCA for some hours and the bilges showed traces of long departed breakfasts as the entire group had progressed to the dry-heave stage of misery. MacDonald soon joined them. Then he noticed that the bilge was littered with leaflets from General Ike Eisenhower. A collector of military memorabilia, MacDonald struggled to retrieve a leaflet but later admitted he just didn't have the guts. However, he did come up with a copy from the National Archives some years later.

The 7th and the 8th Canadian Infantry

***Having reached the shores and taken this concrete pillbox from the Germans at Juno Beach, the wounded are cared for by the medics before being loaded onto LCI and their return to England for medical treatment.* (NAC)**

ONE COMPANY CAME UNDER FIRE 700 YARDS FROM SHORE AND MANY WERE KILLED CHEST HIGH IN THE WATER. EVERYBODY WAS HIT IN THE FIRST SECTION TO LAND AND ALL BUT TWO IN THE SECOND.

brigades were to attack on either side of the Seulles river with the 8th going in between Courselles and St. Aubin-sur-Mer on the left and the 7th landing to the right. The target area was dominated by four resistance nests spaced about every 2,000 yards and located at Vaux, Courselles, Bernières and St. Aubin.

Translated into regiments this meant that the Winnipeg Rifles and C Company of the Canadian Scottish faced a 75 mm gun at Vaux while two companies of the Winnipegs and the Regina Rifles at Courselles faced heavy fire from three 50 mm, two 75 mm and one 88 mm gun and 12 machine guns. They were supported by 1st Hussar tanks.

RESISTANCE NESTS HOLD FIRM

Bernières, where the Queen's Own were assigned, was protected by two 50mm guns and seven machine guns. At St. Aubin the North Shore faced one 50 mm gun and several machine guns. In addition, the enemy had seven mortars and several flame throwers overlooking Juno beach. They were originally supported by the Fort Garry tanks and later the Sherbrooke Fusiliers. Hours of bombing and naval bombardment failed to knock out most of the resistance nests but it did alert the occupants in their cement emplacements. The Royal Winnipeg Rifles and the Canadian Scottish on the far right landed with little trouble as a 75 mm gun had been wiped out. But the two companies on the left of Mike beach at Courselles ran into heavy fire. One company came under fire 700 yards from shore and many were killed chest high in the water. Everybody was hit in the first section to land and all but two in the second.

FIGHTING WITH BARE HANDS

The earlier bombardment "failed to kill a single German or silence one weapon." The Hussars tanks had not arrived and the infantry huddled under fire for six minutes before seven surviving tanks floated ashore. By the time B Company fought its way into Courselles, its strength was down from 120 to 27 men. Bull Klos took a burst of machine-gun fire from a pillbox but continued to clear it with his bare hands. Then he died.

The Regina Rifles weaved through tank-traps and huge shards of metal with Teller mines attached. They came under heavy fire from the strongpoint at Courselles but the 1st Hussars managed to land their tanks ahead of the infantry and a duel developed between a tank and an 88 – the latter was knocked out. A second gun fired 200 rounds before it was knocked out. The infantry, meanwhile, had divided Courselles into 12 sections and clean-up began.

No one knows exactly when Gib Boxall, a stretcher-bearer, picked up his first wound. He was cut down while answering the call for a stretcher and friends found five dried dressings on his body where he had been shot but refused to stop.

NAN SECTOR

On Nan sector, to the left, waves broke over the doors of the LCT's and the swim-in of DD tanks was abandoned. The Duplex-Drive tanks had a screen which normally enabled them to swim ashore where the screen was lowered and the enemy engaged. In the attempt to beach the tanks, four were knocked out of the water, three hit mines and eventually 13 got ashore, but not until after the infantry had landed.

Wind and tide carried the Queen's Own Rifles 200 yards east of their landing, into the fire of two 50 mm guns and seven machine-guns. Brothers Hume and Charles Dalton commanded the two first wave assault companies. Major Hume Dalton's landing craft weaved through mines and obstacles but drifted a bit too far left. Dalton bent over to tell the coxswain to bear right and discovered a dead hand at the controls. The coxswain had been hit between the eyes. By the time A Company hit the beach, one platoon was virtually wiped out. The 30-man platoon was down to about five survivors who drove the enemy out of the buildings and into the woods beyond Bernières.

In D Company Major Charles Dalton had 65 casualties by the time they reached the headwall. Lieutenant W.G. Herbert, Lance Corporal Rene Tessier and Rifleman W. Chicoski neutralized a machine gun nest after Dalton placed charges and the Queen's Own moved inland.

GUN SHELTERS UNTOUCHABLE

The New Brunswick North Shore touched

down at 07:40 hrs on the eastern flank of the Canadian beachhead and adjacent to where the British 3rd Division was landing at Lion-sur-Mer. The seawall at St. Aubin, where they landed, was dominated by a concrete gun shelter which the naval bombardment failed to touch. Tanks from the Fort Garry Horse swam in but two tanks were knocked out before the emplacement fell to a Royal Marine Centaur tank mounting a 95mm gun, two Shermans, and the prodding of a petard on an AVRE.

Although the 9th Brigade's three reserve battalions were ashore by 12:30 hrs, the beach and streets leading through Bernières were so jammed that there was a critical delay of three hours in moving inland. It was this delay, and not enemy resistance, which resulted in failure to reach D-Day objectives. A number of factors contributed: rough seas and delayed landings; inability of AVRE craft to clear beaches in time; wreckage blocking access and rising tides which obscured mines and narrowed the beach.

The beaches of Normandy and the man-made harbours on the English Channel would serve as a landing area for weeks to come as troops, tanks and vehicles continued to disembark on the continent.

MINES TAKE TOLL

There were between 12,000 and 14,000 mines on the beach fronting Courselles and Bernières, a distance of about two miles, and they took a heavy toll after the original touch-down. The landing craft which had delivered the first wave of the North Shore and Queens Own began setting off mines as soon as they went into reverse. One quarter were sunk. Reserve battalions such as the Canadian Scottish at Courselles were held up on the beach because of minefields and came under heavy mortar fire. The leading company of Le Régiment de la Chaudière, which followed the Queen's Own, lost all but five landing craft.

In Courselles, there was continued fighting in both the Winnipeg and Regina sectors. One 1st Hussar squadron lost half its tank strength on the beach and nine surviving tanks rumbled inland to support infantry. They hadn't cleared the village before five more were knocked out.

Sergeant Leo Gariepy suspected that the road flanked by a continuous brick wall was mined so he swung off. However, the only course open to him on the other side of the wall was to smash through 17 property walls which ran out to the road. Gariepy was so attracted to the walls of Courselles that he returned after the war and took up residence. For decades he was a friend and guide to visiting Canadians.

A LEARNING EXPERIENCE?

The North Shores touched down about 19:40 hrs on the left flank of Juno at St. Aubin where an enemy strongpoint consisting of one 50 mm gun and several machine guns dominated the beach. The New Brunswickers moved inland to Tailleville where they fought for six hours before taking it. Although 6 June was a learning experience for every man on the beach, Jack Marshall was probably the only one there in an official learning capacity. The future senator landed with the North Shores as a pre-officer cadet assigned to a Bren carrier platoon.

Somehow this experience was designed to help him with officer training if he survived. Much of the day was a blur as they drove from point to point but one aspect stands out. A German prisoner on the carrier tried to turn the gun on Marshall. The young trainee from Cape Breton responded with a rifle butt and the German departed the speeding carrier.

The 9th Brigade with the Sherbrook Fusiliers landed at Bernières-sur-Mer and by late afternoon the Canadians were firmly anchored on the continent. Forward elements such as the North Nova Scotias were within three miles of Caen. A 19-man platoon of the Winnipeg Rifles dug in at dark. During the night they heard a force marching towards them. They sent up a flare and within a few minutes collected 110 prisoners.

GLIMPSE OF THE FUTURE

Although they had not achieved the objectives set in quiet contemplation, the Canadians made as deep a penetration as any army along the invasion front with a loss of 358 dead and 715 wounded. Most of the engagements beyond the beach were skirmishes and houseclearing. But on the afternoon of 6 June, a hint of things to come occurred to the left of the Canadians. The 21st German Panzer division exploited the gap between the Canadians and the British until the Shropshires and the Staffordshire Yeomanry's anti-tank guns inflicted heavy losses on their Mark IV's. They withdrew, failing to reach the coast, but their presence set the tone for what was to follow beyond the beaches.

REPRINTED FROM:
Esprit de Corps, *Volume 4 Issue 1*
AUTHOR: *Norm Shannon*

SEALANES TO NORMANDY

Canada's navy assisted in mine sweeping preparations for the D-Day assault. They also provided troop transport and covering fire for the landing.

ABOVE: *Mulberry harbours – man-made harbours complete with piers, docks and quays – were of great strategic importance during the Normandy invasion because the Germans believed the Allies needed a major port to invade.* (U.S. NATIONAL ARCHIVES)
LEFT: *In heavy seas whipped by strong winds, anxious troops made their journey for shore aboard LCAs (Landing Craft Assault) from HMCS* Prince Henry. *(NAC/PA 132790)*

LATE IN THE AFTERNOON of 5 June, the HMCS *Caraquet* slipped out of port and led nine Canadian minesweepers across the English Channel. Six more were working with the Royal Navy that afternoon. Their task was to clear the turbulent channel of mines and prepare lanes for the invasion fleet of 6000 ships.

Canada's contribution to the naval operation was 107 varied vessels and some 10,000 men. As swift Canadian Motor Torpedo Boats (MTBs) swept the channel to the north, the coxswain of clumsy infantry landing craft prepared themselves for the much less glamorous work of landing a barge in rough seas. The sweepers were closely followed by trawlers loaded with dan-buoys which marked the route to Normandy and whose bobbing lights guided ship after ship through the proper lane. The Canadian sweep flotilla finished its job about 03:00 hrs on D-Day a mile and a half off Omaha beach.

Within two hours, 366 vessels of all sizes churned through a rough area ten miles deep and five miles wide off Juno beach where the Canadians were to land. Canada's naval responsibilities fell into several broad areas. Troop transport was first, as the *Prince Henry* and the *Prince Robert* dropped anchor and prepared to transfer the Canadian Scottish and the Chaudière into landing craft. Destroyers HMCS *Algonquin* and *Sioux* formed part of the transport escort and soon would provide covering fire for the landing.

CHOPPY SEAS

Eight Landing Craft Assaults (LCA) were dropped into choppy seas and coxswains and crews fought to keep the clumsy machines steady while a platoon of 30 men filled each of them. They followed a wave of Landing Craft Tanks and were followed by a flotilla of larger craft which came directly from England loaded with AVRE tanks, breaching vehicles, guns and an assortment of Hobart's funnies.

As the assault force moved towards shore, warships saturated the beaches with thousands of shells and several small craft with heavy loads and small engines failed to cope and had to be towed. One out of nine reached the right of Mike beach.

As the tide started to drop, the mines on

Mike beach and heavy machine-gun and mortar fire raked craft from the *Prince David*. Only one reached the beach undamaged yet they got the troops ashore.

LCAs ATTACKED

The commander of a group of five Landing Craft Assaults (LCA) reported three quarters of the troops had been disembarked from one craft when an explosion blew in the port side. On another the port side was blown away after one-third of the men were evacuated. A third was holed and suffered a damaged starboard bow, and an explosion ripped the bottom out of a fourth and a fifth suffered the same damage. Yet, somehow, the Royal Canadian Navy survived the day without a fatal casualty and with only a few wounded.

When the beachhead was established, the navy's job had just begun. The Canadian flotillas had put 4600 men ashore but even before nightfall a shuttle service to England had been established and it was to grow to prodigious proportions in the following weeks. Mulberry harbours were established and a massive build-up of men and equipment proclaimed that the allies were in France to stay.

REPRINTED FROM:
Esprit de Corps,
Volume 4 Issue 1
AUTHOR:
Colonel (ret'd)
Strome Galloway

NEWS AT NINE

The best in army public relations soon brings out the best in Canadian war correspondents as they combine to bring the war news to Canada.

NINE MEN TOLD CANADIANS all they needed to know about the biggest invasion in history. They landed after the first wave at various places along Juno beach, each looking for his own war to report to the Canadian people.

The Canadian Press was represented by Ross Munro and William Stewart. Marcel Ouimet and Matthew Halton were from the CBC, while Ralph Allen of the Toronto *Globe and Mail* was selected to represent combined daily newspapers. Lionel Shapiro was with the North American Newspaper Alliance and a fuzzy-cheeked Charles Lynch covered for Reuters. Ron Clark was with British United Press and Joe Willicombe represented International News.

In addition to War Correspondents (WARCOs), the CBC fielded a battered recording van and technical staff.

Considering the hand-to-hand combat seen nightly in media scrums on Parliament Hill in the 1990s, one has to conclude that there is a strong element of competition in news gathering. That element existed on D-Day, but the men in a fiercely competitive business became partners in history once they dropped off the landing craft.

THE PRESS CORPS

The story of the Press Corps is also the story of army Public Relations and a dedicated group of conducting officers who literally went ashore hand-in-hand with the WARCOs and guided them around Normandy.

For Marcel Ouimet, later president of CBC, dropping off the landing craft was part of what war correspondents had been trained to do. At Bernières-sur-Mer, Ouimet dropped off with a typewriter in his left hand and his right hand holding that of conducting officer Captain Bill Cornforth. Ouimet dropped into water up to his chin. Alas Cornforth was a shorter man and soon Marcel was looking at a helmet, trying to break water like a turtle.

Ouimet recalled: "When we got a few paces forward and his head emerged, salt water was coming out of his ears, out of his nose and out of his helmet."

ABOVE: *Lieutenant Colonel Richard S. Malone hangs the sign over the editorial offices of the Canadian Army's newspaper,* The Maple Leaf.
(CANADIAN ARMY PHOTO 36423-N)

Some of the correspondents were veterans of Sicily and Italy where Colonel Dick Malone brought together the public's desire to know with military security. A pre-war journalist and militia officer, Malone was wounded in Sicily but later, as advisor to Montgomery, greatly influenced Canadian Army and allied PR policy. By D-Day Malone was in charge of Canadian army PR and his influence also enlightened the British army.

Colonel Malone believed WARCOs to be vital members of the armed forces with the right to report what they saw, provided it didn't jeopardize security. He insisted on formal and informal briefings for WARCOs along with conducting officers, transportation, food and accommodations. They could also go into a battle zone if accompanied by a conducting officer. Such were the ground rules already established in Sicily and Italy. In Normandy they revolutionized war coverage.

FILING COPY

Ross Munro started his first story in a wardroom aboard ship on the night before the landing. He worked all night and two hours after the Canadians hit the beach the first was complete, but Munro was confronted with the problem of getting it back to CP in London. An obliging naval officer got the story onto a destroyer leaving for England. Somehow it was fast-tracked through the Ministry of Information to the Canadian Press and thence to Canada.

In the hours after the invasion, the only sure way of getting copy to England was to hand it to somebody on a craft returning to England. During this period, Canadian army PR Captain Jack Wilson became a virtual copy boy with wet socks who spent most of his time wading out to craft with copy for England.

Charles Lynch had taken the precaution of bringing a number of homing pigeons with him. It worked for Reuters during the Crimean War but to Lynch's dismay his pigeons, when released with dispatches, flew gleefully towards Paris as if keeping a rendezvous with pigeon pie.

With camera in hand, war correspondents and photographers experienced the mix of exhilaration and apprehension of the D-Day landings. The blurriness of the photo adds realism as the first wave of soldiers disembarked from their landing craft at Courcelles. ***(NATIONAL FILM BOARD)***

WRITING IN TRENCHES

Ouimet landed at Bernières-sur-Mer with the Chaudière and although heavy shelling had subsided, they were still getting fire from 88's. Ouimet sat with his back to the seawall and banged out his first piece. Bill Stewart landed at Courselles, where western units had taken heavy casualties. He dug a slit trench on the beach and wrote his first story as wounded were brought down from the town where fighting continued.

Conducting officers Roy Oliver and Placide Labelle dutifully sought out a house for press headquarters at Courselles. They entered and found the place full of Germans who were even more surprised than the Canadians. They surrendered. While Oliver rushed out for reinforcement, Labelle held the enemy captive with a shovel as his gun was in the jeep. Labelle, Matt Halton and Stewart later worked their way inland where they spent the night between sheets as guests of a French farmer.

INSOMNIA

Correspondents in Bernières didn't have it quite so lucky. They spent the night in slit trenches in an orchard which was part of divisional headquarters. They tried to sleep but warnings of possible German parachute attacks induced insomnia. Then they were bombed in the heaviest enemy air action seen that day. Within a week, enemy action forced the press corps to abandon two headquarters. When the Château at Courselles was hit, the WARCOs were in shelters but much of their transportation was damaged. A Château outside of Beny almost seemed a step up until a British armoured brigade moved in and became the object of attention by German artillery. After heavy shelling, and loss of equipment, the WARCOs withdrew.

During the next month, WARCOs combed the front individually or in pairs in the company of conducting officers. Ross Munro was able to get to the 1st Canadian Parachute Bn after three attempts to cross the Benouville bridge which was under persistent enemy shelling. He found the men who were to hold the vital positions on the Orne for 11 days.

AFTERNOON FOOTBALL?

Beyond Beny-sur-Mer some 200 Germans held out in a fortified radar station. It was bypassed by the Canadians on D-Day. Highlanders of the 51st Division failed to take it a few days later and 12 days after the invasion the Royal Marine Commandos and assault engineers took a hand in neutralizing the station which was already not functioning. It was like a Saturday afternoon football game. Invitations went out to the press and seats were provided in a church steeple. Charlie Lynch unlimbered his portable and waited for the games to begin.

Artillery blasted the massive strong points. Assault engineers moved flails through the barbed wire and minefields, exploding a path for the marines. Some German tanks responded but were soon knocked out. The marines moved in shooting from the hip and then the German garrison surrendered. The sight of marching prisoners was to become very familiar to WARCOs in the months ahead as they followed the Canadians into Germany on the *Maple Leaf Up* route.

While the performance of Canadian troops on this long march was laudatory and in the best of military traditions, it was matched by that of the war correspondents and army PR which brought the war home to the people of Canada.

REPRINTED FROM:
Esprit de Corps, *Volume 4 Issue 1*
AUTHOR: *Norman Shannon*

REMEMBER THE D-DAY DODGERS

The D-Day landings upstage the occupation of Rome and the questionable Italian campaign is soon forgotten as well as the heroism of the men who fought there.

LEFT: *Almost 6000 Canadians lost their lives in Sicily and Italy. Padre Roy C.H. Durnford conducted numerous burial services during his tour of duty, this one after the heavy fighting at San Leonardo in December 1943.* (NAC/PA 167913)

THE OLD CONTEMPTIBLES, Kitchener's Mob, the Red Chevrons and now the D-Day Dodgers. These were in their times British and Canadian warriors of special note. The first three have passed away, but the thinning ranks of the D-Day Dodgers should not be ignored.

As of midnight on 4 August 1914 the British and German empires were at war. Within 19 days a British expeditionary force of 80,000 regulars was engaging the German invaders of Belgium along the Mons-Condé canal. The Kaiser called his British opponents a "contemptible little army." The name stuck as a title of honour and after the war the surviving British regulars who had fought so gallantly at Mons gloried in their name of The Old Contemptibles.

On the outbreak of World War One Lord Kitchener was appointed War Minister and immediately called for 100,000 volunteers. Britain's young manhood responded and without uniforms or weapons began to turn from civvies into soldiers, calling themselves "Kitchener's Mob." Thousands of them died at Loos and in the Battle of the Somme.

RED, WHITE AND BLUE CHEVRONS

Meanwhile, in Canada the first 30,000 volunteers mustered at Valcartier, sailing for England within two months of the declaration of war. Later in the war Canadian soldiers were issued with coloured chevrons indicating years of overseas service. These chevrons were sewn on the right cuff, red for the 1914 men, blue for subsequent years. The 1914 men dubbed themselves "the Red Chevrons" and organized post-war Red Chevron clubs where they, "the first to fight," could gather as a select group of veterans. A similar system was adopted in the Second World War, a white chevron being awarded for overseas service during the first year of the war, red ones for each of the five following years of overseas service. The 1939 volunteers did not apparently value their white chevron as much as the 1914 veterans valued their red one. This was probably because the first year of the war saw no fighting for Canadian troops, though the men who wore it were proud enough of it during the war, it was not of sufficient meaning to remain a symbol of anything special. The first year of WWII had seen no battlefield epic for Canada's soldiers, such as the magnificent stand by the Red Chevrons in the face of the gas attack at Ypres in April 1915.

OLD CONTEMPTIBLES

To the man in the street "D-Day" means only one thing, the day the British-Canadian-American forces under General Eisenhower landed on the Normandy coast – 6 June 1944. But to many Canadian soldiers this date has little, if any, significance. They are the "D-Day Dodgers" – something like the Old Contemptibles, the Kitchener's Mob, the Red Chevrons of 1939-45. They are the survivors of the 93,000 Canadians who served in Sicily and Italy months before the Normandy landings – especially those assault troops who waded ashore on the two D-Days of 1943.

These "D-Day Dodgers," some of them with these two other D-Days to their credit, suffered more than 26,000 casualties, which is one in every four who served in Sicily and Italy. Of these, almost 6,000 were killed-in-action. When one realizes that thousands of men are back-of-the-line troops the ratio is higher.

DODGING RISK?

The term "D-Day Dodger" is attributed to Lady Astor, a British Member of Parliament, who, in the House of Commons spoke of the campaign in Italy as being, in her opinion, of limited value to the Allied cause. She claimed that the troops in that theatre were "dodging" the greater task by not being back in England to increase the invasion force being assembled to land in Normandy.

Having conquered Sicily and most of Italy in co-operation with their allies, and having suffered in loss of life and limb long before the Normandy D-Day, the "D-Day Dodgers" came to glory in their ill-sound-

ABOVE:
For the 93,000 Canadians who served in the Italian and Sicilian campaigns Lady Astor's belief that they were "dodging" the war because they were not part of the Normandy force was an unintended insult to the valour and honour earned in battle.
(NATIONAL FILM BOARD)

ing nickname. Later in the war the Canadian government decided to withdraw the Canadian troops from Italy. After 22 months away from their own Canadian Army they rejoined it in the Rhineland for the final victory campaign in Holland and Germany. But they remained proud of their accomplishments in Sicily, in the Daunia Mountains, at Ortona, on the Hitler and Gothic Lines and in the winter campaign in the Po Valley.

IT'S ABOUT TIME

Perhaps the feeling of the D-Day Dodgers as to their role in the war and the part played by those Canadians who up to then had remained in the United Kingdom until the Normandy invasion, was best expressed to the writer on 6 June 1944, when, after the Dodgers had broken the Hitler Line, and thereby assisted in the capture of Rome, it was announced that 3rd Canadian Division had that day landed on the coast of France.

"Well, Sir," the Orderly Room Sergeant said to me, as he sat typing out our battalion's casualty list, "It's about time those bastards did something."

Spur of the moment remarks often offend and they usually are regretted as no doubt this remark was. The 3rd Division did 'something' on 6 June 1944, and did a lot more in the following 11 months. But the D-Day Dodgers had done something during the previous 11 months, and continued to do something during the following 11 months as well.

When honouring the memory of those Canadians who, with their British and American allies, stormed the Normandy beaches, and those who followed them in post-invasion operations in France and Holland, also pause and remember the D-Day Dodgers, especially those nearly 6000 who lie in their graves in Sicily and Italy. Lady Astor's insult ended up as a badge of honour.

REPRINTED FROM:
Esprit de Corps, *Volume 4 Issue 1*
AUTHOR:
Colonel (ret'd) Strome Galloway

BEYOND THE BEACH

The days following the D-Day landing were no less difficult for the Canadians as they moved slowly toward Caen.

OBJECTIVES FOR THE CANADIANS on D-Plus One were to reach the original D-Day objective which was a line running south of the Caen-Bayeux highway extending from Carpiquet airport to Putot-en-Bessin. On the right the Winnipegs and the Reginas moved forward to take Putot-en-Bessin while a company of the Reginas got a bit further south to Norey-en-Bessin. The Canadian Scottish moved up to the rear of these units and shortly after noon the objectives were secured.

On the left flank elements of the North Nova Scotia Highlanders and the Sherbrooke Fusiliers rolled towards Carpiquet. During the night there had been skirmishes with troops of the 21st Panzer Division and a tank threat on the exposed Canadian left flank. The North Novas rode universal carriers behind the Fusiliers' tanks followed by a platoon of machine-gunners from the Camerons and a troop from the 3rd Anti-Tank Regiment. Three companies of Highlanders on Shermans brought up the rear. As they approached Buron enemy fire intensified and they also came under mortar fire from nearby high ground.

LONGEST THREE MILES

Elements of the North Nova Scotia Highlanders and the Sherbrooke Fusiliers got to within a mile of Carpiquet. Three miles to their right stood Caen. It was the longest three miles in either regiment's history because the enemy had launched his first major counter-attack. It caught C Company of the North Novas in the village of Authie where they underwent heavy shelling with no hope of defensive fire, having outrun the range of their artillery and being unable to call up naval fire. In the tall grass outside

***ABOVE**: Infantry and tanks make their way into Normandy. Heading towards Caen, they would encounter heavy resistance from German forces.* (CAMERA PRESS)

the village tanks swirled in combat and the village was overrun. Although some members of C Company escaped to Buron less than a mile to the north, most of the Company was killed or taken prisoner.

The enemy had penetrated Buron and it was noon before the Highlanders won a precarious victory. Although the village was reasonably secure, the surrounding area was awash with enemy troops and tanks. Survivors from Authie made their way back in ones and twos and throughout the afternoon there was hand-to-hand fighting in the fields and by late evening the relentless enemy tide pushed into Buron and captured A Company positions.

The village of Les Buissons, a mile north of Buron, now became the fall-back position for the Canadians. That morning they had moved off in an offensive war. By evening they were digging in, desperately trying to keep the enemy's infantry and armour from breaking through to the beach beyond. As the North Novas and Fusiliers prepared for their second night in Normandy, the North Novas counted 84 killed and 158 wounded or missing. The Fusiliers had 21 tanks knocked out, seven damaged and 60 men killed. But they had knocked out more than 30 tanks during the day and this was probably a factor in a relatively quiet night.

THE THREE MILES TO CAEN WERE THE LONGEST IN EITHER REGIMENT'S HISTORY DUE TO THE FACT THAT THE ENEMY HAD LAUNCHED HIS FIRST MAJOR COUNTER-ATTACK.

WITHDRAWAL UNDER SMOKE

On the morning of 8 June, the enemy applied pressure to the other flank of the Canadian line held by the 7th Brigade. The 25th Panzers virtually encircled the Winnipegs and then with tanks made the final attack. The Winnipegs fought until ammunition was running low, then three companies withdrew under smoke and the Germans occupied most of Putot.

Rifleman Bob Smellie and John Thompson lay down covering fire to allow the remains of their C Company to escape. Then they put down smoke and escaped across a field to later join their platoon. Thompson, however, was soon dead, one of 58 Winnipeggers murdered by the 12th SS.

One company of the Reginas had moved to Norey-en-Bessin, to the east and south of Putot, while the rest of the battalion was at Bretteville. By mid-afternoon a large force of enemy tanks formed behind the Canadians but failed to attack when a squadron of Sherbrookes, with tanks fresh off the landing craft, rumbled towards Camilly. Norey was attacked in the afternoon and at dusk a large force struck at Bretteville. The 3rd Anti-Tank Regiment threw up defensive fire but some tanks penetrated to within 300 yards of the Canadian headquarters and for an hour and a half shot up the town. During the night of wild shoot-ups, 22 German tanks circled battalion headquarters but the Canadians managed to hold Bretteville.

EXCELLENT EXECUTION

When the Reginas became exposed on D-Plus 1, Lieutenant Colonel F.N. Cabledu of the Canadian Scottish was detailed to take Putot. He was assigned tanks from the 1st Hussars, two artillery field regiments and machine-guns and 4.2 mortars from the Camerons of Ottawa. Bringing all elements

RIGHT:
Bailey bridges were erected by engineers across the Odon River so that tanks and infantry of the 2nd Canadian Division could move into position south of Caen.
(PAC/PA 131392)

together at the precise time, especially with pockets of fighting throughout the area, was a stroke of excellent execution and luck.

The artillery barrage started at 08:30 hrs and a squadron of tanks rolled down from the north just as the infantry companies moved to the start line. The Scottish moved off, breasting fields of grain as enemy fire tore gaps in their ranks. Artillery and Cameron mortar fire responded as well as the Sherman tanks and the Canadians once again fought their way into Putot. Here they rescued some of the Winnipegs who had remained behind and had fought down to virtually the last round of ammunition.

STATIC WAR

Two days after the landings, the war of movement became static with both sides hinting at victory: the allies had landed but were unable to advance; the enemy counter-attacked furiously but was unable to break through to the coast. The war evolved into company or even squad actions at crossroads or villages Canadians had never heard of but would never forget.

At Le Mesnil-Patry 1st Hussar tank crews learned the bitter lesson of German 88mm efficiency when they roared into the west of Carpiquet airport without even pausing to arrange fire support. The lead squadron lost 19 of 21 tanks. The tanks had 80 casualties while the Queen's Own lost 55 dead and 44 wounded.

By now the facts of life were known to Canadian tank men. Their Shermans were very vulnerable to enemy 88mm shells especially in the weak lower front section which became a popular target.

Sherman 75mm shells simply bounced off the enemy Panther tank. One variety of Sherman with a 17 pounder gun was able to cope with the German tanks but they were not in wide distribution. It was during this period that the PIAT anti-tank gun came into its own.

TEN-DAY CLEANUP

For about ten days after the landing, action in the British sector consisted of cleaning up isolated strong points or fighting a defensive war. This was followed by a period during which units regrouped and supplies poured in. The battered Winnipegs became reserves and training schools were set up at depots where cooks were taught how to handle a rifle.

When there was not significant Canadian or British movement for a month, there was grumbling at SHEAF by Americans disenchanted with Montgomery's lack of progress. General Montgomery countered with the rationalization that he was deliberately drawing enemy strength to the British sector to give the Americans a chance to break through.

He never did indicate how he would oppose the massed German forces if it started to move against him. Fortunately, the Germans believed that the entire Normandy operation was a feint to draw forces from the Pas de Calais. The Eisenhower-Montgomery war raged for over a month before the Canadians and British moved against Caen, an objective some Canadians had been looking at since D-Day.

TOP LEFT:
The crew of a German Tiger tank, hidden inside a shattered building, lie in wait, ready to pounce on their unsuspecting enemy.

TOP RIGHT:
As the Germans retreated further inland, snipers were left behind to slow down the advance of the Allied forces.
(PIX)

REPRINTED FROM:
Esprit de Corps, *Volume 4 Issue 1*
AUTHOR:
Norman Shannon

WHEN THE DEVIL CAME TO THE ABBEY

In its 800-year history the Abbey of the Ardennes saw no crimes to match the murder of Canadian prisoners-of-war.

SWALLOWS HAVE TAKEN OVER the Abbey of the Ardennes and perhaps they can put it to better use than man has for the past 800 years. With vaulted dome and clean gothic lines, the chapel is a textbook of how Europe emerged from the dark ages. But there are names scrawled on stone pillars which date back to the 13th Century; names of friars whose chants filled the Abbey for centuries. Across the courtyard, in what was once a stable, you'll find other names carved on stone, Canadian soldiers executed in the Abbey in June 1944.

June 6 was a day of confusion and frustration for SS Colonel Kurt Meyer. Because nobody dared wake Hitler from a drug-induced sleep, orders for German troops were not cut until at least six hours after the landings. Meyer's first orders were to attack British and Canadian paratroops who had landed during the night and held bridges over the Orne and the Caen Canal. Meyer's regiment started towards the enemy strong points but heavy bombing and strafing forced them to spend four hours in a ditch. Then the orders were changed. Meyer's men were poised for an attack in the fields of St. Germain.

HITLER YOUTH FANATICS

Meyer's regiment was composed of Hitler Youth fanatics and seasoned killers from the Russian campaign where the regiment had distinguished itself as an extremely tough opponent. His headquarters set up in the Abbey, Meyer mounted the winding stone steps of the chapel tower. Through field glasses he saw the Canadians moving rapidly down the road from Buron to Authie.

LEFT: *The smiling face of innocence belies the evil actions the fanatical young soldiers of the Hitlerjugend were capable of carrying out. War correspondent Ralph Allen described the Hitler youth who served with Kurt Meyer's 12th SS Panzer Division as "beardless killers whose highest aim was to die, whose only God was Hitler."* (ULLSTEIN)

THE DEVIL HAD HIS HOUR AND IT SET UP A SAVAGE SEASON OF KILLING. CANADIANS HAD THEIR LONG KNIVES OUT FOR ANYONE IN SS UNIFORM.

Three companies each of Tiger tanks and panzer units waited in concealed positions. The North Novas, supported by the Sherbrooke tanks, got to Authie but Col Charles Petch decided to withdraw to higher ground. Then, Meyer ordered the attack. The next six hours set the tone for the bitter fighting which was to follow. The most savage aspect came that evening as the Canadians withdrew leaving behind wounded and prisoners. Bodies littered the square at Authie, some deliberately dragged into the road where they were crushed by passing trucks and tanks. Twenty-three Canadians were shot after capture, the start of a gruesome campaign of terror.

The incidence of prisoner shootings jumped at an appalling rate as the SS attacked other Canadian units the next day. In one, 40 members of the Winnipeg Rifles and Cameron Highlanders were herded into a field and shot. Five escaped. A padre was taken prisoner unwounded but was found a month later with a bayonet gash in his chest. Within ten days, the SS shot 134 prisoners, most within the shadow of the Abbey.

The best documented case occurred in the Abbey on 8 June when seven Canadians were brought in for interrogation. They were taken to the stable. Meyer was heard to ask one of his officers: "What shall we do with the prisoners?" Then, according to a Polish conscript, Meyer spoke to the officer in a low voice. The officer and a guard then walked to the stable where the officer spoke to the prisoners in English and sneered at one who had tears in his eyes.

An SS corporal went through into a garden, surrounded by a high wall and about the size of the average living room. The officer collected identification papers and then called out the names. As his name was called, each Canadian shook hands with the others and was directed into the garden up six stone steps to where the corporal waited. Seven men marched up the stairs and seven shots exploded, reverberating in the confines of the garden. Occasionally, there was a scream or the crunch of a heavy blow.

DEVIL'S HOUR

The devil had his hour and it set up a savage season of killing. Every Canadian in France seemed to know what happened, and they lost all interest in taking prisoners. The long knives were out for anything in SS uniform. Records indicate how many Canadians were murdered: there is no record of how many SS were killed in retaliation.

One tank commander is still haunted by the ghastly dawn. After a night battle, he saw Canadians crawling amongst the enemy wounded slitting throats. This terrible

THE DEVIL THEY DIDN'T KNOW

BELOW: *Tried for the murder of Canadian prisoners of war, the commander of the 12th SS Division, Major General Kurt Meyer, was found guilty by a military court and sentenced to be shot. However, Canadian Major General Chris Vokes later commuted his sentence to life imprisonment. (DND)*

ABOVE: *As Canadian soldiers advanced inland, they were met with stiffened resistance from SS Panzer Divisions. (CAMERA PRESS / PIX)*

dimension of war applied only to SS and by the middle of August they ceased to exist. Kurt Meyer was later convicted on three counts as a war criminal and sentenced to be shot. He served some time in New Brunswick's Dorchester penitentiary and was transferred to a prison in Werl, Germany. After about nine years he was released and ended up selling beer to another generation of Canadian soldiers.

At the Abbey of the Ardennes, Jean Marie Vicos has turned the property into a prosperous farm. He and his brother Michael were not there at the time of the shooting, but with the Underground. Michael later found 19 bodies in his garden which has become part shrine, part chamber of horrors. As if to exorcise the devil, the Vicos brothers have erected a shrine of a crucifix, cut flowers and a rusted helmet. Vegetation has grown thick and dark, shutting out the light. The shrine does not penetrate the gloom but it does say something for man's anguish.

REPRINTED FROM:
Esprit de Corps, *Volume 4 Issue 1*
AUTHOR: *Norman Shannon*

On the second day of the invasion Jack Veness and Jack Fairweather were captured at Buron but later escaped and joined an under-ground unit led by an underworld figure.

WHEN KURT MEYER CLIMBED the Abbey steps, he came to "prey" and his victims were Canadians. Lieutenant Jack Veness was leading a platoon on the outskirts of Buron when Meyer's tanks and artillery opened fire. The encounter was swift and savage but the North Novas had fought their way down the road to Authie when they were overrun. Veness and fellow New Brunswicker Lieutenant Jack Fairweather were among the first to go into the bag and were marched to the Abbey of Ardenne. At Authie, Veness had seen one prisoner shot and another run over by a truck. The body of a friend was desecrated when the enemy put a beer bottle in his hand and a German helmet on his head. Within hours hell would be in session for many POWs, but Veness and Fairweather were lucky.

"We were marched out of the Abbey to a school on the outskirts of Caen," Veness recalls. "We spent the night there without incident and the next morning started a march 144 miles to Rennes." They covered about 35 miles a day for four days and rested on the fifth. American Mustangs strafed the column, killing 25 and wounding 12. After a month in the camp at Rennes, 31 prisoners were put onto a train.

"We were put into a boxcar and shunted around France, spending a lot of time in sidings under allied bombing and strafing," he said. The heat, the close quarters and the air attacks frayed nerves. During a bombing about two weeks later, one of the officers went berserk and tried to kick his way through the front of the boxcar. By the time he was restrained his comrades noticed that shrapnel had weakened the spot where he had been kicking. One man's outburst of agony

LEFT:
Fairweather and Vaness joined the French Maquis resistance organization known as the Groupe Le Coz. Named after its leader, Captain Georges Lecoze (standing at left) who had at one time been an officer with the Foreign Legion.

eventually led to escape as others worked the spot with a knife, a spoon and a hammer. German guards occupied the next car so all the work had to be done while the train was in motion.

SUDDEN FRESH AIR

The interior of the car was cramped and stuffy. Veness remember he had dozed off when a sudden rush of fresh air and the clatter of wheels woke him. A form slipped through the opening. He shook Fairweather awake and they agreed to jump five seconds apart. Veness crawled through the opening headfirst and straddled the buffers which were jumping like pistons on the rough roadbed. Three other officers were standing on the buffers waiting for the train to slow down. Then they disappeared into the night like chewing gum wrappers discarded from a speeding car.

Fairweather got stuck in the opening but finally edged free in time to kick Veness' hand away from the buffer disks as he tried to get a footing. Veness was seconds away from being handless as the disks smashed together on the rough road. Then Veness stood briefly, took a deep breath and vanished. Sparks traced his passage in the dark as boots slammed into the roadbed. His roll ended in a ditch, chest burning, hands wet with blood. Fairweather landed in a pile of nettles. They lay there for some seconds watching the light on the last car disappear.

But a crisis was building in the prison car. The 16th man to try to escape was a portly American colonel who got stuck in the hole. The next morning an irate German major lined up the 16 remaining prisoners and selected ten for execution. The sentence was not carried out but the 15 escapees soon had prices on their heads and German troops had orders to shoot them on sight.

Veness and Fairweather wandered aimlessly for eight days, sleeping in barns, sheds and a church steeple. Eight years ago Veness got a card from a villager of Luizelle, a panoramic view which features the church where the Canadians hid. French civilians managed to get food to them. "But we didn't make much progress," Veness remembers, "because after a week we were still only about a dozen miles from where we jumped."

BIZARRE ADVENTURES

Near Tours they joined a Maquis band, as did most of the escapees, and began one of the most bizarre adventures of the war. Although thousands of allied evaders worked with the underground under difficult circumstances during the war, most worked with people they could trust. But while the group to which Veness and Fairweather turned for help attracted some patriots, it also attracted brigands and thieves; the biggest of which was its leader who was then going by the name of George Lecoze. At the time, the band offered the hope of freedom but Lecoze's personal agenda soon raised fears that perhaps all the escapees had exchanged a devil they knew for one they didn't.

The band they joined was led by a brutal, psychopathic killer who according to one of his own men had more atrocities to this credit than Himmler, (he'd only been in the Maquis business seven weeks). A de Gaulle lookalike in a rented or stolen uniform, he was chosen to lead the newly-formed Maquis group although some protested that they knew nothing about the man who wandered into the locality the previous March. When confronted by the fact that the man, then known as Dr. Jan, was a swine, a politician agreed but argued that France had great need of such swine. It was the classic Western scenario of the gunfighter being hired to clean up the town and then turning on its wimpish citizens. This is essentially what happened at Loches where the plot was complicated by the fact that Dr. Jan (or Captain Lecoze) was George Dubosq, a small-time thief with a long criminal record, including being a *Gestapo* informer.

ABOVE LEFT AND MIDDLE:
Captured when the 12th SS Panzer Division overran the North Nova Scotia Highlanders at Authie and Buron on 7 June 1944, Lieutenants Jack Vaness (left) and Jack Fairweather (middle) would spend the next six days in a boxcar with other Allied prisoners.
(WILLIAM R. BIRD, JACK VANESS)

ABOVE RIGHT:
Simple coded messages were relayed to resistance groups through the news broadcasts of the BBC. Members of the French resistance listen intently for the transmission of coded information.

THEFT AND MURDER

On the day of the invasion, Lecoze and two other musqueteers set up headquarters in the outbuildings of a Château near Loches. Their first sortie was to steal a car from a doctor in a nearby village. Then they returned two days later and riddled him with machine gun fire. About a week later they shot a farmer. Two days before Veness and Fairweather were picked up, German troops swept in on Loches and Beaulieu, arresting 60 people, most of them police. Lecoze was suspected of being a double-agent who had a score to settle with most of the people arrested. But as the politician said, France needs its swine and the Maquis Lecoze prospered.

Veness and Fairweather knew nothing of Lecoze's background but soon became suspicious. One evening the band was having dinner in a clearing. Tables consisted of planks drawn up on sawhorses and food and wine was plentiful. Suddenly sentries came out of the woods with six prisoners; young men who were accused of trying to leave the group. Lecoze lined up the prisoners and after kicking and punching them ordered two to be shot. Then after the shooting, he raised his glass, "Vive la France!"

LECOZE CHALLENGED

The new arrivals were soon doing "expeditions": armed sorties of limited military value. One member of the group, a former Legionary, challenged Lecoze's leadership adding that, "I came here to fight Germans not the people of the region." They fought and Lecoze shot him.

At one village the enemy had demanded 50 horses and when the detachment arrived to collect the horses, they were hit by 30 of Lecoze's group. By 16 August, German strength had been drained from Loches. A Maquis convoy paused outside of town and the men formed up in three ranks. Lecoze insisted that Veness and Fairweather march with him at the head of the column as they liberated the town. But the brief moment of victory soon ended in another outburst of terror. Suspected collaborators were lined up in the town square and Lecoze worked himself into a frenzy as he kicked and beat them. One man denied being a collaborator and struck back. He was shot after an ugly scene in the square, a scene which haunts Veness to this day. He wonders if he could have done more.

The liberation of Loches was an ego trip for Lecoze and military insanity. When the enemy mounted a counterattack, Veness was given 20 men to defend a position outside of town. As on all the "expeditions," language was a problem as only two of the 15 escapees spoke any French. The main force of Maquis withdrew from Loches and the town came under heavy fire as the enemy brought up 600 men. After a delaying action, Veness and his group escaped beyond Loches and gradually joined up with survivors at a farm. Thirty Maquis were killed and over 50 wounded, Veness and Fairweather decided to leave and told Lecoze who scowled and said, "Pass over your weapons!"

These were the longest seconds of Jack Veness' life. Although he had not heard of the summer of atrocities, they were marked for instant death if picked up by the Germans. They had joined a band of brigands but there was some protection in numbers. The killings and the blind rages convinced Veness that it was time to leave although a few weeks ago, Lecoze brutally had two men shot for trying to do just that. Veness looked at the faces around him; some were armed punks, some true patriots, but a madman led them. Veness and Fairweather knew how they wanted their war to end and it wasn't with Lecoze. They handed over their weapons and Lecoze finally extended his hand and wished them well.

RESISTANCE ORGANIZERS

The two Canadians and an American pilot worked their way south, meeting other Maquis bands and eventually being brought to the provincial Maquis headquarters. Here they found Major Crown of the Welsh Guards who was a liaison officer organizing resistance.

When Veness told him they had been with Lecoze, the major showed considerable interest because they had been trying to locate him for weeks, but their interest was in burying Lecoze not in praising him. Crown operated a nearby airstrip. Two nights later, he received a message, "Two Daks and a Hudson 12:30." Later that night, Veness and Fairweather were flown to England where their scruffy appearance caused chagrin to well-turned out MP's. Veness later joined his unit in Holland and as a major was the first Canadian army in Germany. Fairweather also returned to action, the youngest major in the Canadian army.

The spring the war ended, French authorities caught up with Lecoze. French justice was slow in its process but swift in execution; that fall a man called Lecoze or Dr. Jan or George Duboscq was tied to a post and shot.

REPRINTED FROM:
Esprit de Corps,
Volume 4 Issue 1
AUTHOR: *Norman Shannon*

MYNARSKI EARNS THE VICTORIA CROSS

Below are the last known words of Andy Mynarski, who sacrificed his life for a friend in a blazing Lancaster.

"AND A GOOD NIGHT TO YOU, SIR"

ABOVE:
His Lancaster shot down by night-fighters as they approached their target just after midnight on 13 June 1944, mid-upper gunner Andy Mynarski risked his life to save a friend. Badly burned and with his parachute on fire, Mynarski died shortly after hitting the ground from his burns and wounds. For his actions he was awarded the VC posthumously.
(PAINTING BY PAUL GORANSON, CWM)

D-DAY WAS SIX DAYS old when the crew of A-Able at Middleton St. George sat on the grass or clowned on the hardstand as the shades of evening deepened and they waited for take-off. Flight Officer Art de Breyne waited impatiently to get his hands on the new Lancaster with 25 hours on her lean frame. The Moose Squadron was converting from Halifaxes to Lancs, and for pilots like de Breyne the new bomber handled like a fighter. Tonight the proximity of the target meant less fuel and even better handling.

The two gunners lay on the grass, enjoying the spring evening. Yesterday Andy Mynarski had been commissioned, and as he chewed grass he probably wondered if this would destroy the private joke he shared with Pat Brophy. Since Mynarski joined the crew as a Sergeant in April, Flight Officer Brophy had become one of his best friends and drinking partners. Evenings at the *Unicorn* in Stockton-on-Tees invariably ended with a ceremony as they headed for different quarters. Brophy would bid Irish, or O'Mynarski, goodnight while the other would solemnly stand to attention and salute, and with a heavy Polish accent proclaim, "Good night, sir."

They had flown 12 operations together, mostly on communications targets. None had been particularly long or difficult although there were indications that German fighter strength was being moved from the defence of Germany to France and Belgium where the allied air forces had been hammering communications. Andy had found a four-leaf clover that he handed to Pat, a gesture that became one of the most symbolic of the war. Deeply touched, Pat conceded that he could use a good omen. After all, it was their 13th operation and they would be over the rail yards at Cambrai minutes into 13 June.

The crew which boarded the aircraft was a particularly close one because of previous linkages. Bob Bodie, the navigator, and Brophy had been roommates at Bournemouth when they first arrived in England, and Jack Friday, the bomb-aimer, came from Pat's hometown of Port Arthur. Friday and Jim Kelly, the wireless air gunner, shared a room, which led to his joining the crew. Roy Vigars, the only British member of the crew, was the flight engineer. When Mynarski joined, he replaced Ken Branston (sidelined with a fractured jaw) as mid-upper.

A-Able lifted off the deck as part of 671 Bomber Command force that was sent against six communications centres in France. From his rear turret, Brophy reported light flak at the coast. Then suddenly they were coned by searchlights. Art de Breyne took evasive action, throwing the Lancaster into a dive and descending into darkness. As they approached the target area, they were still descending when Brophy reported a bogey which struck from six o'clock low.

De Breyne corkscrewed but cannon shells ripped the bomber knocking out both port en-

ABOVE:
Andy Mynarski and his crew had this photo taken upon their return from an air test flight on this newly-built Halifax 2 Series 1a bomber. Front row: Pat Brophy, Roy Vigars, Andy Mynarski. Back row: Jim Kelly, Art de Breyne, Jack Friday, Bob Bodie.
(PHOTO FROM R. BODIE AND ART DE BREYNE)

gines and setting a wing tank ablaze while another shell started a fire between the mid-upper and rear turrets. As the aircraft plunged, the crew listened for orders but the intercom was dead. Then the red light in both turrets blinked dit-da-da-dit which meant P for parachute.

Art de Breyne fought to keep the machine out of a death dive and Jack Friday yanked at the forward escape hatch. When it opened, the up draft smashed it against his head and knocked him unconscious. Roy Vigars struggled to the hatch, pushed Friday through while holding the D-string of his parachute. As Vigars said later, "He floated down in a state of slumber."

Then Vigars fought his own war with the hatch which again jammed in the opening and the Flight Engineer kicked at it for an eternity as Bob Bodie watched from behind de Breyne. Vigars kicked the hatch free and jumped as Bodie and Jim Kelly quickly followed.

ART DE BREYNE FOUGHT TO KEEP THE MACHINE OUT OF A DEATH DIVE AND JACK FRIDAY YANKED AT THE FORWARD ESCAPE HATCH. WHEN IT OPENED, THE UP DRAFT SMASHED IT AGAINST HIS HEAD AND KNOCKED HIM UNCONSCIOUS.

HYDRAULICS KNOCKED OUT

They were now very low. De Breyne jumped and landed abruptly. Four members of his crew had escaped through the forward hatch and this gave the pilot hope that his gunners might also have escaped through the rear hatch. But the cannon shell which started the fire between the turrets knocked out the hydraulics which controlled the rear turret. Brophy was locked at an angle where he could not get out or even reach his parachute in the aircraft. He pried open the doors far enough to get his parachute and tried to hand-crank the turret to a beam position. Then the crank handle broke as the flames swept down the fuselage.

Mynarski climbed down from the mid-upper and struggled to the escape hatch. He was about to jump when he looked and saw Brophy through the flames and read the situation. He crawled on hands and knees through flaming oil.

"By the time he reached me in the tail, his uniform and parachute were on fire," Brophy later reported. I screamed, "Go back, Andy! Get out!" Andy grabbed a fire axe and smashed at the turret. He tore at the doors with bare hands, now a mass of flames from the waist down. "When I waved him away again he hung his head and nodded as though he was ashamed to leave."

GOOD NIGHT SIR

Finally, he was forced to crawl backwards through the flames but his eyes never left

his friend. At the escape hatch, he stood up. "Slowly, as he'd often done before in happier times together, he came to attention. Standing there in his flaming clothes, a grimly magnificent figure, he saluted me…just before he jumped, he said something. Even though I couldn't hear, I knew it was 'Good night, sir.'"

Mynarski jumped and Brophy rode the burning bomber and its five tons of bombs on the short trip to the ground. Its flaming port wing hit a tree and snapped the turret doors open, hurling Brophy to safety. Then two of the bombs exploded.

THE REAL STORY

The real story of Andrew Mynarski was not concluded until 13 September when Brophy made it back to England. Two of the crew were taken prisoner and four evaded. Jim Kelly was among the latter. After he came down, while hiding out, a Frenchman reported finding a parachutist who died of burns shortly after landing that night. Painted across the front of his helmet was the name "Andy."

When Brophy documented the story of what happened that night, Andrew Mynarski became one of the few to get the Victoria Cross on the testimony of a single witness.

"SLOWLY, AS HE'D OFTEN DONE BEFORE IN HAPPIER TIMES TOGETHER, HE CAME TO ATTENTION. STANDING THERE IN HIS FLAMING CLOTHES, A GRIMLY MAGNIFICENT FIGURE, HE SALUTED ME... [SAYING] 'GOOD NIGHT, SIR.'"

REPRINTED FROM:

Esprit de Corps, *Volume 5 Issue 8*

AUTHOR:

Norman Shannon

ABOVE:

De Breyne's Lancaster is shot down by a Junkers JuM88 at 13 minutes past midnight on 13 June 1944. This 13th mission would be the last for Andy Mynarski.

(PAINTING BY DON CONNOLLY)

PRAYERS BEFORE CAEN

Canadians spend a month within sight of Caen, a British objective on D-Day. Soon after landing they are engaged by savage SS troops who murder prisoners.

THE FIRST CANADIAN Army that formed up in northwest Europe in 1944-1945 was the largest military formation ever to be commanded by a Canadian. It surpassed in size (if not skill) the magnificent Canadian Corps of 1917-1918 and, like it, was destined to strive across the same region of France and Belgium that claimed so many lives only 26 years before. Flanders and the Somme valley would have to wait, however, until the job of putting a "cork" in a bottled up collection of angry Germans was accomplished in Normandy.

The sons of Great War veterans spent much of their time defending England against an invader who would not show up. When they did see action it tended to be bloody, as at Dieppe, or plain bloody awful, as in Italy after 1943. The government of Mackenzie King was very careful about committing Canada's soldiers to the global conflict, but knew enough to up the political stakes when national prestige was on the table. The Americans were expanding their forces rapidly, and Canada could not be seen as a laggard. Canadian troops in England needed battle experience for the inevitable return to France, and what better way than to commit the 1st Division to Sicily and Italy, the "soft underbelly of Europe." Shipping in 1943 was scarce, but a way was worked out to also transfer the warm bodies of the 5th Armoured Division into the tanks of the 7th British Armoured Division when they were in Italy. Canadians and British agreed the experience would be helpful, and that the resulting Corps formation could be returned to England in time for the Normandy

***ABOVE LEFT:** The Queen's Own Rifles of Canada use their Wasp flamethrower vehicles near Vaucelles in July 1944. (PAC/PA 130187)*
***ABOVE RIGHT:** In preparation for Operation CHARNWOOD, the city of Caen came under heavy artillery fire and was the target of Allied bombers. This destruction reduced the city to rubble, making the streets virtually impassable but providing snipers with ideal coverage. (NAC/PA 116510)*

invasion. Ironically, the opposite effect was achieved: 1st Canadian Corps was tangled in the Italian campaign until the winter of 1944, and all their hard-won battle experience was sorely missed by their colleagues in Normandy.

MAGNIFICENT CANADIANS

Canadian soldiers, overwhelmingly amateur and recently civilian, performed magnificent feats nonetheless. Third Division troops accomplished the furthest penetrations of D-Day, 6 June 1944, and seemed poised to conquer the important city of Caen. What was mere miles away at midnight 6 June, however, ended up costing a month of bloody fighting, hundreds of Canadians dead, and a series of painful lessons on interservice cooperation.

The city of Caen counted 55,000 souls before the Allies and Germans made it their killing ground. Theatre commander General Montgomery would explain that he had every intention of using Caen as an anvil against which to hammer German Panther tanks, ostensibly to draw them away from the American front. If his purpose was to simply draw strength, his attacks succeeded, but some historians suggest it is an excuse to explain the clumsy use of tanks, heavy bombers, and exposed infantry in numerous piecemeal thrusts. At ground level individual Canadian soldiers could think only of the next farmhouse or hedgerow, and try not to think of the horrors they often witnessed there.

On 7 June the North Nova Scotia Highlanders, supported by gasoline-powered Shermans of the 27th Armoured Regiment, Sherbrooke Fusiliers, drove up the road into the villages of Buron and Authie. The Sherman was a reliable if underpowered and outgunned tank of American design, and its gasoline engine tended to ignite easily when struck by enemy shells. Tank crews began to refer to them as "Ronsons" after a popular brand of cigarette lighter; using black humour to cover up for the fact that they would prefer not to be caught dead in one. Tanks were in plentiful supply, however, even if experienced crews were not.

Lack of experience may account in part for the bloody repulse experienced by the North Novas and Sherbrooke Fusiliers that day. D-Day casualties had been made up by green reinforcements who were then sprinkled among tank crews in the hope of averaging out the inexperience. On the fateful day, few crews were composed of battle-hardened veterans, but had trainees at various positions. (Till the end of the war, few Canadian infantry units had the luxury of breaking in their reinforcements either.)

VICIOUS STREAM OF BULLETS

As the North Novas advanced, the gap between themselves and the 7th Brigade opened up. Artillery cover failed to keep pace, and naval guns offshore were out of touch due to radio failure. To the left, British troops had been ordered elsewhere, and unbeknownst to the Canadians, evil eyes followed their progress into Authie. Lieutenant Colonel Charles Petch sensed his vulnerability and ordered his troops to higher ground, but the moment had passed. From the alleys and hedgerows of Authie issued a vicious stream of machine-gun bullets, tank shells, grenades and the blood-curdling screams of the 12th SS Panzer Division led by SS Colonel Kurt Meyer's *Panzergrenadiers*. Shermans brewed up on the spot and infanteers either scrambled across an exposed wheatfield or died where they stood. The North Novas were strung out along the road, and now Buron to their rear was under renewed attack. Captain Hank Fraser, with machine gunners of Ottawa's Cameron Highlanders, fired till their barrels glowed and flung every grenade at the onrushing enemy. His position was overrun.

A Company, under Major Leon Rhodenizer, held a hedgeline throughout the day as Germans bombed and shot their way around them. Surrounded, Rhodenizer was invited to surrender at sundown, but the killings had only begun.

LEFT: *The Fusiliers Mont-Royal take cover behind a Sherman tank as they carefully make their way towards Caen.* *(DND)*

SYSTEMATIC EXECUTION

Incensed SS troopers shot prisoners on a whim at first, and then systematically. The garden of the Abbey of Ardenne was silent witness to dozens of executions, and the blood feud between SS soldiers and Canadians was born. Prisoners of war became an instrument of revenge.

On the 8th, Meyer's 25th SS *Panzergrenadier* launched themselves at the 7th Brigade at Putot-en-Bessin. It was the turn of captured Royal Winnipeg Rifles to be shot, including a stretcher-bearer. 1st Battalion Canadian Scottish retook Putot and stabilized the Third Division front, but for establishing the blood-thirsty ground rules of the next month, the decision went to the *Schutzstaffeln* and *Hitlerjugend*.

In the ensuing weeks, the Allies strove mightily to build up their men and resources within the beach head on Normandy. Flanks were secured and contact was established with neighbouring units until, by 12 June, a bulge of 50 miles wide by 7-10 miles deep was reasonably secure. Over 300,000 men and 54,000 vehicles had been landed, and overhead, Spitfires and Typhoons operated with relative impunity. Hitler cooperated in this consolidation by holding the German 15th Army in the Pas de Calais until it was too late. Canadians satisfied themselves with patrols, preparing for the day they would once again face their tormentors of the SS. On 12 June, the Queen's Own Rifles took up the challenge, but inexperience and bad habits learned in training took their toll. At Les Mesnil-Patry, soldiers rode into town on the hulls of their accompanying armour. The Germans took full advantage by blasting the 1st Hussar tanks with machine guns and their famous 88 mm guns. D Company of the Queen's Own Rifles was shattered, though some Canadians did reach the farmhouses in front of them. The Hussars limped back with two Shermans out of 19 committed to battle.

SHORT REPRIEVE

Third Division was given a two-week reprieve and a chance to contemplate 1017 dead and 1814 wounded for a week of intense combat. Artillery from both sides ensured that there was no rest, nor a day when another casualty did not sadden a family back home. The fighting had been frustrating, and it was time to finish the job regardless of the opposition. The frustration of the slow, slogging match reached into the highest strategic consideration.

At Carpiquet Airfield, 150 *Hitlerjugend* prepared to lay down their young lives for their beloved *Fuehrer*. Opposite them, 428 field guns in concert with naval cannon up to HMS *Rodney*'s 16 inch guns, prepared to send them to the Valhalla they so richly deserved. The North Shore (New Brunswick) Regiment, Queen's Own Rifles and Régiment de la Chaudière of the 8th Brigade with the Royal Winnipeg Rifles and flame-throwing Wasps followed the bombardment on 4 July.

CANADIANS GET HELL

Even with three guns trained on every defender and outnumbered 20 to 1, the Nazis gave the Canadians hell. From well-sited block houses and taking advantage of an excellent trench system, the enemy inflicted terrible casualties. The Canadians had no features to hide behind and only the iron will of highly-trained soldiers to drive them into the maelstrom of fire. The North Shores lost 46 dead and the Winnipeg Rifles left even more of their mates among the shattered hangars. At night the SS swooped down on the Chaudière and bound and shot many of their captives. Canadians hung on grimly to their bloodied prize (although part remained in German hands). On 7 July, 467 RAF and RCAF bombers plastered Caen in preparation for its capture. They succeeded in destroying a medieval town, killing hundreds of its inhabitants, and providing rub-

***ABOVE**: Performing the most dangerous part of mine-clearing, this Royal Canadian Engineer carefully lifts this mine to diffuse it. Mines and booby traps were left behind by the German Wehrmacht, requiring a careful advance. (PAC/PA 132918)*

ble for the German defenders who had withdrawn during the raid.

Once more the North Novas and the 9th Brigade battered their way into Buron and Authie. It was the turn of the Highland Light Infantry to get the bloody nose. Sixty-two Highlanders dead and 200 more were wounded in one day's battle. Objectives were taken even at this great cost, and on 9 July the Stormont, Dundas and Glengarry Highlanders accompanied the Sherbrooke Fusiliers and two British divisions into the ruin of Caen.

The battles for the suburbs of the city had only just begun. Over the ensuing week, Third Division would spend its precious human resource at a prodigious rate; on some days suffering a higher rate of casualties among riflemen than that experienced in World War I. Advances to Colombelles and Giberville were paid for in Canadian blood and still the ultimate objective remained over yet another ridge: Verrieres or Bourquebus. Canadians were racing against time to reach Falaise and trap 300,000 enemy soldiers between themselves and the advancing Americans. They were also racing against the cruel calculation of war: battle experience increases as the number of surviving veterans decreases.

REPRINTED FROM:
Esprit de Corps, *Volume 4 Issue 4*
AUTHOR: *James G. Scott*

***RIGHT:** Attempting to flee Falaise before the Allied assault, this German column was hit by a squadron of Typhoons. They, along with U.S. Air Force aircraft, were responsible for "friendly fire" attacks on Allied vehicles because of confusion related to coloured smoke signals. (IMPERIAL WAR MUSEUM)*

***OPPOSITE PAGE:** The rockets that were mounted on rails under the wings of the Typhoon were key to this fighter-bomber's tank-killing ability. RCAF armourers are loading the aircraft's small calibre cannon with ammunition. (PAC/PL 30936)*

THE TRAGIC SUMMER OF FRIENDLY FIRE

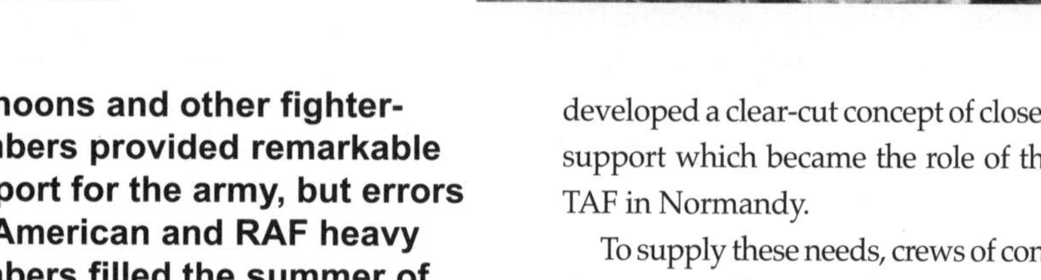

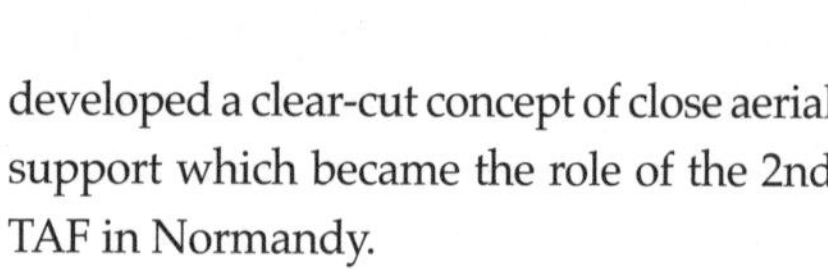

Typhoons and other fighter-bombers provided remarkable support for the army, but errors by American and RAF heavy bombers filled the summer of 1944 with tragedy.

THE TYPHOON WAS A questionable machine when it was introduced in 1942: when 135 of the first 142 delivered succumbed to accidents. Intended as a fighter, it was never a contender because of engine and structural problems. Ironically, one of these failures was the thickness of the wing which eventually made the single-seater capable of delivering 2000 pounds of bombs, mounting four 20 mm cannon or a devastating array of rockets. In Normandy, the Tiffies soon established themselves as bad news for the enemy, and along with Spitfire squadrons, worked with the troops from the beaches to Falaise and far beyond.

Canadian Raymond Collishaw was the first to relearn forgotten lessons of the past when he transformed Kittyhawks and the few Hurricanes available into fighter-bombers in North Africa. When Collishaw was posted out, Air Marshal Arthur Coningham developed a clear-cut concept of close aerial support which became the role of the 2nd TAF in Normandy.

To supply these needs, crews of construction commandos moved into Normandy the day after D-Day. At Ste-Croix-sur-Mer they bulldozed a landing strip under fire and soon England-based fighters were skidding in to refuel, re-arm and return to combat. It soon became home to Johnny Johnson's Canadian 144 Spitfire Wing. By the 18th of June, 126 and 127 Wings were also in place nearby, and, although enemy aircraft were hard to find, in less than three months the three Canadian Wings scored 262 victories.

SURFEIT OF PRIMA DONNAS

In the days following the landing, it became manifest that never before in human conflict had such a surfeit of prima donnas in senior commands been crowded into such close quarters. The bridgehead some 60 miles long and averaging ten miles in depth not only contained about one million men, 200,000 vehicles and vast store of equipment, it was also dangerously over-burdened with egos.

General Montgomery was rivalled by George Patton who upstaged him in Sicily and promised to do the same in a rush for Paris. Arthur Coningham's association with Montgomery in North Africa had not been a happy time for the egotistical New Zealander.

As the Norman summer lengthened, Coningham's voice became one of many urging Montgomery to get on with the war. Coningham needed potential landing sites south of Caen and is alleged to have despised Montgomery to such an extent that he refused to operate on the same continent with him. However, Coningham was extremely fortunate to have Air Vice Marshal Harry Broadhurst as his deputy in France to keep army-TAF communications open. Unfortunately, no such communications existed between the army and Bomber Command and this may have been a factor in the tragic summer of 1944.

PERSONAL AGENDAS

The negative impact of high ranking officers of various services and countries, engaged in a common cause, but pursuing personal agendas and petty jealousies, has never been evaluated. Nowhere is this more tragically recorded than during the summer of friendly fire and in the personality of Air Marshal Arthur Harris, head of Bomber Command.

Broadhurst and his men worked and lived close to the army. This gave them a new perspective on the war and what was required of them. What evolved was a pattern: on any given night RAF and army officers met to study bombing objectives for the following day, often based on photos brought back by Spitfires. A general program for the day would be established with the understanding that a considerable amount of freelance air support would be required during the day. After initial objectives were hit, the taxi rank on fighter bases came into play to support army needs. Instead of calling up a cab, the army called up a Typhoon.

RESENTFUL INTRUSION

When the army moved on Caen, General Montgomery demanded support from Bomber Command. Harris not only resented an intrusion into his headline-grabbing campaign of bombing German cities but was apprehensive about his ability to provide precision bombing. It was this inability which led to the phrase "carpet bombing" but now his crews were being asked to bomb within yards of allied troops without additional training.

THE SIGHT OF MASSES OF BOMBERS POUNDING ENEMY POSITIONS FIRST BROUGHT CHEERS FROM TROOPS WHICH SOON BECAME DEATH SHRIEKS.

He sent 416 machines against the northern section of Caen but the bombing took place six hours before the infantry moved. By then the enemy had recovered and Canadian and British troops had to poke their way through the rubble as they confronted entrenched troops.

Wing Commander Johnny Johnson flew escort and reported: "It was quite apparent that a number of bombs had fallen well outside the target area and…we were using a sledge hammer to crack a nut."

REFUSAL TO CO-OPERATE

Neither Montgomery nor Harris addressed the problem of how to move troops into an area fast enough to take full advantage of bombings' effect on the enemy. A simple phone call or message could have done it. But somehow this solution evaded both. Montgomery insisted on again using a 'sledge hammer' in Operation Goodwood. Heavy bombers mounted a massive ground support raid, but the army failed to follow through soon enough and operations stagnated.

The sight of masses of bombers pounding enemy positions originally brought cheers from troops which soon became shudders of apprehension or death shrieks. It came first in the American sector shortly after the Op GOODWOOD failure. On the first day of the American assault, 25 soldiers were killed and 115 wounded by friendly fire as the USAAF bombed through overcast skies. Shocked troops returned the fire on American bombers. The next day 1800 Fortresses and Liberators wheeled towards the men on the ground and bombed short, killing 111 and wounding 490.

FRIENDLY FIRE

On the British front, the RAF bombed at night and more than half of 1100 were called off because of smoke and dust. Troops milled about in the dark and smoke for some hours and it was noon before they were ready to exploit a gap. Shortly afterwards, some 500 USAF heavies bombed short causing 300 casualties among the Canadians and Poles. Richard Bison of the North Shore regiment was one of them. The images of that day still haunt him. "They flew across our flank and seemed to leave something behind. Then we saw but couldn't believe it. Bombs! Hundreds of bombs sliding across the sky right at us."

Major General Rod Keller was also hit that day, an accident which apparently spared Lieutenant General Simonds the task of relieving him of his command. One week later, 14 August, Bomber Command again inflicted casualties on Canadian and Polish troops. This time the tragedy deepened because 44 of the 77 erring aircraft were Canadian. Confusion over smoke signals was key to the disaster and Harris divested himself of responsibility by blaming his crews and hinting that the army was at fault. Actually, Bomber Command was ignorant of a five month-old standing order.

A Supreme Headquarters Allied Expeditionary Force standing order issued five months earlier proclaimed that yellow smoke, flares and panels would be used for identification purposes between air and ground units. Yellow was not to be used for any other purpose. This order got to all allied services, but, according to Harris, never showed up at Bomber Command. The bombers used yellow target markers while the men on the ground, according to the order, also used yellow flares and smoke.

The closer the first waves of bombers got to the troops, the more smoke the army sent up to identify their positions. The result was creeping chaos and faulty identification of targets as on at least four occasions groups bombed the wrong aiming points. They had yellow smoke to aim at, but it was marking Allied troops.

Having given but a passing interest to the ground war, Harris was now on the defensive. In a 12-page document, he responded to criticism, insisting that no one had told Bomber Command about the standing order. His Senior Staff Officer had assured him that there would be no possibility of conflicting pyrotechnics. Harris concluded: "To that extent therefore, the First Canadian Army themselves subscribed to the errors which were made."

CRITICISING A HERO

A lone Auster pilot gallantly flew his small observation aircraft into the bombing stream, firing red verey flares in an unsuccessful attempt to divert the bombers. Instead of recommending the army pilot for an award, Harris not only accused the pilot of compounding the confusion but questioned at some length how such a sensational story could be released to the press, calling for an investigation.

Harris then went to great lengths to spread the blame to his crews. He observed: "Air bombers as a whole are by no means of outstanding intelligence. They are in the main selected as such because, although passing other standards for aircrew, they are the least likely to make efficient pilots or navigators."

PUNISHING CREWS

He took action against crews involved for not following a timed run from Caen. This included revoking any acting rank for squadron and flight leaders involved and banning all crews to other squadrons. When many crews approached the target area, they heard the master bomber describing the target and flares.

Unfortunately, what he described was duplicated some distance nearer at hand and that's where the crews bombed. It was a quarry which contained Canadian troops. While failure to complete the timed run was a breach of discipline, over-reacted in an effort to divert attention from the essential problem of lack of communication between Bomber Command and the army.

The incident failed to improve communications. While 2nd TAF had a mechanism in place whereby the army at brigade level could halt air bombing in an emergency, it was and remained, impossible for the army at any level to interfere with Bomber Command operations. Although Gen Crerar, commanding the 1st Canadian Army, expressed confidence in Bomber Command, Harris soon went back to bombing German cities. 2nd TAF helped restore army trust in air support and became a major force in closing the Falaise Gap. The day before the gap was closed, 2nd TAF claimed 3000 vehicles.

As the war moved inland, Mitchell and Boston medium bombers would continue to hammer tactical targets until they operated on a bombline of 1,000 yards. On one such operation, the captain of a B-25 huddled with his crew before take-off. He made a quick calculation. The squadron would be dropping 144 bombs. "Let's think about where these buggers drop!" he urged. "My brother will be a thousand yards away."

REPRINTED FROM:
Esprit de Corps, *Volume 4 Issue 2*
AUTHOR: *Norman Shannon*

THE HIT AND RUN WAR

Canadians on loan to the Royal Navy write a dashing page in the history of Motor Torpedo Boats.

THE ROYAL NAVY HAD 18 Motor Torpedo Boats in service when war came in 1939. They carried two 18-inch torpedoes slung from reins in the engine room, and a quick burst of power was necessary to send the torpedoes sliding out the ports. Then, as the torpedoes picked up speed, the coxswain had to dipsy-doodle to avoid having their collective asses shot off.

For obvious reasons that model's career was rather short, but British coastal forces grew from a Mrs. Miniver jumble of leaky boats and tweedy, pipe-smoking gentlemen who popped off to Dunkirk to an effective fleet of motor torpedo and motor gunboats which gradually spread operations from the Channel to the Mediterranean, the Aegean and the Adriatic Seas.

Their swift, deadly encounters with the enemy attracted a number of Canadians in much the same way as the Spitfire beckoned to their airborne brothers. By March 1940, some 40 pink-cheeked RCNVR officers were loaned to the Royal Navy. Tony Law was among those who ended up in the Coastal Force and, about a year later, he was appointed navigator on Motor Gunboat 53.

OPPOSITE PAGE: *Lieutenant Commander Anthony Law was awarded the Distinguished Service Cross for his actions on the night of 23 May 1944. Law also served as an official war artist, recording many of his experiences as a captain of the Royal Canadian Navy.* (NAC/PA 144588)

LEFT: *Although introduced in 1936, the Fairey Swordfish remained a reliable carrier-based bomber throughout the war, having a good record against the German, Italian and Japanese fleets. Armed with rockets and torpedoes, the Swordfish went up against numerous German convoys during their "Channel Dash."* (IMPERIAL WAR MUSEUM)

He saw little action but was given command of MTB 48 which was shot up one night by a German R-boat off Dover, wounding a crew member.

WOLF PACK

MTB's and MGB's were like packs of hungry wolves which struck suddenly, savagely and withdrew. They hit enemy convoys, protected their own and engaged in a perpetual battle with enemy E-boats which were usually faster, more heavily armed and not prone to burn because they used diesel fuel instead of high octane.

These encounters again resembled those of the Me-109 and the Spitfire, and the men who operated the short boats had much in common with fighter pilots: they were individuals, not big on discipline and anxious to get on with the bloody war.

Sometimes this was easier said than done. During the Battle of France, Corny Burke led a group to The Hague to blow up the locks. They had demolished some of the lock gates, but were then left behind by the main party which went off to rescue members of a trapped 52nd Highland Division.

INEBRIATED PARTY

Burke and another man joined a small party of soldiers whose duty seemed to be to consume a stock of booze before the enemy took The Hague. They had achieved a victory of sorts when their inebriated party was rescued by a trawler as German tanks rolled into the city.

Later, as navigator of MGB 42, Burke set course for Penzance and ran over an acoustic mine which blew the stern off. However, he managed to beach the wreck before it sank. Later, when he took command of MGB 90, he felt confident that a new boat and a new crew would usher in a new era. After sea trials, the boat was about to join a flotilla and Burke was making a few last notes below while a rating examined a Lewis machine-gun on deck. He pulled the trigger to see if it was working. It was.

HUGE EXPLOSION

The bullet hit a box of ammunition on the next boat and explosions ignited 200 gallons of high octane. Two boats were destroyed and, with three MTB's to his credit, Corny Burke was well on his way to being a German ace and he hadn't been in action yet.

The fourth occasion was a near miss. As a member of 20 MGB flotilla, Burke and Doug Maitland were lying overnight off the Hook of Holland. A line joined the two boats which lay silent. At dawn, Burke gave orders to start engines, but while the three engines screamed there was no reply from the gears. The boat refused to move and a man was sent over the side to examine the three propellers. He emerged somewhat dazed to gasp that they had no propellers. Maitland towed the boat back to Lowestoft while Burke entertained unkind thoughts about the dockyard where Curly or Moe had installed the three new wheels that afternoon but had not tightened the nuts.

Tony Law's MTB 48 was one of five in a flotilla which set out from Dover to intercept the *Scharnhorst*, *Gneisenau* and *Prinz Eugen* which were protected by six destroyers, 24 E-boats and a screen of air cover.

SCREEN IMPENETRABLE

Amid heavy smoke and tossing about in heavy seas, the MTB's were unable to break through the E-boat screen and launched torpedoes over two miles from their target.

Overhead, six Fairey Swordfish led by Esmonde flew through a wall of flak to make an equally futile attack on the battleships. They fell one by one until there were no aircraft still aloft while the German flotilla sped away. Spitfire pilot Omer Levesque was also shot down, but was later picked up by a German boat as the enemy flotilla steamed northward at 30 knots.

Tom Fuller, another Canadian loaner to the Royal Navy, was one of three skippers who had just completed mine laying off the coast of France when they encountered a German convoy of some 22 ships, including eight fast E-boats. Somehow, Fuller became disengaged from the others when he decided to attack. His MGB stood on its tail under full power and pounded down the lane between two columns of enemy ships.

Gunners laced enemy ships to port and starboard, but by the time the enemy returned the fire, they were firing at themselves.

The significance of the attack in terms of damage to the enemy was obviously light, but the *elan* and derring-do fuelled talk around mess bars for weeks and also earned Fuller a Distinguished Service Cross. Along with Tom Ladner, Doug Maitland and Corny Burke, Fuller was soon bound for the Mediterranean for a new phase of the hit-and-run war.

FIFTY FOOT FLAMES

As part of the flotilla on the 1600 mile journey to Gibraltar, Maitland's 657 was hit by submarine fire which penetrated a gasoline tank. Fifty foot flames gushed upwards. Maitland jammed throttles to the wall and turned into the rolling sea which washed the burning petrol away.

Meanwhile, a second submarine surfaced but did so into the first. Fuller and another MTB stood by to collect survivors.

Among those collected and not immediately bound for a prison camp was a cook who became Able Seaman Jock MacPherson and Fuller's personal chef.

Two days into Operation Torch, Fuller led two MTB's into the Messina Straits where they destroyed two German E-boats, but most MTB captains found the Sicilian campaign disappointing. As the Italian operations lengthened, most stayed in the Med but Fuller drifted east to the Aegean and Adriatic. There he took part in some 105 gun and torpedo actions as well as a number of adventures which earned him the name "the pirate of the Adriatic." Thus he somehow got involved with Tito's Yugoslavian partisans. The Coastal Force sank 269 ships and lost 76 of which Fuller and Burke shared at least 21.

BACK TO THE CHANNEL

Late in 1943, the RN provided the boats to man two Canadian flotillas. Lieutenant Commander Tony Law took over eight 72-foot 'shorts' of the 29th Canadian MTB Flotilla while Lieutenant Commander J.H. Kirkpatrick commanded ten 115-foot boats of the 65th Flotilla. It was back to the Channel in preparation for D-Day.

***ABOVE:** Illustrating one of his many patrols in the English Channel, artist and MTB captain Tony Law experienced several close calls in actions against the Germans. Capable of destroying warships – as they were armed with four torpedoes, pom-pom, Oerlikon and machine guns – MTBs were best-suited to attack swiftly using "hit and run" tactics.* *("PATROL OFF LE HAVRE," BY TONY LAW, CWM)*

Flotilla 65 covered the west flank of the invaders and then struck enemy convoys inside the Channel Islands. Shoot-outs with enemy E-boats was like the OK Coral on water, and casualties ran to 30 percent. Law's 29th Flotilla, meanwhile, was assigned to the The Hague sector, home of E-boats, R-boats, destroyers and accurate coastal guns. They worked the sector for almost two months during which Lieutenant Commander Law's 459 was hit and almost sunk. David Killam's 460 struck a mine and there were few survivors, while Glen Creda's 463 was also blown up by a mine.

BATTLE OF THE SCHELDT

With the failure of Operation Market Garden in September, the port of Ostend became critical to Allied supply. As Canadian troops fought the battle of the Scheldt to secure the 40-mile estuary to Antwerp, MTB's and MGB's were very active in attacking shipping and coastal installations. They became a critical weapon in securing the entrance to the port which had been captured earlier. Then the angry little boats escorted precious convoys to Antwerp where, ironically, the story of Flotilla 29 came to a disastrous end.

One afternoon in February 1945, the crew of one of seven Canadian boats, rafted together in harbour, pumped 50 gallons of contaminated gasoline from the tank. For weeks they had been trying to have it done by shore maintenance and were finally told to do it themselves.

The job was complete when suddenly fire broke out among three rows of boats. Explosions which were heard in England ripped the afternoon as fire spread to other boats. When it was finally over, 23 Canadians were among the 79 dead and 12 MTB's were demolished. Bad luck had finally won.

REPRINTED FROM:
Esprit de Corps, *Volume 5 Issue 12*
AUTHOR: *Norman Shannon*

PLODDING THE POLDERS

After fighting their way up the coast, Canadians are assigned to clearing the flooded Scheldt estuary.

ABOVE: *The heavy floods turned the flat ground of Breskens Pocket into a waterlogged battleground. Their universal carriers stuck in the mud, men of the 3rd Canadian Division were nicknamed the "water rats."* *(NAC/PA 131252)*

CANADIAN TROOPS HAD THREE months of combat following D-Day. There was a moment of satisfaction at Dieppe when the 2nd Division staged a ceremonial parade. But as the Canadians fought their way up the coast in a critical but isolated campaign, their war took on the quality of a time warp: they were assigned the task of clearing the Scheldt Estuary, with little support, fighting waist deep in water for almost two months. In September 1944, the Canadians stumbled onto a war.

The mud of Passchendaele and rotten death was the Canadian legacy of poor leadership in 1917. Field Marshal Haig was obsessed with breaking through from Ypres to the coast and the dreary winter of stagnation followed. General Montgomery was obsessed with capturing bridges over the Rhine and launching an immediate attack into Germany. Whereas Haig, prior to the Somme, promised his men that after the breakthrough the cavalry would trot to Berlin, the speculation around Montgomery's headquarters was that the war would be over by Christmas.

Having talked Eisenhower into Operation Market-Garden, the airborne assault on Arnhem, Montgomery did a second take with respect to the task of the Canadians.

DON'T WASTE RESOURCES

Lieutenant General Crerar had been ordered not to waste resources in clearing channel ports north and east of the Ghent canal. Then on 13 September, presumably under pressure from Eisenhower, Montgomery ordered Crerar to open up the Antwerp port which had been taken by the British on 4 September. Montgomery's order came almost as an aside because his attention was then focused on the Rhine crossing and the poorly planned operation of a bridge too far.

The British went into the Arnhem drop with either incredibly poor intelligence or a disregard for reality. The only area in which gliders could be reasonably landed was eight miles from the bridge at Arnhem and two Panzer divisions were regrouping between the site and the bridge. These critical factors were overlooked, and became fatal flaws as almost 8000 of 10,000 gallant Airborne were killed, wounded or captured.

FAILED THRUST

The Americans were successful at Nijmegen and at a series of bridges to the south. Montgomery covered his failure with percentages, pointing out they were 90 per cent of the way to their objective which was a bridge over the Rhine. But the thrust into Germany had failed and it became apparent that the war would not be over by Christmas.

This created immense problems in logistics and the 1,000 berth port of Antwerp became critical. While the port was cleared the 45 miles of estuary leading in to it were heavily defended by the enemy and the waters mined.

Meanwhile, Canadian troops captured Boulogne, cleared coastal strong points at Cap Griz Nez and prepared to move on Calais. The 2nd Division was ordered to the Antwerp sector to relieve the British the day before the airdrop at Arnhem. With his troops spread from Boulogne to Antwerp, Crerar got orders to clear the Scheldt estuary but illness forced him to withdraw and Lieutenant General Simonds put his plan into action.

FAT CAT CORRESPONDENTS

The 2nd Division swept around Antwerp and to the northern suburb of Merxem. For a period correspondents could live like fat cats in the luxurious Century Hotel in Antwerp and take a streetcar out to the scene of the action. The Royal Regiment and the Essex Scottish cleared Merxem but pockets of resistance remained in other suburbs.

Strong resistance along the Turnhout canal slowed progress, but the 2nd Division with the 4th Canadian Armoured Division gradually drew a net northward to trap the enemy in the Scheldt. The Polish Armoured Division and the British 49th Division were also major players in the encirclement.

The 3rd Division moved up to the Leopold canal to the west prior to an attack on the enemy strongpoint in the Breskens Pocket, and the 4th Division held a line in the Bruges-Eecloo sector.

LEFT: *Paratroopers from British and American airborne divisions parachute into the Low Countries on 17 September 1944 as part of Operation MARKET GARDEN.* (U.S. AIR FORCE)

ONE MORE BLOODY CANAL

To the Canadians the war became one more bloody canal to cross. CorporalAndre Fevre was wounded in an early crossing where enemy fire slashed the canal like lacework. Fevre lay mortally wounded on the north bank, exhorting his companions to brave the fire. He yelled at them and then he sang to them but his voice grew weak and he was dead by dawn.

Some of the German forces escaped from the coastal area across the Scheldt to the isthmas of South Beveland but two strong divisions remained behind to man the defences on adjacent Walcheren island and the Breskens pocket on the south bank of the Scheldt. The land was flat, below sea-level, and slashed with canals and dikes some which were 15 feet high and up to 250 feet in width. With a determined, well entrenched enemy following orders to defend their positions to the last man the Polder battle soon became a nightmare.

STORMING THE LEOPOLD

The 3rd Division made its move over the Leopold canal before dawn on 6 October. The Regina Rifles, the Canadian Scottish, the Royal Winnipegs and a company from the Royal Montreal Regiment stormed the canal north of Maldegem. The RMR's insisted on action after a stint at headquarters. They got it.

The Scottish landed shortly after the flame-throwers brought initial panic and seared defenders in their trenches. But by the time the Reginas crossed their boats were riddled with heavy fire. The enemy brought down fire on both sides of the canal, including precise fire from coastal batteries and the bridgehead went to ground.

A gap existed between the two Canadian positions on the north side and the Winnipegs bridged it. The Canadians fought off attacks for five days and withstood enemy fire although the three battalions suffered 533 casualties.

PLODDING ACROSS THE POLDERS

One of the 2nd Division's first tasks was to seal in the enemy at the eastern neck of the South Beveland isthmus. The 5th Brigade plodded across the polders without much resistance until they reached Woensdrecht which rose like a giant boil in the mud near the entrance to the isthmus.

The enemy had reinforced the area with four battalions of paratroopers in addition to the two entrenched battalions dominating the crossroads which led north to Bergen-Op-Zoom and the entrance to the isthmus.

LAND OF SLIME

For six days the Canadians fought against murderous firepower and appalling conditions which brought high casualties. It was a land of rain, mud and slime where stinking corpses blew up if you attempted to administer a bit of dignity. The Canadians made no ground for three days. Then things got worse. In an attack against the dikes of Woensdrect on Walcheren island, over a 1200 yard causeway, every rifle company commander of the Black Watch was wounded and there were 146 casualties.

Meanwhile the 9th Brigade mounted an amphibious attack accross Braakman Inlet which opened onto the south shore of the Scheldt and the Breskens Pocket.

GROUND HELP FINALLY ARRIVES

Breskens was cleared on 21 October and ten days later, the Canadians received their first significant ground help although the RAF had bombed the sector 11 times during the month. Two amphibious assaults were made by the British on flooded Walcheren Island and by 8 November the Scheldt was finally cleared.

The operation cost the Canadians 6367 casualties but the port of Anwerp was opened. A ship loaded with allied brass steamed in on 28 November for a ceremony of national anthems and speeches. There were delegates from SHEAF, the Royal Navy, the 21st Army Group and Belgian and Dutch officials.

Nobody had bothered to invite the weary Canadians.

REPRINTED FROM:
Esprit de Corps, *Volume 4 Issue 6*
AUTHOR: *Norman Shannon*

RIGHT:
A squadron of Curtiss P-40 Kittyhawk fighters are ready for action. On 21 February 1945, a Kittyhawk shot down a Japanese fire balloon about 50 miles from Vancouver.
(DND/PMR 80-197)

WHEN JAPANESE MISSILES ATTACKED CANADA

In 1942, following the Japanese attack on Pearl Harbour, Canadians on the west coast were on alert. However, the expected "assault" did not occur until late 1944.

FOUR DAYS AFTER THE Japanese hit Pearl Harbour, the U.S. Army in Seattle reported that the main Japanese fleet was 154 miles west of San Francisco and heading northeast. The crews on Esquimalt harbour's two Bofors guns stood briskly at the alert for some hours, but nothing developed. This was the start of a strange psychological battle that was to characterize 44 months of war.

On 23 February 1942 a Japanese submarine fired some 20 shells in the direction of an oil refinery at Ellwood, California. Two days later anti-aircraft gunners in Los Angeles blasted off over 1400 rounds at an unseen enemy who might have been up there. Public opinion along the west coast of both the United States and Canada was now reaching panic proportions, and Japan had won the first round in the psychological war.

PSYCHOLOGICAL DAMAGE

Things changed when Colonel Jimmy Doolittle led 15 B-25 bombers off the American carrier *Hornet* on 18 April 1942. Shortly after noon his bombers hit Tokyo and four other cities in a raid which did more psychological than physical damage to the enemy. One aircraft managed to land in Vladivostok, but all others either crashed or were abandoned. The raid was a tactical disaster but it proved to the Japanese that they were not invulnerable.

The Japanese responded by launching 80 ships and a diversionary force against the Aleutian Islands in June, at the time of the Battle of Midway. Canadian military circles saw Prince Rupert as the next possible Japanese target.

The next round in the psychological war came as the Japanese sub I-26 surfaced and shelled a wireless station and lighthouse at Estevan Point on Vancouver Island. Again, little physical damage was done, but tensions ran high along the coast.

On 6 June 1942, the Japanese suffered a defeat at Midway and, gradually, the momentum of the war came to favour the Americans. But for almost two years, the Japanese worked on a secret weapon designed specifically for the west coast of Canada and the United States. On 4 November 1944, a U.S. Navy patrol boat found a large piece of tattered cloth with something attached to it floating on the sea. Within a month, they had picked up enough fragments to conceptualize that a new weapon was in use.

SIMPLISTIC MISSILE

The balloons were 33 feet in diameter and made of mulberry bark. A combination of incendiary and antipersonnel bombs made them simplistic unguided missiles. Launched from the Kanto district on the island of Honshu, they were swept northeastward on the jet stream at 200 mph and dropped on the west coast from Alaska to Mexico.

Of the 9300 released, at a cost of about $900 each, some 300 reached North American soil and at least 90 were recovered in Canada although many more might still be scattered about the bushland. Some were located as far east as Saskatchewan.

The missiles were ingeniously simple. Each balloon carried some 30 six-pound sandbags that were released by barometric pressure whenever the balloon dropped

TOP: *On 20 June 1940, the lighthouse and wireless station at Estevan Point on Vancouver Island were shelled by an I-class Japanese submarine. Although little damage resulted, it sparked a growing fear the war would breach our borders. This fear of invasion led to the internment of Japanese citizens in Canada.*
ABOVE RIGHT: *Men of the Royal Canadian Engineers inspect an unexploded firebomb balloon on a British Columbian hillside. Beginning in late fall 1944 and over the following several months, Japan released some 9000 balloons although only 296 reached North America. Made of mulberry bark paper, each balloon carried about 120 kg of high-explosive or incendiary bombs. (DND)*
ABOVE LEFT: *A Japanese balloon bomb photographed as it descended on the British Columbian coast. (U.S. AIR FORCE)*

below 30,000 feet, the lower level of the jet stream. A similar device opened a valve to let hydrogen escape if the craft rose above 35,000 feet. These two devices ensured that the craft rode the jet stream and maintained the desired course and at a reasonable rate of speed.

Each balloon carried an assortment of fragmentation and incendiary bombs. The release mechanism for the bombs was designed to operate after all ballast bags had been dropped. The Japanese calculated that, at this point, the balloon would be over Canadian or American territory.

FLASHES IN THE SKY

The first balloons were launched on 1 November 1944. Three days later a U.S. patrol boat fished a large fragment of cloth out of the sea. In order to retrieve it, they had to cut away at something dangling from a rope deep in the water, presumably the bombs. The first hard evidence that Japan had launched a new secret weapon came early in December when observers in Montana saw an explosion in a balloon. Flashes in the sky were later reported and it is estimated that at least 100 balloons exploded while airborne.

Authorities in the U.S. soon identified the weapon and its fundamental operation. They were able to confirm the detail of how the missile worked when a pilot pushed a balloon towards open country by repeated blasts from his propeller. The rocking balloon released the hydrogen-controlled device and the craft dropped to the ground where the destruction device fortunately failed to work.

A news blackout immediately descended over future sightings in both Canada and the U.S. At the RCAF stations in Pat Bay and at Toffino on Vancouver Island, Kittyhawk fighter crews were on constant alert. On 21 February 1945 a Kittyhawk scrambled from Pat Bay, intercepted and destroyed a balloon about 50 miles east of Vancouver. It was one of three missiles destroyed by RCAF aircraft during the five-month campaign. Because the attacks came during the winter months, the hazard of forest fires was greatly diminished. The news blackout was also very effective. The Japanese General Staff heard of only the first landing on the continent and, as a cone of silence descended, it decided the campaign was a failure and ceased operations.

Had the timing of the attacks coincided with warm weather, the first unguided intercontinental missile attack might have been much more successful.

REPRINTED FROM:
Esprit de Corps, *Volume 7 Issue 8*
AUTHOR: *Norman Shannon*

1945 - VICTORY

With the defeat of Germany's last-ditch gamble in the Ardennes and the failure of Japan's "Divine Wind" suicidal Kamikaze attacks, the Allied advance proves unstoppable. Under Hitler's directive to "fight to the last German" the Third Reich resists the inevitable until 7 May. Isolated and battered, Japan fights on for three more months. Following the U.S. detonation of two Atomic bombs, the Japanese emperor agrees to an unconditional surrender.

1 JANUARY The Luftwaffe mounts its last major offensive effort against Allied airfields in France and Belgium.

28 JANUARY Battle of the Bulge concludes with Germans pushed out of Ardennes.

13 FEBRUARY The Royal Air Force mounts a controversial bombing attack against Dresden, killing thousands of civilians.

23 FEBRUARY United States marines plant the flag atop Mount Suribachi on Iwo Jima.

22-23 MARCH Allies mount major effort to cross the Rhine – the last German defensive line.

15 APRIL Canadian troops conclude a successful drive to the sea in Northern Holland.

16 APRIL Russian troops launch their asault against Berlin.

30 APRIL Adolf Hitler commits suicide in his bunker as Russian troops close in on Berlin's city center.

7 MAY Germany capitulates.

11 MAY United States marines launch a major attack on Okinawa.

22 JUNE Resistance on Okinawa ceases after the Japanese suffer 120,000 casualties.

6 AUGUST The Enola Gay drops the first Atomic bomb on Hiroshima.

8 AUGUST The Soviet Army declares war on Japan and invades Manchuria.

9 AUGUST A second atomic bomb is dropped on Nagasaki.

14 AUGUST Japan surrenders unconditionally.

BELOW:
The "Fatboy" Atomic bomb detonates on Nagasaki on 9 August 1945. With a week, on 14 August, Japan had surrendered.

RIGHT:
Allied prisoners in Japanese camps suffered from disease, torture, malnutrition, and rigours of slave labour at the hands of their captors. Conditions have been described as "hell on earth." (IMPERIAL WAR MUSEUM)

FAR RIGHT:
U.S. Marines plant the flag atop Mount Suribachi on Iwo Jima.

THE DAY THE LUFTWAFFE WAS OUT AT THE "BODENPLATTE"

The Luftwaffe celebrated New Year's Day 1945, by sending 1000 aircraft against allied air bases on the continent. It became their last stand as they lost 300 machines and irreplaceable pilots.

THERE WERE WORSE places to be during the war than in the shadow of Brussels, and most of the crews who flew Mitchells and Bostons out of 139 Wing took it all with a good deal of fortitude. By December of 1944, many were looking forward to sharing Christmas with friendly natives of the opposite sex, and their families in Brussels. Then along came Gerd von Rundstedt, the Field Marshal whose bold drive in the Ardennes made him the grinch who stole Christmas for allied airmen, and immeasurably enlivened New Years for Second Tactical Air Force personnel in France, Belgium and Holland.

On 16 December, von Rundstedt's armour started rolling under cover of fog, snow, and sleet which kept aircraft grounded. Within a week his panzers had driven a wedge 45 miles into allied lines. His plan was to drive that wedge to the coast and cut off the British from the Americans. Our base at Melsbrook lay in his path some 70 miles distant. This created a great incentive among the aircrew, but deplorable weather continued for almost a week. Rumours of German parachutists infiltrating the lines were rampant, and everybody became a strategist. Some questioned why Montgomery's forces hadn't turned south to help the Yanks. Others, remembering the screw-up at Caen and the debacle at Arnhem, took little comfort from the prospect of being rescued by Montgomery. George sipped creme de menthe and came up with a masterful suggestion: "Get a newsreel crew into Bastogne and Montgomery's bound to show up."

HEAVY FLAK

Bastogne was the village in the Ardennes where outnumbered Yanks slowed Rundstedt's drive. On 23 December we got off to bomb a crossroads at Schmidtheim, about 45 miles north-east of Bastogne, where Patton's tanks were then engaging the enemy. We went weaving down a valley through heavy flak, and one got the impression of every flat car in Germany mounted an 88 or a 105 mm flak gun. Schmidtheim Charlie came into our lexicon that day, a term which recognized the professionalism of the German gunners. On subsequent days the war became a simple contest; Schmidtheim Charlie vs the Mitchell's ability to take a pounding.

On Christmas Eve, Bradford kept talking about the Virgin of Albert who hung precariously from a church tower throughout WWI. This led to speculation on what might happen on Christmas and a hint of derision from George.

He wanted to know if Bradford expected the Virgin to appear in the battered church tower at Bastogne and yell. "Knock it off fellas!" It should be added that George was not the most sensitive member of the squadron. His father, an Anglican minister from Newfoundland, closed off a letter admonishing him to go with God. George replied, "Sorry, we've got a full crew."

The battle order was posted, but most of us went to bed thinking of another war, with

ABOVE: *When the German Luftwaffe launched Operation BODENPLATTE on New Year's Day, 1945, their goal was to destroy as many Allied fighters as possible, while they were still on the ground at bases in Holland, Belgium and northern France. Here, an aircraft burns on the tarmac at Eindhoven, Holland.* (DND PHOTO)

OPPOSITE PAGE, TOP:
With smoke and flames rising skyward after the surprise, large-scale strike by the Luftwaffe in the "Hangover Raids" of 1 January 1945, the Allies would lose as many as 180 planes destroyed, with another 100 damaged. However, the losses for the Luftwaffe would be crippling. Losing 277 planes and 232 pilots, including most of the group and wing commanders, Germany's air force would never recover from this loss. (DND/PMR 74318)

LEFT:
Launching more than 1000 sorties, the Luftwaffe gathered all available fighter-bombers in this last great effort to eliminate Allied fighters that served as escorts on bombing raids, thereby improving the Luftwaffe's ability to defend Germany. A squadron of Heinkel He III bombers proceed to their targets. (DND PHOTO)

ABOVE:
Germany's most versatile aircraft of WWII, the Junkers JU 88 served the Luftwaffe as a level bomber, dive-bomber, reconnaissance machine, ground-attack aircraft, trainer, day and night fighter, minelayer and torpedo-bomber. Designed as a fast bomber, it was equivalent to Britain's de Havilland Mosquito. (DND PHOTO)

visions of a few German soldiers tramping through the Ardennes snow singing Christmas carols. The Yanks would join in, setting in motion a day of goodwill and high living. What actually happened on Christmas morning was that an orderly woke us in the dark, we had breakfast of burnt bread fried in grease in a cheerless mess, and then we went out and bombed a crossroads at Stadkyll. By noon we'd abandoned the theory of divine intervention.

Two days later weather closed in as we returned from another target, and we were diverted to Lille. All it had to offer was a place to park the Mitchells. A strange procession of airmen in flying kit made their way into town. About six of us were discussing options for an overnight stay. The cafe was comfortable but the horseshoe booth was hardly overnight accommodations. Jan van Over-scheldt kept glaring at a man standing near the booth. Suddenly, he growled something in his native Belgique, jumped up and jammed a .38 into the man's stomach.

When the police came, Jan explained that the man had been listening to our conversation for ten minutes. Unable to produce papers, the man was hustled out. "A spy or a parachutist," Jan explained, "so where are we going to sleep?" Jan was tuned into a war we knew nothing about. He grew up in the Ardennes, escaped from a German labour camp and made his way to England. He wore an RAF uniform, but I think he belonged to the Belgian Air Force. When our squadron came to the continent, Jan got a weekend pass to visit his parents. He came back early, crushed by the fact that his parents had become collaborators.

DRUNKEN PILOTS

Our target for 1 January was Dasburg, a railroad junction about 25 miles east of Bastogne. The flight out was routine but we sensed an undercurrent of tension in the British voice on the RT, which told us that our little friends would not be with us. We entertained dark, envious and erroneous thoughts about fighter pilots who got so drunk on New Year's eve they couldn't get off the ground in the morning. This was the opening moments of the *Luftwaffe*'s Operation Ground Plate. Between 900 and 1,100 enemy fighters were sweeping towards 17 allied bases in Holland, Belgium and France. Had they been looking up, the day would have started with the great Mitchell turkey shoot, but they didn't and we went on to bomb Dasburg.

On the return, we saw an incredible pall of smoke. It was a beacon of disaster; black coils in the morning sky was a distinctive signature of burning aircraft lining the runway and perimeter track. I lost count at about sixty, and as we rolled towards our dispersal, bullets exploded like popcorn, and skeletons of proud aircraft sank wearily away. Even today details of that half hour are elusive. The British fudged figures. It seems some of their damaged aircraft were actually beyond repair. Best estimate at actual loss is 225 planes while the enemy lost 300.

The *Luftwaffe* also lost heavily during the two weeks of fighting in the Ardennes, and the question which haunts history is what would have happened if a stronger *Luftwaffe* had attacked on the first day of the Rundstedt offensive? For some strange reason, the enemy mounted its air offensive when it had already lost hundreds of fighters, and Patton had turned the tide in the ground war. While enemy jet fighters continued to harass bombers for the rest of the war, the *Luftwaffe* literally struck out at 'ground plate.'

One history of the *Luftwaffe* claims the sky over the Ardennes was empty of British and American planes for a week following Ground Plate. They wish! (A curious statement in view of the fact that the Mitchells were out two days later.) On 5 January, we bombed St. Vith. Perhaps this crossroads in Belgium was not one of the most important targets of the war, but it was important to Jan van Overscheld. That's where he bombed his parents.

REPRINTED FROM:
Esprit de Corps, *Volume 2 Issue 2*
AUTHOR: *Norman Shannon*

CROSS CHANNEL FERRY

The Shelburne escape line for downed airmen, operated by two Canadian soldiers, becomes a highly successful and popular route to freedom for evaders.

SERGEANT MAJOR LUCIEN Dumais splashed ashore at Dieppe on White Beach, landing between two wrecked landing craft. With other members of the Fusiliers Mont Royal, he immediately came under heavy fire from the nearby headland and castle which dominated the beach. He then stumbled towards the Casino over large rocks where for five hours Canadians sniped at Germans from the first and second floors while Germans sniped at Canadians from the third.

When withdrawal came, at about 11:00 hours, Dumais stumbled over a wounded man in the dash to the landing craft. He was too heavy to lift and Dumais returned to the Casino where he collected two prisoners and used them as stretcher-bearers to get the man to the departing boats. In the chaos of the evacuation, he found himself in a beached LCT with Padre Foote who was shuttling wounded out to the assault craft. It was Foote's decision to stay behind with the wounded, but Dumais made no conscious decision to do so: he was among the abandoned as the last craft left.

ON ONE OCCASION, WHILE TRANSPORTING 20 AMERICANS, KARAMBRUN'S TRUCK BECAME IMPALED UPON A TANK-TRAP SPIKE IN BROAD DAYLIGHT. WHEN ACCOSTED BY GENDARMES, HE DECIDED HE WOULD HAVE TO TELL THE TRUTH AND EVOKE PATRIOTISM.

UNDERGROUND CONTACT

He later jumped from a train bound for a German POW camp, and managed to establish contact with the underground. Eight weeks after coming ashore, Dumais was flown out of Gibraltar and became a high prospect at MI9 as a potential operator of an escape line.

About the time Dumais went to Dieppe, the British agency was recruiting Sergeant Ray LaBrosse for a mission to France where they would set up an escape organization for downed aircrew. LaBrosse and a partner were parachuted into France where they operated an escape line for six months until it was infiltrated. The partner was arrested but LaBrosse escaped across the Pyrenees.

LEFT:
Prior to every mission, maps were carefully studied not only for orientation but also so that each member could familiarize themselves with possible escape routes should they be shot down.
(IMPERIAL WAR MUSEUM)

OPPOSITE PAGE:
Before being set ablaze by the Germans, la maison d'Alphonse was a temporary refuge for downed Allied airmen.
(COURTESY RAYMOND LABROSSE, VETERANS AFFAIRS)

TAG TEAM

Back in England, he was made an offer most men would have gladly rejected out of hand: MI9 wanted him to go back to France to establish another escape line. This time LaBrosse teamed up with Dumais and their Lysander touched down some 50 miles north of Paris in November 1943. Their mission came as the German net was closing around escape lines, and it almost ended the day after they arrived when a contact and several airmen were arrested. But gradually the two Canadians developed the Shelburne line which consisted of several safe houses and small colonies of evaders or downed airmen. These were fed through Paris and then out to the coast of Brittany near the village of Plouha. In six months Shelburne evacuated over 300 airmen by various routes, and the key to the channel route was Bonaparte beach in Brittany and the House of Alphonse.

ENEMY TERRITORY

La Maison d'Alphonse sat on a cliff in the heart of enemy-occupied territory. A minefield ran between the house and the cliff which descended to the beach which was flanked on the left by a German outpost containing searchlights, cannon and machine guns. The Giguel's house was a small cottage but it became the key assembly point for evaders about to become escapers.

As the backlog of evaders built up in houses along the line and camps in the woods, LaBrosse finally got word from the BBC on 29 January, which announced: "Good evening to everyone in the House of Alphonse." This told LaBrosse that a British Motor Torpedo Boat (MTB) had left Portsmouth and would soon be standing-by off the beach for the first pick-up of 18 men bound for England.

La Maison d'Alphonse was the end of the line for evaders who had been shuffled from point to point like pawns in a chess game.

The packages were moved from place to place until they graduated to the modest cottage near Plouha. Many Frenchmen, like Francois Kerambrun, were involved in the process. Kerambrun lived in the village of Guingamp, the second-last stage in the escape route, and delivered dozens of evaders to La Maison d'Alphonse.

EVOKING PATRIOTISM

On one occasion, while transporting 20 Americans, his truck became impaled upon a spike of a tank-trap in broad daylight. When accosted by Gendarmes, Karambrun decided he would have to tell the truth and evoke patriotism. If patriotism failed, he would have to shoot men in blue. Fortunately, they were patriotic.

The success of the line and the Bonaparte operation was due to the courage of natives who undertook great risks and the strong sense of discipline provided by LaBrosse and Dumais. Many of the airmen ultimately rescued by Shelburne were Americans who were suffering heavy bombing casualties. In one week, in this period, they lost over 4000 airmen. Ralph Patton was among the missing and gradually ended up at La Maison d'Alphonse. But he and a companion arrived unannounced and this set alarm bells ringing at the crowded cottage in Brittany.

"What was your last stopping point before you left USA?" The GI .45 was pointed at Patton's gut and the interrogator barked, "Where were you stationed in England?"

A motley bunch of English, French, Canadians and Americans crowded the small room. Most had no idea why they were there and a voice broke out in my defence. "You don't have to answer any of those questions. You're an officer in the US Air Force...name, rank and serial number!" There was a loud mumble of assent.

"Shut up!" snapped the interrogator. "It's my job to get you back to England. Some of you may have holes in your bellies but you'll get back." The man who called himself Captain Harrison didn't stand on protocol. Patton later learned he was Sergeant Major Lucien Dumais, head of the Shelburne Line.

But the stranger who glared at Patton wanted to know how two extra airmen had arrived at La Maison d'Alphonse. Lieutenant Jack McGough and Patton had been on the run since their B-17 was shot down eight weeks ago. All of the men crowded into the tiny stone building had undergone similar experiences. But McGough and Patton were the uninvited because Dumais had not known they were coming from Guingamp, a staging centre up the line.

They had been transported by François Kerambrun's truck, but apparently were not scheduled to arrive until the next major mission. Finally convincing him they were genuine, Dumais explained the plan.

A corvette was enroute from England and boats would pick the men up on Bonaparte Beach, less than a mile away. Dumais was emphatic: "This is the most dangerous part of your escape. Do exactly as you are told. Follow the man in front of you very closely. Don't deviate one step, left or right. When you get to the cliff, sit down. Dig your heels and hands in tightly. Don't slip or you might take the whole line down with you. And, above all, keep your damn mouth shut!"

A TIDE OF DOUBTS

Enemy patrols, mines, coastal defences and weak hearts were obstacles encountered en route to the beach. A French pilot located the mines while organizer, François Le Cornac, had patrols timed so 35 men could slip through.

Reaching the beach, Dumais flashed a "B" in Morse code. Minutes dragged and doubts swept in with the tide. Then the night was ripped by fire and the roar of cannons on the left. It came three times, then there was silence. More signals to see, more impatience, more waiting and more grumbling. At about 3 o'clock, we heard the first faint sound of oars as five plywood skiffs drifted in on gentle swells.

They boarded the boats and, as they cast off, Dumais and his band of French patriots waved adieu, then turned wearily to climb the cliff and prepare for the next mission. After the war, Dumais admitted that the hardest part of his job was climbing the cliff instead of getting into a boat.

REPRINTED FROM:
Esprit de Corps, *Volume 5 Issue 11*
AUTHORS:
Norman Shannon and Ralph Patton

CANADA'S WINGS FACTORY

BELOW: *As the recruits in the BCATP graduated to flight training, accidents sometimes happened. In this bizarre instance, a pilot somehow managed to park his Avro Anson on top of another. (BCATP MUSEUM)*

Canada's greatest contribution to allied victory, the British Commonwealth Air Training Plan turned out 131,000 aircrew.

MOST OF THE BRITISH Commonwealth Air Training Plan existed only on paper by the end of 1939, but even before it was removed from political posturing, the first few steps on a long complicated journey had been taken as site selection for aerodromes had begun. Much of the survey work and planning was done in the winter so that bulldozers moved in during the spring of 1940.

AERODROME CONSTRUCTION

The RCAF's strength at the declaration of war was 4,061 personnel and the training plan called for a tenfold increase in size merely to provide trained personnel to keep things moving at 74 depots and flying schools. Canada's Minister for Air, Chubby Power, was responsible for recruitment and training. Transport Minister C.D. Howe energetically directed aerodrome construction, and 17 civilian flying clubs agreed to provide elementary flight training. The aircraft program was directed by Ralph Bell, an executive who reported to Howe. Bell experienced his first setback when Britain was unable to deliver 1500 Ansons promised as advanced trainers.

England stood alone in 1940 and the gravity of the situation hit those in the know when a shipload of Ansons was ordered back to England in mid-Atlantic. If Britain depended on the Anson for defence then the situation was indeed even worse than the new Prime Minister's promise of blood, sweat and tears. Howe attacked the problem by buying up all the engines an American firm could produce and establishing Federal Aircraft to produce the Ansons for training potential bomber pilots.

He solved the problem of training fighter pilots by having Noorduyn Aviation produce over 100 Harvards a month. And if there was one sound which came to say it all about Canada's war effort, it was the sound of a distant Harvard changing pitch in the frosty air anywhere from Summerside to Medicine Hat. Air Commodore Leckie came over from England to become another key player as he was named the RCAF's director of training. Seven Manning Depots began to receive recruits during the winter and by April 1940, the first draft of BCATP students arrived at the Eglington Hunt Club in Toronto which had been turned into an Initial Training School.

FIRST STOP ON THE WAY

From the perspective of the new recruit, the Manning Depot was the first stop on his

ABOVE: *As the BCATP took shape, extensive planning was required to manage the complex organization in which 51 air training schools were created between April 1940 and December 1941. By May 1942, the BCATP had taught 39,000 students, over 80 per cent of them Canadian, with the balance coming from Britain, Australia and New Zealand.* (DND)

way to war. Here he got a haircut, a winter cap which slid down over his ears when he bashed the parade square which was often. He learned to make his bed with tidy corners and if he happened to be at No. 1 Manning Depot in Toronto, he quickly adjusted to the permeating stench of cattle manure. The bull pen at the Canadian National Exhibition grounds was a major centre of activities. Generations of cattle had left happy mementos of better times in various patterns on the floor. It was this build-up which the RCAF considered as an ideal marching surface.

Later in the plan, those recruits parading outside were constantly exposed to aircraft doing circuits and bumps from nearby Toronto Island. The endless stream of aircraft were flown by tall, blond Norwegians who would soon be swaggering around Sunnyside wearing a white aircrew flash in their caps which became a beacon for women.

The time an individual spent at Manning Depot depended on how well the entire training treadmill was moving and also the demand for certain trades. Most were assured that the Airforce would find some backwater shack which needed guarding and this meant a period on guard duty and a chance to become familiar with the Southern Cross or the Big Dipper.

Although a recruit may have originally been selected as pilot or observer when he signed up, some unwritten law or Catch 22 gave the RCAF authority to con certain groups into other trades. This exercise went according to demand. One group had successfully completed training at Initial Training School but, instead of going through as pilots or observers, all were packed off to become Wireless Air Gunners.

THERE WAS THE CONSTANT DANGER OF OBSCURE INTERVIEWS. BLAND FACED, WINGLESS ADMINISTRATIVE OFFICERS ASKED HYPOTHETICAL QUESTIONS, THE ANSWER TO WHICH ASSUREDLY DETERMINED IF ONE BECAME A PILOT OR OBSERVER. TALL CANDIDATES TENDED TO SCRUNCH DURING SUCH INTERVIEWS BECAUSE EVERY NOW AND THEN RUMOUR HAD IT THAT THE RCAF WAS ONLY TAKING SHORT PILOTS.

A KNOWING SQUINT

In the spring of 1941, there was a sudden demand for radar mechanics. The exercise went something like this: a recruit was examined and tested for aircrew. Then some genial administration person congratulated him and said: "By the way there's another course coming up...most interesting... good possibilities of commissions... dealing with radar." The word radar was usually uttered with a knowing yet secretive squint. The deal was if the applicant didn't like the course, he could always remuster.

Hundreds, later thousands, took the difficult course and went on to vital groundcrew work. But a number followed Slim's lead. Slim wrote the final exam at the University of New Brunswick in less than 30 seconds.

A stunned physics professor read the paper to the class which hadn't completed the first question on a superheterodyne: "There'll always be an England and I intend to buy lots of war bonds.

Somewhere there's a Spitfire waiting for me and I damn well want to find it."

By fall, Slim had hundreds of followers who returned to Manning Depots. Some, like Slim, got to remuster but as candidates were reviewed alphabetically many of those in the bottom half of the alphabet came a cropper on 7 December when Japan hit Pearl Harbour. The priority became defence of the West Coast and the RCAF responded by sending bodies with no training and less aptitude. Presumably, numbers alone solved a public relations problem.

One group whose first experience with boats was the one which took them up the Inland Passage to absolute isolation at Alliford Bay in the Queen Charlottes. On their second aircrew interview, they had inadvertently selected duty on high-speed rescue launches as a second choice. But instead of streaking across the English channel, this group's first encounter with war was to scrape barnacles and paint buoys and themselves with red, lead paint. However, in spite of many detours, the flow to Initial Training Schools grew steadily. For potential pilots the schools were a psychological obstacle course. The idea was to emerge with a recommendation for pilot training. It wasn't enough to flex one's muscles like Buster Crabbe or memorize where each valve was during the intake stroke.

NOT VERY TALL

There was the constant danger of obscure interviews. Bland faced, wingless administrative officers asked hypothetical questions, the answer to which assuredly determined if one became a pilot or observer. Tall candidates tended to scrunch during such interviews because every now and then rumour had it that the RCAF was only taking short pilots. The conveyor of such information usually confirmed it with: "Billy Bishop wasn't very tall was he?"

Those who survived I.T.S. and the demon link trainer experience took either of two routes: they went to one of 26 Elementary Flying Schools or became observer trainees at one of ten schools. At EFTS the trainees did battle with the mighty Tigerschmidt (Tiger Moth) or Fleet Finch and counted off the hours to solo. If they counted above 13, it usually meant an interview with the terminator.

Those who survived EFTS moved to Service Flying in either Harvards or Yales if streamed as potential fighter pilots. Bomber candidates trained on Ansons or Cranes. After cross-country flights on the prairies, English students often returned in confusion and abject fear of being washed out because of poor map-reading.

Ogilvie Oats had grain elevators sprinkled all over the prairies with the name "Ogilvie" standing distinctly tall. British student-pilots checking landmarks invariably saw Ogilvie but failed to find it on a map. Confusion grew by the second because there were few other landmarks as distinctive as the elevators. Canadians later nodded sympathetically as the distraught Brits told their story, but there is no record of anybody ever telling a Brit that Ogilvie was the guy who made oats.

Observers started the war as jacks of all trades: they acted as navigators, bomb-aimers and nose gunners. In September, 1942, the march of technology induced the RAF to limit the function of the navigator to navigation.

A PRIMARY SOURCE OF PERSONNEL

The original BCATP was to be phased out in March, 1943, but by 1942 it became obvious that the end of the war was nowhere in sight and the scheme was expanded. At its peak, the plan operated 97 schools with 184 support units. It turned out 131,000 aircrew graduates in eight categories from the Commonwealth and France, Belgium, Holland, Norway, Czechoslovakia and Poland. Of the 72,835 Canadians there were 25,747 pilots; 12,855 navigators; 6,659 air bombers; 12,744 wireless air gunners; 12,917 air gunners; 1913 flight engineers. The significance of the BCATP was the significance of the RAF's air war itself and its cost. The BCATP became a primary source of personnel for Bomber Command which lost more than 55,500 aircrew in the campaign to defeat Hitler, and most of Canada's 13,589 fatal casualties were drawn from British Commonwealth Air Training Plan graduates.

REPRINTED FROM:
Esprit de Corps, *Volume 6 Issue 10*
AUTHOR: *Norman Shannon*

PUSH TO THE RHINE

Canadian water-rats of the 3rd Division devour enemy strong points along 25 miles of water.

WITH THE ENEMY THREAT in the Ardennes removed and the *Luftwaffe* virtually wiped out on New Year's Day, the allies returned to plans for a break-out from Nijmegen.

From mid-January the Medium bombers and fighter-bombers of the Second Tactical Air Force worked enemy communications centres between the Rhine and the Maas. Then on 7 February, Goch was hit by 464 heavies and the next night 295 Lancasters destroyed Cleve. The last Lanc had not left when artillery, south of Nijmegen, started a five hour barrage from 1700 guns which hurled 160,000 shells south-eastward through the corridor between the Rhine and the Maas. It was the start of Operation Veritable, the drive to crack the Siegfried Line.

Canadians who wanted to kick the mud of Nijmegen from their boots had to be patient. There was plenty of mud ahead. Gen Crerar's First Canadian Army, strengthened by eight British divisions, numbered some 450,000 men, the largest force ever assembled under Canadian command.

CANADIAN OBJECTIVE

It moved south-eastward on a six-mile front which expanded to 20 miles in the flooded corridor. Their objective was the shell of the town of Wesel on the west bank of the Rhine. Here they were to link up with the Americans, scheduled to move up from the south. The First Canadian Army moved off on 8 February 1945, but the United States' Ninth Army was delayed for two weeks by severe flooding.

The weather was bad, the terrain soggy and about 25 miles of land adjacent to the south bank of the Rhine was a lake, in many places four feet deep. The British moved

LEFT: *Beginning on 8 February 1945, Operations VERITABLE and BLOCKBUSTER were designed to push the Germans back into the Reichwald Forest – thereby clearing the land between the Maas and Rhine Rivers. Moving along the flooded riverbanks, the amphibious Buffalo, the water rats of the 3rd Canadian Infantry Division move into position. (DND)*

against the Reichwald Forest on the left, and the Canadian 3rd Division's initial course was over the flooded area to the right of what began as a six-mile front. Mild weather and the fact that the enemy had breached dykes days earlier, made it necessary to substitute amphibious Buffalos and Weasels for tanks.

THE WATER RATS

But the water rats who landed in Normandy and fought their way through the Scheldt were probably the most accomplished troops in Europe at soggy warfare. They moved towards their objectives in water and took Leuth, Zandpol and other villages which were underwater. Then, like the Loch Ness Monster, the 3rd Division devoured enemy strong points along 25 miles of water.

On the first day of the attack, the 2nd Division took Wyler and units to the south and moved on to their objectives, wiping out six enemy battalions which screened the 'Siegfried Line.' The 53rd Welsh Division spent the first night of Operation Veritable on the northern fringes of the Reichwald Forest, hard against the 'Siegfried Line' while the British 51st Highland Division moved to the south. The Canadians lost many vehicles and attack battalions were sometimes marooned as they cleared Millingen and moved towards Cleve. At Rindern, they fought off a strong counterattack by enemy paratroopers and the pillboxes at Duffelwald told them they had reached the 'Siegfried Line'.

LOGISTICAL PROBLEMS

Meanwhile, the enemy threw three additional divisions into the Reichwald battle. Major roads such as the one leading from Nijmegen to Cleve were under four feet of water, creating massive logistical and communication problems. In spite of this, the centre was reinforced with three British divisions which cleared the Reichwald five days into the operation. But ahead lay the centre of Goch and more heavily defended forests.

The Canadians swung in from the manmade lake to clear Moyland Wood, a strip reinforced by the Panzer Lehr Division and another infantry division. On the second day of the encounter, the enemy's shelling was the heaviest the Royal Winnipeg Rifles had yet encountered and the diary of the Regina Rifles agreed that it was as bad as anything in Normandy.

During one night, the Canadian Scottish beat off six savage counterattacks. While the 3rd Division struggled in Moyland Wood, the 2nd Division swung south to the Goch-Calcar road which was critical and heavily defended. Battalions of the Essex Scottish and the Royal Hamilton Light Infantry swept across open ground in Kangaroos, supported by Fort Garry tanks and artillery.

The tanks bogged down, and German 88's on the road took their toll. The infantry reached its objective but came under heavy fire. The Essex Scottish was overrun and, at one point, it was feared the battalion had been lost. After three days of heavy fighting, the Canadians controlled the road while in the Moyland Wood the Winnipeggers achieved their objectives.

The American attack to the south got underway on 23 February – three days later Crerar sent the 2nd Canadian Corps, plus three British divisions, against the Hochwald Forest. The 2nd Canadian Armoured Brigade and the RCA provided support. On the advance's left flank, the Queen's Own Rifles of Canada were tasked with gaining positions on the road from Calcar to Udem. Two companies moved up a slope towards the objective at 04:30 hrs and met resistance from paratroopers.

Sergeant Aubrey Cosens' platoon twice attacked three farm buildings but were repulsed. The enemy struck back and only five men from the platoon survived the attack. Cosens found himself in command of the survivors who huddled under intense fire. When a Canadian tank appeared, Sergeant Cosens ran 25 yards across open ground, climbed aboard and began directing fire onto the three strong points.

HEROIC ACTION

The enemy tried another counterattack but Cosens scattered the paratroopers with the tank. He rode the tank as it rammed the first building, jumped off and neutralized the occupants. He repeated the process at the second building and then again across the road, leaving 20 dead and 20 captured in his wake. As Cosens left to report to his company commander, a single shot rang out. Cosens fell from a sniper's bullet, but was posthumously awarded the Victoria Cross.

Three days later, Major Frederick Tilston led a company of the Essex Scottish over

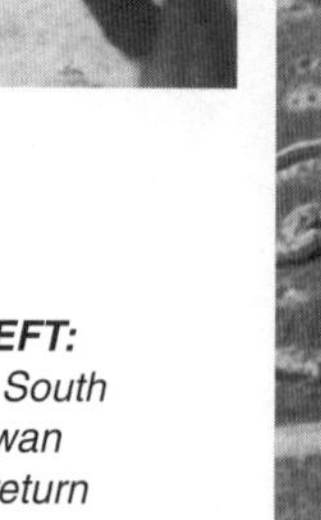

ABOVE, LEFT: *Men of the South Saskatchewan Regiment return enemy fire. (NAC)*

ABOVE: *This aerial photograph clearly shows the trench system of the Siegfried Line near Cleve, which the Canadian 3rd Division reached in February 1945. Built before the outbreak of war, the Siegfried Line would be dismantled to create a supposedly impregnable Atlantic Wall. The ditches were dug parallel to the line to impede the use of tanks. (NAC/PA 145751)*

500 yards of open ground a few miles south of where Cosens had fallen. They attacked under intense fire through ten feet of barbed wire into the enemy trenches.

Tilston wiped out a machine-gun nest with a grenade and was hit in the hip as he leaped into a network of trenches. He led his men in hand-to-hand combat but three-quarters of the company was gone. Major Tilston organized his 26 survivors and made several trips across bullet-swept ground. Wounded three times, he finally turned over command to the one remaining officer. In the skirmish on the brink of the Hochwald Forest, Frederick Tilston lost both legs but won the Victoria Cross.

FANATIC ENEMY

Late in February, the 3rd Division captured Kepplen and Udem and the 4th was positioned on slopes overlooking the Hochwald. Infantry and tanks of the 4th Armoured Division were halfway through a gap between the Hochwald and the Balberger Wald forests when they came under intense fire. The battle in the forest raged for several days and all Canadian formations were engaged. When they fought their way out, veterans once again compared it to Caen or the Scheldt. For the fanatic enemy, the shadows of the Hochwald were the final stage on the road to Armageddon.

The 4th Armoured Division fought its way through the gap, turned south and fought another fierce engagement at Veen. Then they closed with other formations on Wesel where the British and Canadians linked up with the US Ninth Army. The enemy blew the bridges and withdrew to the east bank of the Rhine.

RIGHT: *Carefully making their way across open ground, a company of the Essex Scottish comes under intense fire from the heavily fortified farm buildings occupied by the German Wehrmacht. (IMPERIAL WAR MUSEUM)*

WELL EXECUTED OPERATION

The operation was perhaps one of the best executed of the war, under extremely difficult circumstances against a determined enemy. General Eisenhower wrote to Crerar: "Probably no assault in this war has been conducted under more appalling conditions of terrain." The cost was high. The First Canadian Army had 15,634 casualties of which one-third were Canadian. The Americans had 7300 and the Germans 90,000.

The Canadian Army – with strong support from the British – had broken the 'Siegfried Line.' Within two weeks there were no German troops west of the Rhine and the allies were ready to spring across. On the evening of 23 March, 1300 guns opened up. It was the overture to the last act of the Third Reich.

REPRINTED FROM:
Esprit de Corps, *Volume 4 Issue 9*
AUTHOR: *Norman Shannon*

RAIDERS TWILIGHT

The end came suddenly for submarine crews. Three weeks after they sank HMCS *Esquimalt* near Halifax, the crew of U-190 surrendered in Bay Bulls, Nfld.

ABOVE: *Lying in the shallow waters of the Grand Banks, U-190 spotted the Bangor-class minesweeper as she sailed towards Halifax on calm seas in the early morning hours of 16 April 1945. Firing a Gnat Torpedo weapon the U-boat hit HMCS* Esquimalt *directly on her starboard side. Within four minutes, she was gone. Only 26 of the 70-man crew survived. These men were rescued at sea after surviving several hours in frigid water. (PAC)*

AMERICAN FORCES CLOSED ON Berlin and the Allies thrust across the Elbe in mid-April of 1945. Then politics took over and the Yanks were warned off Berlin and the Canadians and other allies were slowed down out of deference to the Russians approaching from the East. The blue skies above a devastated Germany turned milky white at height, a result of contrails from an announced 10,000 allied aircraft.

Hamburg, Kiel, Wilhelmshaven and Lubeck lay in rubble, but a deadly array of new German submarines still roamed the Atlantic and inland waters. The resurgence started about the time von Rundstedt's troops pushed towards Malmedy in mid-December of 1944, but this time Germany's second wave of 445 improved submarines was taking the war to inland waters and became active in the English Channel.

Among the first victims was a British ship sunk in St-George's Channel and another off Cornwall in spite of the presence of eight RN support groups. Six more ships were sunk and two damaged before the end of December. One was the US troopship *Leopoldville* which went down with an estimated 2500 lives.

TORPEDOED IN HALIFAX

Two days before the *Leopoldville* went down, the Canadian freighter *Samtucky* was torpedoed at the entrance to Halifax harbour. Officials thought she struck a mine but when a torpedo was found in her beached hold, an alarm of sorts went out. Patrols were stepped up and the *Clayoquot*, *Transcona* and the frigate *Kirkland Lake* were sweeping off the Sambro Light Vessel.

It was all in the line of duty but nobody took the threat too seriously. On the *Clayoquot* at noon on Christmas Eve, off-duty seamen lined up for a shot of grog in the best Nelsonian tradition. Then a torpedo struck and blew the *Clayoquot* out of the water, and the RCN into the real war.

It was launched by Kauptman (Captain) Claus Hornbostel of the U806 who, three days earlier, had sunk the *Samtucky*. Admiral Murray did not have a response team, as everything was out on patrol elsewhere. But he put together a small array of boats and ships which predated a scene from "The Russians Are Coming." It was a scrub force of launches, corvettes and minesweepers which carried out asdic sweeps. The operation was screwed up by the Nelson tradition when a shore-based RN officer took over the search from Commander N. Clarke, of the *Kirkland Lake*. The RN's assumption of superiority on traditional grounds without pacing the war on technical grounds was a major factor in the RCN's questionable performance at this time. While Claus sat on the bottom, the search grew and moved out to sea. Hornbostel had dropped to the ocean floor, shut off all systems, had a cold Christmas dinner and waited 14 hours before moving on. This was the pattern of the schnorkel war.

RADAR TURNED OFF

Captain Robert MacMillan sailed the *Bangor Esquimalt* through Halifax's approaches in the early morning 16 April. The radar was switched off because it wouldn't detect a periscope or a U-boat snorkle.

At 06:20 hours, the sweeper was pinging along on old asdic near the Sambro Light Vessel. The U-190 rose to periscope depth and immediately fired a torpedo. The ship's asdic operator reported nothing and the *Esquimalt* continued on a straight course.

The torpedo struck and two of the carley floats refused to release through poor maintenance. Within four minutes the ship went down in a bright, calm sea and within sight of shore.

An RCAF aircraft overflew. The crew saw the men in the floats and thought they were fishermen. The Light Vessel was silent and later two minesweepers swept by and also failed to see the waving survivors.

SURVIVAL GEAR INCOMPLETE

Presumably, a Verey pistol or flares was not

part of the *Esquimalt*'s survival gear and for seven hours men drifted away from the rafts and died. Three weeks before the end of the war, 44 of the 70 man crew died almost within earshot of land.

The sad incident dramatized two things: the German success at moving its undersea war to inland waters and the RCN's failure to come to grips with training, equipment and a concerted plan for the second phase of the submarine war. A large part of this failure was probably due to the influence of the RN and its lack of aggression as it continued to fight a defensive war against U-boats in the mid-Atlantic.

Canadian ships with inferior asdics — and relatively few fully trained asdic officers — were in a no-win position both in mid-ocean and in inland waters.

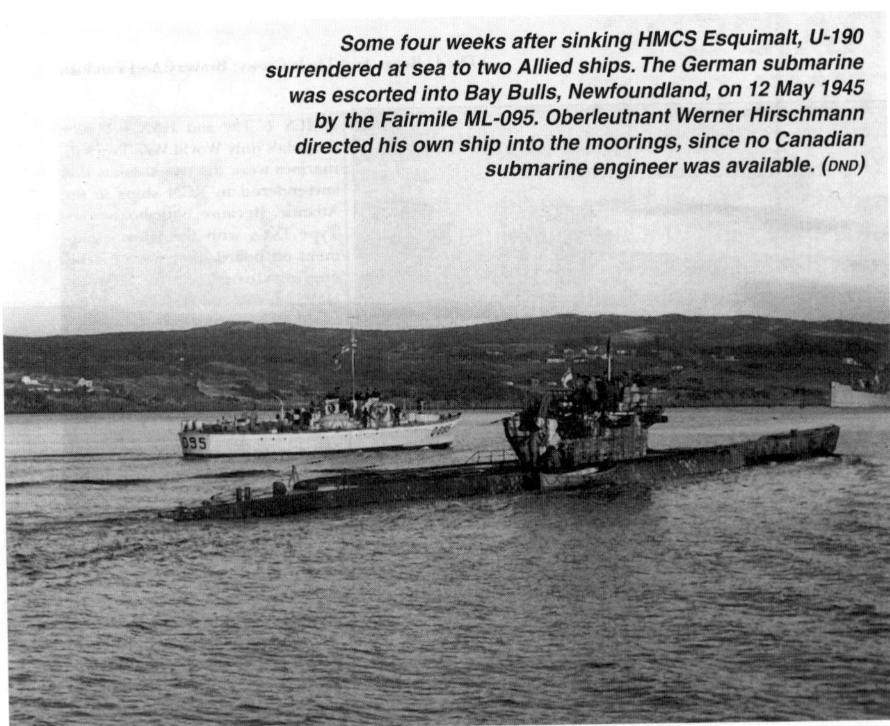

Some four weeks after sinking HMCS Esquimalt, U-190 surrendered at sea to two Allied ships. The German submarine was escorted into Bay Bulls, Newfoundland, on 12 May 1945 by the Fairmile ML-095. Oberleutnant Werner Hirschmann directed his own ship into the moorings, since no Canadian submarine engineer was available. (DND)

ASDIC LIMITATIONS

In the cold northwest Atlantic, asdic would not penetrate with accuracy to 200 feet because of temperature variations which bent the waves. In shallow waters, the reverse was true but these scientific truths were not discovered until 1944 and few Canadian ships were equipped with compensating asdics before the end of the war.

Yet the RCN accounted for 19 submarines during the last two years of the war, the last encounter taking place in March 1945. It was an engagement which definitely fell into the 'you lose some you win some category.' On the night of 26 March, the *New Glasgow* slipped out of Londonderry with a group bound for training in Loch Alsh. Four ships steamed north line abreast. A lookout on the *New Glasgow* warned: "Low flying aircraft approaching!" Suddenly the lookout did a second take: "Object in the water!" he yelled. Seventy-five yards away the periscope and schnorkel of a submarine closed at speed. The *New Glasgow*'s Captain ordered a shallow depth charge pattern but it was too late.

NOT A GOOD NIGHT

Oberleutenant zur See Struebing, Captain of the U-1003, was not having a good night either. While his sub ran on schnorkel, their radar operator failed to report a contact dead ahead. There was violent contact and Struebing's boat was pushed down out of control. Struebing ordered all engines cut; the engineer ordered full ahead. The U-boat hit the bottom some 200 feet down.

THE U-190 ROSE TO PERISCOPE DEPTH AND IMMEDIATELY FIRED A TORPEDO. *ESQUIMALT*'S ASDIC OPERATOR REPORTED NOTHING AND THE SHIP CONTINUED ON A STRAIGHT COURSE. THE TORPEDO STRUCK [AND] WITHIN FOUR MINUTES THE SHIP WENT DOWN IN A BRIGHT, CALM SEA AND WITHIN SIGHT OF SHORE.

New Glasgow circled and the word went out that she had rammed a U-boat. She was leaking and the asdic was damaged. Other ships in the group dropped depth charges.

Although they shook up the U-1003, an hour later Struebing was able to move away. Some 40 hours later the crew scuttled the damaged sub. After due deliberation, the Admiralty credited the *New Glasgow* with the RCN's last kill of the war.

STATISTICS

The enemy lost 632 U-boats but sank 2600 merchant ships and 175 allied warships. The Royal Canadian Navy was credited with 33 enemy submarines and lost 24 ships to undersea action. The defiant U-boat fleet lost 28,000 men, some 70 per cent of their crews, and were active until 8 May when Admiral Dönitz ordered them to surrender. Over 100 submarines were scuttled and the last surrendered at sea. Then the last of the raiders were brought into Canadian ports. The U-190 was brought into Bay Bulls by the RCN and the U-889 was escorted to Shelburne, Nova Scotia

Years later, the commander of a Canadian Corvette recalled that period at Brest as they watched the crew of a submarine officially surrender. They had been at sea for some time and had that blue, scruffy feeling. On the submarine deck, a nattily attired crew marched into captivity with a flourish. The officer standing next to the Captain muttered in amazement: "And we won the bloody war?"

REPRINTED FROM:
Esprit de Corps, *Volume 4 Issue 11*
AUTHOR:
Norman Shannon

D-DAY DODGERS LIBERATE DUTCH

LEFT: *On 5 May 1945 Lieutenant General Charles C.C. Foulkes (left), commander of the 1st Canadian Corps, accepted the formal surrender on the Canadian sector, from the 25th German Army's commander, General Johannes Blaskowitz (second from right), who commanded the German forces in the Netherlands.* (NAC/PA 138588)

The 1st Canadian Corps moves from Ravenna, Italy, to the Nijmegen sector of Holland.

IN 1945 1st Canadian Corps saved the people of Amsterdam, Rotterdam and the Hague from starvation and took the surrender of General Johannes Blascowitz and the remnants of his German 25th Army in Holland. May is pay-back time as the Dutch once again open their hearts and homes to thousands of Canadian veterans and their families.

The 1st Corps' D-Day came 11 months earlier than 6 June 1944, when they landed in Sicily and fought fierce battles against a relentless enemy up the spine of Italy to the Po Valley. But after Rome fell—the day before the Normandy landings—they were bypassed; ignored, forgotten. I was with them most of the way from the beaches of Pachino to the Lombardy Plain, and I know how they felt.

HEAVIEST CASUALTIES

They suffered the heaviest casualties in cracking the 'Gothic line,' but no one noticed or seemed to care. Then Lady Astor dubbed them the D-Day Dodgers and her attempt at humour stuck in their craw. Yet shortly afterwards they turned mortification into defiance, and sang a bitter little ditty to the tune of *Lili Marlene*:

We are the D-Day dodgers, way out in Italy,
We're always tight, we cannot fight,
What bloody use are we?

THE VICTORY PARADES BEGAN. THE D-DAY DODGERS WERE TREATED LIKE CONQUERING HEROES; THEY WERE MOBBED BY AN ADORING PUBLIC, CARRIED SHOULDER HIGH, KISSED BY PRETTY GIRLS AND EVEN HAD TO SIGN AUTOGRAPHS.

Today Canadian veterans of the Italian campaign wear a cap which proclaims "I am proud to be a D-Day Dodger." But today such veterans appear to be more isolated than their British counterparts who served in the Eighth Army. During the celebrations in 1995, marking the 50th Anniversary of the Normandy landings, the Dodgers felt slighted and ignored.

FOR THE RECORD

Sir Alex Guiness, who served in the Mediterranean during the war, protested. In a letter to *The Spectator* (Hamilton, Ontario), he said:

> *...All praise and homage to the men who finally took northern France, but I think it would be appreciated if those involved in the softening up, and indeed the defeat, of Mediterranean Europe, which enabled 6 June 1944 to go ahead successfully, were not totally forgotten. If children are to be taught some military history, it would be good if it is fairly accurate...*

Fifty years ago in April, the 1st Corps completed its long trek from Ravenna, Italy, to the Nijmegen salient and came under Gen Harry Crerar's command. "For a little more than a month, the 1st Canadian Army fought as a truly Canadian Army instead of a mixed allied force under Canadian command." [From *The Sound of War.*] Ironically, the newly arrived 1st Corps, which had been all but forgotten, was given the job of liberating Holland. One suspects that this had nothing to do with a consolation prize but followed the military tradition of having the 1st Corps on the left flank.

CREDIT DUE

As it developed, the 1st Corps advanced into Holland while the 2nd Corps swept to the right and advanced along the Dutch-German border. Veterans of the 2nd Corps were indignant, if not somewhat miffed. They claimed they did the dirty work, the harsh fighting on the cold, wet banks of the Scheldt and later on the Nijmegen front and beyond. With justification, they felt they had been a major force in the enemy's withdrawal and deserved the honour of liberating Holland. But they mistakenly transferred their frustration to a group of men who had also fought a bitter war with no credit.

At the time, few members of the 2nd Corps took any comfort from the fact that the blame for the mess fell squarely on the shoulders of the Mackenzie King Government which, for domestic political reasons, broke up the Canadian Army and put one of its two corps in Italy.

CHILLED RELATIONS

While relations between the two corps were somewhat chilled, it soon became apparent that priority had to be given to feeding the Dutch in the great cities where they were dying of starvation. I was the only Canadian correspondent to wangle his way into a food conference with the enemy, held some ten days before D-Day. It arranged dropping zones and other ways of getting food to the cities and the D-Day Dodgers played an important role in the operation. A second conference was held in a hotel at Wageningen and the Germans surrendered to General Foulkes on 5 May.

Then the victory parades began. No one who was in the Fortress Holland area 50 years ago will ever forget the huge, excited crowds everywhere, cheering and throwing flowers. I can testify that a well-aimed bunch of tulips could hit with quite a smack. As for the D-Day Dodgers, they were treated like conquering heroes; they were mobbed by an adoring public, carried shoulder high, kissed by pretty girls and even had to sign autographs.

The love affair between Canada and Holland has not only endured but has grown over the years. Generations of school children have adopted Canadian graves which they decorate on the soldier's birthday and 5 May, the Dutch Liberation Day.

REPRINTED FROM:
Esprit de Corps, *Volume 4 Issue 11*
AUTHOR:
Peter Stursberg
(Mr. Stursberg is the author of *The Sound of War.)*

LEFT:
Food parcels and supplies are dropped by an Avro Lancaster bomber to a cheering and grateful Dutch populace in May 1945. (IMPERIAL WAR MUSEUM)

OPPOSITE PAGE:
A thankful Dutch farmer sends a message to the Allied pilots who dropped food rations to the starving people below, and who helped to liberate their country from German occupation.

For the starving Dutch, it was food from heaven but for pilot Paul Burden, the first RAF food drop over Holland was hell.

MANNA FROM HELL

THE DANGER OF widespread starvation in the cities of Western Holland became more acute as the war wound down. And while my Pathfinder Squadron started the month of April with raids on German targets, we ended up flying Operation Manna. A truce had been arranged with the German commander in Holland which allowed the RAF and the USAF to fly food to the Dutch people. For them, it was manna from heaven. But my first operation turned out to be manna from a personal hell. With 38 operations in my book and sensing the end of it all, I was not disturbed when I read the Battle Order for 405 Sqn for 30 April. I was not on it. I stood in the mess pondering the Battle Order, wondering if it was all going to end simply by not having your name posted on a Battle Order.

Charlie rushed up well beyond the brink of despair. Charlie belonged to Meathead's crew. " Paul," he gasped, "we need a driver. God, do we need a driver!" My friend Meathead had 'expired' from bottle fatigue. He was on the battle order and his aircraft awaited out at dispersal.

When you prepared for an operation, clerks with sharp pencils figured out the cost of your flying gear, parachute, sidearms... whatever you drew and signed for before a flight and somehow you figured they would charge it back to your insurance if you went missing. So, in response to Charlie, I casually made my way out to V-Victor without any of that high-tech flying stuff.

ONE ABNORMALITY

I fired up the Lanc in routine fashion. The only abnormality was the 'body' lying on the floor in the area normally occupied by the flight engineer.

We warmed up and then the navigator reported the Gee wasn't working. Gee was some kind of electronic device, the knowledge of which enabled navigators to assume a fleeting degree of superiority over pilots.

In retrospect, the Gee failure was a mere bagatelle because any navigator who could not find Amsterdam or The Hague on a clear day would get lost on the way to the men's room and had no business on a pathfinder squadron.

The other curious aspect of the flight was that radio silence was being observed even though the flight had been planned *with* the Germans and a bunch of them were sitting in the bleachers waiting for us to appear at a racetrack near The Hague.

ONE MORE CRISIS

But old habits die hard and we observed radio silence and shot off a red flare to indicate a malfunction. Pip-Squeak came careening down the perimeter track in a battered Austin to investigate the Gee failure, and this brought us face to

face with another crisis.

As Pip-Squeak approached, I embraced the floorboards and the crew propped Meathead into the pilot's seat, coaching him. Meathead's lips were blue as he looked down at Pip Squeak and laboriously formed the words: "Gee U/S." Pip Squeak yelled up: "Take X-Ray the spare kite!" Then he crunched gears on the Austin and was gone.

Meathead's crew managed to trundle him down the taxiway while I darted behind parked aircraft like an Indian stalking a wagon train.

Soon we were all assembled in X-Ray. Once again, I fired up and we took off. It was all done observing proper radio silence. The approach to the coast in daylight brought a strange lack of flak.

OVERCOME BY DRAMA

Meathead and I had shared many ops together and I was overcome by the drama of the moment: this was our first flight into peace. I think Meathead was similarly moved because he snorted and rolled over on his shoulder.

We found the racetrack and dropped two target indicators at 100 feet and German troops sat in the bleachers waiting for showtime. No shots were fired and I was startled at the sight of hundreds of Dutch citizens on the streets and in windows waving flags and bunting.

This was the first of some 3000 sorties during which Bomber Command delivered 6670 tons of food, but my memory and the official RCAF record are at odds on this first operation. As we approached our home base at Gransden Lodge, I encountered another problem: the normal request to join the circuit. If I used the RT my voice would be recognized.

As I approached base, a wartime career flashed before my eyes with a deep sense of foreboding. Mine. The Canadian government had been making seductive sounds to servicemen about gratuities and other goodies. I was 90 seconds away from destroying it all if I spoke.

I looked down at the body which was now starting to look like a living thing, a freshly caught Miramichi salmon twitching in the bottom of a boat.

REHEARSAL

Meathead even managed to smile although he still showed signs of acute discomfort. "Get him awake!" I said. I would be flying the plane but we needed Meathead alert and within reach of a mike, or RT as we called it then. We rehearsed it and then Meathead came through as he had done on so many operations. He found the strength to mutter into the Mike: "Chisel X-Ray to Ardmore... downwind out."

I flew the downwind leg. Then Meathead managed: "Chisel X-Ray funnel!" Ardmore replied: "Land now." Which is what we did.

Like a bubonic rat, I scurried to my quarters while Meathead's crew celebrated its mission of mercy. Aside from having two pilots for one Lancaster, the lack of flak, the Germans in the bleachers and the Dutch people in the streets, it was a routine operation.

OP CHOW HOUND

When the next Battle Order was posted, I was officially assigned my first Manna mission. The Yanks called it Chow Hound. When I told my crew about the reaction of the Dutch citizens and what to expect, they gathered up all their goodies from parcels and quickly raised scrounging to a fine art as they prepared a special parcel to fit between the guns of the rear turret.

As we approached our target, our air bomber took over the aircraft, directing me: "Left, left steady!" Then we were over the target, hundreds of kids. The bomb-aimer yelled to the rear gunner: "Now!" I banked away blinded by tears and a snotty nose as Tomlinson, the rear gunner, reported: "The parcel hit the ground...it ricochetted off the wall of that apartment building...and Jesus Christ, I've never seen so many kids!"

INCREDIBLE THANKS

Our third sortie was to Rotterdam on 7 May. By now, without official blessing, we were taking groundcrew as spectators. A ladder was placed across the open rear door to provide an excellent view, and one of the passengers was Freck, a diminutive WAAF bat-person who had faithfully brought two buckets of hot water on the handles of her bicycle to our digs each morning for washing and shaving. I like to think that the flight to Rotterdam and the sight of hundreds of happy Dutch people was Freck's great event of WWII.

Even though Bomber Command and I differ on how many Manna operations I flew, somehow they stuck with me for half a century, long after the other operations were pushed to the back of my mind.

REPRINTED FROM:
Esprit de Corps, *Volume 4 Issue 11*
AUTHOR: *Paul Burden*

***RIGHT**: When victory in Europe was announced, celebrations in Halifax turned into drunken revelry accompanied by looting and rioting. Many storefront windows were broken and looters swarmed the liquor and beer stores. (DND)*

Threats to "take Halifax apart" were ignored by civil and naval authorities. On VE Day, the city paid the price.

MURRAY'S FOLLY

IT WAS NOT ADMIRAL Murray's finest hour. On VE Day, the Commander-in-Chief North-West Atlantic was reduced to navigating a sound van through the streets of Halifax bellowing into a loud-hailer: "This is Admiral Murray speaking… in person… Go to your billets, your ships, your homes…. Don't stand about the sidewalks…. This is an order! It is not a joke!" From time to time, as the van swerved around servicemen and civilians loaded down with looted clothing, furniture, tinned goods and liquor, he pleaded: "Go back to your ships boys! You don't want to get caught do you?" Crunching through broken glass, the Shore Patrol followed him, unceremoniously dumping the bodies of drunken sailors into a convoy of trucks. By nightfall, hundreds had been laid out in rows in the Stadacona Drill Hall. "An unfortunate incident," the Admiral concluded, and chided the citizens of Halifax for leading his men astray.

A SOLEMN PROTEST

Haligonians were outraged. As the rest of Canada celebrated VE Day with parades and picnics, fireworks and street dances, Admiral Murray's "boys" had inflicted the greatest damage on their city since the French munitions ship *Mont Blanc* blew up in the harbour in 1917. Scores were injured, 564 businesses wrecked or damaged, and thousands of plate glass windows shattered. Liquor stores and breweries lost 5000 cases of wine and spirits and 8000 cases of beer to looters. "I must solemnly protest against the Canadian Navy," Mayor A.M. Butler said in a radio address. "It will be a long time before the people of Halifax forget this great crime."

There had been storm warnings. Both civic and naval authorities were aware of repeated threats to "take Halifax apart," but did little to prevent it. The threats were born of frustration. The population of Halifax had doubled to 120,000 during the war, and sailors and civilians alike were fed up with overcrowding, blackouts, extortionate rents, rotten service, and antiquated liquor laws. On any weekend, it was normal for thousands of sailors to roam the streets with precious little to do. On pay nights, they drank their wet canteens dry then headed downtown to fight, break windows, and harass women – as if rehearsing for what was to come.

On 7 May, the news of Germany's surrender set ship whistles and sirens blowing and happy crowds filled the streets. Trouble began when it was discovered that liquor stores, restaurants and theatres were closed. A mob of boisterous sailors, trailed by civilians returning from a fireworks display on Citadel Hill, broke into the Sackville Street liquor store and began passing out bottles. Several other stores were looted, trams were overturned, and a police car set afire. Many of the revellers lurched into St. Paul's Cemetery where they drank them-

selves into a stupor. By midnight, the looting was over and the situation seemed to be under control.

BEER IN THE GUTTERS

All was calm on the morning of 8 May. Despite the looting of the liquor stores the night before, Admiral Murray refused to rescind an order granting his men "open gangway" leave. In the early afternoon, a great wave of seamen surged into the heart of the city, tearing down flags, breaking windows, setting fires, and wrecking shops along the way. Trams collided and careened into buildings. Thousands broke through the gates of Keith's Brewery as the police and Shore Patrol stood by helplessly. Beer ran in the gutters. Goods were hauled out of the stores along Barrington Street in baby carriages and handcarts while a Petty Officer sat drunkenly at a desk in the middle of the street signing imaginary discharges. A nude sailor rode a horse through a Wren's bar-

ABOVE:
Drinking their loot, these sailors and their female friends enjoy their Keith's beer in a Halifax park.
(NAC C 79578)

OPPOSITE PAGE, BELOW:
The first, and only, Canadian to command a theatre of war in WWII, Rear Admiral Leonard Murray (left) would be unceremoniously dismissed and forced to resign for his inability to control his men. Pictured with Murray is Lieutenant Commander John H. Stubbs who died on 29 April 1944 when his destroyer HMCS Athabaskan *was torpedoed in the Bay of Biscay.*
(ROYAL CANADIAN NAVY)

BEER RAN IN THE GUTTERS. GOODS WERE HAULED OUT OF THE STORES ALONG BARRINGTON STREET IN BABY CARRIAGES AND HANDCARTS WHILE A PETTY OFFICER SAT DRUNKENLY AT A DESK IN THE MIDDLE OF THE STREET SIGNING IMAGINARY DISCHARGES. A NUDE SAILOR RODE A HORSE THROUGH A WREN'S BARRACKS AND COUPLES MADE LOVE IN THE PARKS.

racks and couples made love in the parks.

Word of the riots reached Murray at a thanksgiving service on the Garrison Grounds. He ordered the sailors, soldiers, and airmen present to form up behind a navy band and march through the city as a diversion and show of strength. Pelted with empty beer bottles, about half melted into the crowds. At 1800 hours, he met with civic leaders, declared a curfew, then set out aboard a sound van. Order was not fully restored until a contingent of paratroopers was brought into the city from Camp Debert late in the day.

A Royal Commission headed by Justice R.L Kellock of the Supreme Court of Canada, blamed the riots on "the failure of the naval command to keep their personnel off the streets." Admiral Murray was quietly relieved of his command, resigned from the navy, and sailed for England where he became a successful barrister. He died in 1971. Many feel that he was a scapegoat, that he was poorly informed and took the blame for junior officers who failed to contain the situation. The report also pointed out that a good part of the civilian population joined in the mayhem. Nevertheless, the riots are remembered in Halifax as "Murray's Folly" and he was never publicly honoured for his role in winning the Battle of the Atlantic. That was his finest hour.

REPRINTED FROM:
Esprit de Corps, *Volume 4 Issue 11*
AUTHOR:
Bill Twatio

THE FOG OF WAR

A low-key War Museum exhibit sparks a national debate about the Holocaust.

THROUGHOUT RECORDED history people have used the past, or at least their interpretation of the past, to justify their own views and actions. The 1998 debate as to whether a Holocaust exhibit was appropriate at the Canadian War Museum triggered such a response. It is evident that in this country, because of fragmentary knowledge of our military history, anyone can infuse his or her own personal agenda into a debate on pseudo-historical grounds. With passions so high, the aim became not to search for the truth or listen to a different point of view but simply to outdo contrary arguments. Any means to win an argument seemed justified. The debate became a trial in the court of public opinion. Phrases such as the "Fog of War" come to mind.

'Truth is the first casualty of war.' In a heated personal argument, does the truth win out? History and its interpretation in this country varies from one community to another. One missing piece of the puzzle in this episode was the experiences of Canadian troops in The Netherlands and Germany in the spring of 1945. Many Canadian troops involved in the fighting in the last weeks of the war in northern Germany and The Netherlands learned, if they did not already suspect, the ruthlessness of the enemy in its treatment of subject peoples. Emphasis on the Holocaust and its connection or, as some insist, non-connection with Canadian military experience has obscured the liberation by Canadian troops of camps in which POWs and political prisoners had been treated with similar brutality. Neither this aspect nor the Holocaust is separate from the Second World War.

What seemed to strike home the most to many Canadian soldiers in Germany as evidenced from war diaries, photos and radio broadcasts was what they saw of the treat-

ment of Russian, Polish and even Italian prisoners of war. Matthew Halton broadcast from the north German town of Meppen, within a 30-mile radius of which there were political prisons, and POW camps. He spoke of 2,000 Russians in one of the camps, most of them dying.

"We came too late to save them…In another camp which I saw, there are 12,000 Italians in the same condition. When Italy went out of the war those Italian soldiers came over to our side, and were captured by the Germans. They're not human beings any more, to look at…"

In late April Matthew Halton sent the following broadcast;

"Your hate rises, of course, when you see, as I saw the other day, Dutchmen who had been tortured to death. And it rises again when you see the streams of freed slaves thronging down the roads. This astonishing sight is one we see every day. In the areas we've already overrun in Germany we've liberated over a million of these slaves, chiefly Russian and Polish but also French, Czechs, Yugoslavs and others… what an extraordinary thing this is, in the twentieth century. You see these things and wonder if you're not back in the pages of an historical novel, back in the Thirty Years' War. Freed bondsmen – ten or twelve million men and women of Europe have been uprooted by the Germans and enslaved." According to Dr. William McAndrew in his book *Liberation*, "In 2 Canadian Corps area alone there were 42 prisoners or displaced person camps containing Russian, Polish, Czechoslovak, Yugoslav, Italian and other inmates, in which the most appalling conditions were typical."

This aspect of the war was to be shown in a low-key Canadian War Museum exhibit of 2,000 square feet at the end of the Second World War display. How this "Holocaust" exhibit tripled in size and grew into a national debate remains open to question.

In the end, it seems that many people believe what they want to believe about the past. The press reports what it chooses usually in a partisan manner, rather than investigate. A public debate may establish majority opinion but not necessarily the facts.

LEFT: *Female guards at the notorious death camp of Bergen-Belsen unload bodies from a wagon into a mass grave. Within the camps, conditions were appalling: overcrowding, starvation and sickness were made worse by lack of sanitation, violence, forced labour and medical torture.*

TOP LEFT: *When men of the U.S. 42nd Division of the 7th Army liberated the concentration camp at Dachau in May 1945, they were greeted with cheers and jubilation.*
TOP RIGHT: *Along with the estimated six million Jews who died in the death camps, some five million other people also died in camps, including communists, gypsies and homosexuals. Not all of the POWs and political prisoners – those who represented a resistance to the Nazi regime – interned at the Nordhausen camp in Germany lived to see liberation by Allied troops.*

REPRINTED FROM:
Esprit de Corps, *Volume 7 Issue 1*
AUTHOR: *Fred Gaffen*

BEYOND THE PACIFIC

LEFT: *Small groups of four or five men would be dropped into the Burmese jungle to set up networks of resistance against the Japanese. Wading across a river in the jungle areas of highland Burma, these native detachments helped to break down Japanese defenses.*

As the war spread into south-east Asia, Canadians of Chinese and French ethnic backgrounds were in demand as secret agents to work behind enemy lines.

CANADA WIMPED OUT OF the war in the Pacific because the Mackenzie King government feared a conscription backlash and pulled the HMCS *Uganda* out of the British Pacific Fleet late in July 1945.

King organized a Parizeau-type referendum whereby sailors could decide if they still wanted to volunteer. While King was politicking and the *Uganda* came back to Canada under a cloud, another group of Canadians were on operations in South-East Asia. Most had worked so hard to get there that they probably would not have withdrawn at the point of a gun.

About 140 Chinese-Canadians volunteered to serve in South East Asia although few had any idea of what they would be doing as agents of a British undercover agency known as the Special Operations Executive (SOE). The French-Canadians who volunteered for Pacific duty had a pretty good idea of what to expect because, since Gustave Bieler first jumped into France in 1942, French-Canadians were very active in training the underground and carrying out subversive activities in France.

TENUOUS RELATIONSHIP

Canadians also served with the SOE in Yugoslavia, Italy and the Balkans. When the agency turned its attention to South East Asia, it naturally sought volunteers from appropriate ethnic backgrounds, and Chinese-Canadians were suddenly much in demand after having been ignored or discriminated against for most of the war. The relationship between the British and groups in Asian countries were tenuous at best because a strong tide of nationalism and communism was sweeping the colonies of Britain, France and Holland before and during the Japanese invasion.

A year after France fell, the Japanese occupied Indo-China and turned it into a major naval and land base for its later invasion of Malaya. But few Indo-Chinese felt any remorse at exchanging one conqueror for another.

NATIONALISM

The only sense of nationalism came from Ho Chin Minh who managed to get the support of China's Chiang Kai-shek to establish his Viet Minh (Independence League) party. Considering that Chaing represented the Nationalists and Ho Minh the communists, this was no mean accomplishment. Later Ho Minh sent a number of his agents into Japanese occupied north Vietnam and gradually gained control of key installations.

The world saw a measure of his success some 30 years later when the United States lost the war in Vietnam. While Ho Minh's legacy crushed American hearts in 1975, in 1941 he was a slippery ally.

The American OSS (Office of Strategic Services) and the British SOE worked at recruiting allies in the war against Japan, but they weren't always singing from the same song sheet. The American position in Indo-China was that we should not prop up the French after the war. Britain was more inclined to pursue the status quo but she did eventually withdraw from colonialism. However, in seeking allies to fight the Japanese, both countries enlisted patriots, communists, cutthroats and even bands of headhunters.

COMPLICATED TRADE-OFFS

In Burma, trade-offs were complicated by the fact that both the Communist party and the Thakins, an influential group of intellectuals, sought independence and were anti-British. In fact a year before the Japanese invasion, the British were throwing Thakin leaders in jail. One leader, Aung San, evaded British arrest and went to Japan where he trained for six months in leading a revolutionary army. By the time the Japs hit Pearl Harbour, Aung San had 1000 in his Burmese Independence Army.

When the Japanese invaded British Burma in January 1942, Aung San's 4000 troops helped. Then the BIA took to looting and was disbanded by the Japanese, but when Burma was granted a degree of independence in 1943, Aung San was permitted to form a larger, more disciplined Burma National Army. While spreading throughout the country, the BNA made secret contacts with the SOE and became an underground organization. The Communist party and the Thakins secretly formed the Anti-Fascist People's Freedom League in August, 1944, and the SOE promised support for anti-Japanese activities.

In Malaya, the Chinese population already had reason to hate the Japanese and became eager members of the Communist underground or the Malayan People's Anti-Japanese Parti (MPAJP). Japanese reaction was swift and severe as cells were broken up and members forced to scatter to the jungle. They were able to form a network in the jungle and soon the MPAJP was receiving money and equipment from SOE in return for co-operation with the British after the war, but in the first days of peace the MPAJP tried to seize control.

When the Japanese advance in Burma was checked in the spring of 1944, the SOE's campaign in south east Asia became more aggressive. By the spring of 1945, routine drops were being made behind enemy lines, the first being a party of four men into the mountains of Borneo. Here they precariously negotiated with headhunters in seeking support against the Japanese.

Ray Wooler, a Canadian veteran of North Africa and Italy and many months in Britain where he did 300 parachute jumps, dropped out of the sky with three Australians about four months later. His orders were to clear the lower Rejang river of the enemy and he chose the Ibans, a head-hunting tribe, as his escort.

As SOE agents cleared the river, the Ibans wondered at the fickleness of the white man. The British had previously frowned on the custom of taking heads, but now the strangers encouraged a brisk trade by offering a Sarawak dollar for each Japanese head.

Wooler's party worked their way down the river and about a month later he got news that a Canadian team headed by Roger Cheng would touch down by flying boat.

Their job was to infiltrate and keep the Australians aware of Japanese movements on the Sarawak coast and the Rejang delta.

OPERATION CHARACTER

Meanwhile in Burma, Jacques Taschereau, a veteran of the French Resistance, was dropped into the highlands where he linked up with guerrilla tribesmen on a mission of ambushing Japanese attempting to cross into Thailand. Rocky Fournier and Jean-Paul Archambault were also part of Operation Character as were Joseph Benoit, Pierre Chassé, Paul Meunier and Bentley Cameron Hunter.

LEFT: *To claim a victory in Burma and force a retreat of the invading Japanese force, a motley group of international units was sent to help the Chinese to regain this area. By 1945, the amount of supplies required grew from 600 tons of food and ammunition a day to some 8600 tons daily.*

They were assigned to or led different teams whose objective was to cleanse Burma of Japanese. Fournier's expertise with a radio enabled jungle groups to keep in touch with SOE in Calcutta and call up air strikes on Japanese columns. Eventually, Fournier and Thibeault linked up with the British 14th army at Sittang and were flown to hospital suffering from dysentery and malaria which was more formidable to most Canadians than Japanese resistance.

Paul Meunier jumped into the mountains on the other side of Sittang with a five-man team which climbed for nine days before reaching Pegu tribesmen. A recruiting campaign soon had 150 volunteers who became part of an information network which spread out over a 100-mile radius. They called up bombing strikes on enemy food and ammunition dumps and took the garrison at Lelpadan without firing a shot.

Chassé's team went into the flatlands of the Irrawaddy as the 14th Army moved on Rangoon. Charlie Chung jumped with the team near the Thai border. Essentially, their task was to pave the way for the 14th Army's movement south from Rangoon. Chassé linked up with the Burmese National Army. But they didn't have much to do. The day the team moved eastward, a Mosquito pilot did a low level on Rangoon and saw a sign: "Extract Digit Japs Gone."

Henry Fung jumped near Kuala Lampur in Malaya late in June 1945 as part of a team headed by a prewar planter. They joined up with the MPAJA and organized air drops to guerrillas and blew up a railroad bridge, destroyed telephone lines and attacked convoys. The 19 year-old Canadian remained in the jungle for three months and, like many Chinese-Canadians who followed, found that his mission changed when the bombs fell on Hiroshima and Nagasaki.

As the war wound down, SOE teams continued to be dropped into the hinterland of South East Asia but now the orders were to destroy remnants of Japanese resistance. When Japan surrendered, saboteurs became sheriffs and became responsible for the surrender of isolated Japanese garrisons, the release of prisoners and their transportation to India for treatment. There was also the very delicate matter of trying to disarm tribes bent on communist revolt or with a propensity to take heads.

Probably the most effective role of the SOE in that forgotten campaign was the contribution members made to the outposts which helped establish and maintain a critical air link with India.

REPRINTED FROM:
Esprit de Corps, *Volume 5 Issue 1*
AUTHOR: *Paul Burden*

RIGHT:
Typical of the thousands of Canadians who served with RAF squadrons are (left to right) Sergeants W. Gosling, R. Cramer, C. Smith and F. McDonald, pictured while on the Arakan coast of Burma. (DND)

Once some 7500 Canadian airmen were posted to the South-East Asia Command it was a matter of being...

OUT OF SIGHT OUT OF MIND

ALTHOUGH AN ESTIMATED 7500 Canadian airmen, all trades, served in South East Asia, as far as the Canadian public was concerned, it was a matter of being out of sight and out of mind.

When the Japanese first attacked in 1941 about 35 Canadian aircrew were serving with the RAF which had 233 serviceable aircraft in Singapore and Malaya. The rest was junk, scattered over 25 poorly maintained airstrips.

Not only were air defences scattered, coordination between the RAF and the navy was so poor that one night-fighter squadron was forbidden to fly over the naval base at Seletar (Singapore) for any reason whatsoever. The heroism of RAF crews was not enough to stop the Japanese, who sank the *Prince of Wales* and the *Repulse* within 48 hours and went on to spread across the China Sea and into the Indian Ocean.

Five Canadians were searching for Japanese fleets as crews of Catalina flying boats by the end of the month. On 24 December P/O D. Babineau was navigator on a Catalina out of Seletar It was shot down while searching for a Japanese convoy. The crew managed to escape before the Cat blew up, but they spent 11 hours in hostile waters supporting two airmen who had not worn life jackets.

Within five weeks Japanese air attacks forced evacuation of the vulnerable flying boats which were retired to Java where they took up night bombing without much success. Hopes were high when the first of 51 Hurricanes arrived to replace the ineffective Brewster Buffaloes, but they were no match for the Zeros, as Sergeant R. Mendizabel discovered when his machine was badly shot up and he was wounded. Four days later, Sergeant J.P. Flemming destroyed an enemy fighter over Japanese-held Malaya but was immediately shot down himself. It took six days for Flemming to get back to the base at Tengah.

The following day the battered No. 232 squadron was withdrawn to Sumatra, and another Canadian, Flight Lieutenant T.W. Watson, flew the last aircraft off. Unfortunately two Canadian radar technicians didn't make it. Flight Lieutenant L. Montgomery and LAC E. Graham became prisoners.

Watson flew to Palembang, Sumatra, about 1200 miles to the south, but Japanese paratroops hit the field four days later and two Canadian pilots, Sergeants W.H. James and H. Low, were captured while leading ground crew in defence of the base. Watson managed to get off and flew to Java where No. 205 Catalina squadron was then based.

Three days before Sumatra fell, Sergeant R.D. Bonnar, a Canadian navigator with No. 203 Squadron, spotted the approach of a large Japanese fleet. The Cat made a pass and withdrew after sending out a warning. Although it provided the British with an estimated time of arrival of the enemy, it was all academic because the British had no way of stopping the Japanese.

As Java fell, Sergeant R. Mendizabel saw the last of the serviceable aircraft leave. The pilot started building, from scrap at hand, a bunch of Lockheed trainers long pronounced dead. With four other pilots, he flew 2600 miles to Ceylon.

STRUGGLE TO CANADIANIZE

Meanwhile in Scotland, No. 413 Squadron became a battleground in the struggle to Canadianize squadrons. When ordered to Ceylon about 50 per cent of the aircrew and 70 per cent of the ground crew were Canadian but Coastal Command only sent four Catalinas to Ceylon.

Two days after his arrival, Squadron Leader L. Birchall was concluding a 12-hour patrol when he spotted a Japanese fleet in the moonlight. Birchall dove closer to identify and count the enemy ships and was immediately attacked by carrier fighters.

Birchall's Wireless Air Gunner was halfway through a third transmission when a shell killed him and destroyed the radio.

LEFT:
A Catalina flying boat is readied for its next mission on a beach in Ceylon as part of Coastal Command.
(DND)

Under further shelling, fire broke out and pieces fell away from the flying boat.

Birchall reported: "I got the aircraft down on the water before the tail fell off."

OCEAN OF FIRE

A gunner went down with the aircraft. Survivors swam through an ocean of fire, dragging two unconscious crewmen in life jackets. Enemy fighters strafed the survivors, killing the two with life jackets who were now unable to dive under water. Birchall and five of his crew were picked up by a Japanese destroyer.

Next day, 127 carrier-based aircraft attacked the harbour at Columbo which had been cleared of merchant vessels after Birchall's warning. The Japanese force was met by 42 Hurricanes and Fulmars which destroyed 18 aircraft, three of which were brought down by Canadians.

Flight Lieutenant R.G. Thomas of 413 Squadron spotted the Japanese fleet again on 9 April. He was shot down before completing his message. This time there were no survivors and 120 Japanese aircraft hit the port of Trincomalee where 24 were shot down. RAF losses were heavy but the enemy also lost 60 aircraft in the two engagements.

The sad footnote to these heroic actions by the RAF is that while the attacks went in, most of Navy Commander Sir James Sommerville's ships were holed up in Adau Atoll under orders to stay put. Then they withdrew to eastern Africa and India. But RAF air action so depleted Admiral Nagumo's air power that he sent five carriers back to Japan to regroup.

By spring Burma, Malaya and the Dutch East Indies were in Japanese hands, and most of the allied ground action for the next two years saw the allies on the defensive. When Lord Mountbatten took over South East Asia Command in November 1943, one of his first actions was a push on the Arakan coast of Burma.

RAF aircraft struck from treetop height at Japanese supply and communication centres, helping the army hack out a tenuous footing. The monsoons of the following June washed out the operation but in the meantime a new pattern of warfare had developed. Wingate's Chindits launched a new type of invasion deep into enemy territory. Seven columns of commandos slashed their way through 1000 miles of jungle, spreading confusion and panic, and every ounce of food, ordinance and ammunition was supplied by air.

By the end of 1943, Beaufighters and Hurricanes dominated a 700-mile front across Burma. But if a pilot had trouble beyond the front, he inherited big problems not only from the enemy, but from the climate, the jungle and any number of hostile critters therein.

Flight Lieutenant Bob Johnson was shot down on a fighter-reconnaissance mission and managed to jump near a Burmese village. He was pursued by villagers, dogs, and Japanese during his 21-day trek to freedom. On one occasion, he unexpectedly came upon a group of Japanese soldiers on a narrow trail. He met 20 armed enemy as he walked head-down at arm's length. Then he cut for the hills and, after 21 days in enemy jungle, got back to allied lines.

ATTACKING FORCE DECIMATED

When the enemy started its invasion of India in 1944, they laid siege to Kohima and Imphal. The 80-day siege was broken by allied air drops and disease which decimated 75 per cent of the attacking force. Prior to November of that year, with the exception of No. 413 Squadron, thousands of Canadian airmen had served with the RAF. Then 435 and 436 Canadian Transport Squadrons were added and became important elements in Lieutenant General William Slim's 14th Army push into Burma and the capture of Rangoon and Bangkok.

Airdrops were the key to the scattered British defence and later enabled offensive forces to maintain momentum over vast distances. This not only had a tactical impact on the Japanese but also had a profound effect on morale. Supplies were literally dropped into allied foxholes within yards of the Japanese, one of whom complained: "It broke our hearts to see the stuff dropping on British troops day after day while we got nothing."

REPRINTED FROM:
Esprit de Corps, *Volume 5 Issue 1*
AUTHOR:
Norman Shannon

***RIGHT:** On the 25th sortie over south-east Asia, author Harry Smith, bandaged, and his Flight Sergeant Curley Copley (right) were shot down over present-day Thailand on 30 May 1945. After three harried weeks, the wounded crewmen were airlifted to India. (RCAF)*

The first good weather in 18 months came as Harry Smith was over the drop zone some 600 miles in enemy territory, but the weather also attracted nine Zeros.

DOWNED IN SIAM

OUR 25TH AND LAST briefing at Jessore, India, took place after lunch on 29 May 1945. It went something like this: "Smith you will be dropping three OSS [Office of Strategic Services] agents and 14 containers onto a DZ near Korat. There will also be an OSS observer along to witness the drop. Takeoff time will be 00:00 hrs to place you over the DZ at dawn. Your aircraft is 'P' Peter and the I.O. will brief you on enemy activities."

For 18 months we had been flying special duty missions with 358 Squadron, Royal Air Force, dropping British, American and French agents and supplies behind enemy lines in Burma, Malaya, Siam, French Indo China and the Dutch East Indies. Our Liberators ranged more than 1000 miles into enemy territory. Now on our last sortie our time over the DZ meant we would be flying 600 miles of enemy territory in daylight with no fighter escort and only the tail and mid-upper turrets manned.

We were airborne at 23:59 hrs and six and a half hours later began our descent from 6000 feet to reach the DZ at drop altitude. This is when things started to go wrong. The sun over Siam rose earlier than expected. For the first time in 18 months ceiling and visibility was unlimited. Then CAVU soon became SNAFU.

Then bomb-aimer Jack Draper warned: "Enemy fighters at two o'clock." Nine Japanese Oscar fighters closed fast. Three set up a race track for head-on attacks; three hit the starboard quarter and three strafed from above and below but avoided the tail turret.

WITH THE LAST OF OUR AIR SPEED BLEEDING OFF, I GAVE CRASH-LANDING ORDERS, A DRILL WE HAD REHEARSED MANY TIMES. WE WERE TOO LOW TO PARACHUTE AND THE ONLY HOPE OF SURVIVAL WAS IN A TREETOP LANDING... THE PLANE RIPPED THROUGH TREES WITH A COLOSSAL RENDERING OF METAL.

I began violent evasive action and dove for the deck. The frontal attacks were devastating and we were systematically shot to pieces. "Lofty" Brenchley, our navigator, was killed in one of the first attacks. Bill Pinckney, our mid-upper gunner, fired steady bursts until he was hit. Then co-pilot Bob Poole was hit while jettisoning containers. The flight deck was a shambles with cannon shells and bullets slamming about everywhere, and the fighters continued their attacks gradually destroying virtually everything including the engines.

TOO LOW TO PARACHUTE

With the last of our air speed bleeding off, I gave crash-landing orders, a drill we had rehearsed many times. We were too low to parachute and the only hope of survival was in a treetop landing such as Canadian bush pilots used. At the last minute, I lowered the flaps to reduce airspeed and dropped the undercarriage to absorb some of the impact. When trees brushed along the bottom of the aircraft, I braced both feet against the instrument panel and hauled back on the control column with all my might. Even with Bob Poole's inert body draped over the controls, strength born of desperation helped me put the B-24 into a full stall.

The plane ripped through trees with a colossal rendering of metal. The wings sheared off with their load of fuel and I was glad to see them go. The impact folded me around the control column. Recovering, I noticed a small hole in the side of the fuselage which I ripped wider until I could crawl through. Bill Pugh, the 2nd Wireless Operator, followed but his foot caught in the jagged metal so he ended up hanging upside down.

A bullet had gone through his hand, rendering it useless and I released him and low-

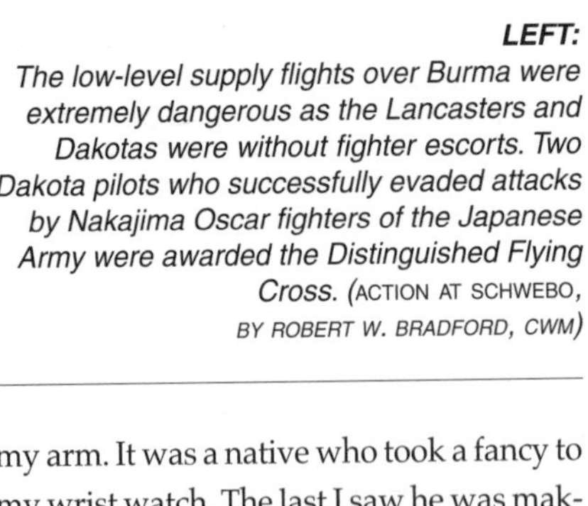

LEFT:
The low-level supply flights over Burma were extremely dangerous as the Lancasters and Dakotas were without fighter escorts. Two Dakota pilots who successfully evaded attacks by Nakajima Oscar fighters of the Japanese Army were awarded the Distinguished Flying Cross. (ACTION AT SCHWEBO, BY ROBERT W. BRADFORD, CWM)

ered him to the ground. Then I made my way to the aft section of the Liberator amid a hail of exploding bullets from the burning bomb bay while enemy fighters added to the chaos by strafing us. Curley Copley approached from the remains of the tail section and we made two trips into the fuselage to help the OSS agents remove the wounded.

The list of injuries was daunting. Corporal Naparolski of the OSS had a gaping hole in his abdomen and would not survive. Major Gildée had a broken collar bone while Sergeant McCarth had a fractured back and other injuries while Lieutenant Reid, also of the OSS, suffered leg burns. Bill "Taffy" Parsons our air gunner/dispatcher had a bullet through his foot while Curley Copely, our tail gunner, was relatively unscathed. In addition four of our crew had died in the crash. Flight-Sergeants Poole, Brenchely, Draper and Bill Pinckney were later buried at Kanchanaburi War Cemetery in Malay near the River Kwai.

HEAD SOUTH

I had started to cut small trees to make a litter when we heard voices. Fearing Japanese troops, we left the crash site and hid in the jungle. After assessing our injuries, we decided that McCarty could be carried out but not Naparolski. That's when I decided

FIVE OF US DROVE THROUGH BANGKOK SHORTLY AFTER MIDNIGHT THE NEXT NIGHT. THE OLD BUS STARTED BACKFIRING IN THE CENTRE OF THE CITY AND A JAPANESE PATROL CLOSED IN. THE PATROL LET US PASS AS THE DRIVER EXPLAINED HE WAS TRANSPORTING SOLDIERS TO JAIL.

to stay behind with the OSS man and gave my revolver, compass and a map to Maj Gildee. I also told him to head south because there were 300,000 Japanese on the run to the north of us.

After they left, I tried to comfort Naparolski but he died without waking. I had lost a lot of blood from a head wound and dozed off resting against a tree and cradling a Sten gun. Suddenly, I jerked awake. Voices again! Fortunately, they were natives who had found our main party and were now looking for Nap and me.

FLAP OF SCALP

During the walk to the village I stopped for a rest and woke when I felt a tugging on my arm. It was a native who took a fancy to my wrist watch. The last I saw he was making off with it on a white horse. A mirror was produced and I soon realized the extent of my head wound. I got the flap of scalp more or less in place and wrapped it with a bandage. By evening our party was reunited at a village which was just like something out of National Geographic with its thatched huts mounted on spindly legs.

Next morning we were startled awake when a Thai police lieutenant led a group of horsemen into the village to warn us that a Japanese patrol was approaching. With Thai police as guides, we left as fast as the ox carts would carry us to a hiding place nearby, and ate our last K-ration and shared our last four Camel cigarettes. In spite of our circumstances, we got a chuckle from the greeting inside a book of matches. It read: "Jolly good luck to you wherever you are from Dromedary Foods."

DREAMS OF HOME

We travelled two days with the wounded on bullock carts and eventually came to a river where a boat waited to take us to Bangkok. The first night we stayed with a Chinese couple who fed us and gave us huge cigarettes. Next morning Reid told of a dream he had where they were taken to a BOAC counter, fed ice cream, had baggage weighed and boarded a flying boat for home. All this after only one smoke.

We spent two days crouched low on an old motor launch and worked our way to Bangkok where 15,000 Japanese soldiers manned the local garrison. Our ancient bus rode through the city. On several occasions a breeze blew the straw blinds back and we looked out at Japanese soldiers who stared at us from arms length. We ended up at the Thai police headquarters.

Our presence there placed the whole

Thai underground, including the armed forces and police, in serious jeopardy. The patrol which found us ordered to prevent our capture at all costs and now a plan was drawn up whereby the OSS agents would be dispersed. As captain of the aircraft, I would also be placed out of reach and Curley Copley would accompany me.

CREW ACCOUNTED FOR

There were now six graves at the crash site, including an empty one and with four members of the crew in a Thai prison — under the eye of the OSS — the entire Liberator crew would be accounted for. Our smaller party of five were moved out to OSS headquarters located in the palace of the Regent of Siam where two Thai doctors worked on our wounds. The hospitable Regent offered a few days of R and R in his luxurious surroundings and when the offer was declined he retorted: "But Dick, even I can't afford these women."

Five of us drove through Bangkok shortly after midnight the next night. The old bus started backfiring in the centre of the city and a Japanese patrol closed in. Breach blocks clicked behind the straw curtains of the stalled bus as the driver explained he was transporting soldiers to jail.

The patrol let us pass and we later turned into an old race track and hid in the stalls. With a tow truck and spare bus following, we drove to the village of Pan-Pe where an old Fairchild, a twin Beechcraft and a Taylor Craft were used to get the group to a rendezvous with a DC-3 from 357 Squadron. With a refuelling stop in Rangoon, which had just been captured from the Japanese, we flew on to Alipore Airport in Calcutta. It is still difficult to believe that the entire operation took three weeks.

For the surviving crew, the period was about two months. Then we were reunited in India for the mother of all celebrations.

REPRINTED FROM:
Esprit de Corps, *Volume 5 Issue 1*
AUTHOR:
Harry V. Smith, DFC, Croix de Guerre

CROSSING THE IRRAWADDY

BELOW: *Coming out of the Irrawaddy River, men of the Sea Reconnaissance Unit (SRU) carefully make their way up the enemy's riverbank as they scout possible landing locations for an upcoming attack. (BRUCE WRIGHT, READERS DIGEST)*

Harry Avery commanded a section of underwater specialists who swam so close to the Japanese they could have dropped grenades into their boats.

WHEN LORD LOUIS Mountbatten sent out the word that top swimmers were needed in 1942, it filtered into the most unlikely places. Flight Lieutenant Harry Avery of the RCAF, a swimmer of note at Ottawa's Lisgar Collegiate, was stationed at the RAF base at St Albans in Wales. Employed in installing radar sets on bombers, the radar officer maintained his fondness for swimming by frequent excursions into the nearby Bristol Channel. One day, the adjutant's assistant brightly told him that she had put him down for something. "We volunteered you for a special unit," she beamed. Two weeks later, Harry Avery was on his way to Portsmouth where 400 marines and 100 officers were about to undergo tests for a Sea Reconnaissance Unit.

ONE DAY, THE ADJUTANT'S ASSISTANT BRIGHTLY TOLD HIM THAT SHE HAD PUT HIM DOWN FOR SOMETHING. "WE VOLUNTEERED YOU FOR A SPECIAL UNIT," SHE BEAMED.

BRAINCHILD

The SRU was a brainchild of then S/Lt Bruce Wright of the RCNVR. One night in 1941, while guarding the entrance to St. John's harbour, Wright was impressed by how easy it would be for strong swimmers to penetrate the submarine nets. Wright put his idea on paper and it went through channels, eventually ending on Mountbatten's desk at Combined Operations. The gathering at Portsmouth was the raw material from which Wright would form his unit.

Mountbatten's call also summoned RCNVR Lieutenant Bruton Strange, who mysteriously went from cold nights in the North Atlantic to the near-tropic splendour of Camp Pendelton, California, where four squads were then assembled from some 50 surviving volunteers.

A former football player Strange, an American, outflanked a recruiting officer by giving as his place of birth some unpro-

LEFT:
Japanese infantry move into position. With their crucial defeats at the battles of Imphal and Kohima, the Japanese lost their only chance of securing western sea routes through India. As the months passed, they would continue their retreat from advancing Allied forces.

nounceable community in British Columbia where he once had a fishing vacation. His skill as a swimmer and rugged physique was a comfort to Wright who still had concerns about the suitability of some of the volunteers. According to Wright, the short, underweight Englishmen appeared ready for hospital. Training on the high board and pounding through 10-foot breakers on surfboards and paddleboards took a toll of about ten trainees but Wright emerged with four sections of ten.

LENGTHY TRAINING

Harry Avery and Strange each commanded a section as the group moved on for more training in the Grand Bahamas. Long periods of training followed and by the winter of 1943, Lieutenant Commander Wright's group were in England searching for employment.

Parachute training lessened the boredom somewhat but frustration built up as the D-Day landings went in without the Sea Reconnaissance Unit. Wright's efforts to be transferred to Mountbatten's command in southeast Asia finally paid off when they were ordered to Ceylon. Here they spent more time on training, adapting to jungle conditions and getting to know its inhabitants such as crocodiles and pythons. The Japanese had withdrawn their ships from the Bay of Bengal and the SRU's search for employment continued until early in 1945.

WHEN THEY SURFACED, THE ROWBOATS, FILLED WITH JAPANESE, WERE SO CLOSE THAT AVERY REACHED FOR HIS GRENADES. "I WAS SURE WE COULD REACH OVER THE GUNWALES DROP GRENADES INTO THEIR BOATS," AVERY STATED.

FIRST ASSIGNMENT

By mid-February 1945, the British 14th Army was approaching the Irrawaddy which angles through Burma. Four assaults were planned along the river which ran through Mandalay in the north and Rangoon some 500 miles to the south. Another assault was planned on the Arakan coast to the west where Indian and British forces had landed on Ranree Island some three weeks earlier. The river formed a water barrier up to two miles wide which protected the Japanese and the SRU drew its first operational assignment after a long wait.

Four sections of SRU were flown from India to Shwebo Airport where they were then dispersed to different army units. Sections 1 and 4 were allocated to units assembling to attack near Mandalay. Section 2 began its work further south at Pagan where Wright joined the team because Strange was ill. Harry Avery's Section 4 drove for hours and arrived at 2nd Division HQ about 03:00 hrs where he was immediately taken to Major General C.G. Nicholson.

ASSAULT OUTLINED

Nicholson pointed to a map, indicating an area about 30 miles downstream from Rangoon. The British were on the north side and in five days would be launching an attack across the river in Divisional strength. Near dawn, at the river bank, the General indicated that the Camerons would assault from where they stood; the Worcesters would hit two miles to the west and the Royal Welsh two miles to the east. Avery's section had four nights in which to reconnoitre three beaches and their approaches.

That night Avery led a party of four, two on paddleboards and two in a canvas canoe, into the swift current where the Worcesters were to cross. Aside from a six mile an hour current, there were no problems with the approach or the landing area on the south shore.

The following night, they ran into a sandbar and Avery left two men to check it out and went on with another man to examine the beach but suddenly a light blinked and boats appeared. Avery and Bombardier Grindland froze and dropped to the bottom. When they surfaced, the rowboats, filled with Japanese, were so close that Avery reached for his grenades. "I was sure we could reach over the gunwales drop grenades into their boats," he said recently. "But that would have given away our mission."

BACK TO THE SANDBAR

Eventually Avery and Grindland swam back to the sandbar. Then they spotted Bailey and Sellers who had explored the sandbar which ran 600 yards downstream. As they met, an explosion rolled across the water from the northeast as 150 enemy hit the Worcester's outpost, where the SRU operated from the previous night, and killed about 100 at the advanced post.

The following night Avery and Sellers swam across to find a route for the Camerons. They plotted a course which took them beyond the sandbar and then cut back up the river to a narrow, sandy beach. There was firing to their left where Lt James Turpin, the second in command, and the rest of the section set up a diversion. Back on the north shore, Avery waited until 5 hrs for signs of Turpin who finally appeared with mortar shells bursting around him.

Churning the water like a porpoise, he finally dragged himself onto the friendly beach, a briefcase strapped to his waist. Turpin got it from a Japanese officer who bolted at the sight of him. It contained orders-of-the-day which simply said the British were to be pushed back into the river when they attacked.

NERVOUS ALERT

On the final reconnaissance at Pagan, just before the assault, men in a canoe came upon two Japanese swimming just off the far shore directly in the area where a landing was hours away. They were eliminated by a blast of a Tommy gun but the noise sent both sides into a nervous state of alert.

The next phase of the SRU operation was to lead the assault across the swiftly flowing river and engage in traffic control. Wright and one of his men swam out to two sandbars to guide the force to the enemy shore. But a snag had developed and there was a long wait. The troops were using old canvas boats with balky outboards. Prior to departure there had been no run-up of engines and when the loaded boats were pushed out into the six-knot stream they drifted into chaos. Standing off a sandbar on the enemy bank, Wright finally saw boats approaching in the first light. Suddenly they turned and headed back towards the allied shore. Later, he learned that these were the reserves whose engines worked better than those of the assault force, and they were trying to get into position.

ABOVE:
With Burmese at the helm, British soldiers patrol an enemy outpost along the Irrawaddy.

ONLY THREE WORKING ENGINES

Of the 23 boats which Wright guided past the sandbar, only three had working engines. Some of the others were being towed but most were being propelled by tin hats, rifle butts or floorboards and the enemy opened fire in broad daylight.

The 2nd British Division crossing came 11 days later. Avery, Grindland and Bailey slipped into the water and some 20 assault boats followed across the moonlight water. As they rounded the sandbar, tracers ripped the water near Avery's head. He waved the paddle boards for the others to follow.

"I looked back and saw them all coming, digging hard and fast. I lowered my head and paddled," he said.

The first wave landed without much trouble but of the 30 reinforcements who followed only ten reached shore alive and they were all wounded. Shells began to fall on the beachhead and while crouched in elephant grass, Avery heard somebody crawling towards him. It was a young Cameron whose foot had been blown off. As Avery dropped to help him, the soldier said: "Help someone who needs it, sir. I can still crawl!"

Avery swam back to report conditions to General Nicholson when the radio failed, and by morning with reinforcements and air support all beaches remained in British hands. It was the first and last operation for the SRU although Avery and three others were briefed for a mission whereby they would land behind Japanese occupied Signapore, move through the city at night and invade the harbour. Here they would swim around and identify Japanese warships. The operation was scrubbed when the atomic bomb fell. Harry Avery's family celebrated the 50th anniversary of the Irrawaddy crossing by presenting him with a magnificent cake which featured a map of Burma. It was given with love and well received, but there was a hint of irony to it all. The SRU's operation on the Irrawaddy was anything but a piece of cake.

REPRINTED FROM:
Esprit de Corps, *Volume 5 Issue 1*
AUTHOR:
Norman Shannon

RIGHT:
On 9 August 1945, just three hours before the U.S. would drop the second atomic bomb on Nagasaki, Robert "Hammy" Gray received a change of orders. Departing the British carrier HMS Formidable *in his Chance-Vought Corsair, the RCN Volunteer Reserve would be awarded Canada's last VC when he was shot down after successfully sinking the Japanese escort vessel* Amakusa *in Onagawa Bay.*
(FINALE - 1945 *BY DON CONNOLLY, CWM*)

HAMMY GRAY'S LAST RAMROD

One day after the atomic bomb fell on Hiroshima and while a second was en route to Nagasaki, it was time for Hammy Gray's last mission

FOR FOUR YEARS ROBERT Hampton Gray played the old service game of hurrying up and waiting. He left the University of British Columbia in 1940 to join the RCNVR and later transferred to the Fleet Air Arm. Although his brother John was killed returning from a mine-laying mission early in 1942, the closest Hammy got to action was flying ancient Skuas out to sea to test radios.

There was a brief tour in the Mediterranean and a period in South Africa where the mild mannered pilot distinguished himself by reporting from a Christmas party with a black eye.

Back in England, he missed action on D-Day and it seemed that the war might run its course without him. But during the years of frustration,Gray showed promise at administrative duties and, when posted to 1841 Squadron aboard the HMS *Formidable,* he was made senior pilot. On 22 August 1944 Hammy Gray finally flew out to action.

Well, near action. An airstrike of Barracudas and Corsairs set out for the German cruiser *Tirpitz* which was holed up in a Norwegian fiord, but the first mission was aborted because of weather.

ON 9 MAY FOUR BOMBER STRIKES WERE MADE ON ANOTHER AIRFIELD BUT LATE IN THE AFTERNOON THE FLEET WAS HIT BY KAMIKAZES. ONCE AGAIN AN ENEMY AIRCRAFT WAS HIT JUST OFF THE *VICTORIOUS'* STARBOARD QUARTER AND SMASHED INTO THE FLIGHT DECK

Two days later, the *Formidable* launched 18 Corsairs and 16 Barracudas. Gray led a flight of Corsairs down into Kaafjor where the *Tirpitz* was lying surrounded by numerous destroyers and shore-based flak batteries. At low-level the Corsairs endured intense flak but they drew fire from the Barracudas which bombed without success. Seven Fleet Air Arm machines were lost but another strike went in five days later.

ARMOURED DUD

This time an armour-piercing bomb sliced through eight decks of the *Tirpitz* but failed to explode. Hammy again led his flight on water-level attacks on three destroyers which returned heavy fire.

Once again, the Corsairs drew fire away from the Barracudas and Gray was mentioned in despatches for his leadership. The *Formidable* left the task force and the *Tirpitz* was later sunk by Bomber Command.

Gray underwent another period of enforced boredom as the carrier underwent a refit and spent months being readied for service in the South East Asia Command. The *Formidable* joined Task Force 57 of the British Pacific Fleet. On 4 May 1945, the Fleet was attacking an airfield and flak positions on the island of Miyako Jima. Vice Admiral Rawlings decided to disengage the fleet consisting of two battleships, five cruisers and several destroyers from the four aircraft carriers. One of the cruisers which disengaged was the HMCS *Uganda.* His rationale was to send the carriers in close for fire support, but the plan backfired when *Kamikaze* struck.

KAMIKAZE FIGHTERS

The guns and radar of the cruisers were not available to the aircraft carriers when needed. A *Kamikaze* got through to crash on the flight deck of the HMS *Formidable.* He dropped his bomb at the last minute killing eight, wounding 47, wiping out 11 aircraft and putting most of the radar out of action, but fires were brought under control and the flight deck was patched in six hours.

On the HMS *Indomitable,* a *Kamikaze* pilot literally bounced across the deck, wiped out radar equipment and crashed into the

RIGHT:
Fire crews of a carrier extinguish the blaze after an attack by Kamikazes in the Pacific. The suicide missions of the Japanese pilots could inflict much damage and numerous casualties if their fuel tanks exploded on impact.

sea where the bomb exploded.

Sweeps against the airfields continued, in spite of damage, and by the end of the day runways at two fields were unserviceable, and the *Formidable* was soon making 24 knots. The fleet then sailed to a refuelling area where the crew of the *Uganda* underwent an emotional spasm as Captain (later Admiral) Edmond Mainguy read the result of a strange referendum: 605 members of the crew of 902 had elected to sign a separate peace and the *Uganda*'s days were numbered.

MAJOR DAMAGE

On 9 May 1945, four bomber strikes were made on another airfield but late in the afternoon the fleet was hit by *Kamikazes*. Once again an enemy aircraft was hit just off the *Victorious*' starboard quarter and smashed into the flight deck where an exploding bomb holed the deck and did other damage. A second *Kamikaze* crashed and bounced off the stern. A third crashed before reaching its target and a fourth hit the after deck part of the HMS *Formidable*, wiping out six Avengers and one Corsair. The fire quickly extinguished, within an hour the *Formidable* was operational but now had only four bombers and 11 fighters serviceable. An accidental fire in the *Formidable*'s hangar later reduced aircraft strength to 11 Corsairs and 4 Avengers and the carrier sailed to Sydney for repairs and replacements.

By mid-July the British task force joined the American 3rd Fleet for assaults on the Japanese mainland. On 28 July Hammy Gray led a low-level strike against the naval base at Maisuru and sank a Japanese destroyer for which he was awarded the Distinguished Service Cross. His victory came the day after Canada withdrew the HMCS *Uganda* from the war.

On 6 August, Colonel Paul Tibbets, Jr pulled the Enola Gay off the runway at Tinian and flew almost 3000 km north-west to Hiroshima, a city of 245,000. They were accompanied by two other B-29's which recorded what happened when bombardier Major Thomas Ferebee tripped the release which sent "Little Boy" plunging from 31,600 feet. The bombers were 15 miles away when the flash and concussion from the atomic bomb struck.

Three days later the HMCS *Formidable* scheduled three Ramrods or fighter sweeps against targets. The first Ramrod went out early and Hammy Gray walked to his aircraft with Lieutenant Bill Atkinson sometime before 08:00 hrs.

Gray was to lead the second Ramrod against airfields on Honshu. Atkinson strapped Hammy into the Corsair and waved as they started engines. Suddenly a messenger made his way through propellers and shouted up to Gray: "The target's been changed." The second Ramrod would hit shipping in Onagawa Bay.

GRAY SINKS THE *AMAKUSA*

About an hour and a half later, Hammy Gray led eight Corsairs down from 10,000 feet to water level in an approach which came from inland. The Bay was surrounded by hills but the entrance provided an exit to an approach which offered pilots a four-second level bomb run. Gray plunged through the hills to water level and ran into a blast of cannon and machine-gun fire from three ships. The pilot behind him saw flames as a bomb was shot off and Hammy dove towards the *Amakusa*. Gray's second bomb penetrated the engine room of the *Amakusa*, blowing up an ammunition magazine. The destroyer quickly capsized and sank.

Gray flew towards the exit but the Corsair suddenly trailed smoke and flame. Then it rolled to the right and hit the water. One of the pilots nearby gasped over the RT: "There goes Gray!"

Later that morning another atomic bomb destroyed Nagasaki and the Japanese surrender came six days later.

That afternoon Gray's stunned squadron flew another Ramrod and Lieutenant G.A. Anderson's aircraft was damaged by flak and lost fuel. His engine cut out on the landing approach and Anderson crashed into the stern of the *Formidable* and was killed. Lieutenant Anderson was probably the last Canadian to die in action in World War Two.

REPRINTED FROM:
Esprit de Corps, *Volume 5 Issue 1*
AUTHOR:
Norman Shannon

AFTER THE BOMB – VJ DAY

V-J Day was an anti-climax for most Canadian troops. By September 1945 the most important years of their lives had ended without a whimper.

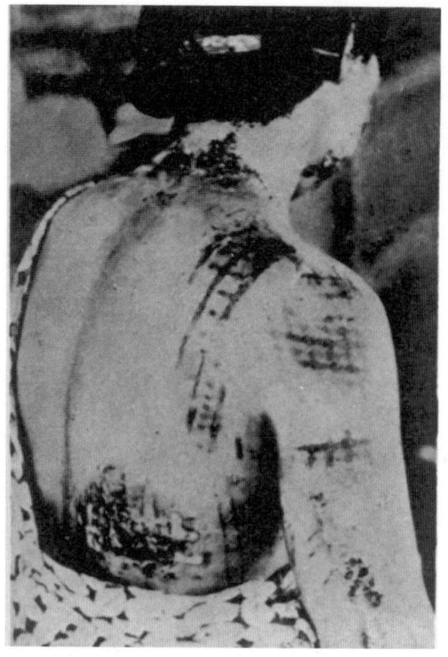

LEFT:
Although they had already suffered mass destruction from years of U.S. strategic bombing. The horrific casualties caused by atomic bombs forced Japan to capitulate on 14 August 1945. The pattern from her kimono has been burned onto this Japanese woman's skin.

THREE HOURS BEFORE THE atomic bomb known as "The Fatman" dropped on Nagasaki on 9 August 1945, Canadian Hammy Gray led a flight of Fleet Air Arm Corsairs off the deck of *HMS Formidable* to attack shipping in Japan's Onagawa Bay. Diving down through the hills, Gray approached at water-level as three ships laced his approach with flak and machine-gun fire.

Cannon-fire ripped a bomb from the gull-wing of Gray's Corsair and flames spread along the belly, but Gray continued to dive toward the destroyer *Amakusa* and his second bomb scored a hit on the engine room which blew up the destroyer's ammunition magazine. The destroyer quickly capsized and sank, but Gray's burning Corsair plunged into the water and he was killed. He was later awarded the Victoria Cross.

That afternoon, Lieutenant G.A. Anderson – another Canadian – flew another raid from the Formidable. His aircraft lost power on the approach when landing and Anderson crashed into the stern of the carrier and was killed. He was the last Canadian to die in the Pacific war because the Japanese surrendered five days later.

Although Canada had relatively little involvement in the Pacific fighting, its presence was haunted by poor political decisions. Some six weeks before Japan bombed Pearl Harbour, Canada sent some 1,975 ill-trained and ill-equipped men from the Winnipeg Grenadiers and the Royal Rifles to Hong Kong, a spot which Prime Minister Winston Churchill had previously declared indefensible, but the Canadian goverment was quick to respond to the British military requests for help.

Many were recruits whose only experience was garrison duty. But for 17 days they withstood attacks until on Christmas Day when they were overrun and only 1,420 were alive in Japanese prisons in 1945.

Squadron Leader Leonard Birchall was one of some 7,500 Canadian airmen who served in the Pacific theatre. Most, unlike Birchall, did not belong to a Canadian squadron and their deeds were soon lost to Canadian history. Birchall and his Catalina crew distinguished themselves by intercepting and reporting the presence of a Japanese task force some 350 miles south of Ceylon. Their aircraft was shot down and the crew taken prisoner. During almost four years as a POW, Birchall's leadership became an inspiration to others. But the war bypassed most of the Canadian airmen who operated in South East Asia as it did a number of Chinese Canadians who operated with the British underground.

The day after the atomic bomb was dropped on Nagasaki, the *HMCS Uganda* slipped into Esquimalt, British Columbia, riddled by a strange sense of shame, frustration and defiance. The cruiser had been providing fire support to an American flotilla in the Pacific which was striking at Japanese held-islands. In May it underwent an attack by Japanese Kamikaze planes and later was flagship in an attack on the heavily fortified island of Truk. This came at the time of an election in Canada in which Mackenzie King tried to atone for the previous year's conscription legislation. He promised that any Canadian serving in the Pacific war would do so voluntarily. When this was translated into action it resulted in a referendum on the *Uganda* in which 556 votes were against volunteering and 344 opted to stay on. Canada officially abandoned her allies in the hour of victory and ordered the ship home.

In Canada, the Japanese surrender came as an anti-climax because virtually our total war effort had been in Europe. By VE-Day the Americans were not only on the verge of producing the atomic bomb, they had the island of Japan under assault with conventional weapons. In March of 1945, without great enthusiasm, the Yanks accepted the Canadian offer of a force for the invasion of Japan but they insisted that the equipment and training had to be American. Major General B.M. Hioffmeister, who distinguished himself in Italy, was to be in command and some 39,000 veterans had volunteered.

Throughout the war, the British had relatively little presence in the Pacific but the RAF was to be strengthened there after VE-Day. The RCAF was to contribute eight heavy bomber squadrons and three transport squadrons as well as 2,000 construction engineers which it didn't have. These elements washed back on thousands of individual airmen who had returned from overseas after VE-Day. Some, like Omer Levesque and Tony

Little, had just been released from POW camps. Others had flown their last operation a week before the European war ended and were now enjoying the Canadian summer, a brief leave before reporting to British Columbia for training in the Tiger Force.

Then their war ended with a dull thud. In terms of the aircrew team, it meant that the most important people in their lives had suddenly dropped out of sight. Instead of meeting as planned in Abbotsford or elsewhere, each was suddenly discharged. The bonds forged through nights of fire and ice, of shared terror and sacrifice over the Ruhr were suddenly severed. By September, thousands of new civilians left a strange discharge centre to buy a new set of clothes and the most important years of their lives died without a whimper.

The Department of Veterans Affairs met the onslaught of almost one million service people suddenly seeking discharge, and thanks to earlier briefs by the Canadian Legion, the transition from war to peace was much more efficient than in 1919. Some 33,000 took up holdings under the Veterans Land Act and tens of thousands soon found their way to university. Others took advantage of business loans or industrial training and for thousands there was still a long period of hospitalization ahead. The total DVA program with its gratuities, training and treatment placed Canada in the forefront of allied nations in the treatment of its veterans, and the government also provided transportation and other help for 47,000 war brides.

AUTHOR:
Norman Shannon

CANADIAN VICTORIA CROSS WINNERS: 1939-45

BAZALGETTE, SQN/LDR IAN, RAF
Volunteer Reserve. Posthumous award.
On 4 August 1944, Bazalgette piloted a Lancaster bomber over France. On approaching the target two engines were out of action due to heavy AA fire and serious fires broke out in the aircraft. Despite this, he carried on to bomb his target and later tried to return to safety, after ordering the unwounded crew members to bale out. His aircraft exploded on landing.

COSENS, SGT. AUBREY
Queens Own Rifles of Canada. Posthumous award.
In February, 1945, in Holland, Cosens took command of the remaining four unwounded members of his platoon and ran forward to a friendly tank, directing its fire from a position in the open. He followed the tank into an enemy strongpoint, killing or capturing the defenders, and repeated this action twice more before being killed by a sniper.

CURRIE, MAJOR DAVID
South Alberta Regiment. In August 1944, in the Falaise area, Currie commanded a small force of infantry, tanks and anti-tank guns, with the mission of cutting a main German escape route. After establishing a position in a village his unit tenaciously held it for 36 hours. In the course of the battle seven enemy tanks, twelve 88mm guns and many vehicles were destroyed while almost 2000 enemy were killed, wounded or taken prisoner. (Colonel Currie subsequently became Sergeant-at-Arms of the House of Commons).

FOOTE, HON. CAPT. JOHN
Canadian Chaplains Service. On 19 August 1942, at Dieppe, Padre Foote constantly worked with the wounded of the RHLI, providing comfort and medical care, saving many lives by his efforts. When the remnants of his unit were evacuated, he left the landing craft which would take him to safety and gave himself up to the Germans in order to help his comrades in captivity.

GRAY, LT.(N) ROBERT
RCNVR. Posthumous award - The last award from the Second World War. On 9 August 1945 Lt. Gray, flying a Fleet Air Arm Corsair, led an attack on a Japanese destroyer off Honshu, Japan. Although he was wounded, and his aircraft in flames, he pressed home his attack, sinking the enemy vessel before crashing into the bay. (Lt. Gray's medals, including a previously-earned DSC, are held in the Canadian War Museum.)

HOEY, MAJOR CHARLES
The Lincolnshire Regiment. Posthumous award.
In the area of Arakan, Burma, Major Hoey's company came under heavy machine gun fire. Although twice wounded, Major Hoey advanced alone on a Japanese strongpoint, destroying it. He was mortally wounded in the action. Major Hoey was born in Duncan, British Columbia.

HORNELL, FLT. LT. DAVID
RCAF. Posthumous award. On 24 June 1944, while on patrol over the North Atlantic, Flt.Lt. Hornell's Canso aircraft was fired on and badly damaged by an enemy U-boat. Despite the damage, Hornell pressed home his attack, sinking the submarine, but was forced to bring down his burning aircraft in the sea. The crew had to take turns using the only serviceable dinghy - when they were picked up the next day Hornell was blinded and weakened so badly that he died shortly afterwards. (The remaining crew members all received gallantry awards).

MAHONY, MAJOR JOHN
The Westminster Regiment. On 24 May 1944, on the Melfa River, Italy, Major Mahoney's company established and held a bridgehead alone for several hours. Although Mahoney was three times wounded, he refused medical aid and continued to command the defence.

MERRITT, LCOL. CECIL
South Saskatchewan Regiment. At Dieppe on 19 August 1942 Colonel Merritt's battalion was to advance across a bridge under heavy mortar, artillery and small arms fire. Merritt personally led several charges, eventually succeeding in his mission. Although wounded twice, he continued to control his unit and later prepared a covering force to enable his unit to withdraw from the beach. (At the time of writing, Cecil Merritt is one of the two surviving Canadian V.C. winners).

MYNARKSI, W.O. ANDREW
RCAF. Posthumous award.
On 12 June 1944, over France, W.O. Mynarski was the mid-upper gunner on a Lancaster bomber. The aircraft was attacked and set on fire by enemy fighters, and the crew was ordered to bail out. Observing that the tail gunner was unable to leave his turret, Mynarski went to his assistance, although his own clothing was on fire and he was severely burned. At the last minute, his efforts unsuccesful, he saluted his comrade and left the escape hatch, but died from his burns. Ironically, the tail gunner survived the crash of the aircraft. (W.O. Mynarski had been promoted to Pilot Officer effective 11 June 1944 but died before being notified of his promotion).

OSBORN, W.O. II JOHN
Winnipeg Grenadiers. Posthumous award.
In December, 1941, in Hong Kong, a sub-unit commaded by WO Osborn captured and held Mount Butler until the overwhelming odds forced the Canadians to retire. CSM Osborn, under heavy fire, assisted his men to comparative safety. Later the enemy threw grenades at his unit - after hurling several back he threw himself on one of them, saving his comrades at the cost of his own life. (Although gazetted after the war, CSM Osborn's action was the first to merit a Canadian V.C.).

PETERS, CAPT. FREDERICK
Royal Navy. On 8 November 1942, in Oran, North Africa, Capt. Peters commaded *HMS Walney*. He led his vessel into action towards the jetty, facing fire from two larger vessels as well as shore batteries. Badly wounded, Capt. Peters was the only survivor of nearly 20 men on *Walney*'s bridge, but his burning vessel managed to reach its objective before sinking. A few of the crew managed to reach shore, but Capt. Peters died in an aircraft crash soon afterwards. Capt. Peters was a Native of Charlottetown PEI.

SMITH, PTE. ERNEST
Seaforth Highlanders of Canada. On the night of 21 October 1944 Pte. Smith was in the forefront of an attack which established a bridgehead at the savio River, in Italy. He neutralized an enemy tank using a PIAT (the platoon anti-tank projector) at a range of ten yards - later he took out another tank and two self-propelled guns as well as several German infantry. He exposed himself to heavy fire continually while protecting a wounded comrade. ("Smokey" Smith is the last of Canada's surviving V.C. winners. He continues to be active in the support of veterans' interests).

LEFT:
Sergeant Ernest 'Smokey' Smith, VC.

TILSTON, MAJOR FREDERICK
Essex Scottish. In the Hochwald Forest, Germany on 1 March 1945 Major Tilston, already wounded, led his company to its objective, personally destroying a machine gun position. He continued to lead his men to take the enemy's second defence line, which his company held against heavy odds, inspired by their leader. Despite severe hip wounds he refused medical attention until he was certain that the defence was adequately organized. (Major Tilston, a double amputee, remained active in the cause of veterans and the St. John Ambulance Society until his death).

TOPHAM, CPL. FREDERICK
1st Canadian Parachute Battalion.
On 24 March 1945, after crossing the Rhine, two medics had already been killed while attending to a wounded man lying in the open. Cpl. Topham went to attend the casualty under heavy fire and received a facial wound. Despite this, he treated and recovered the casualty, refusing to have his own wound treated until all the casualties had been cared for. He later rescued three men from a blazing and exploding bren gun carrier.

TRIQUET, CAPT. PAUL
Royal 22nd Regiment. At Casa Berardi, Italy, on 14 December 1942 Captain Triquet, with the remnants of his company (over half of whom had been killed or wounded)broke through strong enemy resistance to seize a strong-point, which he held with seventeen men against vastly superior German forces until they were relieved the following day. (It is part of the "Van Doo" folklore that Capt. Triquet encouraged his men forward by crying that "the safest place to be is on the objective." Brigadier Triquet, a pre-war RSM, became President of the Royal 22nd Regiment Association).

THE BEGINNING OF THE END

WEAPONS AND UNIFORMS

BELOW:
The .50 calibre (12.7-mm) M2 was developed by John M. Browning at the end of WWI, and was adopted by American forces in 1933 as the Browning M2 water-cooled machine gun. Subsequent models (.50 calibre M2 aircraft gun and M2 heavy barrel gun), using the same receiver, were later adopted. During WWII, almost two million M2 machine guns of all variations were produced before production ceased in 1946. Additional M2s were built in the 1970s to supply America's and Israel's wars. The Browning M2 is chiefly an automatic, belt-fed, recoil operated, air-cooled, crew-operated machine gun. The ammunition belt may be fed from either the left or right side. A disintegrating metallic link-belt is used to feed the ammunition into the firearm. The M2 is usually mounted on vehicles or ground mounts as an anti-vehicle and anti-aircraft weapon. The .50 calibre entered Canadian service in 1942.

ABOVE, LEFT: *Ortona is said to have been a town destroyed by hand, one brick at a time. A battle fought entirely in a built-up area, Ortona was nicknamed "Little Stalingrad." A Sherman tank of the Calgary Regiment drives through the rubble of the Piazza Plebescito. Primarily an infantry battle, armour was still essential but vulnerable in such terrain. When fighting in close confines, the tanks were susceptible to assault by infantry with hand-held anti-tank weapons (such as the PIAT, Bazooka and German Panzerschreck) or hand-placed satchels of explosives. ("CANADIAN ARMOUR PASSING THROUGH ORTONA" BY CHARLES COMFORT, CWM 12245)* ***BOTTOM***: *The 5.5-inch (140-mm) gun was classed as medium artillery and generally became a divisional asset. It could fire a 100-pound round more than 14 kilometers in distance. At the beginning of the Second World War, most of the available artillery was of WWI vintage. The addition of the 5.5 in 1941 gave the Commonwealth armies additional medium-range punch. The gun's crew is conducting maintenance under the watchful eye of their sergeant. ("MAINTENANCE ON A 5.5" BY W.A. OGILVIE, CWM 13438)*

TOP LEFT: *To be torpedoed during an ocean crossing was the worst of fates for mariners. In the first years of the war, standing orders for convoys precluded any ship from stopping to pick up survivors. And in the cold Atlantic waters, survival was often a matter of minutes. In greatest danger were the men who served on ships carrying fuel or ammunition because the ships often exploded or burst into flames upon impact of a torpedo or bomb. Only in the latter part of the war were convoys assigned a rescue ship that followed behind to pick up survivors. ("PASSING?" BY HAROLD BEAMENT, CWM 10055)* ***SECOND FROM TOP:*** *Manufactured in Canada, the Sten was the simplest mass-production submachine gun (SMG) used during WWII, evolving from a more complex and expensive Lanchester. Made entirely out of metal and made to generous tolerances, it was much faster and cheaper to make than an Enfield rifle. It cost $6 to make at the time. While its sights were rudimentary, the low recoil of its 9-mm round and controllable rate of fire enabled even poorly trained soldiers to use it effectively. World War II was a great testing ground. By the mid-1950s, the Sterling SMG was introduced in Britain to overcome the Sten's shortcomings, primarily the occasional jamming of its single-row feed, which necessitated a special loading tool after hand inserting the fourth cartridge. To its credit, the Sten Mk II was the perfect partisan weapon, and was also airdropped into Europe for that purpose. By removing the barrel retaining lug/handguard and the buttstock, the Sten could easily fit into a briefcase.* ***THIRD FROM TOP:*** *The Bren .303-inch Mark IV light machine gun (LMG) is considered a reliable, accurate and simple weapon. The Bren was a legendary weapon in its time, and even some Germans, when given a choice, favoured the Bren over the MG42 because of its accuracy and reliability. The Bren light machine gun was adopted for service by the British forces in August 1938 as a successor to the Lewis. It is a modified version of the Czech ZB26, firing .303 calibre ammunition from a curved 30-round box magazine. Air-cooled and gas operated, it weighed 10.10 kg with a rate of 500 rounds per minute. Canada was soon producing Brens for the war effort. Of note, during the first year of the Korean War some Chinese units used the Bren Mark I. These weapons were probably captured from the Japanese, having originally been taken by the Japanese from British forces at Singapore and Hong Kong. Ironically, Canada also supplied the Chinese with 43,000 of these LMGs during WWII through a Lend-Lease program. The Chinese Brens made by John Inglis featured the CH serial number range like the Inglis Browning Hi Powers. (PAC)*

The four Tribal class destroyers acquired by the Royal Canadian Navy in 1942-43 were small but powerful vessels, involved in numerous skirmishes including night battles with German warships in the English Channel. Of the four ships (HMCS **Athabaskan, Huron, Iroquois** ***and*** **Haida*****), only the*** **Haida** ***remains. Her final duty station is as a memorial, tied up in Toronto's harbour at Ontario Place. ("CANADIAN TRIBAL DESTROYERS IN ACTION" BY TONY LAW, CWM 10248)***

RIGHT: *Motor Torpedo Boats (MTBs) were small, swift and manoeuverable. They were used to attack German Kriegsmarine vessels and to protect larger ships. Used in great numbers during the D-Day invasion of Normandy, they were also employed to put small commando units ashore in France. ("PATROL OFF LE HAVRE, FALL 1944" BY TONY LAW, CWM)* ***BELOW:*** *Friend and fellow war artist Charles Comfort did this painting of Carl F. Schaefer. Although painted three years after WWII, it still captures Schaefer as haunted by his wartime experiences. Assigned to Bomber Command, Schaefer learned all he could about aircraft, navigation and gunnery, shared tension, fatigue, danger and tremendous fellowship with the bomber crews. Tense and foreboding, Schaefer's war paintings were executed in dark monochromatic colours. Wounded on a mission with the RCAF, he was injured a second time when a V-1 "Buzz bomb" hit the London pub he was in. The war had a profound effect on his art. Schaefer later confided that it took him 10 years to get over the war. ("FLIGHT LIEUTENANT CARL SCHAEFER" BY CHARLES COMFORT, ART GALLERY OF ONTARIO)*

BOTTOM RIGHT: *The night raids over Germany by the RAF and RCAF were truly battles in the sky. Searchlights would attempt to illuminate the bombers so that German anti-aircraft artillery fire could bring them down. At the same time, Luftwaffe night-fighters such as the Me-110 would hunt the defenseless bombers that, at this distance from their base in England, no longer had the protection of their fighter escorts. ("NIGHT TARGET, GERMANY" BY MILLER BRITTAIN, CWM 10889)*

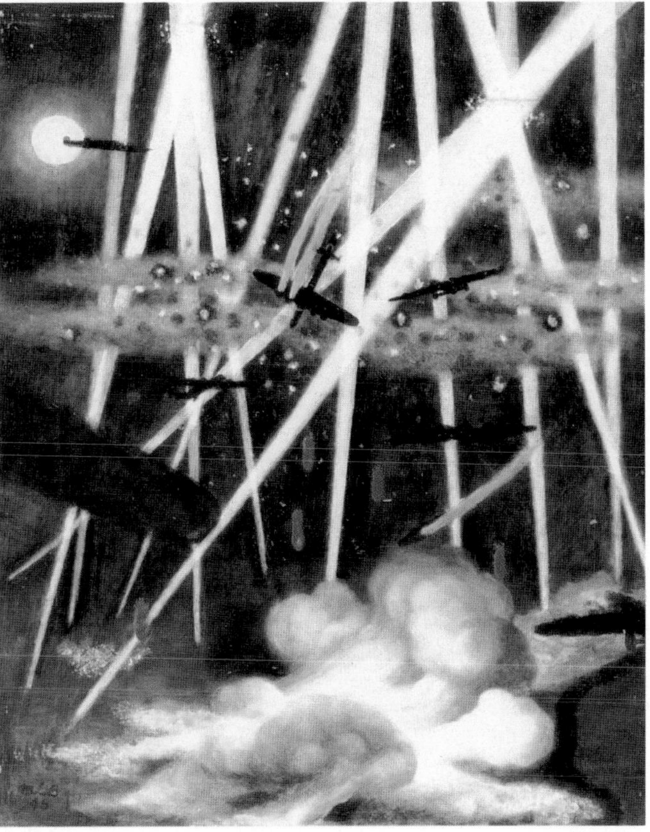

TOP LEFT: *"Ugly as hell, cranky as hell – but efficient as hell" was how sailors described the Rhino ferry. Carrying enormous loads of vehicles, these ferries quickly unloaded them at the beachheads. These craft pioneered the concept of the Ro-Ro (role on, roll off) ship as a military tool. For the D-Day invasion, a white star inside a white circle was painted on the tops of vehicles and ship decks as a (by today's standards) crude method in preventing fratricide by having a common identifier for all Allied forces' equipment. However this was not a sure means of avoiding friendly fire as the weeks following D-Day saw several incidents of bombing of Allied ground forces by Allied aircraft. ("RHINO FERRY TO NORMANDY" BY ORVILLE FISHER, CWM)* ***BOTTOM:*** *There were dozens of Canadian Sherman tanks destroyed in the battle for the airfield at Carpiquet. The heavily defended field had numerous dug-in 88-mm anti-tank guns that brought devastation upon Allied armour. The desperate struggle for this airfield lasted from 4 to 9 July 1944. ("CARPIQUET AIRFIELD, NORMANDY" BY ORVILLE FISHER, CWM 12439)*

OPPOSITE PAGE, TOP RIGHT: *Air cover was absolutely essential to the success of the Allied invasion of Normandy on 6 June 1944. A North American P-51 Mustang in its D-Day colours (all aircraft involved with Operation OVERLORD were painted with black and white stripes) flys over the coast of Normandy shortly after the landings at Graye-sur-Mer, transports and MTBs visible below. The Mustang was used as both a low-level fighter-bomber and as a long-range high-altitude escort fighter. During D-Day, it was one of 11,000 Allied planes used in the Tactical Air Force. Some 4000 ships also made the Channel crossing that day.* (*"INVASION PATTERN NORMANDY" BY ERIC ALDWINCKLE, CWM 10679*) ***RIGHT:*** *One objective of the D-Day landings was the town of Caen. Before reaching it, the 8th Canadian Infantry Brigade of the 3rd Canadian Infantry Division, with elements of the 2nd Canadian Armoured Brigade, had to take the heavily fortified airfield at Carpiquet, some five kilometers from Caen. The airfield was defended by troops and tanks of the German 12th SS Panzer Division. Seen here is a section of the Queen's Own following a Fort Garry Sherman tank through a destroyed aircraft hanger.* (*"BATTLE FOR CARPIQUET AIRFIELD" BY ORVILLE FISHER, CWM 12421*)

The Highland Light Infantry of Canada advances toward Wessel in 1945. Note the lightly armoured Bren gun carriers. These universal carriers were used in a multitude of roles by Canadians throughout the Second World War. Small with no roof, they provided minimal protection but were of great assistance in moving troops, supplies and ammunition over rough terrain. They were sold off as surplus after the war and many ended up on farms as a mechanized workhorse. (***"INFANTRY ADVANCING" BY ALEX COLVILLE, CWM 12171***)

ABOVE: *The Supermarine Spitfire is arguably one of the most effective fighters of WWII. Receiving constant updates and design improvements, the Spitfire remained in service throughout the war. With a 500-pound bomb attached to the center of its fuselage, this late model Spitfire is dive bombing a German V-1 "Buzz bomb" site in France. By June 1944, almost 40 per cent of Allied ground and air war efforts were directed at neutralizing the V-1 flying bomb threat. The artist was also an experienced RCAF Spitfire pilot.* *("DIVE BOMBING V-1 SITES, FRANCE" BY ROBERT HYNDMAN, CWM 11532)*

LEFT: *In 1950, a second battalion was raised by each of the three Permanent Force infantry regiments that remained after the Second World War – the PPCLI, RCR and R22eR. Known as the Special Force, these new recruits formed Canada's commitment to the UN's Commonwealth Division in Korea. Equipped primarily with American weapons during training, upon arrival in Korea the Special Force would have a mixed bag of Canadian, British and American weapons and equipment, as depicted. The weapon carried is the WWII-era Bren gun.* *(ILLUSTRATION BY KATHERINE TAYLOR)* ***BOTTOM:*** *The liberation of Holland near the end of WWII was one of the Canadian Army's finest hours. As a result, the Dutch venerate all Canadians for their hard-fought battles in the Low Countries and continue to show their gratitude even today. The most visible gift is the yearly delivery of thousands of tulip bulbs which are planted throughout Canada's capital, Ottawa. In early March 1945, it was a tough slugging match over dykes and around flooded areas. The Wehrmacht were still putting up stiff resistance and Canadians suffered more than 6000 casualties in liberating The Netherlands.* *("INFANTRY NEAR NIJMEGEN, HOLLAND," BY ALEX COLVILLE, CWM)* ***OPPOSITE PAGE, BOTTOM:*** *Much of the Korean War experience for Canadians was a defensive one. The Canadians endured winters that were as harsh as those of their grandfathers during WWI. Korea resembled not so much the mechanized fighting of WWII, but rather the more static positions of WWI. Edward Zuber, a member of the Royal Canadian Regiment, recalled this quiet evening spent in a tunnel by candlelight.* *("NEW YEAR'S EVE" BY EDWARD ZUBER, CWM 1986-158/7)*

***RIGHT:** VE-Day sparked an enormous outpouring of relief and joy throughout the Allied world. The city of Halifax saw the biggest spontaneous party ever on 8 May 1945 to celebrate the victory in Europe. The merchants of the city closed down their shops, hoping that partying servicemen would go elsewhere. The result was more than 65,000 stolen bottles of liquour along with 100,000 "liberated" quarts of beer, fueling the most destructive celebration in Canadian history. Although the celebrations for VJ-Day on 15 August 1945 were no less joyful, they were more controled, as the war in Japan had not affected Britain and Canada to the same degree as that in Europe.* ("V.J. CELEBRATIONS, PICCADILLY CIRCUS, LONDON," BY CAMPBELL TINNING, CWM 14029)

BELOW:
Chinese preparations for their attack on the Jamestown Line held by B Company, 1RCR, included a tremendous concentration of artillery fire just after sunset on 23 October 1952. B Company had moved into forward position at last light and found these defensive works badly damaged by previous artillery barrages. Chinese artillery fire began but lasted only ten minutes, before shifting their attention to neighbouring companies for a further 45 minutes. B Company was essentially sealed off. When the artillery barrage shifted, the Chinese began their assault and the Canadians withdrew to neighbouring company areas. By 19:40 hours, "no friendly troops remained in action," and divisional artillery began to pound the enemy in B Company's vacated position. At 01:10 hours on 24 October, the RCRs counterattacked and, by 03:30 hours, had resecured their positions on Hill 355. Most of the casualties were sustained by the beleaguered B Company. The battalion lost a total of 18 killed, 35 wounded and 14 captured by the Chinese. *("INCOMING" BY EDWARD ZUBER, CWM 90328)*

ABOVE: *The Royal 22nd Regiment defended against repeat Chinese assaults on the night of 23 October 1952 in Korea. The American position on Hill 355 had been overrun and the Vandoos, on the neighbouring saddle, had to hold their line until a counterattack by U.S. forces finally resecured the hill. ("CONTACT" BY EDWARD ZUBER, CWM 90033)*

BOTTOM: *At the end of November 1952, the Commonwealth Division, parent formation to Canada's 25 Brigade, redeployed the Canadians to the left front sector where the key terrain was the high ground known as The Hook and allowed observation into the lower Sami-ch'on valley. The Canadian engineers of 23 Field Squadron dug extensive tunnels and defensive works during December 1952 and January 1953, linking firing bays to company locations and providing cover against incoming artillery fire. Once in position, the conflict assumed a WWI quality with sniping and patrolling being the main activities. ("FIRST KILL, THE HOOK" BY EDWARD ZUBER, CWM 1986-158/9)*

UNEASY AFTERMATH 1946 - 1950

As aircraft and ships are scrapped and the Canadian Army is reduced from two corps to a single brigade group, over a million servicemen and women settled back into civilian life. A new Department of Veterans Affairs administered what has been described as the best rehabilitation package in the world. An exhausted world paused to take a deep breath.

1947 The first session of the United Nations General Assembly opens in Brooklyn, New York. ▪ Former Prime Minister Winston Churchill declares that "From Stettin in the Baltic to Trieste in the Adriatic, an Iron Curtain has descended across the Continent," in a speech at Fulton, Missouri. ▪ Nine Nazi war criminals are hanged following the Nuremberg Trials. ▪ Igor Gouzenko, a cypher clerk in the Soviet embassy in Ottawa who had defected the year before, exposes a widespread espionage network.

1947 With civil war raging in Greece, President Truman pledges U.S. aid to countries fighting communist aggression. ▪ As a corollary to the Truman Doctrine, Secretary-of-State George Marshall announces a massive assistance plan to facilitate the economic recovery of Europe. ▪ Britain grants independence to India and Pakistan. ▪ French government proclaims martial law in Vietnam. ▪ Canadian veterans triple pre-war university enrolments. ▪ "Baby Boom" begins.

1948 Mahatma Ghandi assassinated. ▪ Communists stage a coup against the Czech government. ▪ The U.S. and Britain mount an airlift to thwart a Soviet blockade of Berlin. ▪ Tito of Yugoslavia breaks with Moscow. ▪ State of Isreal comes into existence and is immediately attacked by its Arab neighbours. ▪ Canada rejects a draft free-trade agreement with the United States. ▪ Mackenzie King announces his retirement after 22 years in power and is succeeded by Louis St. Laurent.

1949 Chinese Communists march into Peking, ending a long civil war, Chiang Kai-shek's Nationalists retreat to Formosa (now Taiwan). ▪ Berlin blockade ends and Soviets explode their first atomic bomb. ▪ German Federal Republic proclaimed by Konrad Adenauer, the Chancellor-in-waiting. ▪ Dutch yield independence to Indonesia. ▪ Newfoundland comes into Confederation. ▪ St. Laurent wins election, taking 192 of 262 seats. He and his foreign minister, Lester B. Pearson, lead Canada into the North Atlantic Treaty Organization (NATO).

1950 Soviets walk out of UN Security Council to protest the presence of Nationalist Chinese delegates. ▪ Senator Joe McCarthy of Wisconsin launches "anti-Red" crusade. ▪ Viet Minh attack French forces in Indochina. ▪ North Korea invades the South. ▪ Mackenzie King dies at Kingsmere. ▪ St. Laurent presides over Canada's greatest peacetime military buildup, sending an infantry brigade to Korea and another to Western Europe along with an air division of fighter aircraft.

***LEFT:** On a Formosa dockside (now Taiwan), an officer awaits evacuation following the defeat of Chiang Kai-shek's Nationalist forces by the Communists in 1949.* (HENRI CARTIER-BRESSAN, MAGNUM)

***LEFT:** U.S. President Harry S. Truman and Winston Churchill are welcomed in Fulton, Missouri on 5 March 1947. In his speech, Churchill warned: "An Iron Curtain has descended across the continent of Europe, dividing east from west."* (GEORGE SKADDING, LIFE)

HOMECOMING

Our victorious troops danced the Hokey-Pokey, and returned home to a heroes' welcome. Veterans would receive excellent rehabilitation packages.

LEFT: *Veterans wait at one of the demobilization centres set up by Mackenzie King which were to assist returning soldiers to once again adapt to civilian life. The centres were not nearly as efficient as the Prime Minister had envisioned. In some, it took hours just to get a bowl of soup and months to receive an initial pension cheque.* (NAC C-49434)

FOR MOST VETERANS, THE euphoria of Victory in Europe was short-lived. While many joined the throngs in London to dance the Hokey-Pokey and sing "Knees Up Mother Brown", the prospect of service in the Pacific took the edge off VE-Day celebrations.

In Halifax, however, things were different. Mayor Allan Butler's committee decided that an appropriate way to observe victory would be to close liquor stores. Somehow restaurant owners took this as a cue to close their establishments. Some 30,000 uniforms with nowhere to go except the Sally Ann roamed the streets looking for a hint that their victory in the longest battle was recognized.

Haligonians had almost six years of rationing, uniforms, crowding and increasing pregnancy rates. The flash point came with the questionable decision to close liquor stores. Mobs of civilians and sailors looted a brewery and stole 119,000 bottles of beer and raids on liquor stores produced 65,000 bottles of hard liquor. Some $5 million in damage and theft was inflicted on downtown stores. As word of the riots spread across the country, it diminished the glory of a victory in Europe.

Many of the first veterans to reach Canada were bound for the Pacific. Canada's Pacific Force was to be drawn from 30,000 men serving in Europe who were to receive training in the United States. Airmen, slated for the Pacific, were destined for Abbotsford. Then the bottom dropped out of the Pacific war while thousands were home on a month's leave.

SLEAZY HANDLING

Prime Minister Mackenzie King's handling of the conscription issue was a matter of resentment until the dying days of the Pacific War. In November 1944, King capitulated to the reality of possible manpower shortages and conscripted 12,800 Zombies for overseas service. Under the National Resources Mobilization Act, these men had previously been selected for home service only. The first draft arrived in Europe in February. An election was slated for June, and as if to atone to Quebec for his November decision, King then decided that all service in the Pacific would be voluntary. The Prime Minister made that announcement in the House of Commons on 4 April 1945. It created considerable resentment because it meant that the men who had fought in Europe would be the ones who would also 'volunteer' for the Pacific War.

At the time the Yanks were pushing towards Japan while heavy bombing had done extensive damage and most of the once powerful Japanese fleet was at the bottom of the Pacific. A Canadian cruiser HMCS *Uganda* was part of an American operation off Okinawa. As a result of King's decision, many of the ship's crew elected not to pursue the war in the Pacific and the humiliated captain was forced to abandon the operation and sail home.

VETS GET THE BEST

In spite of the negative aspects of King's politicking, over a million Canadian veterans received what was probably the best rehabilitation package in the world. Much of the preparatory work was contained in Canadian Legion briefs throughout the war; the veterans of WWI were meticulous in outlining the deficiencies of an earlier attempt at rehabilitation.

The needs were carefully evaluated and a new Department of Veterans Affairs had a program which covered gratuity, clothing allowance, pensions, medical treatment, vocational training, land settlement and higher education. A period of remarkable social adjustment followed as 200,000 returned to pre-enlistment occupations; 250,000 used re-establishment credits to buy tools or as working capital for small business; 22,000 took up farming and 23,000 had small holdings under the Veterans' Land Act.

LEGION FOLLOWED SERVICEMEN

Throughout the war, the Legion had provided correspondence courses which followed Canadians wherever they served: on a rolling corvette, in a frozen slit trench or in an aircraft over Germany.

One navigator actually recalls the difficulty he had reading at night while orbiting Berlin. Others remember the disdain of one potential student who leafed through a text on Theology and muttered, "Nothing in this damn thing but religion."

Over 50,000 such veterans created a revolution at Universities and provided Canada with a nucleus of professionals who became key players in the post-war period as Canada moved onto the world stage. The government paid out $775 million in gratuities and credits but it was money well spent because it not only provided the country with stability but with winners.

AUTHOR: *Norman Shannon*

MUTINY – THE NAVY'S SECRET SHAME

Navy downsizing and class bitterness caused three shipboard revolts officially called 'incidents.'

CANADA'S NAVY WAS BUILT following the lead and traditions of its parent service, the Royal Navy. The Royal Navy, the "Senior Service" of Great Britain's Forces, was long the upholder of a rigid class system wherein the lower decks were treated with the disdain shown the lower classes. From a history which included press gangs and the lash, it was the usual course of events to ignore the living conditions and aspirations of the enlisted man.

Following the First World War, the class system of Great Britain began a steady, inevitable decline, and this erosion of the power of the privileged few was greatly speeded up after WWII. The Royal Navy was one of the few bastions resisting these changes.

It only followed that the Royal Canadian Navy, whose officers were, for the most part, trained in Britain, would be indoctrinated into the Royal Navy way of running their ships, with little or no concern for the enlisted ranks. The post-War Canadian sailor was not prepared for a return to the strictures of the pre-war navy particularly when the "King's Regulations" were seen to belong to another time, and another country. Like their American cousins of another era they took the only course of action they could – they mutinied.

INEVITABLE BURDEN

The year 1949 saw the Royal Canadian Navy in the midst of consolidating its forces from the world's third largest fleet into a smaller more manageable fleet that the post-war government was willing to sustain. With the pressures involved it was perhaps inevitable that most of the burden should fall on the shoulders of the Navy's most common resource, the enlisted man.

On 26 February 1949, 90 men of the destroyer HMCS *Athabaskan* mutinied by locking themselves in their mess deck and refusing to report for duty. On 15 March, a second mutiny occurred on board HMCS *Crescent*, this time involving 83 enlisted men using similar tactics. Yet another mutiny took place on board the aircraft carrier HMCS *Magnificent* stationed in the Caribbean on 25 March 1949. Again the tactic of locking themselves in their mess deck and refusing to report for duty was used, this time, by 32 crew members.

EXPRESS GRAPEVINE

The fact that the same method was used by the lower decks on all three incidents has been "explained" officially by the news of *Athabaskan's* mutiny travelling the "express grapevine" that exists in all large organizations. Crews on board the *Magnificent* and the *Crescent* already knew of the mutiny on board the *Athasbaskan*.

ABOVE: *The crew of the Canadian destroyer* HMCS Iroquois *mutinied in July 1943.* *(NATIONAL ARCHIVES OF CANADA)*

Aggressively concealed was the fact that two similar incidents had previously occurred. In July 1943 the crew of the destroyer HMCS *Iroquois* mutinied and the cruiser HMCS *Ontario* had experienced a lower deck mutiny in 1947. It has been presumed, but never officially confirmed, that crewmembers from the *Iroquois* and *Ontario* were serving aboard other mutinied ships and therefore "knew the ropes."

FULL IMMUNITY

Three mutinies in the space of three weeks at the height of the Cold War (see page 288) so concerned the Canadian Government that the Navy Brass was pressured to act quickly and convene a Board of Inquiry. Such was the concern for Communist subversion that full immunity was granted to all participating mutineers in order to obtain complete and full voluntary co-operation so the board could quickly reach its conclusions.

Admiral Rollo Mainguy was selected to chair a three member panel. The investigation was held *in camera* and those testifying were assured of complete anonymity. Witnesses ranged from the Naval Chief of Staff down through the ranks to the lowest level

of enlisted man. Everyone who wanted to be heard, was. Testimony showed two very dissimilar attitudes, a thriving class system and a history of complaints from the lower decks being ignored by the "officer class." No evidence was found to support the theory of Communist involvement.

SUBJECT SENSITIVITY

Results from the Inquiry had several officers transferred summarily without benefit of an inquiry into their performance. No actions were taken against the enlisted ranks. Such was the sensitivity of the subject of mutiny, and the well known consequences of such actions both by the public and by those in the services, that all references to, and use of the word mutiny were avoided by the use of the term "incidents." Had it been shown that mutiny could go unpunished in the Canadian Armed Forces, it would have meant the end of any hope of discipline and the legal chain of command.

The Board of Inquiry Report was published as "The Mainguy Report on Certain Incidents Which Occurred on board HMC Ships *Athabaskan*, *Crescent* and *Magnificent* and Other Matters Concerning the Royal Canadian Navy."

DESTROY ALL PROCEEDINGS

In keeping with the promise of complete anonymity of those participating, all transcripts of the proceedings were ordered destroyed. However, one of the Board members, retired Commander L.C. Audette kept his copy of the 3600 page transcript and 25 years after the publication of the Mainguy Report he donated it to the Public Archives of Canada!

ABOVE LEFT:
HMCS Crescent *experienced a mutiny in 1949. (DND PHOTO)*

ABOVE RIGHT:
Admiral Rollo Mainguy (1901-1979); he was chairman of the board of inquiry into the "incidents." (CF PHOTO)

LEFT:
The crew of cruiser HMCS Ontario *refused duty in 1947. (DND PHOTO)*

The action taken in the wake of the Mainguy Report has ensured that the modern-day Canadian Navy is second to none in its operations and in enabling its personnel to progress to the limits of their desire and ability. Adm Mainguy is revered as the "Father of Today's Navy" and the new Maritime Command Headquarters Building in Halifax, Nova Scotia, bears his name.

Thanks to the Maritime Command Museum for its assistance in providing photographs.

REPRINTED FROM:
Esprit de Corps, *Volume 2 Issue 11*
AUTHOR: *David Smart*

[DURING THE INQUIRY] ALL REFERENCES TO, AND USE OF THE WORD MUTINY WERE AVOIDED BY THE USE OF THE TERM "INCIDENTS." HAD IT BEEN SHOWN THAT MUTINY COULD GO UNPUNISHED IN THE CANADIAN ARMED FORCES, IT WOULD HAVE MEANT THE END OF ANY HOPE OF DISCIPLINE AND THE LEGAL CHAIN OF COMMAND. IN KEEPING WITH THE PROMISE OF COMPLETE ANONYMITY OF THOSE PARTICIPATING, ALL TRANSCRIPTS OF THE PROCEEDINGS WERE ORDERED DESTROYED.

RIGHT: *HMCS* Quebec. *Previously named HMCS* Uganda, *she joined the British Pacific Fleet after being commissioned by the RCN in 1944. After the war,* Uganda *spent the rest of her career as a training ship, having been renamed the* Québec *in 1952. (PUBLIC ARCHIVES)*

A PERSONAL REMINISCENCE OF THE RCN

BETWEEN THE WARS

Too young to serve in WWII, Jim Lister joined the Navy as a "boy" seaman in 1945. Not much had changed.

WHEN THE TERM "BETWEEN the wars" is mentioned, most people think of between WWI and WWII. But the period between WWII and the Korean War (1945-1950) is hardly ever brought to mind. This was the time when, after the end of WWII, most servicemen were returning to civilian life. But for some of those who were too young to serve in WWII, this was a time for *them*. There were also many who had joined the Permanent Force as early as the 1920s, who were still serving, plus those who had joined the RCN in the early part of the war, when seven year hitches were the norm.

There was still a job to do, even after Germany (and later Japan) surrendered. It was the time when Winston Churchill made his famous speech "an iron curtain has descended,"etc. There were still enough ships in commission to give everyone who wanted (and some who did not) the chance for sea time. We used the same ships (those still sea-worthy), the same tools and weapons, even the same duffle coats. The meals were the same, lots of sauerkraut, beets, red lead and bacon, and the old reliable, powdered eggs. There was also hard tack on occasion. Did we get steak? It looked like steak, but the few times we ate it we would have found a hack-saw useful. However, the rum issue made up for a lot.

It would really be interesting to know the cost of 'vitilling' in the naval budget in 1946, compared to the previous war years. Probably about the same per person. The Korean War changed a lot of things for the better, including the living conditions on board ship, and clothing issue.

In 1945 the government announced a recruitment drive for the Royal Canadian Navy. Any male at least 17 and a half years of age was welcome to apply. Having served a couple of years in the sea cadets (44-45) I was prepared, with my father's consent, to join up. So I became a 'boy seaman.'

I was sent to *HMCS Cornwallis*, at Deep Brook, Nova Scotia, for my basic training. Actually, things in Cornwallis were winding down and many RCNVR, hostilities-only personnel under training, were sent home and we commenced our basic training. The base finally closed in December 1945, and we were sent to *HMCS Naden* at Esquimalt, BC, to complete our training, with a two-day stop-over at our homes for Christmas. It was here I met my brother, newly-arrived home from Europe (Royal Regiment). He could not believe that I had joined up. Anyway, on our trip west we picked up a lot more new recruits from across Canada. Many were RCNVRs who had joined during the war and had signed up to stay until September 1947. Most of our instructors were Permanent Force RCN who had joined as early as the 1920s and 1930s. But lots of people were, like myself, new entries. They called my type "VJ 60s" in that we had joined within the period, 60 days of VJ Day. We arrived in *HMCS Naden* on New Year's Eve 1945.

After completing our basic training in *Naden*, most of us were sent to serve in *HMCS Uganda*, one of Canada's two cruisers. Aboard *Uganda* were many of the original crew who had stayed in her, including Captain E.R. Mainguy. The new guys were mixed in with the "old hands." Their experience certainly helped us, and we learned fast – especially from our many mistakes. But a trip to South America and around Cape Horn, for an 18-year old, was quite an event.

Those like myself, who served their time between World War II and Korea, never received, or expected, any awards or medals – the experience and comradeship of those five years was priceless. I got out in 1950, but many of those I had joined up with went on to serve in Korea and with NATO in other trouble spots, some making a full career in the Navy.

Every kid should have that chance.

REPRINTED FROM:
Esprit de Corps, *Volume 7 Issue 2*
AUTHOR: *Jim Lister*

THE COLD WAR YEARS

After the Second World War ended in 1945, another, more subtle conflict began. Ex-allies became potential enemies and vice versa.

ABOVE: *In the post World War II partitioning of Germany, the Brandenburg Gate soon came to symbolize the division boundary of eastern and western Europe.* (DND PHOTO)

OPPOSITE PAGE, LEFT: *The roadblocks, erected by the Soviet Union, which shut down all traffic between Berlin and the West are about to be dismantled on 14 May 1949. For the better part of a year, Western airlifts supplied Berliners with essentials.*

ALTHOUGH THE MEN WHO died at Dieppe in 1942 were very much part of a shooting war, there is a strong suspicion that they were the first victims of the Cold War. Russian forces had suffered a disaster on the Don less than a month before the Dieppe raid and the Germans were at the gates of Stalingrad. Soviet Leader Joseph Stalin had been most vocal in his criticism of the Allied failure to get on with a second front.

There is ample evidence that the disaster at Dieppe on August 19th was an ill-conceived attempt to appease him. It became the first of several attempts to appease a calculating despot and each attempt added to the fabric of the iron curtain which would eventually descend over Europe and bring on the Cold War.

BETRAYAL AT YALTA

The appeasement of the Soviet Union led to an agreement at Yalta in February 1944 by Britain and the United States which was a betrayal of the Polish government in exile and the thousands of Poles who had fought in the Allied cause. In drafting the post-war areas of influence, the Russians insisted on setting up a puppet regime in the territories of Poland it had occupied since 1939-40, and the Western allies withdrew their support of the exiled Polish government in England. As a trade-off, Stalin agreed to discourage Greek communists from seizing power and the West anticipated an agreement with Communist Marshal Tito in Yugoslavia.

The outcome of the Yalta agreement and the Potsdam declaration a year later was that a line of demarkation ran south along the Elbe River and Stalin had access to much of central Europe and the Balkans.

As the Russian armies moved west in 1945, within one month a million German refugees were either killed or disappeared. Germans fled from Rumania, Yugoslavia and Hungary and were replaced by communists. This form of political cleansing reduced the German population East of the Elbe by over 14 million in four years.

DRESDEN

In February, 1945, some 350,000 such refugees had fled to Dresden, a city whose population was 650,000. Although Dresden contained little of military value, it was destroyed as Allied bombers struck seven times and induced firestorms which killed an estimated 135,000 people. The most devastating air attack in history surpassed casualties at either Tokyo or Hiroshima.

Winston Churchill had impatiently urged the RAF to get on with the job before the raid, but a few weeks later, as a shocked reaction spread throughout the West, Churchill decided:" The destruction of Dresden remains a serious query against the conduct of Allied bombing." Dresden apparently was another misguided attempt to impress the Russians.

After Germany's surrender, the United States, Britain, Russia and France controlled a divided Berlin. Russia occupied the Eastern half and as relations between the conquering powers deteriorated and a psychological wall separated the East and the West. The Russian policy was twofold: to maintain a perceived pressure at the line of demarkation while working to expand communism in eastern Europe and around the world. In February, 1947, the Communists staged a coup in Czechoslovakia and a year later took over the government.

BERLIN AIRLIFT

Stalin arranged a blockade of Allied trains into Berlin that year and the Western section of the city faced starvation. It needed at least 2500 tons of food a day and this was provided in a dramatic show of defiance by an airlift to the besieged city. The blockade went on for 328 days and the USAF and RAF more than met the minimum food requirements. On one day alone 895 aircraft flew in 7000 tons of supplies. It was the first clear-cut Allied victory in dealing with the Russians who abandoned the blockade and later agreed to the formation of the West German Republic. Two months after Konrad Adenauer won a free-election in the

ABOVE:
The escalating nuclear arms race between the United States and the Soviet Union placed Canada squarely on the frontlines between the two Cold War belligerents. (US NAVAL INSTIT.)

West, Stalin set up a Soviet-controlled German Democratic Republic in the East. The Russians also developed an atomic bomb and the Cold War became a hard reality by the fall of 1949.

The United Nations was formed in 1945 but, with Russia on the Security Council with a veto, it was hardly more effective than the League of Nations. As more countries joined, each brought its agenda and the UN became a money-consuming, bloated bureaucracy where many programs proliferated but effective peacekeeping was slow to take root.

The pattern of Russian domination was to seize resources rather than improve the economy. It was a fatal flaw which led to the implosion of the Soviet empire in the early 1990s. In the West, the US Marshall Plan provided a major impetus to an economy shattered by war, and became one of the key elements in eventually winning the Cold War.

CANADA ON STAGE

Canada emerged from WWII the fifth Allied military power with a commendable war record, having achieved tremendous industrial growth. But nobody abroad took it seriously. During the first year or so of peace, Canadians just wanted to get back to the good life. Armed Forces of more than 700,000 were allowed to dwindle to about 8000 by 1947. At first this was a natural course, but the establishment of the United Nations and the concept of collective security raised a few doubts among some. Then as tension grew between Russia and the United States, it became quite clear that in a shooting war, Canada might well be the shooting ground. After VE-Day a Canadian Occupation Force remained in Europe but was withdrawn by stages over the next two years. As numbers dwindled in the forces, some militia units were hard-pressed to muster a platoon, and the threat of Russian bombers, immediately converted infantry militia into anti-aircraft units.

The threat had a positive effect on militia recruiting while the regular army developed a Mobile Striking Force. The fundamental concept was a swift-moving force capable of meeting pockets of enemy invaders in the north. Several exercises were mounted in cooperation with the Yanks, the first being an airborne attack by the Princess Patricia's Canadian Light Infantry on Fort St John.

The operation gave new meaning to the cold war and while DND was quick to extol the effectiveness of the MSF, it soon became clear to all that rather than a quick-action force, the group was nothing but ordinary troops in long-underwear. Furthermore, if the Russians had the Atomic bomb, it seemed logical that Washington, New York or Chicago should be a bomber or missile target rather than Le Pas, Manitoba. The concept of MSF remained but numbers dwindled and by the early 50's the only troops involved in Arctic defence were from the Western Command militia.

A Russian cipher clerk, Igor Gouzenko, came in from the cold with documents which proved that the Soviets had been spying on Canada. An ally of both the United States and Britain, Canada took a somewhat perverse pride in being spied upon. This may or may not have been in the minds of diplomats at External Affairs who got tired of Canada's lack of international recognition. But Canadian planning at External Affairs was soon designed to give Canada a place at international tables. This concept, related to defence, led to the idea of a North Atlantic Treaty Organization.

NATO was first conceived by Escott Reid of External Affairs in 1947 and became a reality two years later. In spite of the contribution of Canadians such as Escott Reid, Lester Pearson and Hume Wrong in the establishing of NATO, the DND had neither resources nor enthusiasm for sending troops abroad. But when Communist North Korea, with Russian and Chinese backing, launched a strong attack on South Korea, the so-called Cold War warmed up.

AUTHOR: *Norm Shannon*

THE BERLIN BLOCKADE AND THE BIRTH OF NATO

When the Soviets shut down land access to the Allied-controlled sectors of Berlin, the only way into the surrounded city was by air. For nearly a year, tensions ran high as the Western powers struggled to maintain their vital "air bridge."

ABOVE: *Children gather on a mound of rubble to watch as an American C-54 Skymaster carrying assorted supplies sweeps low over West Berlin on its way into Templehof Airport, July 1948. Templehof would soon be one of the busiest airports in the world.* (BBC/BETTMAN ARCHIVES)

ON 16 APRIL 1945, three red flares lit up the night skies over Berlin, signalling the start of a grim and bloody battle. As hundreds of thousands of Berliners sheltered in the U-bahn, railway tunnels and cellars, Marshals Konev and Zhukov of the Soviet Union launched their final offensive. Remnants of the once-mighty Wehrmacht, old men and boys fought street by street and building to building – to no avail. Thirteen days later, Hitler wakened to reality and, oblivious to the lives of civilians and fighting men alike, took his own. The next morning, a red flag fluttered from the Reichstag.

A young Soviet soldier thought the city looked like a picture of Hell. "Starving people shambled about in the ruins," he wrote. "All of them looking terribly tired, hungry, tense and demoralized." Over 300,000 Soviets had been killed or wounded in the battle for Berlin, 480,000 German soldiers were taken prisoner and 100,000 Berliners perished. The city was reduced to rubble with no electricity, little drinking water and even less food.

To General Lucius D. Clay, newly-appointed to the Joint Control Commission, Berlin was "the city of the dead." An engineer, well-versed in politics, he hoped to establish a peace without malice, much like the peace Lincoln had envisaged for his native South. The Soviets, however, had other plans.

THE IRON CURTAIN

The Grand Alliance of the Western powers and the Soviet Union, which had led to victory over Hitler's Germany, did not long survive that victory. Strains in the alliance were apparent even before the war ended when it became clear that the Soviets were determined to impose communist-dominated regimes in Eastern Europe. Watching the process, Winston Churchill remarked that an "Iron Curtain" was descending across Europe, a phrase that would enter the English language.

At the Potsdam Conference, Germany had been divided into four zones – British, French, Soviet and American – with a Joint Control Commission in Berlin, 160 kilometres inside the Soviet zone of occupation. The four-power administration had worked reasonably well throughout 1946 and 1947 and Berlin was on the verge of an amazing economic recovery. But as the Soviet grip on eastern Europe tightened and East-West relations deteriorated, the city, isolated and vulnerable, also came under threat. At midnight on 23 June 1948, in a major test of western resolve, the Soviets announced that "passenger and freight traffic to and from Berlin will halt at 0600 hours because of technical problems." The next day, they cut all rail and road connections.

General Clay's immediate reaction was to call the Soviet bluff and send an armed convoy down the Helmstedt-Berlin autobahn. Persuaded that such an act might lead to war, he accepted a British proposal to mount an airlift, informing the mayor of Berlin that "I may be the craziest man in the world, but I'm going to try the experiment of feeding this city by air."

Code-named "Operation VITTLES," the airlift began on 26 June when 12 C-47's swooped over the rooftops into Templehof airport to deliver 80 tonnes of milk, flour and medicines; far short of the 4,500 tonnes needed daily to support Berlin's 2.5 million inhabitants. In the months to come, British and American aircrews, taking off and landing at five minute intervals day and night, would deliver an astounding 2,325,000 tonnes of supplies to the beseiged city. Templehof, Tegel and Gatow became the busiest airports in the world.

Although they indulged in a good deal of harassment, buzzing aircraft and jamming radio frequencies, none of the relatively few crashes that took place during the airlift were attributed directly to Soviet interference. Ever the realist, Stalin recognized

LEFT: *The desperate conditions following the Second World War, prior to the airlift, forced many to seek food handouts at refugee camps.* (HUTTON GETTY)

ABOVE: *Foreign Minister Lester B. Pearson welcomes former British Prime Minister Winston Churchill to Ottawa following the signing of the NATO treaty, August, 1948.* (HUTTON GETTY)

that he was involved in a confrontation he could not win and lifted the blockade on 12 May 1949.

The crisis in Berlin led to the permanent division of Germany. In May 1949, a few days before the blockade ended, Konrad Adenauer, an extremely able politician who had been imprisoned by the Nazis, was appointed Chancellor of a German Federal Republic. Five months later, the Soviets responded by forming their zone into the very undemocratic German Democratic Republic.

The Soviet threat prompted Western European governments to take collective defence measures and seek American assistance. The process began with the singing of the Treaty of Dunkirk, an Anglo-French mutual aid agreement, in March 1947. Encouraged by President Truman's commitment to Greece and Turkey against Soviet encroachment and the implementation of the Marshall Plan, the foreign ministers of Belgium, France, Luxembourg, the Netherlands and the United Kingdom moved the process along with the Brussels Treaty. Although the objective of both treaties was to contain Germany, the Communist coup in Czechoslovakia shifted the focus of concern. On 22 March 1948, secret talks began in Washington with a view to broadening the alliance which now included Denmark, Norway, Iceland, Italy and Portugal.

PEARSON REPRESENTED CANADA AT THE TALKS DESPITE KING'S RESERVATIONS THAT "HE MAY GET US MUCH MORE DEEPLY INVOLVED WITH WORLD SITUATIONS THAN WE EVER SHOULD BE."

The American, however, remained cautious about becoming directly involved in any permanent European defence agreement. So too was Canada, with Prime Minister Mackenzie King confiding to his diary that "it would be a mistake to make Canada a sort of apex to a movement which would link us to other nations in a project that is intended to offset the possibility of immediate war with Russia."

THE CANADA ARTICLE

Canada was represented at the talks by Foreign Minister Lester B. Pearson despite King's reservations that "He may get us much more deeply involved with world situations than we ever should be." An ardent supporter of an Atlantic treaty, Pearson insisted that economic, social and cultural issues be considered, "otherwise it would be considered as merely another old-fashioned military alliance." His concerns were addressed in Article 2, referred to as "the Canadian Article" in NATO lore.

The NATO Treaty, which came into force on 24 August 1949 and consists of 14 articles, is dedicated to the defence of the territories of the member states. An international military agreement for collective defence as defined in Article 15 of the United Nations Charter, its aims are set out in the preamble: "to safeguard the freedom, common heritage and civilization of their peoples, founded on the principles of democracy, individual liberty and the rule of law."

The Korean War hastened the creation of an integrated military structure with the appointment of a Supreme Commander Europe (SACEUR) with Headquarters (SHAPE) at Rocquencourt near Paris. In October 1950, Greece and Turkey became associate members in preparation for their eventual entry into the alliance in 1952. West Germany became a member on 5 May 1955.

NATO would become "an old-fashioned military alliance" after all, much to Pearson's disappointment. Slyly, he wrote: "And so we signed the North Atlantic Treaty on a pleasant spring day in Washington while the band of theU.S. Marines played soft music, including two selections from *Porgy and Bess*: "I Got Plenty of Nothing" and "It Ain't Necessarily So." Appropriately, he thought.

AUTHOR: *Bill Twatio*

CANADA'S SAS COMPANY

Canada's first post-war airborne unit was a company-sized group led by a hero of the Resistance in the Second World War. They pioneered the way to an expanded airborne role for the Canadian army,

ABOVE: *Members of Canada's Special Air Service (SAS) company practice their aircraft exit from a mock tower. The first and only commander of this elite commando unit was the legendary Guy d'Artois. (NAC/PA 166961)* ***OPPOSITE PAGE.*** *When the SAS company was disbanded, d'Artois returned to serve with the Royal 22nd Regiment (Vandoos). (NAC/PA 189545)*

OVER 400 AXIS AIRCRAFT were destroyed by the Special Air Service or SAS in the Desert War of 50 years ago. This is a higher total than was achieved in aerial combat by the Royal Airforce in the same theatre. The total of kills by Commonwealth anti-aircraft units in Africa doesn't even come close. The Royal Navy up to 1943 in the Mediterranean destroyed far fewer enemy aircraft. The men with parachute wings, not pilot's wings, were the most successful in depriving Rommel of his much-needed air support from the Luftwaffe. Ironically, in the North African campaign, the SAS were delivered into action in most cases by the vehicles of the Long Range Desert Group, not aircraft. Not surprisingly, Canada, Australia, New Zealand, South Africa, France, Belgium and Rhodesia went on at war's end to create a national organization carrying the name made famous by the SAS.

THE SAS APPROACH

The SAS, which at war's end consisted of over a brigade, started in the mind of an officer recovering in a Cairo hospital from injuries received while parachuting. David Stirling, knowing that a mere subaltern would not get anywhere near the Commander in Chief of British forces in the Middle East, had to resort to an SAS approach to expose Sir Claude Auchinlek to his ideas. He left his crutches outside the wire surrounding the Middle East Headquarters and was able to confront the Deputy c-in-c, Lieutenant General Ritchie before security staff were alerted to his presence. He sold his heresy. It remains one of the unanswered questions of history whether Montgomery would have supported Stirling's proposal. Stirling deliberately rejected the basis of the standard infantry battalion, sections of eight to ten men led by a Non-Commissioned Officer, for an organization based on modules or sub-units of four. The SAS concept did not call for a leader to emerge in this group. Rather, each was trained to a high level in all SAS skills while having one special area of expertise. In an operation each individual exercised his own perception and judgement. The risk that discipline would break down was recognized. In fact a British writer has suggested the functioning of a module of four was "anarchy" based on the dictionary definition that relates the word to regulation or laws being unnecessary. Stirling's success in destroying over 100 aircraft with only 20 men within months of forming the SAS ensured the survival of his idea, at least for the duration of the war. The SAS was one of a whole range of small, highly effective elements created, particularly by the British, in World War Two. The Sea Reconnaissance Unit, the idea of a Canadian Sub-Lieutenant Wright, is an example. The name "Special Air Service" had been chosen to deceive the Germans into thinking an airborne unit was stationed in North Africa. Canadians served in many of these organizations, so it was to a veteran of one of these that the Canadian Army turned in 1946 when forming the Canadian SAS Company.

Captain Guy d'Artois was the first and only Officer Commanding of the Canadian SAS Company. He had served with the British Special Operations Executive (SOE). The SOE mandate was to encourage resistance in Fascist occupied Europe and Asia by sending agents to assist in organizing and training locals in sabotage. D'Artois had joined the Royal 22nd Regiment in Southern England following study at the University of Montreal early in 1940. He had returned to North America to join the Canadian-American SSF in 1942 and participated with the Special Service Force in their Kiska operation in the Aleutians. In the autumn of 1943 he was recruited and trained to work for the SOE in France. Dropped in April 1944 into the Burgundy countryside, by D-Day d'Artois had helped in the creation and equipping of two underground battalions, one of which he commanded himself. From 6 June 1944 onwards no German troops or supply convoys could enter d'Artois' area without being attacked. The contribution of d'Artois, others like him and the French Resistance contributed immensely to the break-out at Normandy. By the autumn of 1944 the work of the SOE in France was no longer required. D'Artois' work was recognized by awarding him the DSO.

TRAINING BEGINS

There were many Canadians with SOE experience including some who first served in France and then went on to Asia. D'Artois was probably good choice as first OC of the Canadian SAS Company because he had challenged even the somewhat eccentric bureaucracy of the SOE by marrying a fellow agent before parachuting into France. (His wife, Sonia, was the youngest female agent sent to France.) The first members of his Canadian SAS began arriving at the Canadian Joint Air Training Center in Rivers, Manitoba in the spring of 1947. The Company was under command of this Center for administration, discipline, rationing and quartering, but was under the operational control of Army HQ in Ottawa. The company second-in-command has said that much local freedom of action was taken, or given by d'Artois.

The roles of the Canadian SAS never seem to have been enunciated clearly. In 1946 Canadian Defence policy-makers were having difficulty identifying a threat to the North American mainland, so it was probably a question of preserving unique skills acquired in war-time before they became lost. The actual roles as understood by members of this SAS organization seemed to be undertaking "Otto Skorzeny" type operations, sabotage activities and raids in section or platoon-sized groups, reconnaissance or information gathering in rear or remote areas, or support to guerilla factions. While many of these roles were undertaken by the SAS in the Second World War it can be seen that there was a return to the conventional army basics of platoon and section, a departure from Stirling's principles and present British SAS practice. Moreover the suggestion of supporting guerillas has a strong SOE overtone reflecting the OC's

CAPTAIN D'ARTOIS EARNED A GEORGE MEDAL WHEN HE HELPED RESCUE AN ANGLICAN MISSIONARY IN THE HIGH ARCTIC IN THE FALL OF 1947

SOE background in France with the French Resistance. The training not only had an SOE flavour but some subjects, such as Spanish language, appears hard to relate to any possible post-war Canadian defence policy consideration.

BASIC LESSONS

In common with the British SAS model and indeed all specialist units, physical fitness was stressed. All were parachutists and the original members were also trained to be parachute packers. Air portability courses were given to all. All ranks learned knots, lashing and ropework. Demolition training described as similar to that which would have been used in the "maquis" was undertaken. Morse Code was also taught, again perhaps a reflection on one of the Resistance's main tasks before the 1944 invasion, that of information gathering. D'Artois is said to have made the training highly imaginative and creative, perhaps necessary with war veterans who had already seen combat forming the basis of the SAS company. There was also said to be a strong element of risk in some of the training. Like the SAS training, there was a strong emphasis on development of personal initiative and self-reliance. This was needed not only operationally but because the unit appears to have lacked Senior NCOs. At one point there were four officers, one sergeant, two corporals, four lance-corporals and 60 private soldiers.

The Canadian SAS Company, at least on paper, returned to a traditional infantry subunit organization in having three platoons. Army politics was perhaps reflected in that there was a RCR platoon, a PPCLI platoon, and a R22eR platoon. Late in 1948 a "services" platoon was added. Contact with the rest of what was basically a small Canadian army (15,000) was limited. The SAS Company did a summer concentration in August 1948 at the Cadet Camp at Clear Lake, Manitoba. Although several company level paradrops were conducted, these were all in the vicinity of Rivers with the scenario generally being that of an airborne raid against a key enemy installation. Airlift resources were to some extent concentrated at Rivers at this time making this a logical approach in time of fiscal constraint. Half the SAS Company did a barnstorming tour of eastern Canada apparently making jumps at Camp Petawawa, Camp Valcartier, and Debert. The only known fatality occurred in an accident during one of these demonstrations. Operationally the SAS Company was only deployed as a unit in the Spring of 1948 when it formed the basis of the Joint Training Center's contingent fighting floods in the Lower Mainland of British Columbia. Captain d'Artois himself went on to earn a George Medal when he and three other members of the Company were involved in the rescue of an Anglican missionary in the High Arctic in the fall of 1947. The unit was disbanded in September 1949 with members forming the nucleus of instructors and trained personnel within their respective battalions for conversion of these units to an airborne role. In keeping with policy, developed by 1949, it had been decided to convert the three Active Force infantry battalions to a parachute role. Conversion of the PPCLI, the first unit to this airborne role was complete the same month the Canadian SAS Company disbanded.

The return to conventional military organizations that predated the Second War was also completed by this step. Field Marshall Slim, who had said that any well-trained infantry battalion should be able to do what a commando can do, no doubt would have approved. In any case it does not appear that the Canadian SAS Company made an attempt to graft the module of four principle into Canadian Army practice. The SAS Company instead, served as a reservoir of airborne personnel who could serve as the basis for the Mobile Strike Force parachute battalions, once that concept received approval.

The Mobile Strike Force (MSF) was to be a distinctive Canadian force which could operate in the North in conjunction with much larger American forces. It was thought that the airborne role would give Canada the desired degree of influence even though the US forces were much more numerous. The perceived threat was a hostile airborne lodgement which was to be countered by a MSF paradrop on top of the enemy. There was no place for specialists such as the SAS in this concept, if indeed the Canadian Company had specialists on the scale of their British counterparts. Korea, then the commitments to NATO, never brought forward a Canadian requirement for a SAS type element. The Canadian Airborne Regiment, when created, continued to be organized in the traditional Army manner. In 2001, as matter of survival, the Army was struggling to keep alive the General Purpose Capability of Canada's ground forces. Stirling's module of four was unlikely to receive consideration in that Force Development climate. The only opportunity for the SAS concept to be adopted by a part of the CF appears to have disappeared in September 1949 when the Canadian SAS Company was dissolved, if it was ever there at all.

REPRINTED FROM:
Esprit de Corps, *Volume 3 Issue 3*
AUTHOR:
Roy Thomas

AFTERMATH OF 1945

For some, Japan's surrender in 1945 was an ending. For Korea and the United Nations, it was a new beginning.

ABOVE: *Students protest as American troops enter Seoul in August, 1945. The U.S. antagonized many Koreans by maintaining Japanese administrative and police forces.*

WHENEVER WE CELEBRATE THE anniversary of VJ day, we often forget that the conditions of Japan's surrender led directly to another major war, half a decade later.

For centuries Korea, described by John Toland as "the crossroads of Asia," had been the scene of local wars by various warlords. The "Land of the Morning Calm" finally achieved stability under the benevolent protection of its Chinese neighbours for twelve centuries, acquiring a reputation for culture and, when occasion demanded, proving well capable of defending its borders against outside aggression. In the late sixteenth century Japan attempted to invade China via Korea but was repelled, largely through the efforts of Admiral Yi Sung Sin, whose revolutionary "turtle boats" – the world's first "ironclads" - soundly defeated the Japanese fleet.

From the start of the twentieth century, Japan exerted more control on Korea, until the latter became virtually a vassal state. Though Korea was nominally independent, Japan's sovereignty was evident in the 1936 Olympics, when Kijung Son, of Korea, won the Marathon but was obliged to receive his gold medal under the Japanese flag.

FOR A TIME THE POLITICAL SITUATION IN THE SOUTH WAS EXTREMELY VOLATILE. AT ONE TIME OVER 140 "PEOPLES COMMITTEES" CONTROLLED VARIOUS AREAS OF THE ZONE.

MIXED BLESSING

Japan's 'protection' was a mixed blessing. While many bright young Koreans were sent to Japan for education (many of them attained high rank in the Imperial military forces) other Koreans were treated as virtual slaves. Many were conscripted into the Army (several of whom served as guards in POW camps). The Japanese government recently formally apologized to Korea for the abduction of 200,000 young females for use in Japanese Army brothels.

During the Second World War, Korea's postwar future was discussed briefly by the Allies. In 1943 Roosevelt, Chiang Kai-shek and Winston Churchill agreed in Cairo that following an Allied victory, the country would become independent, but this was almost an afterthought to other and more vital matters discussed. In July of 1945 the Allied leaders – who now added Stalin to their group – again raised the issue briefly in the Potsdam conference, when it was decided that the Soviet Union, which was no longer threatened in the West, would join the war against Japan. Ironically, while division of the spoils was discussed, the fate of Korea was left to a comparatively low-level military group, whose main concern was to define a boundary determining where in the Korean peninsular Japanese troops surrender would be accepted by either the Soviets or the Western allies. Eventually a US Colonel and his Soviet counterparts, with the blessing of Secretary of State Dean Rusk, arbitrarily drew a dividing line at the 38th Parallel of latitude – a boundary which not only had no geographical features, but which in fact isolated part of the "southern" zone from the rest.

***ABOVE:** After a 40-year absence, Syngman Rhee returned to Korea as an uncompromising anti-communist. Although backed by the Americans in UN supervised elections, he did not enjoy popular support.*

SOVIET LIBERATORS

In the North, the advancing Soviets – who had hardly fired a shot against the Japanese – were welcomed as liberators. The closest US troops were a thousand miles away in Okinawa, and it was some time before they arrived. When they did so, it was as an 'army of occupation' rather than restorers of freedom. Nevertheless, on 15 August 1945 Korea was again a free country, after nearly 36 years of subjucation to Japan. (This date is now celebrated annually as "Liberation Day" by Koreans.)

Political struggles however, began soon after. In the North, the Soviets welcomed a reputed anti-Japanese guerrilla leader, Kim Il-Sung and when they left Korea in 1947, Kim became prime minister of the "Democratic People's Republic of Korea" in a manner familiar to many East European satellites – after an 'election' during which his principal opponent had disappeared and in which only one name appeared on ballot sheets.

The South was politically active, too. Against the wishes of the US State Department, General MacArthur (now Military Governor of Japan) brought in the aging Syngman Rhee, who had lived in exile in the US for over 40 years. Another leadership contender was the head of the ad-hoc government-in-exile, Kim Kyu-Sik (the preponderance of "Kims" in the political and military field was due to the fact that about 25 per cent of Koreans from both areas shared that family name, which means "golden one").

For a time the political situation in the South was extremely volatile. At one time over 140 "peoples committees" controlled various areas of the zone. The US occupation forces antagonized many Koreans by restoring Japanese-organized administrative and police forces, and rioting and civil disorder occurred frequently. Problems increased with the arrival of over a million discontented 'refugees' from the North, most of whom settled in or around the capital city of Seoul.

LIBERATION DAY

In 1947, the United Nations had voted for an "all-Korea" election, supervised by a supervisory commission (UNTCOK). Canada was represented in the nine-nation group – one of our first but far from last 'peacekeeping' operation, earning inclusion of "Korea" on Ottawa's National Peacekeeping Monument. The North refused to admit the teams, but in the south Syngman Rhee eventually took office as President of the Republic of Korea on 15 August 1948. ("Liberation Day" anniversary.)

There were now two Koreas – although both sides hoped for unification. The North (with about one third of the total population but almost all of the industry) would have liked a united Korea – under Kim Il-Sung. Not surprisingly, Syngman Rhee had the same goal, with himself as President. The Soviets evacuated their sector; two years later the Americans followed suit. The Communists were generous with military aid; artillery, aircraft, vehicles and hundreds of the famed T-34 tanks found their way to North Korea. The Western allies, who were afraid that the fiesty Rhee would invade the North if he had the resources, were more sparing. Only infantry small arms were allocated to the raw South Korean army, with an "Air Force" consisting of three elderly training aircraft.

BORDER CLASHES

Following the departure of the last US occupation troops in 1949 – leaving behind a few hundred "advisers" – both sides began preparing defences along the 38th Parallel. There were several border clashes and raids by communist guerrillas.

On 19 June 1950, John Foster Dulles addressed the Korean National Assembly and pledged US aid, if necessary, in defence of South Korea. Meanwhile, North Korean armies, who hopelessly outclassed their southern neighbours in numbers, equipment and training, conducted "exercises" in the border areas. In the morning of Sunday 25 June 1950 the roar of Communist artillery and the presence of hordes of T-34 tanks south of the parallel showed the world that this was NO exercise. The rest is history.

REPRINTED FROM:
Esprit de Corps, *Volume 5 Issue 1*
AUTHOR: *Les Peate*

THE KOREAN WAR 1950 - 1953

15 AUGUST 1945 Japan surrenders. 38th Parallel is dividing line between U.S. and U.S.S.R. areas of influence.

NOVEMBER 1947 UNTCOK formed to supervise elections in Korea. (First Canadian participation in UN mission)

APRIL 1948 Elections held in U.S. Truman elected.

15 AUGUST 1948 Republic of Korea proclaimed – Syngman Rhee is President.

9 SEPTEMBER 1948 Democratic Peoples Republic (North Korea) inaugurated under Kim Il Sung.

25 JUNE 1950 North Korean troops invade across 38th Parallel. UN Security Council meets. North Korea named "aggressor" and UN support sought to repel invaders.

29 JUNE 1950 RN, RAN and RCAF units committed to UN Command.

12 JULY 1950 Three Canadian destroyers committed to UN.

27 JULY 1950 Airlift by 426 Sqn. RCAF begins. U.S. government requests Canadian Brigade.

7 AUGUST 1950 Canadian Army Special Force proclaimed.

8 AUGUST 1950 Brigadier J.M. Rockingham appointed Brigade Commander.

16 AUGUST 1950 First Canadian "shots fired in anger" by *HMCS Cayuga*.

AUGUST 1950 90 per cent of South Korea in enemy hands. (Allies hold Pusan Perimeter)

15 SEPTEMBER 1950 Inchon landing. HMCS *Athabaskan* will later receive ROK Presidential Citation for her part. (The only such award to a Canadian unit)

25 OCTOBER 1950 Chinese enter the War.

21 NOVEMBER 1950 Canoe River train wreck in British Columbia.

18 DECEMBER 1950 2 PPCLI disembark in Pusan, join 27 BRITCOM Brigade.

22 FEBRUARY 1951 First Canadian battle casualties.

7 MARCH 1951 Private Barton, MM, first Canadian decoration.

22-25 APRIL 1951 The Battle of Kapyong.

28 JULY 1951 First Commonwealth Division formed. Includes 25 (Cdn), 28 (Comwel) and 29 (UK) Brigades.

4-11 OCTOBER 1951 Operation COMMANDO.

23 NOVEMBER 1951 2 R22eR defence of Hill 227.

25 MAY 1952 B Coy, 1 RCR arrive on Koje-do.

SEPTEMBER 1952 HMCS *Nootka* captures enemy vessel at sea – the only such capture by UN Navies.

23-24 OCTOBER 1952 1 RCR defence of Hill 355.

2-3 MAY 1953 Attack on 3 RCR. Heaviest casualties in single action.

27 JULY 1953 Cease-fire declared

ABOVE, RIGHT: *When General MacArthur's UN troops landed at Inchon on 15 September 1950, they discovered evidence of a massacre by the retreating North Koreans.* (DND PHOTO)

RIGHT: *In response to the invasion of South Korea, Canada sends* Cayuga, Sioux *and* Athabaskan *to the Far East.* (DND PHOTO)

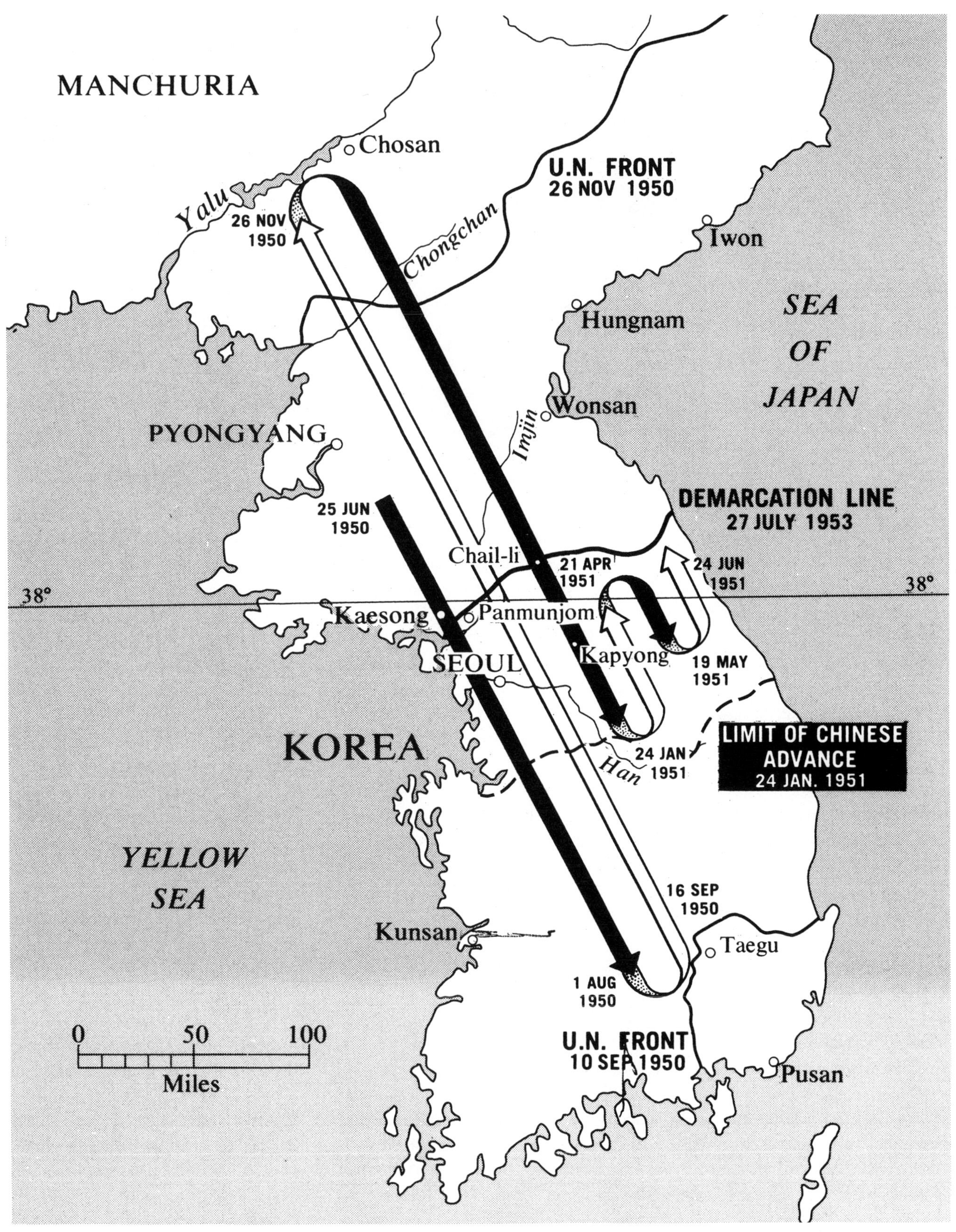
MANCHURIA
Chosan
U.N. FRONT
26 NOV 1950
Yalu
26 NOV
1950
Chongchan
Iwon
Hungnam
SEA
OF
JAPAN
Wonsan
Imjin
PYONGYANG
DEMARCATION LINE
27 JULY 1953
25 JUN
1950
Chail-li
21 APR
1951
24 JUN
1951
38°
38°
Kaesong
Panmunjom
Kapyong
SEOUL
19 MAY
1951
LIMIT OF CHINESE
ADVANCE
24 JAN. 1951
KOREA
24 JAN
1951
Han
YELLOW
SEA
16 SEP
1950
Kunsan
Taegu
1 AUG
1950
0
50
100
Miles
U.N. FRONT
10 SEP 1950
Pusan

RIGHT:
Canada's first reaction to the events in south east Asia was to provide humanitarian relief through an airlift. Here a Royal Canadian Airforce plane lands in Tokyo (1950) with supplies. (DND PHOTO)

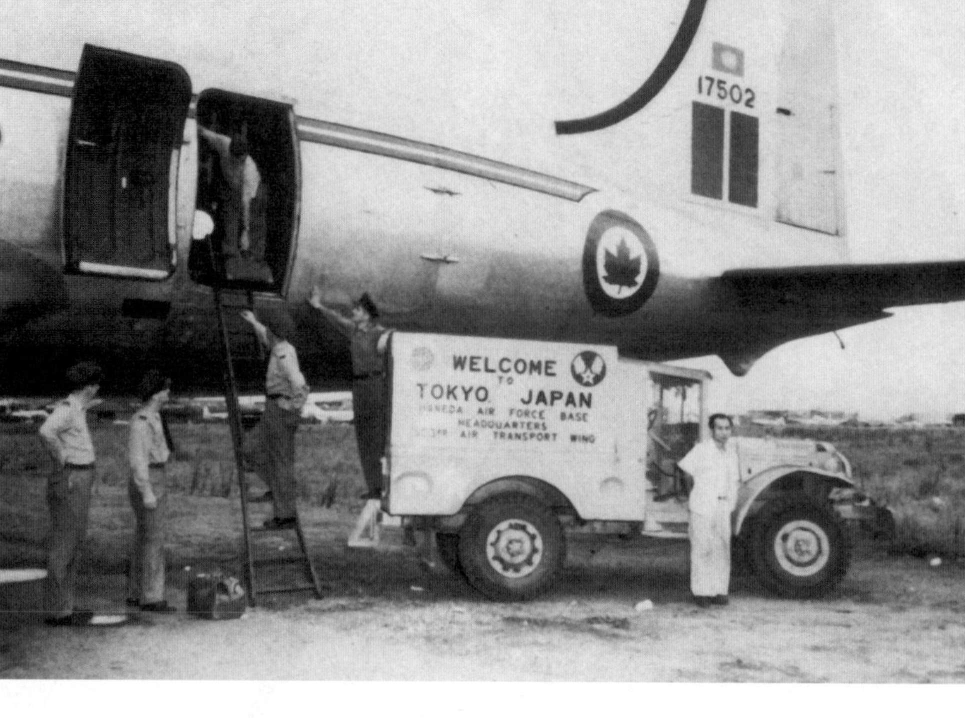

When the United Nations called, "Stand up and be counted," Canada answered – at a heavy cost.

CANADA'S RESPONSE

WHEN NORTH KOREA LAUNCHED its invasion of the South on 25 June 1950 western leaders were universally dismayed. Most though, including Canada's Prime Minister St. Laurent and the Minister for External Affairs Lester B. Pearson, were initially cautious in their reactions to the crisis as they knew only the United States possessed the military capacity to halt the aggression. This meant America must lead the response and determine the extent or really active opposition to the invasion. When U.S. President Harry S. Truman committed increasing levels of American forces over the next three days, gaining approval for this assistance from the United Nations, Canada's leaders were both relieved and impressed. They felt his actions were important for the 'Cold War' confrontation with Russia, which was thought to be the real power behind the North's attack, and also for the credibility of the UN, to which they also attached great importance.

America, though, was only a decade away from the isolationist policies of the 1930s and Truman feared that if American opinion felt it was carrying the load of containing communism alone it would be unwilling to bear the burden. This apprehension had resulted in strong pressure on America's European allies and Canada to increase their defence effort before the NATO Treaty was signed, committing the United States to their defence. It also meant that within days of the start of the Korean War America was pressing its allies for assistance.

STRONG PRESSURE

This pressure was particularly strong on the small circle of countries which America felt were its truly reliable allies – Britain, France, Australia and, of course, Canada. However, the Canadian government was resistant to this pressure. It felt Canada had relatively small interests in the Far East compared with the NATO area, the theatre which it felt would be decisive in the Cold War and where Canada's security contribution could best be made. There was also the ghost of the Canadian experience at Hong Kong in the background.

On a purely practical level Canada's response was also determined by the limited size of its Armed Forces. In 1946 the government had established a ceiling of 51,000 for the forces (Army 25,000, RCN 10,000, and RCAF 16,000) but in March 1950 the reality was still nearly 4,000 short of this figure, with the Army accounting for virtually the whole shortfall. These figures reflected a very understandable desire for low defence expenditure after the Second World War and a belief, commonly held with the US and Britain, that Russia would be unlikely to go to war with the West before about 1956 or '57 due to her wartime devastation.

NO ALLOWANCE MADE

No allowance had been made for the early dispatch of forces overseas by 1950. Canada's Army was designed to provide the framework for an expeditionary force of six divisions in a general mobilization for a major war. Its only active units in 1950 consisted of three infantry battalions and two armoured and one artillery regiment. The infantry were assigned to the Mobile Striking Force (MSF), a brigade group designed as a response to Canada's new post-war danger, that of air or airborne attacks by the Soviets in the North West. In June 1950 though the MSF was still more impressive in title than reality. Its understrength units were scattered across the country, it lacked a proper headquarters and no exercise had ever been undertaken at more than battalion level. The Chiefs of Staff reported it would take six months to turn it into a battle ready brigade group. Sending it to Korea would also leave Canada with no units at all for its own defence.

Faced with this reality the government limited its initial response to naval forces, ordering three destroyers to the Far East on 30 June. Minister of National Defence Brooke Claxton though, had few illusions about the usefulness of this relatively painless and risk-free contribution. He told the Cabinet, 'While it was considered that more naval forces would probably be available than necessary, nevertheless a Canadian contribution might be a desirable gesture.'

NO AVAILABLE GROUND FORCES

But as the crisis continued, with the North Korean forces making great advances, the issue had to be considered again. On 19 July the Cabinet Defence Committee definitely decided that no Canadian ground force could be made available. It also failed to endorse Lester Pearson's suggestions that Canada might allow recruiting for 'some kind of international UN force' or send a medical unit. It did, though, recommend that a squadron of North Star transports be made available to the UN airlift. These planes of 426 Squadron were the first Canadian forces actually in the theatre. (Interestingly, their comrades from 435 and 436 Transport Squadrons had been Canada's last operational units in the Second World War, through their flights over Burma in 1945.)

THREE TOKENS

However it was ground forces that America was really pressing for. Pearson described Canada's three destroyers as 'no mere token' but an official of the U.S. State Department supposedly quipped back, 'Okay, let's call it three tokens.' When Britain, Australia, and New Zealand all announced they would be contributing ground forces on 25 July the pressure on Canada was greatly increased. Returning from Washington after consultations with his American counterpart, Dean Acheson, Lester Pearson was now convinced Canada must send troops. He felt such support was vital both for the alliance with America and for Canada's credibility as a leader at the UN. In a memo to Canadian Prime Minister St. Laurent on 3 August 1950, he stated that if the decision was still not to send troops he would, 'have great difficulty in reconciling it with my views on the menace which faces us'. This left the door open for his resignation. After a series of four Cabinet meetings stretching over a week St. Laurent announced on 7 August the decision to recruit a new infantry brigade group, the Canadian Army Special Force, for use by the UN or NATO, but in all probability for Korea.

ABOVE: *US Naval Ship* James O'Hara, *loaded with American and Canadian soldiers en route to Korea, departs Seattle harbour, October, 1950.* (PAC CA-115034)

OVERWHELMING RESPONSE

Much of the reluctance to mobilize such a force undoubtedly came from fears that it might not be possible to recruit and sustain it through voluntary recruiting, thus raising the divisive spectre of conscription, particularly if other commitments arose, as indeed became the case in 1951 when the 27th Brigade was raised specifically for NATO. The first poll of Canadians with regard to the war that July had shown two-thirds of Quebecers opposed to the dispatch of Canadian troops. However the initial response was excellent, with the new battalion of the Vandoos swiftly up to strength. Overall in fact, the numbers of volunteers were so overwhelming that the tiny Army recruitment machinery, set up to cope with only a trickle of Permanent Force recruitment, was hard-pressed to cope. The resulting mismatch between the eager queues and the small numbers actually led Brooke Claxton to reverse the normal procedures so that men were attested instantly with checks and medical examinations coming later. In this way he hoped to capitalise fully on the initial enthusiasm.

Captain Bill Sutherland of the PPCLI was at this time seconded to the Royal Canadian Engineers as a recruitment officer. Suddenly confronted with 299 recruits for 59 Field Squadron he only had time to ask them three questions: "Have you ever been convicted of a criminal offence? Do you come from a broken family? Why do you want to go to war?", instead of the normal 40 minute interview. As he told me, his assessments had to "rely a great deal on intuition."

CLAXTON CRITICIZED

Claxton's intervention in the recruiting has

RIGHT: *Men of Lieutenant Colonel "Big Jim" Stone's 2nd Battalion, Princess Patricia's Canadian Light Infantry (2PPCLI), begin patrolling exercises shortly after their arrival in Korea.* (NAC PA 128820)

FAR RIGHT: *Colonel Bill Sutherland* (COURTESY HELEN SUTHERLAND)

since been criticized for the many administrative problems and inefficiencies it later caused. Famously, a 72-year old and a man with an artificial leg were enlisted. By the end of March 1951, when the bulk of the force went to Korea, over one third of the 10,000 Special Force recruits had been discharged or had deserted.

However, the recruitment did quickly provide sufficient manpower for the 5,000 strong brigade and its support and reinforcement elements, as well as some of the manpower for the Army's general expansion, despite all its losses while in training. Of the new recruits, 47 per cent were Second World War veterans and 20 per cent were tradesmen, for whom there was a lower loss rate. According to Captain Sutherland only 5 of the 299 recruits for 59 Field Squadron were eventually rejected.

WINTER TRAINING

Initial training quickly began at various bases throughout Canada and the Army estimated a minimum of five months was required to achieve acceptable standards of readiness. Soon, though, the problems of concentrating the brigade and continuing its training through the winter was being considered. This issue was settled in the last week of October when it was agreed that 25 Canadian Infantry Brigade, as the force was now known, should use the US Army's Fort Lewis in Washington State for advanced training. The move to America was carried out from the 11th-21st of November, a transfer most remembered for the Canoe River Train Crash resulting in the deaths of 17 members of the RCHA.

UNCERTAINTIES

For the new 2nd Battalion PPCLI, however, the visit to Fort Lewis was in transit only. This was the result of the course of the fighting in Korea – by October the war seemed to be almost over. General MacArthur felt he no longer required Canada's Brigade for operations but did desire a Canadian presence to stress the UN character of the war. Thus, while the rest of the Brigade continued training with their eventual destination – Korea or the Rhine – still uncertain, 2 PPCLI was despatched to the Far East only three months after its formation. This was considered acceptable as it was thought they would be required for occupation duties only. The part-trained battalion sailed in the USNS *Joe P. Martinez* on 25 November. This was the very day the Chinese launched their first major offensive in Korea.

That intervention quickly called Canada's bluff over the deployment of 2 PPCLI. The battalion arrived in Korea on 18 December and on the 20th its CO, Lieutenant Colonel J. Stone, met his new American commander, General Walker, who wanted the PPCLI to immediately join Britain's 29th Independent Infantry Brigade in the line. Stone had to refuse, having been given a written order that his unit should not be engaged until he felt they had had sufficient training. While this was a reasonable order, especially remembering the Hong Kong experience, the government had decided not to communicate it to the UN Command before Stone's arrival, despite the changed situation with Chinese intervention, thus leaving him to explain to Walker. Stone later praised the General's understanding over the issue but the situation reflected little credit on the Canadian government.

AWKWARD POSITION

That Stone remained in an awkward position, training his troops while others, sometimes with less training, fought desperate battles against the Chinese, is shown by the battalion War Diary. The entry for 5 January 1951 shows he was once again asked to commit the battalion at once, and that for 7 July records, "Lieutenant Colonel Stone is under heavy pressure to commit the battalion early". The diary also reveals the level of preparedness at the time, with the entry for 3 January stating:

"Questions were raised by platoon and company officers regarding the method and speed with which this battalion was raised particularly when a battalion is sent overseas with some men who have never fired their weapons."

It was to Stone's credit that the battalion was ready to move to reinforce the 27th British Commonwealth Brigade on 15 February, a month before the Directorate of Military Training in Canada had thought it would be prepared. Their arrival meant 27th Brigade contained troops from five coun-

tries. The Princess Pats soon added to the Brigade's excellent record in Korea by winning, together with the 3rd Battalion, Royal Australian Regiment, the US Distinguished Unit Citation at Kapyong.

ARRIVAL DELAYED

Arrival of the remainder of the Brigade was delayed both by the proper completion of training and vacillation over whether it was to go to Europe or Korea. Finally, on 21 February 1951 it was announced the Brigade was to go to Korea, and on 4 May it arrived in Pusan. The last major UN reinforcement, it allowed the establishment of a proper three brigade Commonwealth Division that July. The decision to group the brigade with the Commonwealth had originally been made strictly on practical logistic grounds, given the fact Canadian troops were still using British pattern small arms and artillery. By the time 25 Brigade arrived, Lester Pearson had also decided it would "be safer and more efficient in a Commonwealth Division," given the U.S. Army's mixed record in the fighting thus far.

Canada's response had been inevitably slow due to the lack of ready forces, a lesson for any government, and because of vacillation due to the unpredictable course of the war and the higher priority given to the still 'cold' conflict in Europe. Canada's specially recruited force was deployed later than the equivalent New Zealand's unit, which arrived at the end of December 1950. However, this owed much to the fact the

ABOVE:
Brooke Claxton, Minister of National Defence, visits troops of 2PPCLI on 12 September 1950 prior to their departure for the Korean War. General Charles Foulkes looks on. (DND PHOTO)

New Zealand's unit consisted of gunners while Canada's self-contained force centred around that most dangerous and demanding of military roles – infantry.

TAKING UP THE SLACK

Also it should be remembered that once the Canadian troops were in position, they were kept fully up to strength in order to fulfil their role. By December 1951 Brig Rockingham had to tell the Canadian Liaison Mission in Tokyo that 25 Brigade was providing "over half the infantry on the line [within the Commonwealth Division]", as well as undertaking 50 per cent of the service and engineering work, rather than the third which should have been their share. This was largely due to manpower problems among the other Commonwealth contributors, especially Britain. Ironically, given government worries at the outset, of all the problems associated with Canada's response to the war, quality and quantity of its newly recruited manpower was the one that had given it no real worries.

REPRINTED FROM:
Esprit de Corps, *Volume 4 Issues 11 &12*
AUTHOR: *Stephen Prince*
(Excerpted from the author's thesis on the role of the Commonwealth nations in the Korean War.)

TRAGEDY IN THE ROCKIES

Heroism and suffering borne by 2RCHA was not confined to Korea.

IN ALL, 516 CANADIAN servicemen gave their lives in the Korean War. Not all of them saw Korea. Seventeen members of the Second Field Regiment, Royal Canadian Horse Artillery (RCHA), died before they had even left Canada - more than the total number of Gunners who were lost in the Far East.

During the months of October and November 1950, the soldiers of the newly-formed "Special Force" travelled by rail from all parts of Canada to Fort Lewis, Washington, to train and organize for their role in Korea.

One of the last of the 22 troop trains carried 340 members of 2 RCHA. On the morning of 21 November, the "special" had just crossed a trestle close to the Alberta-B.C. border, near the small community of Canoe River, BC. As it began the climb into a long curve, the eastbound Transcontinental Express sped into the same curve on the single-track railway. At 10:35 hrs the trains collided.

CATASTROPHIC CRASH

The crash was catastrophic. The locomotive of the troop train was hurled into the air and landed on the coaches behind it. Several of the train's cars derailed, some of them falling down a steep embankment. The wooden coaches twisted and shattered, and the bodies of dead and wounded soldiers and railroad staff were entombed in the wreckage.

At first, many of the soldiers thought that their train had been caught in an avalanche or rock slide. Those in the rear of the train were horrified by the carnage that they encountered when they ran forward. Several victims were trapped in one of the coaches

LEFT: *On 21 November 1950 a troop train carrying men of the Royal Canadian Horse Artillery, bound for the west coast on their way to Korea, collided with a Transcontinental passenger train near Canoe River, BC. Seventeen soldiers were killed and 52 injured in the crash.* (JOHN STABLES)

beneath the remains of the two locomotives.

Rescue efforts were hampered by steam which was gushing everywhere – eventually freezing in the sub-zero climate. A number of casualties, some of them fatal, were caused by scalding. Clouds of steam reduced visibility in the crash site, and rescuers were working in waist deep snow.

RESCUE ATTEMPTS ORGANIZED

Most of the Regiment's officers were in the rear of the train, and together with the NCOs, quickly organized rescue attempts. To quote Jack Skinner, a former officer with 2 RCHA, "Like good leaders, we had allowed the men to eat first and most of us were in the dining car."

The spirit and discipline of the Gunners was exemplary. Although some of them were veterans of the Second World War, many had been in uniform for only a few weeks. A Transcontinental passenger recalled, "The first reaction of the injured soldiers was to ask if any of the women and children on our train had been hurt. They ignored their own injuries and, if trapped, waited quietly for their comrades to come to their rescue."

The dining cars on the troop train became a makeshift hospital. An Alberta doctor, Patrick Kimmett, himself a veteran of the Second World War, was a passenger on the Transcontinental, and aided by his wife and a nurse whose name he never knew ("We were too busy to get acquainted then") took charge of the injured until the arrival of a medical team from Jasper, Alberta, several hours later. Fortunately, in addition to the regular first aid supplies carried on the trains, the unit equipment included medical items such as bandages, morphine and antiseptics. These were put to good use.

Meanwhile, the troops, many of them injured or scalded themselves, worked feverishly to extract their dead and living comrades from the wreckage. One NCO recalled that he saw a shoe with a foot in it, a severed head and part of a torso pulled out of the wreckage; another Gunner helped to remove six bodies and had to leave three more pinned under the locomotive boiler.

Although first reports denied this, it was later confirmed that fire had broken out in two of the shattered wooden coaches, adding to the difficulties.

LUCKY FEW

Some soldiers were lucky. Gunner Boutillier, slightly injured by flying wreckage, credits his survival to the fact that at the time of the crash he was purchasing a pack of cigarettes from the news vendor, whose portable cart provided a few square feet of cover. James Thomas recalled that he was pinned to the floor by a detached upper berth, but his car was less battered than those in front and he survived without serious injury.

Improvisation was the order of the day. Somehow the news vendors were able to produce a little coffee to warm the rescue workers. Towels, table linen and even white seat covers were pressed into service as improvised bandages and dressings.

LIGHTER MOMENTS?

Even in the midst of the tragedy, Jack Skinner recalls there were lighter moments. He remembers that while most of the passengers and train crews were busily engaged in rescue operations, a number of the dining car staff were frantically searching the wreckage and the surrounding area for dining-room silverware. When he tried to remove a fire-axe from its clips to help to free his troops from the wreckage, he was severely chastised by a train man, who told him to leave it alone as "it was for emergency use." His reply is not recorded!

Eventually help arrived. The train crew had "hooked in" to the telegraph lines, and a relief train arrived from Jasper. Eventually, the serviceable cars of the troop train were hauled to Edmonton, arriving early in

ABOVE AND OPPOSITE PAGE: Injured soldiers are attended to, while others try to clear away portions of the wreckage. *(JOHN STABLES)*

the morning of 22 November. A special train containing military medical staff met the train at Edson, where the redoubtable Doctor Kimmett and his family left for a well-earned respite. On arrival in Edmonton the dining car windows were smashed to allow the removal of the stretchers with over 50 injured soldiers. More quietly, 12 blanket-wrapped bundles were carried off, the bodies of the 12 dead who had so far been recovered from the wreckage. Every available ambulance in the city was pressed into service to convey the injured to military and civilian hospitals.

The less-damaged Transcontinental, meanwhile, was towed into Kamloops. Ironically, of the only two casualties on that train requiring hospitalization, one was an Army Staff-Sergeant posted east with his family.

SEQUELS...

There are sequels to this tragic story.

2RCHA arrived in Korea on 5 May 1951 and served with distinction in support of Commonwealth Division units. The first Canadian artillery shell fired in the Korean War was from one of the 25-pounder guns of "E" Battery. Five more members of the Regiment lost their lives before the unit returned, a year later. While in Korea they were redesignated "Second Regiment, Royal Canadian Horse Artillery." During their tour, 2 RCHA members received 25 awards for gallantry and distinguished services.

Canadian National Railways eventually attempted to pin the blame for the disaster on a young telegrapher, Alfred Atherton. CNR officials alleged that he had omitted part of a message ordering the westbound train onto a siding, to permit the passage of the Transcontinental. Atherton was tried for manslaughter in Prince George, BC. He was defended by an upcoming politician and lawyer, John Diefenbaker (who was admitted to the BC bar for the occasion by passing a simple, one-question, oral examination).

OFFICIALS LIE

The defence was based on the fact that snow on the wires may have caused an incomplete transmission of the message. The key point of the case, however, occurred when Diefenbaker was examining a senior CNR official. Although at the time of the disaster the railroad had denied that obsolete wooden cars had been used for the troop train, it was established that this, in fact, had been the case.

The prosecution was put on the defensive, and finally an exasperated Crown Attorney – a former First World War colonel – remarked that they were "not concerned about the deaths of a few privates going to Korea" (referring to the fact that Atherton was being tried for the deaths of the four railroad employees killed on the troop train). This was Diefenbaker's opportunity; "You're not concerned with the killing of a few privates? Oh, Colonel!"

ATHERTON ACQUITTED

Some old soldiers were on the jury, and their reaction to this exchange was undoubtedly a factor in Atherton's eventual acquittal. Diefenbaker, of course, went on to greater things, including, unfortunately, the scrapping of the Avro Arrow programme.

A minor mystery surrounds the memorial cairn which was erected a few hundred yards from the crash scene. The RCHA had applied for permission from CNR to place a memorial at the disaster site, but was turned down. Instead a monument was unveiled at the nearby Valemount Royal Canadian Legion in May 1989. Gunners visiting the crash area were surprised to find a memorial cairn there. It had been erected there by the Canadian National Railway.

FINAL COUNT

When the final count was taken, 17 gunners lost their lives in the train wreck. In 1992 a Canadian Volunteer Service Medal for Korea was initiated. The Korea Veterans Association of Canada has attempted – so far unsuccessfully, at time of printing, 1998 – to obtain this medal for the families of Gunners Atchison, Barkhouse, Carroll, Conway, Craig, George, Levesque, Manley, McKeown, Orr, Owens, Snow, Stroud, Thistle, Wenkert, White and Wright, the RCHA's first casualties in the Korean War.

The Artillery's motto is *Quo Fas et Gloria Ducunt* – "Everywhere Right and Glory Lead."

REPRINTED FROM:

Esprit de Corps, Volume 3 Issues 8

AUTHOR:

Les Peate

KAPYONG'S TORTURED SLOPES

How 2PPCLI became the only Canadian unit ever to receive a U.S. Presidential Unit Citation.

WHEN THE PENDULUM OF offensive action swung back in favour of the United Nations' armies in the spring of 1951, it was not charged with the same over-confident exuberance that had led to disaster the previous autumn. Despite steady progress back up the Korean peninsula, with air superiority and uncontested control of the sea, the UN high command could not discount unsettling reports of the enemy's gathering strength. The Communists were falling back on their land-based supply lines and inching closer to the vast pool of human resources in China. Over all, the UN was outnumbered two-to-one.

Since February 1951, 2nd Battalion Princess Patricia's Canadian Light Infantry (2PPCLI) had been leading the UN advance as an element of the 27th Commonwealth Division. In April, 2 PPCLI, 3rd Battalion Royal Australian Regiment (3RAR) and 1st Battalion the Middlesex Regiment were placed in reserve as the 6th Division Republic of Korea (6th ROK) continued the advance. The "rest area" chosen for the Commonwealth Division troops was the Kapyong Valley. The village of Kapyong was a road and rail centre able to reach the entire 9th US Corps area, and sat astride one of two major routes down to Seoul. 2PPCLI sought to get comfortable on Hill 677, while 3RAR, separated by the Kapyong River, settled onto Hill 504. The Chinese had other plans.

CRUMBLING FRONT

Just before midnight, Sunday 22 April, a quarter of a million Chinese soldiers smashed into the UN's unconsolidated line and broke over two regiments of the 6th ROK. The Koreans were bloodied and then beaten as the magnitude of the opposition became apparent. The front began to crumble, and all day Monday a stream of panicked soldiers poured past the Commonwealth positions.

Colonel Jim Stone, officer commanding the Canadians, took an opportunity to view his position from the north. Knowing a battle was imminent, he carefully sited his men in obvious attack corridors. The Patricia's dug in overnight, and when they witnessed the firing on Hill 504, they dug in a little deeper.

PPCLI SPECTATORS

At 22:00 hrs the Australians across the river were confronted with the human waves of a Chinese attack. The Patricia's had a higher (677 metres versus 504) vantage point and the dubious luxury of being spectators for the opening rounds. For 16 hours, the Aussies flung back wave after wave with Bren gun, grenade, and rifle butt. Tanks of the US 72nd Regiment fired point blank into the attackers, but still they came on. Ammunition ran low, exhaustion was taking its toll, and after calling artillery down on their own position, the Australians were forced to withdraw. Tuesday evening, at 17:30 hours, smoke obscured the valley as American tanks, carrying Aussie wounded, rumbled southward. Forty miles to the west, a second prong of this massive offensive was testing the Gloucester Regiment on the Imjin River. It was a night for Last Stands. Consolidation was never a lengthy chapter in the Chinese training manual, and within hours they turned their attention to the Canadian positions.

Facing north, Colonel Stone had positioned A Company on his right, C Company in the centre, and D Company on the left. B Company was moved to a salient in front of D after Stone observed the intensity of the Communist attack. From their new position, B Coy. could overlook the valley.

The dramatic prologue across the Imjin did nothing to relieve the sense of foreboding that now crept into young Canadian minds. Fortunately or not, they were given little time to contemplate their exposed position. From the gathering gloom came a bizarre cacophony of bugles, whistles and screaming soldiers in their quilted cotton uniforms. Hand grenades flew in both directions, mortar shells crunched into the earth, and artillery sought to cut the enemy threat off at its root. Rifles flashed; Chinese 'burp' guns spat out their venom as the Canadian Brens barked their deadly response. In the darkness, the sporadic fire from all sides created local strobe effects; one second the enemy was in front, the next tumbling back down the hill or behind you with his bayonet. Mates were hit and went down, or were dashing forward to rescue another. The waves were incessant and nearly irresistible.

A group of enemy managed to skirt B Coy's position and infiltrate a ravine where the headquarters was located. Massed machine guns and mortar fire blasted them back out with terrible losses. From dozens of gun pits and slit trenches, the Canadians fired all they had and still had to fight their way out or hang on grimly for whatever fate had in store.

Firing down shallow ravines, D Coy mowed down untold numbers, but was faced with an enemy possessing inhuman determination. Canadian gunners died at

their post surrounded by enemy corpses. One by one they were overwhelmed or driven back to the company area. B Coy, running low on ammunition, was leapfrogging back by platoon. Private Wayne Mitchell earned a Distinguished Conduct Medal (DCM) and Private Ken Barwise a Military Medal (MM) as they fought like lions to assist their fellows. Barwise accounted for at least six with grenades, rifle fire and even with the enemy's own guns. Mitchell was wounded twice but stayed at his post until medevaced by helicopter.

WITHDRAWAL NOT AN OPTION

The Chinese were everywhere but they were exposed to the bullets and shells. D Coy commander, Captain J.G. "Wally" Mills was informed by Stone that withdrawal was impossible: if they lost the hill, they could lose Seoul. Mills responded that his men were dug in and that the only salvation was to fire artillery down on his own positions. The New Zealand gunners obliged and not a single Canadian was lost. The Chinese, however, were starting to lose momentum.

Throughout the terrifying night small units braced themselves against the onslaught and held on. The Communist forces managed to surround Hill 677 but its Canadian defenders had not given it up. Colonel Stone planned on extending their stay, and aware that the supply line was cut, ordered an airdrop at 04:00 hrs. From a Japanese airbase four C119 "Flying Boxcars" delivered the entire order ten hours later.

Communist artillery shelled Hill 677 most of 25 April, but the Patricia's re-occupied their forward trenches and began to clean up the battlefield. Air strikes and daylight artillery shoots took their toll and the Chinese offensive ground to a halt. From the south, the Middlesex cleared the road and relief from the US 5th Cavalry Regiment arrived. Snipers were dealt with and casualties were tallied up.

Amazingly, the Canadians lost only ten killed in action and twenty-three wounded. The violence of the battle highlighted the value of being properly dug in, but it was difficult to ascertain what effect it had on enemy numbers. The Chinese were in the habit of retrieving wounded and dead from a battlefield to confound opposing intelligence. In this case, however, the job seemed a bit too much; in one section of Hill 677 over 50 corpses were counted, and hundreds more littered the entire area.

***ABOVE:** Captain Mills calls in artillery on his own D Company positions, as the Chinese overrun his forward trenches.* (ILLUSTRATION BY SCOTT R. TAYLOR)
***OPPOSITE PAGE:** A weary Private John Hoskins, 2PPCLI, during the advance on Hill 419, 24 February 1951.* (PPCLI MUSEUM)

PRESIDENTIAL CITATION

The importance of the Patrician stand at Kapyong was illustrated by the award of an American Presidential Citation for "outstanding heroism and exceptionally meritorious conduct." Few of these are handed out, and rarer still is its award to a foreign unit. Ironically, it had only been December 1950 when the same Colonel Jim Stone of the newly arrived Princess Patricia Canadian Light Infantry had convinced General Walton "Bulldog" Walker that he would not commit his men to action until properly trained. Fortunately, his point had been taken.

REPRINTED FROM:
Esprit de Corps, *Volume 2 Issue 12*
***AUTHOR:** James G. Scott*

RIGHT:
Sergeant John Richardson and Sergeant Prentice engage a Chinese platoon while trying to assist the wounded Corporal Hastings.
(ILLUSTRATION BY SCOTT R. TAYLOR)

The Brigade War Diary for 15 October 1952 describes "a quiet night." For Sergeant John Richardson and his patrol it was anything but.

A QUIET NIGHT IN KOREA

ONE OF THE PRINCIPLES of War constantly drummed into junior tacticians was "maintaining the Offensive" - in other words, forcing the enemy to act in a responsive way rather than letting him determine the conduct of operations. During the lengthy "static" period of the Korean War, UN policy was to maintain the initiative, and hopefully dominate "no man's land," by intensive patrolling.

The U.S. Eighth Army planned to conduct at least one major patrol every 24 hours by each battalion-sized unit. The Commonwealth Division commander, however, felt that this practise would result in unnecessary casualties with doubtful results, and the British, Canadian and Australian infantry were reluctantly exempted from this order. Nevertheless, units sent out nightly ambush and standing patrols, and every few days fighting patrols were ordered, usually for the purpose of capturing prisoners or destroying enemy installations. Fighting patrols were usually at platoon strength – about 25 men – and according to the rules, should be commanded by an officer. This was not always the case, as evidenced by a fighting patrol conducted by the First Battalion, Princess Patricia's Canadian Light Infantry in October of 1952.

The patrol was commanded by Sergeant John Richardson, who had enlisted in 1945, soon after his 18th birthday, and remained in the Army after the Second World War.

OFFICIAL REPORT

The night's activities can best be described in an official report:

"On the night 15 October 1952 a fighting patrol of 25 men was sent out from the 1st Battalion, Princess Patricia's Canadian Light Infantry, the task of the patrol being to search out the enemy and capture a prisoner. The patrol limit was the base of a strongly held enemy feature some 2800 yards by patrol route from our forward defended localities over very rough, broken terrain. The patrol was commanded by SergeantRichardson. Having established firm base, this non-commissioned officer with the assault group of 16 men proceeded a further 150 yards. He then, with two snipers, detached himself from the main group and reconnoitred forward searching out the enemy.

Having observed a small party of enemy digging, Sergeant Richardson withdrew to the assault group, where he called for supporting artillery fire to cover the sound of his intended attack on this enemy party.

Suddenly, in pitch blackness, Sergeant Richardson and his men were assailed on two sides, over-run and cut off from the firm base by an enemy force estimated at 35 to 40, which apparently had been lying in wait. Eleven of his men were wounded by the first volleys of small arms and grenade fire, and the patrol wireless set was destroyed. However, the enemy were beaten off temporarily and heavy casualties were inflicted.

Sergeant Richardson, himself severely wounded in five places, reorganized his group and began a withdrawal with his wounded in the face of continuous enemy small arms fire. Although pursued by the enemy, this courageous non-commissioned officer personally carried Sergeant R.A. Prentice, a seriously wounded comrade, a distance of over 100 yards to the firm base. Despite the severity of his own wounds, on regaining wireless communication at the firm base, Sergeant Richardson called down artillery, mortar and machine gun fire on the pursuing enemy while supervising and encouraging his men in the difficult task of carrying back the wounded a further 800 yards where they were met by a carrying party sent out from the battalion."

The above quotation is taken from the citation for the award to Sergeant Richard-

ABOVE LEFT:
Prior to every patrol, a briefing between the officer and his NCOs would be held to plan the night's objectives.
(NAC/PA 129739)

ABOVE RIGHT:
Members of the Princess Patricia's Canadian Light Infantry move up to the front in Korea.
(DND PHOTO)

son of the Distinguished Conduct Medal.

The official Patrol Report paints an even more vivid picture, parts of which are refuted by Richardson. According to the report "both sides used a number of automatic weapons" in the fire-fight; in fact, the Canadians had only a Bren, a Sten machine carbine, a Thompson sub-machine gun and two US semi-automatic carbines. The rest of the patrol carried standard .303 rifles. The Chinese assailants were, however, equipped with several Soviet-made sub-machine guns – the "burp gun." The report also stated that the Chinese attackers employed concussion grenades – to which Richardson replies "'Concussion grenades' my *&#@! They were all the standard Chinese potato-masher type. I have the marks to prove it!"

Two members of the patrol were reported missing – later to be presumed Killed in Action. One was seen to fall, and the other was hit by a burst of fire and went down close to Richardson. To quote the Patrol Report, "Lance Corporal Hastings was being carried back by Sergeant Richardson… Sergeant Richardson saw Sergeant Prentice, also wounded and unable to move. Though Sergeant Richardson had now been wounded in the stomach and leg… he began to carry them both back, Prentice by his left arm and Hastings by his right, when (he was again wounded) by a concussion [sic] grenade."

Richardson disputes this – in fact, after ascertaining that Hastings was apparently beyond help, he was firing his carbine at the enemy and attempting to half-carry Sergeant Prentice to safety at the same time.

RICHARDSON EXTENDS CREDIT

While he is justifiably proud of his award, one of the last DCMs presented to a Canadian, Richardson's personal account gives credit to others whose part went unrecognized.

"I tried to pass the word that my Bren gunner, Private Chute from Nova Scotia, should get at least a Mention in Despatches," he said. "He'd taken over the section and done a fine job from start to finish!" Private Chute was wounded in the action.

Richardson also acknowledges the part played by his unit's Pioneer Platoon commander, who on his own initiative, organized a stretcher party to bring in the wounded.

Sergeant "Rocky" Prentice survived a broken hip, and was himself a recipient of the Military Medal a few months later.

Sergeant Richardson recovered from his wounds, completed a second Far East tour, and retired from the PPCLI as a Sergeant-Major.

The PPCLI museum has Richardson's "Cap, Field Service, Olive Drab" with a bullet hole in the peak. He still regrets that his US carbine which he had borrowed for the patrol was not returned to its owner, Second Lieutenant (now Major General) Pitts, MC who later became Colonel of the Regiment.

John Richardson also regrets that, under the Canadian Order of Precedence, his hard-won DCM is now placed below all Canadian awards, despite the fact that it is second only to the Victoria Cross as a Commonwealth military award. Incidentally, the Brigade War Diary for the night 15 October 1952 begins "A quiet night . . ."

REPRINTED FROM:
Esprit de Corps, *Volume 2 Issue 10*
AUTHOR: *Les Peate*

THE LAST BIG PUSH

After a year of alternately advancing and retreating, the United Nations allies finally seized their "home" for the next two years – the "Jamestown Line."

ABOVE: *Although achieving its objective on 4 October 1951 by taking the area surrounding Hill 187, members of 2RCR (seen here enjoying a quiet moment in their front-line dugout) came under heavy enemy fire.* (DND PHOTO)

DURING THE EARLY DAYS of the Korean War there was a great deal of "coming and going." The North Korean army was slowly being rolled back from the Pusan perimeter, and the first Commonwealth land forces (27 Brigade HQ, the Middlesex Regiment and the Argyll & Sutherland Highlanders) moved into the line on 5 September 1950. Following the Inchon landings, the jubilant UN troops quickly pushed into North Korea. The tables were quickly turned. In October patrols reported contact with Chinese troops south of the Yalu River, and soon the United Nations forces were forced to withdraw under heavy pressure.

The Chinese offensive finally petered out some miles north of Seoul, where four Commonwealth units, including the 2nd Battalion PPCLI, earned US Presidential Unit Citations for their part in the battles.

OPERATION COMMANDO

By the end of the summer the Commonwealth Division was established more or less on the line of the Imjin River. In September a bridgehead was established north of the river, and it became the jumping-off point for "Operation Commando." This was to be an advance of 6 – 10,000 metres, with the intention of securing the left flank of the US 1 Corps.

On 3 October 1951, 28 Commonwealth Brigade reached its objectives on the right flank after a desperate battle. The next day, 2 PPCLI captured Hill 187 following heavy fighting and 2RCR seized neighbouring high ground but was very heavily shelled. B Company of the Royal Canadian Regiment, in particular, came under especially heavy fire. Not until four days later did the British and Australian units achieve their final objectives.

Lieutenant Eric Devlin, a former Platoon Commander with 2 RCR, recalls, "B Company was committed to a leading role. We reached our objective successfully. In the second phase my platoon was in reserve. I learned that (6 Platoon Commander) had been wounded and his platoon had suffered a good many casualties. My platoon lost two wounded at this time." Lieutenant Devlin recalls that the company 'medic,' Corporal Ernest Poole, was in the thick of the action. Corporal Poole's participation was of such a high standard that I can only quote the words of 2RCR Commanding Officer Lieutenant Colonel Bob Keane;"

CITATION

"On 3 October 1951 the 2nd Battalion, The Royal Canadian Regiment, was moving forward against Enemy opposition as part of a general attack launched by our own forces.

"B Company was ordered forward from the Naechon feature, an intermediate objective, to the final object on the right flank of the Battalion, the feature Nabu'ri.

"At 17:45 hours, No 6 Platoon came under very heavy and accurate enemy small arms and mortar fire from the left flank and intense machine gun fire from the right flank. Within a few minutes, a dozen casualties had been suffered by the platoon, some of them critical. Because of the steep slopes and thick underbrush it was not possible to determine precisely the nature and location of all the casualties, and there was a real danger that some of them would be lost to the Enemy where they fell.

COURAGE OF THE HIGHEST ORDER

"L 800192 Corporal Poole, W.E., RCAMC was the NCO in charge of stretcher-bearers with B Company during this operation; his actions in dealing with the casualties suffered gave evidence of courage of the highest order under Enemy Fire and contributed very markedly to the ultimate success of the operation.

"Corporal Poole proceeded forward through intense Enemy mortar and shell fire to render first aid and arrange for the evacuation of the wounded. He was warned that he could be killed but he insisted, 'I have a job to do and I am going to do it.' He searched meticulously the whole area and did not stop until satisfied that all casualties had been accounted for. Enemy artillery and mortars were harassing the area, and Enemy snipers and machine gunners made any movement hazardous, but nothing could deter him in his search for the wounded. Two of the casualties were again hit while he was tending them, but he continued with unruffled calm to render aid.

ATTACK MOMENTUM

"While still under fire Corporal Poole improvised stretchers from rifles and branches of trees; he bound the casualties securely by using thick vines. He moved from man to man with complete disregard for his own safety; his steady hand and quiet courage brought relief to all the wounded. No. 5 platoon was ordered to pass through No. 6 platoon in order to maintain the momentum of the attack. They, too, came under heavy fire and suffered serious casualties. Corporal Poole was on hand at once and urged the Platoon Commander, 'Go on, I will see that your men get good care.'

"When the wounded had been prepared for evacuation, Corporal Poole led his party of bearers back some 3000 yards in the dark to the Regimental Aid Post. The route was subjected to continuous shell fire. Enemy patrols had infiltrated along both sides, the area was heavily mined, and even the natural hazards were enough to deter any but the very brave. But Corporal Poole led his party with confidence and all the casualties were borne safely to the Regimental Aid Post. Undoubtedly his leadership and the persistence with which he carried out his duties against any odds was vital in saving the lives of one Officer and three other Ranks and in preventing two of the wounded from falling into the hands of the Enemy.

"Throughout the day of 3 October, all that night and the next day, Corporal Poole continued his task of attending the needs of the wounded. Whenever first aid was required, he was present to administer it. He was utterly tireless in his work. During the operation one thought only dominated his action: That his duty was to tend his wounded comrades. No obstacles, no hazard, no personal danger, was allowed to stand in his way; his selfless devotion to his work was in the highest traditions of Military Service.

"Corporal Poole's conscientious determination to carry out his duties, his complete disregard for his own well being, his exemplary conduct under the most adverse conditions and his outstanding leadership resulted not only in saving the lives of five men and making possible the evacuation of and treatment of many others, but, even more, inspired his comrades to maintain the fight and contributed largely to the successful attainment of the objective."

SAD ENDING

Colonel Keane recommended Corporal Poole for the Victoria Cross. This was concurred with by Brigadier John M. Rockingham, but the award was subsequently downgraded by the Divisional Commander, Major General Cassels (UK), and the overall commander, (Australian) Lieutenant General Bridgeford. The reason given was that, 'Corporal Poole's action did not have a direct effect on the battle.' Sadly, when Ernest Poole was contacted by writer John Gardam, he simply wanted to forget his decoration, so gallantly earned over forty years ago. "When I see what is happening in the Canadian Forces today, I do not want to be associated with it or the past."

Canadians were short-changed again. The British and Australian units who participated in 'Operation Commando' were each awarded a battle honour commemorating their role. Although, arguably, the men of 25 Canadian Brigade fought just as hard, they did not receive this recognition. The reason for this, surprisingly, was not an Aussie/Brit effort at one-upmanship, but a refusal by Canada's Battle Honour Committee to approve the awards.

Meanwhile, the ground seized by the efforts of 25 and 28 Brigades (plus the Royal Ulster Rifles of 29 Brigade) became the Commonwealth positions for the remainder of the Korean War. Heavily attacked over the next two years, the Canadians, Brits and Aussies would continue to hold fast until the final 'ceasefire' on 27 July 1953.

REPRINTED FROM:
Esprit de Corps, *Volume 5 Issue 12*
AUTHOR: *Les Peate*

Canadian wounded are evacuated following the fight for the high ground around Hill 187, October 1951. (DND PHOTO)

CANADIANS ON KOJE-DO

"If you see a prisoner trying to escape – help him!" The story of 'Peterforce.'

LEFT: *A typical Koje-do guard tower surrounded by barbed wire. These guards seem relaxed, but events were soon to take a much more violent twist. (PAC PA - 180376)*

KOREA, MAY 1951. The Warning Order sounded ominous. "B Coy 1 RCR will proceed to an unidentified destination on an unspecified mission. Transport will be by truck, train and boat. Extra Brens will be carried." Speculation intensified when the Royals Arrived at Tangkok railhead and joined a green-bereted British contingent. Rumours of island raids, and even a second "Inchon landing" spread, before the destination was finally announced as the troops had boarded the train. We were going to Koje-do.

The island of Koje-do, off the coast of Pusan, held over 150,000 North Korean and Chinese prisoners-of-war. The North Koreans, concerned over the number of defectors to the south, and seeking to gain a propaganda victory in the truce talks under way at Panmunjon, infiltrated the camps with hardcore political officers to encourage resistance to the US and South Korean guards. They were very successful.

PRISONERS GAIN CONTROL

After a number of bloody riots, the prisoners gained complete control within the compounds. Finally, on 7 May 1952, they seized the Camp Commander, Brigadier General Dodd and held him hostage; they presented a series of demands, including "confessions" of ill-treatment, to which General Dodd's successor acquiesced. General Dodd was then released.

The U.N. Commander, General Ridgway, and his successor General Mark Clark, were appalled and reacted promptly.

The former camp commanders were removed and summarily demoted, to be replaced by an experienced veteran of the Far East service, Brigadier General H.L. "Bull" Boatner. The guards were replaced or reinforced by field troops from the United States and other national U.N. contingents.

The Commonwealth Division was represented by B Coy, 1st Battalion, The Royal Canadian Regiment, commanded by Major Ed Cohen, and B Company of The King's Shropshire Light Infantry. Despite the secrecy accompanying the move, Peterforce, (as the group was known) was greeted on Koje-do on 25 May by POW's brandishing welcome banners and singing a very catchy song, later identified as "The Big-Nosed American."

Following a speech of welcome by General Boatner, the troops received a few days training from the Americans. The "Bull" cautioned the newcomers against indiscriminate use of firearms, although advocating us to "slash them, use the rifle butt or knee in the groin" if necessary.

To the Commonwealth soldiers, used to weapon training conducted in small groups, the U.S. method of teaching the use of shotguns, tear gas grenades, riot drill and other subjects was a startling contrast. The Americans adopted an en-masse "lecture-demonstration" approach. The Military Law lectures were particularly disappointing: a U.S. officer read for hours from a manual, and even the explicit descriptions of sexual offences failed to keep the troops awake.

After a week Peterforce took over guard duties on Compound 66, which held about 3500 prisoners. No-one was sure of the exact number, because during the period of misrule, prisoners moved fairly freely between compounds.

The compound was surrounded by double-apron wire and seven two-storey watchtowers alternated with sandbagged guard posts. Roving guards patrolled the area between the two barbed wire fences, while the towers and ground posts held light machine-guns (including the extra Brens we had brought).

The guards' orders were unusual. Besides keeping the POW's in order, they were instructed to assist, where possible, any prisoners trying to escape. To discourage defectors, hardcore Communists guarded the inner perimeter and used all means – including killing – to stop prisoners from leaving. In fact, most of those defecting to Peterforce did so by quitting working parties, mostly the "honey-bucket" latrine emptying details, outside the compounds.

The North Koreans were most ingenious. From ordinary materials such as ponchos, tent fabric, food products and scrap lumber they fabricated national flags, realistic U.N. uniforms and badges, dummy firearms and real lethal weapons. Compound 66 even had a functional ironworker's shop created from misappropriated US materials. Colorful female costumes surfaced in a corner of the compound, worn by soldiers who were variously identified as either

FAR LEFT: *Prisoners held on Koje-do were ingenious in their creation of weapons. Using everything from steel shoe supports to oil-drum metal, POWs made knives, daggers and hand grenades. Here, a South Korean military policeman guards some of the seized contraband.* (U.S. ARMY)

LEFT: *A prisoner of war (POW) worries about his now uncertain future as he is herded into Compound 66. In May 1951, anarchy reigned supreme on Koje-do.* (U.S ARMY PHOTO)

LESS AMUSING WAS THE DISCOVERY, FOLLOWING A FORAY BY THE U.N. TROOPS INTO THE COMPOUND, OF A NUMBER OF DISMEMBERED BODIES, PRESUMABLY OF POTENTIAL DEFECTORS.

amateur actors, potential spies or inmates of a homosexual brothel.

REPORTS OF TUNNELS

Alarms and excursions were frequent. The POW's drilled with dummy rifles and bayonets, and from time to time would "charge" the perimeter guards, stopping just short of the wire. A report of a tunnel system between compounds resulted in the arrival of a large mechanical shovel, which dug a large trench round the compound. It attracted many interested spectators, but revealed no unauthorized excavations. (Later, when the compound had been evacuated, the beginning of a large tunnel *was* discovered.)

Less amusing was the discovery, following a foray by the U.N. Troops into the compound, of a number of dismembered bodies, presumably of potential defectors. A number of vicious–looking spears, hatchets and other weapons also came to light.

There was a bright side. To quote one Peterforce member: "It was a hell of a sight better than the sharp end. The Airborne (187 Regimental Combat team) had loads of beer and gave it away freely. The Dutch had gin in their canteen for ten cents a shot and the Red Cross clubs and PX had all the coffee, donuts and ice-cream you wanted." Peterforce long remembered the hospitality of the U.S. troops.

LUCRATIVE ACTIVITIES

One especially lucrative activity involved the British company, who were paid in "Baffs" – British cash vouchers. With the connivance of the Canadians, the bootleggers on Koje were led to believe that a 6d. (sixpence – worth about 15 cents) was a six-dollar bill. Until the bubble burst, fortunate Peterforce members were buying bottles of "moonshine" for 15 cents and getting four dollars change.

In early June the prisoners were moved into new, smaller compounds. A few days earlier, attempts by the US troops to clear another compound resulted in strong resistance and several casualties. This time, there were few problems. Tear gas effectively removed the hard-core prisoners, and the compound was surrounded by tanks, half-tracks mounting heavy machine guns, and what seemed like a whole regiment of U.S. troops in full battle order, supervised by "The Bull" himself (the Commonwealth troops were particularly intrigued by one hefty second lieutenant whose sole function appeared to be to photograph the General giving orders).

In contrast, when the prisoners had marched to the "half-way" point, they passed between a double line of lightly-armed and equipped Shropshires and Royals, spaced at intervals of about 20 yards.

MISCONDUCT NOT TOLERATED

On arrival in their new compound the prisoners' representatives were advised by the Peterforce commander, Major D.R. Bancroft of the KSLI, that they would be treated fairly but that no misconduct would be tolerated. Major Bancroft had already gained the respect of the prisoners, if not his allies, when he forced an American driver to return a home-made cap badge which the latter had ripped from a North Korean's cap.

The rest of the tour passed smoothly. Our riot drill training proved unnecessary – while our American allies would enter the compounds in a "flying wedge" of troops with fixed bayonets, visitors to the Commonwealth compound would be escorted by an unarmed N.C.O. – a practise which discouraged visits from our allies. One minor rebellion was quickly quashed when the instigators were forced to remain outside on parade during one of the frequent rainstorms. An RCR member successfully removed a rebellious prisoner from a hut roof with a charge of birdshot.

The prisoners ate well, receiving an issue of vegetables and rice supplemented by time-expired K-rations. As cigarettes could be used as "currency" they had to be removed from K-rations before the meals were passed to the POWs. The removal and theoretical destruction of the smokes was a chore which never lacked volunteers, especially among the British, whose daily pay was roughly the cost of 30 cigarettes at home.

LACK OF COURTESY?

Even monotonous tasks had their moments. One Peterforce NCO, unaware that US Warrant Officers rated salutes, was rebuked for his lack of military courtesy. From then on he would make a point of marching the "nightsoil party" complete with filled containers of latrine waste all over the area until he found the offending W.O. Then he would holler in stentorian tones "S***-House Detail, Eyes Right!" Nevertheless, B Company made a good impression on the island. Canadian Press reports indicated that "the smartly turned-out Canadian soldier on the parade square, in the canteens or PX's, proves he can also be a top representative among the Allied armies."

With the pacification of the prisoners, Peterforce's work was done. On 12 July the Commonwealth troops had left the island – following farewell parties hosted not only by the U.N. troops, but by our involuntary North Korean guests, who held a sports meet in our honour.

En route back to rejoin our units at the "sharp end," derisory calls from passing troops, no doubt envious of our stay in the island paradise, gave us our new nickname – "The Koje Commandos."

The Koje–do saga was not quite over. In *Strange Battleground*, Lieutenant Colonel H.F. Wood's official history of the Canadian Army in Korea, the author reports that Chinese interrogators singled out 1 RCR prisoners for special attention, and those identified as B Company members were unsuccessfully pressured to give details of U.S. "atrocities" on Koje-do.

REPRINTED FROM:
Esprit de Corps, *Volume 1 Issue 12*
AUTHOR:
Les Peate

THE VANDOOS IN KOREA

The fight for Hill 355 was possibly Canada's hardest battle in Korea. However, for the R22eR, 'ce n'était pas un problème.'

NOVEMBER 1951 WAS A busy month for the First Commonwealth Division in Korea. The Division had just successfully completed "Operation Commando" and was now occupying the new "Jamestown" Line between the Samichon and Imjin rivers.

In the early part of the month the enemy began a series of attacks in an attempt to drive the Australians, British and Canadians from their newly-won positions. On the night of 31 October a small attack was launched against 2PPCLI, who were due to be relieved by their First Battalion in a few days. "Artificial moonlight," was used to good effect, and the Chinese were repulsed. Two nights later it was the turn of A Coy, 2 RCR, who beat off a Battalion-strength attack, inflicting heavy losses on the enemy.

During the next five days 28 (Commonwealth) Brigade bore the brunt of enemy activity. Following intense artillery fire, strong enemy forces attacked the King's Own Scottish Borderers and 3rd Royal Australian Regiment, and later assaulted the Brigade's other battalion, the King's Shropshire Light Infantry. It was during this battle that Private Bill Speakman, of KOSB, won the fourth and last Victoria Cross of the Korean War.

On the morning of the 5th, the enemy were in possession of Hills 217 and 317, on the right of the division front. An attempt to retake 217 was unsuccessful. The newly-arrived 1PPCLI received a welcome from the Chinese in the form of two battalion-strength attacks on the night of 5 November, but beat off both.

RAIN ADDS TO DIFFICULTIES

To add to the problem facing the Division, heavy rain set in. Not only did this hamper communications and make the task of the Korean porters who brought up the supplies of food, water and ammunition more difficult - it also grounded the aircraft whose support role was critical. On the "plus" side, it was raining on the Chinese, too, which may have been the reason for a couple of comparatively quiet days.

The final fling against 28 Brigade was a brigade-strength attack against 3 RAR, supported by artillery and tanks. The Aussies beat off the enemy, inflicting heavy casualties.

OPPOSITE PAGE:
"D" Company is briefed before a patrol along the slopes of Kowang-sang (Hill 355).
(DND PHOTO)
RIGHT:
A machine-gun crew of the R22eR discusses peace rumours in their position overlooking the Imjin River, June 1951.
(DND PHOTO)

A comparatively quiet week followed. This time it was the turn of the Canadians to be aggressive, and a raid was carried out by a reinforced company of 2 R22eR on Hill 166. After four hours of confused fighting, the Vandoos returned with their casualties – seven wounded.

From 17 to 19 November it was again the turn of the British. A full-scale attack was carried out on KSLI and the Royal Leicesters. The Shropshires were driven off Hill 227 but recovered the position at dawn next day. During this period a probing or diversionary attack was launched against 1PPCLI. It was during these attacks that the legend of the "Lady in black" originated. Reports were received that some of the most pressing enemy attacks were led by a glamorous female, waving a pistol and clad in close-fitting black silk pyjamas. These stories were never confirmed, but continued to circulate, including a sequel in which the "Dragon Lady" was captured by the Vandoos and suffered several "fates worse than death" before being handed over to the POW cage.

On 22 November a shuffle took place. General Cassels, the Commonwealth Division commander, had frequently asked for a shortened front, and the U.S. 3rd Infantry Division took over the area from Hill 355 east to the Imjin, while the British 29 Brigade moved west of the Samichon.

D COMPANY MOVES

Hill 355 (Kowan-sang) was held by the 7th US Cavalry Regiment. The right-hand unit of the Commonwealth Division was 2R22eR, whose forward company, "D" Company commanded by Major Réal Liboiron, occupied a saddle between Hills 227 and 355. The company moved in, replacing the KSLI, on the morning of 22 November. During the afternoon they were heavily shelled, forcing Major Liboiron to move the company command post from its position on the flank of Hill 355.

The effectiveness of the Chinese intelligence was demonstrated when a number of enemy patrols approached the Van Doos position with cries of "Hello, Canada!"

Heavy snow and more artillery fire on the Canadian and US positions marked 23 November. Sporadic attacks on the left of the line took place. To quote 11 Platoon's commander "the Chinese began running down the hill towards the platoon position in twos. They were like sitting ducks and the men shot them down...with ease." Later, it was the turn of 12 Platoon, on the right, who were able to bring effective fire into the rear of Chinese troops attacking the Americans on Hill 355.

CHINESE ADVANCE HALTED

Meanwhile, the centre platoon, commanded by Lieutenant Mario Côté, was under heavy attack by at least two enemy companies. The Canadians held, and the Chinese were brought to a halt just short of the Vandoos lines. For a whole hour, Corporal Earl Istead, although wounded, held a critical point of the line with a Bren Gun, while another corporal, Joseph Harvey, under heavy fire, used a pick-axe to destroy fortifications left by previous "tenants" which had become a danger to the defenders.

The battalion was now exposed on both flanks, as enemy had taken over the unoccupied Hill 227 on the left, and had driven the Americans from 355. The R22eR Commanding Officer, Lieutenant Colonel (later General) J.A. Dextraze had a choice – to hold firm or to withdraw, perhaps jeopardizing other UN troops. "Jadex" was a tough, experienced soldier who had already earned a DSO in Europe – there was no question, the troops would stay put.

During the night, attacks on the two flank sub-units were repulsed. A dawn assault by about 400 enemy on 11 Platoon was broken up by effective fire from 2RCHA's 25-pounders and the Battalion's own 81 mm mortars.

HELL BREAKS LOOSE

At about 16:20 hrs on the afternoon of 24 November "all hell broke loose." A force estimated at about 500 enemy swarmed down Hill 227. The concentrated enemy made an ideal artillery target, but they still kept coming. In the words of Lieutenant MacDuff of 11 Platoon "the first row was armed with burp guns, the second with

LEFT:
Even well dug in positions such as these would be overrun by the fanatical Chinese attacks. The equally resolved Vandoos however (here, members of 1R22eR on reconnaissance patrol), refused to be ejected from their trench lines.
(DND PHOTO)

heavy matting carpets and the third with bayonets on sticks…they came over the wire like buffaloes over a bridge." When more Chinese approached from another flank, MacDuff ordered his men to pull back. This was no discredit – the platoon left-forward Bren was knocked out, the only NCO left was a lance-corporal and several reinforcements who had only been in the line for a few days. MacDuff himself had been wounded.

When Major Liboiron heard of the situation, he immediately called down tank, mortar and artillery fire on 11 Platoon's position. Meanwhile, MacDuff and the few survivors of his platoon had reached 12 Platoon's positions. They were assisted by the indomitable Corporal Harvey, who had been dispatched by his platoon commander to their rescue.

Another decorated Second World War veteran now enters the picture. Corporal Léo Major had already earned a Distinguished Conduct Medal in Holland with Le Régiment de la Chaudière. His part in the fight that night was to win a bar to that coveted Decoration – one of only two awarded in the whole Korean War. (The other recipient was Sergeant Bill Rowlinson of the Royal Australian Regiment who was awarded both the Medal and the Bar in Korea.)

Corporal Major commanded a "platoon" of 18 scouts and snipers. Dextraze ordered him to recapture the ground lost by 11 Platoon and to restore the defences. The history of the Commonwealth Division states simply "One platoon position was overrun, but was recaptured soon after midnight."

The citation for Corporal Major's award is a little more explicit. It reads in part, "Although he had no previous knowledge of the ground, Corporal Major led his platoon in the dark over the wind and snow swept hills firing his Sten…as he advanced. Dugout by dugout, slit trench by slit trench, using grenades and bayonets the platoon cleared the enemy from the position. By sheer determination and courage and because of great confidence in their leader, this small group overran an enemy six times their number causing them to fall back. Corporal Major hastily organized the defence. So expertly did he direct fire of supporting mortars and artillery that the platoon was able to repulse four separate enemy counter attacks.

MAJOR REFUSES TO GIVE GROUND

Running from one point of danger to another under heavy small arms fire from his flank he directed the fire of his men, encouraging them to hold firm against overwhelming odds. While under a heavy attack a part of his platoon was overrun. Corporal Major left his wireless set…to fire his personal weapon to assist in restoring the situation. He was credited with killing four enemy during this attack.

Against a force superior in numbers Corporal Major refused to give ground. His personal courage, coolness and leadership were an inspiration to the men of his platoon."

The long battle was not quite over. Lieutenant Nash, commanding the right-hand Platoon, recalled that the Americans were counter-attacking and forcing the enemy down the West ridge of Hill 355 into his position. At one time the Company Commander had to order artillery and mortar fire onto 12 Platoon position. The Vandoos could see the Chinese on Hill 355, but could not get clearance from the Americans to fire on them. Nash was short of water and ammunition. One unnamed soldier typifies the fighting spirit and tenacity of the troops. In Lieutenant Nash's words, "[Three soldiers] left the company supply point to carry ammunition and water to the platoon position. Shell fire wounded one man and the other took him back…The other soldier picked up both his loads and continued on his way. His load consisted of ten loaded Bren magazines, two boxes of grenades, a four-gallon jerrican of water, a can of oil, a large can of "four by two" flannelette cleaning strips, a rifle and two bandoliers of .303. He arrived at my position…after taking nearly four hours to crawl half a mile under heavy shell fire…right through the Chinese…who had the platoon surrounded. He then helped to man the position and then carried one of our dead part way out until he was forced by heavy shelling to leave the body."

Incidentally, during the attacks, several members of 12 Platoon claim to have encountered the "Dragon Lady."

On the evening of 25 November, the Chinese attacked again. They swarmed towards the left and centre platoons, and Lieutenant Côté called for immediate artillery support. Dextraze ordered all the UN artillery within range to bring down fire and very shortly afterwards 3500 artillery shells broke up what was to be the last large-scale attack against the Vandoos.

By now, D Company had been without sleep for four days, and had undergone atrocious weather conditions in addition to their other privations and dangers. Food and water were in short supply. Nevertheless Lieutenant Colonel Dextraze's "advice" to have the troops shave was a real morale-booster and helped to sustain the regimental pride which so far, had not been lacking.

Just before dawn on 26 November, the weary members of Dog Company were relieved by Baker Company and were able, at last to rest and lick their wounds.

NO BATTLE HONOURS?

There were no battle honours for the R22eR. During their six days of battle, they had lost 16 killed, 36 wounded and two captured. A number of participants received individual awards. Corporal Harvey received a DCM – this was the only Canadian action for which two DCMs were awarded. Major Liboiron was awarded the DSO – one of the only two such awards to sub-unit commanders in the Korean War. Lieutenant Colonel Dextraze added an OBE to his DSO and went on to become Chief of the Defence Staff. Lieutenants MacDuff and Nash, together with Corporals Istead and Prud'homme were Mentioned in Despatches.

For six days the Vandoos, newly arrived in their position, endured everything that the enemy could produce and held their own. Perhaps their Regiment's fighting prowess is best typified by Corporal Major's laconic response to his CO's request for a SITREP when his newly-won position was being heavily attacked – "No Problem!"

REPRINTED FROM:
Esprit de Corps, *Volume 4 Issue 5*
AUTHOR: *Les Peate*

ALL ASHORE

BELOW: *HMCS* Sioux, *pictured here in 1944, was one of the first three ships which Canada dispatched into Korean waters.* (KEN MACPHERSON)

While they lacked much of the Army's publicity, the 'Senior Service' established an enviable reputation in Korean waters.

CANADA'S INITIAL RESPONSE to the outbreak of open warfare in Korea was to commit three destroyers of the Royal Canadian Navy. HMC Ships *Athabaskan*, *Cayuga* and *Sioux* sailed across the Pacific to a little known corner of the globe, while politicians in Ottawa argued over whether it would be enough. In the ensuing months, the Korean War was to confound more than just Prime Minister Louis St. Laurent and his cabinet.

During the 25-day crossing there was, no doubt, a great deal of speculation as to the sorts of operations the ships might undertake. The Soviets had developed a nuclear bomb in 1949 and possessed a fleet of submarines; would they get involved? Would we have to contend with hostile aircraft or motor torpedo boats?

HMCS *Cayuga* was first in action on 15 August when she bombarded the port of Yosu. One hundred thirty thousand more rounds would follow from Canadian ships, aimed at everything from field guns to trains and sailing junks. North Korea gunboats were few in any case and their early departure from the war ended ship-to-ship encounters for the duration. Of course, this only became apparent in time.

OPERATIONAL DANGERS

HMCS *Athabaskan* was among the busiest of the RCN ships and ran the full gamut of activities on the island-studded west coast of the Korean peninsula. Republic of Korea (ROK) marines and guerillas were transported and supported by the RCN. On one patrol *Athabaskan* put ROK forces ashore, landed a party of her own, bombarded shore installations and a radio station, illuminated a raid with star shells, intercepted small coastal craft, and took off and treated casualties.

The absence of equal opposing naval forces did not lessen the danger to UN ships of operating off the Korean coast. Mines, in particular, proved a hazard as they were randomly anchored offshore by otherwise harmless looking junks. Ingenious methods were devised to destroy them when found at low tide. *Athabaskan's* Gunner David Hurl would cautiously approach the device in the ship's dinghy and attach a TNT charge. After the oarsman applied "full astern" with alacrity the charge detonated. Only the Australians aboard HMAS *Bataan* imitated this

HMCS Athabaskan *steams for duty in the far east.* (DND PHOTO)

crazy Canuck method.

The British dominated the Commonwealth forces in Korea as their navy traditions dominated the post-World War Canadian Navy. The average Canadian sailor chafed at the petty discipline and feigned class distinction which was the hallmark of the RN, and officers who attempted to transfer their Royal Navy training to Canadian ships met with stern opposition (up to and including mutiny). British officers insulted their Canadian counterparts when they admonished them for conducting a private war among the strategic coastal islands. After a visit by Rear Admiral Wallace Creery in September 1951, however, the snooty Brits were put in their place and the innovative and courageous tactics of the Canadian Navy reached new heights.

The battle for the islands occurred largely at night and with commando-style forces. The possession of the innumerable features and islets of the west coast provided intelligence bases, protected harbour approaches, and allowed the enemy to float mines against the UN navy. As bases for guerilla operations they were indispensable and the significance of the battles fought for them is attested by the Distinguished Service Cross awarded to Lieutenant Donald Saxon. As a liaison officer to the ROK Army, he was detached from *Cayuga* to help the South Koreans carry out small-scale offensive operations. He coordinated their small craft fleet, organized big ship support, including medical evacuation, and participated in planning raids. With the opposing armies locked in linear stalemate inland, the island campaigns took on greater importance.

BONE OF CONTENTION

The Chorusan Peninsula stretches 65 kilometres due south from the Yalu River. Being Communist territory, it was with a large degree of annoyance that the Chinese regarded enemy occupation of the neighbouring islands. Taewha-Do formed a particular bone of contention and in November 1951 the Chinese began a systematic reduction of the garrison on the island.

The protection of Taewha-Do was the responsibility of UN naval forces and irregular troops recruited from the local inhabitants. US-led groups were under the command of army NCO's, code-named Leopards. (ROK equivalents were "Salamanders.") The Leopards would feed information as to enemy emplacements and troop concentrations which were promptly shelled by UN ships. Of course, the action was not always one-sided.

UNEXPECTED ACTION

Cayuga, under the command of Commander James Plomer, was anchored off Amgak when she was bracketed by shells from an enemy 75mm battery. The action was totally unexpected even though *Cayuga* was there to destroy these very guns. A much-chastised ship reversed out of harm's way, leaving an anchor behind and crushing two of her own boats which had been tied on her stern. When *Athabaskan*, under Commander Dudley King, replaced her sister a few days later, she showed more caution. The second ship did not anchor and was surreptitiously backed up by HMS *Belfast*, a light cruiser with eight-inch guns. *Athabaskan* pounded some buildings and a junk, but did not receive a reply. She left the area unmolested and returned to Cho-Do.

As she was refuelling, *Athabaskan* received an urgent message that Taewha-Do

KING CIRCLED THE ISLAND LOOKING FOR AN OPPORTUNITY TO RESCUE SURVIVORS; ...[HE] REQUESTED PERMISSION TO PUT A PARTY ASHORE TO ASSIST ANY POSSIBLE EVACUATIONS, BUT HE WAS ORDERED TO LEAVE. THERE WAS NOTHING LEFT TO DO THERE.

LEFT: *Cayuga's B turret fires back at an unseen gun along the Korean coast, January 1951.*(DND PHOTO)

was under air and sea attack. Upon arrival she learned that Chinese bombers had devastated the island, though the invasion had not occurred. Commander King felt that a pre-emptive sortie against this possibility was called for, and moved to shell the enemy-held island of Ka-Do only a few miles north. In the darkness, guided by maps and information supplied by the local agents, the Canadian ship rocked enemy installations.

PERMISSION TO EVACUATE

Back at a rendezvous with CTE (Commander, Task Element), King got permission to evacuate wounded villagers from Taewha-Do in the company of *Cayuga.* He raced back, but found the Leopard's soldiers reluctant to take their sampans into shore in the dark, choppy seas. Time was wasting as the reluctant transport waited for calmer water before carrying out their task. If daylight found the destroyers sitting in shallow water, surrounded by Korean boats, disaster could surely be expected. By 04:00 hrs, however, King managed to get 47 wounded aboard and head south. The next night the loss of Paegun-do and Sowhado tightened the ring around Taewha-Do.

UN ships continued shelling Ka-Do to forestall any further Chinese adventures. As November drew to a close it seemed to be a successful tactic and there was every indication that the enemy could be delayed into the new year.

DREADED REPORT

During that final month, the Canadian destroyers had stood guard over Taewha-Do, but they did have other duties to perform. HMS *Cockade* had relieved *Cayuga,* and *Athabaskan* found herself off Cho-Do on the night of 30 November when the dreaded report came in: Taewha-Do was under attack by Chinese infantry. *Cockade* lacked the more sophisticated radar of the Canadian destroyers and had failed to detect the assault boats crossing the channel. Responding immediately, she sank one large junk and damaged others, but was soon struck by shore-based fire, losing one man.

Athabaskan arrived in time for the denouement. King circled the island looking for an opportunity to rescue survivors; his guns were useless lest they kill friend as well as foe swarming over the island. The Chinese brought a field gun down to the beach with the intention of assaulting the Canadians, but were quickly despatched. An armed junk was also dealt with in a similar manner. King requested permission to put a party ashore to assist any possible evacuations, but he was ordered to leave. There was nothing left to do there.

TAEWHA-DO LOST

A number of reports from agents and naval commanders had warned Tokyo Headquarters the Chinese had designs on Taewha-Do, but no measures had been taken to bolster the defence. The absence of the Canadian ships was a coincidence. Their bigger guns and superior radar might have changed the course of events. In any case, it now became a priority to defend the remaining islands further to the south. Though some important "horses" had already left, the barn door would now be locked.

REPRINTED FROM:
Esprit de Corps, *Volume 1 Issue 6*
AUTHOR: *James G. Scott*

THE TRAIN BUSTERS CLUB

How HMCS *Crusader* acquired the codename 'Casey Jones:' Canadian destroyers prove their worth off the Korean coast.

WHEN THE GOVERNMENT OF Prime Minister Louis St. Laurent finally gathered its members to deal with the crisis in Korea, it was widely agreed that a contribution to the growing UN effort was a foregone conclusion. The situation had broken over a sleepy weekend in summertime Ottawa; during a sleepy period in our history. Korea certainly didn't seem to merit much attention at the time. In any case, the post war Canadian Army was a shadow of its former greatness, destined for European garrison duty and home defence. The Royal Canadian Air Force was also suffering from the Canadian inclination to wipe out wartime establishment with unseemly haste; it was a transport service with inadequate combat capabilities. Only the Royal Canadian Navy was anywhere near ready, and the government quickly offered three destroyers to the UN mission.

NOT IMPRESSED

UN commander in chief, Gen Douglas MacArthur, was not as impressed with the Canadian contribution as he would have been with troops. Warships he had in plenty, but his ground forces were in definite need of professional stiffening . His communications to the RCN flotilla were polite, but basically intimated that he would have to find a place for them in the line-up. In the end result the sterling service and unmatched record of the RCN ships which served in this theatre made them the envy of every other navy.

In actual fact, the RCN was not officially ready when the balloon went up. The Pa-

RIGHT:
HMCS Nootka.
(DND PHOTO)

cific Destroyer Command, from whence the three would come, was caught without a fully operational ship. HMC Ships *Crescent* and *Crusader* were out of commission, while HMC ships *Cayuga, Athabaskan,* and *Sioux* were in refit to prepare for an upcoming European tour. Pneumatic hammers, welding torches and miles of electrical cable were strewn about the decks when the new Commander Destroyers Pacific (COMDESPAC) showed up to get them ready for war.

LEFT:
HMCS Crusader, *a former British 'C' Class Destroyer, became the lead scorer in train 'kills. (DND PHOTO)'*

EXEMPLARY COMMAND

On 29 June 1950 Captain Jeffry Vanstone Brock arrived at Esquimalt, BC. He was to take over command of *Cayuga* as well as the entire task force, but an arrangement with the serving COMDESPAC, Capt M.A. Medland was necessary to smooth the transition. Medland's command only ended on 4 July, and he was allowed to oversee activities aboard *Cayuga* until then. Brock was only 36, but had been in the navy for half of his life. His WWII experience was aboard RN vessels and he had excelled in tactical skills. He also held a deep respect for RN routines and class distinctions, which may have served England's "wooden walls" for centuries, but didn't sit well with the more democratic Canadian sailors. Onerous disciplinary measures and petty commands brought back from the RN after WWII led to a series of "incidents" in the RCN. Brock was in command of HMCS *Ontario* when she experienced a mutiny off the Mexican coast in 1948. His reputation among the lower-deckers preceded him, and was not helped by an overzealous Lieutenant Commander who ordered full uniforms be worn in Hawaii's tropical heat in July of 1950.

ONEROUS DISCIPLINARY MEASURES AND PETTY COMMANDS BROUGHT BACK FROM THE RN AFTER WWII LED TO A SERIES OF "INCIDENTS" IN THE RCN.

Cayuga's Welfare Committee got the order rescinded and the situation defused without further trouble. Brock's exemplary command while in Korean waters slowly brought his men around and, eventually, mutual respect led to smooth, professional operations.

SHORE LEAVE

The three ships arrived at Sasebo, Japan on 30 July. No immediate operational orders were available, so shore leave was granted to all crews. In this case it was a dubious pleasure, as Sasebo had little to offer except diseased "Butterfly Girls" and trinket shops. An American naval club, the Anchor Club, offered a smoky, raucous environment and cold beer, while the British version was decorated with wooden benches and served pints of warm Bass and Worthington. The Canadians were too "North Americanized" to really appreciate the latter.

The UN naval forces consisted of Task Groups broken down into Task Elements and further into Task Units under the overall command of USN Vice Admiral C. Turner Joy. The Canadians were originally intended to operate in a group, but the nature of the naval war around the Korean peninsula, and the specialized skills possessed by the Canucks, led them to perform a variety of functions under many commanders. The RCN participated in mine-hunting, commando operations, blockade functions, carrier escort, shore bombardment, evacuations and strangest of all, "trainbusting."

FIRST SHOTS

HMCS *Cayuga* had the privilege of firing the first shots in anger when she and HMS *Mounts Bay* bombarded the southern port of Yosu on 15 August. *Cayuga* laid her 6 x 4" guns (three twin-barrel mountings) along the harbourfront and blasted petroleum stocks, ammunition and North Korean artillery into oblivion. The first shell casing was made into a commemorative ashtray for the Prime Minister.

Athabaskan was next in action at Kunsan

and Popsong'po where she bombarded shore batteries. RCN ships engaged in all naval activities over the ensuing three years, primarily on the west coast. This side of Korea, the Yellow Sea coast, was the closest to Red China and the responsibility of the British. They had diplomatic relations with the Chinese, and before the invasion of December 1950, the Americans felt any incidents in Chinese coastal waters could be sorted out. Canadians preferred to operate on the east coast where there was more action – and more trains.

CLUB ORIGINS

The Trainbusters Club began as an American morale boosting activity in July 1952. The trains operated on tracks high up in the Taebeck Mountain range and were often hidden by fog and numerous tunnels. It was luck that brought one within range of a destroyer's guns off the coast, and excellent gunnery that knocked the North Korean trains of the tracks.

Other navies had recorded kills prior to the competition, but the Yanks only set up the Club after USS *Orleck* destroyed two trains in a two week period in July 1952. Only ships serving under Task Force 95 (TF95) could qualify for membership and only after hitting the engine of the initial victim. What started out as a morale boosting gimmick for the USN turned into a free-for-all with His Majesty's Canadian Ships leading the pack.

GUNNERY SKILLS IN DEMAND

HMCS *Crusader* was on her first tour under the command of Lieutenant Commander J.H. Bobey when she joined the Club. East coast service did not automatically mean duty with TF95, and even this did not allow full time attention to trainbusting. Opportunities were rare, and gunnery skills had to be exceptional. *Crusader* got her opportunity on the night of 26 October 1952. Anchored 10,000 yards off the coast, the night was passing uneventfully when gunnery officer Lt Copas spotted a likely victim. *Crusader* laid her 4.7 inch guns on the target, but only snapped the tail off this dragon. The engine managed to escape into a tunnel.

LEFT:
Captain Jeffry Brock. Later, as Rear-Admiral, Brock would serve with distinction as Flag Officer, Atlantic Coast.
(DND PHOTO)

OPPORTUNITIES FOR TRAINBUSTING WERE RARE, AND GUNNERY SKILLS HAD TO BE EXCEPTIONAL...THE USN WAS TRYING MANFULLY NOT TO HAVE JOHNNY CANUCK MAKE OFF WITH ANOTHER REWARD, BUT WAS HAVING LITTLE SUCCESS.

The next night another opportunity presented itself and no mistakes were made. Range was reduced to 3,000 yards and shells hammered the unfortunate communist train. Smoke obscured the whereabouts of the engine and it was not until the next day that a spotter plane made the kill official. *Crusader's* gunners had spent the night picking off the remaining cars.

NEXT ROUND

Canadian ships either missed their few chances or were generally not on west coast patrol again until early 1953. *Crusader* once again led the way and established the mark which no other ship equalled. On the morning of 15 April she bounced a train off a high trestle, though the engine escaped (it was no longer a prerequisite anyway). The same afternoon another train was spotted at extreme range. Even hugging the shore the distance was estimated at 13,000 yards. The second salvo found this victim and *Crusader* bumped off her fourth victim. This ship with the hawk-eyed gunners spent an enjoyable afternoon demolishing what was left of their enemy. *Crusader's* codename was changed from "Leadmine" to "Casey Jones."

The rest of the RCN could not allow the champion's laurels to fall on their sister ship without challenge. HMCS *Haida,* already possessed of the finest record in the fleet, was not above adding Club membership to the list. The USN was trying manfully not to have Johnny Canuck make off with another reward, but was having little success. *Haida* arrived off the golden coast on 26 May and at 23:20 hrs her first night, bagged a train with excellent marksmanship. Three days later, also at night, she recorded a second kill.

***ATHABASKAN*'S RECORD**

HMCS *Athabaskan* was the only other Canadian member of the Trainbusters Club. Her entry fee was paid on 24 June when her "A" gun knocked a train off the tracks. She returned later to deliver the coup de grâce.

On 30 June she damaged a train; which did not count, but on Dominion Day, 1 July 1953, she cashiered her second, and the RCN's eighth train.

Like our Gulf War contribution of 1990, the Canadian ships of 1950-55 never made up a significant part of the numbers of ships involved, but made a disproportionate impact on overall operations. Korean War vets did not sail "rust-buckets" (the average ship age was just over five years), but they often had to scramble for supplies. Another difference was government recognition: the Gulf War ships got theirs right away.

REPRINTED FROM:
Esprit de Corps, *Volume 2 Issue 7*
AUTHOR: *James G. Scott*

CASE OF THE SPURIOUS SAWBONES

The popular surgeon, Lieutenant Cyr was not all that he appeared to be.

IN THE FALL OF 1951, a lady glancing through her daily newspaper inadvertently unmasked one of the most unusual deceptions in Canadian naval history.

She was the mother of a doctor, Joseph Cyr, who was practising medicine in Grand Falls, New Brunswick. To her astonishment, she read an account of an emergency operation performed on the deck of a Canadian destroyer off the coast of Korea – apparently by her son. She contacted Dr. Cyr, who, after reassuring his mother he was indeed still in civilian practise, called the RCMP. A bizarre story unfolded.

It began in early 1951, when an American named Ferdinand Waldo ("Fred") Demara entered Canada and became a novitiate monk in Grand Falls. For more than a decade, Demara had held positions in a number of religious orders, and as a psychologist, university lecturer, college department head, school teacher, and prison warden. Despite this impressive employment record, Demara – later to become famous as "The Great Imposter" – had obtained and held these posts on the basis of forged, stolen or non-existent qualifications.

Demara became friendly with Doctor Cyr, and often visited the latter's offices. Eventually the visits ceased.

LEFT: *Fred Demara, the 'Great Imposter' posing as Dr. Joseph Cyr.* (DND PHOTO)

OPPOSITE PAGE: *HMCS* Cayuga *takes on supplies in Korean waters.* (DND PHOTO)

DOCTOR CYR VOLUNTEERS

In March 1951, a Doctor Joseph Cyr appeared at the Naval recruiting office in Saint John, NB, and offered his professional services to the RCN. He hinted that if the navy couldn't use him, the Army or RCAF would be glad to accept him. At this stage of the Korean War and with Canada's new NATO commitments, qualified medical officers were desperately needed by all three services, and no time was lost in processing this valuable recruit.

"Cyr's" credentials were accepted without verification, and three days after his visit to the recruiting centre, he was commissioned into the RCN as a Surgeon-Lieutenant. The normal two-month enlistment process took about one day.

AMERICAN ORDERLY

Had a thorough background investigation been conducted, the authorities would no doubt have discovered that 'Dr. Joseph Cyr' was none other than the ubiquitous Fred Demara, whose medical experience was limited to a few weeks as an unskilled hospital orderly in the United States.

The bogus doctor was assigned to the naval hospital at HMCS *Stadacona* in the Halifax area. Retired naval Captain 'Mack' Lynch, who was a department head in Stadacona at the time, recalls 'Cyr' appeared to be a fairly competent medical officer, and a pleasant enough individual, although not a great mixer. Captain Lynch remembers that 'Cyr' showed a great deal of interest in adapting aircrew selection psycho-physical test methods (which Lynch had taken in WWII) as a naval screening procedure.

'Cyr's' hospital patients apparently survived his ministrations by a combination of generous use of penicillin, referral or consultation with other medical officers and, no doubt, a combination of physical fitness and sheer luck!

IDYLL ENDED

This idyllic existence ended on 16 June 1951, when 'Cyr' joined HMCS *Cayuga* in Esquimalt, BC – leaving three days later for the destroyer's second tour of duty in Korean waters.

"Surgeon-Lieutenant Cyr" managed to cope effectively with the few minor injuries and ailments which occurred en route to the war zone. He was fortunate in that he had a capable Sick Berth Attendant, Petty Officer Bob Hotchin, who handled most of the routine cases. Hotchin was surprised, and gratified, by the way in which he was allowed to work with a minimum of direction and interference from his medical officer.

'Cyr's' biggest challenge came when he was forced to act as a dentist. His patient was none other than the *Cayuga's* commander, Captain James Plomer. In the rush to prepare his ship for her return to Korea, Plomer had no time to obtain treatment for an infected tooth, which became a problem during the westward voyage.

WINGING IT

The bogus doctor, highly perturbed, feverishly studied his manuals and racked his brain to recall any dental surgery that he had witnessed in the past. He eventually gained the courage to collect his dental gear, a large supply of anaesthetic and make his way to the Captain's cabin.

After administering a hefty dose of local anaesthetic, 'Cyr' successfully removed the offending tooth, and by all reports, Plomer had no further trouble with it.

His confidence no doubt restored, the bogus doctor continued to handle routine shipboard injuries and minor ailments as *Cayuga* entered the war zone.

On arrival off the West coast of Korea, *Cayuga* and her crew became involved in operations that smacked more of the "gunboat diplomacy" of the nineteenth century than the traditional picture of naval warfare. Captain Don Saxon, who was a Lieutenant Commander at the time, recalls that the Canadian vessels would take part in commando-type operations against enemy-occupied islands. Selected members of the ships' crews would accompany members of US or Korean marines ashore and with their weapons and demolition charges generally create "alarm and despondency" in enemy circles. While our own casualties were light, the amount of "hairiness" involved was evidenced by a number of gallantry awards, including a Distinguished Service Cross for Saxon.

One of these "commando" raids led to Demara's unmasking.

MASK REMOVED

Following a highly successful foray on the West coast of Korea, the only three seriously-wounded casualties – all South Korean guerillas – were brought back to *Cayuga*. One apparently had a bullet embedded in his lung. He was operated upon on the spot by the ship's medical officer, by all accounts successfully, although no one ever saw the bullet which was supposedly extracted. (Other reports indicate that 'Cyr' also amputated a foot during these naval operations.) Whatever his qualifications, it would appear that the patients survived the attentions of the bogus doctor.

Unfortunately for the masquerade, news from Korea was scarce at that time. A pair of war correspondents snapped up the story of the "open deck" surgery – the account found its way into the Canadian papers, and the real Doctor Cyr began asking questions.

He remembered that his medical credentials were missing, but attributed the fact to a recent move. He also recalled that "Brother John"(Demara) disappeared at the same time.

UNQUALIFIED IMPOSTER

Eventually, in October 1952, Captain Plomer received a signal to the effect that his medical officer was an unqualified imposter. He found this hard to believe, as in the opinion of the ship's officers, 'Cyr' was a capable and popular doctor. Another message received the following day removed all doubts, and 'Dr. Cyr' was transferred to a British cruiser, HMS *Ceylon*, for transfer to Japan and subsequently to Canada.

Lieutenant Commander Saxon, with another officer, was detailed to search the doctor's cabin, and found letters and other documents which confirmed the imposture. Demara – there was no question of his identity by this time – had apparently taken an overdose of drugs that day. Whether or not this was a suicidal attempt is questionable, although Captain Plomer felt that it was.

BACK TO RELIGION

On arrival in Canada, Demara appeared before a naval board of inquiry. There appears to be no record of disciplinary proceedings, and service records indicate that 'Cyr' was given an honourable release and several hundred dollars in back pay. He left Canada (some reports indicate that he was deported) and returned to the religious field, eventually becoming a bona-fide clergyman under his own name.

John Melady, author of *Korea, Canada's Forgotten War*, recalls a telephone interview in which Demara "had good things to say about Canada, the Canadian Navy and the officers and men he knew on the *Cayuga*." Demara supposedly participated in a *Cayuga* reunion in Victoria in 1979. The Reverend Ferdinand Waldo Demara died in 1982.

CASTING MISTAKES

One minor deception remained as a result of Demara's escapade. In 1961 Hollywood made a movie, *The Great Imposter*, starring Tony Curtis in the title role. "He was nothing like the real thing," chuckled Don Saxon. "Cyr, as we knew him, was a pretty chunky 200-pounder – nothing at all like Curtis. And Edmund O'Brien was just as much out of place in the role of Captain Plomer."

'Commodore Plomer' was listed in the film credits as "technical adviser" but Saxon feels that his "technical advice" was not always heeded. Even I, as a "brown job" noted the incongruity of a Canadian naval board of enquiry consisting of group of officers properly clad in RCN uniform, but with every member sporting a black pencil moustache.

ON ARRIVAL IN CANADA, DEMARA APPEARED BEFORE A NAVAL BOARD OF ENQUIRY. THERE APPEARS TO BE NO RECORD OF DISCIPLINARY PROCEEDINGS...

In one case, apparently, Plomer had his way. He was able to ensure that the correct hull number was used for his ship. This generated a deception which Demara would surely have enjoyed.

THE SECOND IMPOSTER

Cayuga (hull number 218) was on the East coast – the film crew was working out of Esquimalt, British Columbia. As George Guertin, a naval veteran of the Korean War recalls, "In 1961 I was out west on *Athabaskan*. We got an unusual order to 'paint ship.' We had to close up the '9' on our side number to make our '219' read '218.' We were told that it was something to do with a movie – when we saw "The Great Imposter" we realized that there were really two imposters, Demara and *Athabaskan*!"

REPRINTED FROM:
Esprit de Corps, *Volume 3 Issue 5*
AUTHOR: *Les Peate*

IN KOREAN SKIES

The group of Canadian F-86 pilots were a match for North Korean (and Soviet) jet jockeys.

ABOVE: *Flying the rugged and versatile F-86 Sabre, 22 RCAF pilots saw action with American Squadrons.* (*U.S. ARMY PHOTOS*)

HE WAS MISTAKEN FOR A NORTH KOREAN AIRCRAFT AND SHOT DOWN BY AN AMERICAN PILOT. HE WAS CAPTURED BY THE CHINESE AND SURVIVED IMPRISONMENT, INTERROGATION, SOLITARY CONFINEMENT, LACK OF FOOD AND MENTAL TORTURE.

CANADA'S CONTRIBUTION TO the Korean War was exemplary in every way. Her ground troops, eventually numbering 26,791, were third largest in number behind the US and UK, but were second to none in professionalism. The Thunderbirds of 426 Squadron ended up flying nearly 600-round trips between McChord AFB and Japan. Not a life or load of cargo was lost in 34,000 flying hours. At sea, the Royal Canadian Navy dispatched a total of eight ships over four years, and these too deported themselves with skill and dedication. Though they were requested by the U.S., Canada's fighter squadrons did not put in an appearance in Korean skies. Europe was deemed more important and the few fighter squadrons available were sent there. However, 22 RCAF fighter pilots did see action with American Squadrons.

Flight Lieutenant J.A.O. Levesque, on exchange duty with the American Air Force in November 1950 became the first Canadian pilot to see action in Korea. Believing that RCAF pilots would gain valuable experience, the Defence Department required that pilots have 50 hours of solo jet flying in order to volunteer for 50 combat missions or to remain in Korea for six months. One officer eventually completed 82 sorties with an American unit. Andy MacKenzie, a veteran of ten years was forming 441 Sabre Squadron in St. Hubert, Quebec. A former Spitfire pilot with 8 $^1/_2$ kills and DFC in World War Two, Squadron Leader Mackenzie DFC served with 51st Fighter Interceptor Wing in Korea and experienced four uneventful sorties. On his fifth in an F-86 Sabre, while attempting to catch up with his flight leader, he was mistaken for a North Korean aircraft and shot down by an American pilot. He was captured by the Chinese and survived imprisonment, interrogation, solitary confinement, lack of food and mental torture.

TWO DFC'S

Another veteran pilot was Flight Lieutenant Glover. He had flown Hurricanes for the Royal Air Force over France during the WWII. In Korea, Glover successfully completed his tour, racking up three enemy fighter kills and damaged three others. After his return to Canada, Flight Lieutenant Glover received two Distinguished Flying Crosses; one Canadian and one American.

The Korean War was the site of many firsts. The Lockheed F-80 Shooting Star triumphed in the first jet battle in history when on 7 November 1950, an F-80 shot down a MiG-15 as it crossed the Yalu River. In time, however, the MiG-15 aircraft proved to be more maneouvrable, and against it the F-80 sustained a loss ratio in air combat of seven to six.

BRUTAL AMBUSHES

Sabre was an appropriate name for the premier fighter as air combat in that time still depended on the "tally ho" of a visual sighting of the target. The brutal ambush of enemy fighters, which was the surest guarantee of returning from a sortie, could not always decide the victor. The slashing melee of the dogfight require a stout heart, quick reactions and an almost supernatural awareness. In this, the F-86 fighter pilot was assisted by many aids, but the most important was a radar computing gunsight which assisted in aiming.

The North American F-86 Sabre was a classic postwar first generation jet fighter. Derived directly from German research into subsonic flight, it was produced in larger quantities than any other aircraft since the end of the second world war. The F-86 Sabre was the pride of the United States Air Force during the Korean War, and the front line interceptor in most NATO and SEATO countries during the 1950s. A swept-wing version of the US Navy's straight-winged FJ-1 Fury, the $232,000 Sabre first flew in 1947, entering service with the US Air Force in 1949. The early versions which received their air combat baptism in Korea were armed with six M-3 .50 calibre machine-guns, each with 267 rounds, mounted forward on either side of the nose. They could also carry eight five-inch rockets or two 1000-pound bombs for ground support.

PILOTS' FAVOURITE

The E and F models of the Sabre were the favourite with the pilots in Korea, capable of a maximum speed of 687 miles per hour. Though unable to climb as rapidly or to as high an altitude as the Soviet MiG-15, they were rugged and versatile, and quickly established their superior manoeuvrability, with a kill ratio of seven to three against Soviet aircraft. By the war's end, Sabres had shot down a total of 814 enemy aircraft. This in spite of it's lacking in weight of air-to-air armament represented by cannon.

SABRES HEAVILY TRADED

In Canada, between 1950 and 1958, a total of 1815 Sabres were produced by Canadair to various standards, including Mk2, Mk 4, CL-13 Mk 5 and CL-13 Mk 6. Some of this production was undertaken for the Royal Canadian Air Force, and the rest were exported. None of these aircraft served in Korea during the conflict. Produced also under licence in Australia, Italy, and Japan, it has also been heavily traded and retransferred throughout the world, and at time of printing, 34 countries still use them.

The well-armed MiG-15 swept-wing single-seat fighter was the Sabre's best opponent over Korea, and served in great numbers both with the Red Air Force and with the air forces of the Russian satellites. It had a better rate of climb and ceiling than the Sabre, as well as a tighter turn and superior speed. Armed with a single 30mm and two 20mm cannons, the MiG-15 had a top speed of 746 mph. The main drawback of this plane was that it was short-ranged at 560 miles. The North Korean Air Force of initially 132 MiG-15s was knocked out of the war due to UN strikes on Korean airfields and transportation and the short-ranged MiG-15 rebased in China could do little to support the North Korean Army against UN airpower.

FORCES FORBIDDEN

UN forces were forbidden to travel north of the Yalu River – the border between North Korea and China – furthering the frustrations of UN pilots. On the ground, as in the

RIGHT: *with a better rate of climb, a tighter turn and more firepower, the MiG-15 (here with North Korean markings) was a match for the Sabre. By war's end, however, the Sabre had a kill ratio of seven to three against the Soviet-built aircraft.*
(U.S. ARMY PHOTOS)

air, patrols and reconnaissance were undertaken over "bastard-steep hills" to determine the intentions and dispositions of the enemy. These deadly games of hide-and-seek took place in all kinds of weather, and their essential purpose was to penetrate the fog of war and bring back information. As a defence, skilled troops on both sides practiced effective camouflage in order to hide. The practice of Chinese troops and their uniform's dirt colour made it difficult to identify targets. Through mist, rain and clouds troops and pilots searched for an elusive enemy. Air support made the difference to the troops on the ground. From the conflict's early stages, the UN fought to maintain air supremacy over the battlefields. Heavy bombers struck as far north as the Yalu River and inflicted heavy casualties and damage on airfields, bridges, railways and tunnels. The fighters hammered the enemy's forward positions and forced them to move supplies and troops at night, while air reconnaissance aided the UN ground troops. The 22 RCAF fighter pilots and technical officers serving with the US Fifth Air Force were credited with 20 enemy jet fighters destroyed or damaged, as well as the destruction of several enemy trains and trucks.

ONE CAN BUT MARVEL AT THE COURAGE AND DEDICATION OF THE CANADIAN PILOTS DURING THE KOREAN WAR.

THE VALUE OF A REGULAR

While the Chinese and North Koreans could not match the UN in the air, they defended with a surprising amount of anti-aircraft artillery for the pilots whose job it was to fly through it. Anti-aircraft artillery was responsible for over 70 per cent of the planes lost. One can but marvel at the courage and dedication of the pilots who, while riding the cutting edge of an emerging technology, depended on the Mark I eyeball (not lasers and TV) for target identification, dodging killer flak to accomplish their missions. For the RCAF pilots, their professional fighting qualities displayed the value of a Regular. Now, in an environment of restraint just as acute, and a political scene not as black and white, the traditions upheld and new ones forged in the Korean War are vital and may perhaps shine as a beacon.

Continuing their exceptional performance from World War Two, Canadian pilots found themselves in very different machines only five years later, in a different corner of the world.

One of the best was Flight Lieutenant Ernie Glover with three kills, but Squadron Leader J.D. Lindsay, DFC (US) got two, plus three damaged, and Squadron Leader J. Mackay got one, the last of the war.

Flight Officer A. Lambros got the US Air Medal for damaging two MIG's. Squadron Leader J.C.A. LaFrance received a DFC and one kill to his credit.

The most unfortunate of the Canadian pilots, (beside Joe Liston whose scout plane was shot down on his 13th day and 13th mission), was Andy Mackenzie. As he was swooping to catch up with his leader, an American pilot fired a burst. Mackenzie caught it in the canopy and spent two years as an uninvited guest of the Chinese.

TOP:
Communist MiGs were not the only threat to American Commonwealth air forces over Korea. This light observation plane suffered severe damage from groundfire.
(US ARMY)

ABOVE:
Squadron Leader Andy MacKenzie poses with his F-86 Sabre. Accidentally shot down by a U.S. jet, MacKenzie was the only Canadian fighter pilot taken prisoner during the Korean War.
(DND/PL 52195)

REPRINTED FROM:
Esprit de Corps, *Volume 1 Issue 6*
AUTHOR:
John Coffey

MOSQUITOS OVER THE IMJIN

Slow and noisy, the World War II Harvard trainers proved their worth over hostile areas in Korea.

While UN air superiority allowed light aircraft to fly relatively safely, low, slow, spotter aircraft like this American L-19 were frequent targets for Communist ground troops. (US ARMY)

SPEAK TO A WWII aviator about "Mosquitos" and you would probably generate stories of the versatile De Havilland "wooden wonder." (One of the best of which is Dave McIntosh's *Terror in the Starboard Seat.*) Mention the "Mosquito squadrons" to a Korean War Veteran, and in many cases you would receive only a blank look.

Exploits of the F-86 Sabres, F-84 Thunderjets and F-80 Shooting Stars, together with their naval counterparts the Phantoms and Corsairs, and the Commonwealth's Mustangs and Meteors have been well-documented. Even Hollywood got into the act with such classics as "The Bridges at Toko-ri." One lesser-known organization, vitally important to our front-line infantry, was the Fifth Air Force's 6147 Tactical Control Group.

While the UN forces enjoyed air superiority there was one significant limiting factor when it came to the provision of close air support to our ground forces. During WWII, many tactical air force targets consisted of vehicles and troop concentrations which were comparatively easy to spot from the air. In Korea the ground support aircraft were required to knock out well-concealed gun positions and bunkers in mountainous terrain with few distinctive landmarks. In addition, with the exception of the Mustangs, which were soon replaced by jets, the higher speeds allowed little time for pilots to locate and identify their targets. (One unit of 27 Commonwealth Brigade suffered heavy casualties from an attack by "friendly" aircraft.)

The solution to the problem was the introduction of an unusual type of aircraft to the front lines. An innovative genius decided to take a number of AT-6 Texan trainers out of mothballs, and send them to Korea as spotter and ground liaison aircraft. Anyone who has heard the AT-6 (the "Harvard" in Canada) would recognize the distinctive drone of its Pratt & Whitney "Wasp" engine – hence its nickname "The Mosquito."

The AT-6 was ideal for its new role. Its maximum speed of 212 mph gave the pilot and observer much more time to search for targets – this compared with 580 mph for the F-80 and over 600 mph for the Sabre and Thunderjet. The rugged construction, designed to take the rough handling of student pilots, enabled it to withstand a great deal of ground fire. Finally, it was capable of carrying a supply of rockets (used to mark targets), armour plate and two or more radios. The "greenhouse" cockpit provided a wide field of vision for a pilot and observer. As we will see later, the fact that the Harvard was originally built as a training aircraft proved vital to one Canadian officer.

TEAM EFFORT

The AT-6 pilots and support personnel became established as 6147 Tactical Air Control Group. They soon realized that close air support was a team effort, and USAF personnel underwent tours of duty with ground units, while the combat units from more than a dozen UN provided airborne observers. The teams were in contact with the ground units and with the controllers of the "strike aircraft."

Generally, targets would be called for by the ground commander, through his air control team, or spotted by the pilot or observer in the AT-6. The spotter aircraft would call in a strike and if necessary fire smoke rockets to indicate the target's location. (This usually brought out the friendly infantry, who had a front-seat view of the ensuing air strike – bombs, rockets, cannon-fire or, the most spectacular of all, napalm.)

DARING STRIKES

Perhaps the most daring 'strikes' were conducted by the Mustangs of the South African Air Force. The Springboks would approach their targets by following the valleys, then open fire from below the objectives, which were usually on hilltops or ridges. This approach proved costly – the SAAF's Second Fighter Squadron (the 'Flying Cheetahs') lost 42 pilots during their Korean tour.

Canadians had their share of 6147 Group's activity. Eight Canadian Officers were decorated by the United States for gallantry in the air. Four of these, Capt J.R.P. Yelle and Lt J.F. Plouffe of the R22eR, Lt A.J. Magee of the Royal Canadian Regiment, and Capt Bill Ward of LdSH received the U.S. Distinguished Flying Cross. (As an aside, Capt Peter Tees, Royal Canadian Artillery, was the only Canadian Army officer to receive the Commonwealth DFC, awarded for his deeds as an Auster pilot with the British 1903 Air OP Flight.)

AWARD CITATION

Lieutenant Plouffe's experience typifies the

hazards of the operation. The citation for his award reads as follows: "Captain Plouffe (who had apparently been promoted since his exploit) directed his pilot through intense enemy ground fire in a low reconnoitering pass to discover the location of six camouflaged enemy bunkers, four mortar positions and an artillery position behind a key hill. Disregarding his personal safety he directed the pilot in making these passes to mark individual targets with smoke rockets, for orbiting fighter aircraft. One of the fighters was hit by ground fire during the attack and Captain Plouffe's pilot escorted it to the nearest emergency strip.

"Upon returning to the area he continued to direct the fighters on to the targets, resulting in four bunkers, two mortar positions and one artillery position being destroyed. By his high personal courage, aggressiveness and devotion to duty Capt Plouffe brought great credit upon himself, the Commonwealth and the US Air Force."

START PUMPING!

The citation did not tell the full story. Plouffe recalls that his aircraft was hit, and the fuel pump was damaged. The pilot instructed his observer in the use of the manual pump, and Plouffe was told to "start pumping." As the aircraft made its way back to friendly territory, Plouffe recalled that "every time the propeller seemed to slow down, no matter how tired I was, I found the energy to pump harder!"

Despite the damaging effects of Capt Plouffe's efforts on the Chinese mortars, he was presumably readmitted to the mortar fraternity, serving at the School of Infantry as a senior instructor on that weapon. One can be sure that concealment of mortar baseplate positions from the air was a significant part of the course syllabus.

Another Vandoo officer who underwent a hair-raising experience in the back seat of a Harvard was Capt J.P.R. (Pat) Tremblay, a liaison officer at 25 Canadian Infantry Brigade headquarters.

OBSERVER

Tremblay was flying as an observer in an AT-6 piloted by a USAF officer, Capt Wittom. As a qualified parachutist, he was no stranger to air-ground operations.

LEFT:
An observer with a K-20 camera in hand sits in the rear seat of an L-5 aircraft in preparation for a reconnaissance flight.
(U.S. ARMY PHOTO)

When they arrived over the forward areas Tremblay was able to identify several key features in the Commonwealth Division sector. He was able to locate the enemy trench systems, but could not spot any activity. As the pilot descended to make a more detailed search, the aircraft ran into a burst of light anti-aircraft fire. The Vandoo officer saw that some of the rounds had entered the pilot's cockpit.

Wittom was obviously seriously wounded – he was unable to speak coherently and was bleeding badly. Meanwhile the AT-6 was bouncing around in the air, with no one at the controls.

FIRST TIME PILOT

This is where the Harvard's previous role as a trainer paid off. Although some of the aircraft had been denuded of the rear-seat student's controls, Wittom's plane still had these in place. Recalling his basic knowledge of aviation, Tremblay (who had never before touched the controls of an airplane) knew that he could control the rise and fall of the machine by pushing the joystick forward or back. This enabled him to avoid the plane's ploughing into the terrain.

By trial and error, Pat Tremblay was able to gain some control over the aircraft and made his way back towards the UN lines. He was now faced with another problem – should he bail out or attempt to land the plane? Although his pilot was badly wounded, he was obviously still alive. There was no question of abandoning the aircraft.

After flying around for a while Tremblay recognized familiar landmarks and eventually located the Kimpo airstrip, close to Seoul. Wittom had now regained consciousness, but due to his injuries was unable to operate the stick and rudder bar in the front seat. As the "back-seat driver" approached the strip, and began a steep descent the Air Force pilot realized that Tremblay did not know how to throttle back, and Wittom was able to slow the aircraft by activating the landing flaps. He was also able to drop the retractable undercarriage.

ON THE GROUND AND ON FIRE

After a series of bounces and zig-zags, the AT-6 finally came to a stop with the assistance of a four inch wall. Despite flames licking around the aircraft engine, Tremblay lifted Wittom from the cockpit – no easy task, as the USAF pilot was over six feet tall.

Captain Wittom recovered from a number of shrapnel wounds in the spine. Although many of his comrades felt that Pat Tremblay deserved a Distinguished Flying Cross for his coolness and courage he did, in fact, receive a Military Cross for his efforts. Surprisingly, he did not receive an American award.

The "Mosquito" Group holds a reunion annually, and despite its decreasing numbers there is usually some Canadian participation. While the 6147th's role may have been overshadowed by the more spectacular fighter and bomber units, in one way it has achieved immortality. Comic book aficionados will recognize Steve Canyon at the controls of an AT-6 over the Korean front.

REPRINTED FROM:
Esprit de Corps, *Volume 3 Issue 9*
AUTHOR: *Les Peate*

THE STORY OF "BED-CHECK CHARLIE"

PLYWOOD AND FABRIC

They were ancient crates reminiscent of World War One days, but still proved effective in the jet age.

Two Soviet Polikarpov Po-2s take off on a training flight. Entering service in 1928, the biplanes became known as "Bed-Check Charlies" during the Korean War.

THE PRIMITIVE BIPLANE, a melange of fabric, plywood and yards of bracing wire, powered by a rackety 100-horsepower engine, chugged through the darkness towards the enemy's rear areas. On arrival at the target, the pilot dropped two small bombs, which destroyed a fuel dump and thousands of tons of fuel. This sounds like the climax of "Dawn Patrol" and Errol Flynn's last flight, but in fact it describes a typical mission of one of the Korean War's unsung air heroes, "Bed-check Charlie." Thanks to Hollywood – and the stories of the exploits of Omar Levesque, Eric Smith, Andy MacKenzie and the other Canadians who were attached to USAF Sabre squadrons – aviation enthusiasts tend to regard the Korean air war as the milieu of jets or, at the very least, high performance propellor-driven aircraft. Nevertheless, a number of pre-World War antiques played a their part in the conflict.

Esprit de Corps has already related the adventures of several Canadians who flew as observers in the 1938-vintage AT-6 (Texan or Harvard) trainers which were removed from mothballs to serve effectively as target-spotters in the forward areas. Piper Cubs and their spin-offs, Taylorcraft Austers, served as air observation posts and on liaison duties. (These were even used on at least one occasion to drop ammunition – although not always required – and desperately needed rations to isolated units.)

THE FLYING PORCUPINE

Another early aircraft which saw extensive, if comparatively unrecognized service, was the 1937 Short Sunderland flying boat (the 'Flying Porcupine') which the RAF operated on maritime patrols from its base in Iwakuni, Japan. Nor can we forget the C-47 which circled overhead in the darkness, scaring the living daylights (nightlights?) out of isolated listening patrols with a loudspeaker burst of propaganda in Korean, apparently right beside us.

When North Korea invaded its neighbour, the North Korean People's Air Force consisted of almost 200 planes, including 40 YAK-9 fighters (considered by experts as on a par with the Me-109 and Spitfire) and 70 of the much-vaunted Stormvik ground-attack aircraft. After initial successes against the badly-outnumbered South Korean air force they were virtually annihilated by the US Navy and Fifth Air Force. Later, the Chinese Communist Air Force entered the fray with MiG jet fighters, but that is another story.

KOREAN DETERMINATION

Despite the loss of most of their combat aircraft, the North Koreans did not give up completely. In a war which featured jets and high-performance propellor-driven aircraft such as the Sea Fury, Corsair and B-29, they turned to what was almost a museum piece, the Polikarpov Po-2. This antique machine first went into service in 1928, and was built for simplicity. For instance, the upper and lower wings of the biplane were interchangeable. The "Kukuruznik," or *corn-cutter*, as it was nicknamed, was powered by a 100 h.p. motor which gave it a maximum speed of 170 km/hr (103 mph). The wood and fabric-covered Po-2 served in the Second World War as a trainer and in many other roles, coming into its own as a nuisance raider in support of Russia's guerrilla forces. One of its main advantages was an ability to operate from small grass airstrips near the front, which helped overcome its fairly limited range of 430 km. Its ability to operate on low-grade "regular" gasoline was an asset to the North Koreans in light of the constant interdiction of supply lines by UN aircraft and naval vessels.

During the "static" phase of the Korean War (from late 1951), North Korean counterparts of Errol Flynn would climb into the open cockpits of their biplanes and head south. Sometimes they would be accompanied by an air gunner armed with a machine gun or, in at least one instance, a "burp gun" machine carbine. The intrepid duo would fly "low and slow" between the mountain crests, usually at dusk or in darkness, seeking targets of opportunity, dropping their bombs (or in some cases leaflets) and making their way home.

"MAYTAG" PLANES

The M-11 engine sounded like a washing machine motor, which resulted in the U.N. nickname of "Maytag Charlie," although the habit of droning overhead after last light earned these raiders the more familiar sobriquet of "Bed-check Charlie." Their low altitude and wooden construction negated the effectiveness of allied radar, and their low speed, small size and manoeuverability frustrated the efforts of the higher- powered UN aircraft. Despite this, several of the biplanes and other more modern "bed-checks," such as the YAK-18 trainer, fell to the guns of the U.S. fighters. Three of the latter were credited to the U.S. Navy's only Korean War ace, Lieutenant Guy Bordelon. Nor did the American fighters escape unscathed. Aviation historian Mike O'Connor, as reported in *Military History* (March 1998), stated that at least six high-performance aircraft, including three jets, met disaster at the hands of "Charlies." At least one of these, flown by an experienced jet jockey, stalled and crashed in a low-altitude attempt to outmanoeuvre a Po-2. On the "plus" side 13 "Charlies" were confirmed as destroyed in aerial combat.

During the last year of the war the "Kukuruzniks" were reinforced by another, slightly faster, training aircraft, the Yakolev YAK-18. Developed in 1946, the YAK-18 monoplane boasted a closed cockpit and retractable undercarriage. Its bomb-aiming "equipment" consisted of the observer dropping the light missiles overside. Like the Po-2, this aircraft could operate from primitive airstrips. Occasionally these aircraft were heard (but seldom seen) over Commonwealth Division lines. Although they had some success (*Military History* reports that, in the last month of the Korean War, a raid by a few YAK-18's destroyed 5.5 million gallons of fuel), their main achievement was their nuisance value. While some casualties were inflicted on the ground troops, perhaps "Charlie's" most significant effect was the loss of sleep by rear-echelon troops (a hardship which the sharp-end sufferers who had heard the sounds of a washing-machine rinse cycle overhead heading south did not always appreciate).

REPRINTED FROM:
Esprit de Corps, *Volume 6 Issue 11*
AUTHOR: *Les Peate*

OPERATION HAWK - THE KOREAN AIRLIFT

ABOVE:
The North Star provided Canada's Air Force with a long range transport capability. During the Korean War 12 of these aircraft flew regular resupply missions.

426 (Thunderbird) Squadron had an impressive record in the Second World War – revamped as a transport unit, it upheld the tradition in the Korean War.

WHEN THE KOREAN WAR broke out on Sunday, 25 June 1950, No. 426 (Thunderbird) Squadron based in Montreal was engaged in routine flights, mainly of a domestic nature, which included scheduled runs to Whitehorse and Goose Bay. Apart from northern destinations, special flights included the movement of Air Force and Army Reserve personnel to and from their summer camps. On the squadron's agenda were a series of long range overseas training flights utilizing the unit's recently acquired fleet of eight (later 12) Canadair North Star aircraft. As Canada's only long range transport squadron, there was a strong possibility that the unit might be called upon to support United Nations operations in Korea. The squadron immediately initiated plans to meet such an eventuality.

SQUADRON PLAN SUBMITTED

Responding to a 12 July letter from the Chief of the Air Staff, A.M.W.A. Curtis, a squadron plan endorsed by Air Transport Command (ATC) was submitted to Air Force Headquarters on 18 July. The plan called for the arrival of the squadron at a base in the Western United States within 18 hours of notification from where the unit would undertake sustained airlift operations for a period of one year. With six of its North Stars and 12 crews, the squadron's operational element was to consist of 50 officers and 200 airmen taking with them 100,000 pounds of ground handling equipment and spares. Five of the North Stars were to be made available for operations, supervised by the USAF's Military Air Transport Service (MATS), by 36 hours after notification. The 6th North Star was to be utilized in providing logistics support for the squadron.

Following a Cabinet meeting on 19 July, the Prime Minister announced that the Government had decided to immediately provide a long range transport squadron for service in the Pacific airlift. The next day the Chief of the Air Staff issued a directive ordering immediate action to be taken to integrate No. 426 Transport Squadron operations with those of US MATS in support of the United Nations campaign in Korea. The squadron was placed on alert 20 July for a move to a west coast base and the unit's Commanding Officer, W/C C.H. Mussells,

RIGHT:
A North Star of 426 (Thunderbird) Squadron attached to U.S. Military Air Transport Service is towed into a hangar at McChord Air Base, Tacoma, Washington. The Squadron flew 600 round trips over the Pacific, carrying more than 13,000 passengers and three million kilograms of freight – without loss.
(JOHN RUTHERFORD, CXC 93 2165)

accompanied the commander of ATC and several staff officers to Andrews AFB near Washington, D.C. There they met with Lieutenant General L.S. Kuter, Commander of MATS, and members of his staff. Amongst other issues in the day-long discussions was that the squadron was to be based at McChord AFB which was located near Tacoma, Washington, and that the unit was to depart Dorval on 25 July. Canada's participation in the airlift operation was given the code word "Hawk" by Air Transport Command.

THE FORMATION HEADED WEST FOR OTTAWA AND, AS THEY FLEW OVER PARLIAMENT HILL, DIPPED THEIR WINGS IN SALUTE TO THE LATE PRIME MINISTER WILLIAM LYON MACKENZIE KING.

LOADED, SERVICED AND READY

By late afternoon of 25 July, six North Stars had been loaded, serviced and made ready for departure. A brief farewell ceremony was held at Dorval; it was attended by senior officers from the three services and several hundred family members and friends. At 19:02 hours W/C Mussells lifted North Star 17514 off the runway, closely followed by the rest of the squadron detail. Shortly after takeoff the squadron sorted itself into two VICs of three and flew in formation at 1200 feet over Montreal, dipping their wings in farewell as they passed over Dorval. The formation then headed west for Ottawa and, as they flew over Parliament Hill, dipped their wings in salute to former Prime Minister W.L. MacKenzie King who had died on 22 July, his body laying in state in the rotunda beneath the Peace Tower.

From Ottawa, the squadron proceeded to Toronto, flying over the waterfront and, as it was dusk, all aircraft had their navigation lights on. The unit then broke formation and the aircraft climbed to their assigned altitudes and headed for their first refuelling stop at Winnipeg. After another brief stop at Vancouver all aircraft were at their new operational base by noon on 26 July. Some 18 hours after leaving Dorval, 258 squadron personnel, of which 72 were flight crew members, set about getting themselves ready for an airlift operation which, unknown to them at the time, was to least nearly four years.

Although given a week by the Base Commander to get settled, Mussells advised him that if loads were available three North Stars would be ready to depart for Japan within 36 hours. During the afternoon of 27 July a logistics run, captained by Flight Officer Dean Broadfoot, was despatched to Montreal. That evening three squadron aircraft, captained by Squadron Leaders Harry Lewis and Don Dickson and Flight Lieutenant Art Byford, each carrying 34 US Army personnel, were on their way to Japan. Taking the North Pacific route to Tokyo, stops were made at Anchorage, Shemya and Misawa. Lewis and Dickson returned to McChord after a refuelling stop at Adak in the Aleutians. Both aircraft were back at base on the morning of 31 July after nearly 50 hours in the air and an elapsed time of 82 hours. Byford and his crew returned to base via Misawa, Shemya and Anchorage arriving at McCord early on the morning of 1 August. Their elapsed time was 103 hours of which 50 were spent in the air.

While the bulk of the squadron's missions were carried out using the North Pacific route, the unit also utilized the southern route particularly when carrying out medical-evacuation flights. This took squadron aircraft to Wake Island, Honolulu and Travis AFB (near San Francisco). At various stages of the airlift, servicing and slip crews were positioned at Anchorage, Shemya, Tokyo and Honolulu as well as at McChord. Within a year the squadron returned to its home base at Dorval and its airlift commitments were met by despatching individual aircraft to McChord. In total the squadron completed 599 round trips to Japan carrying troops, high priority cargo and mail. When Flight Officer Bruce Ingall and his crew returned to Montreal on 9 June 1954 in North Star 17510 RCAF, participation in the Korean Airlift ended.

Extracts from *Thunderbird at Peace: Diary of a Transport Squadron*.

REPRINTED FROM:
Esprit de Corps, *Volume 7 Issue 12*
AUTHOR:
Larry Motiuk

CODE WORD IRONSIDES

The frequently-overlooked role of the Lord Strathcona's Horse's Shermans in the Korean War.

ABOVE: *In Korea armour was rarely used other than in a static support fire role.* (SF 5914)

ANYONE WHO USED A radio set in the Korean War era will recognize the "Appointment Code" designation for Armour.

Although Canada's part in the Korean War was primarily an infantry role, the tankers of Lord Strathcona's Horse were an important element of 25 CIBG.

Unlike previous (and subsequent) wars, the fairly static situation in Korea following the formation of the Commonwealth Division, and the very nature of the terrain, neither called for nor favoured the tanks' greatest asset, their mobility. Their other characteristic – fire-power – was often put to better use.

In initial stages of the Korean War, with successive advances and withdrawals for the whole length of the peninsula, both sides made good use of armour. The North Koreans' invasion was spearheaded by Russian-built T-34's, arguably the most effective all-round AFV of the Second World War. With over 200 of these formidable machines, against four U.S. companies equipped with light Chaffee tanks, the North Koreans had a fairly easy ride at first. Not only were the outnumbered UN and ROK forces hopelessly outmatched in armour, but the refusal of the US to provide the South Korean armies with anything but small arms prior to 1950 meant that other anti-tank weapons were few and far between.

REINFORCEMENTS

Eventually, the beleaguered Pusan Perimeter troops were substantially reinforced with more, and heavier, tanks, until the American forces outnumbered the North Koreans by five-to-one in armour, the bulk of it in the form of M4A (Sherman), Pershing and Patton tanks, which proved more than a match for their opponents. By late 1950 the NVA's 105th Armoured Division was no more. After the Inchon and Pusan Perimeter breakouts, 239 destroyed T-34's were found, almost half of them knocked out by aircraft. Only 39 had been destroyed in tank-to-tank action.

The first Commonwealth armour to arrive in Korea were the 8th King's Royal Irish Hussars and a Royal Tank Regiment squadron. These units were soon in action in support of 29 British Brigade, covering the withdrawal of the Royal Ulster Rifles at Chunhung Dong. The tank detachment – "Cooperforce" – suffered 20 killed (including its commander) as well as some of its tanks. The fighting was so fierce that some Centurions evacuating Riflemen from the battlefield were awash with blood from their wounded passengers. The Hussars later saw action in a vain attempt to extricate the Glosters from their Imjin position in April of 1951, and in November of that year supported 1 KSLI in a successful counter-attack on Hill 227.

THE TANK DETACHMENT – "COOPERFORCE" – SUFFERED 20 KILLED (INCLUDING ITS COMMANDER) AS WELL AS SOME OF ITS TANKS. THE FIGHTING WAS SO FIERCE THAT SOME CENTURIONS EVACUATING RIFLEMEN FROM THE BATTLEFIELD WERE AWASH WITH BLOOD FROM THEIR WOUNDED PASSENGERS.

PRESIDENTIAL CITATION

Perhaps the first major Canadian connection with armour occurred at Kapyong, where 2 PPCLI shared the distinction of a US Presidential Citation for their role with Company A, 72nd Heavy Tank Battalion of the US Army. In the words of the Citation, "Company A … supported all units (PPCLI and the Australians) to the full extent of its capacity and in addition kept the main roads open and assisted in evacuating the wounded."

Meanwhile, back in Canada, an armoured element was being prepared for Korea. Major "Jim" Quinn, an officer with a reputation for being "firm but fair," was tasked with forming what was originally entitled the "1/2 Royal Canadian Armoured Corps Squadron" in Camp Borden, Ontario. Major Quinn was lucky enough to be given carte blanche to select his own officers and senior NCOs. He was less fortunate in his allocation of weapons; despite protests the 1/2 Squadron (so named to represent the two Canadian armoured regiments at that time) was to receive the US M-10 seventeen-pounder, which was actually not a tank but an open-turret self-propelled tank-destroyer.

SLOW-ON-SIR

Major General Bruce Legge recalls how the squadron commander obtained one of his nicknames en route to Fort Lewis for training. The major asked one of the dozing troopers on the train how he was doing.

"All right, I guess," was the reply. The indignant Quinn hauled the unfortunate soldier to his feet and roared, "All right, Sir! I won't have any troopers in my squadron who are slow on the 'sir'." From then on, the chastised soldier and his buddies nicknamed their leader "Slow-on-sir Quinn."

REPRINTED FROM:
Esprit de Corps,
Volume 6 Issue 6
AUTHOR:
Les Peate

***Canadian tanks move up to the front lines.** (DND PHOTO)*

IRONSIDES:
SHERMANS AT THE SHARP END

The Strathcona story continues.

IN THE PREVIOUS SEGMENT we left the newly-designated C Squadron, Lord Strathcona's Horse in Fort Lewis.

In April of 1951, the squadron arrived in Korea under Maj Quinn, who had now acquired another nickname – "February." This arose from his penchant for awarding a standard punishment of 28 days in the slammer to the unfortunate troopers found guilty of military transgressions.

Both Quinn and Brig Rockingham had to resist efforts by the British divisional commander to exert the UK influence on the unit. General Cassels would have liked to see the Strathcona's used as an additional squadron under command of the 8th King's Royal Irish Hussars, but Rocky was successful in keeping them in 25 Canadian Infantry Brigade. (The Order of battle for 1 COMWEL Division lists LdSH(RC) as Divisional Troops, but apart from occasional fire support to other UN units they remained more or less under Canadian control.)

IMMEDIATE DELIVERY

More significant was the choice of tanks. Britain hoped that they would adopt the Centurion, used by the British armoured units, in place of the M-10 SP anti-tank weapons. This was no doubt influenced not only by standardization, but by the fact that the UK was desperate for dollars to pay off the World War II debts and could use the bucks (for the same reason the Aussies tried to inflict THEIR rations on Canadian troops). As it might have taken up to a year to obtain the Centurions, Quinn insisted on – and got – M4A Shermans, delivered immediately from US stocks. It was a good choice. While the British tank had, arguably, the best tank gun of its time, the Sherman was far more able to deal with Korea's rugged terrain.

A week after the Shermans arrived, C Squadron was in action. On 25 May they accompanied R22eR on a general advance, sustaining their first casualty and later acquitting themselves well on a nine-mile reconnaisance north of the 38th parallel, returning with a number of Chinese prisoners. The mixed nature of the UN forces was apparent when the Straths were called upon to support the Phillipine Battalion (whose members included a future national president, "Eddie" Ramos).

HEROIC DEFENCE

During the summer, many UN units carried out probes and "reconnaissance in force". The Straths worked very well with the Canadian Infantry battalions; with effective fire support from the tanks always forthcoming. Major Quinn and his successor, Capt (later Major) V.W. Jewkes, developed and used infantry-tank liaison techniques and target indication procedures that later became the model for COMWEL

Division. In particular, the rapport with Lieutenant Colonel Dextraze ("Jadex") of the Vandoos proved most effective, especially during the battle for Hill 227 in November of 1951, where the infantry's heroic defence was bolstered by the Strathcona's tanks.

In October of 1951 the Squadron effectively supported 25 CIBG during Operations MINDEN and COMMANDO – the last significant mobile operation on the Commonwealth front. During the advance, the Brigade War Diary reports: "C Squadron was in support and under the able direction of the (R22eR) company commander, literally fired the troops down the slope, across the valley, and on to the objective."

ABOVE: *A Sherman tank of the Lord Strathcona's Horse negotiating rough terrain.* (DND PHOTO)

MOBILE PILLBOXES

From October 1951, until the ceasefire in July 1953, the infantry dug in on the "Wyoming Line" and most tanks were moved into the forward positions and dug in as "mobile pillboxes." A small reserve of British Centurions remained as a counter-attack force.

During the closing months of the war, A Squadron of the Strathcona's (which had relieved C and later B Squadrons) was used effectively in a sneaky scheme to neutralize Chinese pillboxes. The targets would be plotted, the Shermans would move into forward valleys overnight and would open fire on the enemy at first light, leaving before counter-artillery fire could be brought to bear.

LOSS OF MEN AND MATERIAL

Although the very nature of the war spotlighted the foot-soldier, the Straths had their share of the action. The Sherman proved to be an excellent weapon – it was able to get into spots inaccessible to most other vehicles and its multi-bank engine performed well under the adverse weather conditions. Even so, the regiment suffered losses in men and material. Five troopers died and tanks were destroyed or badly damaged by mines and shell fire.

There were lighter moments. Retired Major General Phil Neatby remembers one time when troops were awaiting inspection by Major Jewkes, a stickler for efficiency. The tanks were spotless an hour before the OC's arrival. However, during that fatal hour an energetic Korean sparrow was able to build a nest in the muzzle of one of the 75 mm guns. Jim Quinn, (who retired as a LGen) recounts the story of Squadron Quarter Master Sergent Doug Everleigh, who contrived to draw rum rations for a non-existent tank delivery troop for a year.

Individual honours were bestowed on Major Jewkes (DSO) and his successor, B Squadron's Major Roxborough, who with his SSM, Warrant Officer Armer received the MBE. "A" Squadron's Major Ellis was awarded the Military Cross, and MM's went to Trooper Roy Stevenson and Sergeant Allen – the latter for his work in supervising the recovery of a tank while under heavy artillery fire. The resourceful SQMS Everleigh and Trooper Wyatt received the MBE; 14 members were Mentioned in Despatches. Perhaps the most unusual award was the US Distinguished Flying Cross, presented to Captain Bill Ward for 81 missions as an observer in the back seat of an AT-6 Harvard with 6147 Tactical Control Group.

The involvement of the Strathconas during the Korean War can be judged by the fact that the Regimental Committee on Battle Honours listed ten engagements between May 1951 and July 1953 in which squadrons took part. Admittedly, in three of these the tanks neither fired nor were fired upon. Other claims were refused as they did not involve "a major part of the unit" – most involved only one or two troops. However, Lord Strathcona's Horse proudly display the theatre honour "Korea 1951 – 1953" on their Guidon – and well deserve it. *(Thanks to Colonel John Gardam for permission to refer to his book* Korea Volunteer.*)*

REPRINTED FROM:
Esprit de Corps, *Volume 6 Issue 7*
AUTHOR: *Les Peate*

ALTHOUGH THE VERY NATURE OF THE WAR SPOTLIGHTED THE FOOT-SOLDIER, THE 'STRATHS' HAD THEIR SHARE OF THE ACTION. THE SHERMAN PROVED TO BE AN EXCELLENT WEAPON – IT WAS ABLE TO GET INTO SPOTS INACCESSIBLE TO MOST OTHER VEHICLES AND ITS MULTI-BANK ENGINE PERFORMED WELL UNDER THE ADVERSE WEATHER CONDITIONS. EVEN SO, THE REGIMENT SUFFERED LOSSES IN MEN AND MATERIAL. FIVE TROOPERS DIED AND TANKS WERE DESTROYED OR BADLY DAMAGED BY MINES AND SHELL FIRE.

OF MINES AND MAYHEM

A mix of leftover mines from several armies and Chinese ingenuity, made mine-clearing a hazardous task.

ABOVE, LEFT:
Chinese troops were skilled at penetrating the UN frontlines at night in order to lay minefields. These soldiers are using Russian-made box mines.
ABOVE, RIGHT:
A graphic road sign welcomes approaching infantry to the Main Line of Resistance.

ONE STORY THAT WENT the rounds shortly after the Second World War told of a visitor to the Middle East who found that the inhabitants had changed their customs, and, instead of the male head of the household leading the way on the narrow trails, he now let his wife precede him. "Western courtesy?" he asked. "No, landmines!" was the response.

When I joined the Army, it was forcibly brought home that landmines were no laughing matter. A shattered hut in my basic training unit bore witness to an incident where a senior NCO instructor, seeking to demonstrate that a "75 Grenade" (which was really a messtin-size anti-tank mine) would not explode if a human individual trod on it, was proven wrong the hard way.

The first RSM of 2PPCLI, "Jim" Wood, DCM, was demonstrating a captured Chinese landmine in January of 1951, when that, too, exploded, making RSM Wood the Patricia's first fatal casualty in Korea.

Mine-clearing in Korea was a hairy task for our field engineers, pioneer platoons and, in some cases, even members of rifle companies. A multiplicity of anti-vehicle and anti-personnel mines were to be found. The North Koreans and their Chinese allies used a mixture of WWII relics (many of them already unstable due to age) and Russian or Chinese manufactured mines. Some had wooden bodies, reducing the effectiveness of magnetic detectors. Others, perhaps those most feared and detested by our troops, were known as "de-bollockers" because, when detonated, they would spring about two feet in the air before exploding. In addition, both sides would improvise various ingenious mines and booby-traps.

TWO STRETCHER-BEARERS, CARRYING OUT ONE OF THE WOUNDED, SET OFF ANOTHER MINE. BY THE TIME THE HELPERS HAD BEEN ORDERED TO "FREEZE" PENDING THE ARRIVAL OF BATTALION PIONEERS, SIX OF THE PLATOON HAD BECOME CASUALTIES

One Chinese innovation which I remember well consisted of a 36 type grenade which would be plastered with mud or clay. When the mud had set, the pin would be removed but the striker would be held in place by the gunk. Anyone treading on or kicking the "mud-ball" would break the mould and allow the thing to detonate. They would also be dropped behind our lines by enemy patrols and, when it rained heavily (a common occurrence in Korean summers), the mud would melt away and we would be subject to mysterious explosions which, if nothing else, disturbed our meagre sleep.

The most tragic experience I had with mines was one summer evening in 1952. We heard several explosions in front of our neighbouring platoon and, soon after, were ordered to send a section to take over their position. It turned out that the inner minefield marker had slipped down a slope and a patrol, thinking that they were skirting a minefield laid by the previous occupants (1PPCLI), were in fact inside the deadly area. Two members were injured, one killed.

Subsequently two stretcher-bearers, carrying out one of the wounded, set off another mine. By the time the helpers had been ordered to "freeze" pending the arrival of Battalion pioneers, six of the platoon had become casualties, and the platoon was finished as an effective fighting unit. Luckily, the Chinese did not catch on to what was happening, and so we were spared the additional ordeal of harassing artillery fire during the rescue process.

NO PLACE FOR THE FAINT-HEARTED

Despite comments made by General Maurice Baril (Chief of the Defence Staff) in 1998, that anti-personnel mines are "cowardly weapons," most field engineers would agree that the tasks of laying and clearing minefields are not jobs for the faint-hearted. Unlike the anti-personnel mines which are scattered randomly by various militant fac-

ABOVE, LEFT: *Next to artillery fire, landmines were the number one cause of casualties during the Korean War. (NAC)*
ABOVE, RIGHT: *A recuperating Vandoo and buddy share a lighter moment at a military hospital in Japan. (DND PHOTO)*

tions, allied minefields were laid in accordance with strict rules. They had to be approved by higher formation and located by grid reference on special maps. Each minefield was surrounded by barbed wire and warning signs in applicable languages prominently displayed. Within the field, the mines – be they anti-vehicle, anti-personnel or a mixture of the two – were laid in set patterns. (The Lord helps fools: One area near a NAAFI canteen by the Main Supply Route was nice and level and someone had conveniently wired it off. British troops used it as a soccer field for weeks, until a horrified Engineer pointed out that their "arena" was a minefield, which was quickly neutralized without casualties.)

Defensive minefields are a useful weapon and, if used properly, can, in fact, reduce casualties. Their purpose is not so much to "kill" as to slow or halt enemy advances, or to channel them into "killing grounds" where they can be dealt with by more discriminating weapon systems. Tactical doctrine usually requires that they be covered by fire, to further delay an advancing foe.

Anyone in his right mind would condemn the indiscriminate anti-personnel mines which kill and maim soldiers and innocent civilians alike. Like the bombs and booby-traps used by terrorist groups, they are an unnecessary abomination of doubtful military effectiveness. Canada, rightly, has taken the lead in demanding the abolition of these. However, there is another side to the coin.

DESPITE GENERAL BARIL'S COMMENTS THAT ANTI-PERSONNEL MINES ARE "COWARDLY WEAPONS," FIELD ENGINEERS BELIEVE THAT THE TASKS OF LAYING AND CLEARING MINEFIELDS ARE NOT JOBS FOR THE FAINT-HEARTED.

Both the US and South Korea, among others, have been under fire because they feel that they cannot discontinue the defensive minefield which form part of the defences south of Korea's demilitarized zone.

REPRINTED FROM:
Esprit de Corps, *Volume 6 Issue 3*
AUTHOR:
Les Peate

There is blood on the hills of Korea
The blood of the brave and the true…

BLOOD ON THE HILLS

The medics' 'Geneva Convention cards' were of little use under heavy artillery fire. It wasn't like M.A.S.H. – these doctors were serious!

SO BEGINS A WIDELY-circulated poem, known to most members of the Commonwealth forces in Korea. There was indeed blood – at times a great deal of it – spilt in many areas of Korea known only by nicknames (such as "Pork Chop Hill", or "The Hook") or by contour references (Hill 355, Hill 187). Many of the Canadians whose blood enriched the soil of the Korean peninsula did not return. Five hundred and sixteen Canadian servicemen gave their lives in the Korean War.

A surprisingly high number of Canadian casualties survived their wounds, and in many cases, returned to their units to continue the fight. Over 1000 servicemen were wounded – in some cases more than once. Despite the primitive and unhygienic living conditions in the Korean battle area, the fatality rate of the injured "backloaded" to hospitals was little over half of the Second World War figures.

INNOVATIVE EVACUATIONS

A very significant factor was the speed in which a casualty could be given specialized surgical treatment. One innovation of the Korean War was the use of helicopters for casualty evacuation. It was in Korea that the chopper proved its worth. Instead of a long, dangerous and uncomfortable trip over substandard roads, the wounded soldier could be taken directly to a field surgical hospital in a few minutes. The US Army helicopter pilots would bring their choppers right into the front-line positions, and the medics quickly became skilled in providing emergency treatment en route. Despite the fact that the earlier S-52 models airlifted the

RIGHT:
Korean porters bringing a wounded Canadian from a forward position.
(DND PHOTO)

wounded in stretcher pods outside the fuselage, the medics were able to perform life-saving work in the air, even providing blood transfusions.

In the book *At War in Korea*, George Forty, a former tank officer, himself a "client" of the service, recalls that "the casevac chopper, with its...external pods (containing stretchers) became a regular sight in the battle area. It was estimated that they could normally get a casualty on to an operating table within an hour of his being wounded."

Unfortunately, not everyone could be evacuated by helicopter. Lack of suitable helipads in the rough terrain at the sharp end, enemy artillery and mortar fire, weather conditions and, sometimes, heavy casualty loads and limited numbers of aircraft were all factors. Often it was necessary for harassed medical officers or orderlies to establish triage systems to ensure that the air evacuation could be most effectively utilized. Abdominal and head wounds, and those requiring immediate surgery, normally got priority. There were still cracks in the system. One Korean farmer was treated at an advanced dressing station for minor injuries, and went to sleep on a stretcher outside. Unfortunately, he chose a bed at the "Category A" section of the triage area and awoke from his slumbers to find himself strapped to the side of a Sikorsky helicopter, hundreds of feet in the air. On landing at the Mobile Army Surgical Hospital (MASH) unit, he reportedly broke all speed records in fleeing to his native hillside.

EFFICIENCY SAVED LIVES

Even without the helicopters, the professional and efficient casualty-handling procedures undoubtedly saved many lives. Clovis Bordeleau was one of a number of PPCLI soldiers wounded in the forward area by Chinese artillery. Despite the severity of his wounds, he was conscious enough to be amazed at the speed and efficiency with which he was treated and backloaded.

Bordeleau's experience was typical of many. As soon as he was hit, he was treated by unit stretcher-bearers. (In some cases a Royal Canadian Army Medical Corps (RCAMC) orderly would be located in a rifle company, but there were not always enough of these specialists to go around.) Field and Shell dressings were applied to stop the bleeding. "Our troops are trained to use the *victim*'s dressing – none of the heroic use of your own – which you might need yourself next," Bordeleau recalls.

The next – and perhaps the most uncomfortable – part of the backloading process was the trip to the Regimental Aid Post (RAP) on a stretcher (I believe that the expression is now a "litter.") This took place over undulating ground, through narrow communication trenches and possibly as far as a mile or more. While the unit supplied stretcher-bearers (often a secondary role of the battalion musicians) most casualties were carried back by Korean Service Corps porters – the overworked, underpaid and unsung heroes who kept the troops in the line supplied with the necessities of life.

MEDICAL PROCEDURES

At the RAP, Corporal Bordeleau was examined by the unit medical officer, who diagnosed his injuries, changed his blood-soaked dressings, and despatched him by ambulance to the Advanced Dressing Station (ADS) – a part of the Canadian Field Ambulance. In some cases the Field Ambulance might set up Casualty Collection Points (CCP) close to the line. Les Pike, a RCAMC veteran of Korea, remembers that these were so far forward that he and his colleagues often found themselves in the PPCLI or RCR lines.

Bordeleau recalls, too, that he was fortunate in that he travelled to the ADS in the relative comfort of a "real, box ambulance" rather than one of the Battalion's litter jeeps which may have been handy but were decidedly uncomfortable and exposed to all weathers. 28 Commonwealth Brigade was served by an Indian Field Ambulance which eventually became the longest-serving Commonwealth unit in Korea.

CONVERTED COACHES

From the ADS, Corporal Bordeleau was transported directly to the Commonwealth Military Hospital at Seoul. One of Canada's significant contributions to the Commonwealth Division was a 200-bed Casualty Clearing Station (CCS) near the Tangkok railhead. Casualties were sent back from Tangkok by road or rail – one US innovation was the conversion of civilian-type coaches for rail use, with provision for stretchers – a distinctly smoother ride.

After treatment in Seoul, Bordeleau was airlifted to Kure, Japan, to the Commonwealth Base Hospital – a permanent building with every available facility. Following a lengthy stay there he was considered sufficiently recovered to be given "recuperative duties". The light duty in question was a spell at the Haramura Battle School in the hills, and the Corporal was no doubt relieved to eventually return to his battalion!

I can almost hear the TV addicts crying "What about the M*A*S*H? You haven't mentioned the M*A*S*H!" Like all of the formations in Korea, the Commonwealth Division was served by a Mobile Army Surgical Hospital. "MASH" fans, if they could be transported back in time, would be disappointed with our facility – Norway's contribution to the Korean War effort. There were no unprofessional shenanigans, none of the male members of the unit paraded in female dress and the dedicated surgeons and medical staff carried out their duties in a professional and efficient manner. The Norwegian flag in the Pusan military cemetery commemorates two Norwegian MASH members who gave their lives in Korea.

FORWARD LOCATION

The 60 to 70-bed MASH was the most forward location where major surgery could be regularly performed, and patients usually remained there until they could be removed to other hospitals. During its stay in Korea the Norwegian MASH treated almost 100,000 military and civilian casualties, many of them Commonwealth troops.

Overall, the Royal Canadian Medical Corps, together with their fellow-medics from other Commonwealth countries, the RCASC ambulance drivers, the casevac helicopter pilots and our Scandinavian allies constituted a complex but highly efficient medical system. Many times equipment was in short supply and improvisation was the order of the day – the extremes of climate were a problem, as was the ever-present dust from paddy-fields fertilized with human waste.

The value of the work of the RCAMC members in Korea is reflected in the fact that they were awarded 15 decorations, (including one of the only eight Distinguished Conduct Medals awarded to Canadians in the entire war) as well as 14 "Mentions in Dispatches." However, the evacuation process began at the unit level, and it is perhaps fitting that the verse at the start of this story is attributed to a RCR stretcher-bearer, Pat O'Connor who was killed in the line of duty on 30 May 1951.

On 3 October, 1951, 2 Battalion, The Royal Canadian Regiment, was moving forward against enemy opposition as part of a general attack launched by our own forces. "B" Company was ordered forward from the Naechon feature, an intermediate objective, to the final object on the right flank of the battalion, the feature Nabu'Ri. At 17:45 hrs No. 6 Platoon came under very heavy and accurate enemy small arms and mortar fire from the left flank and intense machine-gun fire right flank. Within a few minutes, a dozen casualties had been suffered by the platoon, some of them critical.

CASUALTIES LOST

Because of the steep slopes and thick underbrush it was not possible to determine precisely the nature and location of all the casualties, and there was a real danger that some of them would be lost to the enemy where they fell. Corporal Poole, of the Royal Canadian Army Medical Corps was the non-commissioned officer in charge of stretcher bearers with B Company during this operation; his actions in dealing with the casualties suffered gave evidence of courage of the highest order under enemy fire and contributed very markedly to the ultimate success of the operation. Corporal Poole proceeded forward through intense enemy mortar and shell fire to render first aid and arrange for the evacuation of the wounded. He was warned that he could be killed but he insisted "I have a job to do and I am going to do it." He searched meticulously the whole area and did not stop until satisfied that all casualties had been accounted for. Enemy artillery and mortars were harassing the area, and enemy snipers and machine gunners made any movement hazardous but nothing could deter him in his search for the wounded. Two of the casualties were again hit while he was tending them but he continued with unruffled calm to render aid. While still under fire he improvised stretchers from rifles and branches of trees; he bound the casualties securely by using thick vines. He moved from man to man with complete disregard for his own safety; his steady hand and quiet courage brought relief to all the wounded.

OPPOSITE PAGE:
Despite being wounded by enemy shrapnel, Sergeant Neil McKerracher (of Thamesville, Ontario) remained at his frontline post. (NAC PA 128818)

RIGHT:
Canadian medics treat a wounded soldier at a forward casualty clearing station. In all, the Canadian Army suffered 1588 battle casualties in Korea. Of these 516 were killed in action. (SF 1811)

MAINTAINING THE MOMENTUM

No. 5 Platoon was ordered to pass through No. 6 Platoon in order to maintain the momentum of the attack. They too came under heavy fire and suffered serious casualties. Corporal Poole was on hand at once and urged the Platoon commander "Go on, I will see that your men get good care." When the wounded had been prepared for evacuation, Corporal Poole led his party of bearers back some 3000 yards in the dark to the regimental aid post. The route was subjected to continuous shell fire, enemy patrols had infiltrated along both sides, the area was heavily mined, and even the natural hazards were enough to deter any but the very brave. But Corporal Poole led his party with confidence and all the casualties were borne safely to the regimental aid post. Undoubtedly his leadership and the persistence with which he carried out his duties against any odds was vital in saving the lives of one officer and three other ranks and in preventing two of the wounded from falling into the hands of the enemy.

DUTY TO THE WOUNDED

Throughout the day of 3 October, all that night and the next day, Corporal Poole continued his task of attending the needs of the wounded. Whenever first aid was required he was present to administer it. He was utterly tireless in his work. During the operation one thought only dominated his action: that his duty was to tend his wounded comrades. No obstacle, no hazard, no personal danger, was allowed to stand in his way; his selfless devotion to his work was in the highest traditions of military service. Corporal Poole's conscientious determination to carry out his duties, his complete disregard for his own well being, his exemplary conduct under the most adverse conditions and his outstanding leadership resulted not only in saving the lives of five men and making possible the evacuation and treatment of many others, but, even more, inspired his comrades to maintain the fight and contributed largely to the successful attainment of the objective.

This is the citation submitted for the award.

Corporal Poole was awarded the Distinguished Conduct Medal for his courage and devotion to duty.

REPRINTED FROM:
Esprit de Corps, *Volume 4 Issue 2*
AUTHOR:
Les Peate

FOOD FOR THOUGHT

As Napoleon said, "an army marches on its stomach." How this author gained 80 pounds on C-rations.

TO AVIATION BUFFS A P-38 is the twin-boomed Lockheed Lightning fighter, while small-arms experts may identify it as an effective sidearm. Korea veterans may not recognize it by this nomenclature, but it is in fact a piece of equipment which they have probably used more than any other. This is the identification code name for the C-Ration can opener, that little hinged metal 'doohickey' which most of us wore beside our dogtags.

Feeding the multi-national troops of the First Commonwealth Division was an achievement second only to the miraculous use of loaves and fish over 1900 years earlier.

The overall Commonwealth commander in the theatre was Lieutenant General Sir Horace Robertson, an Australian. Naturally, he hoped that the Commonwealth troops would use Aussie rations – Australia, like most Commonwealth countries, could use the dollars. In fact, after the limited British scale of issue, I found that Aussie food was excellent (including breakfasts of steak and eggs). However, Brigadier Rockingham dug in his heels, insisted that his troops were used to American food, and Canadians spent most of the Korean War on American rations.

PROBLEM COMPOUNDED

The overall supply problem for the Division was complicated by the fact that generally the British, Australian and New Zealand troops lived on US "C-Rations" in the line and a combination of Australian and locally purchased fresh rations and British "compo" rations in reserve. The Canadian Brigade enjoyed US rations, while the Indian Field Ambulance had its own special food. This problem did not apply only to rations. Equipment, weapons and ammunition varied between the national units, necessitating, among other things, an additional 120 vehicles to pick up and deliver these from different supply points.

While C-Rations undoubtedly had a high caloric value (the author gained almost 80 pounds during the 18 months that they constituted most of his diet), they tended towards monotony. They arrived in cartons of six individual boxes, each of which contained one day's ration. (The large cartons were much sought after for lining bunker walls or for fuel.) Each individual ration contained "meal" units, which included such delicacies as ground meat and spaghetti, hamburger patties, chicken stew, beans (allegedly) with pork and ham and lima beans.

LEFT: *Soldiers of 2RCR line up for a rare dessert treat at the appropriately named "Duke's Donut Dive." Field kitchens such as this were a rear area luxury.* (PAC PA 191156)

AND THE BEST PART...

There was also a "B" Unit, which included a jelly or chocolate disc, a small tin of jam and some crackers. A can of fruit was also included, as well as a "goody" package which contained matches, chewing gum, coffee, sugar, powdered milk, a disposable can-opener and – a real treasure to those so addicted – a package of 20 cigarettes. To complete one's dining pleasure, three plastic spoons were also included in the box. (As the food could be heated and eaten straight from the can, and the "B" unit cans made good drinking cups, dish-washing in the line was reduced to a minimum. The opened tops of the cans also made ideal "measures" for the rum ration.)

C-rations could be eaten cold, heated over sterno cans or solid fuel "tommy-cookers" or, in bulk, immersed in dixies of boiling water until they were hot. My first experience of these was on the train from Pusan to the front, where the "dining car" proved to be a US cook-sergeant dishing out a can apiece (there was no choice – you got what came up in the draw).

MAGICIANS

Out of the line Canadians were usually well fed. Where possible, fresh meat and vegetables were provided, and the cooks worked wonders on the M-39 cookers and anything else that they could improvise. Occasionally British "ten-in-one" rations would find their way into Canadian hands. These were designed to feed one man for ten days, ten men for one day or any combination in between. While many of their contents were unpalatable to Canadian tastes, they did contain several tasty items, such as oatmeal cookies and canned bacon. The ubiquitous "bully beef" was a British staple, and, of course, lots of tea (boiled with condensed milk).

OUT OF THE LINE CANADIANS WERE USUALLY WELL FED. WHERE POSSIBLE, FRESH MEAT AND VEGETABLES WERE PROVIDED, AND THE COOKS WORKED WONDERS ON THE M-39 COOKERS AND ANYTHING ELSE THAT THEY COULD IMPROVISE.

MORE TREATS

Another treat was the US "101-pack" ration supplement. This contained all sorts of 'goodies' including candies, more canned fruit, razor blades, lighter flints, candles, cigarettes and even chewing and pipe tobacco. The effect of chewing tobacco on unsuspecting novices to this addiction was awesome. Also included were Hershey chocolate bars (this gave rise to a derisive mocking of our US allies "goddamn, the Fourth of July and NO Hershey bars"). Less popular were "K-Rations" which were supposed to provide one meal. The omelettes were tasteless and almost impossible to heat over our "sterno" burners without becoming charred on the outside and cold in the centre. Fruit, other goodies and seven cigarettes came with these. To Koje-do North Korean POWs were given "time-expired" K-Rations (minus the cigarettes) to supplement their rice and vegetable rations. Some of us felt that, like Peter Worthington's "gift" of ham and lima beans to the Chinese, this may have constituted cruel and unusual punishment.

Occasionally, too, we would receive cans

of British self-heating soup. This consisted of a can of tomato or oxtail soup with a chemical heating agent in the centre, which could come to boil in a very short time. It was ideal for wet and wintry nights in the slit trenches.

GIFT BOXES

Thanks to organizations at home, food packages came along from time to time. (I remember one especially appetizing gift box from an Australian ladies' patriotic association.) When we were out on the line, we also visited the NAAFI "road-houses" for "tea and buns," or the US Red Cross mobile canteens which provided free coffee and donuts. Nor must we forget the staple beverage of North American troops. Its importance was evident on arrival in Pusan where, on the quayside, a large sign proudly proclaimed the presence of a numbered Quartermaster Co., a Coca-Cola bottling unit.

All in all, our cooks and supply services did a pretty good job of keeping us well fed. I would be remiss if I did not also credit the porters of the Korean Service Corps who carried the C-Rations, water and, of course, the Asahi beer quota to our forward positions. To our Service Corps and unit cooks and their British counterparts of the Army Catering Corps (ACC), whose initials were unjustly interpreted as "Any C*** can Cook," a belated "thank you" from a grateful – and well-fed – Korea vet.

REPRINTED FROM:
Esprit de Corps,
Volume 5 Issue 9
AUTHOR: *Les Peate*

RIGHT:
Canadian breweries would often donate their products to the troops in Korea - much to the soldiers' delight.
(BOB MAHAR)

Drinking is the soldier's pleasure... Of booze and bootleggers.

HOLD THE KIMSHI

THE SOMEWHAT ODD TITLE refers to a book by Robert Peacock, entitled *Kimshi, Asahi and Rum.* The book recounts Colonel Peacock's experiences in Korea with PPCLI.

Kimshi, for the benefit of the uninitiated and unwary, is a particularly potent form of Korean "sauerkraut". Each family had its own jealously-guarded recipe, but normal additions included garlic, hot peppers, other spices and perhaps dried fish. It was an ideal food additive during the Korean winters and there is little doubt of its effectiveness as a blood purifier in summer.

ASAHI AND RUM

While some brave Canadians would obtain Kimshi from the Korean porters to supplement their C-Rations, my article deals with Colonel Peacock's other ingredients - the Asahi and the Rum.

Over the centuries, soldiers and booze have been closely associated - sometimes unjustly. Certainly the ingenuity of Canadian soldiers over the last three wars in obtaining and concealing intoxicants of all kinds is almost legendary. (One popular story from Korea tells of a British medical officer who reported to his CO that he had discovered two cases of beri-beri. The alleged response was to "give it to the Canadians, they'll drink anything".)

While some of the legends may be based on fact, in most cases the troops, particularly those in the "sharp end" have often been sorely maligned. Perhaps the most sobering influence on our troops in Korea was lack of opportunity. While the troops in the "A" and "B" echelons and the supporting units were able to establish "wet canteens," these were lacking in the forward company areas. In the first place, after digging weapon pits, communication trenches, mortar positions, living bunkers and latrines, very few infantrymen had the energy, the space, the time or the materials to construct a suitable "drinking hole."

The nature of the job itself discouraged excessive drinking. A soldier on watch in his weapon slit would often find it difficult enough to stay awake for his two-hour "stag" without the soporific effects of over-indulgence. Although a number of unsubstantiated stories continue to make the rounds regarding heroic deeds performed under the influence of "Dutch Courage"

a cool head and quick reactions were essential in battle.

The most deciding factor, however, was one of supply. Not only was the quantity "rationed" by the supplier, but every bottle had to be carried to forward positions by Korean porters. Their numbers were limited, and other items such as ammunition, food, defensive stores, fuel and water were also back packed by these unsung heroes on primitive wooden "A"-frames. The beer ration was often superseded by more operationally-vital supplies.

The prevalent brand of beer was Japanese Asahi lager distributed through the British Navy, Army and Air Force Institutes – the NAAFI. (An acronym which detractors said was short for "No ambition and f- - - all interest!"). This nectar was packed in cases of 24 quart bottles, each individually covered with straw. The wooden cases were greatly prized as makeshift furniture, fuel for wood-burning space heaters and (as I mentioned in a previous article) toilet seats in field latrines. Asahi beer cost about 18 cents a bottle (even so, the impecunious British troops soon discovered that NAAFI would replace any broken bottles in exchange for bottlenecks with the caps still intact. They learned to remove caps without a mark, drink the beer, replace the caps, smash the bottles and return the necks for replacement.)

The bottles, too, had a certain value. By tying a piece of gasoline-soaked string around the body of the bottle, lighting it and, when it had burned out, tapping the head of bottle sharply, one would be left with a fairly serviceable drinking glass. Manufacture of these items was a fairly lucrative "cottage industry" among the few Korean residents remaining in the forward areas. Unsubstantiated legends also credit one Victoria Cross winner with retaking a Chinese-held position by throwing empty "Asahi" bottles at the enemy when he ran out of grenades.

Occasionally beer from home arrived. Particularly generous in shipping samples of its product to Canadians in the field was John Labatt's brewery. In fact, one Royal Canadian Engineer (RCE) unit expressed its appreciation by naming one of its bridges "Mr. John Labatt's Anniversary Bridge. " Other sources of the beverage were the UK brewers (through NAAFI) and, in Japan and some base areas, the Australian forces' brewery.

THE INFAMOUS RUM RATION

Perhaps the most potent "legal" beverage was the Rum Ration, which came in stone crocks marked "S.R.D.". There were many versions of the meaning of "SRD", the most common being "Service Rum, Diluted." If SRD was "diluted" I would caution anyone against drinking spirit neat! It was normally issued in cold or wet weather, and each platoon would receive about a quart daily. Logistical problems precluded the use of regular "mixes," although the US Army Quartermaster Corps did in fact have a Coca-Cola bottling unit in Pusan! The recipient would usually drink his rum "straight" or add a mix of (chlorinated) water and lemonade powder, or to coffee or tea. In my platoon most of the members were teenagers, and despite the pleas of the old sweats, we would add the ration to a dixie of hot tea and issue a mug of the brew on conclusion of a sentry's watch, or on return from patrol.

In addition to the rum ration, senior NCO's and officers were allowed to purchase a bottle of whisky and a bottle of one other beverage (gin, rum, brandy etc) each month. The cost was about a dollar a bottle. Although, theoretically, the rank and file were not allowed spiritous liquors, the ingenuity of the Canadian soldier came to the fore. Large loaves of bread in parcels from home were not intended to provide relief from "C" ration crackers and hardtack, but often, hollowed out, concealed bottles of stimulating beverages.

DEMAND OVERESTIMATED

While the NAAFI controlled most spiritous liquors, they frequently over-estimated the demand for more exotic potions and were left with large stocks of Grand Marnier, Apricot Brandy, Creme-de-Menthe and similar fancy drinks. In exchange for a few bucks, the dollar-starved NAAFI staff might be prepared to let thirsty soldiers have a few bottles of these.

I remember on one occasion watching with admiration and horror as a Kiwi gunner "chug-a-lugged" a whole bottle of Benedictine. I once made the mistake of ordering a case of 96 bottles of Guinness for my platoon and found that the beer drinking minority had become so addicted to Asahi that I could not unload any of it. The laxative effect of the stout alone (see use of Asahi beer box, above) necessitated mixing it and

OPPOSITE PAGE:
One bottle per man per day was the beer ration permitted for men in Korea. Here troops of 3R22eR eagerly receive their allotment of beer from the British NAAFI (Navy, Army, Air Force Institutes) supply centre.
(R22ER MUSEUM)

RIGHT:
Canadian ration packs arrive at the front. Bottles of 'issue' rum were often traded to the alcohol free (dry) U.S. soldiers in exchange for a variety of creature comforts.

I was able to obtain a case of Moët & Chandon champagne at about 60 cents a bottle. This resulted in what would undoubtedly be a godsend to the detractors of the military today – a scruffy-looking infantryman digging out pork and beans from a can and washing it down with mess tins full of "Black Velvet."

DRY ALLIES

One aspect of our access to alcoholic beverages affected most of the troops in the line. For some reason – I believe that it was pressure on the US War Department by womens' temperance groups – our American allies were "dry." This may have been to provide business for the Coca-Cola Bottling Company mentioned above. In any case, they had the "good stuff" – space heaters, flashlights, batteries, .45 calibre pistols and other items which made life in the line more bearable. They also had lots of disposable income – a particularly attractive consideration to the British troops who were officially forbidden to possess the US "scrip" which was a necessity for making PX purchases or using the US clubs in Tokyo on R&R leave. Bootlegging operations reminiscent of the Capone era were commonplace – you had only to visit a US supply depot with a partly-concealed bottle of Scotch and the world was your oyster! The impecunious British found to their delight that the going rate for Asahi beer was the then unheard of $1.00 for a quart bottle.

THE AMERICANS HAD LOTS OF DISPOSABLE INCOME – A PARTICULARLY ATTRACTIVE CONSIDERATION TO THE BRITISH

UNAUTHORIZED SOURCES

Not all the beverages came from authorized sources. Former RCEME member Don Randall, writing in the "Uijongbu Club" newsletter recalls that "those of who, against orders, tried the Korean home-made spirits kept in a crock in farmhouse kitchens will not even yet forget its fragance, taste and kick. Surely some of you... have experienced unsteadiness and perhaps a fall into a moonlit rice paddy or worse after a night foray into the boondocks!"

In some cases the results were more severe. John Melady in *Korea, Canada's Forgotten War*, relates that after celebrating St. Patrick's Day with a concoction of wood alcohol-based spirits, several members of 2PPCLI succumbed – four of them fatally. The Patricia's Commanding Officer, Lieutenant Colonel "Big Jim" Stone, reportedly had the battalion pass in front of the bodies in single file – a brutal but salutary object-lesson. Certainly the effects of locally-produced liquors were not to be ignored and signs such as "Korean Whisky KILLS" were prominently displayed along roads in the Division area.

To quote Don Randall once again: "It is difficult... for many of the Korea vets to think of their general experiences in the war in terms which are unrelated to alcohol... In my unit, non-drinkers were rare and suspected of being possessed of other unsociable habits." Don recalls that, while in Japan, his group added another dimension to their imbibing experience by sending their houseboy to purchase supplies of saki. Notwithstanding these experiences and the undoubted excesses which occurred on R&R leave and in transit, alcohol abuse by the line troops was fairly rare. As Don Randall recalls "we Canadians were trusted with alcohol to a greater extent than were American soldiers."

To quote John Dryden "Drinking is the soldier's pleasure!" Thanks to NAAFI, the Canadian brewers and those intelligent supply authorities, that pleasure was not denied to our troops in Korea.

REPRINTED FROM:
Esprit de Corps, *Volume 3 Issue 6*
AUTHOR: *Les Peate*

CALM RESTORED

Despite the ceasefire in 1953, all was not peace and harmony around the DMZ.

COLONEL BILL SUTHERLAND well remembers the morning of 27 July 1953. "It developed into a really nice day," he recalls. Not only did the sun break through the heavy overcast, but unknown to the troops in the line, this was to be the last day of the Korean War.

It was not a complete surprise - ceasefire negotiations had been under way for over two years. In some ways these were as acrimonious and bitter as the fighting in the line.

Before the Korean War was a year old, Yakov Malik, the Soviet Ambassador to the UN, agreed with US proposals that an attempt should be made to cease hostilities. In late June of 1951 the UN Commander, General Ridgway, invited the Chinese and North Korean military leaders to meet and discuss armistice terms.

TEAHOUSE TALKS

The talks began on 10 July 1951 in a teahouse in Kaesong (a few kilometres south of the original border between the two Koreas, the 38th Parallel) at that time held by the Communists. The UN negotiating team was headed by US Admiral C.Turner Joy, while North Korean General Nam Il was the senior Communist negotiator.

From the start it was obvious that the North Koreans and Chinese were fighting a psychological "war-within-a-war." Communist "escorts" adopted a belligerent attitude to their "guests" and at the negotiating table Admiral Joy and his team were directed to chairs placed in unfavourable locations, and which had their legs shortened to place their occupants in humiliating positions. One North Korean general lengthily harangued the UN team, ignoring a horde of flies which crawled over his face. This effort to demonstrate self-control backfired, as the UN officers concluded that this indicated that he was used to being insect-infested!

A nine-point agenda put forward by the UN team was rejected; the Communists countered with a simple proposal to return to the *status quo ante bellum* with both forces withdrawing to their own side of the 38th Parallel and all "foreign" troops leaving Korea. Although the latter point was later conceded, the North Koreans and Chinese adamantly insisted in the adoption of the Parallel as the demarcation line.

It soon became evident that talks were fruitless - the pressing question of prisoners-of-war was brushed aside. Several allegations of violation of the "neutral" Kaesong area by United Nations aircraft were presented - most if not all of them patently unfounded. Finally, on 22 August 1951, General Nam Il abruptly broke off negotiations.

Talks resumed on 25 October of that year at nearby Panmunjon. The new site was close to the Commonwealth Division area, and the balloons that marked the location by day and the night-time searchlights provided excellent navigational aides to our patrols.

Discussion dragged on; the three main issues being the location of the Cease Fire line, withdrawal of "foreign" troops and repatriation of prisoners of war. The latter was a major concern – over half of the North Korean prisoners interviewed wished to stay in the South, and their numbers far exceeded those of the Republic of Korea and UN troops held by the Communists.

TALKS SUSPENDED

The "face-maintaining" battle continued. Surreptitious introduction of ever larger national flags on the discussion table, acquisition of prestigious seating locations and carefully orchestrated news photographs were normal occurrences. The talks were again suspended for a six-month period (ironically at this time an exchange of sick and wounded POWs was arranged by the field commanders).

Finally, by June 1953 (three years after the North Korean Army invaded the South) the negotiators reached an acceptable agreement. POW repatriation would be handled by Indian troops (although India had contributed a Field Ambulance as part of the Commonwealth Division, her impartiality was accepted). The boundary would conform to the current front lines and the US would be allowed to maintain a military presence in South Korea.

While this accord was acceptable to the Communist and UN governments, South Korea's President Syngman Rhee adamantly opposed the arrangements and

OPPOSITE PAGE:
Canadian soldiers in the line were relieved to hear that an armistice had been signed on 27 July 1953. Here, American General Mark Clark pens the cease-fire agreement.
(U.S. ARMY)

RIGHT:
Aerial view of Panmunjon, site of the signing.
(U.S. NAVY)

NEXT PAGE:
Members of the Lord Strathcona's Horse celebrate news of the armistice.
(JIM LYNCH)

threatened to continue the war alone if they were accepted. He was especially stubborn regarding the proposal to forward all prisoners for screening at Panmunjon, as the majority of prisoners held in South Korea had indicated no desire to return home. Rhee engineered the mass "escape" of over seventy thousand North Korean captives. A shooting battle erupted between US guards and ROK military police freeing the prisoners, most of whom were never recaptured. While continuing to express his disapproval, Rhee finally, grudgingly, agreed not to stand in the way of the proposed armistice arrangements.

Through the night of 26 July 1953, carpenters in Panmunjon worked feverishly to construct a special building for the signing of the armistice agreement.

At precisely 10:00 hrs on the following day, Generals Nam Il and Harrison (who had replaced Admiral Joy as the UN representative) signed copies of the agreement, which were later ratified by their respective commanders. To allow time for the word to reach all units, the ceasefire was set for 22:00 hrs that evening. Max Hastings, in *The Korean War*, estimates that 18 million words had been exchanged in the years of talks.

When the word reached the Canadians it was still pretty much "business as usual." Colonel Sutherland (who was a company second-in-command with PPCLI at the time) said: "We'd been hearing rumours and were more or less expecting something of the sort to happen. We didn't take things for granted as the enemy had recently launched heavy attacks on the South Korean and US Marine divisions on our flanks. The Battalion sent out a strong patrol well forward of our positions as we could not predict the enemy intentions. I remember that they were told to be prepared to stay out past the official 'ceasefire' time if they had to."

A 'FEU-DE-JOIE'

"Understandably, this was a matter of some concern," he continued. "One could not possibly predict what the enemy might do should the patrol be discovered there after the time set for hostilities to cease. There was also the matter of random artillery fire - a 'feu-de-joie' as it were."

Exchange of artillery fire continued almost until the last minute. In some cases, especially on the front held by our neighbours, the US Marines, the intensity equalled that of any time during the war. The last Canadian rounds were fired by 81 Field Regiment, RCA.

While the last efforts undoubtedly had a psychological impact, there may have been a subconscious practical reason for the utilization of the ammunition. As part of the agreement, all weapons, ammunition and warlike stores and equipment were to be removed two miles behind the forward positions. Of course, every round fired was one less to backload! Bill Sutherland parsimoniously considered this to be wasting good ammunition and recalled that every 25-pounder shell cost the Canadian taxpayer about 80 dollars.

On 27 July the troops felt relief, rather than elation. After many false hopes of an armistice over the years, there was some scepticism that this was for real. Two years of stalemate deprived the UN troops of the jubilation of victory. With a three-day deadline to withdraw themselves and all their equipment from the positions that they had held at great cost for over two years, they were too busy to celebrate.

At 22:00 hours flares and verey lights shot up from both sides of the line. One PPCLI officer stated, "We were astonished at the number of Chinese who came out of their holes! Intelligence summaries had indicated a suspected regiment on our front, but there must have been at least a division." It was later revealed that, during the final hours, a massive reinforcement by Chinese and North Koreans took place; whether for propaganda purposes, or to counter a possible last-minute UN offensive, is uncertain.

Although many Chinese approached the Canadians with candy, cigarettes and other gifts, there was little fraternization.

READY FOR RE-OCCUPATION

In some cases the Canadians abandoned their forward positions with more expediency than thoroughness. Colonel Sutherland recalls his surprise and embarrassment when he conducted a senior staff officer to a supposedly "cleaned out" position. "There were primed grenades and ammunition all over the place," he remembers. "About the only thing that they'd taken were their weapons. It seemed ready for re-occupation!"

Perhaps the most emotional Canadians were the POWs repatriated in August under Operation "Big Switch." They were quietly shipped home with little fanfare. One of them, Lance Corporal Paul Dugal, of the R22eR, who had been repatriated with other wounded prisoners a few months earlier, earned the rarely-awarded British Empire Medal for his efforts in maintaining information on his fellow captives.

The Royal Canadians, Vandoos and Patricias as well as their supporting elements remained in the area beyond the Demilitarized Zone (DMZ) for some months until they were relieved by the Canadians Guards, Queens Own Rifles, Black Watch of Canada and other units. Almost 50 Canadians subsequently died in Korea *since* the ceasefire.

The troops returned to Canada with little ceremony. There were no "Victory Parades." As Bill Berry, a former infantryman remembers: "My best buddy John and I, having been together from the day we joined up, got off a bus at the old Colonial Coach terminal and simply went home. After that it seemed that we were expected to apologize for having been soldiers . . . the job market was no place for a 20-year old whose background . . . consisted entirely of a high proficiency for killing. All too many drifted into despair, became alcoholics or derelicts . . ."

One significant ceremony did take place. En route home the battalions stopped off at the UN military cemetery in Pusan to pay

their last respects to the 516 Canadians who would not be returning.

TALKS CONTINUE

It would be pleasant to report that the 1953 cease-fire brought an end to the tension in the troubled Korean peninsula. Unfortunately, this is not the case. The UN and North Korean delegates still meet and talk in Panmunjon, which is now a major tourist attraction, although "out of bounds" to South Korean nationals. The discussions are now held before an audience of foreign tourists peering through the windows while the deliberations take place.

Sabre-rattling, allegations, countercharges and in some cases armed clashed still occur. In 1976 two American officers were attacked and killed by North Korean troops while pruning a tree in the DMZ. (A subsequent attempt to trim the tree was supported by several battalions of infantry, Special Forces troops and a US aircraft carrier. The operation was described by the commander of the US guard force at Panmunjon as "the most expensive tree-trimming in history.")

A number of tunnels constructed under the DMZ by the North Koreans have been unearthed (I visited one of these; it could accommodate a jeep-sized vehicle with ease). Their purpose was apparently to facilitate large numbers of their Special Forces troops to infiltrate the South. At least one of these tunnels is a tourist attraction - visitors may descend below "no mans land", eventually coming face to face with a metal barrier behind which a North Korean guard glares menacingly.

South Koreans are concerned over a large dam which their neighbours have built close to the border - they feel that it could be used to flood their strategically-important and fertile lands close to the Parallel. The tension remains high as a result of more sabre-rattling by North Korean President Kim Il Sung, who declared in the early 1990s that "a state of semi-war now exists between the two Koreas."

From 1950 - 1953 over 26,000 Canadians served in the Korean War. Most remaining veterans of that War (and despite the tendency to refer to it as a "police action" or "conflict" it *was* a war) hope that their grandchildren will not have to complete the job that they began – 40 years ago.

REPRINTED FROM:

Esprit de Corps, *Volume 3 Issue 2*

AUTHOR: *Les Peate*

SALUTING THE RICE-BURNERS...

The Korean porters were the unsung heroes of the Korean War. They have no known memorial.

LEFT: *Canadian soldiers developed a strong affinity towards the hard working South Korean peasants – in particular the labourers who toiled on behalf of the UN.* (U.S. ARMY)

PRIOR TO OUR ARRIVAL in Korea, the British units of 27 Commonwealth Brigade, and its successor, 28 COMWEL Bde, had spent over a year preparing to defend Hong Kong against a Chinese invasion which, fortunately for us, never happened. One of the advantages of this was that when we left for Korea we had lots of experience in climbing up and down the many mountains in that colony – training which stood us in good stead later.

As there were no roads to the mountain tops where we dug in our positions, equipment, weapons and supplies were carried up either by the long-suffering infantry or by those four-legged friends, the pack mules. (There is no feeling quite like struggling up a precipitous mountainside, slick from monsoon rains, under a blazing sun and following a train of incontinent equine hybrids.)

NO MULES

For some reason we saw few, if any, mules in Korea. Perhaps some veteran may be able to tell me why. On the other hand, the amount of materiel needed for permanently-occupied positions on the heights was far more than we used in our Hong Kong exercises. Moving into position with our basic arms, ammunition, rations and bedding was in itself a challenge. Obviously, we needed help to bring up from the jeepheads the supplies, water, ammunition, equipment and defensive stores for life in the line (not forgetting, of course, the 24-quart-bottle cases of Asahi beer).

The answer lay in an organization of unsung heroes of a "forgotten war." Just as Kipling's India had its "Gunga Dins," the UN forces in Korea had the Korean Service Corps (KSC) and its predecessors.

Millions of Koreans served in the ROK Army, which, by the War's end, developed from an ill-equipped and poorly-trained body into a fighting machine second to none by the War's end. Others served in a less spectacular, and poorly rewarded, fashion.

At first, units "recruited" civilian porters to carry supplies to forward positions. "Recruited" is perhaps a euphemism. Able-bodied Koreans were simply rounded up and put to work. Niceties such as pay, uniforms and even rations were incidental. Many of the "rice-burners" (as opposed to "hay-burners") were entirely dependent on the generosity of their employers.

THE PORTERS' EQUIPMENT

Porters were expected to carry a minimum of about 25 kilos for 25 kilometres each day. While this may not seem a lot, most of those kilometres were usually through very hilly and rough country. This feat was achieved with the aid of what many Korea veterans consider to be the most important piece of equipment used in Korea, the A-frame. (Others hold the view that the P-38 C-Ration can-opener has that distinction.)

An A-frame consists of three poles lashed together to form a crude triangle with shoulder straps of roughly-woven straw. A load, often far in excess of the standard 25-kg, was attached and carried on the porter's back. This primitive apparatus, together with the incredible stamina of the bearers, led rise to the boast "give a Korean an A-frame and he could move the world".

Heavy and awkward loads were not the only problems facing the Korean porters. As their ultimate destination was the Sharp End, they shared the dangers of the line infantry, without the protection of steel helmets or defensive weapons. They were frequently called on to accompany "reconnaissance in force" or other combat operations. I can remember patrolling in front of my own position seeking a suspected enemy patrol in the area, accompanied by a very unwilling porter whose function was to demand the surrender of any enemy encountered. Many a Canadian, wounded in the line, was carried to the helicopter or jeep ambulance on a stretcher borne by Korean porters, frequently under fire.

In the early days, Korean porters developed strong affinities with their parent units. Some acquired cast-off or donated uniform items and proudly wore the unit shoulder-flashes and other insignia. They worked with designated porter guides from the

Commonwealth units, who usually established an excellent rapport with the Koreans. Most Korea veterans will recall the sight of a train of perhaps 50 porters, heavily-laden with the necessities of frontline life, steadily making their way over rough mountain tracks through atrocious weather, to our forward positions.

A VARIETY OF JOBS

Gradually, they were joined by other Korean nationals who worked for the units on an informal basis. Abandoned or orphaned youngsters worked as houseboys, mama-sans served in rear-echelon units as laundresses and the more educated Koreans were in great demand as interpreters. Food and accomodation were provided in porter villages and units would often arrange for those helpers fortunate enough to be able to visit their families, to take along gifts of food, cigarettes and other "luxuries." Some of the well-established porter villages were equipped with moonshine stills which would be the envy of Ozark mountaineers, producing a foul-tasting but potent brew. Many Canadians, at one time or another, sampled this oriental version of "Kickapoo Joy Juice," to their cost.

FATIGUE DUTIES

By 1951, the Korean Service Corps was established on a more military basis. Organized KSC units served under Republic of Korea army officers and NCOs. The 120th KSC Regiment was assigned to the Commonwealth Division. It had three battalions, each of up to 2000 men. One was assigned to the divisonal engineers and worked on road repairs and other tasks – the rest were allotted to other units as carriers, vehicle loaders and for other "fatigue" duties.

Discipline was strict and summary. At least three veterans write of occasions where Korean workers were accused of minor thefts and executed on the spot by one of their officers (Ron Larby, in his *Armoured on the Left, Signals on the Right* remembers that an accused, who had apparently taken a few cigarettes, was first ordered to dig his own grave, and then despatched with a pistol shot.) Robert Hepenstall, in *Find the Dragon*

***Unarmed, and technically non-combatants, many of the Korean labourers became casualties or refugees during the fighting.* (W.H. OLSON)**

quotes a Canadian NCO who felt that sometimes the loyalty of porters was suspect, and believed that North Korean sympathisers in the KSC ranks had removed mines by night which he and his comrades had previously laid during the day.

CASUALTIES AMONG PORTERS

Nor were the porters unscathed by war's perils. At least five of their number died when 3 RCR were heavily attacked in May of 1953. One of Ted Zuber's Korean War paintings displayed in the Canadian War Museum shows a Korean porter bringing a box of No. 36 grenades into a bunker. What it doesn't show is what happened immediately afterwards. Corporal Roy Reid of the Royal Canadian Engineers (RCE) recalls that the Korean dropped the box. The grenades, which were primed, exploded and the porter died together with his Canadian allies.

By the war's end, the Korean Service Corps had a strength of over 100,000. There are memorials in Seoul to the famed "Capitol Division" and other distinguished Korean units and formations, but nothing to commemorate the unsung heroes of KSC and their predecessors.

REPRINTED FROM:
Esprit de Corps, *Volume 5 Issue 5*
AUTHORS: *Les Peate*

THE AMAZING TOMMY PRINCE

The most decorated native soldier in World War II returned to Korea... twice.

PRINCESS PATRICIA'S CANADIAN Light Infantry served with distinction in Korea from 1950 to 1953. Several members went on to greater things, including Jack Shields (who became a member of Parliament) and *Toronto Sun* editor emeritus Peter Worthington. One notable member of the Regiment died in poverty, but is still remembered in his home province as one of Manitoba's war heroes.

Thomas George (Tommy) Prince was born in Manitoba in 1915 – a descendant of notable Ojibwa chiefs. The story of his amazing military career begins well before the Korean War – in 1940. Tommy was one of the many thousands of Canadian Indians who volunteered to serve in Canada's forces during the Second World War.

After two years in the Royal Canadian Engineers, Prince volunteered for parachute training, and in 1942 was posted to the First Canadian Special Service Battalion – part of the famous Canada-US "Devil's Brigade."

FIRST DECORATION

The unconventional warfare practised by the Special Service Force suited Tommy well. The SSF specialized in reconnaissance and raiding operations, although when operational necessity resulted in their use in a "straight" infantry role their tenacity was a byword. Promotion came quickly and by the end of 1943 Tommy Prince was a sergeant in Italy. Early in 1944 his courage and initiative earned him his first decoration, the Military Medal.

Tommy had set up an observation post (OP) in an abandoned farmhouse just 200 yards from the German enemy. During his all-day watch his telephone line was sev-

RIGHT:
Sergeant Tommy Prince (second from left) earned a reputation for fearlessness in World War II, which served him well during his two tours of duty in Korea. (SF 853)

ered by artillery fire. Donning some old clothes abandoned by the previous residents he took a hoe and, posing as an Italian farmer, traced the line on the pretext of weeding his plants until he had found and repaired the break. Returning to his OP, he directed artillery fire, which destroyed several enemy positions.

In the fall of 1944, the SSF participated in the invasion of Southern France, and Prince once more distinguished himself. Bruce Sealey and Peter Van de Vyvere have written a short biography of Tommy Prince in the *Manitobans in Profile* series. In their words, "Sergeant Prince and a private, scouting deep behind German lines… located [an enemy] gun site and encampment area. Prince walked 70 km across rugged, mountainous terrain to report…then led the brigade to the encampment."

MORE HONOURS…

Prince joined in the battle, in which the enemy were wiped out. This act was to earn the Ojibwa soldier one of the few US Silver Stars awarded to Canadians. The gallant sergeant was later decorated by HM King George VI with the Military Medal and, on behalf of U.S. President Roosevelt, the Silver Star, becoming the most decorated Canadian Indian of the War. Soon after the war ended, Prince returned to Canada.

In 1950, the Korean War broke out, and in August the government put out a call for volunteers for a Special Force to serve there. One of the first to sign on was the comparatively "old" Tommy Prince. He was assigned to the 2nd Battalion, PPCLI as a platoon sergeant.

In Korea in early 1951 Prince was in his element. He distinguished himself as a patrol leader, although his officers were concerned that his daring could result in unnecessary casualties, and tried to restrict his activities. When 2PPCLI fought their battle at Kapyong in April of 1951, Tommy Prince was there, and earned the right to wear the insignia of the US Presidential Citation – the only such award to a Canadian unit.

But Tommy was a sick man. In addition to being older than most of his comrades, he suffered severely from arthritis – a condition aggravated by the hilly nature of the Korean terrain. Reluctantly, he left the line for duties in the rear and was eventually returned to Canada.

He served as a platoon sergeant at the Camp Borden Officer Cadet School. He did his job well but, in the words of one of his former officers, was not a great mixer and felt more at home in the field. In late 1952 he got his wish, and returned to Korea, again with PPCLI, but this time with the 3rd Battalion.

BAPTISM OF FIRE

Arriving in early November, the battalion soon received its baptism of fire. On the night of 18 November the (British) Black Watch was attacked by the Chinese, on a key position, "The Hook," and the Patricia's were called to their assistance. The Canadians lost four killed and several wounded, including Sergeant Prince.

For the next few months, the sergeant was in and out of hospital; in addition to his wound his arthritis had recurred. He was able to remain in Korea and returned

IN KOREA IN EARLY 1951 TOMMY PRINCE WAS IN HIS ELEMENT. HE DISTINGUISHED HIMSELF AS A PATROL LEADER, ALTHOUGH HIS OFFICERS WERE CONCERNED THAT HIS DARING COULD RESULT IN UNNECESSARY CASUALTIES, AND TRIED TO RESTRICT HIS ACTIVITIES. WHEN 2PPCLI FOUGHT THEIR BATTLE AT KAPYONG IN APRIL OF 1951, SERGEANT PRINCE WAS THERE, AND EARNED THE RIGHT TO WEAR THE INSIGNIA OF THE US PRESIDENTIAL CITATION – THE ONLY SUCH AWARD TO A CANADIAN UNIT. BUT TOMMY WAS A SICK MAN. IN ADDITION TO BEING OLDER THAN MOST OF HIS COMRADES, HE SUFFERED SEVERELY FROM ARTHRITIS – A CONDITION AGGRAVATED BY THE HILLY NATURE OF THE KOREAN TERRAIN. RELUCTANTLY, HE LEFT THE LINE FOR DUTIES IN THE REAR AND WAS EVENTUALLY RETURNED TO CANADA.

ABOVE:
Lieutenant Colonel 'Big' Jim Stone had already served his country with distinction during the Second World War. He was managing a summer resort in British Columbia when a friend convinced him to rejoin the army in the summer of 1950.
(NAC/PA 142233)

ABOVE:
Tommy Prince was a member of Lieutenant Colonel 'Big Jim' Stone's 2nd Battalion, PPCLI, when they moved up into the lines at Kapyong. On his second tour of Korea, he served as the platoon sergeant for a young lieutenant named Peter Worthington (later founding editor of the Toronto Sun*).*
(PAC PA 115564)

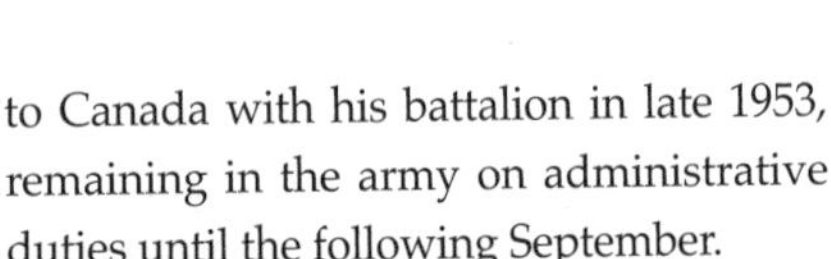

to Canada with his battalion in late 1953, remaining in the army on administrative duties until the following September.

On leaving the service, Tommy encountered a series of misfortunes. In addition to domestic difficulties, he lost his medals and other memorabilia in a house fire in Winnipeg. His health continued to plague him and, in the words of a Winnipeg newspaper, was "a man who earned fame fighting in war but ultimately lost his battle with the bottle." Some of his former comrades felt that he deserved more help. Jim Summersides, a "Devil's Brigade" veteran feels, "It's a crying shame what happened to Tommy. I think that the country could have done more to help him, especially considering what he did for his country."

Tommy Prince died in the Deer Lodge Veterans' Hospital in Winnipeg in 1977 – a 62-year old pauper.

RECOGNITION DELAYED TOO LONG

Recognition, perhaps, came too late. His funeral was attended by over 500 people, including Manitoba's Lieutenant-Governor, consuls from nations who had participated in the Korean War, representatives of the Armed Forces – past and present – and many other citizens. Princess Patricia's Canadian Light Infantry provided pallbearers, and a traditional dirge was chanted by members of his own Brokenhead Indian Reserve.

Fifty years ago, Tommy Prince was decorated by his Sovereign. Ten years later he had left the army, for the second time. Although recognition came too late, he will long be remembered by his comrades in the Special Service Force and PPCLI. To quote another Manitoba aboriginal language, that of the Cree, "Kahgee pohn noten took" – "*The Fighting Has Ended.*"

STORIES TOLD

Janice Summerby, in *Native Soldiers, Foreign Battlefields* (produced by Veterans Affairs Canada) tells the stories of Tommy Prince and other native Canadian veterans. She concludes with the statement that "...[in the World Wars and Korea]...Canada's Native soldiers overcame cultural challenges and made impressive sacrifices and contributions to help the nation in its efforts to restore world peace." Sergeant Thomas Prince, MM, Silver Star, is an excellent example.

REPRINTED FROM:
Esprit de Corps, *Volume 4 Issue 6*
AUTHOR: *Les Peate*

PRINCE WAS DECORATED BY HIS SOVEREIGN BUT TEN YEARS LATER HE HAD LEFT THE ARMY, FOR THE SECOND TIME. HE DIED IN THE DEER LODGE VETERANS' HOSPITAL IN WINNIPEG IN 1977 – A 62-YEAR OLD PAUPER. ALTHOUGH RECOGNITION CAME TOO LATE, SERGEANT THOMAS PRINCE, MM, SILVER STAR, WILL LONG BE REMEMBERED BY HIS COMRADES IN THE SPECIAL SERVICE FORCE AND PRINCESS PATRICIA'S CANADIAN LIGHT INFANTRY.

THE COLD WAR 1954 - 1989

1954 Krushchev wins power struggle in Kremlin. ■ Red-baiting Senator Joe McCarthy censured by U.S. Senate. ■ French defeated at Dien Bien Phu.

1955 Western Allies formally end occupation of West Germany and Federal Republic admitted to NATO. ■ Soviets respond with formation of Warsaw Pact.

1956 Hungarian Uprising brutally suppressed by Soviets. ■ UN General Assembly adopts Lester B. Pearson's Suez peacekeeping plan.

1957 Diefenbaker defeats Liberals. ■ Arrow program cancelled. ■ NORAD Agreement signed. ■ Soviets launch Sputnik. ■ Pearson wins Nobel Peace Prize.

1958 U.S. launches first satellite, "Explorer I." ■ Increased emphasis in Canada and the U.S. on civil defence.

1959 Castro takes power in Cuba.

1960 U-2 shot down over Soviet Union. ■ UN Secretary General Dag Hammarskjöld dies in plane crash in Congo. ■ John F. Kennedy elected U.S. President.

1961 Bay of Pigs. ■ Kennedy and Krushchev meet in Vienna.

1962 Cuban Missile Crisis.

1963 Lester B. Pearson elected Prime Minister of Canada. ■ President Kennedy assassinated in Dallas, Texas.

1967 Centennial Year. Expo '67 a huge success in Montreal. ■ Six Day War in Mideast.

1968 Tet Offensive in Vietnam. ■ Warsaw Pact crushes "Prague Spring." ■ Pierre Elliott Trudeau succeeds Pearson as Prime Minister.

1970 FLQ Crisis. Trudeau invokes War Measures Act.

1973 Yom Kippur War.

1975 Last American troops leave Vietnam.

1979 Carter and Brezhnev sign Salt II Agreement in Vienna. ■ Soviets invade Afghanistan. ■ Sandinistas take power in Nicaragua as civil war rages in neighbouring El Salvador.

1980 Iran-Iraq war. ■ Rise of Solidarity Movement in Poland.

1982 Falklands War. ■ Argentinians surrender at Port Stanley.

1984 Last nuclear weapons leave Canadian soil. ■ Gorbachev introduces glasnost and perestroika to Soviet Union. ■ Brian Mulroney elected Canadian Prime Minister.

1985 Reagan-Gorbachev summit in Geneva.

1989 Tiananmen Square Massacre. ■ Soviet Union retreats from Eastern Europe. ■ Berlin Wall falls.

BOTTOM LEFT: *On 21 November 1963, President John F. Kennedy was assassinated in Dallas, Texas. Arrested for the crime, Lee Harvey Oswald was himself shot to death by Jack Ruby, on live TV.* (ART RICKERBY, LIFE)

BOTTOM MIDDLE: *On 8 January 1958 Fidel Castro, the lawyer who had become a rebel, celebrated with his people his victory over deposed dictator Fulgencio Batista. More than 43 years later, Castro still rules Cuba, the only Communist country in the Americas.* (GREY VILLET, LIFE)

BOTTOM, RIGHT: *Protesting government policies, a young Buddhist monk immolates himself on a Saigon street in 1963.* (CORBIS-BETTMANN/ UPI)

CANADA'S ROLE: THE COLD WAR

As the Cold War heats up, Canada sends a Brigade to Europe and bolsters its defences.

ABOVE:
Had the Avro Arrow fighter jet been allowed to proceed beyond the prototype stage, Canada's air force would have been equipped with an aircraft generations ahead of its time.
(PRIVATE COLLECTION)

THE KOREAN WAR WAS a page from the Russian textbook for world domination. The United States led the charge into Korea and Canada later raised a brigade, a decision apparently taken on a train by members of Louis St. Laurent's Cabinet as they returned from Mackenzie King's funeral. Some members interpreted the Korean crisis as a prelude to Communist action in Europe, and this brought forth a decision to send a Brigade to Europe as a contribution to NATO. An Order in Council was passed on 18 October 1951, which authorized sending the Brigade and the first of the RCAF Squadrons to Europe. Until fields became available in France and Germany, the first of the Air Division was sent to England. The Brigade was recruited from the militia and had some of the characteristics of the formations put together by Sam Hughes in 1914. Few militia units could raise a complete battalion and the Brigade was drawn from six composite infantry, rifle and highland battalions. The Brigade was based in Hanover, a hostile haven of neo-Nazis and Communists. Morale sagged as the Brigade began its training and shortages of clothing and equipment persisted throughout the winter. The disparate organization of the group had also created an uneven standard of performance, but after initial problems were overcome the Brigade saw 42 years of service in a frustrating but successful endeavour.

BROOKE ANNOUNCES EXPANSION

The Berlin Airlift touched a nerve with the Minister of National Defence Brooke Claxton in 1948 and he announced an expanded program for the RCAF. Enlistments were to increase, airfields were to be refurbished and jets manufactured. A team studied Canada's need to replace the aging CF-100 and came up with specifications of an all-weather interceptor which surpassed anything in the air. The team from the RCAF, Defence Research, the National Research Council and the National Aeronautical Establishment handed the requirements to A.V. Roe Canada. Designers fashioned a machine designed to fly at twice the speed of sound at 60,000 feet with a combat radius of 200 miles. The USAF became interested in the machine and original sessions in which their weapons experts provided advice soon led to strong interest if not domination of the project. Although costs were born by the Canadian government, the project was optimistically viewed as a North American Defence initiative whereby senior American Airforce officers would plan on using the Arrow or CF-105 on their squadrons. The first machine was rolled out and preliminary tests indicated the Arrow was craft ahead of its time. Five aircraft were produced and testing proceeded. Pilot Spud Potocki took one to 1300 miles an hour at 58,000 feet without pushing the envelope. A Mk2 CF-105 was already in the planning stages which would boost speed on the level to about 1650 mph. Such a machine was produced but never left the ground. Prime Minister John Diefenbaker not only ordered production stopped but all aircraft were scrapped and records destroyed.

AMERICAN PRESSURE

Dozens of theories have emerged on why the Arrow was scrapped. The Canadian Government obviously succumbed to American pressure which in turn was applied by lobbyists for American aircraft firms. As a result of the cancellation, Canada lost not only a chance to produce the best aircraft in the world but a promising team of experts.

At the time, some observers were acutely reminded of the other occasion Canadian leaders lacked the courage and the conviction to pursue a world-class idea. Canadian Casey Baldwin was the first citizen of the British Empire to fly in 1908. With John McCurdy, he was part of Alexander Graham Bell's Aeronautical Experimental Association. In 1909 a demonstration flight for government officials was arranged at Petawawa. The night before the flight, the Deputy Minister of Militia and National Defence, Colonel Eugene Fiset, told the *Ottawa Journal*: "You cannot expect a young country like Canada to strike out and adopt a military aeroplane policy. We will probably follow the footsteps of England along this line." Casey Baldwin had flown a year before the first Englishman. Canada simply

RIGHT:
When Egyptian President Nasser seized the canal that joined the Red Sea to the Mediterranean on 26 July 1956, Britain, France and Israel made a secret pact to attack and bomb the Canal Zone on 31 October 1956. But, before the UN could step in, British paratroopers dropped into the zone on 4 November. A cease-fire was agreed to two days later. (POPPERFOTO)

did not have the initiative to push on and some 40 years later the only difference was that it was being dominated by the United States instead of Britain.

The advent of NATO, the following year, saw the rebirth of a training program as Canada once again became the Aerodrome of Democracy. This time trainees were students from eight NATO countries. An expanded RCAF now had three roles: defence of Canadian skies; participation in UN. operations; and, most pressing, support of NATO where Canada soon operated four wings out of France and Germany. As the 27th Brigade and the Air Division established a strong Canadian identity in NATO, events to the south brought forth a remarkable yet bizarre crisis in which Canada played a major role.

SUEZ CANAL CRISIS OF 1956

Egypt's President Nasser had dreams of increasing cotton production by building the Aswan Dam for irrigation. He appealed to Britain and the U.S. for funds, but when he elected to buy $200 million worth of arms from the Russians, no funds were forthcoming. Nasser nationalized the Suez Canal, creating a furor in England and France as the canal was a vital route for European oil.

Within a month, British and French troops were sailing for Cyprus, a British Crown Colony. Two months later heavily armoured Israeli forces crossed the 120-mile border into Egypt and drove towards the Suez Canal. British Valiant and Canberra jets bombed military airfields and the Canal zone. A week later, Royal Marine Commandos fought their way to the centre of Port Said.

While this was going on, alarm bells had been ringing at the United Nations in New York. Canada's Foreign Minister, Lester Pearson, had been shuttling from delegation to delegation and back to Ottawa with a plan to set up a UN peace force. On the day the Royal Commandos struck at Port Said, Pearson presented a document to the General Assembly.

FIRST UN PEACEKEEPERS

It asserted that the British and French would have no role in the United Nations Emergency Force. Political control would be in the hands of Dag Hammarskjöld, secretary-general of the UN. Within days helmets had been painted blue and the first UN peacekeeping force was on its way. Two days after Pearson made his presentation, all military operations by the British and French came to a halt. When the first UN Peace Contingent arrived in Egypt to restore order, the Queen's Own Rifles represented Canada. Nasser then posed a legitimate question: What's wrong with this picture? Britain had invaded Egypt but among the international troops in the UN force was a regiment from Canada called the Queen's Own which marched behind a flag which had the Union Jack in the corner.

Nasser's argument, while logical, posed political problems in Canada. It was resolved by assigning an RCAF transport squadron and substituting administration, signal and supply personnel to General E.L.M. Burns' UN force. British Prime Minister Anthony Eden resigned in the wake of the British action and although Lester Pearson won the Nobel Peace prize for his work, it was downplayed by or even criticized by pro-British elements in Canada.

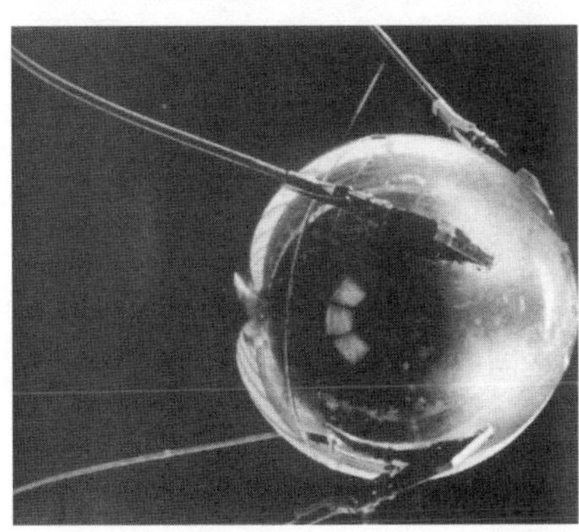

ABOVE:
Launched by the Soviets in 1957, the tiny Sputnik *was joined in space the following year by the American satellite,* Explorer I.

When the U.S.S.R. launched the first satellite in 1957, the cold war went into space. It marked a definite victory for the Soviets in what became known as the battle of the missile gap. The Soviets felt secure enough to attend a rapprochement summit of the Big Four two years later but 12 days before the Paris summit the Soviets shot down Gary Powers who was flying an American U-2 spy plane over Soviet territory.

AUTHOR: *Norm Shannon*

RETURN TO GERMANY

After defeating the Nazis in 1945, few Canadian soldiers would have envisioned redeploying into Germany just six years later. This time, Russia was the threat and the Germans were our allies.

WHEN THE LAST CANADIAN troops left Germany in 1946 they had no idea that many of them would return half a decade later. Yet in 1951, Canadian soldiers were once again on German soil, this time not as a conquering army, but as defenders of their former enemies.

Following the Second World War it appeared possible that the U.S.S.R. and its allies might try to overcome the remainder of Western Europe. To counter the threat, in 1949 a treaty was signed in Washington establishing the North Atlantic Treaty Association, in which forces from Belgium, Canada, Denmark, France, Italy, Luxembourg, the Netherlands, Norway, Portugal, the United Kingdom and the United States would operate under a single command in defence of estern Europe. In 1950 General Dwight D. Eisenhower was appointed Supreme Allied Commander Europe (SACEUR).

PLANNING PROBLEM

While Canada had developed a contingency plan to mobilize forces for NATO, the Canadian Government responded to requests for a more viable presence. A Canadian infantry brigade would be sent to Europe in 1951.

This posed a problem for the planners. At the time Canada's regular army consisted mainly of the Mobile Strike Force - a brigade-group-sized formation. These professionals were tasked with the defence of Canada, although most of them were to find their way to Korea early the following year. The flood of volunteers for the "Special Service Force" enlisting for the Korean War had dried up. Eventually, as they had done on in earlier crisis situations, the authorities turned to the Militia.

Because it would be almost impossible to embody Militia units en bloc, three composite infantry battalions would be formed. The organization of the new force, to be known as the 27th Canadian Infantry Brigade Group, was carried out under the codeword PANDA. As we will see, to some regular soldiers, mention of PANDA might provoke a violent reaction.

Five Militia regiments each contributed one company, the whole forming the First Canadian Infantry Battalion. Similarly, five Militia rifle regiments and five Militia highland regiments formed, respectively, the First Canadian Rifle Battalion and the First Canadian Highland Battalion. Artillery and Engineer units were combined in a similar manner, while the regulars of the Royal Canadian Dragoons provided the armoured element. Like their predecessors in Korea's 25th Brigade, these were "unaccompanied" postings.

The volunteers were something of a mixed bag. While many of them were war veterans, others had little or no long-term military experience. The regulars who helped swell their ranks were sometimes discouraged to find themselves placed in subordinate positions to "weekend warriors" whose skills and knowledge were far less than their own. A number of unsatisfactory NCOs were weeded out, but the problem still rankled for a number of years.

Meanwhile, the Royal Canadian Air Force, too, was preparing to take its place in the NATO defence picture – that is another story in itself.

DISCORD DEALT WITH

In late 1951 the Brigade reached its new home, in Hanover. SACEUR had decided to place the Canadian force under command of the British Army of the Rhine. This could have caused problems, but did not - BAOR was still technically an occupation force and its members were subject to different rules, while the Canadians were German "allies." (By the time that I arrived in Germany the peace treaty had been signed and the Budeswehr were part of NATO.)

While there was some discord at first between the Canadians and the British troops and the German populace, this was quickly remedied and 27 Brigade soon made themselves at home. Partly because of the damage caused by Allied air raids earlier, and the necessity to retain accommodation for the British troops who remained in the city, the Canadians could not be concentrated in one area, and spread around the surrounding countryside. The 58th Field Squadron RCE was especially fortunate, locating in the historic town of Hamelin (of pied piper fame).

The Brigade was unique in that its equipment was a mixture of British and U.S. material. Most vehicles and some of its weapons came from American sources (to the relief of the Canadians, most vittles were purchased locally- British rations were not popular). The Dragoons were equipped with Centurion tanks, while the Gunners' original U.S. 105-mm weapons were later replaced by British 25-pounders.

OPPOSITE PAGE: *On 21 November 1951, soldiers of 1st Canadian Infantry Battalion disembarked in Rotterdam. Part of NATO's commitment in Germany, they are inspected by General Dwight D. Eisenhower, Supreme Allied Commander Europe (SACEUR).* (LEX DE HERDER) ***LEFT:*** *Having arrived in West Germany as part of NATO's commitment, Canada's infantry brigade parades through Hanover's Waterloo Platz in 1952.* (DND PHOTO)

WET AND DRY CANTEENS

The tour was not a holiday. Plans for a "mobile defence" against a possible invasion by the nearby Bloc forces included a first-line role for 27 CIBG, and contingency plans were prepared and practiced. Intensive training was conducted at Putlos (on the Baltic) and later at the Rhine Army centre in the Sennelager area.

All work and no play makes for a tired soldier. The British NAAFI provided "dry" and "wet" canteens, while BAOR came up with movie theatres and a radio network. Perhaps the most pleasant surprise was the low cost of entertainment - the Deutschmark was available at four to the dollar and alcoholic beverages and female company came cheaply. Many young Canadians were led on the "road to ruin" following their introduction to Steinhager, Dopplekorn whisky and a variety of excellent beers. (In later years, when the families arrived, the beer salesman cruising the married quarter area like an ice-cream salesman was a familiar sight). Sean Maloney, in his excellent account *War Without Battles* [McGraw Hill-Ryerson, Limited] indicates that sometimes temptation was too much, and describes a parade of over a hundred defaulters from one unit paying for their misdemeanours with pack drill.)

In 1953, 27 Brigade came home. The Infantry, Highland and Rifle battalions were renamed, and became the Canadian Guards, Black Watch and Queen's Own Rifles respectively. They were replaced by the Second Battalions of the Royal Canadian Regiment, Princess Patricia's Canadian Light Infantry and Royal 22e Regiment. The new formation, the 1st CIBG, moved to the Soest area, where the concentration of barracks in the neighbourhood were named for historic Canadian forts (Brigade HQ was located in Fort Henry, close to The RCR's Fort York). The Second Battalions had originally constituted part of the Special Service Force for Korea but now consisted of regular soldiers.

By now, provision was made for dependents to join their husbands and fathers in Germany. Married quarters were constructed, Maple Leaf Services family stores and food outlets replaced the NAAFI, while churches, cinemas, bingo halls and all the comforts of home became available. (While many families took advantage of the opportunity to experience the European way of life, many missed this golden opportunity and confined their activities to the North American atmosphere of "Klein Kanada.") The practical and moral support provided by the "Sally Ann" was appreciated by all – their Volkswagen canteen buses were familiar in all fielde exercises.

EVER PRESENT THREAT

Complacency didn't set in. The threat of invasion was ever-present. Evacuation exercises for dependents were conducted, and many a night's sleep was disrupted by a knock on the PMQ door and the cry of "Fishing Pole" – the codeword for families to assemble to await transportation to Bremen for a rapid return to Canada. However, the opportunities were there for a wonderful family experience. Travel to NATO countries was easily arranged, often subsidized. The Mark was still trading at 25 cents, and everyday items such as coffee and cigarettes were exchanged for treasured souvenirs or domestic services. The British Military Hospital at Iserlohn established a Canadian wing, and many families returned to Canada with an increase in the number of their dependents, courtesy of BMH.

In 1955 2 CIBG took over – consisting of the First Battalions of the three regiments, with supporting arms. They were succeeded over the years by other groups, until in 1970 it was decided to concentrate all Canada's forces – land and air, in Lahr, Germany. But that is another story. NATO service was finally recognized in 1992, when the Canadian Special Service Medal was initiated, with bars for "service performed under exceptional circumstances." One of the bars reads "NATO-OTAN."

AUTHOR: *Les Peate*

SALLY RANDS

Fondly known as the Sally Rand, HMCS *St. Laurent* was the first anti-submarine vessel designed and built in Canada.

HMCS **St. Laurent** *was the first of her 20-ship class – a custom-built Canadian anti-submarine destroyer escort.* (DND PHOTO)

INSET: Prime Minister Mackenzie King was a reluctant supporter of Canada's naval refurbishing post-World War II. (PHOTO NATIONAL ARCHIVES OF CANADA)

WILLIAM LYON MACKENZIE King, Canada's perpetual Prime Minister, was most emphatically not a sailor. After a visit to the Esquimalt naval yard in November 1920, while serving as Leader of the Opposition, he confided to his diary that "the whole institution with the *Rainbow* at the wharf seemed a great waste of public money. Idle officers and 15 mounted police, etc. It is shameful the waste on these military and naval fads."

Fads maybe, but a navy is a continuing and wise investment for a trading nation bordering three oceans. In time, King would come to see the RCN as the safest form of military expenditure, and naval policy became part of his "liberal nationalist" scheme of achieving domestic political power and independence from Britain. Without much public enthusiasm, the Navy survived the lean years between the wars. An admiral felt the Canadian public "would be quite pleased if someone would take the whole navy out to the middle of the ocean and sink it without trace or memory."

The *St. Laurent*, a River class destroyer dispatched to England in the early days of the war, almost saved that "someone" the trouble when she tried to torpedo herself and her sister ship *HMCS Skeena*. Sailing up the west coast en route to Pentland Forth in July 1940, with the *Skeena* astern, the crew was busy cleaning and painting the torpedo tubes when a young seaman accidentally lifted a safety catch with his paint brush and pulled back the firing lever. With an explosive WHOOMP! a torpedo leaped free and hit the deck.

Fired towards the stern, it struck a ladder to a gun platform then knocked over ammunition boxes before crashing into the aft superstructure. As sailors raced from one side of the ship to the other, *Skeena* turned smartly away. The torpedo continued on its way, its propellers racing madly with a shattering din on the steel deck.

"It would lurch forward with each heave of the deck," the captain said. "Then, as the deck came level, it would stop, like a bull in the ring, undecided in which direction to make its next charge."

He and a crewman finally straddled it and held on for dear life. "With the next roll of the ship, it rolled away and we galloped along with it," he recalled. "Our only concern was to keep clear of the propellers, which were close behind us."

Coralled along a guardrail, the torpedo was deactivated when a crewman turned off the compressed air. The *Sally Rand*, as she was affectionately known, sailed safely on to a magnificent wartime career.

DRAGONS IN ACTION

When her namesake was launched on 30 November 1951, at the height of the Cold War, Mackenzie King was no longer around to complain about the cost. The designers had, for all intents and purposes, been handed a blank cheque when the Soviets exploded an atomic bomb in the autumn of 1949. The first anti-submarine ship designed and built in Canada, she was the prototype of 20 destroyer-escorts which entered service between 1955 and 1964.

The RCN's wartime expansion had been phenomenal. From a pre-war force of 1,800 all ranks, it grew to nearly 100,000 and served in every theatre of operations. It assumed resposibility for escort duties on the vital North Atlantic trade routes. Most of the 25,000 merchant ships which crossed the Atlantic during the war were escorted by the RCN. In doing so, it sank or shared in the sinking of 31 U-boats and 42 surface ships. By 1945, it was the third largest navy in the world, with over 400 warships.

But King was tiring once again of the navy's ambitions and the cost of maintaining a fleet. Ships were sold or scrapped and bases closed. A new spirit of internationalism and peaceful cooperation dominated the immediate postwar world, and he was anxious to return to the "old Liberal principles of economy, reduction of taxation, antimilitarism, etc." Disabusing the naval staff of its larger ambitions, he committed himself to no more than maintaining a minimum force. Admirals, with visions of crusiers and carriers dancing in their heads, were sorely disappointed.

King's postwar euphoria was quickly swept away by events. In early 1948, a Communist coup in Czechoslovakia, and the Berlin crisis that followed, raised concerns about the Soviet Union's intentions. When a cipher clerk by the name of Igor Gouzenko defected in Ottawa with word of traitors and Soviet spies, he concluded that his wartime ally was "a dragon in action" and a "menace to be stopped." Purse strings were loosened and the RCN reinvented itself to meet the growing Soviet challenge.

In 1954, while still in the builders' hands, the St. Laurent *showed a unique profile, with rounded lines designed to shed ice and nuclear contaminants.* (NATIONAL ARCHIVES)

THE CADILLAC DESTROYER

In 1947, the RCN estimated that the Soviet Union had about 300 submarines. Planners noted that "if it insists on building a very strong submarine fleet, then we in turn must immediately commence the building or acquiring of an equally strong or stronger anti-submarine force." With its long-cherished vision of a large conventional fleet gone, the RCN grasped at anti-submarine warfare as its salvation.

Building plans were announced the following year for a fleet of seven ships to be designed and built in Canada under the direction of Captain Rowland Baker, on loan from the Royal Corps of Naval Constructors. No one, including Baker, knew what the ships would cost. In one of the most remarkable industrial and technological commitments Canada ever made to its Navy, he would supervise the construction of a remarkable futuristic ship which would soon be praised as distinctly Canadian in appearance, as distinctive as the maple leaf.

Baker completed a rough sketch of the ship in 1949, based on a design that had been rejected by the British Admiralty. The end result was a Canadian hybrid – a mixture of British hull and machinery and American weapons and electronics. Work began at the Canadian Vickers Yard in Montreal using an innovative technique known as unit construction. The hull and main components were built elsewhere in units ranging in weight from five to 25 tons, and then transported to the ways, thereby greatly reducing building time in the shipyard. The hull was then built up by sections, a sea change from the traditional method of laying a keel and building a ship plate by plate.

As the building program expanded to include the Burrard Yard in Vancouver, Halifax Shipbuilding and MIL at Sorel, sections were designed to go through any rail tunnel in Canada. In an emergency, it was expected that steel manufacturers across the country would be assigned specific sections for prefabrication. At long last, a built-in Canada Navy, employing Canadian industry, was coming into being.

A 'BUCK ROGERS' FEEL

The new *St. Laurent* had a Buck Rogers look to it, old-timers said. It had smooth, rounded lines designed to shed heavy seas, ice and nuclear contaminants. There were no superfluous fittings or scuttles, no portholes and the anchors were stored in recesses behind heated, mechanically-operated doors. Weight-saving aluminum was used extensively in the superstructure, funnel casing, masts, storerooms and magazines. It was the first ship to introduce an operations room away from the bridge and she could be sealed off from the external environment. It was possible to walk from bow to stern without going on deck. A Cadillac, she was air-conditioned and was the first ship in the RCN to be furnished with bunks instead of hammocks.

Below decks, 50 miles of cable were installed along with 300 motors and generators. An "electrical wonderland," she had 12 separate telephone systems for internal communications and specialized lines for docking, damage control and radar maintenance. Propelled by a boiler design of much-reduced size and weight, she was fitted with twin screws and rudders.

Bofors and two three inch .50 calibre guns fore and aft made up the main armament, and she boasted state-of-the-art radar and sonar and the latest in anti-submarine weapons, including triple-barrelled limbo mortars and homing torpedoes.

The *St. Laurent* was commissioned on 29 October 1955. Evaluated at the U.S. Trials Centre at Key West, Florida, she then sailed up the Potomac to Washington to show herself off. She was praised by the American Secretary of the Navy as the finest warship of her kind ever built, before sailing on to England to escort the *Britannia* on a royal visit to Sweden. An admiring Lord of the Admiralty remarked: "Why couldn't we come up with a ship like this?"

Rebuilt in 1959, the *St. Laurent* and her sister ships were outfitted with improved weapons systems, and flight decks and hangers to accomodate helicopters. The funnels were twinned to make room on deck and all were fitted with new variable-depth sonar. The *St. Laurent* served with distinction until she was paid off on 14 June 1974.

The *Sally Rand* left Halifax for the last time on New Year's Day 1980, under tow by the tug *Odin Salvator*. Bound for a scrapyard in Brownsville, Texas, she foundered in a gale off Cape Hatteras 12 days later.

REPRINTED FROM:
Esprit de Corps, *Volume 8 Issue 3*
AUTHOR: *Bill Twatio*

THE 1956 SUEZ SUCCESS: PEARSON'S LEGACY

A year later, Pearson won the Nobel Peace Prize and Canada was committed to the business of peacekeeping.

TO HAVE PLAYED A major military role within NATO would have cost Canadians far more in defence dollars than the electorate was ever prepared to pay. However, it was once again Prime Minister Lester B. Pearson who first realized that a maximum of international clout could be gained through a minimum of military input — provided the mission was right. When the Suez crisis erupted in 1956, it quickly ensnared Britain, Israel, France and Egypt with the United States and the Soviet Union waiting in the wings. Given the potential for the "regional" conflict between Israel and Egypt to escalate quickly into a global nuclear holocaust, the United Nations moved with unusual speed to broker a settlement. It was Pearson who successfully proposed the deployment of an international peacekeeping force. (Ironically, it was not unlike the plan he'd suggested for Korea six years earlier, which was shot down by his own government.) Since Canada put forward the idea, the UN decided it would be up to Canada to command the mission — and to contribute a sizable portion of the troops.

A COMPLETE SUCCESS

Because these "peacekeepers" were not intended to engage in combat, they needed to be only lightly armed and highly mobile. Their mission in the Suez was to replace the British, French and Israeli troops who had successfully captured the Sinai Peninsula, and to monitor this newly created no man's land. Thanks in large part to the very willing cooperation of the French and British, who wanted to speedily extricate themselves from a delicate situation, Pearson's United Nations Emergency Force (UNEF) was hailed internationally as a complete success.

However, from a front-line perspective, the UN's Suez venture was plagued by the confusion and corruption born of a lack of experienced leadership and unified command. Among the UN soldiers, including nearly 1000 Canadians, there were chronic logistical screw-ups, which had created an almost laughable situation. When Canadian medical officers had requested 1500, five ounce bottles of cough syrup for the detachment, the supply depot had been unable to fill the order, all they had were five gallon jars of cough syrup. So 1500 of these oversized containers had been forwarded to Egypt. The ecstatic peacekeepers had promptly made vast quantities of homemade booze with the medicinal elixir. The cheap white paint purchased locally to convert the vehicles to their now traditional UN "colour" would never seem to dry properly. Sand stuck to everything and water washed the paint right off. On a more macabre note, a cheap coffin, acquired from an Egyptian shop, was used to bury a combat engineer who had been killed in a minefield. During the funeral, the casket began to leak blood onto the shoulder of the shortest pallbearer. Noticing the drips, the soldier raised his end higher, causing the same result at the opposite end of the coffin. When Peter Worthington, then a young reporter for the *Toronto Telegram* (and a veteran of the Second World War and Korea) wrote about the situation, it sparked an angry response from the army brass. Major General E.L.M. Burns, the Canadian Forces Commander in Egypt, had been John Bassett's brigade commander throughout the Italian campaign in the Second World War. Bassett had left the military after the war, and went on to become the *Telegram*'s publisher. Burns wrote an angry letter to Bassett suggesting his old comrade "fire" Worthington. The general did not dispute the accuracy of the reports, he simply felt that Worthington should have known better than to cast the military in a bad light. Bassett ignored the letter.

THE NOBEL PEACE PRIZE

Despite the bad publicity, one year later Lester B. Pearson won the Nobel Peace Prize for this diplomatic triumph in Suez. Thereafter, the Canadian army was extensively committed to the business of peacekeeping as successive Canadian governments tried to emulate Pearson's formula for getting a maximum political return on a minimal military investment. As a result, in just over four decades, nearly 100,000 Canadian troops have participated in 31 United Nations missions.

The first opportunity to duplicate the

LEFT: *Canadian members of the United Nations Emergency Force (UNEF) patrol the dunes of the Sinai desert in Egypt. Serving under Major General E.L.M. Burns, the Canadian Force Commander, the troops suffered chronic logistical screw-ups during the 1956 mission.* (DND PHOTO)

Suez "success" came in 1960, when a full-scale civil war erupted in the Congo. The UN decided to intervene in what soon became the largest, most controversial operation to date for Canada. The request for participation could not have come at a worse time. The economy was in a recession and our meagre military resources were overextended. As the political pressure from New York mounted and public opinion swayed, John Diefenbaker's Progressive Conservative government reluctantly agreed to provide a 280-man signals squadron.

Shortly after a contingent of our first troops arrived at the Congolese city of Stanleyville, they were immediately taken into custody, stripped and beaten with rifle butts. "Better beaten than eaten," one of the victims bravely told Canadian reporters after the incident. The officer in charge of the Canadian detachment, Captain John Pariseau, chose not to raise the issue with the Congolese commander, or the United Nations. As a result, the much relieved Congolese general provided every possible concession to these Canucks for the rest of their deployment. Like the Suez operation, the UN's Congo foray broke down into chaos. There were 20,000 UN troops from 30 different nations and even their Swedish commander, Major General Carl Carlsson von Horn, described his force as "an armed mob in which logic, military principles — even common sense — took a second place to political favours." Of the mission itself, the general likened it to giving first aid to a rattlesnake. For everyone involved, the UN Congo operation was mercifully short-lived — from 1960 to 1964.

REPRINTED FROM:

Tested Mettle:

Canada's Peacekeepers at War

AUTHORS:

Scott Taylor & Brian Nolan

PEARSON'S PEACE PRIZE

ABOVE: *Lester B. Pearson*

"LESTER PEARSON IS A big man from a country that is a small power," the *New York Times* declared. "He is probably better known abroad than in Canada." So it seemed to his colleague, John Holmes, when he arrived at the United Nations on the afternoon of 1 November 1956, at the height of the Suez crisis. He marvelled at Pearson's reputation as he was swarmed by anxious diplomats asking, "What's he got? We hear Mike's got a proposal. Can he do it?"

Both the *Times,* which extolled his virtues, and Holmes, may have exaggerated Pearon's importance, but Canada's Minister of External Affairs was highly regarded in U.N. corridors. He had kept Canada uncommitted since the crisis began, had consistently urged that the U.N. was the proper forum for negotiations, and scribbling notes amid the din of delegates sipping whiskey sours in the North Lounge, had worked out a plan of action. Dismissing previous resolutions as no more than a return to an unacceptable status quo, he strode to the podium and called for a "United Nations force large enough to keep the peace while a political settlement is being worked out." It was, Holmes said, "one of the most potent conditional sentences in U.N. history."

AVOIDING A DISASTROUS SETBACK

Five days later, Pearson secured an agreement to establish a United Nations Emergency Force (UNEF) under the command of Major General E.M.L. Burns of Canada. Speaking with deep conviction, he told the General Assembly that "if we can exploit the possibilities of a U.N. force quickly and effectively we may not only find a way out of present difficulties and have saved the U.N. a disastrous setback, but also have paved the way for U.N. progress in the whole field of collective security."

The idea of a U.N. presence in areas of conflict was not a novel concept. Some 500 military observers had been sent to the Mid-East in 1948-49 to supervise armistice agreements between Israel and the Arab states and a smaller number, including five Canadians, were observing a ceasefire in Kashmir. Canada also had a battalion still serving with U.N. Forces in Korea and was beginning to shoulder the burden of peacekeeping duties in Indochina.

Pearson took no special credit for having advanced the proposal for a U.N. police force. He told the House of Commons that he had discussed the idea with the British as early as 1953, when it was judged to be impractical, and again in 1955. His immediate objective had been to work out "an enduring and honourable settlement for [the Mid-East]," and, just as important for Canada, to "restore unity amongst the allies." He did concede, however, that "we may have started something of immense value for the future... a step to put force behind the collective will of the international community under law." A pragmatic idealist, he had joined together the principal imperative of Canadian foreign policy at that time - transatlantic unity - with his own vision of a more secure world.

When informed that he had won the Nobel Peace Prize, Pearon's only comment was a modest and memorable "Gosh!"

AUTHOR: *Bill Twatio*

NORAD

Geography and history have bred a long tradition of Canadian and American military co-operation. Not, however, without concerns for our sovereignty.

WILLIAM LYON MACKENZIE KING, Canada's perpetual Prime Minister, once remarked that Canada has too much geography and too little history. In the postwar years, both would assert their importance in forming a realistic defence policy.

Geography is an immutable part of any strategic appreciation and imposes constraints on the formation of policy it would be dangerous to deny. The undeniable reality is that Canada is a vast and sparsely populated country bounded on three sides by oceans and on the fourth by the United States. Historically, that reality has led to a long tradition of military co-operation with our American neighbours. Not, however, without concerns about Canadian sovereignty.

"I give to you assurance," President Roosevelt told an audience at Queen's University in August 1938, as war clouds gathered in Europe, "that the people of the United States will not stand idly by if domination of Canadian soil is threatened by any other empire." His speech was an echo through time of Washington's farewell address and the Monroe Doctrine of 1823. Three days later, Mackenzie King responded, in his convoluted style, in a speech at Woodbridge, Ontario.

"We too have our obligations as a good and friendly neighbour," he said, "and one of them is to see that, at our own instance, our country is made as immune from attack or possible invasion as we can reasonably be expected to make it and that, should the occasion ever arise, enemy forces should not be able to pursue their way, either by land, sea or air, to the United States across Canadian Territory."

The danger at hand brought King and Roosevelt together at Ogdensburg, New York, in August 1940. As the Battle of Britain raged, they issued a statement which came to be known as the Ogdensburg Declaration, providing for a common defence of the northern half of the Western Hemisphere and the establishment of a Permanent Joint Board on Defence. The Declaration constituted the first mutual defence agreement by the United States with a belligerent nation

ABOVE: *As part of the early warning system established across northern Canada during the Cold War years, this RCAF radar station was built on the Pinetree Line.* (DND PHOTO)

ABC-22

The formation of the Permanent Joint Board on Defence (PJBD) was the first step toward continental integration in military affairs. Meeting in Ottawa on 26 August, the Board presented a defence plan to deal with the alarming possibility that Britain might be defeated. In the spring of 1941, the Board met again to prepare the joint Canadian-United States Basic Defence Plan No. 2. Dubbed ABC-22, it outlined five joint tasks for continental defence to remain in effect for the duration of the war.

As the war wound down, it became evident that postwar defence policy would demand close attention to American security requirements, particularly as the growing antagonism between the United States and the Soviet Union could lead to confrontation. One of the first documents on the subject was submitted by Lieutenant General Maurice Pope, chairman of the Canadian Joint Staff Mission in Washington, and a member of the PJBD.

"In such circumstances, our position will be a difficult one," he wrote. "To the Americans the defence of the United States is continental defence, which includes us, and nothing that I can think of will ever drive that idea out of their heads. Should, then, the United States go to war with Russia they would look to us to make common cause with them and, as I judge their public opinion, they would brook no delay."

General Pope recommended the renewal of ABC-22 and emphasized the importance of maintaining a strong defence establishment "not so much as to defend ourselves... but to ensure that there was no apprehension as to our security in the American public mind."

Standing across the shortest air routes between the Soviet Union and the United States, Canada now acquired immense strategic importance to the Americans. Air power opened the continent to attack. Not only was Canada vulnerable to direct attack, it was also thrust into even closer defence ties with the United States.

Efforts to revise ABC-22 continued into 1946, culminating in a Joint Canadian - U.S. Basic Security Plan. The authors of the Plan noted that modern aircraft, missiles and

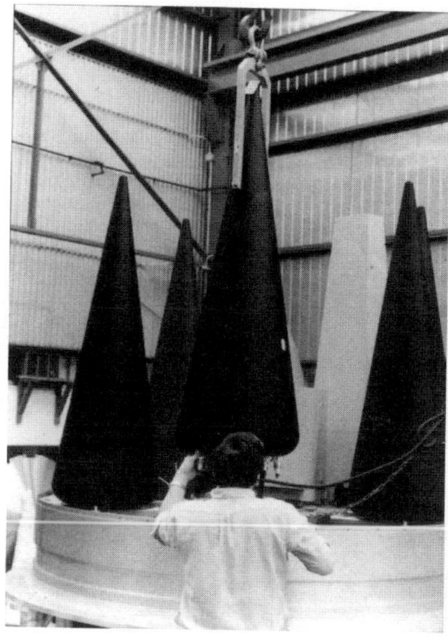

RIGHT: *Warheads are carefully loaded onto an American Inter-Continental Ballistic Missile (ICBM).* ***FAR RIGHT:*** *This MGM-118 Peacekeeper ballistic missile, test-launched in the 1980s, is but one type of ICMB developed by the U.S.. Others include the Minuteman, Titan and Pershing missiles. (BOTH U.S. ARMY PHOTOS)*

submarines had rendered the continent more vulnerable than ever. Around 1950, they warned there would be an additional threat posed by missiles with nuclear warheads targeted against "executive, military, and industrial centres." An attack would come over the polar regions, particularly in the northeast, and an effective defence would have to barricade those routes. They concluded that this would entail a comprehensive warning system with suitable interceptor aircraft and air bases

RADAR LINES AND TEXAS TOWERS

The Basic Security Plan was a boon to A.V. Roe Aircraft – and to the RCAF, which was soon allotted the lion's share of the defence budget. CF-100s rolled off Avro's production lines at Malton to equip nine new air defence squadrons and plans were being developed for a supersonic fighter, the CF-105 Arrow.

Canada's few radar installations were merged into the Pinetree Line straggling along the 49th parallel, Canada paying a third of the cost and sharing operating and personnel costs with the United States. The Mid-Canada Line or "McGill Fence" was completed in 1955, the same year that work began on a Distant Early Warning (DEW) Line in the Arctic stretching from Alaska to Greenland. As Canada had accepted responsibility for the Mid-Canada Line, American taxpayers bore the enormous cost of the DEW Line. These radar lines were supplemented by offshore long-range radars on platforms, called Texas Towers, ship-borne radar and airborne early warning (AEW) radar flown around the clock aboard USAF Super Constellations.

It was now virtually impossible for a bomber to penetrate North American airspace undetected. In the unlikely event that one did, it would have to run a gauntlet of all-weather interceptors from Alaska down through the lower states. F-89s, F-102s, F-106s,Skyrays, CF-100s and batteries of Nike missiles were on constant alert.

It was a formidable operation, yet it was soon challenged by a weapon it could do nothing to stop – the Inter Contintental Ballistic Missile (ICBM).

The radar lines were built on American initiative with Canada's half-hearted cooperation. Ottawa skirmished endlessly with Washington over issues of cost, jurisdiction and control of the facilities. The DEW Line was of particular concern as the installations, most on Canadian territory, were restricted to American personnel. Although the Americans attempted to placate Canada by recognizing long-standing Arctic claims, their presence in the north raised the most serious questions about Canadian sovereignty since the construction of the Alaska Highway.

The Louis St. Laurent government reluctantly granted interception rights over Canada to the USAF, and Diefenbaker's extended the agreement to allow the use of air-to-air nuclear weapons. By the mid-1950s, there was a widespread public sense that Canadian independece was being compromised.

WAR AND PEACE

But the Americans wanted more. In December 1956, they proposed a fully unified operational command. The newly-elected John Diefenbaker government indicated that it accepted Canada's place in the Western alliance in principle and had no desire to challenge the relationship either in North America or Europe. Diefenbaker was easily convinced by the Chief of Defence Staff, General Charles Foulkes, that delay was unacceptable. "I am afraid," he later told a House of Commons committee, "that we stampeded the incoming government with the NORAD agreement." With little time for reflection, the appropriate documents were signed and the North American Air Defence Command came into being on 12 May 1958.

It was agreed that NORAD would operate with an American commander and a Canadian deputy commander from headquarters at Colorado Springs, with separate regional headquarters. All data from the DEW, Mid-Canada and Pinetree lines would be processed through these centres and North Bay would be equipped with the Semi-Automatic Ground Environment (SAGE) interpretation equipment. Diefenbaker told reporters that "the appointment of a Canadian as Deputy Commander-in-Chief will give Canada a proper measure of responsibility in any decision that might have to be taken to defend North America against an attack. "

The prime minister might not have been stampeded, but he missed the implications of his decision. He had approved a tightly centralized defence system in which the Americans could order Canadian forces into action without the consent of Parliament.

If Robert Borden and Mackenzie King had stuggled for Canada's right to control its destiny, Diefenbaker had unwittingly signed it away.

AUTHOR: *Bill Twatio*

THE CLUNK

The CF-100 all-weather interceptor was superior to any aircraft in its class and secured Avro's reputation for excellence in design.

ABOVE:
The first CF-100 Mk1. One of two prototypes powered by Rolls-Royce Avon engines, it made its first flight on 19 January 1950 with test pilot Bill Waterton at the controls. (PRIVATE COLLECTION)

WAR HAD CREATED A modern aircraft industry in Canada. Peace almost destroyed it. An industry that had produced 16,400 military aircraft came to a standstill. Boeing faded away in Vancouver; Noorduyn in Montreal. Canadian Vickers reorganized as Canadair. Victory Aircraft in Malton, which had started out as National Steel Car with a contract to build Lysanders and moved on to Lancasters, sent 10,000 workers home without notice. Only 300 stayed on to clear out the production bays.

The federal government, which owned the largest aircraft plants, was anxious to get out of the business as soon as the war ended. War surplus and Crown Corporations became the biggest bargains in the country. Tireless and single-minded, Roy Dobson of the British Hawker-Siddely Group, managing director of A.V. Roe, Manchester and the driving force behind the Lancaster, was not a man to miss a bargain.

Dobson had visited Canada during the war to welcome the "Ruhr Express," the first of 422 Lancasters to be built at Malton. His business instincts told him that the Canadian aviation industry had tremendous potential. "It opened my eyes, I'll tell you," he later confessed. "If these so-and-so's can do this during a war, what can't they do after it." With some expertise in aeronautical engineering, Dobson believed that Canada would have all the necessary elements to compete in the postwar international market. Design and development talent and getting it to Canada was precisely what he could arrange. Before he returned to England, Dobson managed to convey his enthusiasm to C.D. Howe, the Minister of Reconstruction and Supply.

On 1 December 1945, with Howe's blessings, A. V. Roe Aircraft of Canada acquired the Victory plant and set to work storing Lancasters, making forms for plastic brushes, fenders for cars and trucks and saucepans; taking on any job that would help it through the difficult transition period. Generous capital assistance from the government, accelerated depreciation allowances and cost-plus contracts, gave the company the edge it needed to expand. Within 12 years, Avro, as it came to be known, would grow into a diversified complex of nearly 40 companies with 41,000 employees, becoming the third largest corporation in Canada and the industrial arm of the RCAF.

Far from being a dependent branch-plant operation, Avro engaged Canadians in research and development that would put the company in the forefront of aviation technology. It would build the world's first commercial jet transport, the Canuck, the Arrow and the Orenda and Iroquois engines in a country that seemed to hold unlimited promise. That promise died in the winter of 1959

LEFT:
The Avrocar was a vertical takeoff and landing aircraft developed for the U.S. Department of Defence. It was capable of wobbly flight at very low levels. (PRIVATE COLLECTION)

THE AVRO JETLINER

While Avro was making pots and pans, Dobson was haunting the Department of National Defence in search of aircraft contracts. "Oh, lumme, I got a cold reception there," he said. "Canada doesn't want to embark on aircraft design and research they told me. Canada is too small and should only build on licence. That's rubbish, I said, Canada does want an aircraft industry. What you want to see is poor old Bob here being a kept woman and having to rely for his livelihood on other people's resources." Dobson, with characteristic tenacity, would not be moved until he had an agreement to design and develop two prototype jet fighters. Nor did he stop there. In March 1946, he secured a letter of intent from Trans-Canada Airlines to purchase a 30-seat jet airliner.

Seven days a week, for two years, Avro engineers had laboured with the revolutionary idea of using jet engines in a commercial transport. "I've worked on a few airplanes and I've never before seen such an emotional involvement," Project Manager Jim Floyd said. "They were going to make it fly, make it a good one, and they did."

The C-102 Jetliner, powered by four Roll-Royce Derwent engines flew for the first time on 10 August 1949, two weeks after the de Havilland Comet was unveiled in Britain. On 18 April 1950, it completed the first international jet transport flight in North America by flying from Toronto to New York. With a cruising speed of 500 m.p.h., it covered the distance in just seventy minutes, impressing passengers with the lack of noise and vibration. A New York newspaper wrote: "The Canadian plane's feats accelerated a process already begun in this nation – a realization that Uncle Sam has no monopoly on genius."

Avro was soon busy showing off the Jetliner to interested parties all over the continent, including the USAF and the U.S. Navy. Unfortunately, interest did not translate into sales. American airlines were committed to the Super Constellation and the DC-6B. TCA expressed concern about the Jetliner's fuel consumption. With the outbreak of war in Korea, C.D. Howe ordered Avro to concentrate production on the CF-100 interceptor.

ABOVE:
North America's first jet transport, the Avro Jetliner, was successfully tested on 10 August 1949. A victim of the Cold War and the need to focus on CF-100 procurement, it was scrapped in 1970 without ever having gone into production.
(PRIVATE COLLECTION)

The Jetliner flew for several more years on projects relating to the development of the CF-100. It flew for the last time on 23 November 1956, then was grounded as maintenance costs soared and spare parts became scarce. It was offered to museums, but there were no takers. The Jetliner was sold for scrap and cut up. Its main wheels ended up on a farm wagon.

THE AVROCAR

The demise of the Jetliner was a disappointment, but it did not dampen spirits at Avro. 1956 was a vintage year for the company. Early problems with the CF-100 and Orenda engines had been overcome and the CF-105 was on the drawing boards. Work was also underway on a "flying saucer" for the U.S. Department of Defence.

In the early fifties, the U. S. military commissioned Avro to build a plane capable of vertical takeoff and landing. The result was project Y, fondly known as the Avrocar. It was an intriguing machine which resembled a partially flattened doughnut. Circular, with a hole in the middle, it was powered by a central fan driven by three Continental J69 jet engines. It was capable of wobbly flight at very low levels, but was deemed too unstable. When the project was cancelled, two prototypes were sent to the United States. One is now in the U.S. National Air and Space Museum in Washington, D.C., while the other, in poor condition, is on display outside the U.S. Army Transportation Museum at Fort Eustis, Virginia.

It was an exciting time at Malton and even C.D. Howe was feeling effusive. "I congratulate you," he wrote in October "on having assembled a very efficient organization and on having achieved your production objectives. You certainly have a fine lot of top executives as well as a highly efficient labour force."

THE CF-100

The CF-100 was the only one of Avro's postwar designs to reach production. Affectionately dubbed "The Clunk" or "The Lead Sled," it was also the only jet fighter ever completely designed and built in Canada. Between 1950 and 1958, 692 were built to equip nine home-based RCAF all-weather fighter squadrons and four in Europe. In addition, 53 American-financed CF-100's were sold to Belgium under the terms of the NATO Mutual Aid Plan.

The CF-100 made its first flight on 19

January 1950, with test-pilot Bill Waterton at the controls. The black prototype was powered by Rolls-Royce Avon engines, although work was well underway on a Canadian engine, the Orenda. Observers were impressed. At 16 tons, it was the world's heaviest fighter and with a speed of 600 m.p.h., one of the most formidable. Waterton said that "this is the first aircraft I have flown for some time that I wouldn't mind going to war in."

C. D. Howe was on hand at Malton a year later when the RCAF formally took possession of the CF-100, remarking that "the aircraft as it stands before us is a notable achievement... a milestone in Canadian industrial development." Soon after, the RCAF formed its first CF-100 unit, No. 3 All-Weather Operational Training Unit at North Bay.

Armed with a 50-calibre machine gun pack and later with 2.75 inch rockets in wing pods, the CF-100 had a ceiling of 60,000 feet. It had a good rate of climb, excellent radar and fire-control systems and very reliable engines, much-needed over the vast expanse of northern Canada and in the fog and murk of France and West Germany. On 18 December 1952, Chief Development Pilot Jan Zurakowski took a Mark 4 into a dive and exceeded Mach 1, making the CF-100 the first straight-winged aircraft to break the sound barrier without rocket power.

ABOVE:
A CF-100 Mk 3a used by the RCAF Central Experimental and Proving Establishment for testing Velvet Glove missiles.
(PRIVATE COLLECTION)

Zurakowski had nursed the CF-100 through its development phase. The process was laborious, tedious and sometimes terrifying. In the summer of 1954, while testing a fuselage rocket-pack, he was forced to eject when a fuel leak caused an on-board explosion. His observer was killed.

The CF-100 was superior to any aircraft in its class, largely due to the performance of the Orenda engine. Orendas were also installed in Canadair F-86 Sabres and sold abroad. A total run of nearly 4,000 engines secured Avro's reputation for production efficiency and excellence in design.

Avro's next undertaking, a gleaming-white, delta-winged supersonic interceptor, indicated that the company was not content to rest on its laurels. More than an aircraft, the CF-105 Arrow would become the stuff of legend.

AUTHOR: *Bill Twatio*

FALLEN ARROWS

Hailed as a technical masterpiece, the gleaming white CF-105 Arrow was a legend in its time... No aircraft in the world could match it.

AT THE FARNBOROUGH AIR show in 1951, Jan Zurakowski astonished observers with his "Zurabatics" in a ground attack variant of the Meteor F-8. Each day of the show, he would pull up into a steep climb and by throttling back one engine with the other at full power, execute one-and-a-half vertical cartwheels.

He had honed his flying skills in the RAF and the Empire Test Pilot's School. Flying Meteors, Javelins and the GA.5, he established a reputation as the best test pilot in Britain. Peter Cope, a fellow pilot with Hawker-Siddely remarked that he had a "built-in ability to diagnose airplane responses in terms of its performance and handling ability." This, and infinite patience, made for a test pilot of incomparable skill.

Jan Zurakowski was at the controls of the Avro Arrow as it turned to line up on a runway at Malton on 25 March 1958. Rescue vehicles and fire trucks stood ready as he opened the throttles and released the brakes. Accelerating to 150 knots, the nose wheel lifted off and he was suddenly airborne. A controller radioed a terse message; "Avro 201 off at 9:51 and cleared to company tower." Thousands of Avro workers cheered.

There were few surprises as the Arrow climbed to 11,000 feet on that first brief flight. Zurakowski's snag list consisted of a brief comment about two electrical switches. There was more tension on the ground than in the cockpit when he turned into his final approach. Tension gave way to elation when he landed smoothly and deployed the drag chute.

THE BOOMING FIFTIES

The Avro Arrow was born on the crest of an

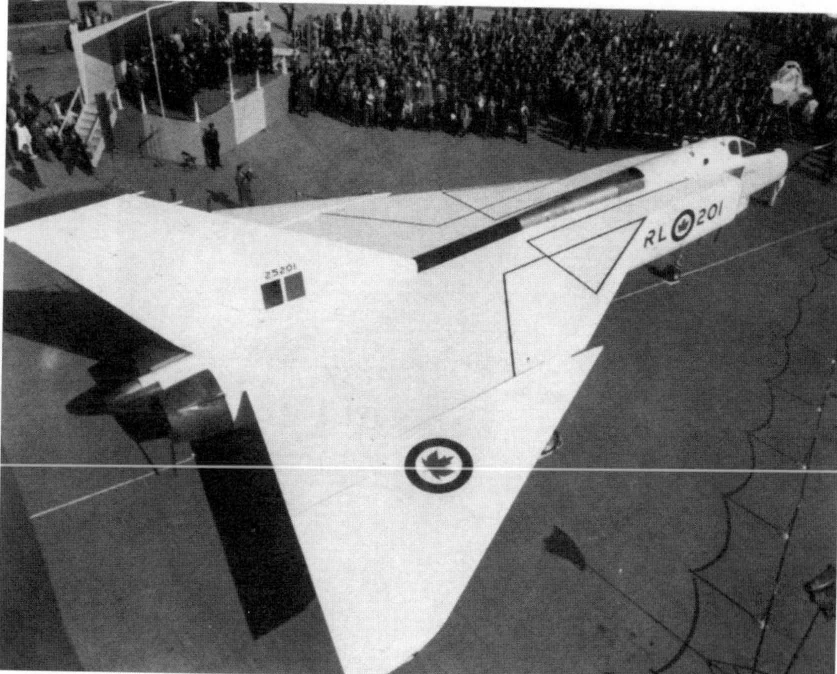

ABOVE, RIGHT: *The roll-out of the first CF-105 Arrow at Malton, 4 October 1958. Within months, prototypes, parts and drawings were destroyed and Canada's national pride had been dealt a savage blow. A superb aircraft, the Canadian air force would not see its like again until the 1980s and the acquisition of the CF-18 Hornet (**ABOVE, LEFT**).*

economic boom. To the amazement of most Canadians, years of scarcity, war and rationing had been followed by a time of rising incomes and full employment. Sprawling suburbs seemed to spring up overnight in farmers' fields surrounding the cities. Every household came equipped with new appliances, remorselessly advertised on the equally new medium of television. New cars sped along new highways. A subway was under construction in Toronto to ease traffic congestion in the streets. The manufacturing sector expanded rapidly and free-flowing American capital stimulated the development of oil and gas reserves, iron ore, nickel and uranium mines.

The fifties were also a time of fear. The Soviet Union, an esteemed wartime ally, was now regarded as a renegade state and threat to world peace as it subjugated the nations of Eastern Europe. Winston Churchill spoke of an "Iron Curtain" and the phrase, "The Cold War," entered the international political and military lexicons.

In Ottawa, Igor Gouzenko, a cipher clerk at the Soviet embassy, had dismayed Canadians in September 1945, with evidence of widespread espionage activities. That dismay deepened in the years to come with news of growing Soviet airpower and the knowledge that the Soviet Union would soon have an atomic bomb. A dispirited Prime Minister Mackenzie King wrote: "it was the most serious situation that we could possibly have imagined and indeed it was altogether beyond anything I had hitherto thought possible. In a word, it came down to this; that within three weeks, there may be another world war. "

THE FIFTIES WERE ALSO A TIME OF FEAR. THE SOVIET UNION, AN ESTEEMED WARTIME ALLY, WAS NOW REGARDED AS A RENEGADE STATE AND THREAT TO WORLD PEACE

Armageddon may not have been immediately at hand, but there was legitimate cause for concern. In June 1950, South Korea came under attack, evidence to some that the Soviet Union was prepared to risk war to further its foreign policy objectives. In response, NATO took on new importance, Germany was rearmed and military spending increased dramatically. Between 1947 and 1953, the defence budget increased from $300 million to $2 billion and the permanent force expanded to 104,000. For the first time in its peacetime history,Canada stationed armed forces abroad. A brigade group was sent to Germany to be followed by the No. 1 Air Division, Europe – four RCAF fighter wings, each with three squadrons of F-86 Sabres. At home, the Air Defence Command grew to 19 squadrons, nine of which were equipped with the Avro CF-100 Canuck.

PAYING THE PRICE

On May Day 1954, less than a year after the Soviet Union exploded a hydrogen bomb, a new strategic bomber, the all-jet, Myasishchev M-4 flew over Moscow. Capable of reaching targets in North America with a nuclear payload, it radically altered strategic planning. Air defence became all-important and the RCAF's budget soon exceeded that of the army and navy combined. A.V. Roe, thrived as defence planners insisted that the air defence of Canada would be seriously weakened without a

strong and independent aircraft industry to support it.

The Soviet M-4 and its successors rendered the CF-100 obsolete. By 1956, it was much too slow to catch incoming bombers. At best, a radar controller could vector the fighter onto the flight path, giving the pilot a single chance to sight and destroy the target. Avro was commissioned to build a successor.

Design studies were already well under way. Like the CF-100, it was determined that its replacement would require a crew of two – a pilot and a specially-trained navigator – and two engines would be preferred for reasons of performance and safety. However, it would not be designed to range across the vast distances of Canada's north. Rather, would have to have the capability to climb high and very fast to guard the avenues to key target areas. Sophisticated weapons systems and counter-measure features would also be needed. Cost soon became a serious concern.

"I understand that your department is planning a substantial development programme for new supersonic jet engines and for a fighter aircraft," C.D. Howe wrote to Minister of Defence Brooke Claxton in the winter of 1953. "Before authorizing these items, I think you should appreciate what has already been spent on the Orenda engine and on the CF-100 to date. I must say I am frightened for the first time in my defence production experience." He would later tell the House of Commons that "we have started on a program of development that gives me the shudders. "

THE SOVIET M-4 AND ITS SUCCESSORS RENDERED THE CF-100 OBSOLETE. BY 1956, IT WAS MUCH TOO SLOW TO CATCH INCOMING BOMBERS.

ABOVE:
An artist's impression of Avro 25201 – the first Arrow to be built and flown.
(ILLUSTRATION BY PETER MOSSMAN)

OPPOSITE PAGE:
Avro 25202 followed by an F-86 Sabre on a test flight, October 1957.
(PRIVATE COLLECTION)

Nevertheless, development and tooling up went forward on the assumption that the aircraft, now known as the CF-105, would go into production. There was no realistic assessment of the costs until the election of a Conservative government in 1957.

AIRBORNE

Under tight security, a prototype was taking shape at the Avro plant in Malton. Sixteen wind-tunnel models were tested and free flight models launched over Lake Ontario. Armament was also tested and work began on the Iroquois engine. Beyond the plant, there were few facts and fewer rumours to go on concerning the aircraft until it was rolled out of a hangar on 4 October 1957.

Christened the Arrow, the gleaming white delta-winged fighter was hailed as a technical masterpiece and Avro could once again boast the world's most advanced all-weather interceptor. Early test flights indicated that the Arrow could easily exceed Mach 2 and climb to 60,000 feet in less than four minutes. It was the first supersonic aircraft to ever fly in Canada and there was no aircraft in the world that could match it.

The Arrow had been designed to perform a highly specialized role, that of intercepting and destroying enemy bombers. That role was now being questioned. Unveiled on the same day that the Soviet's launched Sputnik, experts declared the bomber passé and warned of a new threat, the ICBM. Defence Minister Pearkes told cabinet that "the main threat to North

America will probably be from ballistic missiles with the manned bomber decreasing in importance. Futhermore, ground-to-air missiles have now reached the point where they are at least as effective as a manned fighter and cheaper. "

BLACK FRIDAY

Faced with conflicting advice, complex technology and soaring costs, the Diefenbaker cabinet dithered. As the country slipped into recession, it became increasingly difficult to justify continued work on the Arrow. A single Arrow could now cost $6 million and the entire project was wreaking havoc with the defence budget. The RCAF cut its orders from four hundred to one hundred aircraft and frantic sales efforts produced no foreign buyers. Pearkes recommended that the project be cancelled.

On Friday, 20 February 1959, the Prime Minister rose in the House of Commons and announced "that the development of the Arrow aircraft and the Iroquois engine should be terminated now." The bomber threat had diminished, he said, and "alternate means of meeting the threat developed much earlier than was expected... formal notice of termination now being given to the contractors. "

At Malton, as news of the cancellation reached the shop floor, 13,000 workers downed tools. At 14:00 hours they were sent home. Ironically, the prime minister was shocked. "A more callous act would be hard to imagine," he said.

AFTER NEGOTIATIONS, THE GOVERNMENT ANNOUNCED THAT CANADA WOULD ACQUIRE THE BOMARC-B MISSILE, A MISSILE REJECTED BY THE U.S.A.F.

After complicated negotiations, the government announced that Canada would acquire the Bomarc-B missile, a missile rejected by the United States Air Force, and 66 ageing F-101 Voodoo fighters already relegated to the National Guard. Overseas squadrons were to be equipped with F-104 Starfighters built by licence by Canadair in Montreal.

A few weeks later, as seven Arrows were towed out of the hangars at Malton to be reduced to scrap, Jan Zurakowski was on his way to the Ottawa Valley and a new career. Grounded, Zurakowski was now the proud proprietor of a fishing lodge.

AUTHOR: *Bill Twatio*

THE LATE, GREAT HMCS LABRADOR

A worthy successor to the lengendary *St. Roch*, the *Labrador* earned a reputation as the finest Arctic research vessel in the world.

THERE WAS SOMETHING very special about this journey into Vancouver harbor in the autumn of 1954. As she rounded Point Atkinson, the *Labrador* was joined by Henry Larsen's legendary little RCMP schooner, the *St. Roch*, the only vessel to traverse the Northwest Passage twice: from west to east in 1940-42 and east to west in 1944. As the *Labrador's* helicopters roared overhead, ships' horns blared, fireboats loosed columns of water, and a great cheer went up from the crowds lining the jetties. That evening, the *St. Roch*'s ensign was laid up for the last time while buglers from *Labrador* played a sad refrain.

HMCS Labrador was a worthy successor to the *St. Roch*. In her brief career, she was the first warship to ever circumnavigate the North American continent and contributed more to our knowledge of the Arctic than any single ship in this century.

Laid down in the Marine Industries shipyard in Sorrel, Quebec, in January 1949, she was 369 feet long, 63 feet, 6 inches at the beam, and displaced 6490 tons. Powered by six 2000 horsepower diesel engines, she was capable of 16 knots. Deep-drafted and round-bottomed, with big screws tucked away well below the plimsoll line out of reach of tumbling surface ice, she was fitted with retractable stabilizing fins and heeling tanks on the port and starboard sides capable of pumping water from side to side at the remarkable rate of 40,000 gallons a minute, allowing her to roll in pack ice. With a crew of 225 officers and men and three helicopters, the *Labrador* was not simply an ice-breaker. She was commissioned to pa-

trol northern waters and show the flag, conduct hydrographic and scientific surveys and provide a rescue and salvage service.

Under the command of Owen, "Long Robbie" Robertson, an enormously tall officer and fine seaman who had won the George Medal in WWII for towing a blazing ammunition ship out of Halifax harbour, the *Labrador* set sail on her maiden voyage on 23 July 1954.

ANY DAY IS SUNDAY

Moving north out of Halifax into the Strait of Belle Isle and Davis Strait with ten scientists and 80 tons of coal for the RCMP station at Alexandra Fiord aboard, she ran into dense fog banks. Icebergs and bergy bits - fragments usually not more than 15 feet high and 30 feet across – drifted ominously past in the gloom. Once, 50 icebergs appeared as contacts on her radar screens. The first solid ice she encountered was four-tenths and fairly rotten. Four-tenths to six-tenths ice is normally described as "open pack" while "polar ice" is more than one winter's growth and ten feet in thickness. Her first ice-breaking mission began when she entered Lancaster Sound, churning through fields of rotten pack ice. All off-duty personnel hurried out on deck to watch the ice floes crumple beneath her bows.

GOOFING STATIONS

In the days to come, they would scurry topside again and again to catch a sight of towering blue and white icebergs, seals, walruses and polar bears. This informal sight-seeing was known as "goofing" and "All hands to goofing stations!" was a pipe heard repeatedly at the start of the voyage.

Open water lay beyond Lancaster Sound, and *Labrador* reached Resolute on the southern coast of Cornwallis Island on 1 August, landing a hydrographic party with beacons and enough provisions to last for three weeks. While they were ashore, she carried out her own scientific studies in Barrow Strait. At Craig Harbour, she took Special Constable Arreak of the RCMP aboard along with his wife, four children, and a pack of snarling sled dogs. When a Chief Petty Officer, accustomed to tamer breeds, went forward to give the dogs water, they ignored it and ate his gloves. To his immense relief, they were put ashore at Alexandra Fiord on 8 August along with Arreak, his family and the ship's cargo of coal. The last 15 tons were landed in a race between teams of officers and chiefs. The latter won by less than a minute and were awarded a battered tin plate inscribed, "Presented by the Ellesmere Island Jockey Club."

Using *Resolute* as a base, *Labrador* continued her meteorological and oceanographic studies. Ice, fog and gales dictated when work was possible. The crew worked in shifts during the endless days of the Arctic summer and Sunday was proclaimed whenever work was interrupted by the weather. "Today will be considered Sunday," was piped and the padre held services on the flight deck or in the seamen's mess.

The ghosts of ancient mariners – Roual Amundsen, G. Stefansson, John Franklin and Martin Frobisher – haunted the crew. Sailing in relative luxury, they came to appreciate their trials and triumphs. At Erebus Bay officers and men went ashore to pay their respects at the Franklin Memorial. They were joined by a polar bear, which nonchalantly smashed an oil-drum with his paw before wandering off. Curious bears were a constant menace. A few days earlier, Captain Robertson was forced to shoot a bear, which was stalking a geodetic party. Civilian workers in the area boasted that

ABOVE: *HMCS* Labrador *was commissioned into the Royal Canadian Navy on 8 July 1954 and, until 1957 was Canada's only Arctic patrol vessel. She would make a total of four voyages to patrol and survey Canada's northern border.* (CANADIAN FORCES PHOTO UNIT)

***HMCS* Labrador *returns to the port of Halifax in 1955 after her second Arctic voyage.* (NAC/PA 201412)**

they had the only red-headed polar bear in the Arctic – he had dipped his head into an open five-gallon can of red paint.

After pulling a Boston dragger, the *Monte Carlo*, free from the ice in Baring Channel, the *Labrador* headed west to join the Beauport Sea Expedition – surveying and collecting hydrographic data through Prince of Wales and Amundsen Gulf. Finally, she passed through the Bering Strait to the Pacific and her rendezvous with the *St. Roch*. And then she was off for home by way of Esquimalt and the Panama Canal. As she sailed into warmer waters, hammocks were rigged on the upper decks and a machine-gun sponson was flooded for use as a swimming pool. She sailed into Halifax on 21 November 1954, having established conclusively that it was possible to take a large ship through the Northwest Passage.

ON THE DEW LINE

Re-fitted, the *Labrador* headed north again in the summer of 1955 to carry out survey work in preparation for the sea-lift of materials for the construction of the Distant Early Warning Line, a gigantic project that would employ 25,000 men. In Hudson Strait she encountered ten-tenths ice, approximately 12 feet thick. She broke through the ice at Coal Harbour and as soon as there was enough clear water in which to work, charted the approaches for supply ships, set up navigational beacons and sent a party ashore to clear the beach. At the beginning of July, she set up electronic position indicators at Cape Enauolikon Baffin Island, then anchored four miles off Cape Donovanon Southampton Island, using her helicopters to ferry equipment ashore. At Hall Beach the crew found time to win a softball game on the ice against a team from the civilian contractor, the Foundation Company of Canada. The losers were invited on board for a shower, haircut and break from their bleak and lonely existence.

Captain Robertson was given the command of the Eastern Arctic Task Group with 23 ships, *Labrador* flying the only Canadian flag in the flotilla. Within two years, under the aegis of the U.S. Navy Military Sea Transport Service, 22 radar stations had been completed, stretching from Alaska to Baffin Island.

Labrador, now commanded by Captain T.C. Pullen, whose ancestors had explored the Arctic in the last century, worked the eastern DEW line again in 1956. His executive officer was Athony Law, a former war artist who had commanded motor torpedo boats in the English Channel. Aboard the *Labrador* he would paint some of the most remarkable images of the Arctic in Canadian art.

In addition to sea-lift duties, the *Labrador* under Pullen and Law made major revisions to ten charts and created 12 completely new ones, opening innumerable harbours and channels to deep-draft ships. She navigated and charted Bellott Strait for the first time, discovered a deep channel into Frobisher Bay and surveyed and erected beacons around Foxe Basin making the area safe for navigation. *Labrador* sailed 18,606 miles, more than 12,000 of them in uncharted waters. She took panoramic and radar photographs, salinity and bottom samples. Her oceanographic work constituted the most extensive program ever undertaken in the Canadian Arctic.

MANHATTAN TRANSFER

In March 1957, having earned a reputation as the finest Arctic research vessel in the world, she set off on a triumphal tour of England, Norway and Denmark. The Norwegians, Arctic explorers of note, took great interest in the ship while the crew took the opportunity to visit Nansen's renowned polar voyager, the *Fram*. In Copenhagen, over 8,000 visitors were welcomed aboard. But the *Labrador's* days were numbered.

A victim of spending cuts and a new emphasis on anti-submarine warfare, the *Labrador* was transferred to the Department of Transport on 1 April 1958 and her crew reassigned. As her helicopters formed close escort and all the ships in harbour manned their sides in salute, Tony Law sailed her out of Halifax to the Saint John drydock. She ended her days as an ice-breaker on the lower St. Lawrence.

A decade later, following the discovery of oil in Alaska, the Exxon Corporation sent the supertanker *Manhattan* through the Northwest Passage on a voyage that would raise concerns about Canadian sovereignty in the Arctic. The Icemaster on *Manhattan's* bridge was Captain Tom Pullen, late of *HMCS Labrador*.

REPRINTED FROM:
Esprit de Corps, Volume 7 Issue 4
AUTHOR: *Bill Twatio*

WEAPON PROFILES: ASSAULT RIFLE AND SUB-MACHINE GUN

ABOVE: *An infantry section on patrol in Norway in the early 1980's. These soldiers are equipped with the FN C1 assault rifle and (foreground) the C1 submachine gun. (DND PHOTO)*

The classic post-war battle rifle, the Belgian designed FNC1 was the peacekeepers' weapon of choice.

FABRIQUE NATIONALE'S Fusil Automatique Léger (FAL) has been called the free world's battle rifle, but it is also a great find for collectors and shooters alike. Few other rifles have been adopted by so many of the world's armies. It has served in places as diverse as the Canadian Arctic, the South African grasslands, and even the Falkland Islands, where the FAL was the standard combat rifle of both British and Argentine troops. The FAL is valued for its workmanship, accuracy, reliability and ease of maintenance and, as the C1A1, is part of Canada's military history.

First made by Fabrique Nationale Herstal (FN) of Liege, Belgium, the FAL's gas system was adapted somewhat from the Soviet Tokarev M1939/40 rifle. Dieudonné Saive, a Browning protégé at FN, was the engineer behind its design and development. Saive, who fled the Germans to the UK in 1940, went to work developing a gas operated rod mounted above the barrel. He took his SAFN (FN-49) design, chambered it for the German 7.92mm Kurz round, and gave the new rifle a new profile: a readily detachable magazine, a straight line buttstock with a separate pistol grip and selective fire capability. By 1948 this became the first post-prototype version of the FAL.

The FAL uses the gas from the cartridge's burning powder charge, vented through a small port in the barrel, to drive a piston. The piston then drives the bolt carrier back against a recoil spring to extract a fired cartridge and cock the action. As it returns, the bolt carrier loads a new cartridge into the chamber.

The FAL's piston is a spring-loaded metal rod that rides in a tunnel through the forward part of the receiver. It is not connected to the breechblock carrier like that of the Kalashnikov. The workability of this "tilting bolt" locking and operating system is clear when one looks at how it has been successfully used in the Swedish Ljung-mann, the Soviet SKS, and so on.

The lower receiver is a massive casting machine to shape and, together, the package weighs about nine pounds, a bit heavy for an assault rifle. When the design eventually gained its distinction by chambering the more powerful 7.62mm x 51 (.308 Winchester), this new cartridge all but precluded the FAL from the true role of assault rifle.

FN rebuilt their rifle to fit the new NATO cartridge to create the classic post-war battle rifle. The design quickly cornered the market and was sold to the armed forces of more than 90 countries including Argentina, Australia, Belgium, Canada, India, Israel, Libya, Peru, Singapore and the United Kingdom. Most rifles are capable of automatic fire but are usually used only semi-automatically. Many have been permanently converted to semi-automatic only.

As a fighter, FALs have been employed in diverse wars: Cyprus and Aden, the Congo, the Cuban revolution, in Angola, Guinea, Mozambique, Nigeria, in Israel's Six Day and Yom Kippur Wars, Vietnam, the Falklands, in the fight between Iran and Iraq, Rhodesia, the India-Pakistani War and Operation Desert Storm – not to mention Northern Ireland and countless "peacekeeping" exercises.

Canada adopted the FAL design as the C1 (June 1955), in inch pattern. All were made at Canadian Arsenals Limited, a state

factory. The C1A1 and C2A1 soon followed. The C1A1 (adopted 1959) is a slightly modified version, including a two-piece firing pin and a plastic carrying handle. The C2A1 is a squad auto version of the FAL, with a built-in full auto function, as well as a heavier, longer barrel and a bipod that folds up to become the front handguard. The C2A1 also uses a rear sight mounted on the top cover, not the lower receiver. The Canadian version is the only inch pattern version that lets the last shot actually hold open the bolt. The standard magazine is 20 rounds, although a 30-round straight magazine was made for the C2A1. In addition, the Canadian FAL uses a revolving aperture sight.

Among Canadian soldiers, especially the more seasoned, there was debate as to whether the FN should have been replaced at all. Oh, how they loved that heavy chunk of steel! Canadian history does not offer any battle proof that the FN and its 7.62 NATO round is best for combat, therefore much of the "proof" relies on how the FN was employed by other nations, and on plain old unscientific gut instinct.

7.62 NATO IN COMBAT

What is known is that American GIs in 'Nam used both M14s in 7.62 NATO and M16s in 5.56 NATO and they were tried in tall elephant grass and jungle. Bullets from the M16 went literally everywhere while bullets from the M14 went straight through. Some soldiers reportedly could fire a 14 through a small tree and still hit the guy behind it.

In Rhodesia, 1966-1972, small unit tactics were developed with the four man 'stick,' or half-section, being adopted as the basic formation. Each 'stick' was commanded by a corporal carrying a VHF radio and an FN. The corporal had under him a MAG machine-gunner and two riflemen, one of whom was trained as a medic. Out in the bush, the corporal was autonomous. It was a 'Corporal's War' for he had immediate command on the ground and took the initiative in many instances. Between 1972 and 1974, reconnaissance by the Rhodesian SAS and two-man teams from the Selous Scouts carried FNs with the aim of maximizing the enemy's casualties. A few men, full of confidence in their rifle, up against hundreds of full-auto AK-47 toting rivals? Fire discipline, folks.

American teams with M14s and FN L1A1-armed British SAS in the Gulf War liked how their 7.62mm 'splashes' could be

ABOVE, LEFT:
The compact size and folding stock of the SMG made it suitable for the crews of armoured vehicles.

TOP, RIGHT:
A detailed view of the SMG showing the stock extended and the 30-round magazine detached. The C1 SMG also had a short, ten round magazine.

ABOVE, RIGHT:
The Fabrique Nationale C1 semi-automatic assault rifles. The top version has a flash eliminator and a redesigned forestock. the FNC1 had a 20-round magazine.

CARTRIDGE EFFECTIVENESS

7.62 NATO
Bullet Weight = 150 grains
Nominal Muzzle Velocity@2700fps
Muzzle Energy=2727ft lbs
Muzzle Energy at 500 yards = 1576 ft lbs

5.56 NATO
Bullet Weight = 55 grains
Nominal Muzzle Velocity@3185 fps
Muzzle Energy=1239 ft lbs
Muzzle Energy at 500 yards = 252 ft lbs

7.62 X 39 (AK-47)
Bullet Weight = 125 grains
Nominal Muzzle Velocity@2400 fps
Muzzle Energy = 1598 ft lbs
Muzzle Energy at 500 yards = 414 ft lbs

read more easily at longer desert ranges. There was another reason why the M14 and FN were brought out, once again, for the Gulf War: sand was eating the M16s for breakfast. Picture an aluminum and plastic rifle and a little bit of steel to encourage the grinding. The 7.62s were shipped with no lubrication and were fired with no lubrication. They all functioned flawlessly in a "no lube" sand environment. How many rifles can do that?

While not a battle story, the old pop-up targets used for range practice by the Canadian military would snap down after one hit from an FN. The 5.56mm would pierce this target, making them almost flutter in the wind, but not knock them down. It is enough to say that with a 20 round mag in an FN there is nothing on God's green earth that is getting away. That means, behind trees, behind walls, through brush, and at very long distance.

REPRINTED FROM:
Esprit de Corps, *Volume 8 Issue 2*
AUTHOR: *Warren Ferguson*

C1 (STERLING-TYPE) SMG

This Canadian-made SMG is a variant of the SMG made by the Sterling Engineering Co Ltd, of Dagenham, Essex, England. Its origins in some respects can be traced to the Schmeisser's M.P.18, Lanchester, Sten and Patchett designs. Following Commonwealth tradition, Canada adopted a Sterling variant.

The C1 was manufactured in Canada from the late 1950's at Canadian Arsenals Limited. Externally it looks like the Sterling but almost all are marked "C.A.L." and feature the date of manufacture on the lower side of the magazine housing. Like most other SMGs, the C1 fires from the "open bolt" and has a fixed firing pin. The selector level located on the left side of the pistol grip frame is marked "A", "R", and "S" Automatic, Repetition and Safe.

The modifications which were established in the C1 were a change in the regular magazine capacity from 34 rounds for the Sterling to 30 rounds for the C1. Also, a reduced-capacity ten-round magazine was issued for the C1. The C1 magazines also differ in that they do not utilize rollers as the followers, but instead, a standard stamped follower is used for a two-position feed.

Construction of the C1 is somewhat less expensive to manufacture than the Sterling, especially in the trigger mechanism, barrel and receiver cap. Like all Sterlings, the trigger guard for the C1 may be removed and re-assembled forward of the trigger assembly so winter mitts can be worn.

The C1 uses the standard FN bayonet but the most commonly seen accessory was the yellow blank firing attachment that fits over the muzzle.

AUTHOR: *Warren Ferguson*

CONGO COOKHOUSE

Canada played a major role in the United Nation's ambitious operation in Central Africa. Confusion and power-politics mitigated the mission's success.

DESPERATELY IN SEARCH of a mission, a clutch of Canadian generals dressed in fatigues were photographed milling around in the nooday sun at a dusty roadside in Zaire in December 1996, as tens of thousands of Hutu refugees streamed past to cross the border into Rwanda. The latest victims of Central Africa's endless wars, they were on their way home after spending months in squalid refugee camps around Lake Kivu, brutalized by the Interhamwe, a murderous rag-tag militia. Moved by their plight, the Prime Minister had hurried the generals away to organize a relief effort, which might, incidentally, restore the Army's battered reputation. Fortunately, the crisis resolved itself.

Zaire was known as the Congo the last time Canadians served in that part of the world. Then, as in 1996, the country was sliding into anarchy, riven by warring factions. "I learned something very important in the Congo," a young Canadian lieutenant recalled. "I saw good food, sent by aid organizations, rotting on the docks. I saw fields with wonderfully fertile soil, unplanted. The problem in the Congo was not the lack of potential for feeding the people. It was the chaos caused by fighting."

A PEACEKEEPER'S WAR

A sprawling territory of mountains and equatorialforest, rich in natural resources and inhabited by more than 200 ethnic groups, the Belgium Congo had been ruled with a stern and paternalistic hand since King Leopold acquired it as a personal fiefdom in 1885. Hastily granted independence in June 1960, at a time when there was not a single Congolese in the senior grades of the army or civil service, illiteracy was

LEFT: *Canadians have served as UN liaison officers on numerous peacekeeping missions throughout the world. Here a Canadian Army officer sits with a machine gun unit of Armée Nationale Congolaise.* (DND PHOTO)

universal and the concept of national unity was new and unfamiliar, the country collapsed into chaos as competing factions bid for influence and power.

The civil service, bereft of senior administrators, most of whom had decamped for Belgium, dissolved into impotence. The "national army," little more than a mercenary mob, mutinied. Mineral-rich Katanga province seceeded with the blessing of mining cartels and Kasai followed suit. Fighting broke out and newly-elected President Patrice Lumumba was forced to call for UN military assistance to help restore restore order. A peacekeeping force, the Opération des Nations Unies au Congo (ONUC) was dispatched and soon became involved in the UN's first peacekeeping war as it attempted to crush Katangan separatism. Launched at the height of the Cold War, it was the largest, most audacious and most controversial UN operation to date. Accused of pro-Western bias by the Soviets and condemned for intervening in the internal affairs of an independent country by neutral states, ONUC so divided the UN that its very existence was threatened.

Initially, Canada showed no enthusiasm for participation in ONUC as the economy was in recession, our Forces were already over-extended and short of troops and specialists. But, giving in to almost daily requests from New York and increasing public pressure, the Diefenbaker government reluctantly agreed to provide a signals squadron of 280 officers and men. Designated 57 Signal Unit, the first troops arrived at Léopoldville, the capital, on 15 August 1960 where they were promptly taken into custody by the Congolese, stripped and beaten with rifle butts. "Better beaten than eaten," one battered and bruised trooper told reporters. Despite diplomatic protests from Ottawa, there would be similar incidents in the months to come.

Over 2000 Canadian troops served in the Congo between 1960 and 1964, most in small detachments spread over the length and breadth of the country. Under the command of Major General Carl Carlsson von Horn of Sweden, ONUC's main force, like the Canadians, immediately ran into difficulties. Manned by 20,000 troops from 30 countries, he complained that his command was little more than an armed mob "in which logic, military principles — even common sense — took second place to political factors." Each contingent arrived with different weapons, vehicles and communications systems. "There seemed to be no form of military planning cell in the UN Secretariat which could plan and produce the type of military force required to bring peace to a country which had been reduced to chaos overnight," he said. "Troops arrived, officers arrived and nobody knew quite what they were supposed to do." He likened his mission to giving first aid to a rattlesnake.

Van Horn and most of his staff spoke no French. He was described as "confined to quarters and ...in fact non-effective." Bilingual Canadians handled telephones and codes and were the only officers able to speak to Congolese employees and government officials. His successor conceded that

THE CANADIANS' EFFICIENCY WAS NOT REFLECTED BY THEIR APPEARANCE. JOURNALIST PETER WORTHINGTON REPORTED THAT THEY HAD A REPUTATION FOR BEING FRIENDLY AND CAPABLE BUT WERE THE SCRUFFIEST OF ALL U.N. TROOPS. "IN OLIVE GREEN BUSH PANTS AND SHIRTS, THE CANADIANS RESEMBLE ILL-CLAD REFUGEES – THE ONLY CREASES THEIR TROUSERS HOLD IN THIS STEAMBATH CLIMATE ARE WRINKLES."

ABOVE:
The scourge of UN peacekeepers and the civilian population alike, Congolese irregulars are seen here on the march near Stanleyville, 1960.

"the Canadians were vital to his organization and shouldered more than their fair share of the work."

Flying obsolete North Stars between Léopoldville and Pisa, Italy, the RCAF also provided planes for U.N. transport duty within the Congo. Canadians on the ONUC air staff included the commanding officer, communications officer and chief of air operations.

Individual Canadians served with courage and gallantry. Lieutenant Colonel Paul Mayer and Sergeant J.A.Lessard of the Vandoos were awarded the George Medal for their part in rescuing more than 100 missionaries at Kisadji in early 1964. Lieutenant Terry Liston was decorated for saving a wounded Congolese soldier in a minefield after prodding his way through the mines with a bayonet.

The Canadians' efficiency was not reflected by their appearance. Journalist Peter Worthington reported that they had a reputation for being friendly and capable but were the scruffiest of all U.N. troops. "In olive green bush pants and shirts, the Canadians resemble ill-clad refugees," he wrote. "The only creases their trousers hold in this steambath climate are wrinkles."

CHAOS PILES UP

Chaos was added to chaos as the political situation deteriorated. On September 15, President Kasavubu dismissed Prime Minister Lumumba for allegedly leading the country into civil war "and being a traitor to the state." Lumumba responded by dismissing Kasavubu while General Mobutu, the Army Chief of Staff, a former journalist and sergeant in the Belgian Force Publique, announced that the army was taking over. Lumumba was arrested, tortured and murdered. In Katanga, Moise Tshombe was busy recruiting mercenaries to defend his breakaway state. Known as "les affreux" (the frightful ones), his force included: French paratroopers fresh from defeat in Algeria; South African and Rhodesian adventurers; Italian Fascists; and German veterans of WWII. "No contradiction, no detected lie, caused Mr. Tshombe the slightest embarrassment," said UN Special Envoy Conor Cruise O'Brien. "He had a paternal compassion for the naiveté of anyone who supposed he would tell the truth."

THE UN'S VIETNAM

On 15 February 1961, the Security Council sanctioned the use of force. It had never done so before and would not again until the Bosnian and Somali missions were authorized in the 90s. Katanga was brought to heel after a series of confused and bloody battles which claimed the lives of 126 peacekeepers. Another casualty of the fighting was UN Secretary-General Dag Hammarskjöld, killed in a mysterious plane crash near Ndola. The ONUC mission petered out and the last troops were withdrawn in July 1964. One week later, Tshombe seized power and governed until he was ousted by Mobutu who went on to fashion one of the most tyrannical, corrupt and avaricious regimes in Africa.

Described as "the U.N.'s Vietnam," ONUC violated mostof the principles that had governed previous peacekeeping missions, including impartiality and the consent of all parties involved. U.N. forces were directed "to take all steps necessary in consultation with the Congolese government to provide it with such military assistance as may be necessary." Armed with this vague mandate, the peacekeepers tried to restore order, sometimes by force, provoking bitter disputes in the General Assembly. As the operation became more costly, both in lives and dollars, the Soviet Union, France and others refused to commit their resources and the U.N. was brought to the verge of bankruptcy.

Three decades would elapse before the U.N. dared mount another mission of similar size and complexity.

REPRINTED FROM:
Esprit de Corps, *Volume 5 Issue 11*
AUTHOR:
Bill Twatio

THE CUBAN MISSILE CRISIS

LEFT:
As the military ties between Cuba and the Soviet Union strengthened, so did the U.S-enforced blockade on Cuba. American planes and ships patrolled the seas surrounding the communist island, preventing Soviet ships from supplying Fidel Castro's forces. (U.S. AIR FORCE)

In the 1960s the "nuclear clock" which predicted the possibility of a global nuclear war stood just a few minutes from countdown time. Canadians quietly prepared defensive NBCW measures.

THE MEETING WAS A disaster with Soviet Leader Nikita Khrushchev vilifying President Dwight D. Eisenhower. Krushchev then left the meeting to hand out ball-point pens to children and British Prime Minister Harold Macmillan climbed a garden wall after telling his embassy staff he was going on a pub crawl. The Russians successfully continued to spread the communist doctrine abroad and Cuba became a key centre for launching it into South America. In April 1961, the American CIA responded by sponsoring a group of Cuban refugees in a strike on Cuba. It was ill- conceived and ill- prepared and the Bay of Pigs has since become synonymous with disaster. The Russians responded a month later by erecting a wall of bricks and mortar across Berlin.

A year later Nikita Khruschchev decided to install nuclear warheads in Cuba without notifying the Americans. If another attempt at invading Cuba was made, the Americans would then be told the missiles were at the alert. On 8 September 1962, the first of the medium-range missiles arrived in Cuba and by mid-October some 40 missiles was on hand and construction began on four missile sites.

The Americans became aware of the first of the missiles on 13 September. They identified short-range defensive-type missiles and nothing of major significance was detected until 16 October when U-2 photos revealed a battalion of Soviet medium-range missiles.

No warheads had yet been detected. The US reviewed its options and President John Kennedy opted for a shipping blockade or *quarantine* of Cuba. The Americans then made it clear they knew the Russians trailed in the missile gap. Survival of the world was at stake and yet leaders were forced to resort to the "knock the chip off my shoulder" philosophy. The next step was a speech by Kennedy demanding that the missiles be returned and promising that any attack on the US from Cuba would be responded to with an attack on Russia.

For 13 days the world stood at High Noon. Although Canada was not directly involved, people began figuring their distance from potential impact points. Sales of Spam and bully beef took off and basements became instant but useless bomb shelters. The Emergency Measures Organization remained tight-lipped, and 20 km west of Ottawa Diefenbaker's Cabinet and senior bureaucrats readied a four-storied underground bunker. Throughout this period, Krushchev kept demanding removal of allied missiles in Turkey and other sites which ringed Russian territory. Kennedy's response was that the missiles in Turkey belonged to the UN.

A small group of ships, presumably carrying warheads, accompanied by submarines was spotted approaching Cuba. All NATO forces in Europe were on red alert and WWIII was a button-push away. Kennedy's strategy had been to devise a response which would give Kruschev enough time to consider the full implications of his actions. The ships approached the line where they would have been intercepted. Then they stopped and turned back. The morning of 28 October, Nikita Krushchev announced withdrawal of the missiles.

Although the Berlin wall collapsed in 1989, it was a hollow victory for the allies inasmuch as the decay of communism brought forth economic and political chaos where nuclear weapons abound but responsibility does not.

AUTHOR: *Norm Shannon*

CANADA'S NUCLEAR ARSENAL

Torn between American pressure and domestic opposition, successive Canadian governments vacillated on their policy on nuclear munitions. From 1967-1984 Canada possessed a wide range of these controversial weapons.

ABOVE:
During the 1960s, fear of the Soviet Union's growing arsenal of weapons – an array of missiles on display during Moscow's 1964 May Day parade – justified Canada' s policy on nuclear weapons.
(POPPERFOTO)

PIERRE ELLIOT TRUDEAU denounced him as the "unfrocked prince of peace" and claimed that he was under the influence of "les hipsters" of Kennedy's Camelot. Jean Marchand announced that he would not run as a Liberal and Lloyd Axworthy wrote to say "how very disappointed and saddened," he was "to see a man renege on past principles, and deny the very policies upon which so much admiration and respect have been built." He too declared that he would no longer be active in the Party.

Lester B. Pearson was a man besieged in the winter of 1963. The Diefenbaker government's on-again, off-again decision to adopt weapons systems designed for the use of nuclear warheads had not only angered the Americans, it had also caused a deep rift in the Liberal Party.

The Liberal's policy on nuclear weapons had been almost as confused as the government's. Officially, Pearson had opposed nuclear weapons for Canada's NORAD forces, but accepted them for NATO units if they were under collective NATO control. An unlikely scenario, as Canadian defence planning since the demise of the Arrow had been based on the clear assumption that nuclear weapons would be secured from the United States for the Bomarc, NATO Starfighters and the Honest John surface-to-surface missiles used by the Canadian Brigade in Germany. "The full potential of these defensive weapons," Diefenbaker said, "is achieved only when they are armed with nuclear warheads."

As Diefenbaker developed second thoughts and Pearson waffled, the National Liberal Rally called for Canada to confine its NORAD activities to "identification," leaving the actual shooting to the Americans. "The proposed policy," defence analyst James Eayres wrote, "is a policy for birdwatchers, but bird watchers have more strength and stamina."

The Cuban Missile Crisis stiffened Canadian spines, including Pearson's. On 12 January 1963, in a speech at Scarborough, Ontario, he declared that he was "ashamed if we accept commitments and then refuse to discharge them." By year's end, he was Prime Minister and nuclear warheads were on their way to Canada.

NUCLEAR DETERRENCE

The nuclear debate had raged since the election of Dwight D. Eisenhower as president in 1952 and a shift in emphasis from costly conventional forces to cheaper forms of nuclear deterrence providing a "bigger bang for a buck." As peace activists hit the streets and Stanley Kubrick filmed "Dr. Strangelove, or How I Learned to Stop Worrying and Love the Bomb," defence planners asserted that it was in Canada's interest to do everything in its power to support a credible policy of nuclear deterrence, particularly as the Soviets were testing hydrogen bombs thousands of times more powerful than the bombs that had incinerated Hiroshima and Nagasaki. For the most part, Canadians seemed to agree, supporting the acquisition of nuclear weapons by a margin of two to one.

NATO's military policy was now firmly based on a nuclear response to Soviet aggression. Lacking the quantitative military strength of the Warsaw Pact, the Alliance saw nuclear weapons as a means of making up for its inferiority in numbers. Battlefield or tactical nuclear weapons began to appear, either in the form of nuclear shells fired from 8-inch artillery pieces or short-range rockets.

Although both sides were developing long-range rockets, largely thanks to the expertise of German wartime scientists who had developed the V-2, aircraft remained the principal means of delivering nuclear weapons throughout the 1950's. American B-52's and British V-bombers vied with Soviet Tu-4's and 5's, known respectively as the "Bull" and "Bear." Canadians soon realized that they would be in the direct line of fire in any confrontation between the Soviet Union and the United States and air defence became a major priority. The Pinetree and Mid-Canada radar lines were built along the 49th and 55th parallels, complementing an enormously expensive Distant Early Warning (DEW) Line in the Arctic. The CF-100 all-weather interceptor came into service and work began on the Arrow. Canada and the United States established a formal Defence Sharing Program while the NORAD agreement provided for a tightly centralized bilateral North American Air Defence Command. Bomarcs, Genies and Honest Johns

The launch of Sputnik I on 4 October 1958, the same day that the first Arrow prototype rolled out of a hangar at Malton, ushered in the age of the ICBM or Intercontinental Ballistic Missile. Bewildered by contradictory advice, endless imponderables and soaring costs, Diefenbaker and his Minister of Defence announced that the Arrow was obsolete and would be replaced by the Bomarc missile. Pearson, his successor, ensured that they would be armed with nuclear warheads.

The Bomarc surface-to-air missile deployed by both 446 SAM Squadron at North Bay, Ontario and 447 Squadron at La Macaza, Quebec, was the most visible symbol of Canada's nuclear commitment. Each squadrons was armed with 28 missiles carrying W40 nuclear warheads with an averages yield of ten kilotons. Controlled by a Semi-Automatic Ground Environment computer (SAGE) it could speed along at Mach 2.7 and destroy a bomber 600 kilometres from its launcher. The only SAGE centre located outside of the United States was built into a custom-made cavern beneath Reservoir Hill on the outskirts of North Bay. A duel-key launch procedure was strictly applied, which required an American and Canadian duty officer to use their interlocking switch keys at the same time.

As the missiles were in place for over a year prior to their arming and were useless without a nuclear warhead, cartoonists in newspapers across the country delighted in depicting them topped with bird nests or pots of geraniums. To give the crews the feel of a live system, warhead jumper cables were installed and from time to time they were invited to Elgin AFB in Florida for test launches. Two hours after the warheads finally arrived in North Bay in January, 1964 aboard a USAF Globemaster, an earthquake aroused fears that the Apocalypse had arrived with them. Emergency measures and police switchboards lit up as concerned residents reported a nuclear detonation.

ABOVE:
The Royal Canadian Artillery fires the Honest John, a surface-to-surface missile with a nuclear warhead, while on NATO exercise in West Germany. The use of nuclear weapons remains controversial.
(DND PHOTO)

Nuclear weapons came as part and parcel with the CF-101 Voodoo, the Arrow's replacement. Armed with the Genie AIR - 2A, an unguided, short-range 1.5 kiloton nuclear rocket, Voodoo squadrons were based at Chatham, N.B., Bagotville, Quebec and Comox, B.C. Carried internally, the Genie was a difficult weapon to use as a Voodoo would have to be so close to an enemy bomber to ensure a hit that the blast could destroy it as well. Although the Voodoo-Genie combination was Canada's longest serving nuclear weapon system, the military was loathe to mention it. Official secrecy was pervasive. When a member of Parliament, about to attend a UN Disarmament Conference inquired about the system, he was informed by the Department of National Defence that "it is our policy to neither confirm nor deny the presence of nuclear weapons in Canada."

"Nominal yield" nuclear warheads of less than 20 kilotons were also acquired for use by I Air Division's CF-104 Starfighters bases at Zweibrucken and Baden-Soellingen, West Germany. Here too, secrecy was the order of the day with the military going to great lengths to protect its new weapon systems from what it saw as interfering and possibly hostile politicians. Although the CF-104 was designated as a fighter, it was actually a low-level, tactical bomber carrying four different types of nuclear weapons during its operational life.

The Honest John battlefield rocket was the only nuclear weapon system deployed by the Canadian Army. Between 1964 and 1970, six mobile launchers were in use with the army's only nuclear unit, I Surface-to-Surface Missile Battery, Royal Canadian Artillery, stationed at Hemer, West Germany. Fired from an open truck, the Honest John was a free-flight "Shoot and Scoot" rocket with a range of about two kilometres. An unsophisticated weapon, the Honest John had to be warmed by electric blankets for 48 hours prior to firing to raise the fuel temperature to about 25 degrees Centigrade for an even propellent burn.

Canada's nuclear arsenal was quietly phased out of service in the early 1980's. As a specialized USAF air transport squadron airlifted the warheads away from Canada for disposal, Jean Chrétien rose in the House of Commons to state that "the last piece of nuclear armament was withdrawn from Canadian soil on 5 July 1984." In the only direct statement on nuclear weapons ever provided by the Liberal government over a 20-year period, the future Prime Minister was only off by a week.

***AUTHOR**: Bill Twatio*

CYPRUS

When Canadian troops first deployed to this embattled island in 1964, no one would have predicted that their successors would still be patrolling the buffer zone over three decades later.

ABOVE:
Georges Vanier bids farewell to the men of the Royal 22e Regiment as they board a plane bound for Cyprus in March 1964. The Governor General, a Vandoo, was decorated for his actions in World War I.
(DND PHOTO)

MAKHAIRAS, THE 12TH CENTURY chronicler of Cyprus, wrote that "the poor Cypriots are a much-enduring people, and God in his Mercy avenges them. They make no sign at all." That passivity, nursed through years of foreign domination, vanished in the early 1960s in a civil war which threatened to escalate into a Great Power confrontation. A small island in the eastern Mediterranean, 40 miles off the coast of Turkey, Cyprus has a population of less than a million – 80 per cent of Greek origin and the remainder of Turkish descent. A victim of its geography, the island has been fought over by Phoenicians, Greeks, Romans, Byzantines, Crusaders, Venetians and Turks, to name a few.

In 1878, it was a neglected outpost of the Ottoman Empire, "the sick man of Europe," when Disraeli conceived the idea of acquiring it for Britain. "If Cyprus be conceded to your Majesty," he told Queen Victoria, "the power of England in the Mediterranean will be absolutely increased in that region and your Majesty's Indian Empire immensely strengthened. Cyprus is the key to Western Asia."

WOLSELEY ARRIVES

It was, in fact, nothing of the sort. Nevertheless, on July 12, 1878, the Union Jack was raised in Nicosia, the capital of the island, as British and Indian troops under the command of Lieutenant General Sir Garnet Wolseley, late of the Red River Expedition, marched in. In a welcoming address, the bishop of Kitium, spiritual and temporal leader of the Greeks, told Sir Garnet: "We accept the change of Government inasmuch as we trust that Great Britain will help Cyprus, as she did the Ionian islands, to be united with Mother Greece, with which it is naturally connected." That dream would become known as "Enosis."

Enosis would be the bane of generations of British governors as they attempted to convince a people who had since time immemorial clung to Greek thought, faith and language that they were not Greek. When argument failed, edicts were passed aimed at the suppression of the Enosis movement. In 1925, the island was declared a crown colony and thirty years later became the home of British Middle East Headquarters after it was forced out of Suez by Egypt's President Nasser. But the dream refused to die and became the driving force in the lives of a fiery little colonel with a waxed moustache and a bright young priest, the son of a shepherd.

VICIOUS GUERILLA WAR

George Grivas and Michael Mouskos, later Archbishop Makarios of Cyprus, believed that the passive Cypriot temperament could be fanned into flame by growing discontent with British rule. "The soul of a Cypriot is brave, forward to freedom!" they declared in the spring of 1955 as they launched EOKA - the National Organization of Cypriot Fighters. For the next five years, they would direct a vicious guerilla war of sabotage, mountain sorties, street ambushes and assassinations before Cyprus became an independent state on 16 August 1960.

Independence satisfied neither the Greeks who saw it as a prelude to Enosis, nor the Turks who sought partition of the island. Lumbered with an unworkable constitution that gave the Turkish minority representation far out of proportion to its numbers, conflict became inevitable. In 1963, rioting broke out when President Makarios proposed changes that would enhance the power of Greek Cypriots. As the crisis deepened, Greece and Turkey mobilized and threatened to invade. In response, on 3 March 1964, the United Nations authorized the dispatch of a peacekeeping force for Cyprus bearing the unwieldy acronym UNFICYP.

Canada played an important role in setting up UNFICYP and securing commitments from other participating nations. Within weeks, a battalion of the R22eR and a squadron of armoured cars of the Royal Canadian Dragoons were on their way to Cyprus aboard Yukon transports and the aircraft carrier HMCS *Bonaventure*. They were soon joined by troops from Sweden, Finland, Denmark and Ireland. Under the command of an Indian general, the 7000-man force took up positions between the warring factions and began patrolling communal boundaries.

UN FORCE LIMITED

The UN force was strictly limited in its capacity for action. It was not authorized to try to disarm belligerents or to use force to establish peace. Rather, it would have to stand in the middle and fire only in self-defence while its political arm worked for a negotiated settlement. UNFICYP was only the third mission attempted by a UN force and was to prove the most complex. Unlike Gaza or the Congo which offered distinct ethnic divisions, Cyprus was a land of inextricably mixed communities and the fighting had consolidated scores of embattled Turkish enclaves among a sea of Greeks, each of which required UN protection. "It was no job for a soldier," a Canadian remarked, "but a job that only a soldier could do."

Canada's 1150 soldiers initially had the most difficult task, that of guarding the "Green Line" which divided the Greek and Turkish districts of Nicosia. After the Vandoos took fire from both sides of the line, they adopted a policy of "diplomatic toughness," clearing houses and shops to create a neutral zone, in some places no more than a hundred yards wide. In December, 1964, they were relieved by other UNFICYP units and shifted their operations to the road between Nicosia and the port of Kyrenia. Although a settlement remained out of reach, tensions eased, the force was cut in half and units were rotated every six months.

JUNTA SEIZES POWER

In 1974, a military junta, pledged to the union of Cyprus and Greece, seized power in Athens and toppled the Makarios government. The Turks responded by invoking the Treaty of Guarantee that had sanctioned independence but allowed them the right to act unilaterally to restore the status quo and invaded the island. Turkish jets bombed and strafed Nicosia while paratroopers dropped farther inland to link up with a force of 40,000 troops landed on the northern coast. Fighting was heavy and more than 200,000 were left homeless as the Turks pressed on in defiance of a unanimous UN Security Council call for a ceasefire. Ignoring a hastily-convened peace conference in Geneva, they drove a wedge across the island to seize the port of Famagusta and take control of the entire northern third of Cyprus.

THE BIGGEST HURDLE IN A MISSION LIKE CYPRUS IS STAYING FLEXIBLE,...AS A PEACEKEEPER YOU HAVE TO REMIND YOURSELF TO LOOK AT THINGS WITH THE EYES OF THE PEOPLE LIVING THERE. YOU ARE NOT THERE TO CHANGE THEM, JUST TO HELP. IF NOT FOR THE PEACEKEEPERS, THE KILLING WOULD CERTAINLY RESUME.

The Airborne Regiment, Canada's UN contingent at the time, distinguished itself by assisting women and children caught in the crossfire between National Guard units and Turkish Cypriot fighters and holding the Nicosia airport and other sites as neutral zones. Finnish peacekeepers, pinned down by heavy artillery and mortar fire were evacuated from their camp aboard the regiment's armoured personnel carriers. Two Canadians died in the fighting and several were wounded. Captain (later Major General) Allain Forand won the Star of Courage for rescuing two Canadians wounded by Greek Cypriots.

TWO MEN HIT

"A couple of guys ran up and told me that two of our men, Captain Blaquiére and Private Plouffe, had been hit by a machine-gunner," Forand recalled. "In a situation like that you only think what happens to other guys, not to you." Plouffe, who had been struck by a bullet that deflected off his helmet into his jaw, complained that "they should have hit the other side where I've got a cavity," before Forand dragged him to safety. He then ordered his men to open fire on the Greek position and returned to fetch Blaquière.

With Cyprus effectively partitioned, Canada doubled its contingent size and brought in heavier weapons to preserve a buffer zone running the entire length of the island. Neither side accepted the zone as permanent. Turkish Cypriots saw it as a no-man's-land open only to UNFICYP while the Greeks insisted it remained their territory, temporarily administered by the United Nations. A state of persistent tension punctuated by gunfire resulted, causing enormous stress for the peacekeepers.

Over the next 30 years, every soldier in the Canadian Army could expect to serve at least one tour with UNFICYP with many going back six or seven times. Twenty-seven would die in the line of duty, most in accidents. The peace was kept and Cyprus provided Canadian soldiers with a superb training ground for small-unit tactics, but with costs rising and no political solution in sight, Canada announced it would begin a phased withdrawal of its troops in 1992. Today (1998), only two Canadian intelligence officers are still deployed to Cyprus UNFICYP headquarters.

MISSION SUMMARY

Before his return to Canada, Captain Forland summarized the problems facing United Nations peacekeepers and what he felt the mission accomplished. "The biggest hurdle in a mission like Cyprus is staying flexible," he said. "As a peacekeeper you have to remind yourself to look at things with the eyes of the people living there. You are not there to change them, just to help. That's the thing I hang my hat on: if not for us, the killing would certainly resume. That gives me quite a lot of satisfaction, knowing we've done what we could. After all, what is more important than preventing the loss of even one life?"

From that perspective, UNFICYP was an unqualified success.

AUTHOR: *Bill Twatio*

BRANCH UNIFICATION

Khaki and air force and navy blue equals green! A good theoretical concept that had its proponents and much vocal opposition.

A FRIEND, WHO HAS reason to know, on learning that it was my intention to retire startled me when he said, "one of the things you'll find out is that there won't be time enough to do everything that you intend." How could that possibly be, I thought? Well I discovered that he was absolutely right. Only after a full year had I gotten around to "stripping my files."

I am at present reviewing notes that were made while I was occupying a staff position at Army Headquarters during Paul Hellyer's term as Minister of National Defence. What an interesting insight they provide! The years 1964 to 1966 inclusive were tumultuous ones for Canada and for the Armed Services of Canada in particular. Unification was the central issue.

Coincidentally, the Armed Forces of today are again in a state of uncertainty and crisis and are confronted by many of the same imperatives that we faced then. Given the above, it might be interesting if I were to relate briefly something of my own impressions of those times and of the man who, more than any other, managed to share the lives of a generation of servicemen including my own.

One cannot understand unification and its outcome without knowing something of Paul Hellyer the man. He impressed me as being charismatic, intelligent (though not always wise) articulate, energetic, toughminded and robustly ambitious. He was seen, and wanted to be seen as a political comer. I am convinced that he aspired to become the Prime Minister of Canada.

His appointment as Minister of National Defence seemed to place that goal within his reach. It was the platform he needed – only lacking was a suitable issue to allow him to demonstrate to Canadians that he possessed the leadership potential and qualities to be their prime minister. Unification of the Armed Services became that issue. It was a concept whose time had come. Fortuitously for him, the man and the issue had come together at precisely the right moment.

Mr. Hellyer entered his Ministry determined to shake things up. Canada's defence policy had not seen a comprehensive review since the onset of the Cold War. Such a review, most at that time would agree, was long overdue. Furthermore, the Minister came into office believing strongly that Canada's defence structure was anachronistic and highly inefficient – consisting as it then did of three separate legal entities. The Royal Canadian Navy, the Canadian Army, and the Royal Canadian Air Force with a small and apparently inadequate coordinating mechanism at the top. His conclusion? Integrate the logistical and other common support elements in the interests of achieving economy and greater efficiency; subject all personnel to a uniform code of personnel and management policies and finally unite the three legal entities under a single services head.

It would be incorrect to say that in advocating these reforms Hellyer was ahead of his time – nor can it be said that the ideas

UNIFICATION... *CONTINUED ON PAGE 321*

COLD WAR YEARS

WEAPONS AND UNIFORMS

BELOW RIGHT: *A section of soldiers from the Royal 22e Regiment (circa 1974) moving through a gully at CFB Valcartier, closely followed by an M113A1 Armoured Personnel Carrier (APC). Note the soldiers carrying FN C1A1 rifles and the APC mounting an M2 .50 calibre heavy machine gun. Valcartier remains one of the main training areas along with Gagetown, New Brunswick; Petawawa, Ontario; and Wainwright and Suffield, Alberta. (DND PHOTO)* ***BOTTOM:*** *The series of "Rendezvous" exercises in Canada, starting at CFB Gagetown in 1981, were meant to regain the Army's lost ability to operate at the divisional level. They brought two or three of the Canadian-based brigades together to practice more complicated operations such as assault river crossings. Here, a soldier from the The Royal Canadian Regiment crosses the Battle River in Wainwright, Alberta in 1985, carrying his C1 submachine gun along with a PRC 25 radio on his back. (DND PHOTO)*

The "Flying Boxcar" was the mainstay of tactical airlift for the RCAF in the 1950s. Unusual for its time, the rear opened so that vehicles or cargo could be more easily loaded than on previous aircraft. Seen here dropping supplies by parachute, it was also the main transport aircraft for paratroopers. In the 1950s, Princess Patricia's Canadian Light Infantry became a parachute unit and as part of the Mobile Strike Force logged many hours of flight time aboard the C119. (DND PHOTO)

LEFT: *Patrolling on the Green Line in Cyprus. Two Canadian peacekeepers conduct a vehicle patrol in a "54" pattern jeep. Driving these vehicles on the island required some getting used to because in Cyprus, a former British colony, cars drove on the left side of the road. The left hand drive vehicle the Canadian drivers used made it difficult to pass other vehicles or make turns. At the beginning of each of the almost 60 six-month rotations over 29 and a half years, there were a spate of accidents. (DND PHOTO)*

BOTTOM: *Canadian soldiers along the Green Line in Cyprus man an observation post. The Canadian Army provided a battalion-sized unit that rotated every six months between 1964 and 1993. ("GREEN LINE PATROL, CYPRUS," BY JOAN WANKLYN, MUSEUM OF THE REGIMENTS)*

OPPOSITE PAGE, TOP LEFT: *UNEF (United Nations Emergency Force), the first full scale UN peacekeeping mission, was deployed to Egypt to defuse the Suez crisis. Israel invaded Egypt in October 1956; this was followed by the Anglo-French operation to seize the Suez Canal. The Canadians provided logistical, signal, and ordnance planning that neither the UN nor any of its contingent countries could provide. The assistance of Canadian officers at this point was out of proportion to their numerical representation in the Military Advisory Group to the UN. Canada was to lead the force which was commanded by Lieutenant General E.L.M. Burns, a decorated WWII veteran. Canada provided in excess of 1000 troops, including an infantry battalion, ordnance, logistic, medical, dental, and aviation assets. In all, Canada provided more than one sixth of the force. Seen here, a Canadian signals officer observing from a temporary post with an Indonesian sentry. (DND PHOTO)*

OPPOSITE PAGE, TOP RIGHT: *A Canadian soldier on peacekeeping duty in an observation post along the Green Line in Cyprus. Note the old style ballistic nylon fragmentation jacket, the precursor to the now widely used Kevlar vest. His load-bearing equipment (circa 1985) is designed to carry two C7 5.56-mm 30-round magazines in each of the two ammunition pouches. (DND PHOTO)*

As part of UNEF, Canada provided a reconnaissance squadron from the Royal Canadian Dragoons. The Ferret Scout car was excellent in this role as it was light, quick, silent, and very suited to operations in the desert. The value of UNEF was the demonstration that, in certain circumstances, the UN could move quickly and with strength to halt or prevent fighting. (DND PHOTO)

BELOW:
Soldiers from the Canadian Airborne Regiment march out to their aircraft for a "bare-assed" jump. Note the 1st Special Service Force badge on the right sleeve of the paratroopers. The regiment was officially established on 8 April 1968. Originally a unit with a reputation for highly skilled, disciplined soldiers who undertook tough, demanding, and dynamic activities, the regiment proved itself for the first time in operations with the UN in 1974 during the Turkish invasion of Cyprus. Unfortunately embroiled in the scandals of Somalia during the joint non-UN mission dubbed United Task Force (UNITAF) in 1992-93, the Airborne's reputation was thoroughly sullied. In the spring of 1995, after a series of embarrassing hazing videos, the Minister of Defence ordered the disbandment of the regiment. This loss was felt throughout the Army and was viewed with incredulity by Canadian allies. Arguably, it was the saddest day in the history of the Canadian military when, on 4 March 1995, the CO of the Canadian Airborne Regiment, Lieutenant Colonel Peter Kenward, signed the disbandment documents on parade after one final regimental jump. (DND PHOTO)

ABOVE:
The Chinook, a medium lift helicopter the size of a flying bus, is able to carry 42 fully equipped soldiers and has a ramp at the rear for loading small vehicles and pallets of equipment. This workhorse provided tactical lift for the Army. Built by Boeing, this double-rotor helicopter could cruise at 155 miles per hour, was able to fly more than 1000 miles in ferry mode and could sling a load as heavy as 9000 kilograms or carry 24 casualties in litters. The Chinook was a versatile aircraft. (DND PHOTO)

LEFT:
The Kiowa (photo right) was used as a reconnaissance, command, and liaison helicopter. Flown by one pilot, it was crewed by an observer (normally a combat arms NCO) who assisted the pilot in identifying obstacles while flying NOE (Nap of the Earth). Armed with a 7.62-mm machine gun slung from the belly for defence, it could also launch 2.75-inch rockets for marking targets for artillery or close air support. Equipped with a Radar Warning Receiver (RWR), it could detect when it had been "acquired." Note the scissors-like device above the windshield, a Canadian invention that would automatically cut power or telephone wire in the unfortunate case that the aircraft flew into this type of obstacle. The two other helicopters seen in the rear are British Army Allouettes. This photo was taken over Hohenzolleren Castle in southern Germany. The Kiowa was replaced by the Griffon. (DND PHOTO)

BELOW:
Canada needs an aircraft with some very long legs to patrol the world's longest coastline. The Aurora, a long-range patrol aircraft is Canada's only strategic airborne land and sea surveillance aircraft. Designed originally for anti-submarine warfare, the Aurora is capable of detecting the latest generation of submarines. In 1999, Auroras located several small boats crowded with illegal migrants in the Pacific. Vigilance on the country's coasts, sometimes in concert with NORAD and the RCMP, has also led to the capture of vessels and aircraft smuggling drugs. The Aurora's extreme endurance also makes it a very able search and rescue (SAR) aircraft. In 1996, off Halifax, an Aurora dropped survival gear to 24 crew members of a sinking vessel. The Aurora, purchased in 1980, has a maximum speed of 750 kilometers per hour and a range of 9260 nautical miles. It carries sonobuoys, forward looking infra-red (FLIR) cameras, a magnetic anomaly detector and various cameras and electronic support assets. Carrying MK46 Mod V torpedoes, it is a lethal submarine killer. Ancillary munitions include signal chargers, smoke makers, flares and it can be fitted with air-to-surface missiles. Crewed by 10 to 15 airmen, this four-engined aircraft is a superior surveillance platform. (DND PHOTO)

ABOVE:
Although some confusion may exist, combat divers are soldiers not sailors. The primary role of the engineer is to maintain the mobility of friendly forces and deny mobility to enemy forces. Their secondary role is to act as infantry. Combat divers conduct underwater reconnaissance for the placement of bridges, fording sites and for underwater demolition of piers, bridges, and other infrastructure. (DND PHOTO)

RIGHT:
The Boeing Labrador CH113 was originally purchased by the Canadian Army as a troop transport aircraft. Upon unification of the Canadian Forces, it became the primary search and rescue helicopter. With a cruising speed of 125 knots and a range of 690 miles, this twin-rotored helicopter is a stable platform for rescuing people from rough seas or out of tight locations. Unfortunately, these aircraft have met the end of their useful life and border on being dangerous. A replacement in the form of a modified EH101 and built by Augusta-Westland was originally ordered in 1992 by the Conservative government. However, the Liberal government cancelled the contract after being elected in 1993. Subsequently, after it became glaringly obvious that a replacement was needed for the venerable Labrador, the Liberal government at last ordered 15 EH101 Cormorant helicopters for delivery beginning in 2002. (DND PHOTO)

TOP, LEFT: *Of the three Oberon class submarines built at Chatham Dockyard in the UK to RCN specifications,* Ojibwa *was the first (commissioned 23 September 1965), followed by* Onondaga *(on 22 January 1967), and* Okanagan *(22 June 1968). A fourth sister ship, the* Olympus, *was acquired in 1989 as a dockside training vessel. Somewhat like living in a sewer pipe, this very quiet boat was designed for a crew of 65, but sometimes put to sea with 78 for training purposes. The Oberon subs began to be paid off in the late 1990s and are to be replaced by four Victoria class submarines beginning in 2000. (DND PHOTO)*

BOTTOM: *Operational support ship HMCS* Provider *(2nd), refuels two MacKenzie class destroyer escorts in the Pacific Ocean. Commissioned on 28 September 1963, at Lauzon, Quebec,* Provider *was designated a fleet replenishment ship, and was the largest ship built in Canada for the RCN to date. She enabled ships to remain at sea for extended periods as her tanks hold 12,000 tons of fuel oil, diesel oil, and aviation gas, in addition to spare parts, ammunition and missiles, general stores and food. She could refuel other fleet units at 20 knots, with automatic tensioning equipment to compensate for the ships' motion as fuel oil is transferred at 25 tons per minute. She could also carry three anti-submarine helicopters as spares for the fleet or for transferring pallet loads of solid stores. Paid off in the late 1990s, she is survived by her two sister ships,* Protecteur *and* Preserver. *(DND PHOTO)*

OPPOSITE PAGE, TOP RIGHT:
The Iroquois *or 280 class helicopter-carrying destroyers were the pre-eminent anti-submarine warfare vessel during the Cold War. HMCS* Iroquois *and her three sister ships –* Huron, Athabaskan, *and* Algonquin *– were refitted in the early 1990s, with* Iroquois *and* Algonquin *being further upgraded in the same decade. In the aftermath of the Falklands War and the war in the Persian Gulf where the allied coalition fleet came under attack from surface-to-surface missiles, the problem of air defence became a top priority for the Navy. The Canadian Navy decided to convert the four 280s to the area of air defence. This gave them the self-defensive capabilities they needed to become command and control ships. Thus equipped, the Navy could form independent task groups, responsible for their own security. As well as substantial changes to the vessels, new air defence weapons were installed, including standard vertically launched missiles and a 76-mm Super Rapid gun. The 20-mm Phalanx close-in weapon system provides a final defence against sea-skimming missiles. The ships' anti-submarine warfare weapons – two torpedo-carrying helicopters plus ship-launched torpedoes – were retained, as were their sophisticated, Canadian-designed towed array and hull-mounted sonars. The 280 class also has a variety of electronic jamming and decoy devices and an infra-red suppression system fitted to their new single funnel.* (DND PHOTO)

ABOVE: *By 1976, the World War II designed Centurion tank fleet of the Canadian Army had virtually rusted out and the Leopard I was chosen as the replacement Main Battle Tank (MBT) for the Army. Canada added several modifications and the new Leopard I tanks proved their worth immediately when, in 1977, the Royal Canadian Dragoons won the prestigious Canadian Army Tank (CAT) shoot trophy. This trophy and competition was initiated by Canadians, but with the old Centurion, Canada's tankers were completely out-classed. At 42.5 tons, the Leopard C1 mounts a 105-mm high velocity main gun firing various types of ammunitions and two 7.62-mm machine guns. Powered by a 10-cylinder multifuel 830 horsepower engine, it has a maximum speed of 65 kilometers per hour and a range of 600 kilometers. The tank is capable of firing accurately on the move as its electrical turret and gyroscopically stabilized gun can maintain its aim. Unfortunately, Canada finds itself again lagging in armour as modern tanks have more armour, and powerful, longer range 120-mm guns.*(DND PHOTO)

An infantry section dismounts from its M113A1 APC while on exercise in Germany. First deployed to Europe by Canada in 1965, the M113 was the mainstay of the Canadian Army's mechanized infantry forces. Powered by a diesel engine, this tracked vehicle could climb a 60 per cent grade. The armour protection was minimal as its flat sides could be perforated by small arms fire , although it did offer a modicum of protection against mortar and artillery shrapnel. This was not a fighting vehicle per se, rather it was considered a "battlefield taxi."
(ILLUSTRATION BY KATHERINE TAYLOR)

LEFT: *A soldier of the Princess Patricia's Canadian Light Infantry with equipment used from the 1970s to mid-1980s. His load-bearing equipment did not carry the magazines for his FN C1A1 rifle, rather four 20-round magazines were carried in specially designed pockets in the shirt and jacket of the combat uniform. An emergency field dressing is taped on the upper left of his webbing suspenders. His helmet is the American pattern steel pot.* (ILLUSTRATION BY KATHERINE TAYLOR)
BELOW: *The M113 APC, the mainstay of mechanized infantry, was put into service in the 1960s and is arguably one of the most effective tracked armoured vehicles ever produced. Manned by a crew of two, it could carry a 10-man section of soldiers. Powered by a GMC Detroit 6-cylinder diesel engine generating 215 horsepower, this 11,261-kilogram vehicle could reach speeds of up to 67.6 kilometers per hour. With a maximum range of 595 kilometers, it would ford rivers, climb a 60 per cent grade, climb over an obstacle .61 meters high and cross a trench 1.68 meters wide. In addition, with minor modifications it could be used in an amphibean role. This vehicle also had headquarters, ambulance, recovery, and a TOW missile (Tube launched, Optically tracked, Wire guided) variant.* (DND PHOTO)

The Grizzly Armoured Vehicle General Purpose (AVGP) was a welcome addition to the Army's arsenal in 1980. The steel hull provided better protection than the M113 APC and it had a one man turret mounting a .50 calibre heavy machine gun and a 7.62-mm C5 medium machine gun. Manufactured by GM Diesel from a Swiss design, Canada unfortunately opted for a six- rather than eight-wheel version, which was more stable, however the six-wheeled version had other difficulties. With two doors at the back rather than a ramp, dismounting with equipment was difficult and slower. Originally purchased as a training vehicle, Canada's lack of a powerful armoured infantry fighting vehicle caused these AVGPs to be deployed to the former Yugoslavia. In order to make them effective for operations, numerous modifications, including the bolting on of additional armour, had to be made. **(ILLUSTRATION BY SCOTT TAYLOR)**

UNIFICATION... *CONTINUED FROM PAGE 320*

were his own brain child. Unification had been tried in Canada in 1924 – scant months after Hellyer's birth and had been tried elsewhere in the world following the Second World War. It is, therefore, all the more remarkable that he was able to carry it off. A less determined or a more sensitive man would have failed.

That he did succeed was due in part to the support of Lester B. Pearson, the Prime Minister of the day. Pearson shared Hellyer's vision of a unified defence force as evidenced by the following remark made in speech given by him on 12 January 1963:

"The three Canadian defence services should be fully integrated for maximum efficiency and economy, both in operation and administration. The necessary changes should be made at the National Defence Department for this purpose."

Not all of Hellyer's Cabinet colleagues were similarly persuaded and it has since come to light that even the Associate Minister of National Defence remained doubtful till the end. By mid-summer 1966 unification had become a hot item – an emotion-charged, dominating political issue. Pearson, ever sensitive to the needs and sensitivities of the country urged caution. In a letter to Hellyer he said among other things:

"It is obvious that the successful achievement of the unification of the services, something which no western government has yet achieved, will require careful preparation, and wise and skilful handling, as you say it will have a more direct impact on individuals than integration. It will also arouse emotions and affect traditions... In this connection, I feel strongly, as I know you do, that traditions and past associations which have been a part of the organization of our Defence Forces should be recognized and retained to the maximum extent possible."

Apart from the Prime Minister's support, Hellyer's timing and method had much to do with his success. He began with a thorough going review of defence policy. As it was, his white paper on defence 1964 established a rationale for the reordering of national defence priorities and for a major restructuring of defence capabilities. Scant mention was made of unification. One sentence at the end of a paragraph in the body of the paper revealed his ultimate goal. The sentence stated simply that, "This is the first step toward a single unified service for Canada."

That statement of purpose seems clear and unequivocal, but at the time there was much uncertainty and confusion concerning the Government's real intention. The terms "integration" and "unification" had been used interchangeably. Most understood and supported the concept of integration and the creation of a unified infrastructure for the Armed Services. Unification, on the other hand, was as yet a term without a precise meaning. Many of my acquaintances came, thus, to support the initiative believing unification to be something other than it was. My own first intimation that more than semantics was involved came when a suggested reply to a Naval Officers Association letter that I had prepared for he Minister was returned to me for amendment. I had used the word integration when explaining that it was the Government of Canada's intention to achieve economies by way of integration in order to free up funds for capital investment. Hellyer had underlined the word "integration" and in the margin opposite had inserted the word "unification." When I inquired as to the Minister's meaning I was informed that it had always been the intention to create a single amalgamated defence force. Not many officers of that time were sympathetic to that idea.

Space does not permit the telling of the political donnybrook and mass resignations of senior staff that ensued in the summer of 1966. The story, however, is an enlightening one and is replete with valuable lessons and must sometime be told. Perhaps the outstanding lesson says as much about our political culture as about anything else. The lesson is this – that in a moderate, plural, democratic society such as our own almost nothing is denied the single-minded, charismatic man of conviction. Ambition can inspire – it can also destroy.

REPRINTED FROM:
Esprit de Corps, Volume 1 Issue 5
AUTHOR: *Colonel Bill Sutherland*

PAGE 320, LEFT: *Paul Hellyer, Minister of Naional Defence in the mid-1960s, implemented the controversial unification of Canada's armed forces in 1968.* (DND PHOTO)
PAGE 320, RIGHT: *Unification resulted in all service personnel being issued a standard "CF Green" uniform. In 1984, this decision was reversed and each branch – army, navy and air force – regained their own uniforms.* (DND PHOTO)
LEFT: *The mid-1960s were a tumultuous time for Canada. In February 1965 Canada's new flag is raised, ushering in an era of change – especially for her armed forces.* (DND PHOTO)

RIGHT:
In February 1954, Canadians were sent to the Golan Heights as part of the UN's Truce Supervision Organization (UNTSO). This observation post is located along the border between Syria and Israel. (DND PHOTO)

CANADA'S EXTENDED COMMITMENT TO PEACE IN THE MIDDLE EAST...

THE GOLAN HEIGHTS

A WINDSWEPT, BATTLE-SCARRED plateau overlooking the Sea of Galilee, the Golan Heights rise from Mount Hermon in the north to the Yarmuk valley 45 miles to the south. To the east, the rough, boulder-strewn surface of the plateau rises gently towards the Damascus Plain. To the west, dominating the northern finger of Israel stretching up to the Lebanese border, it suddenly drops down to the Jordan valley. Interspersed with volcanic hills called "tels," the highest, Tel Abu Nidal which looms 3600 feet above Kuneitra, it is a haunted place of abandoned villages, mine fields and burned out tanks. The only permanent residents are snakes, scorpions and United Nations peacekeepers.

HEAVY FORTIFICATIONS

Flanking the 1949 ceasefire line between Israel and Syria, the Golan Heights had been heavily fortified by the Syrian army. Missile batteries, bunkers, mortar and gun emplacements backed up by three brigades of infantry and hundreds of modern Soviet tanks formed a deep defence zone stretching back along the main axes to Damascus. Periodically, the Syrians would bombard kibbutzim in the fertile valley below with artillery fire causing a generation of Israelis to become known as "Shelter Children." Every year brought its shooting season as Israeli farmers ventured forth in their armoured tractors to till the land. There was constant tension on the frontier and incidents without number. It was here that the seeds of the Six Day War were sown.

CONVERGENCE OF ARMIES

In June 1967, Arab armies began to converge on Israel from all sides amid a clamour of boastful rhetoric. President Gamal Abdel Nasser of Egypt closed the Straits of Tiran and the port of Aqaba to all Israeli shipping, sent his armies into the Sinai and demanded that UN observers be removed. When Canadian Prime Minister Lester B. Pearson tried to intervene, he was called an "idiot" by the Egyptian president who then ordered Canadian peacekeepers out of his country within 48 hours. Syria spoke of driving the Israelis into the sea, moved saboteurs into Israel through Jordan and Lebanon and began to mass armour on the Golan Heights.

On the morning of 5 June, the Israelis staged a pre-emptive strike which destroyed the Egyptian air force on the ground. They then turned their attention to the Syrians, Jordanians and Iraqis. By nightfall, 416 Arab aircraft had been destroyed leaving Israel with complete superiority in the air. At the same time, Israeli armour and infantry raced into the Sinai and seized Jerusalem and the West Bank of the Jordan.

The Israeli Minister of Defence, General Dayan, was hesitant about launching a ground attack against the Syrians which might draw the Soviet Union into the conflict. But, as the war progressed, pressure grew from the villages in northern Israel to seize the Golan Heights and put an end to the constant harassment they had been subjected to. Only after the Egyptians had collapsed in the Sinai and the Jordanians ejected from the West Bank were orders given to take the Heights. In fierce hand-to-hand fighting, units of the Golani Brigade overran key Syrian positions to be followed by Centurion and Super-Sherman tanks. After an elite commando unit scaled Mount Hermon, the Syrians broke and ran.

STILL NO PEACE

The Israeli victory did not bring peace to the region. Six years later, in the Yom Kippur War, Syria and Egypt launched simultaneous attacks against Israel from both north and south. Israel, after suffering serious losses, rallied and counterattacked. The Golan Heights witnessed the fiercest tank battles since the Second World War. In what came to be known as the Valley of Tears, the Syrians lost 1150 tanks compared to --- Isreali tanks destroyed before accepting a ceasefire proposed by the United Nations Security Council.

In the wake of the Yom Kippur War, two new UN forces took the field. A large force dubbed UNEF II, which included 1100 Canadians, was positioned between Israel and Egypt, while a United Nations Disengagement Observer Force was dispatched to the Golan Heights. More than 200 Canadians were assigned to UNDOF's logistics unit to service vehicles and electronic equipment and to provide supply, communications and medical services. The airlift required to get the Canadian troops to the Middle East was the largest peacetime operation ever mounted by Air Transport Command.

PEACEKEEPERS KILLED

The mission got off to an inauspicious start. On 9 August 1974, a Buffalo aircraft of 116 Air Transport Unit on a routine flight from Ismailia to Damascus by way of Beirut was mistaken for an Israeli aircraft and shot down by a Syrian surface-to-air missile. All nine Canadians aboard were killed, making it the worst day in the history of the country's peacekeeping efforts.

UNEF II was short-lived, but Canadians continue to serve on the Golan Heights. In May 1974, Israel agreed to withdraw from the ground it had captured the year before, retaining possession only of Syrian lands captured during the Six Day War – lands deemed essential to provide a defence in depth in northern Galilee. The Canadians, along with contingents from Austria, Poland and Peru, were tasked with supervising the Israeli withdrawal and policing a buffer zone, the Area of Separation. At Camp Ziouani, in a barren, treeless landscape on the Israeli side of the line, 180 officers and men of Canlog, continue to provide support for UN patrols. As on all UN tours, they are rotated home every six months.

NO MORE THAN A RUIN

Camp Ziouani, nicknamed 'Camp Roofless,' had been a French Foreign Legion outpost in the 1920s and was little more than a ruin when the Canadians moved in. They were not impressed with either their accommodation or the landscape. Brigadier General Douglas Yuill recalls:

"The Golan is an arid area where poisonous snakes, centipedes and spiders are common and where living conditions are less than attractive no matter what accommodation is available. Summer temperatures in the 40 degree plus Celsius range are common, winds are often very high and the fall and winter rains often turn to snow which is wet, heavy and sometimes very deep. Few winters pass without snow and two to three feet at one time has been known with the usual consequence of a plethora of vehicle accidents, collapsed buildings, including the Canlog mess hall on one occasion and severe flooding."

Minefields were everywhere in this eerily silent place, deserted since more than 70,000 Syrian inhabitants fled the Israeli onslaught. Grass fires, whipped by the wind, sometimes detonated mines and could not be fought until they reached a cleared area. Travel by foot was impossible and the troops never drove alone for fear of bogging down or being mistaken for a terrorist and shot on sight. "You proceed very, very cautiously," an officer said.

ABOVE: *In June 1967, during the Six Day War, some 70,000 Syrians fled from the advancing Israeli army. Canadians, serving with UNDOF, patrolled the war-torn ruins on the Golan Heights. Canada was ordered out of the Sinai one week prior to the War, but sustained no casualties, unlike other UNEF troops.* (DND PHOTO)

CANADIANS HAD OFTEN BEFORE FACED THE PROSPECT OF A LONG AND APPARENTLY FUTILE PEACEKEEPING ENGAGEMENT IN AN INHOSPITABLE PLACE, BUT AT CAMP ZIOUANI MORALE SANK WITH EVERY PASSING MONTH.

Apart from a few shepherds who had UN permits to graze their herds in specified areas, the truce agreement did not allow anyone to enter the Area of Separation. Observers sent patrols to investigate any activity.

OLDEST PROFESSION

"In the peacekeeping business one of the oldest surviving trades is the UN Military Observer, more commonly known as the 'UNMO,'" Captain John McLearn recalled. "To maintain the highest level of impartiality, we staffed our observation posts with two UNMOs from different nations. While one of us is up in the tower the other is doing the chores. Pairs of observers will do one week stints during which they look after all their own housekeeping. So it's one week of lookin' and cookin'."

Canadians had often before faced the prospect of a long and apparently futile engagement with a peacekeeping force in an inhospitable place, but at Camp Ziouani morale sank with every passing month. According to General Yuill, the fault lay with the UN higher command which instituted a person-for-person rotation scheme, instead of sending personnel over in groups and failed to implement effective screening or preparation for "the cultural, climactic and professional challenge of service in the Middle East."

When a Canadian was appointed Deputy Commander at UNDOF headquarters, changes were made. "Better selection and screening, quarterly rotations of half the contingent at a time, pre-tour training, and significant improvements in Camp Ziouani itself were all put in train," Yuill notes. "By the summer of 1987, the contingent was once again an effective unit with high morale, a strong work ethic, and great pride in serving in one of the most operational theatres open to Canadians."

FIRM ROOTS

Today, Camp Ziouani boasts messes and clubs, gym, canteen and water reservoir swimming pool. A monthly newsletter is published and each week the biggest "klutz" is officially recognized by the maintenance engineers for his or her contribution to fouling up equipment. Married personnel have the option of a two week UN leave for which they can choose between a trip home or having their spouse join them in the Middle East. Many take advantage of the latter option to visit nearby historic sites. Damascus is an hour's drive away and Tiberias on the Sea of Galilee is a popular destination.

Boredom remains a problem, but then, boredom on a peacekeeping mission is a sign of success.

AUTHOR: *Bill Twatio*

UNTOLD EFFORT: CANADIANS AND THE VIETNAM WAR

As American draft-dodgers flooded north of the border to avoid service in Vietnam, an equal number of adventure-seeking Canadians entered the United States to enlist in the Army.

CANADIANS LIKE TO THINK of the Vietnam War as an American conflict, one which we were smart enough to stay out of. In the literal sense, this may be true – Canada was never an official protagonist and no Canadian serviceman fought there – but it nevertheless had an impact here.

During the war, Canada became a haven for American draft-dodgers, while Canadian industries waxed fat on military contracts and an entire generation of Canadians grew up watching the fighting each night on their television sets. South Vietnam received economic aid from this country under the Fire Work Assistance Programme. A number of Canadians served on United Nations Commissions in Indo-China, while even more joined the American Forces and wound up in Vietnam.

Canada's official position throughout the conflict was one of neutrality combined with participation in two United Nations Supervisory commissions.

On – August 1954, the first 130 Canadian peacekeepers arrived in Vietnam as members of the International Control and Supervision Commission (ICSC). (Twenty-five more going to Cambodia and 23 to Laos.) With them were members of the Indian and Polish contingents.

PARTICIPATION SCALED DOWN

Initially, their job was to supervise the ceasefire and confirm France's departure. Later, they monitored the relocation of civilians and tried to restrict arms and military supplies crossing between the two countries. Frustrated by a lack of transport, official obstruction and continual violations of the agreement by both sides, participation was scaled down following the 1965 deaths of two Canadian servicemen shot down in a UN helicopter by the Viet Cong.

A handful of Canadians continued to serve on the Commission throughout the war however, later transferring their headquarters from Saigon to Hanoi in order to better facilitate their task. The ICSC was formally dissolved in March of 1973.

OPPOSITE PAGE: *Flying over the Mekong Delta in 1967, this Bell UH-1 Iroquois filled numerous roles and proved to be an invaluable "airborne workhorse" during the Vietnam War.* (FROM "THE VIETNAM WAR")

RIGHT: *The North Vietnamese possessed heavy weapons of their own as this exhausted American reconnaissance patrol discovered. Carrying the 12.7 mm anti-aircraft gun they captured, the troops slog through the Vietnam jungle.* (FROM "THE VIETNAM WAR")

In 1973, Canada was once again asked to involve itself. Under the aegis of the International Commission of Control and Supervision. Canada – with Hungary, Indonesia and Poland – was charged with enuring compliance with the Paris Peace Accords. Operation Gallant began on 29 January with the dispatch of 150 diplomats and servicemen to Saigon. Two destroyers – the HMCS *Kootenay*, and HMCS *Terra Nova* – were sent to the South China Sea in support.

A VARIETY OF CHORES

During the entire six months, over 18,000 incidents were recorded and some 1000 investigations undertaken by Commission members. Canadians flew to remote areas to document violations. They struggled through dense jungle in search of secret arms caches and braved shot and shell recording confrontations. They were plagued by dysentery chased by water-buffalo and subjected to the perils of Saigon nightlife. In a tragic echo of the past, one died when his helicopter was shot down. Two more were abducted by the Viet Cong and held for 17 days.

Overall, they achieved little, American troops were successfully disengaged and 32,000 prisoners of war repatriated, but fighting between North and South Vietnamese continued unabated. The Canadian government eventually withdrew – citing dangers to personnel combined with difficulties persuading the Hungarian and Polish contingents to remain objective – and the last Canadians left Vietnam on 31 July 1973. One disgruntled corporal summed up his experience with the Commission as, "So much B.S. Nobody listened, nobody cared. A bloody waste of time."

A CONTINUOUS SUPPLY

At home, business boomed while the shouts of demonstrators echoed in the streets. Twenty per cent of overall war profits may have gone to Canadian companies. Toronto's *Litton Systems* made bombsights for American aircraft while *DOW Chemical* of Canada refined napalm. 'Agent Orange' the infamous defoliant used on suspected Communist supply trails, was manufactured in Elmira, Ontario, and tested at CFB Gagetown. Ammunition for American rifles and artillery pieces came from Quebec – as did the famous 'green berets' worn by American Special Forces. The Hershey plant in Smith's Falls, Ontario, made "Tropical Chocolate Bars" for the enjoyment of American troops.

The Canadian Armed Forces also supplied incidental assistance of their American colleagues. Under NATO agreement, Canadian pilot instruction replaced American flyers, freeing them for combat duties in Vietnam. US troops trained with Canadian Forces and a number of American officers attended the Staff College in Kingston, Ontario.

MONTHLY DEMONSTRATIONS

Between 1968 and 1973, at least one antiwar demonstration took place at an American Embassy or Consulate office each month. Somewhat more quietly, an estimated 75,000 – 150,000 American draftdodgers took up residence in Canada. (Many remain to this day. As Gordon Bernais of Ottawa put it, "I came here because of the war, and I stayed because of

RIGHT:
Official records show that at least 79 Canadians were killed and over 700 wounded.
(FROM "THE VIETNAM WAR")

the peace.")

On the other side of the coin, many Canadian nationals crossed the border to join the American military. More (10,000 – 15,000) fought in Vietnam than served since Confederation in any other foreign army. At least one Canadian woman, nurse Marsha Jordan from Nova Scotia, went as well.

Carved upon the Vietnam War Memorial in Washington, DC, are the names of 79 Canadians. Some 700 more were wounded in action. Two, Army Warrant Officer Ian McIntosh and Marine Lance Corporal John Reeves, are listed as Missing in Action. No Canadian is believed to have been taken prisoner.

FOREIGNERS LIABLE FOR SERVICE

They came from all walks of life and economic backgrounds, from every territory and province. Most were young (in their teens or early twenties), but some were older men with well-established careers in the American Forces. A few were drafted – at that time, any foreigner in the US on a work visa was liable for conscription – although any Canadian could easily escape induction simply by returning home.

Their reasons were varied as their backgrounds. In *Unknown Warriors*, author Fred Gaffen suggests that one third of these people volunteered for adventure, another third for idealism (to fight Communism) and the remainder for personal reasons. Some lived in the US or had American relations. A number wanted to learn a trade, while others hoped to earn American citizenship (which was offered to all after three years in uniform). A few, unable to join the Canadian Forces, were attracted by the lower wartime standards of the American military.

Canada's Foreign Enlistment Act expressly forbids Canadians from recruiting or joining foreign armies. It is even a criminal offence to fight against a country Canada considers a 'friendly nation.' Although some of the Canadians who volunteered in the Spanish Civil War were tried on exactly that charge, no Canadian was actually prosecuted for fighting in Vietnam.

AS THE LAST CANADIANS LEFT VIETNAM ON 31 JULY 1973, ONE DISGRUNTLED CORPORAL SUMMED UP HIS EXPERIENCE WITH THE COMMISSION AS, "SO MUCH B.S. NOBODY LISTENED, NOBODY CARED. A BLOODY WASTE OF TIME."

JOIN THE CRUSADE

Leniency is perhaps understandable considering the extent of pressures to join the 'crusade' against Communism. Although America technically avoided recruiting in Canada, their media trumpeted the message across the land. Statements from US officials helped. As Ambassador to South Vietnam, Henry Cabot Lodge once said: "If any Canadians wish to go out and help… I can assure them they will be very welcome."

Anyone wanting to enlist found his way made easy. Expanded recruiting facilities were set up in many northern American cities (one near Quebec sported the sign "Beinvenue Canadiens!"). Letters of acceptability could easily be obtained, permitting Canadians to receive the residency visas required for recruitment. (When this writer considered volunteering in 1970, a single call to the American Embassy resolved all questions about how to do it.)

Canadians enlisted in every branch of the American armed forces although most joined the Army or Marines. After induction came basic training followed by advanced individual training and trades training. Then Vietnam, for a 12 or a 13 month tour. (A few extended for an additional six months, or returned later for a second and even third tour.)

While 'in-country,' Canadians drove trucks and flew helicopters, tended the wounded, worked in offices, depots and mess halls, built air fields and conducted Civil Affairs programs amongst the civilian population. They were Huey mechanics, tank crewmen and sailors on small patrol boats, probing Vietnam's many rivers. They also fought, manning artillery pieces in remote fire bases, defending Special Forces camps, conducting search and destroy missions or making long range patrols behind enemy lines. Less credibly, a very few became black marketers or uniformed drug dealers. In short, Canadians in Vietnam did everything their American counterparts did.

CANADIAN PARIAHS

Returning Canadians found themselves virtual pariahs. Not only had they fought an unpopular war for another country, they had lost. Readjustment was a struggle. America accorded them the status of 'veteran,' but many benefits could not be realized outside the United States. Our government ignored them. The Canadian Legion refused permission for Vietnam vets to participate as a group in Remembrance Day ceremonies. Most quickly learned to hide their past and many still do.

A number fell prey to Post Traumatic Stress Disorder (called 'shellshock' or 'battle fatigue' in earlier wars). The initial rate was high (due both to the war's nature and the social antipathy encountered when veterans got home), but most Canadian victims report that problems diminished as the years progressed and public sympathy increased.

Only recently have Canadian vets begun to band together. Vietnam veterans associations have sprung up across the country, providing mutual support and encouragement to their members. Not all veterans become members, but those who do, find the opportunity to relax with others who understand their experiences and problems most helpful.

As time goes on it becomes far easier for Canadians to put that turbulent era into perspective. If nothing else, it was a watershed. Says Canadian Vietnam veteran Michael Touchette: "Then, it was a time to forget. Now, it's time to remember." It is not hard to agree with him.

NOTE: *Today (in 2001) attitudes have changed. A memorial to Canadians killed in Vietnam was dedicated in Windsor, Ontario, and a national memorial is being planned for Ottawa. There is also a small monument in Vancouver, British Columbia.*

REPRINTED FROM:
Esprit de Corps, Volume 1 Issue 6
AUTHOR: *Andrew Moxley*

CANADIAN UN OBSERVERS IN VIETNAM

ABOVE:
The International Commission for Support and Control (ICSC) was the first peacekeeping operation in which Canada participated outside the United Nations. ICSC helicopters were grounded on 8 April 1973 after the Viet Cong shot one down, killing everyone on board, including one Canadian. (DND PHOTO)

As thousands of Canadians "unofficially" fought with the Americans in Vietnam, Canada's Armed Forces "officially" served a brief stint in south east Asia as peacekeepers.

THE INTERNATIONAL Commission for Supervision and Control in Vietnam (ICSC) was unique in that it was the first peacekeeping operation in which Canada participated outside the United Nations. It was also futile; somewhat akin to sending observers into Buchenwald to monitor human rights abuses.

By the mid-1950s, peacekeeping had become fashionable, largely due to the United Nation's success in checking Commmunist aggression in Korea. The concept appealed to other organizations as well, particularly an international commission established at Geneva to bring an end to the long and bloody wars in French Indo-China, a federation of protectorates which included the present-day countries of Vietnam, Laos and Cambodia. When the region was liberated from the Japanese at the end of the Second World War, the French had hoped to restore the prewar status quo, but that hope died when the Viet Minh, a coalition of nationalists and Communists demanding full independence, overran Dien Bien Phu.

In the summer of 1954, all parties in the conflict signed the Geneva Accords which called for an international commission to supervise a ceasefire, monitor the transfer of populations and supervise free elections. Pending elections, a provisional line was drawn at the 17th parallel, separating "North Vietnam" (with its capital at Hanọi), from "South Vietnam" (with its capital at Saigon). A ceasefire would allow the French to withdraw while the Viet Minh pulled back to North Vietnam.

THE TROIKA

Canada had not been represented at the Geneva conference and was much surprised to be invited, along with India and Poland, to supervise the ceasefire. It was

***ABOVE**: By 1972, the ICSC role had become pointless and ended operations following the Paris Peace Accords. However, Canada then joined Hungary, Indonesia and Poland in monitoring the latest cease-fire in South Vietnam and (seen here) supervising the exchange of POWs.* (DND PHOTO)

later learned that Krishna Menon of India had suggested Canada's participation to China's Chou En-lai as a disinterested non-colonial power without military commitments in the region. The commission, he argued, would be balanced, with a Western democracy (Canada), a Communist nation (Poland), and neutral India. In fact, it was a formula for deadlock.

Canada had little knowledge of the region and was concerned with American reaction to its involvement with the commission. Arnold Heeney, Canada's ambassador to the United States felt obliged to assure the State Department that "we would wish to keep the United States Government informed privately of the course of events. This we felt we could do quite properly without impinging on our international responsibilities as members of the Commission." Heeney's assurances would cause Canada considerable embarrassment.

The first Canadians arrived in Indo-China on 11 August. External Affairs provided three officers of ambassadorial rank, 12 political advisers and office staff, while the armed forces contributed 83 officers, including three major-generals and 31 other ranks. Real progress was made in Laos and Cambodia, but the real problem for the ICSC was in Vietnam. External Affairs was soon reporting that "an impartial approach on the part of the Canadians combined with the partisan attitude of the Poles and the middle-of-the-road policy adopted by the Indians did not lead to just decisions. There has been an increasing tendency in the Canadian Delegation to apply pressure against North Vietnam and to defend South Vietnam when it was considered Communist action was unduly harsh." Moreover, there were increasing tensions between the Canadians and the Poles, one officer reporting that "their dress, deportment, cleanliness and observations of local customs leaves much to be desired by our standards. Their table manners and consumption of food and drink is atrocious."

IT IS SIGNIFICANT THAT, ALTHOUGH CANADA'S PARTICIPATION IN THE ICSC PRECLUDED THE COUNTRY'S DIRECT INVOLVEMENT IN THE ESCALATING VIETNAM WAR, VIRTUALLY ALL THE CANADIAN MEMBERS OF THE COMMISSION CAME AWAY FIRM SUPPORTERS OF AMERICAN INTERVENTION.

A PARODY OF NEUTRALITY

In 1954, Vietnam was divided between a Communist regime in the north under Ho Chi Minh and a "democratic" government in the south, and although elections were supposed to create a single government for the country, both sides refused to hold them. As a result, the ICSC was faced with a hopeless task. However, by April 1955, despite bureaucratic obstruction and intimidation, the Commission did manage to oversee the transfer of over 700,000 people from one zone to the other and the exchange of 75,000 prisoners of war. Still, the frustrations were growing. The Poles were openly partisan, the Indians bounced from one side to the other in a parody of neutrality, and the Canadians were coming under increased pressure from the Americans to stem the flow of arms into the south and to monitor the activities of the Viet Cong.

What is significant is that although Canada's participation in the ICSC precluded the country's direct involvement in the escalating Vietnam War – Australia, South Korea and other countries sent troops – virtually all the Canadian members of the Commission came away firm supporters of American intervention. Information collected in the north quickly found its way to Washington. Ottawa's denials of impropriety were always prompt. "Members of the Canadian delegation in Viet Nam are not engaged in clandestine or spying activities," Prime Minister Pearson said in May 1967. "The Canadian delegation reports to the Canadian government only; it is for the Canadian government to decide in the case of these reports... what use is to be made of them in the course of normal diplomatic exchanges." In fact, Canada was passing on information wholesale.

MESSENGER BOYS

Canada had been doing much more than passing on information. In 1964 and 1965 Canadian commissioner Blair Seaborn had made repeated trips to Hanoi as an intermediary for the United States, warning the north that it would be "punished" if its infiltration into the south was not checked. Technically there was nothing improper in Canada acting as it did as the role of diplomatic intermediary is one of long standing. Still, for a member of the ICSC to carry bellicose messages from one warring state to another was surely not what had been intended in the Geneva Accords.

By 1972 the ICSC role had become completely pointless and after the Paris Peace Accords more or less ended the war, the Commission wound up its operations. Canada, however, was willing to join a new commission along with Hungary, Indonesia and Poland to monitor the latest ceasefire in South Vietnam and to supervise the exchange of prisoners of war.

After nearly two decades of unhappy and frustrating experiences in Vietnam, the government had few illusions about the possible success of the new commission and agreed to join only if, as External Affairs minister Mitchell Sharp stated, "the provisions for the operation appear workable and offer some prospects for success." The minister well knew that the peace being established was largely a sham, but considered participation worthwhile as it would help extract the United States from the Vietnam quagmire.

***ABOVE:** Having reluctantly agreed to participate in the new commission for a two-month trial period, ICSC ambassador Michel Gauvin headed a group of 50 officials from External Affairs and a 240-member military team led by Major General Duncan McAlpine (some of whom are seen here inspecting the body of a Viet Cong soldier). Quickly realizing the operation was futile, and, bogged down under complaints (mostly from South Vietnam), Canada announced it would not play a part in such a charade and withdrew on 30 June 1973.* (DND PHOTO)

BUGGING OUT

Canada agreed to participate for a two-month period and the ambassador to the ICSC, Michel Gauvin adopted what was called an "open mouth" policy – if there was interference and obstruction, he would say so. Under the ambassador were 50 officials from External Affairs and a military team of 240 headed by Major General Duncan McAlpine. He and most of his men were on site by late January 1973.

Old patterns quickly reasserted themselves as the ICSC bogged down under a flood of complaints, most of them filed by South Vietnam. The Poles and Hungarians refused to criticize the North and the ceasefire was an illusion, with both sides fighting major engagements. Several Canadian peacekeepers were kidnapped and later released and another was killed when his helicopter was shot down. As one Canadian noted, "a competent ICSC was anathema to the communist side. Investigators might 'discover' North Vietnamese troops."

Reluctantly extending its participation for a further 90 days, Canada announced that it would withdraw on 30 June 1973, refusing to continue to play a part in a charade. In April 1975, with victorious North Vietnamese troops entering Saigon, the Canadian delegation closed its office and personal possessions, including the official car, were flown out. The Vietnam War was finally over.

***AUTHOR:** Bill Twatio*

Although not called upon to go into battle, Bonnie served well in her 12 years with the Royal Canadian Navy – from Belfast shipyard to Taiwanese scrapyard.

HMCS *BONAVENTURE* CANADA'S LAST CARRIER

IN AN AVERAGE YEAR, she handled 3,000 landings and sailed 42,000 nautical miles, or twice around the world. She was away from her home port of Halifax more than 200 days a year – in the far East, the Mediterranean, the West Indies and the North Atlantic.

She sailed tropical seas and storm-tossed seas swept by winds of up to 100 knots. In 1968, she sailed through a hurricane with rollers breaking over her flight deck, tearing a bulkhead loose and punching a hole in her hull. Several crew members were injured and only quick action by damage control teams kept her afloat. She earned a reputation of staying on station long after larger carriers had suspended operations due to heavy weather.

Commissioned at Belfast on 17 January 1957, HMCS *Bonaventure* was too small, too slow and too crowded. Bunks were stacked four high and her thousand man crew froze in winter and sweltered in summer. At 20,000 tons and carrying 34 aircraft - Banshees and Grumman Trackers - she fell far short of U. S. Navy standards. American carrier pilots would not even consider trying to land on her 700 foot flight deck, and, if they did, would have been appalled by the fare offered in her messes. Yet, fondly known as "Bonnie," she was a happy and efficient ship.

BANJOS, HORSES AND STOOFS

Due to her size, only two squadrons of Banshees and Trackers could serve aboard the *Bonaventure* at any given time. Other squadrons were land based when they were not at sea. The Banshee was a reliable carrier aircraft with an all-weather capability, an eight hundred mile tactical radius and Mach .8 speed. Armed with four 20mm cannons and Sidewinder missiles, the "Banjo" flew cover for the Trackers. Known as the "Stoof," the CS2F Tracker was a big, solid ASW aircraft which carried radar, MAD, sonobuoys and homing torpedoes. More than 100 were built under license by De Havilland in Toronto. Bonnie also carried Sikorsky HO4S "Horse" helicopters equipped with dunking sonar.

For more than a decade, she was Canada's major contribution to NORAD and NATO naval defence. Assigned to anti-submarine duties, *Bonnie* excelled at sustained operations or SUSTOPS. With "Pedro," her faithful rescue helicopter hovering overhead, she was the envy of her allies, as she was capable of keeping aircraft in the air around the clock. "She was a really unique ship, and quite capable of flying off when others stood down," a Tracker pilot recalls. "It was a terrifying experience when you were 'catted' off in the middle of the night, especially in stormy weather. "

ABOVE:
HMCS Bonaventure *sails into Malta's Grand Harbour, Valetta, following a 1958 NATO exercise in the Mediterranean. On deck are Tracker anti-submarine aircraft and Sikorsky helicopters.* (DND PHOTO)

Landing a Tracker was just as terrifying, as the slightest shift away from the centreline could result in a crash into the island. On one occasion, a Tracker went over the side, dumping her crew into the sea. As a whale boat from an escort destroyer moved in to pick them up, it was swamped by a wave, dumping its crew as well. "So now we had four of my airmen in the water, plus the full whaler crew," Bob Timbrell, the Bonnie's captain remembers. "The destroyer then started to throw heaving lines to pull out their crew. They were still manoeuvring, and the lines got sucked up into the intakes and water pumps, which resulted in the destroyer becoming immobile." Turning into the wind, Timbrell, who retired as a rear-admiral, recovered the rest of his aircraft then pulled the soggy sailors and airmen out of the sea. Charitably, he left the hapless destroyer unnamed in his official report.

ARRIVALS AND DEPARTURES

Bonnie also excelled at search and rescue. In 1962, she picked up survivors from a

LEFT:
Sailors aboard the Bonaventure *unload equipment at Nicosia 30 March 1964, as part of Canada's initial UN deployment to Cyprus.*

BELOW:
A Grumman C52 Tracker on anti-submarine patrol and a Tracker preparing for takeoff from Bonnie's *flight deck.* (DND PHOTO)

downed Super Constellation off the coast of Ireland and she was called on time and again to come to the aid of fishing vessels in distress. Ever generous, her crew readily contributed to relief funds for the families of missing seamen.

In the winter of 1964, she carried Canada's UN peacekeeping contingent to Cyprus along with 54 army vehicles and four hundred tons of stores lashed down alongside the Trackers. After off loading in Famagusta, she sailed on to Gilbraltar to resume regular operations.

Bonnie's calling card in foreign ports was a party for disadvantaged children. At Portsmouth and Port-of-Spain, Rotterdam, Stockholm and Toulon, wherever she drew alongside between exercises, out came the pirate and clown costumes, a miniature merry-go-round and a train pulled by a tractor. Enthralled children swarmed over the ship and planes and ran races on the flight deck before settling down to gallons of ice cream, soft drinks and mountains of hamburgers.

From time to time, *Bonnie* entertained politicians, celebrities and local worthies. Paul Hellyer, the new Minister of National Defence came aboard at Bermuda to congratulate the crew for a job well done in Cyprus and to familiarize himself with the ship. Reminded of his brief RCAF service during the war, he was kitted out and coaxed into a Tracker for a catapult launch. The pilot, he was assured, would be the most experienced in the navy. Moments later, the deck crew appeared with a white-haired naval aviator wearing an eye patch and tottering along on a cane. Muttering inanities, he was lifted gently into his seat. The Minister was not amused.

Within five years of his flight, Hellyer had merged the navy into the Canadian Armed Forces, admirals were up in arms and the Trackers were operating from shore bases. After a costly and controversial refit, Bonnie was paid off and sold to a Taiwanese shipyard for scrap.

HMCS Bonaventure made her last entrance into Halifax harbour as an operational carrier in December 1969, with four Trackers aboard for a final fly-past. But the wind was wrong and the catapult broke down. Determined not to go out with a whimper, her captain wheeled her down the Bedford Basin like a destroyer and with engines howling and 17 knots of wind sweeping over her deck, the Trackers roared aloft.

AUTHOR:
Bill Twatio

NON-PEACEABLE "PEACETIME"

Canada's military tasks were not all external. From time to time, Duties in Aid of the Civil Power were needed.

A "SPECIAL MILITIA TRAINING PROGRAMME" WAS INSTITUTED IN THE EARLY 1960s. UNEMPLOYED CANADIANS WERE GIVEN SIX WEEKS BASIC TRAINING.

ABOVE:
An armoured infantry company of 2RCR departs from CFB Gagetown, New Brunswick, enroute to Ottawa and Montreal. During the October Crisis, the Army deployed nearly all available troops in response to the separatist threat. These APCs were first loaded onto ships in Saint John and then disembarked in the port of Montreal.
(DND PHOTO)

WHEN CANADIAN TROOPS returned from the First World War most of them felt that they could put away their rifles and equipment, and settle down to a placid life. Indeed, there were several trouble-spots around the world (some Canadians found themselves in Siberia). Iraq, India, the Balkans and other "hot spots" became the focus of the Commonwealth military efforts, but fortunately for Canadian troops (and the Canadian economy) most of these were Britain's concern.

However, from time to time the diminished Canadian regulars, and occasionally Militia units, were called out in support of the authorities against their own countrymen. There had already been one unfortunate incident in Britain in 1919 where Canadian soldiers, impatient to return home, rioted in a repatriation camp, and were fired upon by their comrades with a loss of five lives.

STRIKE VIOLENCE

Two months later, in May 1919, a general strike hit Winnipeg. Violence erupted following an attack by a Mounted Police detachment, and troops were called in to patrol the streets in trucks mounting machine guns. It was unfortunate that many of the protesters were ex-servicemen, but apparently the soldiers carried out their duties without serious incidents.

The army was called in on at least two more occasions between the wars. Colonel Strome Galloway recalls that the Royal Canadian Regiment despatched troops to Cape Breton in 1925, where they remained for two months to assist in keeping order during a coal-miners' strike. In 1933, closer to home, the RCR were again called out for "duties in aid of the civil power" in Stratford, Ontario. Despite their function, the soldiers were well received by the populace - no doubt in part because they took along the regimental band who serenaded the citizens in front of the Armoury.

Between 1939 and 1945 Canada's forces had more pressing business, and after the Second World War their role at home was to defend the homeland. Various alarms and excursions, notably the Korean War, NATO commitments, and numerous peacekeeping operations often placed Canadian soldiers, sailors and airmen in harm's way, but generally things were fairly placid at home.

TRAINING THE UNEMPLOYED

The Cold War, highlighted by the Cuban Missile Crisis, resulted in an emphasis on nuclear survival operations – intensive training on decontamination, rescue and nuclear warning systems took place in both regular and reserve units. A "Special Militia Training Programme" was instituted in the early 1960's, where unemployed Canadians were given six weeks basic training in NBCW techniques and military skills (the scheme had the dual object of providing employment and, hopefully, encouraging suitable entrants to remain in the Militia). Mock "disaster areas" were constructed to train military personnel in rescue and re-

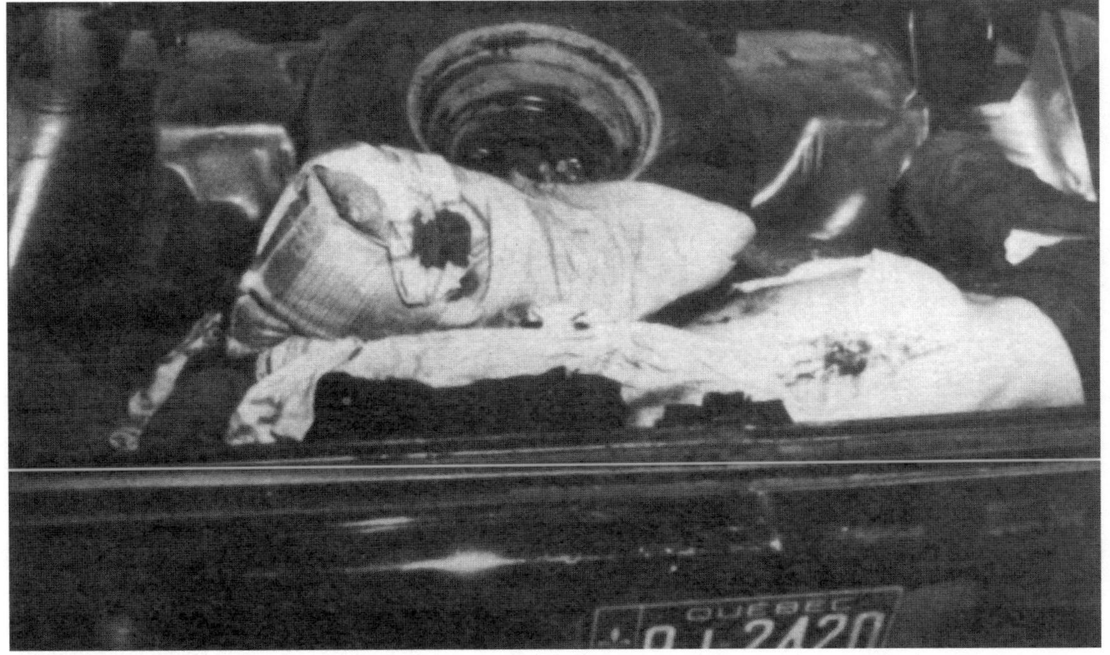

LEFT:
In 1970, Canadians were shocked at the sight of Pierre Laporte's body, stuffed into the trunk of this car. Although largely exaggerated, the threat of further FLQ violence sparked Canada's Prime Minister, Pierre Elliot Trudeau, to invoke the War Measures Act.

covery operations. Ironically, a "ruined" house cost much more to construct than an intact model at that time. These training areas proved useful in later years for street-fighting and house-clearing exercises

Since the Riel rebellion Canadian troops, unlike their British counterparts in Northern Ireland, had not been called upon since the Northwest Rebellion to deal with domestic foes. This was to change in 1963 when militant Quebec separatists, the Front de Libération du Quebec (FLQ) adopted aggressive tactics. Early in the year, bombing attacks targeted military recruiting offices, Legion branches and other symbols of Canadian authority. The first casualties were an army recruiting office employee, killed by a bomb, and Warrant Officer 2nd Class Leja, an Engineer explosives expert who lost both hands in an attempt to defuse a booby-trapped mailbox.

MILITIA INFILTRATED

The following year a branch of the FLQ raided four Montreal militia armouries, stealing a variety of small arms. Some of their members had infiltrated the Militia - these were quickly identified and released, and guarding of the armouries was taken over by the "Vandoos." This had one spin-off advantage for some troops. I was stationed at NDHQ at the time, and each Wednesday we undertook "military training" which consisted almost entirely of tediously marching around the Cartier Square armoury. In response to the threat, weapons held by cadet corps were secured in the armoury, which, to no-one's regret, became unavailable for our drill parades.

The FLQ were not all enthusiastic amateurs. Several had military service; some were graduates of guerilla training cadres in Algeria and Cuba. Nevertheless, at this stage, most of the counter-terrorist operations were conducted by joint RCMP, provincial and municipal police task forces.

Throughout the remainder of the decade the FLQ activities continued, increasing in 1969 with a new offensive, Operation Liberation. The R22eR was again called out, this time to back up the authorities in an FLQ-incited student riot at McGill University. The terrorist efforts did not spare Ottawa – in 1970 NDHQ suffered a bombing attack, in which a public service employee lost her life. The CF, realizing the seriousness of the situation, began counterinsurgency training at all levels.

In October 1970 events came to a head. British diplomat James Cross and Pierre Laporte, Quebec's Labour Minister and acting premier, were kidnapped. Laporte was later murdered by his captors Pierre Trudeau's government then proclaimed the War Measures Act – the first time that this had happened since WWII.

The Canadian Army responded quickly. Two plans were quickly implemented. Operation Ginger oncentrated on the protection of vital points and vulnerable individuals centred on the Ottawa area, while Operation Essay brought almost 10,000 troops into the Province of Quebec in the role of police officers, to aid the hard-pressed constabulary.

Weapon-bearing, combat-clad troops were a common sight on the streets. Virtually all of the troops in Canada were involved in one of the two operations. Rapid deployment by helicopter was a key element in the troops' activity. Major General Dan Loomis was serving with the First Battalion of the Royal Canadian Regiment during the crisis and recalls that the unit's operational area based on the Rockcliffe airfield in Ottawa covered 3200 square miles (General Loomis' book, *Not Much Glory*, graphically describes the FLQ crisis and its effect on subsequent military doctrine in Canada). He fails to mention that within a few days of their arrival from a stint in Cyprus, 1 RCR was actively conducting patrols and cordon-and-search operations on the Ontario-Quebec border. Many of them had not even had time to see their families before they were shipped off to Ottawa.

ABOVE: The October Crisis became the template for a number of major military exercises over the next decade. When the media suggested such actions were provocative, the military claimed their scenarios were coincidental. (DND PHOTO)

THERE IS LITTLE DOUBT THAT THE LESSONS LEARNED IN THE MONTREAL STREETS AND THE QUEBEC FARMLANDS WERE A SIGNIFICANT FACTOR IN SUBSEQUENT "AID TO THE CIVIL POWER" BOTH IN CANADA AND IN THE NUMEROUS AND HAZARDOUS "PEACE-KEEPING" OPERATIONS ABROAD.

TERRIFYING CIVILIANS

The "Essay" forces, as well providing security, conducted raids on suspected terrorist locations. Sometimes the information was faulty, and innocent civilians were scared out of their wits. John Hasek, in *The Disarming of Canada*, describes a hilarious raid on what turned out to be a Montreal pet shop, where the "suspects" included frightened parrots and a monkey. I recall, in the early stages of the crisis, a group of Intelligence Corps friends were enjoying a relaxing beverage in downtown Montreal when they were pounced upon by a squad of city police, after a customer had observed that one of the soldiers (in civilian clothing) was toting a partly-concealed 9mm pistol.

For a couple of months armed troops were a common sight in the sensitive areas. The troops efficiently assisted the police in cordoning-off suspect areas and in searching thousands of buildings and rural areas. Finally, the crisis de-escalated. Laporte's body was found, ironically, in a car trunk close to the St. Hubert military base. Britain's James Cross was released in exchange for safe passage to Cuba for one of the a major terrorist. On 4 January 1971 Prime Minister Trudeau announced that the last federal troops were leaving their support role and returning to their interrupted normal activities.

SIGNIFICANT LESSONS

Dan Loomis attributes the restructuring of the Canadian Forces to deal with counterterrorism to the FLQ threat. Certainly, there is little doubt that the lessons learned in the Montreal streets and the Quebec farmlands were a significant factor in subsequent "aid to the civil power" both in Canada (such as the Oka incidents) and in the numerous and hazardous "peace-keeping" operations abroad.

AUTHOR: *Les Peate*

A REGIMENT WORTHY OF HIRE, 1953 – 1971

Why Canada's youngest infantry regiment was also the Army's most senior. The short but eventful history of The Canadian Guards.

THE REGIMENT OF CANADIAN Guards was brought into being on 16 October 1953. The concept of a regular regiment of Guards in Canada was the result of the Monarch's new style as "Queen of Canada" rather than as "Queen of…her other Dominions beyond the seas," of which Canada had been one of "her other Dominions" until the new style was introduced at the Coronation a year earlier.

Although there were already two regiments of Guards, the Governor General's Foot Guards in Ottawa and the Canadian Grenadier Guards in Montreal, they were modelled on, and affiliated with, the Coldstream Guards and Grenadier Guards in England. It was the view of the then Chief of the General Staff, Lieutenant General G.C. Simonds that there should be a regular regiment of Guards which could stand on its own alongside of the Scots, Irish and Welsh Guards. Her Majesty the Queen consented to this concept and the regiment was born. At the same time the G.G.F.G. and the Canadian Grenadiers were designated the 5th and 6th Battalions of the Canadian Guards with their old historic titles in parenthesis.

CREATION OF NEW REGIMENT

To create this new regiment the 3rd Battalion, The Royal Canadian Regiment and the 3rd Battalion, Princess Patricia's Canadian Light Infantry, two regular regiments dating from 1885 and 1914 respectively, were designated the 1st and 2nd Battalions of the Canadian Guards, while the 1st and 2nd Infantry Battalions, two temporary units

ABOVE, LEFT:
Canadian guardsmen keep a vigilant eye on the streets of Nicosia, Cyprus, from their rooftop observation post. (DND PHOTO)
ABOVE, RIGHT:
The Canadian Guards, 1971. (DND PHOTO)

organized from Militia regiments as Canada's contribution to the newly established NATO forces in Germany, were designated the 3rd and 4th Battalions.

At the time, the RCR and PPCLI battalions were serving in Korea, the 2nd Infantry Battalion in Canada and the 1st Infantry Battalion in West Germany. A regimental depot was established in Petawawa, Ontario, and selected officers and NCOs were despatched to the Guards depot in the United Kingdom to "learn the ropes". In less than 18 months all four battalions were dressed as guardsmen so far as battle dress, badges and Guards' accessories were concerned and full dress uniforms were on order.

Great progress was made in all battalions, but with the Korean conflict ended there were cuts in the defence budget and, in the spring of 1957, both the 3rd and 4th Battalions were disbanded. The 3rd had been raised as a bilingual (essentially a French-speaking) unit, which evoked the following statement from its commanding officer Lieutenant Colonel J.H.J. Gauthier: "I was privileged to prove that as in our Dominion, so too, within the Regiment, our two great peoples, though different in traditions and speech have been brought together to work and possibly to fight as one effective, compact team, united by a common purpose."

In the meantime, the 4th Battalion had served a tour on garrison duty in Korea and soon both the 1st and 2nd Battalions were to see service abroad with the NATO forces in Germany and the UN peacekeeping forces in Cyprus. During the 17 years of their existence, the 1st and 2nd Battalions gained an excellent reputation in all fields of military life. When Her Majesty visited Canada her Canadian Guards, of which she had consented to be Colonel-in-Chief, mounted a Household Guard for Her Majesty's stay at Government House in Ottawa, the first mount taking place in full dress on Parliament Hill on 29 June 1959.

For the next 11 years these public duties were carried out each summer, always before crowds of tourists and citizens to the numbers of four or five thousand surrounding Parliament Hill lawn, where the Old and New Guards changed, prior to marching to Government House to post the sentries.

THE *PRIX LECLERC*

A battalion of the Regiment won the coveted NATO *Prix Leclerc* for excellence, the only Canadian unit to win it in 18 years of NATO competition. The Regiment also fielded the Canadian Army's Bisley team in 1968.

The first Colonel of the Regiment was Major General J.D.B. Smith, CBE, DSO, CD, who was succeeded by Major General Roger Rowley, DSO, ED, CD, in 1966. The only Lieutenant Colonel of the regiment was Colonel Strome Galloway, ED, CD, a former CO of the 4th Battalion. Alas, further cuts in the defence budget ordained that six battalions of the regular army had to be disbanded. Among these were the two Guards battalions, it being considered that although the Regiment was, by virtue of being Guards, senior to the other five multiple-battalion regiments, it, and both battalions of the Queen's Own Rifles and the Black Watch, had to go, leaving the three original regular regiments, all dating from many years before the Guards were formed. As for the Queen's Own Regiment and the Black Watch, their traditions remained inviolate in their militia components, but the Guards, in the official document's wording were "placed in suspended animation." It was said by the Minister of National Defence that this meant, "Should the Regular element of the Canadian Forces expand sometime in the future, the Regiment might again be invited to serve Canada." The Governor General's Foot Guards and the Grenadiers regained their old status.

The Regimental Depot, which had trained 5895 recruits during its existence was closed down in October 1968. The Regimental Band dispersed its members to various surviving bands the same month. In November 1968 the 1st Battalion was reduced to nil strength and in mid-1970 the 2nd Battalion rebadged as The RCR's third battalion. Behind them was a brief 17-year regimental history which saw NATO airlift exercises to Norway and Denmark, jungle exercises in Jamaica and Puerto Rico, and home stations at Petawawa and Picton, Ontario – and in the case of the long-departed 3rd and 4th Battalions, in Valcartier, Quebec and Ipperwash, Ontario. Public duties had been carried out on more than one occasion for the Queen when she visited Canada and for other distinguished Heads of State and statesmen from around the world, including President John F. Kennedy of the United States and Emperor Haile Selassie of Ethiopia, to mention but two of them. Ottawa granted the Regiment the Freedom of the City.

Ceremonial troops in Canada's capital thrilled hundreds of thousands of spectators in their scarlet and gold. As an airportable battalion the 2nd Battalion, the last regimental element to disappear, showed that even Guards' traditions did not hinder the acquisition of state-of-the-art military capabilities. (Two Militia units – The Governor General's Foot Guards and Canadian Grenadier Guards – now carry out the ceremonial duties in the nation's capital each summer.)

THE LAST PARADE

The last Regimental parade took place before the Right Honourable Roland Michener, Governor General of Canada, at Rideau Hall. The Lieutenant-Colonel of the Regiment commanded the parade which consisted of the 2nd Battalion and the Colour parties of both the already disbanded 1st Battalion and 2nd Battalion. The Colours of both battalions, which had been presented by Her Majesty the Queen a mere three years before, were laid up in Ottawa's Rideau Hall, as were also Company Colours of both battalions. The short-lived 3rd and 4th Battalions had never received Colours.

So ended the brief history of a regiment whose motto was *A Mari Usque Ad Mare* - "From Sea to Sea," and of whom it is said on a granite plaque in Petawawa, Ontario, that it was "a regiment worthy of its hire."

REPRINTED FROM:
Esprit de Corps, Volume 7 Issue 3
AUTHOR: *Colonel Strome Galloway*

THE BRAS D'OR

Like the Avro Arrow, Canada's fastest warship was a technical marvel which surfaced before its time.

FAST, FUTURISTIC, AND expensive, the *Bras d'Or* was the navy's answer to the Arrow. She could make 60 knots in a moderate sea and sail rings around a destroyer. Armed with the latest ASW devices, missiles and homing torpedoes, she could cover vast distances quickly atop her hydrofoils and at "jump speed," track and sink the most sophisticated submarine. A subtle blend of marine and aviation technology, the *Bras d'Or,* like the Arrow, was far ahead of its time.

Named after the lake in Nova Scotia where Alexander Graham Bell had first conducted hydrofoil experiments, the *Bras d'Or* was built at the height of the Cold War to counter the threat of a new generation of high-performance Soviet submarines. Costly, but much less so than a conventional frigate or destroyer, she pioneered the use of gas-turbine marine propulsion and pulled the Canadian shipbuilding industry into the computer age.

Bell had been among the first to recognize the potential of the hydrofoil. Convinced that a ship could far exceed known speed and performance limits by being able to rise above the water and plane along on thin strips of metal, he began to experiment with ladder-like hydro-curved surfaces. In 1917, he and Frederick Walker Baldwin developed the HD-4. "She went like smoke," a witness recalled after watching the ungainly craft skim along the Bras d'Or lakes. A year later, with new engines, the HD-4 set a world speed record of 70.86 miles per hour, a record for a hydrofoil which stood well into the 1950's.

In the post war years, the RCN assisted Bell with his experiments by providing high-speed towing behind the destroyer *Puritan*. Unfortunately, there was no money in the naval budget for development work.

Baldwin continued Bell's experiments during WWII, working closely with the American and Canadian navies. In 1943, heeding the lessons learned at Dieppe, he designed a hydrofoil with a V-shaped surface-piercing pod, capable of laying smoke to screen amphibious landings. Trials with a two-man crew were successful and led to the production of the radio-controlled Comox Torpedo smoke-layer.

In the early fifties, scientists at the Naval Research Establishment in Halifax took up Baldwin's design and supervised the construction of the R-100, a 45 foot experimental hydrofoil powered by a Packard-Merlin aircraft engine. On 13 July 1950, it clocked in at 64.28 knots on a measured course in the Bedford Basin.

NRE quietly continued its experiments as navies around the world grew increasingly concerned about the speed of nuclear submarines. NATO demanded naval solutions. As the Royal Navy tested hovercraft and the United States Navy developed a submerged-foil craft, Canada was urged to continue work on the R-100.

In 1957, a teardrop-shaped vessel designated R-103 was build under contract to NRE specifications at Saunders-Roe on the isle of Anglesey. Named the *Baddeck*, it proved unstable in initial trials and fell off its foils at 25 knots. Shipped to Canada aboard the new aircraft carrier HMCS *Bonaventure*, it was put to use as a high speed tug in the development of variable-depth sonar. Tests with the *Proteus*, an acronym derived from the unwieldy name "Propulsion Research and Ocean-Water Testing of Experimental Underwater Systems," were more promising. By 1959, the NRE was confident enough to propose a 200-ton, open-ocean hydrofoil as a practical proposition for anti-submarine duties and work began on the *Bras d'Or* at Marine Industries Limited at Sorel, Quebec.

To the vast amusement of ancient mariners, the *Bras d'Or* was built upside down on a special jig to facilitate welding. Rolled upright, the superstructure was then lowered into place and she was fitted with three-bladed super-cavitating propellers and a propulsion system capable of delivering 25,500 horsepower. The engine was mounted on the upper deck abaft a cockpit-like wheelhouse and coupled to a transmission system through 30-foot shafts which ran down the hull and out into the foils. Accommodation for a crew of 28 was laid out athwartships rather than the traditional fore and aft and equipped with the latest appliances. As the *Bras d'Or* was not just a prototype but a fighting ship, plans were developed to fit her with a complete combat suite including Mark 36 torpedoes.

These pages show a series of photos revealing the Bras d'Or *as she goes through her paces after an extended period of problems – the FHE-400 had a history of breaking down and having to be towed in from sea. However, when Lieutenant Colonel Gordon L. Edwards took command in July 1970, he vowed things would change. He quickly improved morale and restored crew confidence and the* Bras d'Or *performed this, her first foilborne flight of 1970, on 26 October. Executed during sea state four, foilborne flights were exhilirating for those on board.*

Disaster struck on 5 November 1966, when fire raced through the *Bras d'Or*'s hull, setting the project back by a year. As costs rose and questions were asked in the House of Commons, she was floated to Halifax in a slave dock and finally commissioned in July 1968.

In sea trials, the *Bras d'Or* regularly exceeded her design speed of 60 knots. Dancing like a wave on the sea, she sailed figure-eights around lesser craft. Showing off to the fleet at Halifax, her captain conceded that he may have been a tad too enthusiastic. "I overdid it a little," he recalls. "After doing a slalom down the formation, I gilded the lily by going past the flagship; literally waggling my wings. I was accordingly told by the Commodore, 'That will be quite enough.' Any naval officer can quickly grasp the significance of the adjective 'quite' and so I quickly left the Bedford Basin."

As unification of the forces loomed, the *Bras d'Or* met all expectations. She handled 12-foot waves as ably as a destroyer and could cruise at a stable 45 knots in the heaviest seas. At full throttle, she flew.

In May 1971, her crew decked out in green uniforms and army ranks, the *Bras d'Or* set off for Bermuda. At Hamilton, she skimmed up a winding channel past coral heads at 50 knots, dropping down like a great seabird off the Princess Hotel. Thousands toured the ship and the governor came aboard for a demonstration run. Returning home by way of Norfolk, Virginia, she dazzled her escort the USS *Marblehead* with a burst of speed, leaving her far behind in a shower of spray. At Hampton Roads, she roared into Pier Seven, then entertained high-ranking American naval officers. Bands played and flags waved as she returned home triumphantly to Halifax and settled gently into her berth.

But, the *Bras d'Or's* days were numbered. With the defence budget frozen and a White Paper recommending a shift in emphasis from anti-submarine patrol to sovereignty protection, continued development became unlikely. Plagued by delays and technical glitches, she had already cost $52 million and there was little prospect of offshore sales. On 3 November 1971, the Minister of Defence announced that the *Bras d'Or* would be laid up for five years.

Towed to a remote corner of the Halifax dockyard, it soon became evident that five years meant forever. Parts were sold off or scrapped and by 1982 she was little more than an empty shell leaking hydraulic fluid.

The *Bras d'Or* ended her days standing on her foils like a stranded water spider at the Bernier Museum at l'Islet-sur-Mer, Quebec.

AUTHOR: *Bill Twatio*

CYPRUS AIRPORT 1974

ABOVE:
On 23 July 1974, a cease-fire had been agreed to by Turkish and Greek Cypriots a few days after Turkey invaded Cyprus. Broken repeatedly, a permanent ceasefire was agreed to on 16 August.
(DND PHOTO)

When Turkish troops launched their offensive against the Greek Cypriots, Canada's Airborne Regiment chose to hold their ground. They did so at considerable cost.

NICOSIA, THE CAPITAL OF Cyprus, sits on a dusty plain between two mountain ranges, the Kyrenia Mountains to the north of the city and the Troodos Mountains to the south. Both in winter and summer, the weather is guaranteed to be awful — miserably wet and cold from December to February and debilitatingly hot from June to September.

SWELTERING SUMMER

At 08:30 hrs on 15 July 1974, the thermometer was already 40°C when Captain Ian Nicol of 1 Commando Group of the Canadian Airborne Regiment, a composite of 1er Commando Aeroporte and the Airborne Field Squadron, walked to a fired-up Sioux helicopter waiting to take him and one of the unit's company commanders on an orientation flight over the sweltering city. The 486 Canadian peacekeepers, as they had done for the previous ten years, represented the United Nations on the famous Green Line separating Greek Cypriots from Turkish Cypriots in the divided city.

As Nicol's chopper passed over the presidential palace, he noticed smoke coming from one corner of the building. As preposterous as it seemed, Nicol realized that he was witnessing a palace coup, as tanks and armoured personnel carriers surrounded the palace and blocked key intersections in the city. "It was like watching a war game develop beneath us," Nicol later recalled. As in all coups, confusion reigned. In classic fashion, one of the first institutions seized by the rebels was Radio Cyprus. The citizenry learned that the coup had been staged by the Cypriot National Guard. Mainland Greek officers had convinced the Guard to overthrow the Cypriot president, the legendary Archbishop Makarios. The wily, one-time shepherd, known to the international press as "Mac the Knife," had been trying to rid the Guard of its Greek officers whom he suspected were linked to terrorists wanting union with Greece. Soon Radio Cyprus stunned the little island nation with the announcement of Makarios' death.

As the National Guard stormed the palace, a limousine was seen leaving the grounds with a figure in black cleric's robes huddled in the back seat. It turned out to have been a tailor's dummy dressed to look like Makarios. When the car sped by a rebel roadblock, Greek Cypriot guardsmen laced the fleeing auto with a fusillade of bullets. Meanwhile, the real Makarios escaped the palace incognito, becoming the object of an island-wide manhunt until it was discovered that British forces on the island had flown him to safety in Malta.

THE WORLD IN BRIEF...

The world reacted briefly to the coup, but soon it was off the front page. July 1974 was a busy news month. In Washington, a special Watergate prosecutor was seeking a ruling from the U.S. Supreme Court to release evidence that might hasten President Richard Nixon's departure from the White House. In other news, the search for kidnapped heiress Patty Hearst was in full flight; Jimmy Hoffa was still much alive and trying to wrest back control of the Teamsters union. In Canada, the country was getting back to normal following the July 8 federal election that saw Pierre Elliott Trudeau reelected with a comfortable majority. In Cyprus, Captain Nicol recollected that the Canadian UN contingent "adopted a wait-and-see attitude." Although life in Cyprus was hardly ever normal because of the palpable

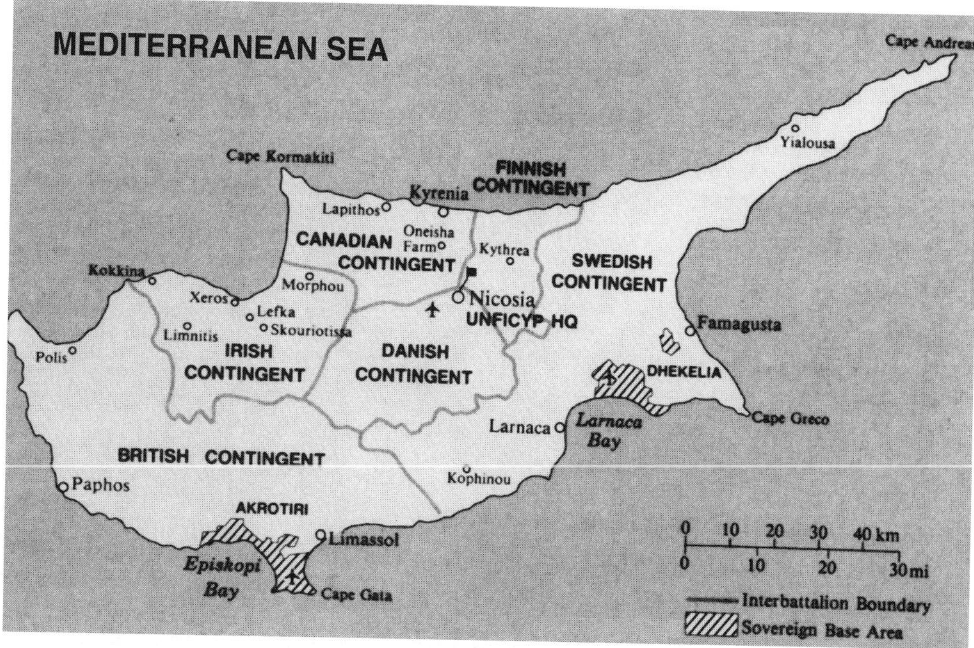

ABOVE, LEFT:
Members of the Canadian Airborne Regiment look towards the Nicosia airport. The summer of 1974 saw numerous cease-fire violations committed by both parties.
(DND PHOTO)

ABOVE, RIGHT:
This map shows the 1965 UN contingent boundaries in Cyprus.
(FROM "IN THE EYE OF THE STORM")

hatred between Greek and Turkish Cypriots, peacekeeping chores became routine again.

All of this changed dramatically on 20 July 1974, five days after the palace coup and the cloak-and-dagger escape of Archbishop Makarios. On that day, Turkey invaded Cyprus, claiming it was doing so to protect Turkish Cypriots. The action brought the world to the brink of war. For Canada, the Turkish invasion changed forever our country's practice of peacekeeping. Overnight, the role of peacekeeper changed to the dangerous and risky undertaking of "peacemaker in a full-scale war," in the words of historian Robert J.A.R. Gravelle.

FAULTY PARACHUTES

The first parachutes of a thousand Turkish paratroopers blossomed in the morning sky at 06:07 hrs. The sticks tumbled from C-130s and C-47s as the aircraft droned toward the hot plain of Nicosia. John "Scotty" Collins, a 34-year old sergeant with the Airborne's 2 Commando, watched with dismay as the Turkish paratroopers dropped from the sky. Many of their parachutes didn't open and they plunged to their deaths. He never found out if the chutes were improperly packed or whether their static lines — which were supposed to pull open the parachutes — were defective. "It was just pathetic," he recalled, years later. Collins kept one memento of the fighting. When a cease-fire was finally arranged, six weeks later, Collins snitched the blue-and-white, bullet-ripped UN flag that had flown over his position at Nicosia airport as a souvenir.

Within 24 hours, 6000 Turkish fighters had seized 40 percent of the island. Two Canadian soldiers, corporals Stan Dolezai and Will Banfield, unexpectedly found themselves with a ringside seat to the invasion. The men were in charge of a boathouse in the picturesque port of Kyrenia on the northern coast, where off-duty Canadian soldiers could go for rest and recreation. As Capt. Nicol recalled: "At 05:00 hrs they were awakened for the red alert and climbed outside to a scene that Dolezai described as the equivalent to a Second World War landing on the beaches in France." Before their very eyes, landing craft were coming ashore, choppers were flying overhead toward Nicosia and jet fighters were swooping over the beach.

THREE TURKISH OBJECTIVES

The Turks had three prime objectives in the first phase of the invasion: to capture Kyrenia; to open a corridor from Kyrenia to the Turkish-occupied section of Nicosia; and to seize Nicosia airport on the western outskirts of the city. They achieved the first two objectives rather readily but failed to capture the airport, mainly because of the initiative of the UN commander Prem Chand and the swift reaction of the commander of the Canadian contingent, Colonel Clayton Beattie the UN's deputy chief of staff on the island.

"When the Turkish forces invaded, we were faced with three options," Beattie recalled 20 years later. "First, we could withdraw into our UN bases and become bystanders and do nothing until UN headquarters decided how to react. Second," he continued, "we could withdraw the force from Cyprus and let the combatants fight it out. Third, we could impose ourselves between the two forces and attempt to negotiate cease-fires and enforce Security Council resolutions which called for the cessation of hostilities. I preferred the last option and the force commander, Prem Chand, was also of this opinion. We chose the third option."

Carrying out that critical decision was a different matter altogether as fierce fighting

RIGHT:
The Airborne Regiment in Cyprus were not issued protective flak jackets until after their battle at the Airport. It was felt that this factor contributed to a higher instance of casualties among Canadians.
(DND PHOTO)

OPPOSITE PAGE:
A Canadian jeep patrol sets out along the Green Line in Cyprus.
(DND PHOTO)

erupted between Greek National Guardsmen and Turkish Cypriots along the entire length of the Green Line. The decision to defend UN property put the Canadians in a hazardous position. Capt. Nicol was at Wolseley Barracks, the Nicosia district UN headquarters, when it was decided to defend it. Fire positions were dug on the grounds along with heavy weapon pits. Everyone was pressed into service, including cooks and clerks. About noon on the first day, the barracks came under mortar attack and four Canadians were wounded. Instead of withdrawing, the Canadians fortified the position.

Elsewhere, some of the UN observation posts manned by Canadians also came under fire. In one incident, Private J. Casse was seriously wounded. When his comrades tried evacuating him through the Turkish lines, they were turned back. They then attempted to take him through the Greek National Guard lines, but the ambulance carrying Casse came under fire. The Canadians didn't hesitate. They returned the fire and got Casse to hospital. It was an important moment in the history of Canadian peacekeeping, marking the first time Canadian soldiers used force to defend themselves.

Another hot spot was the fashionable, first-class Ledra Palace Hotel, located virtually on the Green Line. A favourite of tourists, diplomats and high-ranking UN visitors, it was also the legendary watering hole for the international press corps covering the Middle East. The bar's 'brandy sours' became the signature drink of visiting journalists. With its strategic position overlooking Turkish-occupied Nicosia, the hotel became a valuable UN observation site.

TERRIFIED JOURNALISTS

Shortly after the invasion began, Greek National Guardsmen took over the hotel, drawing heavy fire from Turkish Cypriots. At the time there were about 380 guests staying in the hotel, including a large press corps of over 100 journalists who had rushed to Cyprus following the presidential coup. After coming under fire, the reporters and cameramen demanded UN protection, as did the petrified tourists who huddled in storage rooms for safety. The situation was tense and potentially disastrous. The Canadian initiative in defusing the explosive situation was brilliant.

The Canadian Airborne commander, Lieutenant Colonel Don Manuel, simply informed both sides to hold their fire while the evacuation of civilians was carried out. The first attempt failed when the Canadians were fired upon. The next day they tried again. The situation had become more tense: the hotel had suffered considerable damage from mortar and small arms fire, food was running out and there was no power or water. At 14:30 hrs on 21 July, the Canadians moved quickly. They escorted a convoy of trucks and buses to the door of the hotel and began loading the frightened guests aboard the buses and their baggage aboard the trucks. Then they solved the problem of who would control the hotel by declaring the Ledra Palace a UN position. They dispatched one platoon to secure the ground floor and another to patrol the grounds, capping the operation by placing a UN flag on the roof.

CONFRONTATION

"This incident, and the Canadian Contingent's response, signaled the shift from peacekeeping by observation to peacekeeping by confrontation," said historian Gravelle. "Further, it demonstrated the capability and willingness of the Canadian Contingent to place itself in extreme danger to effect humanitarian assistance under difficult conditions."

Throughout the first three days the Canadians were under direct fire from both sides, so it wasn't surprising that orders were issued to hit back if their lives were threatened. On July 23 the Canadians slugged it out, bullet for bullet, with Greek Guardsmen. The incident began at Camp Kronborg, headquarters for the Canadians who manned the UN observation posts (OPs). The camp was very close to both the Greek and Turkish lines, so much so that three of its buildings had already been demolished by gunfire. On the third day of the fighting, eight Turkish Cypriot soldiers ran into the camp for protection. They could not stay because their presence would draw fire from the Greek Cypriots. Captain Normand Blaquière, the camp's commanding officer, gambled that he could safely escort the Turks to their side at a spot on the banks of the Pedieos River, which separated the warring factions. Under the UN flag, and warning both sides what he intended to do over a bullhorn, Blaquière started wading across the river. In mid-stream, the humid silence was broken by a burst of machine-gun fire from the Greek side of the Green Line, the bullets ripping into Blaquière's legs and wounding Private Michel Plouffe who had accompanied the officer. Plouffe took a bullet in the cheek. Four Turks were killed; the other four managed to make it to the other side. Watching with horror was Captain Alain Forand, a former policeman from Farnham, Québec. Forand was driven back by more gunfire when he attempted to pull Blaquière and Plouffe to safety. Shortly afterward, two UN scout cars arrived and Forand ordered them to return the fire. The Ferret scout cars blasted away at the Greek positions, killing two Greek soldiers, while Forand rescued the two injured soldiers.

There were numerous instances of Canadians being fired upon, but nowhere was more lead expended than at Nicosia airport, held by the Greeks. The runways were left in a shambles as the Turks tried wresting the strategic position from the Greeks. Already, 12 civilians had been killed when a Cyprus Airways van was caught in the crossfire.

TURKS ON THE MOVE

On July 23 at 11:00 hrs, Colonel Beattie received intelligence reports that the Turks were about to mount a do-or-die attack. One battalion of Turkish soldiers with a tank and an armoured personnel carrier were hurtling toward the airfield from the north. At the same time, a company of Greek National Guardsmen were approaching the airport from the south. Beattie, who bears a striking resemblance to Randolph Scott, a western movie star of the 1940s, set out to confront the Turks. Despite being under direct fire by the Greeks, Beattie and his small party made contact with a Turkish infantry company who were holed up out of sight, guarding 35 prisoners, including two women, a child and an old man. Convinced the Turks were going to execute their prisoners, Beattie negotiated their release and put them under UN protection. Then Beattie moved to the Turkish battalion headquarters where he found three rifle companies preparing to attack. The Canadian contingent commander reminded the Turkish commander that both sides had agreed to a cease-fire at the airport the previous day. The attack was momentarily postponed, but at 11:30 hrs, the Turks attacked. Once in open ground, they came under fierce fire from the Greek side. It was a slaughter. After three attacks by the Turks, Beattie was finally successful in getting both sides to stop shooting and withdraw. The UN again declared the strategic location a UN-protected area. When there was another threat of attack from the Turks, Beattie, through UN channels, told the Turks that the Canadian troops now holding the airport would not surrender it to anyone. "I didn't come to Cyprus to surrender Canadian soldiers to ***king Turks and that's it."

MERELY BRAVADO?

Colonel Don Manuel, who commanded the Canadians at the airport, recollected that if they had been attacked, he wasn't sure if they would have been able to hold off a mass attack. The Canadian resolve to hold the airport "was bravado in a way, but it worked." The contingent was in possession of only four 106 recoilless rifles and four heavy machine-guns, weapons which were moved under darkness to different parts of the airport to give the Turks the impression that the UN force was in fact heavily equipped to ward off an attack. Historian Gravelle believes Beattie's decision to protect the airport meant that the UN command in Cyprus had no choice but to defend that position or "fold its tent and go home."

The cost to confront both sides was high, tragically so with the shooting of Private Gilbert Perron, a strapping paratrooper who was about to be released from the army. His future looked bright —he had been drafted to play hockey for the Edmonton Oilers. On the night of August 6, Capt. Ian Nicol was on duty when a report came in that the Turks were reinforcing one of their positions in the vicinity of the Ledra Palace Hotel. Nicol sent Lieutenant Pierre Leblanc, signaler Perron and a driver to investigate this apparent violation of the cease-fire. The patrol drove to the Turkish checkpoint nearest the alleged infraction. As Leblanc talked to the Turks, a shot rang out, but because it was dark, no one was sure where it came from. The bullet found its mark in the body of Private Perron. Leblanc rushed back to the jeep to find Perron bleeding from the chest. After they had raced back to base with the wounded paratrooper, Leblanc reported to Captain Nicol, ashen-faced, his jacket and hands covered with Perron's blood. When

Nicol reached the private's side, he found four or five of Perron's buddies holding him down. "He was a strong man. His chums were saying, 'You're going to make it buddy, you'll pull though.'" He didn't. Perron died in a helicopter taking him to the big British base at Dhekelia on Cyprus's south-east coast.

EYE FOR AN EYE

Perron's death and the wounding of Blaquière and Plouffe were avenged when a burly paratroop sergeant caught and bayoneted an infiltrating Turk commando. For two more days the fighting raged while the Trudeau government heatedly debated the necessity of deploying reinforcements. However, once the political decision was finally made to send in the remainder of the Airborne, the tactical situation in Cyprus had stabilized.

For their heroic efforts in Nicosia, the Canadian Airborne Regiment earned a battle honour and international acclaim. This "glory" did not come without a steep butcher's bill, though: three Canadians were killed in the fighting and seventeen seriously wounded. Some Airborne soldiers felt that these numbers could have been reduced had they been issued protective "flak" jackets from the outset. Although they were in the supply system, the body armour was not made available to Canadian troops until August 6, two weeks after the Turks invaded. Even then they were only issued in direct response to another trooper, Claude Bergeron, being killed, also by a sniper. As for acclaim at home, the Airborne Regiment had to make do with their own private ceremonies. Their dead were buried with full military honours and nine of their comrades were decorated for courage under fire. For the Canadian public, the Cyprus incident went largely unnoticed. Media coverage was focused on the Watergate scandal, and with Prime Minister Trudeau preaching global pacifism, the federal government was not going to go out of its way to play up a successful feat-of-arms.

REPRINTED FROM: *Tested Mettle: Canada's Peacekeepers at War*
AUTHORS: *Scott Taylor & Brian Nolan*

THE CF AND THE RISE OF THE PARTI QUÉBÉCOIS (1968-1976)

ABOVE:
A Canadian soldier and a Quebec policeman stand watch during the FLQ crisis. Throughout 1970-71 over 12,500 soldiers were deployed on security operations in Québec and Ottawa.
(DND PHOTO)

The depredation of the Front de libération du Québec forced Canada's military planners to rethink their strategic and personnel policies.

OVER THE YEARS, THE relatively low number of Québécois in the Canadian Armed Forces (CF) has been a contentious issue amongst scholars, politicians and many Québécois. One reason often cited for the low numbers is that many Québécois have viewed the military as a para-military force the federal government keeps in readiness and reserve for a troublesome colony called Québec. Nowhere was this assertion more visible than between 1968 and 1976 when the Canadian military's involvement in Québec coincided with the creation and subsequent rise to power of a provincial political party called the Parti Québécois.

On 2 August 1968, the Mouvement-Souveraineté-Association (MSA), founded by René Lévesque in 1967, and the Ralliement National (RN) created in 1966 joined together to form the Parti Québécois (PQ) with René Lévesque as its leader. The Rassemblement pour l'Indépendance Nationale (RIN) would later dissolve and join the PQ in 1969. In October 1969, the PQ, representing a merger between three separatist groups, held its first party convention.

OPERATION RIVET – 1968-70

The same year the PQ was born, and five years after the FLQ 100-person terrorist group called the Front de libération du Québec (FLQ) had begun its terrorist campaign in 1963, the Canadian Government created the Canadian Airborne Regiment (CAR). The idea behind its inception, according to David Bercuson in his book, *Significant Incident*, was to create a unit that would specialise in "commando tactics" much like the British Special Air Service (SAS) and counter any potential "...outbreak of revolutionary guerilla war in

Québec..." The Canadian military also became alarmed that separatists might now try to steal nuclear weapons stored in a Canadian Forces Base near Val d'Or, Québec. So it devised a plan called Operation RIVET. Under this operation, troops were issued with live ammunition and tear gas to deal with any threat to the aforementioned base.

OPERATION GINGER – 1970

Only six months after the first Parti Québécois convention on 29 April 1970, the Québec elections saw the PQ receive some 24 per cent of the popular vote. This figure was a substantial jump from the 8.7 per cent of the votes registered by separatist groups in the previous provincial election.

On 4 October 1970, the FLQ kidnapped James Richard Cross, the Senior Trades Commissioner of the British Trade Commission in Montréal. Six days later, the FLQ kidnapped the Deputy Provincial Premier and Minister of Labour and Immigration, Pierre Laporte. On 12 October 1970, the federal government, headed by then Prime Minister Pierre Trudeau, deployed members of the CF to protect diplomats and leading politicians. This deployment from Camp Petawawa to Ottawa was code-named Operation GINGER. It officially ended on 21 November 1970.

OPERATION ESSAI – 1970

On 15 October 1970, Robert Bourassa called on the federal government to deploy the CF in Montréal and other Québec cities to protect "the civil population and public works within the boundaries of Québec." The Québec government request was sent to NDHQ, Ottawa, at approximately 12:45 hours and the Vice Chief of the Defence Staff issued orders to deploy CF personnel at 13:07 hours that same day. This operation was code-named Operation ESSAI. It officially ended on 4 January 1971.

In all, Operations GINGER and ESSAI saw the deployment of some 12,500 troops concentrated largely in the cities of Ottawa and Montréal between 18 October 1970 and 4 January 1971. These forces represented approximately 14 per cent of the entire CF.

Almost two days passed, after calling out the CF, without any news from or activity by the FLQ, so Bourassa requested further powers from the federal government which responded by proclaiming the War Measures Act on 16 October 1970. It was the first time in Canadian history that Canada was put on a wartime footing to face an internal emergency. It was also this decision that allowed people whose membership in the Parti Québécois, a legitimate political party, to become suspects solely on that basis. In fact, during the 1970 October Crisis, some 36 out of the 419 people arrested but never charged were members of the PQ.

The War Measures Act remained in effect until 3 December 1970. It was then supplanted by the less stringent Public Order (Temporary Measures) Act. It was not until 30 April 1971, that the emergency regulations in Québec were lifted.

ABOVE:
Flags fly at half-mast after the murder of Quebec's Minister of Labour, Pierre Laporte, by members of the Front de libération du Québec (FLQ) on 17 October 1970. This event intensified the October Crisis and became the justification for the implementation of the War Measures Act.
(DND)

VIP LIST – 1970

In 1969, according to retired Major General Dan Loomis in his book *Not Much Glory*, "...the military decided to extend counter-insurgency training of army field units from tactical exercises without troops for senior officers to field exercises involving all ranks." One of the first visible signs of this new practise occurred in 1970 when the CF began maintaining a list of VIPs they were supposed to protect during internal security operations. The list contained federal and provincial politicians, as well as some municipal leaders. This revelation would be followed by many more in the press including Exercises NEAT PITCH ('72) and ROYAL FLUSH ('74).

FRANCOPHONE QUOTA – 1970

In the closing days of 1970, DND decided that 28 per cent of the rank structure at all levels, in all areas of responsibility, should be Francophone. Then-Defence Minister Donald Macdonald stated the new policy was to be given the "highest priority."

RIGHT:
For the first time, on 15 November 1976, René Lévesque and his Parti Québécois (PQ) won a resounding 70 seats to their opponents' combined 40 in Quebec's provincial election. The PQ has passed some controversial laws, including Bill 101 which defined the use of the French language in Quebec. (ALAIN RENAUD)

EXERCISE NEAT PITCH – 1972

In 1972, the same year the nine-year existence of the FLQ came to an end, the CF embarked on another operation called Operation NEAT PITCH. Essentially this exercise, held in Montréal on 18 and 19 April 1972, was a "theoretical exercise" where some 65 officers, including approximately eight generals, 14 colonels and 24 lieutenant colonels, met to plan Army strategy to handle civil disorders. More specifically, the purpose of that session "was to determine the function of the armed forces should a civil crisis, similar to the one in October 1970, occur."

When the media questioned the senior officers about the operation, reporters were told that the choice of Montréal as the location for the exercise and the use of the October 1970 crisis as the training scenario were merely happenstance. After all, they added, the scenario did not mention any real names or locations, such as the cities of Québec or Montréal, by name. It is unclear whether or not this exercise was ever dropped from the CF curriculum.

ADSUM – 1973

In 1973, Québec provincial elections were called. The 29 October 1973 results showed an increase in the popular vote for the PQ from 24 percent in 1970 to 30 percent in 1973.

Just prior to these elections, the military base at Valcartier, Québec, made the headlines when its weekly newspaper, the *ADSUM*, refused to accept PQ advertising in its paper. The editor of the paper, Captain Pierre Lachapelle, explained the paper would "not accept PQ advertising because of the party's stand on Québec independence" although he also admitted that he "had no difficulty accepting advertising from the Liberal Party, l'Union Nationale and Le Parti Créditiste."

EXERCISE ROYAL FLUSH – 1974

In 1974, the military announced that it was introducing a new course curriculum for its senior officers at the Canadian Land Forces Command and Staff College at Fort Frontenac, Kingston. This course included, among other things, Exercise ROYAL FLUSH. One document stated the intent of the campaign was to "destroy the First Fantasian Front in CA (Canada), restore the political capital of Ottawa and re-establish the international border along the River Ottawa."

Needless to say the depiction of this scenario – the only one at CLFCSC that delineated between provinces, peoples and languages – created the angst among several military students from Québec: "In these days of political sensitivities between Canada's two founding peoples, I fear that the idea of pushing back the enemy into Québec in order to re-establish Canada's international border may provide some fuel for the Québec separatists."

In contrast to the explanations given by the senior leadership for Exercise NEAT PITCH in 1972, real names, such as the cities of Ottawa and Montréal and the Ottawa River, were now being used for Exercise ROYAL FLUSH. When the media questioned senior military officers about this operation, they were told that the CF was not using the October Crisis as a training scenario for this exercise as in Ex NEAT PITCH. Instead, they were using an imaginary Fantasian army that only happened to be located in Québec. The exercise was only dropped from the CF curriculum in the Fall of 1998.

OPERATION GAMESCAN – 1976

In January 1974, after spending approximately two years preparing an assessment for the upcoming Olympic Summer Games, some 2,000 military personnel were deemed necessary. This was a significant increase when compared to the 600 troops used during the 1973 Canada Games or the 1,000 troops used during the 1967 Pan-American Games (both held outside of Québec).

In February 1976, when the growing popularity of the PQ meant that it could become the provincial government during the next provincial elections, however, the military had a change of heart. It now claimed that the upcoming 1976 Olympics would have to see Canada's biggest combined military force operation since WWII. In fact, this operation saw a bigger deployment of military troops during peacetime on Canadian soil than during the October Crisis when Canada was put on a wartime footing to face an internal emergency. "A well-organized force was needed at the Games in the event of terrorist activity and (that) a clear military presence was (there-

LEFT:
Soldiers prepare for their aid to civil authority duties by practicing the defence of vital installations against mock civilian demonstrations. (DND PHOTO)

fore) required." It was later revealed that the Olympic Games saw the deployment of some 15,763 troops or approximately 20 per cent of the entire CF.

AVGP – 1976

The following month, in March 1976, the CF also decided to revive a project that was stillborn in 1973. The senior defence department leadership now sought the immediate approval to select and purchase some 350 Armoured Vehicles - General Purpose (AVGP).

In the submission to Treasury Board, the Department proposed that: "the first phase of this procurement plan proceed ahead of Cabinet approval of Phase III of the Defence Structure Review." The military's recommendation was also made despite the fact these vehicles (Cougars, Grizzlies and Huskies) had not been "tested under cold weather conditions nor (had) any been fitted with the 76mm gun which has been selected by the Canadian Forces as the most suitable for their purpose."

PQ ELECTION REACTION – 1977

During the Québec provincial election held on 15 November 1976, the PQ formed a majority government with 41 per cent of the vote. Two months after the Québec election, the Trudeau Cabinet began discussing the partition of Québec and the use of the military to defend federal territory.

THE CANADIAN MILITARY'S INTEREST IN QUÉBEC COINCIDED MORE WITH THE CREATION OF THE PARTI QUEBECOIS AND ITS RISE TO POWER (1968-76) THAN THE FLQ TERRORIST ORGANISATION (1963-72).

On 26 November 1976, the federal government announced that the Canadian Airborne Regiment would move from Edmonton to Petawawa and become the Special Service Force (SSF). General J.A. Dextraze described the decision as part of a "military appreciation of a military requirement." From a military perspective, however, the choice of Petawawa, across the river from the province of Québec, was puzzling "because the base had no airfield capable of handling Hercules transport aircraft, the regiment's principal means of transportation." Additionally, the base had no all-weather flying facilities but Edmonton did.

Finally, the Canadian parachute training school was in Edmonton and so were the facilities for drying and packing the parachutes. This meant that after a jump the paratroopers' chutes were bundled up and sent all the way to Edmonton, repacked, then returned to Petawawa.

On 14 January 1977, the CDS spoke at the Conference of Defence Associations' annual meeting in Ottawa and told delegates: "we must insist that this country remains together." Similarly, two days later, the Minister of National Defence stated that the CF must be used as forces for unity and never "to force unity" and that he did not believe "the problems we have in Canada are problems that can be solved by force."

Around the same time, however, the movement of Airborne personnel from Edmonton to Petawawa was unfolding and other military exercises in addition to NEAT PITCH and ROYAL FLUSH were soon being added to the list of exercise scenarios. Unlike previous exercises, however, real troops were now being used to cross the Ottawa River. Perhaps of greater concern was the fact that, when questioned, these troops had no qualms about the validity of their training. In fact, when a journalist questioned some troops during one of these exercises in February 1977, they responded that the "training would not be wasted were war to break out in Canada either..."

CONCLUSION

Clearly, the Canadian military's interest in Québec coincided more with the creation of the PQ and its rise to power (1968-76) than the FLQ terrorist organisation (1963-72). While the military presence in Québec in 1970 did help end Québec terrorism, its *continued* presence proved to be a lame delusion of nearsighted politics that helped bring Québec nationalism to the forefront of the political arena. For this reason, among others, many Québécois have looked upon the plight of the CF with disinterest if not benign neglect.

REPRINTED FROM:
Esprit de Corps, *Volume 6 Issue 12*
AUTHOR:
George Orsyk

CANADA'S NATO BRIGADE

NATO - KHAKI AND BLUE TO GREEN (AND BACK AGAIN)

For nearly 40 years, the Canadian military maintained a presence in West Germany. Known as the 'war without battles,' this era came to an end with the collapse of the Berlin Wall.

AFTER ALMOST TWO DECADES in Westphalia, the 4th Canadian Infantry Brigade Group – since renamed the 4th Canadian Mechanized Battle Group – moved south. There had been a number of changes since their arrival in the Soest area in the early 1950's.

First of all, due to technical improvements on one hand, and reductions in manpower on the other, the face of the formation was drastically changed. Instead of the three infantry battalions, the Brigade had one "regular" battalion of infantry and a similar-sized "Mechanized Commando" - each of which was equipped with M-113 armoured personnel carriers.

The role of the Canadian formation was different. With its reduction in strength and lack of nuclear capability, it was no longer capable of holding its place in the forward areas, and this, coupled with possible financial savings in a unified supply and logistical system (following the integration trend initiated by the Trudeau government) prompted the move of the Battle Group to join the Canadian Air Division in the Lahr and Baden-Soellingen areas. The high level of mobility, with the M-113 and Lynx reconnaissance vehicles, made the Canadian formation a highly effective "rapid deployment" reserve.

While the infantry battalion in Baden-Soellingen were quite at home, as Canadians had been there since the early fifties, the remainder of the Group found that conditions in Lahr were less attractive (the married quarters, especially, were in atrocious condition). Designed strictly for air force operations, the "working quarters" were a system of circular protective revetments arranged in circles nicknamed "Marguerites" after the daisies which they resembled.

Lack of facilities had one positive effect. There was far less accommodation than in Westphalia, and as a result, many Canadians lived on the "local economy," which helped develop friendly ties between the Canadians and their German hosts. While the halcyon days of the 1950s – when the deutschemark traded at four to the dollar – had passed, Canadians still lived well in one of the most attractive tourist areas in Germany, although some Black Forest tourist enterprises did not take kindly to the presence of our armoured vehicles roaring around their peaceful countryside.

Just as integration created new organizations in Canada, so command of the Canadians in Europe fell under a new structure. Canadian Forces Europe (CFE) which controlled both the former army and air force units. This occasionally created "turf" problems, as the Canadian role and activities in their NATO role had to be cleared by CFE.

Nevertheless, for over 20 years, the Canadians maintained their high reputation in the military field. Although no longer tied almost exclusively to the British formation, they were able to exchange training experiences with many other French and German parachutists' wings and insignia, which they had earned during their tour.

Over the year changes occurred. Some were relatively minor amendments to unit establishments; others were more significant. The air force gradually exchanged their universal CF green for their traditional blue, while the land forces' summer uniforms, at least, were once again the familiar khaki. Perhaps the most significant change came with 'glasnost' and 'pere-stroika,' when the Communist bloc finally folded and many of their erstwhile opponents joined NATO. Now Canadians, together with their western allies, participated in training exercise with Czechs, Poles and other former Warsaw Pact members nations.

ABOVE: *Training exercises in Germany were conducted throughout the rural countryside allowing NATO soldiers the rare opportunity to familiarize themselves with the actual ground which they would have fought on if the Cold War had erupted.* (DND PHOTO)

Eventually the time came to leave. Just over 40 years after the first arrival of Canada's 27 Brigade in Hanover, units returned to Canada as the thinning-out process began. Significantly, the "final fling" took the form of a ceremonial parade in Soest in May 1993, where the Third Battalion of the Royal Canadian Regiment exercised their right to the Freedom of the City by marching through the streets of the ancient Westphalian centre with "drums beating, bayonets fixed and Colour flying." Forty years earlier the Regiment's Second Battalion were the first Canadians to occupy Fort York, on the city's outskirts.

Canada's NATO component fought no battles but was an ever-ready and vital component of the western allies' deterrent force. In military professionalism, and on the athletic and social scene, they had left their mark. When the Special Service Medal was approved in 1984, veterans of Canada's NATO forces received the medal and bar "NATO - OTAN."

AUTHOR: *Les Peate*

THE POST-COLD WAR DECADE, 1989 - 2000

1990 Gulf War. ■ German reunification approved following Four Power meetings in Ottawa. ■ Oka Crisis.

1991 Kuwait liberated with de facto surrender of Iraq, 17 February. ■ Boris Yeltsin comes to power in Soviet Union. ■ Yugoslavia disintegrates as Slovenia and Croatia (followed by Bosnia in 1992) declare independence. Four years of civil war and "ethnic cleansing" follow. ■ First newsstand edition of *Esprit de Corps*.

1992 Canada contributes battalion-sized formation to United Nations Protection Force (UNPROFOR) in the former Yugoslavia. ■ Tiring of constitutional debate, Canadians reject Charlottetown Accords in referendum.

1993 Kim Campbell first woman to be appointed Minister of National Defence and first female Prime Minister. Succeeded by Jean Chretien in greatest electoral defeat in Canadian history. ■ EH-101 helicopter contract cancelled. ■ Shidane Arone tortured and murdered by troops from Canada's Airborne Regiment in Somalia. ■ Bases at Baden-Soellingen and Lahr close, ending Canadian presence in Europe.

1994 New emphasis on deficit reduction. Defence spending slashed and Forces reduced to 60,000.

1995 Airborne Regiment disbanded. ■ Somalia Inquiry opens. ■ Sovereignty referendum in Quebec.

1996 Dayton Peace Accords impose settlement in the Balkans. NATO troops replace the UN. Canada reduces troop strength in region. ■ Somalia Inquiry terminated.

1997 Somalia Inquiry presents its final report, "Dishonoured Legacy," severely criticizing NDHQ. Recommendations include the appointment of a civilian ombudsman to hear grievances. ■ Canadian Forces come to aid of flood-stricken Manitoba. ■ Chrétien government re-elected.

1998 More than 14,000 CF regulars and reserves mobilize to help victims of ice storm in Eastern Canada.

1999 Serbs and Albanians clash in Kosovo. Hundreds of thousands displaced as NATO launches 78-day bombing campaign. Serbs withdraw as KFOR troops enter the territory.

2000 Increased pay and benefits announced for Canadian Forces as morale continues to decline. ■ Upholder class submarines acquired from Britain. Slobodan Milosevic toppled from power in Serbia. ■ Chrétien government returned with third majority. ■ Three servicemen and 600 military vehicles returning from Kosovo are held hostage aboard GTS *Katie* en route to Bécancour, Quebec. Caught up in a bizarre contractual dispute, *Katie* drifted listlessly off the Avalon peninsula until she was boarded by the Navy and escorted into port.

TOP LEFT: *A naval boarding party is lowered from a Sea King helicopter onto the freighter GTS* Katie*, in August 2000.* (DND PHOTO) ***TOP RIGHT:*** *A combat engineer prepares Iraqi artillery shells for demolition, in Kuwait, 1991.* (SCOTT TAYLOR) ***BOTTOM:*** *Mohawk warriors line the barricades at Oka, August 1990.* (DND PHOTO)

WEAPONS PROFILES *BY WARREN FERGUSON*

C7 AND C8

It's the 'bells and whistles' version of the popular M16A2. Refined and fine-tuned, the C7 family of rifles has become the mainstay of Western armies. The M16 has gone from mistrusted to prolific after a number of well-known upgrades over the last few decades. But the work of product enhancement is not over, as evidenced by the design input from the Canadian firm of Diemaco, (a division of Devtek), which is located in Kitchener, Ontario.

Diemaco has been serving the international military small arms community since 1976. After a series of trials in Canada and other NATO countries in the late 1970s, the 5.56 mm round was adopted as NATO's standard ammunition. Following this, the Department of National Defence (DND) initiated the Small Arms Replacement Program (SARP) to find the best 5.56 mm weapon for the Canadian Armed Forces. By this time, the Belgian-pattern FN C1, a 7.62 mm semi-automatic rifle, and the Sterling 9 mm sub-machine guns (SMGs) were showing considerable wear.

ABOVE:
The C7 rifle has been in service since 1986. (VIC JOHNSON)

The earliest order was in 1986 for 79,935 copies of the C7 and 1565 (also 800 for the navy) of the C8. The C8 is the shorter carbine version of the C7. Both the C7 and the C8 are fitted with M16A1 sights instead of those adjustable out to 800 meters on the M16A2 version. The A1 upper receiver sports, a forward assist plunger and a case deflector. The fire controls are S-R-F, (SAFE, REPETITION and FULL AUTO). There are two butt lengths (M16A1 and M16A2) and a spacer is available thereby providing four different lengths to suit the user, while the flash eliminator omits cuts on the bottom to keep the muzzle down.

The Diemaco family uses hammer-forged steel barrels with an integral chamber and chrome-lined bores, strictly a Canadian affair. Many firms offer hammer-forged barrels but not with integral chambers because of the large diameter reductions required. But the trouble is well worth the effort and the reward is better performance and longer life. Some of the benefits of hammer-forged barrels with integral chambers that are made of stronger, cleaner material are; greatly improved concentricity chamber-to-bore, and within the bore; a dimensional consistency in the bore, lead and chamber (barrel no. 10,000 is the same as barrel no. 1); when forged in choke, breech-to-muzzle promotes accuracy and longer life; and strength. The forging process refines, aligns and compresses the grain structure of the material in a way that provides a stronger barrel. The aim is to create a barrel with a service life of 30,000 rounds.

C9 - LIGHT MACHINE GUN

Designed by Fabrique Nationale, the C9 was used by Canadians during the Gulf War. *(DND PHOTO)*

The Belgian Fabrique Nationale "Minimi" (French for small machine gun) was standardized as the C9 squad automatic weapon in 1986. The C9 filled the void created by the retirement of the C2 and because other automatic weapons like the C7 lack fire sustainability. The C9 light machine gun is a gas-operated, magazine or disintegrating metallic link-belt fed, individually portable machine gun capable of delivering a large volume of effective fire to support infantry squad operations. The C9 fires the improved NATO Standard SS 109 type 5.56 mm ammunition belts placed in 200-round carrying boxes. If no belted ammunition is available, the C9 will easily accept standard C7 30-round magazines into the left side of the receiver without any modification.

The C9 has seen Canadian modifications over the years, including the addition of the C7-type muzzle compensator, a vertical grip added to the buttstock, and more recently in the A1 model, the addition of the ELCAN Optical Sighting equipment from Armament Technology. The ELCAN C79 sight allows fast target acquisition and significantly improves hit probability at extended ranges and in low light conditions typical in many combat scenarios encountered by Canadian troops in overseas missions. The C9 with the C79 is a light and deadly package and a significant morale booster for our troops.

C7A1 RIFLE / BY SCOTT TAYLOR, ESPRIT DE CORPS

C7A1 AND C8A1

Since the initial contract, Diemaco has continued to offer new products and upgrades. In 1992, a major follow-on contract was awarded for the C7A1 (optically sighted) rifle for the Canadian Forces. Over 50,000 C7s and C8s were converted to A1 configuration by adding a new flat top upper receiver, putting the older upper receiver assemblies in long term storage. Optional are clamp-on handles with A1 or A2 type rear sights and a clamp-on backup sight. DND needed more sighting capability and some magnification for target identification in order to make "shoot, don't shoot" decisions during peacekeeping and other operations, so a modern optical sight was required.

MP5

Widely used by Canadian law enforcment agencies, the German Heckler & Koch MP5 has also become known in military circles as well. The MP5 submachine gun employs the same delayed, blowback operated, roller-locked bolt system that is found in the famous HK G3 Automatic Rifle. Firing from the closed-bolt position during all modes of fire makes MP5 submachine guns extremely accurate and controllable. It is not uncommon to see MP5s sporting advanced optical sights.

The MP5 is extremely accurate, but there's a catch – the so-called cook off hazard. The Sten and Sterling allowed the barrel to cool when the bolt was locked to the rear which means greater sustained fire. However, on the MP5, a live round is usually in the chamber. On full-auto, the chamber gets increasingly hotter until chamber heat can set off the round. Therefore sustained automatic fire (most likely in a heated battle, not during a police action) is not recommended. The MP5's presence in Canada is directly related to the MP5's adoption by the British Special Air Service (SAS).

PHOTO BY HECKLER UND KOCH

DND PHOTO

C6 MEDIUM MACHINE GUN

The C6 is a general purpose machinegun (GPMG) developed in Belgium, where it is known as the Fabrique Nationale MAG. This fully automatic, air-cooled, belt-fed and gas-operated 7.62 x 51 mm NATO weapon entered service in 1978. The C6 fires from the open bolt position and its 21.4-inch barrel is designed for quick-change by the gun crew. Its adjustable gas regulator also permits the cyclic rate to be varied from 650 to 1100 rounds per minute (rpm).

The C6 is used by the Forces as a fire support weapon in the co-axial, sustained or light fire roles. In a co-axial role, the weapon is mounted in a vehicle turret beside the main armament. The C6 is durable and possesses superior reliability and maintainability when compared to most other GPMGs. Metal link belts come in 250 or 500 rounds that can be joined together for good firepower and, at 11 kilograms, is man-portable. So good is the design that American forces have begun purchasing FN MAGs as a replacement for their beleaguered M60s.

STANDOFF AT OKA

In the summer of 1990 the Mohawk Warrior Society set up barricades and blocked highways, prompting a large-scale military response.

LEFT: *Private Patrick Cloutier of the Royal 22e Regiment calmly stands his ground while being threatened by a Mohawk Warrior.* (CANAPRESS PHOTO SHANEY KOMULAILEN)

IMAGES OF OKA LINGERED long after the barricades came down. Masked warriors in fatigues brandishing automatic weapons, angry, stone-throwing mobs, the roar of helicopters and armoured personnel carriers racing down dusty country roads, a young soldier confronting a warrior with the unlikely name, "Lasagna" in a forest clearing. For 78 days in the summer of 1990, Canadians sat transfixed by their television sets as the crisis unfolded.

It was a crisis two centuries in the making. It dated from the time of the French regime when Louis XV granted lands to the Seminary of St. Sulpice north of Montreal where the Ottawa River broadens into the Lake of Two Mountains on the condition that it be used as an Indian mission. The site, a sandy escarpment rising into a forest known as the Pines, was chosen so that the Indians could be quickly called on for military service in the event of war. In 1721, nine hundred Mohawks moved to the site which they named Kanesatake.

BETRAYAL OF TRUST

During the next century, the Sulpicians sold off timber rights and farmland to whites and pressured the Indians to leave. "This land was given you in trust" a chief complained. "And how have you betrayed that trust? By filling your treasury with the proceeds of stolen property. This land is ours - ours by right of possession - ours by heritage." By 1945, when the Canadian government bought what was left of the mission, only a ragged quilt of small lots remained. But the encroachments continued and in 1959 the neighbouring town of Oka acquired title to part of the Pines, felled the trees and built a nine-hole golf course. Mohawk protests again fell on deaf ears. Thirty years later, the crisis came to a head when plans were announced to expand the golf course into an area adjacent to an historic cemetery.

AFTER MONTHS OF FRUITLESS NEGOTIATIONS, BARRICADES WENT UP, MANNED BY LOCAL RESIDENTS AND THE WARRIOR SOCIETY, A GROUP OF RADICAL PARAMILITARIES.

After months of fruitless negotiations, barricades went up, manned by local residents and the Warrior Society, a group of radical paramilitaries including Vietnam veterans from all parts of the Mohawk Nation identifying themselves only by noms de guerre - Lasagna, Mad Jap, Spudwrench, Wolverine, Noriega. They brought weapons and field radios with them and patrolled the barricades on commandeered golf carts, their faces hidden by war paint and masks. Condemned by the Mohawk National Council as a "lawless and terrorist cult, the hired thugs of smugglers and casino operators," the Warriors had been involved in beatings and arson in an escalating wave of violence that had swept across reserves in Ontario, Quebec and New York State, culminating in the shooting down of a National Guard helicopter and the murder of two men at Akwesasne. Oka offered them an opportunity to improve their image as defenders of native land rights.

OFFICERS ATTACK

On the morning of July 11, more than one hundred Sûreté du Québec officers, armed with assault rifles, concussion grenades and tear gas, attacked the Mohawk barricades. In an ensuing shoot-out one officer was killed and the police were forced to retreat. Within minutes of the attack, Warriors at nearby Kahnawake set up barricades on the Mercier Bridge and its feeder ramps, the main traffic artery from the Montreal to the South Shore. Hundreds of feet above the river, they attached what appeared to be dynamite charges to the girders and threatened to blow up the bridge if the police attacked again. "It was an armed insurrection," a top-level aide to Premier Robert Bourassa said. "We didn't know what was coming next. Our police had been defeated and all we heard about was roaming Mohawks with guns. We thought this could be our version of hell - the city shut down, the police in retreat and the Mohawks standing on top of police cars with their AK-47s held high over their heads."

In the days to come, angry mobs gathered at the barricades, shouting obscenities and racial slurs and demanding that force be used to clear the roads. In St. Louis de

LEFT:
A corporal with a Vandoo reconnaissance platoon approaches the barricades at Oka. (DND ISC 90-471)

BELOW:
Native veterans from across Canada form up in a show of support for their people. (DND PHOTO)

Gonzague, police viciously clubbed demonstrators and fired tear gas after they went on a rampage. At Châteauguay, two white youths wearing army-style fatigues were mistaken for Mohawks and beaten so badly that they required hospital treatment. The next day, more than 12,000 residents marched through the town chanting "We want our bridge!" and "Bring in the army!" Two days later, at the request of the government of Quebec, the army began deploying troops.

NO ARMED ATTACK

Operation Salon, under the command of Lieutenant General Kent Foster, marked the first time that Canadian troops had been called out against aboriginal peoples since the North West Rebellion of 1885. At dawn on August 16, tank transporters of the 5th Mechanized Brigade carrying Grizzlies and Leopards fitted with bulldozer blades followed by buses with infantry from the R22eR and Royal Canadian Regiments aboard rolled into Blainville and St. Benoit near Oka and Farnham and St. Rémi across from Kahnawake. By nightfall, more than two thousand troops were in place. Insisting that his mission would not involve an armed attack on the barricades, General Foster announced that all troop positions would be made public and that he would not disrupt ongoing negotiations.

At Châteauguay, crowds cheered as the troops moved in, offering to fetch food and soft drinks from the pizzerias and fast-food restaurants along the highway. "It's so very strange," one soldier said. "Don't these people realize that shooting and killing could start at any moment?" In order to avoid misunderstandings that could trigger a firefight, soldiers walked towards the Mohawk lines to exchange information about their positions with Warriors then shook hands and established a neutral zone. At 17:00 hrs, APCs wheeled into place on the Mercier Bridge. After placing a peace pipe on the pavement, the Mohawks agreed to help the troops remove the barricades.

AUTHORIZED TO FIRE

Violence erupted at Kahnawake several weeks later when the army joined Sûreté du Québec officers to search for weapons. Confronted by a taunting, stone-throwing crowd, the troops were authorized to fire in the air. Seventy-five Mohawks and 19 soldiers required treatment for cuts, bruises and broken bones. Nine others were hurt and a man died of a heart attack when whites attacked a convoy of cars evacuating the elderly, women and children from the reserve.

Marching in to the police lines at Oka, the troops refused to accept the established neutral zone. Rifles at the ready, they moved forward to improve their position, stretching coils of barbed wire across the road in front of the barricades. Questioned about a plan of attack, Prime Minister Brian Mulroney replied that "the army will not fire the first shot."

PRESSING FORWARD

The Warriors understood that the ability to intimidate was their best weapon. An effective tactic in dealing with unarmed civilians, it was lost on the troops who earned considerable respect for their discipline and restraint. Without responding to threats, they pressed steadily forward backed by Grizzlies directed by low flying helicopters. Spreading out among the pines, camera crews in their wake, they approached the Warriors' lines from behind in a wide arc driving them back to a treatment centre, a five-bedroom house near the river. Surrounded with razor wire, searchlights, thermal imaging and light intensification devices, the Warriors were reduced to baiting the troops and playing macho for the cameras before gathering around television sets at night to watch their antics. Meanwhile, combat engineers combed abandoned barricades, bunkers and overturned police cars for explosives and quietly took down the official flag of the Vietnam veterans, respectfully folding it and handing it over to a Warrior representative.

Reaching out to moderates to increase divisions within the Warriors' ranks, the army rejected any discussion of amnesty.

"The army will not get involved in political matters," a spokesman said. "There will be no discussions of Oka land claims by anyone until the Warriors have disengaged themselves in military custody." At sunset on the evening of September 26, the remaining Warriors in the besieged treatment centre compound held a sweetgrass ceremony, burned weapons, tapes, papers and other evidence, then marched out in a column. After a brief scuffle in which several tried to escape, they were herded aboard buses with barred windows and whisked off into the night.

REALLY AN INDIAN PROBLEM

The long, troubled "Indian Summer" of 1990 brought native discontent to wide public attention in Canada and abroad. It seemed to have escaped the notice of members of the Oka Golf Club though. "I'm here to relax and forget about the problems of society," a duffer remarked, oblivious to the drama being played out a few hundred yards from the fairways. "It's really an Indian problem. If the Mohawks want to make their claim, that's fine for the courthouse or parliament. But this is where I want to be in the summer." The officers and men of the 5th Canadian Mechanized Brigade Group, the Vandoos and the RCR would beg to differ.

AUTHOR: *Bill Twatio*

DESERT SHIELD / DESERT STORM

***HMCS* Protecteur *departs Halifax en route to the Persian Gulf, 1990.* (DND PHOTO)**

When Saddam Hussein invaded Kuwait, the United States organized a powerful coalition force to oust the Iraqis. Canada was one of the first to answer the U.S. call to arms.

IN THE EARLY HOURS of 2 August 1990 Saddam Hussein, dictator of Iraq and commander-in-chief of what some called the "fifth-largest army in the world," sent 200,000 troops, 5000 tanks, 4000 artillery pieces and 10,000 armoured vehicles across his south-eastern border into the tiny Emirate of Kuwait.

Four days later, the United Nations imposed sanctions and demanded the Iraqis withdraw. By then, Hussein's troops were imposing a bloody reign of terror – and were firmly in control. A defiant Iraqi dictator, promising to bring glory to Islam and to the Arab world, announced the annexation of the defenceless, oil-rich state on 8 August.

By that time, Prime Minister Brian Mulroney had discussed the crisis with George H.W. Bush, the U.S. President. Britain and the United States had begun deploying troops for the defence of Saudi Arabia and the other Gulf states threatened by Hussein.

Four days later Mulroney announced that Canada would contribute two destroyers and a supply ship to the multinational force being assembled under U.N. auspices and with Bush's leadership.

After hasty training for a mission they had not anticipated and for which the Canadian Forces had not been prepared, Canadian Task Group (CATG) 302.3 – consisting of HMCS *Athabaskan*, *Terra Nova* and *Protecteur* under the moniker Operation FRICTION – sailed from Halifax on 24 August with Commodore Ken Summers commanding. They arrived at the Gulf island of Bahrain on 27 September and undertook their first patrol in the Persian Gulf on 1 October.

On 14 September, Mulroney announced Canada would send a squadron of CF-18s to the region – initially 18 aircraft, 28 pilots and 235 ground crew. They were destined to be the first Canadian fighter squadron to fly into battle since World War II. They were drawn from 439 Tiger Squadron and 416 Lynx Squadron, and placed under the command of Colonel Don Matthews. Operation SCIMITAR required the unit to provide air cover for Canada's naval contingent and to support the massive multinational air forces arrayed against Iraq. Stationed in Qatar, a Gulf peninsula at the western end of the United Arab Emirates, on 6 October. They mounted their first combat air patrol the next day, in what would become an average of 18 flying hours a day during the first phase of the crisis prior to Christmas, 1990.

Security on the ground would initially be provided by a company of the Royal Canadian Regiment. The R22eR (Royal 22nd Regiment) replaced the RCR prior to actual hostilities.

On 27 November the United Nations passed its twelfth resolution on the Gulf Crisis offering Hussein "one final pause of goodwill." This final action also authorized coalition countries led by the United States to take "appropriate actions," including military force, to drive Iraq out of Occupied

Kuwait. They set a 15 January 1991 deadline for Iraqi compliance and the troops hunkered down for Christmas in the desert.

On 11 January, Mulroney, under allied pressure to increase Canada's contribution to the coalition, dispatched eight more CF-18s, a Boeing 707 (equipped for airborne refuelling) and a Challenger jet (to ferry VIPs around) to Qatar.

Hussein's troops now numbered over a half-million, including his crack Republican Guards. He believed they were firmly dug in along the Kuwaiti border and famously promised that the Coalition would face "the Mother of All Battles." He ignored the U.N. deadline.

Canadians came home from work on 16 January to witness glimpses of the incredible air battle underway over Iraq – in the early hours of the morning, Baghdad time. Their pilots were conducting sweep and escort roles in the midst of a fierce and unremitting allied bombing campaign.

GROWING CONTRIBUTION

That same day, Canada's contribution to the coalition grew once again. Mulroney announced that the CAF would deploy a

Surgical Field Hospital to support British forces in Saudi Arabia.

On 23 February the coalition began a massive – but brief - land invasion of Kuwait, retaking Kuwait City on 26 February.

At midnight on 27 February (08:00 on 28 February, Baghdad time), the allies suspended military operations – without occupying Baghdad. The wisdom of that restraint has been questioned and is one reason the problem of Iraq's weapons of mass destruction program remains unresolved to this day.

Canada's ships returned to Halifax on 7 April, 1991. Compared to Saddam Hussein's enormous invasion force – and the massive allied coalition in which Canada took part, the CAF contribution was relatively small.

But in fact, Canada sent one-quarter of its operational warships and deployed virtually all of its modern weaponry. One thousand Canadians took part.

AUTHOR: *Chris Champion*

GENERAL'S OVERVIEW OF THE GULF WAR

A snapshot in time by then-Chief of the Defence Staff, General A.J.G.D. deChastelain, praising the men and women who served overseas as part of the U.S. coalition force.

TOP: *Chief of Defence Staff, General John de Chastelain.* ***ABOVE:*** *The navy's primary role was to hail and search merchant vessels entering the Persian Gulf. The air force contributed a rear area Combat Air Patrol (CAP) which allowed their US counterparts to push forward into the fighting area.* (COURTESY DAVID DEERE)

THE GULF WAR WAS AN extraordinary war for Canada. Not extraordinary in the sense that Canadians went to war once again after a gap of nearly 38 years; but extraordinary in the sense that in this, our fifth war in the space of 90 years, we suffered no casualties.

While that statement is true, a formal ceasefire has not yet been signed and Canada's efforts in the Gulf are not finished. Canada still has engineers in Kuwait City, locating and destroying explosives and ammunition. Further, Canada still has elements of the Canadian Forces Middle East Headquarters (CANFORME) located in Bahrain and rear parties still in Al Jubayl. Finally, HMCS *Huron* is about to enter the Arabian Gulf to continue Multi-National Force interdiction operations.

Nonetheless, from the initial deployment of the Naval Task Group last August, until the interim cessation of hostilities between the Coalition Forces and Iraq on 28 February, Canadian sailors, soldiers, airmen and airwomen took part in a conflict from which they emerged without an injury.

THE CAST

Everyone Canada sent to the Gulf played a demanding and important role. The players included:

- The Commander, Commodore Ken Summers, and staff of CANFORME (including the crew of the Challenger liaison aircraft), in Bahrain, Doha and Riyadh who provided overall control of our deployed units.
- The Naval Task Group, consisting of HMC Ships *Athabascan*, *Terra Nova*, and *Protecteur*. These three ships accounted for a quarter of all naval interdictions, and performed a key role in coordinating the entire logistic effort for the multinational naval contingent in the Gulf during the period of hostilities.
- The artillerymen who served in the ships who provided very low level air defence support; the Infantry Company

and the Platoon at Doha and Bahrain, each of which provided local security to the personnel and material located there; and the Infantry Company with the Field Hospital at Al Quaysuma, which provided both local security and custody of Iraqi prisoners of war.

- The Field Hospital at Al Quaysuma and Al Jubayl, which operated under the control of the British Division, and which saw action in the handling and care of both British and Iraqi wounded.
- The Canadian Medical Teams operating aboard the United States Hospital Ship MERCY.
- The Canadian exhange personnel serving with British, French and American land, sea and air operational units.
- The crews of the Canadian aircraft who moved personnel and equipment into theatre to maintain the combat capability of the forces deployed there.
- And perhaps most visibly, the CF-18 Fighter Squadrons, 409, 416 and 439, and 437 Squadron's Boeing 707 air-to-air refueller, which flew combat air patrol, escort and sweep, and air-to-ground missions during their deployment in the Gulf.

PROFESSIONAL DISTINCTION

The Canadian Forces servicemen and servicewomen who participated in the Gulf War acquitted themselves with distinction and with a degree of professionalism that was much admired by our coalition allies. Their performance was very much in the fine traditions of their predecessors.

And finally, a special acknowledgement to all those Canadian men and women, both military and civilian, from Canada, Europe and other parts of the world, who provided the necessary support to the Canadian forces sent to the Gulf. Without your dedication and consistent efforts, the accomplishments of our Gulf forces would not have been possible. Yours was a service fully appreciated and not to be forgotten.

REPRINTED FROM:

Esprit de Corps, *Volume 1 Issue 1*

AUTHOR:

General A.J.G.D. deChastelain

ATTACKING THE IRAQI PATROL BOAT

ABOVE: *Captain Steve Hill and Major Dave Kendall, the two Canadian pilots who attackd the Iraqi patrol boat – pose beside their CF-18 adorned with the "kill" symbol.*

The solitary act of hostility by Canadian fighter planes was a "qualified success" according to the pilots who flew the mission.

ONE OF THE MORE notable incidents throughout the Desert Cat Deployment was when "Hornet 13" flight was tasked to attack an Iraqi patrol boat. The following summarizes the event.

1. Date: 30 Jan 91, aprox 02:00 hrs
2. Pilots: Capt Steve "Hillbilly" Hill, Maj Dave "DW" Kendall
3. The threat: An Iraqi Patrol Boat designated the TNC-45. It is 145 feet in length and carries the EXOCET anti-ship missile as well as anti-aircraft guns.
4. Debrief: The mission was a night W4 CAP of 2 hrs. The WX was clear with no restriction to us and a full moon. Sea state was "light."

After approx 1.5 hrs on station Papa Bravo (the ship controlling us) asked, "would you like to strafe a boat?" The reply was, "are they defending themselves/ is there any AAA?" PB replied that an A-6 had put two Laser Guided Bombs into an OSA and a dumb bomb onto another vessel. These two were in flames and disabled. The A-6 was "winchester" (out of weapons) and there was a "spitter" (a single target TNC-45) running north that they wanted to hit so that an enroute A-6 could finish him off.

MOONLIT WAKE

PB reported that the A-6 had not received or seen any AAA. As we approached the boat (17 miles) we were informed that a VID (visual identification) was now required prior to being cleared to fire. The vessel was approximately 20 miles south of the Tigris Euphrates Delta and approx 30 miles NE of Piranha heading NNW at 30kts plus. The contact was initially required in Radar SEA mode, however the visual was made possible by the large wake in the moonlight. First pass over at 10,000 ft provided no ID.

On the second pass, flares were dropped over the target to assist in VID. "ID unknown but military and evading." Bear (E-2C), an Airborne radar aircraft monitoring the intercepts replied "cleared to fire" since there were no friendlies in the area. No AAA/RWR indications were noted. Both CF-18's strafed the boat until winchester with observed hits. One subsequent pass per aircraft was made to attempt an air-to-air missile (AIM-9) shot with no success. The boat's heat signature was insufficient for missile guidance. My wingman attempted a radar lock in air-air mode with no success. Lead did the same and received a full system lock. An AIM 7 was launched which impacted the water approx 50 feet to the right of the boat. The flight hit Bingo fuel so the engagement was terminated. The boat was last seen at high speed "jinking."

After further investigation of the incident, it was determined that the TNC-45 was one of four Iraqi surface vessels. The A-6's had engaged three of the four until all ordnance was expended. To fill the gap in armed surface reconnaissance, it was requested that CAP aircraft be used to search for the fourth combatant. Hornet 13 flight was then vectored to engage. Shortly after the CF-18's had expended their rounds of 20mm, the patrol boat was again attacked by US bombers. As such, a seaworthiness kill was awarded to the US bombers with assists to Hornet 13.

REPRINTED FROM:

Desert Cats, the Canadian Fighter Squadron in the Gulf War

AUTHOR:

David Deere

A RETROSPECTIVE LOOK AT THE PERSIAN GULF WAR

ABOVE: *HMCS* Terra Nova *returning from service in the Persian Gulf.* (DND PHOTO)

Looking back at the Gulf War 12 months later, Canada's commitment constituted a herculean effort for our tiny Armed Forces

BY THE SUMMER OF 1992, yellow ribbons no longer decorated trees and homes; the nation flicked past CNN in search of more mindless entertainment, retired General Norman Shwarzkopf earned $50,000 per speech and Saddam Hussein was still the President of Iraq...

Since enduring months of apprehensive waiting and six weeks of emotional tension, one year after coalition forces "suspended offensive combat operations" in the Gulf, most Operation Friction participants had returned to their respective homes and lives. Of the estimated 4000 Canadian Forces personnel who served in the Gulf between August 1990 and April 1991 — with a maximum of 2500 in-theatre at any one time — a small contingent from Valcartier, 5ième Régiment Génie Canada, remained in-theatre throughout 1992 to clean up, monitor and rebuild.

Months of Hussein's threats, criticisms and demands culminated on 2 August 1990 with the Iraqi invasion of Kuwait. The United Nations Security Council immediately adopted Resolution 660, condemning the Iraqi invasion and demanding that Hussein withdraw his troops.

CANADA'S PLEDGE

Supporting a multinational effort to impose strict economic sanctions on Iraq (Resolution 661), Prime Minister Brian Mulroney pledged two destroyers and a supply ship, Canadian Naval Task Group 302.3, to Operation Desert Shield. Two weeks of frenzied activity by Halifax dockyard personnel followed as HMC Ships *Athabaskan*, *Terra Nova* and *Protecteur* underwent extensive refitting before their 24 August 1990 departure. Modern detection and weapons systems were installed on board the Task Group. Simultaneously, the Sea Kings on *Athabaskan* and *Protecteur* were equipped with a variety of defensive equipment and the Forward Looking Infrared (FLIR) system.

Conducting their first Gulf patrol 1 October 1990, the Naval Task Group was only the first wave of the systematic Gulf deployment of Canadian troops which continued through the fi-

ABOVE, LEFT: *A weapons technician loads an AIM (air-to-air missile) aboard a wing pod of a CF-18 in Qatar.* ***ABOVE, RIGHT:*** *Iraqi president Saddam Hussein remained in power even after his country was overpowered by the U.S. and their allies in the Gulf War.*

nal months of that year and into early 1991.

Four months and 12 resolutions after Iraq's invasion, as the 15 January 1991 deadline passed and Hussein's troops remained in Kuwait, Resolution 678 authorized member states "to use all necessary means to uphold Resolution 660." Once it started, the Storm lasted six weeks. Characteristically, Canadian forces quietly and efficiently carried out the tasks set them. Captain (N) Dusty Miller assumed command of the Combat Logistics Force – a multinational force of approximately 24 ships from ten countries – as HMC Ships *Terra Nova* and *Athabaskan* acted as defensive escorts for the Force.

CLOSE TO THE FRONT

In response to a British request for augmented medical resources, 550 staff of 1 Canadian Field Hospital, Petawawa, deployed to Al Jubayl, Saudi Arabia. A subsequent move brought them to within 40 km of the front.

Initially charged solely with Combat Air Patrol for the Naval Task Group, the role of Canada's CF-18's was quickly expanded to include sweep and escort duties "in support of other elements of Allied air forces." A month later, on 20 February 1991, an air-to-ground attack role was authorized for Canadian CF-18's, preceding the ground offensive by only three days. 100 hours later the war was effectively over.

CANADIANS CONCENTRATED THEIR THOUGHTS AND PRAYERS EXCLUSIVELY ON THE TROOPS IN THE GULF, GREETING THEM UPON THEIR RETURN HOME WITH TEARS OF THANKS AND WELCOME.

Typically, it is difficult to pinpoint Canadian accomplishments amidst the records of American and British exploits. Statistics are easy.

- Comprising only 10 per cent of the total interdiction fleet, the Canadian Naval Task Group steamed more than 98,000 nautical miles during their deployment and conducted nearly 25 per cent of all interceptions.
- Sea Kings flew more than 2000 hours.
- 34 CF-18's (a maximum of 26 in-theatre at a time) flew 5730 hours
- one Boeing 707 refueller logged 306 hours
- a Challenger liaison aircraft flew 170 hours
- Air Transport Group ferried more than 2.5 million kilograms of cargo to the Gulf.
- More than 90,000 kilograms of mail travelled to and from Canadians in the Gulf.
- Along with the total 4000 Canadian men and women deployed to the Gulf during the conflict, 2000 Canadian Forces personnel in Germany and Canada operated in direct support of the war effort.
- There were no Canadian operational casualties during Operation Friction.

TEARS OF THANKS

For a month and a half Canadians concentrated their thoughts and prayers exclusively on the troops in the Gulf, then greeted them home with tears of thanks and welcome.

Far from indicating a lack of involvement or skill, the seeming absence of material detailing solely Canadian accomplishments, was instead representative of the quiet confidence of Canadian troops. Certain of their ability, Canadians did not find it necessary to loudly and continually point out their achievements.

REPRINTED FROM:
Esprit de Corps, *Volume 1 Issue 9*
AUTHOR: *Catherine Hingley*

EXPLOSION IN KUWAIT

When the ammo dump of an American Armoured Brigade detonated, Canadian engineers stoically provided assistance to their allies.

ABOVE: *Members of 1 Combat Engineer Regiment relax at an outpost in Kuwait, July 1991... just a few days later they would be called upon to assist the Americans after a massive ammunition dump ignited.* *(SCOTT R. TAYLOR)*

SUNDAY, 11 JULY 1991 was blistering hot, with mid-morning temperatures in Kuwait City pushing the mercury over 50°C. For the sweltering soldiers of the U.S. 11th Armored (Blackhorse) Cavalry Regiment, their live-fire training exercise was already running behind schedule. Heat-fatigued troops soon became careless in marshalling vehicles as they tried to make up for lost time. While sitting in a bumper to bumper convoy, stretching from the compound's front gate back to the ammo dump, one driver, his truck laden with 155 mm howitzer ammunition, watched in horror as his overheated engine burst into flames. When internal fire extinguishers failed to control the blaze, the terrified GI bolted from his truck cab.

Captain (later Major) Fred Kaustinen was the acting commander of the First Canadian Engineer Regiment (1CER) stationed half a kilometre away in the same compound. He had just finished his lunch when he heard, "an explosion like a 16-inch gun." Stumbling from their mess hall, Kaustinen and his men saw a single plume of smoke. However, their experience with explosive shock waves told them that this wasn't a simple garbage dump fire. The engineers quickly donned their protective flak jackets. These sappers were in Kuwait as part of the United Nations force monitoring the post-Gulf War cease-fire between Iraqi and coalition forces. They had been in theatre since April and had gotten used to the gruelling routine: six days clearing unexploded bombs and shells from remote desert tracks, with Sundays reserved for an air-conditioned respite at the Kuwait City warehouse compound. But, on that fateful day, just five seconds after the Yank trucker jumped from his vehicle, all thoughts of R & R disappeared in the earsplitting thunderclap.

AMMUNITION DEPOT IGNITED

Within mere minutes, the ordnance blast from the howitzer shells had ignited the Blackhorse Regiment's entire open-air ammunition depot. Everything started to explode and the terrified Americans fled the scene in panic. Kaustinen steadied his command and quickly briefed them on his intention to remain in place and administer assistance to the U.S. troops as long as possible. The other UN contingents stationed at the compound had no such intentions. To the Canadians' shock, their British, Chilean and Swedish comrades had "bugged out" of their own areas within the complex immediately following the first blast. Only two Canadian UN military observers remained at their posts in the now vacant headquarters building. From the rooftop, they courageously manned a radio throughout the afternoon and sent back the only coherent reports of the situation, including the frantic call for a massive airborne medical evacuation.

Meanwhile, Kaustinen's sappers were shocked at the sight of the first wave of fleeing soldiers. One sapper recalled their being "bug-eyed with panic 'cause the shit was really coming down all over." They looked like lemmings pouring over the compound wall. Some guys were naked, others bleeding, and they literally trampled anybody who got in their way. One shaken U.S. trooper began screaming that there were nerve gas munitions stored at the depot and this set off a second wave of panic. To clarify the situation, Warrant Officer Mike Hartling took the initiative and ordered a couple of "chemical sentries" to dress in protective clothing. These two brave Canadians plunged as far forward into the blast zone as possible to provide an early warning post. Captain Kaustinen eventually pulled aside one frightened Yank captain and managed to get a garbled situation report from him. What was now clear to Kaustinen was that all the senior American officers had fled, making the Canadian engineers the only cohesive unit available to provide aid.

OPERATING IN THE MESS

Kaustinen's men rose to the challenge within minutes. Medical officer Captain Barry Fung set up a makeshift operating room in the Canadian sergeants' mess (it had the best air-conditioning), while triage was carried out in the junior ranks' facility. Of the roughly 1200 American soldiers who

Two of the Lost Boys inspect the destruction left littering the post war 'highway to hell,' just outside Kuwait City. (SCOTT R. TAYLOR)

sought refuge in the Canadian compound, nearly 25 per cent required some form of medical treatment. Wounded were stacked everywhere, screaming in pain as the explosions continued to rock the entire base.

In response to the initial radio request, the U.S. had scrambled a dozen helicopters from nearby Bahrain and they were soon hovering above the disaster scene. Approximately 50 of the injured needed immediate medevac and the choppers had also brought up two surgical teams. However, the only suitable landing strip was an adjacent soccer field with a three-metre-high wall surrounding it. Although this sturdy perimeter would provide the helos with a measure of protection against shrapnel, there was no "safe" entry from the Canadian compound. Sizing up the problem, Cpl. "Smitty" Smith, a likable Maritimer, calmly told Kaustinen that he'd fix the problem, "Right quick!" The only vehicle at hand was an old fork-lift and Smith used it as a battering ram. On his third try, he punched the battered tow-motor right through the wall, making a two-metre-wide hole. Immediately following Smith came a steady succession of stretcher parties, manned by Canadian engineers and cooks, rushing casualties out to the choppers. Still terrified and suffering from shock, few Americans seemed fit enough to assist their own comrades. Instead, they huddled together along the compound's ring road while their non-commissioned officers tried to sort them out. Very few had brought their kit (including canteens) and, inexplicably, a large number of them remained naked. Realizing the heat and exposure could create further casualties, Kaustinen instructed his cooks to prepare a meal and his men to issue water and erect tents for shelter.

ONE CANADIAN INJURY

By mid-afternoon, the blasts had subsided into sporadic explosions and Major Dick Isabel had returned to the compound from leave in Bahrain to assume command from an exhausted Kaustinen. The tired Canuck sappers toiled long into the night administering aid and clearing unexploded ordnance from the compound. In the midst of all this, Captain Kaustinen had retained the presence of mind to send off two Significant Incident Reports to National Defence Headquarters (NDHQ). Only one Canadian had been injured that day — Sapper Paul Leblanc received a gash on his forearm — but the unit had been at the vortex of a major incident. In his second transmission, Kaustinen advised NDHQ that he would follow up with a more detailed account as soon as time permitted. The next day, Maj. Isabel told him, "not to waste [his] time. No one's interested in what happened."

Kaustinen was astounded. An entire U.S. regiment was rendered hors de combat (with more armoured vehicles destroyed in a single hour than the U.S. had lost during the entire Gulf War), and the Canadian combat engineers alone had heroically stayed the course. Yet no press release was ever issued by the Defence Department. Why? The reason given to Kaustinen was that this incident made the Americans look bad, and NDHQ did not want to strain relations with our major ally. So it was decided that the Canadian public would never be told.

The U.S. army quickly issued a letter of appreciation to the Canadian engineers, and at a private November 1991 ceremony, General John de Chastelain issued the regiment with a rare Chief of Defence Staff Unit Citation (CDSUC). Over three years later, Fred Kaustinen, now a major, opened his mail to discover he'd been personally awarded a CDS commendation for his exemplary actions and personal leadership during the Kuwait explosion. "There had been so little officially said about it, I was beginning to question whether it ever really happened, or if it was just a figment of my imagination," Kaustinen recalled.

REPRINTED FROM:
Tested Mettle:
Canada's Peacekeepers at War
AUTHORS: *Scott Taylor & Brian Nolan*

KURDISH AIRLIFT

OPERATION ASSIST WAS THE Canadian contribution to the multi-national relief effort "Provide Comfort" in April and May of 1991. The British, American, French, Italian, and Canadian air forces staged a massive airdrop effort that saved thousands of lives by providing emergency food, clothing, and shelter in the only way possible – aerial delivery.

Two Canadian C 130 Hercules aircraft flew 34 missions delivering a massive 788,000 pounds of supplies over a 23-day period. Tactical airlift crews were able to accomplish this difficult mission because they had spent peace time years practicing and perfecting the skills of supporting ground combat forces in hostile situations. Each mission took four and a half-hours. With each of the four crews flying one mission daily, and nightly maintenance and loading by ground crew, the Hercs maintained a very high operational tempo.

Operating in terrain similar to the Canadian Rockies, many of the drop zones were located at 6000 feet of altitude with the surrounding peaks at as high as 14,000 feet. At these altitudes and with the loads carried, losing an engine – which normally would be easily dealt with – could be catastrophic. There was also the threat of attack by the Iraqi air force. To counter this, F-15s and F-16s flew a defensive Combat Air Patrol (CAP) over the Herc flights to protect them from potential attack. As well A-10 Thunderbolts lead in the Hercs on the drops first identifying the drop zone and then moving to a position to protect the C-130s from attack from the ground.

The biggest problem originated with the Kurdish people, they were understandably eager to recover the loads that were parachuted to them. Since there was no distribution system on the ground, it was first come first served and so the Kurds would swarm onto the drop zone making it extremely difficult to drop the loads with out having them land on the recipients.

As each day passed there became a proliferation of new shelters below and around the drop zones. The landscape became a tapestry of blue, green, and white. The blue shelters were the tents that were dropped, and the green and white ones were made from the actual parachutes. Success however, was difficult to assess as the Hercs returned to their base in Turkey after each sortie. Although there was one informal indicator, word had filtered back that refugees were asking for a change in the menus of the Meals Ready to Eat (MRI).

Canada also had a contingent of 70 medical personnel on the ground from 4th Field Ambulance out of Lahr, Germany providing first line treatment for the Kurds. By the end of the first week in May 1991 the situation had stabilized enough for the Canadian Contingent to begin redeploying home.

REPRINTED FROM: Esprit de Corps, *Volume 1 Issue 3*
AUTHOR: *Air Transport Group*

RELIEF TO ETHIOPIA

RAVAGED BY WAR AND struck by drought the fractured country of Ethiopia was sliding into a famine of immense proportions during the summer of 1991. The UN sponsored and organized emergency shipments of food. The port facilities and the road and rail infrastructure were in such disrepair that the badly needed Canadian and German wheat, and American corn flour sitting at the docks could not be delivered in country from the port of Djibouti.

To transport this food to the main areas of greatest need in Mekele (north), Bahir Dear (west), Jijiga (east) and Kabri Dahar (south) required delivery by air. To assist in this operation, Canada deployed C-130 Hercules aircraft from 435 Transport Squadron along with maintenance and movements units from Edmonton. As well, with the deployment of communications, intelligence, and medical personnel from Ottawa, the CF had 60 members tasked on the mission at any one time.

Operations to deliver food were conducted in daylight as the runways were very rudimentary gravel strips with no navigational aids. Temperatures soared to over 62 C, so hot in fact, that the aircraft thermometers could not read any higher. This did not deter the relief effort. Canadian Hercs delivered 40,000 pounds of food per flight, making an average of seven sorties per day. Upon landing, Ethiopian workers would unload the aircraft, in one case 30 people unloaded the 20 tons of food in 12 minutes flat.

So effective were the personnel of Air Transport Group that in the first 10 days of operations, 2,380,000 pounds of food were delivered. Each aircraft load fed 38,000 starving Ethiopians.

The grueling mission continued into the fall of 1991 when the situation stabilized and the UN continued the operation using ground transport. The Canadian contribution saved untold thousands of lives.

REPRINTED FROM: *Esprit de Corps, Volume 1 Issue 8*
AUTHOR: *Cathy Hingley*

TRAGEDY IN THE BALKANS

"Yugoslavia had tourism, heavy industry; it was a food-surplus nation. Its new freeways linked the rest of the European Community with Greece, Turkey, and the export markets of the Middle East. The totems of an emerging consumer society were everywhere: new gas stations, motels, housing developments, and discos and sidewalk cafés in the villages. Most impressive were the large private houses covering the roadside hills. Before the killing started practically everybody, it seems, was just finishing a new house, or had just bought a new car."

- T.D. ALLMAN, "VANITY RAIR," 1992

Civil War in Yugoslavia was not a foregone conclusion in the aftermath of Communism. Nationalist leaders fuelled old hatreds and destroyed the federation "from the top down."

ABOVE: *Outside the UN press center in Zagreb, Croatia, residents built a wall with each brick enscripted with the name of a Croatian victim. Media were encouraged to photograph this "proof" of Serbian atrocities.* (SEAN CONNOR)

WHEN THE BERLIN WALL, the ultimate symbol of the Cold War, came crashing down in November 1989, it appeared to herald the dawn of a new age of peace, prosperity and hope. Less than two years later, however, a war erupted in Yugoslavia, cruel, pitiless and savage, which shattered visions of a New World Order and cast a long, dark shadow over Europe. To some it appeared absurd that, at a time when other European nations were voluntarily giving up much of their sovereignty to forge lasting bonds with each other, Yugoslavia's republics should be heading in the opposite direction. The collapse of Yugoslavia, the wealthiest and most open society in Eastern Europe, would lead directly to wars in Slovenia, Croatia, Bosnia and Kosovo, throwing some 20 million people into misery unknown since WWII.

Prophets of doom had speculated about Yugoslavia's future since the death of Josip Broz Tito in 1980. Without his charismatic leadership and unifying presence, they argued, the country would surely not survive. Moreover, deep, historical fault-lines divided the Balkans. The north was comparatively rich and the south poor; the difference in per capita income in Slovenia, for example, was six times greater than in Kosovo. Serbs, Montenegrins and Macedonians were Orthodox and had lived under Ottoman rule, while Croats and Slovenes were Catholic and had been subjects of the Habsburg Empire. During World War II, Yugoslavs spent more time fighting each other than they did the Germans. Royalists fought communists, Serbs fought Muslims and Croats fought Muslims and Serbs. The very word "balkanize" became synonymous with fragmentation and strife. In the end, only Tito could impose a semblance of order.

MYTH AND REALITY

The outbreak of war appeared to confirm the pessimists' point of view, that fighting was part of the culture and it had only been a matter of time before Yugoslavia fell apart. As accounts of atrocities and massacres made newspaper headlines around the world and the phrase "ethnic cleansing" passed from Serbo-Croat into the English language and as television viewers tuned in to the destruction of Dubrovnik and Vukovar, most commentators agreed that Yugoslavia had been an historic mistake. The international media had largely ignored Yugoslav affairs until war broke out. Now, as confused as their audience, they examined the war from the propaganda positions of the belligerents, reinforcing myths and historical half-truths.

From the earliest times the Balkans had been a crossroads where different worlds met and overlapped. Yet, for all their differences the people of the Balkans share a common background and before the First World War their history was no more turbulent than other parts of Europe. When the old empires collapsed, the Balkan states were late-comers to the new family of Europe an nation-states, but by no means different in kind.

Yugoslavia had two incarnations, as a kingdom and as a communist dictatorship indelibly linked to the person of Tito. Both

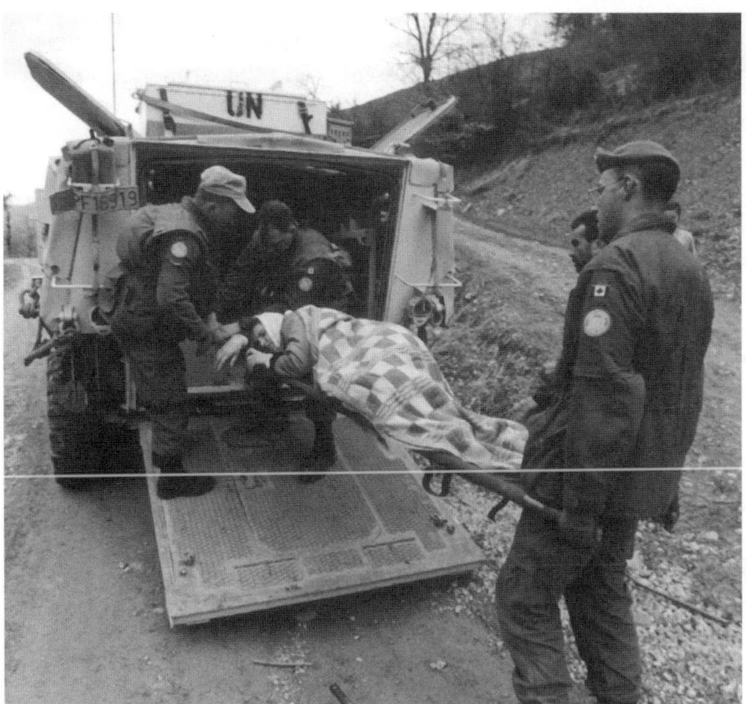

ABOVE, LEFT AND RIGHT: *Peacekeepers were frequently tasked to provide "care and comfort" to the civilian population. A sick woman is evacuated and an abandoned, handicapped child is consoled.*
(SEAN CONNOR)

had merit and were not unmitigated failures in which national tensions were simply swept under the carpet. The Yugoslavia which emerged after the Second World War made genuine attempts to reconcile the interests of all and could boast of a cultural diversity that made the country unique. Though hampered by an ideological commitment to Marxism, living standards rose in Yugoslavia, illiteracy was virtually wiped out, and urbanization radically altered the ethnic map. Workers migrated to the cities and a generation matured which was more aware of its urban roots than its national origins. In the last census before fighting broke out, large numbers identified themselves as Yugoslavs rather than Croat, Serb or any other nationality. A peaceful, proud and prosperous Yugoslavia hosted the 1984 Winter Olympics in Sarajevo and each year hundreds of thousands of foreign tourists flocked to resorts along the Adriatic coast.

The collapse of communism made a major reorganization of the Yugoslav state inevitable. With a modicum of good will it would not have been impossible to build a third Yugoslavia on the ruins of the old. War was not pre-ordained nor was it the result of ancient ethnic and religious hostilities. These factors made things worse, but Yugoslavia's demise and the violence that followed, resulted from the conscious actions of nationalist leaders. Yugoslavia was destroyed from the top down.

On 17 August 1990, Serb and Croat police forces clashed and from that point on, all factions, inflamed by nationalist rhetoric, hurled inexorably toward civil war. Croatia and Slovenia declared independence and troops from the Yugoslav National Army (JNA) deserted to take up arms for their new nations. The remaining JNA forces, largely of Serbian descent, were soon fighting their former comrades along disputed borders. The dregs of society, thieves, thugs and psychopaths also took up arms to become freedom fighters and national heroes, exalted by their respective propaganda machines. The Serbs had Captain Dragan, a soldier of fortune rumoured to be an ex-convict from Australia and Arkan, a home-grown hood boasting a police record in several Western European nations. His penchant for indiscriminate murder was matched on the Croat side by Branimir Glavas, a philosopher of ethnic cleansing specializing in executing Serbian civilians.

Six months of fighting made further efforts to hold the country together pointless and Yugoslavia formally ceased to exist on 15 January 1992 when all 12 members of the European Community recognized Croatia and Slovenia as independent states. Five days earlier, UN special envoy Cyrus Vance had secured an agreement to deploy up to 10,000 troops in Croatia to provide a protection force (UNPROFOR) in three designated areas. Canadians would occupy Sector West near Zagreb.

As the troop trains wound their way down from Germany toward the forward concentration lines, there was an air of confident excitement among the Canadians. Relieved to be leaving endless exercises behind, they talked boldly of the upcoming task and discussed the television images of the war which they had watched on CNN. Morale was high as they rolled into Durovar through rubble-strewn streets presided over by Kalishnikov-carrying Croats, festooned with ammunition belts and rocket-propelled grenade launchers.

"Now that we are on the ground," their commanding officer informed them, "we can expect things to be quiet."

AUTHOR: *Bill Twatio*
PHOTOS: *Sean Connor*

THE BALKAN CRISIS

NOVEMBER 1989 The Berlin Wall comes down.

APRIL 1990 First multi-party elections in the Yugoslav republics. Communists are defeated in Croatia and Slovenia.

17 AUGUST 1990 First armed clash in Yugoslavia between Serb and Croat police in the Krajina.

25 JUNE 1991 Slovenia and Croatia declare independence. Yugoslav federal army (JNA) intervenes in Slovenia. Withdraws ten days later.

JULY 1991 Croat and Serb paramilitaries clash in eastern Croatia.

3 AUGUST 1991 Croatia severs all ties with Yugoslavia.

SEPTEMBER Fighting erupts in Pakrac, Vukovar and Dubrovnik. ■ Peace Conference opens in the Hague. ■ Referendum on Macedonia independence. ■ Proclamation of autonomous Serb regions in Bosnia-Herzegovina. ■ UN Security Council passes Resolution 713 imposing an arms embargo on Yugoslavia.

OCTOBER 1991 Siege of Dubrovnik

NOVEMBER 1991 Vukovar falls to Serbs.

22 NOVEMBER 1991 UN Special Envoy Cyrus Vance proposes peacekeeping mission for Croatia.Three UN protected areas recommended.

10 JANUARY 1992 Vance Plan approved. 10,000 UN troops dispatched to Croatia as part of United Nations Protection Force (UNPROFOR).

15 JANUARY 1992 European Community recognizes Slovenia and Croatia.

29 FEBRUARY 1992 Bosnia-Herzegovina declares independence. Bosnian Serbs proclaim separate state.

APRIL 1992 European Community recognizes Bosnia-Herzegovina. Serbs besiege Sarajevo.

MAY 1992 Government of Bosnia-Herzegovina requests foreign military intervention. Slovenia, Croatia and Bosnia-

Herzegovina admitted to the UN. Security Council imposes an embargo on trade, oil and air traffic on Serbia and Montenegro.

6 MAY 1992 UN Security Council declares six "safe areas" – Sarajevo, Tuzla, Bihac, Srebrenica, Zepa and Gorazde.

JUNE 1992 - Operation CAVALIER. UN troops take up position at Butmir airport in Sarajevo under command of Major General Lewis Mackenzie of Canada.

5 JULY 1992 Sarajevo airlift begins. UN passes Resolutions 770 and 771 authorizing the use of force to protect convoys carrying humanitarian aid

SEPTEMBER 1992 Battle of Medak Pocket. Massive ethnic cleansing of Muslims in Bosnia.

OCTOBER 1992 Security Council Resolution 781 creating a no-fly zone in Bosnian airspace.

1 JANUARY 1995 Four-month truce in Bosnia. Efforts to extend it fail and fighting resumes.

24 MAY 1995 NATO bombs ammunition depot when Serbs ignore a UN order to remove heavy weapons from Sarajevo area.

11 JULY 1995 Serbs seize Srebrenica.

4 AUGUST 1995 Massive Croat offensive in Krajina.

30 AUGUST 1995 NATO bombs Serb positions around Sarajevo.

8 SEPTEMBER 1995 Foreign ministers of Bosnia, Croatia and Yugoslavia agree to divide Bosnia into Serb and Muslim-Croat areas.

NOVEMBER 1995 Peace talks open in Dayton, Ohio.

21 NOVEMBER 1995 Leaders agree to a settlement

16 DECEMBER 1995 NATO-led Implementation Force moves into secure peace under Operation JOINT ENDEAVOR.

20 DECEMBER 1996 NATO-led Stabilization Force (SFOR) deployed under Operation JOINT GUARD.

CANADIANS IN CROATIA

ABOVE: *A Canadian armoured engineering vehicle clears away the battlefield rubble in Sector West, Croatia, April 1992.* (DND)

AS OF 5 APRIL 1992, there were approximately 300 Canadian troops deployed in Daruvar, Croatia. They represented the vanguard of a total 1200 Canadian Forces personnel to be deployed as peacekeepers to war torn Yugoslavia from bases in Germany and across Canada. The bulk of the Canadian service members arrived in Daruvar by train from Lahr, Germany between 8 and 15 April.

Although Daruvar was approximately 20 km from the front line at the time, this town was not long ago a battlefield.

FIRST TO ARRIVE

Bomb-craters, sandbags, and debris littered the streets and, to the uninitiated, provided grim testimony to the random destructiveness of war. Canadian combat engineers were among the first UN troops to arrive in Daruvar and their presence breathed new life into the town. "People are back on the streets and things are returning to normal," said Lieutenant Colonel Michel Jones, Deputy Contingent Commander. "On Saturday they held their first market day since the war started."

There is supposedly a ceasefire in effect, but this was, at the time, a loosely interpreted phrase which limited the fighting to murderous bursts of cannon and rifle fire. "Both sides respect the sanctity of the UN," said Jones. "They have stopped shelling Daruvar now that we told them we are here." Jones thinks this cooperation will continue as the UN troops move into the ceasefire zone itself. "The sooner we get into the line the better for all involved," he said.

Unfortunately, the scope and scale of the UN deployment prohibited any immediate measures. Going into the line with the Canadians will be troops from as far away as Jordan, Nepal and Argentina.

EUROPEAN BASES KEY

Having our forward bases in Europe made the deployment possible on such short notice and enabled Canada to be the first on the ground. Ironically, the Engineer Regiment which provided the vanguard almost did not make it. "We were in the midst of reducing the unit to nil strength as part of the Forces' reduction plan," explained Lieutenant Colonel Mike Gauthier, CO 4CER.

"When the word came through to deploy to Croatia, we had already loaded most of our stores on trains to ship them back to Canada; there was 24 hours of fancy dancing by NDHQ to stop those trains."

Now that they were in Daruvar, 4CER had immediately begun clearing away the rubble and started the work of providing accommodations and checkpoints for the entire contingent. Many of them were stationed in abandoned Yugoslavian army barracks, which, almost without exception, were the scenes of heavy fighting. "There will be some explosive ordnance disposal (EOD) work involved in clearing them up," said Gauthier. "We have just finished three months of intense training for a mission in Cyprus which was scrapped. So my troops are thoroughly prepared and understand the dangers." The Yugoslavians produced quite a variety of sophisticated landmines, and there is reported to be nearly 1 million of them sown across the countryside. With the cooperation of the Serbian and Croatian armies, the engineers of 4CER were soon briefed on their detection and disarming.

For the Canadians who had arrived at that juncture, it took a little adjusting to go from the theoretical to the practical. Although trained with simulation, many Canadians had never been under actual artillery fire. "At first, it was a little unnerving," said Jones. "One night during dinner, they started shelling near the hotel. They were close enough that you could hear the whistle. The hotel staff doused the lights in the interest of our safety, but after a few moments of darkness, we gave in to practicality and ordered the lights back on."

They finished their dinner despite the bombardment and moved one step closer to their acclimatization. Being 'in country' was not without certain very evident dangers, "but," says Jones, "the troops are welcomed here and they know they are making a difference. That in itself makes it worth the risk."

REPRINTED FROM:
Esprit de Corps, *Volume 1 Issue 11*
AUTHOR:
Scott Taylor

RIGHT:
A column of Canadian APCs rolls into Croatia in April 1992.
(G. REEKIE, TORONTO SUN)

Canadian soldiers had trained for decades to fight "the cold war." What no one had prepared for was the reality of horror which they would confront in the former Yugoslavia.

OPERATION CAVALIER - CIVIL WAR IN CROATIA

BISMARCK, THE GERMAN Chancellor, detested the Balkans to the depths of his Prussian soul. "They are not worth the bones of a single Pomeranian grenadier," he thundered in a speech to the Reichstag in 1876. Years later, as he watched tensions mount in Europe, he predicted that it would be "some damned thing in the Balkans " that would lead to war.

War has been a constant in the Balkans, stemming from the mutual antagonism of three disparate ethnic groups – Serbs, Muslims and Croats. Tito had brought a semblance of order to the embattled region, but the fires of hatred had never been banked. The subsequent political upheaval following his death inexorably led to a bloody civil war. As Yugoslavia and its national army, the JNA, disintegrated, thousands of heavily-armed citizen soldiers were soon engaging their former comrades along disputed territorial boundaries. The first clash occurred on 17 August 1990.

Discussions to send UN peacekeepers into the region began in November 1991, with special envoy Cyrus Vance tirelessly attempting to reach a negotiated settlement. Two months later, all parties agreed to the deployment of 10,000 Blue Berets to Croatia to provide a protection force (UNPROFOR). Three areas were designated as UN protected zones, a hastily assembled Canadian continent assigned to the pivotal Sector West, located just south of the Croatian capital, Zagreb.

WELCOME TO F---ING CROATIA

The "battle group" under the command of Lieutenant Colonel Michel Jones, a big, friendly and fluently bilingual officer, was designated as the First Battalion, Royal 22 Regiment (1R22eR), but included 400 troops from the Third Battalion, Royal Canadian Regiment (3RCR) commanded by Major Peter Devlin. His troops were among the first to arrive in Croatia after a long, tiring train ride from Germany. Morale was high, despite widespread evidence of battlefield destruction. Hastily unloading their MII3 armoured personnel carriers in Duruvar, they moved on to the village of Sirac, just behind the Serb-Croat confrontation line. At an orders group the next morning, Jones informed his officers that General

Lewis Mackenzie the deputy commander of UNPROFOR had assured him of the sincerity of all factions to make the ceasefire a success. "Now that we're actually on the ground," he said, "we can expect things to be quiet."

Less than two hours after the briefing, mortar shells began coming down about two kilometres from the Canadian bivouac. Corporal Mack Porter, a vehicle technician, watched as the barrage drew nearer: "They knew where our location was and they just walked the shells in," he recalls. The tired soldiers were given the order to "crash harbour," and armoured vehicles roared to life and rumbled off with troops still boarding them through the combat doors, a procedure they had practised many times on training exercises in West Germany.

By the time the barrage had ended, all personnel were safe, accounted for and manning defensive positions around the town. A few had been nicked by shrapnel and two Croat civilians had been killed. As the sun came up and tension eased, the exhausted men were stood down and sent in relays for a hot breakfast at the field kitchen. As they filed in, they joking greeted each other with, "Hey, welcome to f---ing Croatia."

ABOVE:
Even after the peacekeepers arrived, the killing and ethnic cleansing continued in Croatia. Canadian soldiers would become "witnesses to war." (DND PHOTO)

THE FORGOTTEN FRONT

A few miles away, Lieutenant Colonel Jones and his staff had just sat down for a late supper at the Hotel Therme's dining room in Duruvar when heavy shells came crashing in. A waitress immediately turned off the lights as her guests scrambled under the tables. After moments of fear and anticipation, the Canadians ordered the lights back on, a sign that they were rapidly becoming accustomed to dining in a war zone.

There was no media coverage of the Sirac and Duruvar bombardments - the first occasion that Canadian troops had been shelled since the Korean War. No Canadian reporter had accompanied the troops into Croatia and the CBC relied solely on the BBC and local stringers for information. The ubiquitous CNN was preoccupied with a new development. That same day, Bosnia-Herzegovina had become the new flashpoint in the former Yugoslavia as Serb forces began shelling the capital, Sarajevo. General Mackenzie had hastily departed to assess the situation. Overnight, Croatia became the forgotten front as news crews focused their reports entirely on the situation in Sarajevo.

However, for Michel Jones and his battle group, things remained tense and dangerous. Ordered to establish a strong UN presence in the region, aggressive foot patrols marched over countless kilometres of front-line tracks as engineers de-mined the roads. The workload diminished slightly as other national contingents began to arrive and by the end of May a regular routine had been established and in rotation, troops were sent off on their R&R leave periods.

INTO SARAJEVO

Regular routine, and R&R would soon be things of the past as the troops in Sector West were ordered to provide a 235-man security detachment for General Mackenzie's advanced reconnaissance of the besieged Bosnian capital. Moving into Sarajevo in June under the command of Major J.J. Daniel Beaudoin, their mission was to prepare the ground for a possible UN deployment into the Sarajevo airport to deliver humanitarian aid. A larger force would follow.

The Canadians in Sector West who would make up the force greeted the news with mixed emotions. Beaudoin's party had just returned with their tales of combat and casualties and CNN's nightly broadcast virtually portrayed the Bosnian capital as a second Stalingrad. Others felt that they were missing out on all the "excitement." So, with some trepidation, the battle group readied itself for the long move south.

Jones had to split up his limited forces, not only leaving a rear party in Sector West, but also dividing his troops into two mini battle groups. On Canada Day 1992, 300 set off in a convoy that stretched back two kilometres. After navigating treacherous roads, negotiating their way through barricades and facing down drunken Serb commanders, they arrived in Sarajevo to be greeted as liberators. For many, it was like reliving a scene out of the 1945 liberation of Holland.

Bivouacked at Camp Beaver at the airport, and subjected to sporadic mortar fire, they and their French counterparts began establishing humanitarian distribution centres as medicines and foodstuffs began to arrive in quantity. By the end of their month-long stay, 15 soldiers had been injured in the line of duty.

DOG DAYS

By mid-August, the Canadian battle group had settled into a routine in Sector West. Soldiers were using up their three-week UN mid-tour leave and counting the days until their rotation home. After the strain of Sarajevo, many felt that they could begin to relax a little. Unfortunately, a little too soon.

In the early hours of 17 August, Sergeant Jim Davis was ordered to reconnoitre a possible Croat armour build up in a forest just back of the front lines. Moving slowly along a dirt track in an APC, he hit an anti-tank mine which hurled the 11-ton vehicle four feet into the air. Miraculously, no one was injured. Badly shaken, the crew radioed headquarters for assistance and Sergeants Mike Foster and Mike Ralph were dispatched to sweep the road. Foster was leading the sweep on foot with Ralph following in the section truck when a mine detonated beneath the truck, killing Ralph instantly.

Although Ralph was the first peacekeeper killed in Yugoslavia, his death received scant mention in the Canadian press. In the dog days of summer, Parliament was recessed and most Canadians on vacation.

AUTHOR: *Bill Twatio*

MACKENZIE IN SARAJEVO

General Lewis MacKenzie and his senior staff officers at Sarajevo airport, 1992. (DND PHOTO)

As the eyes of the world were turned to the plight of Sarajevo, a Canadian general would find himself locked in the media spotlight.

HE BECAME CANADA'S BEST known soldier, a national hero as "The Saviour of Sarajevo." A soldier who had never wanted to be a soldier. Athletics and cars were his passions and in later life he would win awards for his exploits on Formula Four racetracks. In Sarajevo, on a day of heavy mortar and artillery fire, his greatest disappointment was not being able to return to a friend's appartment to watch the Spanish Grand Prix on televion. As the commanding general of United Nations forces in Bosnia-Herzegovina, General Lewis Mackenzie had more important business at hand.

Born in Truro Nova Scotia in 1940, his father had served in the Canadian Army in World War II and Korea and, growing up on army bases, young Mackenzie had his fill of things military and had no interest in the profession of arms. But as a young officer cadet, he finally took to the profession with a vengeance, aspiring to lead soldiers, rather just being one.

Described as "a good thinker, cool, iron-willed and brave," Mackenzie became Canada's most experienced peacekeeper, respected and even loved by his men for his affability, empathy and willingness to share in the hardships they face. And he has shared those hardships in every corner of the world. He served three tours of duty in Cyprus, supervised a peace accord in Vietmam, served in Libya and brokered an agreement between the Sandanistas and Contras in Nicaragua. A fellow officer said of him that "he is natural leader, never daunted by difficulties." He would need those qualities more than ever in the most daunting task of his long career on the front lines of Bosnia-Herzegovina where Croat-Muslims were pitted against heavily-armed Serbs in one of the worst outbreaks of ethnic violence in the former Yugoslavia.

A BOSNIAN CHRONICLE

In the early 1990's, the ethnic wars that had ravaged the rest of what had been Yugoslavia found the people of Bosnia, a people plagued with an array of intrangient national leaders vying for position to suplant the old roster of socialist politicans. The most ethically mixed of the former republics, peopled by Muslims, Serbs and Croats, the Bosnians made a determined effort to sus-

tain the Titoist ideal of a multiculuralism. In the election of 1990, Alija Izebegovic, a Muslim, was elected president of a multi-party coalition government. Described by his political enemies as a religious fanatic who represented the threat of Islam in Europe. Few believed that his fractious, divisive government would last. Fewer could imagine how savagely it would be attacked.

Izebegovic's chief critic was Dr. Radavan Karadzic, a psychiatrist and published poet, convinced that the new Bosnian nation could not survive. He had a vision of a united Bosnia, a pure Serb Bosnia which would keep close ties with the regime of President Slobodan Milosevic in Belgrade. Serbs would form a minority in the new Bosnia, he agrued, and would have no guarantee of protection for their religion, culture and property. He proposed ethnic cantons with the Serbs laying claim to the countryside. Muslims and Croats would be allowed to live in specified neighbourhoods in the capital, Sarajevo. Karadzic made it clear, that if Izebegovic unilaterally declared independence, "rivers of blood would flow." And flow they did.

Sarajevo is a densely populated city spread out along a narrow valley surrounded by mountains on three sides and an open plain on the fourth. The proud sponsors of the 1984 Winter Olympics, it is a city of mosques, churches and Orthodox cathedrals, fine shops and outdoor cafes, a cosmopolitan place whose citizens had been living in harmony for 500 years. But on 5 April 1992, as the political situation deteriorated, snipers opened fired on a large peace demonstration in the heart of the city, killing a young woman, the first casualty in a long and bloody civil war. The following day, after Canada and the European Community recognized Bosnia as an independent state, six more were killed by sniper fire and several others wounded. A busy downtown street sooned earned the ominous name – Sniper's Alley.

With no willingness to compromise, Karazdic declared the Serb Republika Srpska and retreated to the mountain village of Pale a few kilometers above Sarajevo, generously suupplied with tanks and artillery of the JNA, the former Yugoslav National Army. They dug in and awaited orders to open fire.

UNPROFOR

Canada was one of the first countries to offer peacekeepers to diffuse the impending crisis. Prime Minister Brian Mulroney had strong personal feelings about Bosnia as his wife Mila had been born in Sarajevo- and they had often visited the country. As Canadian troops were already serving in Croatia, they were placed on standby when the UN decided to locate its Croatian headquarters in Sarajevo hoping that the mere presence of peacekeepers would might avert an all-out war.

ABOVE, LEFT: *Columns of Canadian APCs had to transit through the volatile heartland of Bosnia in order to deploy into Sarajevo.* (TIM NAUMETZ)

ABOVE: *Once inside the besieged Bosnian capital, Canadians had the vital task of securing the airport. Relief flights frequently came under fire from all factions.* (G. REEKIE, TORONTO SUN)

Mackenzie landed in Sarajevo in March, several weeks before the first shots were fired. to set up UNPROFOR Headquarters.- Barricades were going up around the city and President Izebegovic was hurridly raising a Territorial Defence Force (TDA). In a letter home, Mackenzie wrote: "Tragically, there is no solution I can postulate. Hundreds of years of ethnic violence are dredged up at every meeting; everyone thinks theirs is the just cause. From my impartial view, there's more than enough blame to go around for all sides, with some left over." A few days later, full-scale fighting broke out around a JNA barracks and the first artillery shells crashed into the city. In the months to come, the citizens of Sarajevo would be entirely dependent on humanitarian airlifts into the city's airport. Mackenzie had quickly grasped the situation. Returning to the city with a UN force which included a RECCE platoon of the RCR and the Vandoos, he used his considerable military and diplomatic skills to persuade visiting French President François Mitterand that the airport should stay open for business. "When he and I discussed it and I asked him to send humanitarian aircraft, I knew the media would cover it And I knew that every friggin' country in the world watching TV would want to be part of the action." Within days, Mackenzie was able to get the first planeloads of aid into the besieged city, first from the French, and then as predicted, from around the world.

Operating out of headquarters in the city's former telephone exchange, Mackenzie would repeatedly call on those military and diplomatic skills as he attempted to arrange ceasefires and assigned his men to deliver humanitarian aid and help the helpless. A soldier recalls that "our platoon did a variety of escort jobs, usually out to the airport or downtown to the Bosnian Presidency. There was always a lot of shooting going on and we generally dodged bullets every time we went out." Mackenzie's peacekeepers became an essential part of the city's infrastructure, providing services from garbage pickups to dropping off food supplies. No Bosnian politician could move without their transportation and protection.

FIGHTING LEW

Maintaining strict neutrality according to his UN mandate, Mackenzie was subjected to repeated death threats."It never ceased to amaze me," he said, "that the people you were helping wanted you dead." But he continued to his duty. Soldiers who served under him speak fondly of "Fighting Lew" and his constant concern for their personal well-being and safety.

Recently, Lew Mackenzie has been criticized by a prominent Canadian journalist for his policies of accommodation. His comparison of Serbs Croats, and Muslims-as serial killers of 15, 10 and five victims, with none regarded as "good guys" is dismissed. In reality, it's a pretty fair assessment of the Balkans by an officer and gentleman, a good and brave soldier who served his country and the people of Sarajevo with distinction.

AUTHOR: *Bill Twatio*

PAYING THE PRICE FOR PEACE

Canadian armoured personnel carrier edges past a knocked-out Serbian tank. The war still raged throughout the former Yugoslavia, even after the UN deployed the peacekeepers. (DND PHOTOS)

As casualties mounted in the Balkans, Canada's continued commitment became a sensitive political issue. The easiest solution was to hide the truth about the dangers our troops were facing.

DESPITE THE senior staff at National Defence Headquarters being internally polarized and engaged in public debate about the commitment of our ground troops to Yugoslavian peacekeeping duties in 1992, the unit rotation and force build-up there was already complete. As a result, two separate contingents totalling nearly 2400 Canadian Forces men and women were occupying positions in and around the West Slovonian town of Daruvar in the Republic of Croatia.

In early October 1992 the 3rd Battalion, Princess Patricia's Canadian Light Infantry (3PPCLI), under the command of Lieutenant Colonel Nordick, replaced the original Canadian battle-group at the end of their six month UN tour. Since their arrival, the PPCLI had been responsible for enforcing the demilitarization of the devastated region and establishing a sense of law and order. Canada's second contingent, 2nd Battalion, Royal Canadian Regiment (2RCR) completed their deployment on 15 November 1992, but were unable to immediately proceed across a Serbian-held bridge into their area of operations. Once they negotiated this impasse, the RCR was responsible for escorting and protecting United Nations High Commission for Refugees (UNHCR) efforts to distribute relief aid from the town of Banja Luka.

CDS AGAINST THE GENERALS

Headlines at home pitted the Chief of the Defence Staff (CDS) against his generals in a war of words over the ability and conviction of the Armed Forces to maintain a Canadian involvement in the Balkans. During this period there was a virtual media silence on the actual state of affairs in Croatia. To the surprise and disdain of the Canadian troops, the dangers which they faced, and the casualties which they suffered, were not mentioned. "It certainly wouldn't support the official party line if people found out what things are really like over here," said a disgruntled infantry captain. "If this really is part of the 'acceptable risk' and 'price to pay for world peace' to which they so often refer, then why try to keep it a secret?" In a little over two weeks, the replacement troops suffered five casualties ranging from a ruptured spleen, (when a suspect's car ran through a UN checkpoint), to a broken jaw (after an armoured personnel carrier struck a landmine).

Public Affairs Officer Captain (later Major) Rick Jones from the Media Liaison office at NDHQ said that the reason for the delay of information being released was "routine, prior to the notification of next of kin." He added, "We don't wish to alarm family members unnecessarily."

While that may have accounted for the absence of casualty reports, there was also scant to nil coverage of the Canadian successes.

"It is in our mandate to enforce the demilitarization of this sector and we've been aggressively pursuing that aim," said Lieutenant Colonel Nordick. "Since we've been over here, we've more than doubled the seizure of weapons taken in the previous six months."

To achieve this, Nordick and his junior officer used mobile check points, roving patrols and quick reaction forces to keep the radical insurgents off guard.

However, while the UN may ostensibly control the region, Canadian troops did not possess the authority to make arrests. All arms seizures had to be made in conjunction with the Serbian or Croatian police forces within their respective jurisdictions. The ironic and distressing fact is, that 90 per cent of the time, the weapons violators were in fact local policemen themselves. "The UN seizes and retains the weapons, but more often than not the perpetrators are released from custody and back in their police uniforms in a matter of hours," said "C" Company Commander Major Mike Morneau.

"The Croatians are a little more concerned with controlling their own police force at this point because we have a good understanding with their police chief," said Captain Blanc, a platoon commander. To illustrate this, Blanc cited an incident where a Croatian policeman fired his pistol at two Canadian soldiers. "They apprehended him and he's still in jail pending a trial." The motive given for the assault: the policeman was drunk.

Several peacekeepers have died as a result of injuries suffered on UN and NATO missions, but not all have received public recognition for their sacrifice.

The unfortunate result of this situation was that the more successful the Canadians were in enforcing the UN mandate, the more they alienated those with whom they had to co-operate and co-exist.

"On several occasions we've been sent little welcoming packages in the form of rifle grenades aimed at our compound," said Sergeant Trenholm. "However these are largely harmless incidents intended more to intimidate than to injure."

After an 8 November cordon and search operation against a Serbian held house netted a virtual arsenal of automatic weapons, Canadians were once again targeted for retaliation.

Within hours after Major Morneau had met with Serbian militia commanders, refusing their request to return the weapons, Serbian infiltrators booby-trapped a roadway behind a party of UN soldiers and civilians.

Combat engineers had already cleared the road in no-man's-land and were still working only 200 metres from where Captain Blanc detonated the landmine by stumbling over a knee-high tripwire. "He's incredibly lucky that he wasn't killed, " said Master Corporal Devison, the head of the engineer detachment at the incident.

While a suspect was seen leaving the scene, chase was not given as the whole area remains infested with mines and booby-traps. Instead the UN party prudently chose to withdraw.

Perhaps not so surprisingly, the Canadians were able to retain their impartiality throughout their experiences. While taking weapons from both sides, they had also witnessed first-hand the horror and violence of civil war.

"One of our jobs is to escort the forensic team through no-man's-land to recover and perform autopies on the bodies of murder victims, " said Sergeant Wheatley a section commander. "Yesterday we saw them drag up the remains of four bodies, and all had been brutally murdered. Like the overpowering stench, it's something that's tough to get used to."

For the young Canadians serving in the former Yugoslavia, it was certainly an educational experience. "You grow up fast here – you have to," said one soldier, adding, "The biggest irony so far was watching the [1992] Canadian referendum results on television with gunfire rattling over our heads."

REPRINTED FROM:
Esprit de Corps, *Volume 2 Issue 7*
AUTHOR: *Scott R. Taylor*

THE MEDAK POCKET

In Canada's largest battle since Korea, the Princess Pats experienced the horrors of war firsthand in Croatia.

LIEUTENANT TYRONE GREEN, 2PPCLI, was well aware that there was tension between the Serb population and French UN peacekeepers as he deployed Charlie Company in the little town of Medak at the end of August 1993. Earlier that year, the French had denied the local Serb milita access to stockpiled weapons and hundreds had been killed or captured when the Croats launched an offensive. Hoping that the situation had improved, he moved his men into a school less than 200 metres away from a Serbian brigade headquarters.

CALVIN DISPATCHED

The Croat offensive into Serb-held Krajina had not amounted to much, but sporadic shell-fire prevented the UN from a establishing a zone of separation between the two factions. As peace talks got under way in Zagreb, a PPCLI battle group under the command of Lieutenant Colonel Jim Calvin had been dispatched to the relatively quite Sector South and tasked with setting up observation posts and facilitating cease-fire negotiations. Since then, tensions had eased and the mission lapsed into a dull routine of vehicle maintenance and training sessions. An intelligence report indicated that the sector would be quiet for some time to come.

The report was a relief to Warrant Officer Matt Stopford of Delta Company and his company commander Major Dan Drew. As the vanguard of Calvin's force, they had preceded Green into the Krajina to build bunkers at Krosevo and an observation post overlooking a bridge into Croat territory. Now, they and their men, 80 per cent of them reservists, were able to relax over a cold beer and begin to count the days until the rotation home. Three days later, the Croats launched a major offensive.

Minorities in newly-independent Croatia had presented President Franjo Tudjman with an intractable and dangerous problem. In the summer of 1990, Serbs in the Krajina, radicalized by his anti-Serb rhetoric and backed by Belgrade, drove Croatian police out of Knin, the capital, and established an autonomous state which threatened access to the lucrative tourist areas along the Dalmation coast. Tudjman had since itched to use his growing army against the rebellious Serbs. On 9 September 1993, armed and trained by American advisers, the Croatian army struck, ruthlessly driving out the Serbian population, many of whose ancestors had lived in the Krajina for more than four centuries. In Sector South, the Canadians were caught in the crossfire.

At Medak, Tyrone Green was on his way to a morning order's group when a mortar round knocked him flat. Moments later the entire 25 kilometre front erupted as Croatian artillery opened fire in earnest. Dazed, Green picked himself up and set his men to work shoring up bunkers with whatever building material was available, cursing the fact that his platoon had not warranted a much-coveted sea container for use as a portable bomb shelter.

As shells rained down on Krosevo, Stopford and Drew ordered their men to mount their APC's and pull back to a hill some 300 metres away. "This is much safer," Stopford joked as the troops dug in. "The Croats will have to turn their elevation screws at least half a revolution in order to reach us now." Unfortunately, the rocky, barren hillside precluded any sustained digging, forcing the men to fill sandbags with highly-toxic tailings from a nearby mine site.

EYES AND EARS

At battalion headquarters in Cracac, Calvin was trying to determine exactly what was happening in the Medak Pocket as columns of smoke rose ominously on the horizon. He had already radioed in the latest developments to the UN Sector South commander and had briefed Major General Archibald MacInnis, the Canadian contingent commander in Zagreb, but as the day progressed he was flooded with high-level requests from New York for more information. After a hastily-arranged meeting with Green, Calvin ordered him to set up observation posts to monitor the battle. For the next three days, Green's 9 Platoon would be the eyes and ears of the international community.

As retreating Serb soldiers and terrified refugees streamed through Medak, Green interviewed anyone he could stop on the road to gather information. When his position was shelled after each report to

RIGHT: *Sergeant Rod Dearing directs his sections fire as they engage Croatian forces outside the village of Medak. When the four-day firefight was over – 35 Croats were killed or wounded. (ILLUSTRATION KATHERINE TAYLOR)*

OPPOSITE PAGE: *Sergeant Dearing's section after their firefight with Croatian troops in the Medak Pocket. (DND PHOTO)*

Calvin, it dawned on him that the Croats were using radio-direction finding equipment to locate him, mistaking his signals for those of the Serbian headquarters. From then on, he used the radio only in emergencies and switched locations to do so. On 14 September, an exhausted Green reported that the fighting had died down and that both sides were digging in along new front lines.Twenty-four hours later, a ceasefire came into effect, and Calvin was ordered into the buffer zone.

FIREFIGHT

Short of troops and equipment as most of the PPCLI's armoured vehicles had been returned to Germany pending rotation, Calvin was given command of two companies of French mechanized infantry to augment his rifle companies. Informed that he might have to use force, he set off with the French column on the right, Green's platoon in the centre of C Company on the left, and Major Drew's D Company following up. Green's men had barely begun to move forward when a burst of Croat fire cracked through the trees around them. Returning fire, he ran up a large UN flag above his APC then pulled back to radio a situation report.

Rolling in to the village of Sitlik after dark, 8 Platoon also came under fire. Dismounting, as combat engineers moved up to dig fire-pits, Sergeant Rod Dearing ordered his men to fire at the muzzle flashes. Heavily outgunned, they held the Croats at bay as they raked their positions with 20 mm cannon fire and rifle grenades. Dearing and his men repulsed four attacks, killing or wounding at least 30 Croats, before being relieved by French troops.

Nearby, Lieutenant Colonel Calvin and Major Mike Maisonneuve, McInnis's representative from the UN's Zagreb headquarters, were engaged in a heated roadside discussion with the Croat commander. A ceasefire was arranged and it was agreed that the Canadians would advance at noon the following day.

ETHNIC CLEANSING

At first light, Calvin realized the error of not occupying the surrounding villages during the night. Smoke billowed from every house, the aftermath of a frenzy of ethnic cleansing. "The Croats had made sure that the people who had lived there could not return," he later testified. "Either by killing them or by destroying their property." In one village, he came across the still-smouldering bodies of two young women who had been repeatedly raped, tied to chairs and then set afire.

Weighed down with loot, Croat troops were staggling back to the cease-fire line as Calvin's column of APC's moved forward with the infantry sections riding topside, weapons cocked and ready. The shocking sights they were exposed to and the sense that they had somehow failed the people they had been tasked to protect, drove Calvin and his men forward with a reckless sense of purpose. When a Croat company commander refused him passage at a crossroad, Calvin summoned journalists and television crews forward for an impromptu press conference. Quick to grasp the political impact of his move and sensitive to accusations of war crimes, the Croat ordered his troops to shoulder arms and retreat. By day's end, 2PPCLI had reached its objective and began the grisly job of identifying and burying the dead.

DANGER PAY

Throughout the crisis in the Medak Pocket, first-hand reports had flowed into the National Defence operation centre. Although CNN and Reuters had covered Lieutenant Colonel Calvin's progress, there was no mention of the four-day battle in the Canadian media. The parliamentary press corps was preoccupied with a pending federal election and DND refused comment, well aware that Calvin was engaged in a dangerous game of bluff with the Croats in order to establish the UN Protection Force as a credible deterrent – a game that could end in disaster. Once the situation had been successfully resolved, DND saw no need to make the battle public.

Lieutenant Colonel Calvin was awarded the Meritorious Service Cross, Sergeant Dearing and several of his men were mentioned in dispatches and the French gave the PPCLI a unit citation. Several weeks later, the troops were quietly informed that Ottawa had approved danger pay for service in the former Yugoslavia – backdated to 1992.

AUTHOR: *Bill Twatio*

STRETCHED TOO THIN

Unprepared and ill-equipped for the massive commitment of Balkan peacekeeping, the Canadian army soon found itself beyond the breaking point.

ABOVE: *With two 1200-man battlegroups deployed to Yugoslavia, the Canadian Army simply did not have enough manpower (or equipment) to keep up a regular rotation. In the end, politics would prevail and the soldiers would suffer burnout. (G. REEKIE, TORONTO SUN)*

SINCE MACKENZIE KING'S TIME when he described HMCS *Rainbow* tied up at an Esquimalt dock as a "frivolity," successive Liberal governments have been content, except in wartime, to keep the Canadian military impoverished.The once proud Canadian Corps of WWI was allowed to whither away and Walter Hose's fledgling RCN was reduced to a largely land-based training establishment. The St.Laurent government dispatched troops to Korea with antiquated equipment and Pearson and Trudeau were satisfied to keep the military at the minimal level of operational readiness to fulfill our role in NATO. Much to the chagrin of our NATO allies.

In a sudden burst of enthusiasm for things military, the Conservative government of Brian Mulroney changed all that. In I987, Defence Minister Perrin Beatty was to draw up a White Paper, which for generals, admirals and defence lobbyists seemed like a dream come true.The army was to get 400 new tanks to replace its aging Leopards, recruitment was to be increased by ten percent, the naval reserve was to be enlarged and eqipped with new ships, including ten nuclear submarines. But the dream was short-lived. Faced with a mounting deficit and opposition from the electorate, most of the projects were dropped. The only significant acquirement were new uniforms to replace the despised "Jolly Green Jumpers" of Unification days.

TEFLON BOB

Six weeks after Beatty's White Paper was discarded, Robert Ramsay Fowler was appointed to the post of Deputy Minister of National Defence.Describing himself as "a humble public servant," but known around DND – a ferro-concrete bunker looming over the Rideau Canal in downtown Ottawa – as Teflon Bob, Fowler presided over a department where image was allowed to prevail over substance. He and his master, the egregious Marcel Masse, spoke glowing of "Total Force" and a revitalized militia.The reality was that the regular force was about to lose three battalions and to maintain paper strength, the remaining battalions were designated as I0:90 formations, formations that would be fleshed out with ill-trained militia.The effects were soon evident in the field.

CARRYING ON

In the former Yugoslavia, it was clear to commanders in the field that were desperately short of proper equipment and trained men.The situation was soon to deteriorate even further.

Since May 1993, Major General Arch MacInnis, a close friend of Bob Fowler, had been putting forward the opinion that Canada would have to cut its force back to a single battle group, an opinion that was sure to please budget-conscious politicians. Chief of the Defence Staff, Admiral John Anderson concurred, as did Defence Minister Tom Siddon, a featherweight neophyte in the cabinet. Fortunately, the one battle group proposal was turned down but cabinet did impose a ceiling of 2000 troops dedicated to the Balkans. To work within the imposed quota, future battle groups would be reduced to 750 men as opposed to 1100 or more. The fixed limit was to include all headquarters staff, military observers and the logistics battalion required to support the contingent.

Although their professional advice had been ignored, nobody at DND was prepared to fight the issue in an election year. MacInnis, the author of the plan, was appointed to take command of the new reduced formations. He became the Canadian contingent commander of the UN Protection Force (CCUNPROFOR) later that year. Defence Minister Tom Siddon made several half-hearted public statements about the need for a larger budget and more troops.- In the meantime, the Canadians carried on as army officers scrambled to flesh out the two smaller battle groups with reserves.

AUTHOR: *Bill Twatio*

BOSNIA VALOUR AND HORROR

With constantly changing UN mandates and restrictive rules of engagement, Canadian soldiers tried valiantly to do the impossible: bring peace to Bosnia.

SREBRENICA, A ONCE-OBSCURE mining town in the mountains of eastern Bosnia, has now joined the list of place names of tortured towns and cities - Guerinica, Lidice, Oradour-sur-Glane.

The town takes its name from the Serbo-Croat word for silver "srebo," and Srebrenica has been known for its silver since Roman times. Bauxite and zinc are also mined and car-part factories are located in Potacari. Ten miles from the border with Serbia, it is spread out ribbon-like along the bottom of a half-mile wide ravine. The encircling hills give one the sense of being sheltered - or trapped. White houses with terra-cotta roofs, an Orthodox church, a mosque with a hundred-foot minaret, a farmer's market and outdoor cafés grace the town's historic centre. By the early 1990s, Srebrenica with a population of 37,211, enjoyed a standard of living that rivalled that of Western Europe.

That standard of living came to an abrupt end with the collapse of Yugoslavia. Neighbours took up arms against each other and fighting broke out in April 1992. Serb nationalists, intent on incorporating Srebrenica into a Greater Serbia, seized the town, forcing the Muslim inhabitants into the mountains. Rallying around Naser Oric, a charismatic former policeman, they retook the town, indiscriminately slaughtering Serb civilians along the way. Backed by tanks and artillery from Serbia, the Bosnian Serbs counterattacked and by mid-March 1993, more than 60,000 desperate Muslims were isolated in Srebrenica.

THE SIEGE OF SREBRENICA

Food, fuel and medical supplies became scare. Trees were felled for firewood and operations were performed in local hospitals without the use of anaesthetics. On 16 April, fearing the town's fall, the United Nations Security Council passed Resolution 819 declaring Srebrenica the world's first United Nations "safe area." "You are now under the protection of the United Nations," General Philippe Morillon, the UN commander in Bosnia told a crowd in front of the Srebrenica post office. "We will never abandon you."

SAFE AREAS LITE

When UN Secretary-General Boutros Boutros Ghali requested 34,000 peacekeepers to police Srebrenica and five other newly-declared safe areas, member nations balked, but reluctantly approved a second proposal derisively known as "safe areas lite" to deploy a much smaller force. A week later, a company of the RCR moved into the town under the command of Major Perry Poirier.

Although there was nothing that the minuscule force could do to enforce a cease-fire or alleviate the overwhelming misery, they were welcomed by cheering crowds. The stench of death hung over the town and the troops were shocked at the sight of the emaciated inhabitants dressed in filthy, threadbare clothing. Mortar and artillery attacks on the town continued and, without

TOP:
Escorting humanitarian convoys was one of the most challenging jobs undertaken by our peacekeepers in Bosnia. The rapidly changing battlelines and volatility of the belligerents meant that casualties and conflict were inevitable.
(DND PHOTO)

ABOVE:
A Canadian casualty is evacuated by ambulance after being wounded in a firefight. Often, the UN protection force could not use their helicopters to evacuate wounded as a result of hostile ground fire.
(TIM NAUMETZ)

RIGHT:
The evacuated children's hospital in Bakovici proved to be a very emotional tasking for Canadian soldiers. While they were able to save the lives of many, for the others it was a case of too little, too late.
(SEAN CONNOR)

medical facilities, the only hope if a peacekeeper was wounded was a risky helicopter evacuation. Since the Serbs controlled the roads into town, the men would have to become as self-sufficient as possible. Food was carefully rationed. Under the watchful eyes of more than 6000 Serbs in the surrounding hills, Poirier and his 175 men set about the task of demilitarizing Srebrenica.

MANNING APPROACHES

Old tanks and homemade armoured cars, ammunition and antique firearms were brought in to a central collection site. "We were able to establish our patrols and collect a fair number of small arms and ammunition," Poirier said. "It's true though that a lot of the weapons were second-rate and virtually no heavy stuff was turned over." Poirier then allowed an inspection team of Muslims and Serbs to inspect the site. Infuriated at the pitiful collection – "not quite what the Serbs had in mind" according to Poirier – and aware that well-armed Muslims were still manning the approaches to Srebrenica, the Serbs broke off negotiations and cut off all access to the town. The RCR's dug in and prepared for the worse. When informed of the situation, External Affairs Minister Barbara MacDougall, no mean strategist, said: "There should be more people in there."

By 28 April, tensions had eased and two additional platoons were brought into the town. Retired Major General Lewis Mackenzie was instrumental in breaking the impasse, having met with Radovan Karazdic with whom he had established a relationship of mutual trust when he headed UNPROFOR in Sarajevo. His intervention did not earn him brownie points in Ottawa, MPs suggesting that he "quit the freelancing" and leave the job to the proper authorities.

In the meantime, the isolated RCRs had become nearly as bedraggled as the Srebrenicians. Half rations and constant tension had left them looking drained and haunted; their uniforms were in shreds and the UN blue paint on their helmets had been chipped away. They had been under constant artillery and small arms fire. An officer was gravely injured when his APC hit a mine and two soldiers were killed when their Cougar tank-trainer flipped over on an icy mountain road. When a corporal was hit by a sniper's bullet during a night-time fire-fight, it took seven days to arrange a medevac. When the RCR's were finally relieved by the jaunty and smartly turned-out Van Doos, some sporting Ray-Ban sun glasses in their web belts, one soldier recalled that "suddenly there was real fear in their eyes – especially when they saw how fried we were.

RUNNING THE GAUNTLET

The harsh reality of war in Bosnia had soon become evident to Lieutenant Colonel Tom Geburt, the commanding officer of the RCR battle group. Moving from Croatia into Bosnia in mid-February 1993 had been a logistical nightmare, crossing snow-covered mountains and confrontation lines. It took three weeks to move the entire battle group south, with the individual companies managing the trip in three to four days depending on the weather. On arrival in UN Sector Sarajevo, 2RCR established themselves in a former blanket factory in the town of Visoko and a brickworks in Kjiselek- and immediately set to work building sandbag bunkers as Muslims and Serbs shelled each other a few kilometres away. Obsessed with "preventing another Somalia," DND insisted that a nine-metre-high enclosure be built around the camp to deter infiltrators. Dubbed "Fort Apache," Camp Visoko was now looter-proof, but critically short of vital supplies.

Geburt's successors were assigned the task of escorting supplies and humanitarian aid convoys over the mountain passes to isolated towns and villages. As both camps were located in the Muslim-controlled territory just north of Serbian-encircled Sarajevo, this would become a very arduous task indeed. Reaching the embattled Bosnian capital and its vital airport required crossing two confrontation lines over a 30 kilometre stretch of road. Armed with AK47s and rocket launchers, bored Serb militiamen would often halted Canadian columns to initiate "negotiations." Regardless of the time of day this usually involved tough talk and downing generous lashings of Slivovitz, the local homemade plum brandy. With convoys interrupted or delayed, Lieutenant Colonel David Moore was forced to put Camp Visoko on hard ra-

LEFT:
To encourage the ethnic cleansing of opposing factions, civilian accomodations were targetted for destruction. The objective was to force residents to flee – and to ensure they had no home to return to.
(DND PHOTO)

tions and to husband his meagre fuel stocks. Previously, Moore's 12RBC had supplied gasoline to humanitarian convoys. Now the fuel was only authorized for armoured patrols and escort vehicles.

Moreover, Moore was facing manpower-related problems as he had been sent into Bosnia with 500 fewer men than previous battle groups. He was well aware that he was dangerously thin on the ground and lacked the proper equipment to do his job properly.

Manpower problems had plagued the mission from the start. The army high command had committed itself to the concept of "Total Force," an amalgamation of regular and militia units to compensate for a chronic manpower shortage-and the former Yugoslavia would be a test case. From coast to coast, reserve regiments were called upon to select their best and brightest for a month's call-up and 700 volunteers had stepped forward. However, after extensive pre-selection screening and a month of field exercises, nearly half of were rejected as unsuitable. The remainder were inducted as riflemen, but field commanders including Moore, were reluctant to appoint any as NCO's or junior officers.

THE COUGAR

Canadian equipment also left much to be desired. On 18 June, a typical day, there were no serviceable Cougars available for the Visoko-Ksijelek patrol. Of the 24 tank-trainers on hand, 17 were listed as VOR – vehicle off road. There were no spare parts in the supply system and the Cougar fleet based in Canada had already been completely cannibalized. Although its 76mm main gun made the Cougar look like a tank, its low muzzle velocity had a range of barely 700 metres and without high-power scopes and night observation devices, the tank-trainers could not effectively monitor Serb activities. As added protection, the men had resorted to digging in .50 calibre machine guns beside stationary Cougars at checkpoints.

As the fighting intensified around Sarajevo, daily patrols became increasingly dangerous. Twelve peacekeepers were taken hostage on the Ilajas bridge by Serb militiamen, disarmed, beaten and threatened with death following a sniping incident and on the morning of 18 June, Corporal Daniel Gunther – a Vandoo – was killed by an aimed anti-tank rocket as he stood up in the driver's compartment of his APC to scan the surrounding countryside with binoculars. His crewmates were thrown to the ground by the explosion, which lifted the carrier a metre off the ground. As DND knew that the death of a peacekeeper would spark a public outcry and possible backlash against the government's continued commitment to operations in Yugoslavia, Gunther's death was "sanitized" and attributed to a stray mortar round. □

MAYHEM AND MERCY

Five months after Gunther's death, Lieutenant Colonel Moore wrote in his diary that "this is an historic day for 12RBC. Today the regiment conducted its first combat mission since the Second World War." Two days earlier, he had been informed that a massacre had taken place in the Muslim village of Stupni-Do when a retreating Croatian force had laid waste to every living thing in the village, scalping, raping, looting and impaling young children on stakes. As they converged on neighbouring Fornika. Moore dispatched Alpha squadron under the command of Major Randall Thorpe to the town. Eager to exact a measure of revenge for the victims of Stupni-Do, the Canadians engaged the Croats with rifle butts in a flurry of hand-to-hand scuffles, denying them access to the town.

FOOTNOTE ADDED TO ASSESSMENT

Although 12RBC had been declared operationally ready before leaving Canada, senior army officers knew otherwise. To relieve themselves of future liability for the deployment of Moore's understrength unit, they added a footnote to their assessment stating that "the battlegroup has neither the depth nor the resources to meet the demands of both the military and humanitarian tasks for which they are responsible." This became increasingly evident when Moore could spare only 33 personnel, a small platoon and a single medical section to feed and care for 560 mental patients at a hospital in Bakovici while simultaneously guarding the perimeter and escorting hospital staff to and from their daily work.

In mid-July, Moore was informed that during recent fighting between Croats and Serbs in the Canadian sector, two mental hospitals had been abandoned by their staff. At the hospital in Bakovici, the inmates were starving, covered in their own filth and had begun killing each other. At the nearby children's hospital in Drin, the situation was little better. After receiving a full report from Canadian troops, the UN command sent in a British medical team which spent ten days cleaning and treating wounds. It then became the Canadian's responsibility to secure and provision the two facilities, allowing the local staff to return to their jobs.

THE FALL OF SREBRENICA

After 12 desperate months, the strain on Moore's command was considerably relieved when a Dutch battalion took over from the Canadians in Srebrenica - with disastrous consequences. On 11 July 1995, disarmed and humiliated, the Dutch were swept aside by the Serbs in a renewed offensive. Ratko Mladic, the florid, shovel-faced Bosnian Serb army commander swaggered into town proclaiming: "Not Allah, not the United Nations, not anything can help you. I am your God." In the days to come as many as 7000 Muslim men perished in mass executions or ambushes along a 70 kilometre flight one survivor called "The Marathon of Death."

Many years ago, Rebecca West wrote in *Black Lamb and Grey Falcon*, her monumental study of the Balkans, that "only part of us is sane. Only part of us loves pleasure and the longer days of happiness, wants to live in a house that we built, that shall shelter those who come after us. The other half of us is nearly mad. It prefers the disagreeable to the agreeable, loves pain and its darker night despair, and wants to die in a catastrophe that will set back life to its beginnings and leave nothing of our house save its blackened foundations."

With great valour, Canadian servicemen and women rediscovered that truism in the horror that was Bosnia.

AUTHOR:
Bill Twatio

THE KRAJINA COLLAPSE

The collapse in Krajina in 1995 was embarrassing to the point of shameful for our army. Canadian soldiers witnessed terrible things as Serbs fell to a massive Croatian attack. Yet, despite fortress-like bunkers, the 2nd Battalion, Royal 22nd Regiment folded under the pressure and Canadians found themselves prisoners of the Croats.

IT HAD BEEN A blistering hot summer along the Dalmatian Coast, and Major Alain Rochette's soldiers had toiled without respite in the relentless heat. Rochette was the muscular, youthful officer in command of Charlie Company 2R22eR. They, along with the rest of Lieutenant Colonel Jacques Morneau's battle group, had replaced Lieutenant Colonel Skidmore's RCR contingent back in mid-April. The 750-strong Vandoo unit had inherited a formidable task manning a 70-kilometre-long stretch of the Krajina zone of separation. In turn, Rochette's Charlie Company alone had been tasked with manning 38 kilometres of "frontage" defined by seven isolated observation posts.

For months, the Croats had been building up for a major push into the disputed sector, but United Nations intelligence had confidently predicted there would be no offensive launched until "after the summer tourist season." With that time frame in mind, LCol. Morneau had set his men to work "bunkering in." Upon arrival, his Vandoos had been dismayed at the primitive conditions in which their RCR predecessors had lived and worked. While the observation posts were functional, they were by no means comfortable. Morneau and his men set about with a zeal to change that. The Vandoo commander made it his mission to protect his soldiers by not risking their lives needlessly. He and his officers felt that moving troops back and forth from their far-flung three-man posts was inefficient and called for an undue amount of risky transit. To correct this, Morneau had designed a nine-man, section-sized "citadel" mini-fort. Logistically, the construction of a string of complex structures would have been beyond the limited resources of a single battle group. However, with helpful administrative support from their commander, fellow Vandoo General Alain Forand, Morneau was able to obtain over 90 percent of UN Sector South's defensive stores.

Each of the "citadels" required between 30,000 to 60,000 sandbags along with a number of portable ATCO trailers. Like the old Fortress Louisbourg, the corners of the fort protruded to give the defenders an interlocking field of fire. Each section's M113

APC had a walled "garage" that formed the front door of the complex and allowed the .50 calibre machine-gun turret to be used effectively in an all-around defence. The observation tower itself had protected internal access to preclude the occupant from being exposed during shift rotations. Morneau recognized that "Vandoos don't like spiders and scorpions," so creature comforts for the citadels were an integral part of the design. Weight rooms, refrigerators, televisions and VCRs, electrical generators, chemical toilets, independent water supply and even barbecues were all standard items of kit for the 2R22eR OPs.

ABOVE:
Lieutenant Colonel Jacques Morneau returned early from his leave to negotiate the release of his surrendered soldiers. As the Croatian troops advanced, the Canadians had offered no opposition and had been quickly captured and disarmed. As the Croats engaged in a campaign of slaughter, rape and ethnic cleansing, Morneau's Vandoos sat helplessly in their bunkers.
OPPOSITE PAGE:
Soldiers of the Vandoos tear down their Bunkers after the Croatian offensive.

SHARED INTELLIGENCE

The massive construction project launched by Morneau did not go unnoticed. When U.S. intelligence satellites began detecting the series of large white obstacles in the Krajina zone of separation, it caused concern at the Pentagon. It had long been an open secret that the U.S. was sharing its intelligence data with the Croatian high command, but Morneau's citadels forced the issue into the open: By some "coincidence," the Croats, who possessed no space surveillance capability, somehow shared the same concerns as the U.S. authority over the massive bunkers. Morneau had to explain himself to NDHQ, who in turn placated the Pentagon with the assurance that these giant observation posts were intended for "self-protection" only. Morneau had even boasted that his citadels could withstand direct artillery hits.

On the afternoon of 3 August, Rochette hoped that his commanding officer's assessment was correct. Word had just been passed down to the UN peacekeepers to expect the Croat offensive to begin later that evening. Morneau, along with nearly 25 per cent of his battle group, were away on leave as a result of the previous UN intelligence reports. Even two "bricks" of Canadian JTF II operatives had been trying for months, albeit with only limited success, to monitor the Croatian build-up. No action was considered imminent. As a consequence, the UN and the Serbs were taken by complete surprise by the sudden Croat attack.

GERMAN MERCENARIES

At first light on 4 August, a massive artillery bombardment began all along the Krajina frontier. The Croatian guns pounded the Serb positions relentlessly with heavy artillery and mortars. Of the seven "citadel" posts under his command, Rochette had had two sited well forward in the zone of separation overlooking the Croatian front-lines. Shortly after the bombardment began, Croatian soldiers had approached these two observation posts to "recommend" that the peacekeepers "vacate" the bunkers. It was suggested that the Vandoos proceed into the nearby Croatian town of Zadar to wait out the offensive. The Canadian soldiers radioed back to Rochette with this news and asked for directions. It was also noted and passed on to Rochette's headquarters that these "Croatians" were, in fact, well-armed German mercenaries. During the radio exchanges between Rochette and his outposts, the major's intentions became moot. Additional "Croats" had quietly surrounded the citadels and then forced their way inside. Back at Charlie Company headquarters, they were puzzled and alarmed when one of the beleaguered detachment sergeants suddenly went off the air. What they had no way of knowing was that a "Croat" soldier had just placed a primed hand grenade against the NCO's head. The next message Rochette received was that his two units were en route to Zadar under Croat escort.

At the remaining Charlie Company observation posts, months of back-breaking physical labour were proving Morneau correct. Despite enduring a heavy Croat bombardment, the citadels easily withstood the shell splinters. One fortified bunker even sustained a direct hit from a 120 mm mortar round and emerged unscathed.

When Croatian forces threatened to seize a third observation post, Sierra-Charlie 43 (SC43), Rochette dispatched his meagre tactical reserve to reinforce the tiny garrison. The rapid reaction force took some artillery fire en route, but the arrival of these 17 soldiers in four APCs was enough to cause the Croat force to withdraw. Later that day, when the same scene was played out at Sierra-Charlie 50 (SC50), Rochette sent out his last mobile detachment from Recce Platoon.

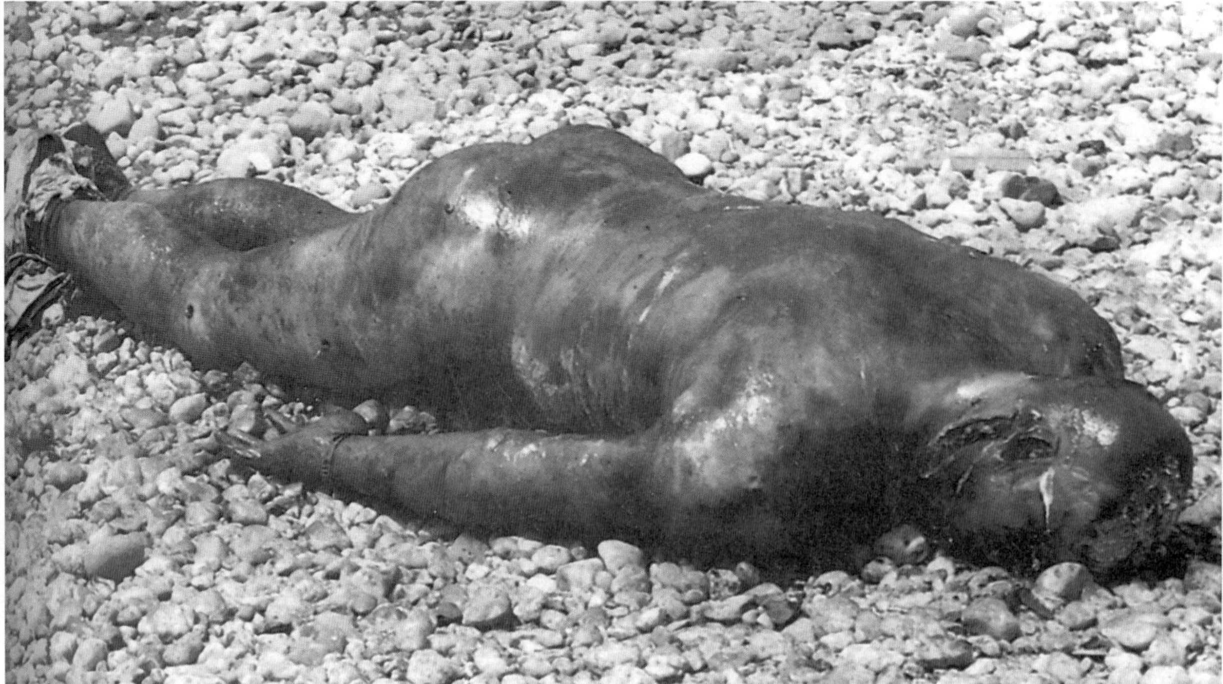

RIGHT: *This old Serb did not stand a chance against his Croat captors. The UN peacekeepers were powerless to stop the slaughter – they could simply record it.*

One of their APCs lost a track to an artillery shell and the disabled vehicle had to be abandoned. With the Recce Platoon reinforcements at SC50, the commander, Lieutenant Michel Godin, put on a show of force. The Vandoos cocked their M-72 rocket launchers and traversed their .50 calibre machine-guns onto the Croat forces. Godin requested and received a low-level "demonstration pass" from two French air force jets. It served to stabilize the situation temporarily.

VANDOOS CAPTURED

Back at SC43, the Croats had returned in force and managed to infiltrate the citadel bunker. With guns at their heads, the Vandoos, including Rochette's reserve force, headed into captivity in Zadar. Up on Sierra-Charlie 57 (SC57), Corporal J.R.D. Pacquin was in command of a five-man section. They had been shelled sporadically and had witnessed the Croats "neutralize" a nearby Serbian defensive position. When a Croatian captain approached SC57 and ordered the Canadians out, Cpl. Pacquin refused to move. The Croat officer then primed and threw a grenade. Fortunately for the Vandoos, the explosive bounced off a sandbag and landed among several Croat attackers. The blast wounded two of the Croats, but the remainder pressed inside and overpowered Pacquin's garrison.

By first light, on 5 August, the situation looked grim for Rochette's Charlie Company. Over two-thirds of his command were in Croatian captivity and all of his observation posts had been overpowered. His remaining 40 personnel at company headquarters were directly in the path of the main Croat axis of advance. At dawn the Croatian armoured columns and infantry had begun crossing the zone of separation and heading into the Serbian sector. Their attack was completely uncontested. Throughout the previous day and all through the night, immediately following the first Croat shells, the Serbians, soldiers and civilians had simply fled the Krajina in a mass exodus. Nearly 225,000 people had packed up whatever they could carry and headed toward the dubious safety of Bosnia.

A SITTING DUCK

Rochette did not know what sort of reaction to expect from the advancing Croats, and he still did not fully believe that the Serbs had left without at least a demonstration of defiance. With so few combat soldiers left, the Charlie Company HQ was a sitting duck, and Rochette had no delusions about defending his position. Throughout the night, his clerks and cooks had been hastily trained to drive APCs and the other assorted vehicles contained in the compound. It was Rochette's intention to man his perimeter with every able-bodied soldier as a show of force to the Croats. If they decided to force the issue, Rochette would mount up his vehicles and depart the camp, destroying whatever he could not drive away. Thankfully, the Croatian juggernaut rolled past the Canadian camp without incident and pressed on into the interior of the Krajina. They were anxious to catch up to the rearguard of the retreating Serb columns.

On 6 August Morneau arrived back in Croatia after cutting short his leave period. Following a hasty briefing, Morneau set out for the Croatian headquarters in Zadar to negotiate the release of his troops. All of the Vandoos were allowed to return to the main Canadian camp in Rastevec the next morning.

The experience of being overrun and held captive temporarily had eroded the morale of 2R22eR, but the next few weeks were to prove far more traumatic for the Vandoo peacekeepers. Immediately behind the front-line Croatian combat troops and German mercenaries, a large number of hard-line extremists had pushed into the

Krajina. Any Serbs who had failed to evacuate their property were systematically "cleansed" by roving death squads. Every abandoned animal was slaughtered and any Serb household was ransacked and torched. Many of these atrocities were carried out within the Canadian Sector, but as the peacekeepers were soon informed by the Croat authorities, the UN no longer had any formal authority in the region. Under the previous agreement, the UN protection force had been tasked with patrolling a zone of separation. It no longer existed. Technically, the Canadian force was now a powerless guest of the Croatian government. The Vandoos were not allowed to conduct patrols without prior approval of the Croat military. Locked down in their camp, the Canadians were well aware of the war crimes being committed all around them, but they were impotent to prevent or even record them.

Just following the offensive, Morneau had been conducting a reconnaissance of an abandoned Serb village when an elderly farmer attracted his attention. The old Serb was terrified at having been left behind and in fear for his life from the Croat invaders. As the Canadian commander talked to the farmer, a Croat military squad arrived and demanded that the Serb be placed in their custody. Morneau inquired as to their intentions and the Croats assured him all refugees were being taken to a camp in Zadar. Convinced of their sincerity, Morneau turned the trembling old man over to the Croat soldiers. Morneau had not gone two blocks when he heard several shots ring out. Racing back, he discovered the bullet-riddled body of the old man. The Croat troops stood nonchalantly, just a few metres away from the corpse. Furious beyond coherent thought, Morneau shouted that he would report the murder to the police. The Croats laughed and held up their metal badges, "We are the police."

REPRINTED FROM:
Tested Mettle:
Canada's Peacekeepers at War
AUTHORS:
Scott R. Taylor and Brian Nolan

ABOVE:
Over its first half century of existence, the United Nations symbol has become synonomous with peacekeeping missions.
(SCOTT R. TAYLOR)

THE FIRST FIVE DECADES

From a shaky start and relative impotence during the Cold War, the United Nations found itself ill-prepared to cope with the peacekeeping demands created by the collapse of the Soviet Union.

WRAPPED IN BLANKETS AND sleeping bags, hundreds of students bunked down outside the gates of Hunter College in the Bronx on the evening of 21 March 1946, vying for tickets to next morning's inaugural meeting of the United Nations Security Council. Statesmen and politicians may have been disillusioned and apprehensive as delegates filed into the gymnasium of the former women's school, but these young people still had the euphoric hope that this new organization would somehow, in the words of its Charter," save succeeding generations from the scourge of war."

Most would carry away a lasting impression of the intrepid interpreters who stood up after every speech to render versions in English, French and Russian as simultaneous translation was not yet available. They would remember the dignitaries too: Lester Pearson of Canada with his trade-mark bow tie; suave, white-haired Edward R. Stettinus, the American Secretary of State; dour, Andrei Gromyko of the Soviet Union and Secretary-General Trygve Lie, a clumsy and confused diplomat with the massive physique of an athlete who had run to seed in middle age, according to an aide, and "apt to go dark red in the face with rage and utter, jowls quivering, complex and ominous Norwegian oaths."

His frequent rages were understandable, however, for the United Nations was off to a shaky start; mired in an acrimonious debate about the continued Russian occupation of northern Iran. Its first days coincided with the advent of the Cold War and postwar rhetoric was turning barbed and mean. "The task of the Secretary-General," Lie soon complained, "is the most impossible job on earth."

THE STAGE

Six years later, there were no idealistic students on hand when the United Nations moved into its permanent home alongside the East River in central Manhattan. Long paralzyed by tensions between the Soviet Union and the United States, it had fallen into bad repute with the Americans, perhaps resentful that it was no longer an extension of the State Department and an instrument of American foreign policy. Nor were Lie's successors - Dag Hammarskjöld, U Thant, the former Nazi Kurt Waldheim, dismissed by some as "a headwaiter standing there as if he were wringing his hands on a towel, asking what he could do for the powerful countries," Perez de Cuellar, and Boutros Boutros-Ghali - held in much esteem.

At the height of the Cold War, the UN was seen as an hypocritical irritant with the General Assembly's Third World delegations, with Soviet acquiescence, blathering on day after day about Western Imperialism while turning a blind eye to the civil war in Nigeria, the blatant genocide of Hutus in Burundi and the unabashed evil of Idi Amin's rule in Uganda. "It is a stage on which certain melodramas are played out," a former American Ambassador said. "It's a simplistic sound and light show in which a country is identified as villain and victim."

Sarajevo 1992: One of the largest and most dangerous peacekeeping operations the UN ever embarked upon was the Protection Force deployed into the Balkans.

CANADA AND THE UN

Canada, on the other hand, considered membership in the UN as central to its foreign policy and would participate in every peackeeping operation. Peacekeeping in its present form had not been envisaged by the founders of the UN, rather it evolved as a response to the world's many messy quarrels. Since 1946, more than 80,000 Canadian servicemen and women have served around the world. They have monitored elections, participated in refugee assistance programmes, overseen prisoner of war exchanges and enforcedceasefires. As David Cox of Queen's University notes: "Peacekeeping which is really the most visible manifestation of Canada's international diplomacy, identifies Canada to Canadians. It makes them aware of our international orientation, of an orientation that is distinctively and perhaps uniquely Canadian."

A mood of optimism swept over the United Nations with the end of the Cold War, culminating with the award of a Nobel Peace Prize on 11 December 1988. The corridors rustled with new confidence and purpose. Twenty-four peacekeeping missions were launched in the 1990's, more than in the first 40 years of the organization's existence. The number of soldiers wearing the UN blue beret rose fourfold and the peacekeeping budget increased from $700 million to $2.8 billion.

Suddenly, there were requests for new new missions in the Persian Gulf, southern Africa, south-east Asia and Central America. For the first time, the UN moved away from its traditional peacekeeping role and began deploying forces as part of political settlements, in some instances helping to disarm belligerents. Missions became much more complex as the UN took on such varied tasks as preventive diplomacy in the earliest stages of conflict, intervention in civil wars, disarmament, verification of arms limitation agreements, anti-terrorism, drug interdiction and administrative and legal aid to civil powers.

The limits of such international efforts soon became apparent. The very complexity of many operations inevitably led to failure, undermining public confidence. The UN was unable to bring an end to ethnic cleansing in Bosnia and genocide in Rwanda. Nor could it cope with the growing number of "teacup wars," defined by Leslie Gelb in *Foreign Affairs* as "wars of deliberation, a steady run of uncivil civil wars sundering fragile, but functioning nation-states and gnawing at the well-being of stable nations."

The high expectations of the early 1990s finally came to grief in Somalia with the death of 18 American servicemen and the torture and murder of a Somali teenager, Shidane Arone, by Canadian paratroopers. Chastened, the United Nations – and the Canadian Armed Forces – wrestled with the nature of its role in a new world order.

THE BLUE BERET

The United Nations does not boast a glorious history. Only chauvinistic nation-states make that dubious claim. But the UN created Isreal, helped preserve the independence of South Korea, put an end to the colonial empires at Suez, ended the secession of Katanga in the Congo crisis of the early 1960s, lobbied for peace in Vietnam, supervised the end of the Iran-Iraq war, authorized thePersian Gulf War and kept the peace in Cyprus, Kashmir, El Salvador, Cambodia, Namibia, Mozambique and a host of other trouble spots. Its specialized agencies have fostered international development and it has been a tireless champion of human rights. Flawed it may be, but over the past 50 years it has served the world nobly and well. Proudly, Canadians continue to wear the blue beret.

AUTHOR: *Bill Twatio*

CANADA'S MILITARY AND PEACEKEEPING MISSIONS, 1947–2000

Home sweet home to a detachment of Canadian peacekeepers in Angola 1992. Note the maple leaf flag below the right window sill. *(DND PHOTO)*

KOREA (UNTCOK) 1947-1948

United Nations Temporary Commission on Korea. Two Canadian officers participated in the supervision of elections in Korea.

KOREA (UNSK) 1950- 54

UN Service in Korea. United Nations wartime service from 25 June 1950 until the armistice on 27 July 1953. Canada had the third largest contingent and 378 Canadian servicemen lost their lives in the fighting. (See pages 238)

KOREA (UNCMAC) 1953-PRESENT

UN Command Military Armistice Commission supervises 1953 armistice. This organization was created after the signing of the Korean War armistice. The Canadian Military Attaché in Korea is Canada's representative.

MIDDLE EAST (UNTSO) 1948- PRESENT

UN Truce Supervision Organization. This was the first peacekeeping operation established by the United Nations. UNTSO military observers (MOs) remain in the Middle East to monitor cease-fires, supervise armistice agreements, prevent isolated incidents from escalating and assist other UN peacekeeping operations in the region. It was established in June 1948 to assist the United Nations Mediator and the Truce Commission in supervising the observance of the truce in Palestine. Since then, UNTSO has performed various tasks entrusted to it by the Security Council, including the supervision of the general armistice agreements of 1949 and the observation of the cease-fire in the Suez Canal area and the Golan Heights following the Arab-Israeli War of June 1967. Canada's involvement began in 1954.

UNTSO assists and cooperates with the United Nations Disengagement Observer Force (UNDOF) on the Golan Heights in the Israel-Syria sector, and with the United Nations Interim Force in Lebanon (UNIFIL) in the Israel-Lebanon sector. Currently, 11 Canadian Forces personnel are assigned to UNTSO. Canadian tasks include the monitoring, supervision and observation of cease-fire agreements and providing observers on the Golan Heights and in South Lebanon. (See page 322)

INDIA, PAKISTAN (UNMOGIP) 1949-1996

UN Military Observer Group in India and Pakistan (Kashmir) supervised cease-fire between India and Pakistan. Initially Canada provided two UNMOs (withdrawn in 1979) but still provides annual aircraft support to move the headquarters.

INDOCHINA (ICSC) 1954-1974

International Commission for Supervision and Control, Laos and Vietnam (non-UN). Supervised withdrawal of French forces and ensure the cease-fire was obeyed. Assisted in restoring order as military forces transferred to their respective areas and controlled the entry of unauthorized military personnel and war materiel. Ceased to function in all areas 17 June 1974. In total, 133 Canadian military observers, staff officers and civilians served. This was the first non-UN peacekeeping mission Canada participated in. (See page 324)

EGYPT (UNEF) 1956-1967

United Nations Emergency Force. Supervised withdrawal of French, British and Israeli forces from Sinai. Secured and supervised the cessation of hostilities, including the withdrawal of French, Israeli and United Kingdom troops from Egyptian territory and, after the withdrawal, served as a buffer between Egyptian and Israeli forces. Canada provided a reconnaissance squadron, signal, engineer, air and land transport, maintenance, movement control, and an infantry platoon. HMCS *Magnificent*, an aircraft carrier, provided deployment transport. Ceased operations 17 June 1967. (See page 298)

LEBANON (UNOGIL) 1958

UN Observation Group in Lebanon. Ensure safety of Lebanese borders. Ensured there was no illegal infiltration of personnel or arms or other materiel across the borders. Ceased operations 9 December 1958. In total, 77 Canadians served as observers, staff officers and support personnel.

CONGO (ONUC) 1960-1964

UN Operation in the Congo. Ensured the

RIGHT: *After an explosion at a American base in Kuwait in July 1991, Captain Fred Kaustinen and his men came to the aid of their allies.* (COURTESY FRED KAUSTINEN)

withdrawal of Belgian Forces, assisted the Congolese government in maintaining law and order, territorial integrity and the political independence of the Congo. (See page 312)

WEST NEW GUINEA (UNSF) 1962-1963

UN Security Force in West New Guinea (West Irian). To maintain peace and security in the territory under the UNTEA established by Indonesia and the Netherlands, Canada's contribution included 13 officers and men of the RCAF and two float equipped Otter aircraft. Ceased operations 20 April 1963.

YEMEN (UNYOM) 1963-1965

UN Yemen Observation Mission monitored cessation of Saudi Arabian support and withdrawal of Egyptian forces from Yemen and observed and certified the implementation of the disengagement agreement between Saudi Arabia and the United Arab Republic (Egypt). Canada contributed observers, six RCAF fixed-wing aircraft and six helicopters with crews.

CYPRUS (UNFICYP) 1964-PRESENT

UN Peacekeeping Force in Cyprus. Its original mandate, in the interest of preserving international peace and security, was to use its best efforts to prevent reoccurrence of fighting and, as necessary, to contribute to the maintenance and restoration of law and order and a return to normal conditions. Since 1974 it was also to supervise the cease-fire line and maintain a buffer zone between the lines of the Cyprus National Guard and of the Turkish and Turkish/Cypriot forces. (See page 318)

DOMINICAN REPUBLIC (DOMREP) 1965-1966

Mission of the Representative of the Secretary-General. Observed cease-fire and oversaw the situation and reported on breaches of the cease-fire between the two rival factions involved in the civil war. Ceased operations 22 October 1966. Lieutenant Colonel Paul Mayer was the only Canadian to serve on this mission.

INDIA, PAKISTAN (UNIPOM) 1965-1966

UN India-Pakistan Observation Mission. Supervised the cease-fire along the India/Pakistan border except for the states of Jammu and Kashmir (see UNMOGIP), and the withdrawal of all armed personnel to the positions they held before 5 August 1965. At its peak the Canadian contribution of 112 was composed of primarily military observers and staff. Ceased operations 22 March 1966.

NIGERIA (OTN) 1968-1970

Observer Team to Nigeria (non-UN). Supervised cease-fire. Authorized in September 1968 and to observe the Nigerian Armed Forces to ascertain if they were following their own code of conduct and to investigate charges that the military had committed genocide. A total of six Canadian senior and general Army officers participated. Ceased operations in 1970.

SOUTH VIETNAM (ICCS) 1973

International Commission for Control and Supervision (non-UN). Supervised truce. Authorized in January 1973 to monitor the cease-fire in South Vietnam, the withdrawal of US troops, the exchange of prisoners; also ensured no build up of military equipment. Over 250 CF personnel and 50 from External Affairs participated. Canada ceased operations in July 1973.
(See page 327)

EGYPT, ISRAEL (UNEF II) 1973-1979

UN Emergency Force II. Supervised the cease-fire between Egyptian and Israeli forces following the 18 January 1974 and 8 September 1974 agreements. Also supervised the redeployment of both Egyptian and Israeli forces, manned and controlled the buffer zone. Canada provided in excess of 1000 logistics troops and staff officers. Ceased operations 24 July 1979.

SYRIA (GOLAN HEIGHTS) (UNDOF) 1974-PRESENT

UN Disengagement Observer Force. Supervise the cease-fire between Israel and Syria and to supervise their forces on either side of a buffer zone in accordance with the Agreement on Disengagement between Israel and Syria. Canada initially provided 226 military personnel when the mission was launched in 1974, but the Canadian contingent has since been scaled down to 187. Canadian Forces personnel serve on the Golan Heights between Israel and Syria, providing second-line logistic support to the force, primarily supply, engineering and

A UN patrol boat approaches a passenger ferry on the Mekong River, Cambodia.
(SCOTT TAYLOR, ESPRIT DE CORPS)

maintenance. Canada also supplies communications detachments to all UNDOF units in addition to first line support to all Canadian Forces personnel. (See page 322)

LEBANON (UNIFIL) 1978-PRESENT
UN Interim Force in Lebanon. To confirm the withdrawal of Israeli forces from Southern Lebanon, to restore peace and security and assist the Government of Lebanon in maintaining authority in the area. From March to October 1978, Canada provided a signal unit and movement control from UNEF II before returning to their parent formation.

SINAI (MFO) 1986-PRESENT
Multinational Force and Observers (non-UN). To prevent violation of Camp David accords. Supervise the withdrawal of Israeli forces from the Sinai and to monitor Egyptian and Israeli compliance with the 1979 peace treaty. Canada provides up to 27 personnel in support and staff positions in the Sinai. From March 1986 until 1990, Canada also deployed a squadron of helicopters.

AFGHANISTAN (UNGOMAP) 1988-1990
UN Good Offices Mission in Afghanistan and Pakistan. Supervised cease-fire and withdrawal of Soviet forces from Afghanistan. To assist the Secretary-General's representative in ensuring the agreements relating to Afghanistan were upheld, and to investigate and report on violations of the agreements. In total five Canadian military observers served on this successful mission. Ceased operations 15 March 1990.

AFGHANISTAN AND PAKISTAN (OSGAP) 1988
Office of the Secretary-General in Afghanistan and Pakistan. Canada provided one observer to assist in planning of future peacekeeping operations in Afghanistan.

IRAN, IRAQ (UNIIMOG) 1988-1991
UN Iran-Iraq Military Observer Group. Verified, confirmed and supervised the cease-fire and withdrawal of all forces to the internationally recognized boundaries following the Iran-Iraq War. In addition to UNMOs, Canada provided a signals unit to UNIIMOG. Up to 525 Canadian Forces personnel were deployed to this mission at any given time. Ceased operations 20 February 1991.

NAMIBIA (UNTAG) 1989-1990
UN Transition Assistance Group. Assisted the Special Representative of the Secretary-General to ensure early independence of Namibia through elections under the supervision and control of the UN. Canada contributed logistics support, civilian police monitors and electoral supervisors throughout the duration of UNTAG. Up to 301 Canadian Forces personnel were deployed to UNTAG at any given time. Ceased operations 21 March 1990.

NICARAGUA (ONUVEN) 1989
UN Observer Mission for the Verification of the Electoral Process in Nicaragua. Five Canadian observers were deployed to observe elections.

CENTRAL AMERICA (ONUCA) 1989-1992
UN Observer Group in Central America. Verified compliance to Esquipulas Agreement. Participated in demobilization of the Nicaraguan resistance forces, and monitored their cease-fire and repatriation. Canada provided UNMOs and a helicopter detachment from December 1989 to January 1992. Up to 174 Canadian Forces personnel were deployed at any given time. Ceased operations 31 January 1992.

NAMIBIA (UNTAG) 1989-1990
UN Transition Assistance Group, Namibia. Assisted in transition to independence. Supported the Special Representative of the Secretary-General to ensure early independence of Namibia through elections under the supervision and control of the UN. Ceased operations 21 March 1990.

GULF WAR (1990-1991)
On the night of 1 August 1990, Iraqi troops deployed along Iraq's southeastern border, mobilizing and attacking Iraq's neighbour, the tiny emirate of Kuwait. Kuwaiti forces put up little resistance and, within a day, Iraqi troops occupied the entire country. This act of aggression brought about immediate reaction from the United States, the United Nations, and from countries around the world. With the support of the UN, the U.S. coordinated a diplomatic and military effort to force Saddam Hussein, the leader of Iraq, to withdraw from Kuwait. The dictator responded to the UN demands by ordering his troops to assume defensive positions along Iraq's borders. In an effort to force Iraq to stand down, the Americans, in coordination with the UN, spearheaded the forma-

tion of an international military coalition. Within a week, coalition forces began to mobilize. Operational flying patrols were put in place, ships set sail for the region and hundreds of thousands of troops were stationed in countries surrounding Iraq. Within days of Iraq's invasion, Canadian Prime Minister Brian Mulroney agreed to Canada's participation in the UN-backed coalition. On 11 August, it was announced that Canada's initial contribution would be two destroyers and a supply ship. On 14 September, Canada dispatched a squadron of CF-18 fighter jets to the area. Tensions in the area increased after November 29th when the UN Security Council agreed to a UN resolution, the last of twelve, authorizing the coalition countries to take appropriate action, including military force, to push Iraq out of Kuwait territory after 15 January 1991. Iraq still refused to back down and coalition forces began their attacks the night after the deadline passed. (See pages 352)

AFGHANISTAN, PAKISTAN (OSGAP) 1990-1993

Office of the Secretary-General in Afghanistan and Pakistan (non-UN). Canada contributed a military advisor to OSGAP from 1990 to 1992.

HAITI (ONUVEH) 1990-1991

UN Observers for the Verification of Elections in Haiti. Monitored 1990 elections. Its mandate was to observe the electoral process in Haiti, assist in electoral security plans and observe its implementation. Canada provided eleven UNMOs to this mission. Ceased operations February 1991. (See page 397)

ANGOLA (UNAVEM II) 1991-1994

UN Angola Verification Mission. Established in May 1991 to verify the arrangements agreed to by the Government of Angola and the Uniao Nacional para a Independência Total de Angola, for monitoring the cease-fire and the Angolan police during the cease-fire period, and to observe and verify elections, in accordance with the Peace Accords. Canada contributed up to 15 UNMOs during that period.

OPPOSITE PAGE:
A Canadian Airborne Regiment trooper goes on a foot patrol in Somalia in 1993 as part of UNITAF. *(DND PHOTO)*

RIGHT:
British armoured cars roll along the Green Line, Cyprus 1994. *(DND PHOTO)*

BALKANS (ECMM) 1991-1994

European Community Monitor Mission (non-UN). Monitoring cease-fires. Maximum of 15 military observers were deployed by Canada.

CAMBODIA (UNAMIC) 1991-1992

UN Advance Mission in Cambodia. Monitored cease-fire and provided land mine awareness. Canada provided up to seven UNMOs between November 1991 and February 1992.

EL SALVADOR (ONUSAL) 1991-1995

UN Observer Mission in El Salvador. Monitored human rights and progress toward military reform, peace. Formed to monitor the cease-fire in El Salvador following 12 years of civil war. Canada contributed up to 55 CF personnel to ONUSAL at any given time, beginning in July 1991. Canada's last five UNMOs were withdrawn in August 1994.

IRAQ, KUWAIT (UNIKOM) 1991-PRESENT

UN Iraq-Kuwait Observation Mission. Post-Gulf War. To monitor the Knor Abdullah waterway between Iraq and Kuwait as well as a demilitarized zone ten kilometers into Iraq and five kilometers into Kuwait, to deter violations of the boundary, carry out surveillance and observe any hostile action. There are four CF members currently serving as United Nations Military Observers (UNMOs) in this observer mission. (See page 357)

IRAQ, KUWAIT 1991-PRESENT

Gulf War Allied Coalition No-Fly-Zone Over Northern and Southern Iraq (non-UN). As part of Canada's commitment to NORAD, approximately 45 CF personnel are assigned to the United States' Air Force Airborne Warning and Control System (AWACS). At any given time, a small number of these CF personnel may be deployed for the monitoring of the no-fly zones over Iraq.

IRAQ (UNSCOM) 1991-PRESENT

UN Special Commission. Post-Gulf War. To inspect and, if necessary, destroy Iraq's biological and chemical weapons as part of the peace accord following the Iraqi invasion of Kuwait. Up to 12 Canadian Forces specialists are authorized to participate in UNSCOM. There are currently three CF members assigned to UNSCOM, two of whom are posted to the UN Headquarters in New York and one who is in Iraq as part of an UNSCOM weapons inspection team.

WESTERN SAHARA (MINURSO) 1991-1994

UN Mission for the Referendum in the West-

ern Sahara. Monitored cease-fire. With the full support of the Security Council and with the full cooperation of the two parties, effected a cessation of all hostile acts. Canada provided observers and movement control personnel. A maximum of 35 Canadian Forces personnel served at any given time as UNMOs, movement control and staff personnel in the Western Sahara from May 1991 to June 1994.

BALKANS (UNPROFOR) 1992-1996

UN Peace Force (UN Protection Force, UN Confidence Restoration Operation). UNPROFOR I, commencing in 1992, involved the protection of Croat and Serbian minorities within Croatia. UNPROFOR II was formed to protect convoys in support of the UN High Commissioner for Refugees and for peace keeping duties in Macedonia. Operation SHARP GUARD was the naval blockade of Yugoslavia in the Adriatic Sea. Canadian involvement included HMCS *Halifax* and HMCS *Toronto*. (See page 362)

CAMBODIA (UNTAC) 1992-1993

UN Transitional Authority in Cambodia. Formed to monitor the cease-fire in Cambodia. Approximately 240 CF personnel served at any given time with UNTAC for the duration of this mission. The Canadian contingent included a 30-person naval observer element, with the majority of the CF personnel deployed with UNTAC providing transport services to the mission. In addition, there were approximately 121 Canadian civilians in Cambodia, with 67 assigned in various capacities to UNTAC. Approximately 50 electoral observers also served.

BALKANS (UNCOE) 1992-1994

United Nations Committee of Experts. Established by the UN Security Council, UNCOE's mandate was to report on the evidence of grave breaches of the Geneva Conventions and other violations of international humanitarian law committed in the territory of the former Yugoslavia. Canada provided up to seven legal and military police officers to UNCOE at any given time.

MOZAMBIQUE (ONUMOZ) 1992–1994

United Nations Operation in Mozambique. Created to monitor and verify cease-fire arrangements, the separation and concentration of forces, their demobilization, the collection, storage and destruction of weapons, the complete withdrawal of foreign forces, and the disbanding of private and irregular armed groups. Canada provided up to four UNMOs to ONUMOZ from February 1993 to December 1994.

SOMALIA (UNITAF) 1992-1993

United Task Force (non-UN). Involving the airlift of supplies and humanitarian relief, the Canadian component (designation Operation DELIVERANCE), involved deployment of a 900-man contingent, HMCS *Preserver* and Hercules transport aircraft. On 30 May 1993, after six months, the Canadian contingent handed their responsibilities over to UNOSOM forces from other countries and returned to Canada. (See pages 390)

SOMALIA (UNOSOM) 1992-1993

UN Operation in Somalia. Headquarters personnel. Involved follow-up of humanitarian assistance after the close out of UNITAF. UNOSOM ended 28 February 1995 as the last United Nations troops were withdrawn from the country. While the impact of the earlier famine had been generally overcome, no political success was gained by the mission and Somalia continued its internal strife with no central government having emerged.

LIBERIA (UNOMIL) 1993- 1997

United Nations Observer Mission in Liberia Established to supervise and monitor the Cotonou Peace Agreement. Brigadier General Ian Douglas was the only Canadian to participate in the UN's early technical reconnaissance of Liberia in 1993. Canada did not, however, participate further in UNOMIL.

HAITI (UNMIH) 1993-1996

UN Mission in Haiti. Implemented the Governors Island Agreement. UNMIH's mandate was to assist the democratic Government of Haiti in sustaining a secure and stable environment, protect international personnel and key installations, to create and train a Haitian National Police Force and to provide electoral support. Canada provided up to 750 military personnel and approximately 100 civilian police at any given time to UNMIH between October 1994 and June 1996. (See pages 397)

ADRIATIC SEA 1993-1996

Enforcement of United Nations Embargo of the former Yugoslavia (non-UN). The purpose of this mission was to enforce UN-imposed maritime sanctions against the warring factions in the former Yugoslavia. Canada contributed a frigate.

BOSNIA-HERZEGOVINA (OPERATION DENY FLIGHT) 1993-PRESENT

The purpose of this NATO-led operation is to enforce compliance of the no-fly zone over Bosnia-Herzegovina. Canada contributes approximately 12 specialists to the crews of NATO AWACs aircraft. Operation DENY FLIGHT is now simply referred to as the air component of SFOR.

THE NETHERLANDS (UN ICTY) 1993-PRESENT

UN International Criminal Tribunal for the former Yugoslavia. Assist in preparing cases against people accused of war crimes in the former Yugoslavia.

RIGHT:
Observer mission in Pakistan: wreckage of a Canadian Twin Otter aircraft that was strafed at Rawalpindi airport.
(DND PHOTO)

RWANDA, UGANDA (UNOMUR) 1993-1994

UN Observer Mission Uganda-Rwanda. Verified that military supplies did not cross border into Rwanda. Established under UN Security Council Resolution 846, UNOMUR was given the mandate to monitor the border between Uganda and Rwanda and verify that no military assistance – lethal weapons, ammunition and other material of possible military use – was being provided across this border. While the tragic turn of events in Rwanda in April 1994 prevented UNOMUR from fully implementing its mandate, the Observer Mission played a useful role as a confidence-building mechanism in the months following the conclusion of the Arusha Peace Agreement and during UNAMIR's initial efforts to defuse tensions between the Rwandan parties and to facilitate the implementation of that agreement. Canada provided three UNMOs between June and October 1993.

RWANDA (UNAMIR) 1993-1996

UN Assistance Mission in Rwanda. Assisted interim government with transition measures leading to elections and commission of inquiry on arms trafficking. The mission was established in October 1993 to monitor a cease-fire in Rwanda. On 6 April 1994, the tragic deaths of the presidents of both Rwanda and Burundi in an aircraft crash sent the country of Rwanda into a frenzy of slaughter and civil war. Since that day, UNAMIR became involved in humanitarian aid, its first supply flight taking place on 11 April 1994. Established under UN Security Council Resolution 918, UNAMIR contributed to the security and protection of displaced persons, refugees and civilians at risk in Rwanda. UNAMIR also provided security and support for the distribution of relief supplies and humanitarian aid, and was authorized to take action, in self-defence, against persons or groups who threatened protected sites and populations, as well as UN and other humanitarian personnel. Canada participated in UNAMIR from December 1993 to February 1996, providing a logistics support unit of up to 112 CF personnel at any given time to the total UN force of approximately 6100. (See pages 393)

OPERATION SCOTCH 1994-1995

Started on 11 April 1994 this operation involved 312 Hercules C-130 flights to Kigali, Rwanda or to Goma, Zaire to deploy 1 Canadian Division Headquarters and Signal Regiment to UNAMIR. The main body of the Regiment returned home at the end of January 1995.

OPERATION PASSAGE 1994

2 Field Ambulance was deployed for humanitarian flights for United Nations High Commission in Refugees (UNHCR) or CIDA from April to October 1994. 8 Air Communications and Control Squadron (8ACCS) was deployed to Nairobi, Kenya and Kigali. On 16 September 1994, the Kigali airport was turned over to civilian control and, by 28 September 8, ACCS had returned to Canada.

OPERATION CADENCE 1994

Multinational Observers Group Dominican Republic (non-UN). Canadian officers were deployed from 1 to 30 September 1994 on Operation CADENCE to assist officers from Argentina, Brazil and the United States in the patrolling of the Dominican Republic/Haiti border. Even though sanctions against Haiti were significantly tightened in May 1994, a great deal of material was being smuggled across the border between Haiti and the Dominican Republic, thus avoiding the naval interdiction operations. In an effort to stem the tide of smuggled material into Haiti, the U.S. initiated a Multinational Observer Group (MOG) on the border between Haiti and the Dominican Republic in August 1994. Canada contributed 15 observers to this U.S.-led force of 88 personnel. The operation was suspended following the permissive landing of American forces into Haiti on 18 September 1994.

OPERATION FORWARD ACTION 1994

UN blockade of Haiti. Canadian participants included HMCS *Terra Nova* and HMCS *Kootenay.* Canadians made 9424 hailings, 1388 armed boardings and diverted 119 ships from making proscribed deliveries to Haiti.

NOGORNO-KARABAKHH (OSCE) 1995-1996

Organization for Security and Cooperation

ABOVE:
NATO troops enter Kosovo 1999.
(SCOTT TAYLOR/ESPRIT DE CORPS)

in Europe (non-UN). Peacekeeping mission in Nogorno-Karabakhh. The purpose of this mission was to monitor the cease-fire negotiated by the OSCE. This was not a UN or NATO endeavor. Canada contributed three staff officers.

BALKANS (UNPREDEP) 1995-1999
UN Preventive Deployment Force. UN Security Council renewed the mandate of this mission until February 1999. The role of UNPREDEP was to prevent any developments that could undermine confidence and stability in the Former Republic of Macedonia or threaten its territory. One Canadian Forces officer served in UNPREDEP as a UN military observer.

BALKANS (IFOR) 1996-1997
NATO Implementation Force in Bosnia-Herzegovina (non-UN). The purpose of IFOR was to enforce compliance by the warring parties in the former Yugoslavia with the Dayton Peace Accord. Canada's contribution consisted of a brigade headquarters, an infantry company, an armoured squadron, an engineer squadron, a military police platoon, and support personnel, for a total of approximately 1030 personnel. (See page 412)

BALKANS (SFOR) 1997-PRESENT
NATO Stabilization Force (non-UN). Responding to United Nations Security Council Resolution 1088 (passed 12 December 1996), the North Atlantic Council authorized the NATO-led operation to support the further implementation of the Dayton Peace Accord. SFOR's mission is to provide continued military presence to deter renewed hostilities and to stabilize and consolidate the peace in Bosnia-Herzegovina in order to contribute to a secure environment for the ongoing civil implementation plans. The current strength of the Canadian contribution to SFOR is approximately 1666. The Canadian contingent includes a mechanized infantry battalion group, helicopter squadron, national support and command elements, and engineer design and works team. The Canadian battalion group is under the operational control of British division in Sector South-West. Canada is also providing 43 CF personnel to various multinational staff positions in SFOR headquarters and is participating in the NATO Multinational Air Movement Detachment (MAMDRIM) that was established to support SFOR in Bosnia-Herzegovina. The Canadian Air contingent in MAMDRIM (CACIM) provides an Airlift Control Element (ALCE) in Rimini, Italy consisting of approximately 12 persons and supporting equipment. (See page 412)

BALKANS (UNMOP) 1996-PRESENT
UN Mission of Observers in Prevlaka. UNMOP's mission is to monitor the situation in Prevlaka at the southern tip of Croatia bordering with the Federal Republic of Yugoslavia. One Canadian Forces officer is deployed as a UN military observer.

BALKANS (UNMIBH) 1996-PRESENT
UN Mission in Bosnia-Herzegovina. UNMIBH is the mission that grew out of the Dayton Peace Accord, having as its main components the UN International Police Task Force (IPTF), Civil Affairs, and Mine Action Centre (UNMAC). IPTF, as the civilian police component, monitors the compliance by competent authorities of the two entities with civic and human rights standards as far as policing is concerned, and provides guidance for police structures and operations. The overall aim of the mission is to promote reconciliation between civilians of all communities, to monitor political developments and inform the Secretary-General, the Security Council and the High Representative of activities, and to assist in clearing the country of mines. Canada contributes a lieutenant colonel to the position of military staff and a liaison officer in the office of the UN Coordinator for Bosnia-Herzegovina, and also provides six Canadian Forces personnel to the Mine Action Center (UNMAC).

BALKANS (UNMACBH) 1996-1997
UN Mine Action Centre, Bosnia-Herzegovina (See above)

HAITI (UNSMIH) 1996-1997
UN Support Mission in Haiti. UNSMIH was established to assist the Government of Haiti in maintaining a secure and stable environment, to support the Government in the professionalization and training of the Haitian national police and to provide support

in the coordination of the activities of other UN agencies to promote institution building, national reconciliation and economic rehabilitation. Canada provided civilian police and up to 750 military personnel at any given time to UNSMIH for the duration of its mandate. (See page 397)

ZAIRE (MNF) 1996

Multinational Force for Eastern Zaire (non-UN). African Great Lakes Multinational Force was to facilitate the return of humanitarian organizations, ensure the effective delivery of aid, and the repatriation of refugees. The purpose of the mission was to bring humanitarian aid to refugees in camps in eastern Zaire, but the refugees returned to Rwanda before the mission was established. Canada contributed about 354 personnel, mostly medics, and some infantry for security.

GUATEMALA (MINUGUA) 1997

UN Verification Mission in Guatemala. Verified implementation of human rights agreements and fulfillment of definitive cease-fire. Canada provided civilian police and 15 Spanish-speaking UNMOs to this mission between February and May 1997. Two RCMP officers were deployed to the follow-on mission in 1997.

HAITI (UNTMIH) AUG 1997-NOV 1997

UN Transition Mission in Haiti. UNTMIH was commanded by Canadian Brigadier General Robin Gagnon and was the final mission in Haiti with a military component. The military's mandate was to ensure the safety and freedom of movement of UN personnel involved with supporting and contributing to the professionalization of the Haitian National Police. Canada contributed up to 750 personnel at any given time to UNTMIH for the duration of the mission. (See pages 397)

HAITI (MIPONUH) 1997-2000

UN Police Operation in Haiti. Canada provided 22 civilian police and 24 police trainers. UN Security Council Resolution 1141 (passed 28 November 1997) established MIPONUH as the follow-on mission for the UN Transition Mission in Haiti (UNTMIH). The Department of National Defence provided six wheeled armoured personnel carriers to this mission as well as Canadian Forces driving instructors and Canadian Forces vehicle technicians. (See page 397)

RIGHT: *Troops of the Royal 22nd Regiment participate in Canada's first operational assault landing since WWII: East Timor, 1999.*

BOSNIA-HERZEGOVINA (OSCE) 1997

(OP Mentor/Bosnia-Herzegovina). The parties to the Dayton Peace Accord concluded an Agreement on Confidence and Security and Cooperation in Europe. This agreement has opened the way for the implementation of Regional Stabilization Measures on arms control. As part of the agreement on CSBMs (article IV of the Dayton Accord), Canada participated, when needed, in inspections for a week at a time.

OPERATION CONNECTION 1998-PRESENT

Secondment to CARE Canada in Kenya (non-UN). One Canadian Forces officer is at any given time, on secondment to CARE Canada in Kenya, participating in a humanitarian assistance program.

CENTRAL AFRICAN REPUBLIC (MINURCA) 1998-2000

United Nations Mission in the Central African Republic. UN Security Council Resolution 1159 (passed 27 March 1998) established the Mission des Nations Unies en République Centrafricaine, or MINURCA, and gave it a three-month mandate, beginning 15 April 1998. MINURCA's mandate was to assist the Central African Republic's national security forces in maintaining law and order, and in protecting key facilities in Bangui. MINURCA also supervised the disposal of weapons retrieved in the disarmament program, and ensured the security and freedom of movement of UN personnel as well as the safety and security of UN property. This mandate was extended until February 2000. Canada contributed a French-speaking signals unit to MINURCA. Its tasks included the operation of radio communications equipment at UN headquarters operations centre on a full-time basis, and the provision of communications between the force headquarters and subordinate contingents. There were about 47 CF personnel assigned to this mission.

ARABIAN GULF 1998

Operation Determination (non-UN). On 10 February 1998, the Canadian government announced that it would provide a Canadian Patrol Frigate and two C-130 Hercules air-to-air refueling aircraft as its contribution to the United States-led, multinational coalition force in the Arabian Gulf. In May 1998, with the continued improvement in the situation, the government announced the reduction of Canadian Forces presence in the Gulf. HMCS *Toronto* left the Gulf in June 1998 while the two Hercules returned to Canada in May 1998. (See page 416)

KOSOVO (KFOR) 1998-PRESENT

Kosovo Force NATO (non-UN). KFOR's mandate comes from a military technical agreement signed by NATO and Yugoslav commanders on 9 June 1999 and from UN Security Council Resolution 1244 of 12 June 1999, which followed a 78-day air campaign. Responsibilities cover the following areas:

- deterring renewed hostility and threats against Kosovo by Yugoslav and Serb forces;
- establishing a secure environment and ensuring public safety and order;

RIGHT:
After the Soviet withdrawal from Afghanistan, Canada provided instructors to teach the Afghan people how to recognize and disable the thousands of anti-personnel landmines left behind. Canada has continued this role throughout numerous countries that are recovering from wars, including Cambodia and the Balkan states.
(DND PHOTO)

FAR RIGHT:
Afghani rebels in 1991.

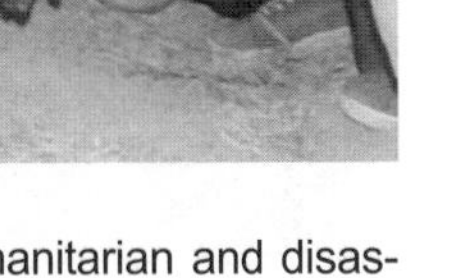

- demilitarizing the Kosovo Liberation Army (KLA);
- supporting the international humanitarian effort; and
- coordinating with, and supporting, the international civil presence, the UN Interim Administration Mission in Kosovo (UNMIK). (See pages 421)

KOSOVO (OSCE) 1999 -PRESENT

Organization for Security and Cooperation in Europe Kosovo Mission (non-UN). The OSCE Mission in Kosovo was established by the OSCE Permanent Council on 1 July 1999 (Permanent Council Decision no. 305). Since then the OSCE Mission has taken the lead role in matters relating to institution- and democracy building, rule of law, and human rights in the province. The Mission forms a distinct component of the United Nations Interim Administration Mission in Kosovo (UNMIK).

KOSOVO (UMMIK) 1999-PRESENT

UN Mission in Kosovo. Mission will:

- promote the establishment of substantial autonomy and self-government in Kosovo;
- perform basic civilian administrative functions;
- facilitate a political process to determine Kosovo's future status;
- support the reconstruction of key infrastructure and humanitarian and disaster relief;
- maintain civil law and order;
- promote human rights;
- assure the safe and unimpeded return of all refugees and displaced persons to their homes in Kosovo.

OPERATION QUADRANT 1999-PRESENT

Designates Canada's overall participation in international organization missions in Kosovo. The seven CF members deployed on Operation QUADRANT fulfil positions as part of:

- the UN Mission Interim Administration in Kosovo (UNMIK); and
- KFOR headquarters.

EAST TIMOR (INTERFET) 1999-2000

International Force East Timor (non-UN). A multinational force under a unified command structure, with the following tasks:

- restore peace and security in East Timor;
- protect and support UNAMET (the UN mission in East Timor) in carrying out its tasks,
- within force capabilities, to facilitate humanitarian assistance operations; and
- authorize the states participating in the multinational force to take all necessary measures to fulfil this mandate.

Canada's one tour commitment consisted of HMCS *Protecteur* (a supply ship/tanker), two Sea King helicopters, a company group from the R22eR, an engineer troop, two C-130 Hercules transport aircraft with support teams, and a national support element. Canada withdrew its troops upon handover to UNTAET (see below). (See page 423)

EAST TIMOR (UNTAET) 2000

UN Transitional Authority East Timor. UNTAET's mandate encompasses the following elements:

- provide security and maintain law and order throughout the territory of East Timor;
- establish an effective administration;
- assist in the development of civil and social services;
- ensure the coordination and delivery of humanitarian assistance, rehabilitation and development assistance;
- support capacity-building for self-government;
- assist in the establishment of conditions for sustainable development.

Immediately following the establishment of UNTAET, the mission established its headquarters in Dili and began the deployment of personnel. The handover of command of military operations from INTERFET to UNTAET was completed on 28 February 2000.

AUTHOR: *Howard Michitsch*

WITH THE CANADIANS IN SOMALIA

A first-hand account of a former military officer who visited the Canadian Airborne battlegroup in Belet Uen.

ABOVE:
An Airborne soldier mans an observation post in the northern area of operations. These paratroopers were not sent in as peacekeepers but rather they were to enforce a cease-fire. (DND PHOTO)

MOGADISHU, THE CAPITAL OF Somalia, isn't the worst place on the planet, but in 1993 it was not far from it. There was no governmental structure, save that due to clan allegiance or imposed by the allied coalition forces. There was no commerce or employment, unless you count collecting garbage and refuse to sell for scrap commerce. There was no electricity or running water, and people lived in whatever makeshift shelter they could find; either in a ruined, windowless building or in a hut made out of corrugated tin or material salvaged from shot-up buildings. There was enough food for everyone, but that was only due to the efforts of the relief agencies and coalition forces, and not because the city or country could feed itself. Not everyone got enough to eat, however, because there were still those too sick or too weak to claim their fair share. The medical aid posts (one could call them hospitals) were under-staffed and suffered from a lack of everything that we take for granted in a hospital; not the least of which were clean sheets and adequate supplies. There was no banking, no foreign exchange, no municipal services and no ambulance or fire service, Conditions throughout the rest of southern Somalia were little better – some places were blessed with a little clean water or some arable land, but everywhere the governmental structure was gone and humans lived in their tribal or clan groups with lawlessness always close by. If it had not been for the presence of the coalition military forces, conditions would have been even worse, because the relief agencies and other non-governmental organisations could only work in the security that the military provides.

WHEN THE CANADIAN SOLDIERS FIRST MOVED IN, INDIVIDUAL SOMALIS COULD BE SEEN MAKING CAREFUL NOTE OF THE LOCATION AND TYPE OF HEAVY MACHINE GUNS AND OTHER WEAPONS THAT THE CANADIANS WERE POSITIONING.

MISSION LIKE NO OTHER

The Canadian Forces played a large part in the international military mission in Somalia, dubbed Operation DELIVERANCE. That mission in Somalia was like no other that our Forces had taken on in recent memory. Our personnel and our equipment on the ground in Somalia faced hardships due to the climate, the terrain and the local political conditions that we here in Canada could ill-imagine. Nearly 1300 Canadian soldiers, sailors and air force personnel were deployed in Africa on this operation. The air force contingent was based in Nairobi where they flew C-130 Hercules transport aircraft into Somalia daily. The navy provided a base-at-sea in the form of HMCS *Preserver* – a supply ship off the Somali coast in the Indian Ocean. HMCS *Preserver* also flew three Sea King helicopters that were used for reconnaissance, resupply, personnel transport and medical evacuation. The army deployed approximately 850 soldiers from the Canadian Airborne Regiment Battle Group to the Human Relief Sector based on the town of Belet Uen (pronounced "Bel-a-Twain"). In March, the Canadian military presence was augmented by a flight of Twin Huey tactical transport helicopters from 427 Squadron at Camp Petawawa in Ontario.

The temperature on the first day that I was in Belet Uen reached 55° Celsius in the sun by mid-day. The Airborne Regiment soldiers had set up a large camp on the eastern side of Belet Uen. The airfield where the Canadian and other planes land operated from the opposite side of the town from the Airborne

ABOVE: *The Canadian Battle Group did not stay long at Mogadishu airport before deploying forward into Belledoggle.* (DND PHOTO)

Regiment camp, and so all military traffic had to pass through the town. The regiment had a platoon of soldiers who remained on perimeter defence duty at the airfield full-time; at night Somali clansmen could sometimes be heard circling the airfield checking to see if the Canadians were alert. When the soldiers first moved in, individual Somalis could be seen making careful note of the location and type of heavy machine-guns and other weapons that the Canadians were positioning. Thankfully, no one attempted to threaten the airfield. The soldiers were kept busy during the day improving the perimeter with trenches and other defensive works; digging earth and filling sandbags was the hottest work that you could imagine. In the town of Belet Uen itself, Airborne troopers guarded the bridges on the road between the Canadian camp and the airfield. At one point, a large group of Somalis became very ugly and started throwing rocks at the Canadians, threatening to overwhelm them. A trooper shot one of the Somalis in the foot; several others were hit as well. The wounded went to the Airborne camp hospital – the fellow hit in the foot refused to come in for treatment at first, but did later on, possibly because he realised that there was no other medical aid to be had. The Somali interpreter working at the hospital said that the locals all hated the gunshot victim and were quite glad that someone had got a "grip on the situation."

THE LOCAL BANDITS IN THE SOMALI COUNTRYSIDE WERE KNOWN AS "TECHNICALS"; UNIVERSALLY HATED BY THEIR COUNTRYMEN, THEY CAUSED MUCH LAWLESSNESS AND RAN THE PROTECTION RACKETS.

BORDER PATROLS

About 90 kilometres to the north and east of the Airborne Regiment location was the small camp manned by A Squadron of the Royal Canadian Dragoons (RCD). This unit was equipped with a six wheel armoured car known as a Cougar which mounts a 76 mm cannon and a medium machine-gun. The RCDs used this vehicle to patrol right up to the Ethiopian border and were sometimes gone for several days at a stretch. They started off with 19 Cougar vehicles, but two were damaged by mines in a week. The last incident was remarkable because the second vehicle that detonated the mine was the one sent to escort the recovery vehicle that had gone out to tow in the first victim, and the other two vehicles had already passed over the exact same track where the mine lay. This recovery task took almost 8 hours to complete and it was done in the middle of a minefield during the night. For the soldiers involved though, this became a regular event.

The local bandits in the Somali countryside were known as "Technicals;" they were universally hated by their countrymen as they caused much lawlessness and they ran the protection rackets to which the relief aid agencies were formerly forced to pay large amounts. When the Canadians appeared in the Belet Uen area, it was important to make an impression and from the start, the Airborne soldiers brooked no bad behaviour. The Canadian infantry conducted vigorous patrols in the countryside, ensuring that everyone knew they were there. Working on little sleep and with minimum equipment, the Canadians covered large sectors quickly and quietly, ensuring that their presence was known and respected. The translators said that the Canadians were called 'the White Technicals.'

NIGHTLY GUNFIRE

At night in Mogadishu airport, gunfire and rocket blasts could be heard. It was impossible to confiscate all of the weapons that each faction keeps, and night seemed to be the time to bring them out again. During the day, the streets were crowded with people and they become used to seeing the coalition military vehicles travelling at high speed between the airport and the former US embassy compound where the Canadian, US and other contingent forces had their headquarters. When you wanted to travel to the headquarters, you had to ride in an eight-wheeled armoured personnel carrier called a "Bison." One rifleman faced outwards on each side of the vehicle and the crew commander manned a medium machine-gun. Barbed wire was strung along the sides of the Bisons to keep people from trying to steal equipment or from climbing up on the sides. Several Canadians were hit by rocks, but none required more than a few stitches. I should add that my use of the word "rifleman" is a bit deceptive because that last time I made the trip the rearward facing machine gunner was a female soldier who was able to stare down the grim looking Somalis as well as anyone.

The Canadian Air Force also flew relief delivery flights into Somalia as part of the United Nations relief efforts. These flights normally consisted of a C-130 Hercules transport plane flying grain or rice into a desert airstrip in places like Baidoa in south-central Somalia. Upon arrival, the planes were laboriously unloaded by hand because there were no fork-lifts to be had. One of the dangers on these flights is dust; frequently the giant Hercules planes were swallowed in dust clouds stirred up by the prop wash upon landing and for a few tense seconds none of the five person crew could see anything. It was a relief to get back up to 12,000 feet where the air was clear and cool.

LEFT: *Paratroopers mounted in a Bison armoured personnel carrier conduct a vehicle patrol through the streets of Belet Uen, Somalia.* *(DND PHOTO)*

THIS GROUP OF CANADIAN MEN AND WOMEN DID THEIR JOB IN A TYPICALLY CANADIAN FASHION – NOT BECAUSE IT ATTRACTED INTERNATIONAL ATTENTION, OR EVEN ATTENTION AT HOME; BUT BECAUSE IT WAS THE RIGHT THING TO DO.

HANDLING OF SUPPLIES

Mogadishu airport had a small detachment of Canadians that formed the national support element. Here, supplies were stockpiled and sorted before being sent forward to the Airborne Regiment by road convoy or – for essential items such as medical supplies or water – by Hercules aircraft. The airport itself was very busy, as all other coalition contingents were also supported by supply flights into Mogadishu. The Canadian camp was between some Americans and the Nigerians. The Americans – the richest military in the world – had some items of kit that the Canadians did their best to scrounge. One of the most popular was the small chemical packet that, upon the addition of water, gave out plenty of heat and nicely warmed either a Canadian or an American individual ration pouch. The Canadians had some advantages though. Our regulations permitted the stocking of beer flown in from Canada and it was available through non-public fund canteens for $1 a can. The American forces were dry when away from garrison, so a visit to our canteen was quite a treat. Also, everyone seemed to like our rations, (based on Magic Pantry foil pouches) better than their own, not least of whom are the French soldiers – they can easily read the bilingual instructions and contents marked on them. A case of Canadian rations was known to guarantee the use of an American forklift for moving shipping containers for at least a day.

This group of Canadian men and women did their job in a typically Canadian fashion – not because it attracted international attention, or even attention at home; but because it was the right thing to do. They risked being shot at, stoned or bitten by a spitting cobra. Yellow fever and malaria were endemic to Somalia. By the time they returned in June 1993, not a few had suffered a prolonged separation from spouses and children - even perhaps the break-up of their marriage. They missed birthdays and weddings and graduations and all those thousand and one other events that give our lives love, meaning and significance. They were heroes, in a distinctively Canadian sense of the word.

REPRINTED FROM:
Esprit de Corps, Volume 2 Issue 12
AUTHOR:
Daniel G. Scuka

Although there were ample warning signs of impending genocide, the United Nations (and Canada) responded too late to prevent the slaughter of 800,000 Rwandans. Canadian General Romeo Dallaire played a central role in the tragedy.

ABOVE:
Tutsi militiamen celebrate their victory over the Hutus on the streets of Kigali.

PRESIDENT HABYARIMANA'S DEATH, PROBABLY AT THE HANDS OF HUTU MILITANTS, WAS THE SIGNAL FOR THE KILLING TO BEGIN.

COMPARISONS TO THE Holocaust are difficult to resist when it comes to Rwanda. Here, in the mountains and hills and gently rolling plateaus of what was once known as the "African Switzerland" one of the great genocides of the century took place. In a frenzy of killing, as many as a million men, women and children were shot, beaten or hacked to death in the course of a a three-month civil war. Traditional objectives of war - to conquer territory or to subject others - were secondary, if present at all. The main purpose of those behind the slaughter was to eliminate an entire population.

The horror that unfolded in Rwanda in the spring of 1994 had been building steadily for many years. A small, densely populated country, Rwanda is peopled by two major tribes of different ethnic origin, the Hutu and Tutsi. Hunters and farmers of Bantu ancestry, the Hutu had originally settled the land only to be reduced to serfdom by the Tutsi, a warrior tribe of Hamitic stock which invaded from the north some four centuries ago. In the heyday of the colonial powers, the Germans and later the Belgians ruled through the existing Tutsi elite which never made up more than fourteen percent of the population, granting it extended powers over the lives of the Hutus. With the coming of independence in the late 1950's, the majority Hutu rose in revolt and slaughtered their former overlords. Great numbers fled into neighbouring Uganda with bitter memories. These "Children of '59" regrouped and formed the Rwandan Patriotic Front, determined to return to the country of their forefathers.

PATH TO CORRUPTION

In their absence Rwanda followed the familiar post-independent path to a corrupt one-party state. There were further outbreaks of violence against the Tutsis in 1967 and 1967 as the condition of the Hutu peasantry went from bad to worse. While senior government officials pocketed vast sums of foreign aid, they encouraged them to blame the Tutsis for their problems. President Habyarimana, who seized power in a coup in 1973, may not have murdered the Tutsis with the same fervour as his predecessors, but he was a master at scapegoating. When the RPF launched cross-border raids in 1990, he began an active campaign to spread hatred and fear. Radio Mille Collines referred to Tutsis as vermin that must be exterminated. "The grave is only half full. Who will help us fill it?" it asked its listeners.

Habyarimana was riding a tiger.

Having done nothing to quell the violence he had unleashed or appease radicals, growing RPF military strength and international pressure forced him to sign the Arusha Peace Accords calling for an interim government in which Tutsis would share power and the establishment of a United Nations Assistance Mission in Rwanda (UNAMIR). The Accords were to be his death warrant. On the evening of April 6, 1994, two missiles were fired at his jet as it landed at Kigali International Airport. The aircraft took a direct hit, crashed in the garden of the presidential palace and immediately burst into flames, killing all aboard.

PLANS FOR MURDER

Three months earlier, Major General Romeo Dallaire, the Canadian commander of UNAMIR had sent a message to UN headquarters warning that detailed plans were being drawn up for the widespread murder of Tutsis. At great personal risk, a Rwandan government official had disclosed the plans and offered to lead him to secret Hutu weapons caches. Dismissed in New York as no more reliable than other rumours circulating at the time, the Security Council refused to act or reinforce Dallaire's force of 2500 lightly armed troops drawn from 23 countries including Bangladesh, Belgium, Ghana, Poland and Senegal. They were now to pay a heavy price.

Habyarimana's death, probably at the hands of Hutu militants, was the signal for the killing to begin. Among the first to die were ten Belgian paratroopers tortured and hacked to death after they surrendered their weapons to the Garde présidentielle in keeping with what they thought was their mandate. No attempt was made to rescue them. When the remaining paratroopers were repatriated they publicly burned their blue berets and the chief-of-staff angrily announced that Belgium would never again take part in peacekeeping operations under UN command.

Unable to protect its own and with no mandate to intervene, UN forces could do nothing but watch helplessly as the slaughter gathered momentum. Death lists had been distributed and the Prime Minister and moderate Hutus who had supported the Arusha Accords were murdered. Interahamwe militia began a house-to-house search for "enemies" and Tutsis were dragged from their cars at roadblocks and shot. Priests, journalists, teachers and civil rights activists were killed. The militiamen quickly understood that they had nothing to fear from UN troops and that they could murder with total freedom from interference. When the Rwandan foreign minister flew to New York to plead his country's case, the UN responded by reducing General Dallaire's force to 270 men.

ABOVE:
Major General Romeo Dallaire the Canadian Commander in Rwanda sent several warnings to the UN in New York of the impending genocide: to no avail.
(DND PHOTO)

SLAUGHTER SPREADS

The slaughter soon spread to the interior of the country. Desperate Tutsis tried to hide in banana groves, swamps, churches, hospitals and schools and almost anywhere where they might not be noticed. Few survived. When sheer numbers proved too much for the Interahamwe to handle, they called in the army. A doctor with Médecins Sans Frontières recalls that "the army men would come inside a hospital, take the wounded, line them up and machine-gun them ...It was also the first time in any of our operations that we saw our local personnel being killed on a massive scale. All our Tutsi medical staff, doctors and nurses, were kidnapped and murdered." Hutu husbands were ordered to kill their Tutsi wives and in schools Hutu teachers denounced their Tutsi pupils to the militia or even killed them themselves. By mid-May, the country reeked of death. Rivers flowing into Lake Victoria were filled with bodies. In Kigali, garbage trucks were used to pick up 60,000 mutilated corpses. The killings only came to an end with the triumph of the RPF.

NO ONE INNOCENT

Bitterly denouncing UN passivity, Vice Secretary-General Kofi Annan declared that "nobody should feel he has a clear conscience in this business. If the pictures of tens of thousands of human bodies rotting and gnawed on by dogs do not wake us up out of our apathy, I don't know what will." After much haggling and faced with a new crisis as hundreds of thousands of Hutu refugees fled into Zaire, the United Nations finally approved the deployment of a 5500-man contingent to join General Dallaire's beleaguered force.

Canada's contribution included the 1st Canadian Division Headquarters and Signal Regiment, 2 Field Ambulance and a protective detachment from the Airborne Regiment. Canadian Hercules aircraft immediately began flying in to Kigali to evacuate foreign nationals and bring in relief supplies while 8 Air Control Squadron took over air traffic control and airport services. Over the ensuing weeks, the Canadians frequently came under mortar and small arms fire and were forced to cancel flights. Nevertheless, as part of Operation Scotch, they were able to fly in 2680 metric tonnes of emergency rations and airlift 6334 passengers.

MASS GRAVE UNCOVERED

As Canadian medical personnel moved into an abandoned milk factory in the village of Mareru to set up a field hospital, they passed continuous streams of refugees being herded towards Zaire by the Interahamwe. The Airborne set up security patrols and cleaned up the area as best they could. Sergeant James Davis recalls uncovering a mass grave: "There were women with babies still in slings on their backs, children with machete wounds, all just piled on top of each other. As the digging progressed we found over thirty heads but could not match up the number of bodies. It was disgusting and sad." Nervous about the presence of Hutu troops in the neighbourhood and mindful of the fate of the Belgian paratroopers, he consulted the Rules of Engagement. "They outlined when we could use force and how much, who we could protect and who we couldn't," he noted. "At the end was a disclaimer that stated that everything in parenthesis was still under review. Everything pertaining to the use of force was in parenthesis. That way, what we did, if it looked bad in the press, the government would be safe in saying we hadn't followed approved procedures and could hang us out to dry."

Inadequate rules of engagement, an unclear mandate, vacillation and cowardice all contributed to the failure of the United Nations Mission in Rwanda. "We were overwhelmed, you see," a Belgian missionary said after being forced to witness the murder of schoolchildren in his care. "We were overwhelmed by this great evil, by these acts of wickedness. Somebody said to me that when they got out of Rwanda they would be insane. As for me ...I am left with lifelong questions. What did I do that I should not have done? What did I not do that I should have done?" Questions the UN should have asked before it placed peacekeepers in harm's way.

AUTHOR: *Bill Twatio*

RULES OF ENGAGEMENT

ABOVE:
A Canadian patrol sets out from Kigali aboard a Cougar – tank trainer – in 1994.
(DND PHOTO)

For the soldiers in harm's way, restrictive policies often proved a hindrance to personal safety. A senior officer reflects upon his experiences in Rwanda.

AFTER MY EXPERIENCE IN Rwanda during the civil war of April–July 1994, I have a rather jaundiced view of the whole idea of rules of engagement (ROE) that only apply to the guys in the middle. I would argue that, in Rwanda, ROE either got in the way, or failed to make any difference because of the insufficient force available.

It is difficult, even now, after nearly two years have passed, to describe my first whiff of African death without wanting to retch. It was a smell that those who had arrived before me knew too well from having spent days cooped up in UNAMIR HQ, Kigali, surrounded by rotting bodies. Most of the dead had been buried shortly before I arrived but still the dogs would fight and snarl all night over the choicest morsels of human flesh left above ground. The scale of the slaughter made any talk of carefully balanced ROE seem absurd.

Unlike Somalia, Rwanda was not made the subject of a CNN blitz until well after the worst of the massacre so there were no coalition forces on the ground to back up the mission. After the evacuation of the Belgian and Bangladeshi battalions shortly after the massacres began, there were only 400 of us left: two armed Ghanian companies, an armed Tunisian platoon and the remainder either armed with pistols or completely unarmed. Either combatant side could, and did, ignore us or shoot at us with complete impunity. As MGen R.A. Dallaire's assistant (OK, his office boy), I had the dubious honour of drafting a strong letter of protest in response to the death of a Uruguayan UNMO as a result of an aimed RPG round. Though the guilty parties made polite noises in response, they knew that they had made a point about where and when the UN could move. They wrote in blood while we had only paper.

In mid-June, MGen Dallaire and many of his staff were waiting on the runway of Kigali airport for an official visit that both sides had agreed to. When the Canadian Herc carrying several Italian politicians taxied up to the terminal, a Soviet pattern 106 artillery round landed about 150 m away. The crew had the ramp down and the loadmaster had just stepped onto the asphalt when the shell hit. The laughter at the sight of the loadie chasing his airplane down the runway and then surfing up the ramp was stifled immediately by the second round impacting only metres from where the Herc had been. I was standing a few feet behind MGen Dallaire when the round hit and was thrown off my feet. The General never budged. Later that night I drafted a second strong letter of protest, this time to the other side, who had chosen this subtle way of letting us know that they disappoved of the visit. Again, we had nothing but paper to express our righteous indignation. I don't think it had much effect. Working under Chapter 7 didn't mean much without the force to back it up.

Over and over again we were forced to rely on wits and sheer bravado to achieve anything at all. For weeks, Canadians like Captain Andre Demers, R22eR; Major Luc Racine, R22eR; and Major Don McNeil, 12RBC made daily trips in and out of zones controlled by drugged and/or drunken, armed militias to check on the fate of the thousands who had sought refuge in churches and orphanages. Daily one would come back paler than they had left – having faced down yet another gang of murderous maniacs armed with grenades, clubs and sundry other instruments of death, but lacking any evident spark of humanity. Under the circumstances, shooting at either side with their little pistols would have been tempting; but suicidal.

A DISTURBING ASPECT

The obvious lesson to be taken from this longwinded war story, is that having the right ROE is only half the battle. Understanding the game the protagonists are playing, having the wit and courage to play it better and having the firepower to back up any attempt to change the way they play are also necessary. But there is another aspect of this business that disturbs me deeply.

ROE are a device by which the actions of troops on the ground can be controlled by political forces a great distance away from the action. In Rwanda, the rules in place were developed for conditions that changed dramatically overnight. The morning after the massacres started, the rules became an affront to common morality and to the most basic sense of humanity for which the UN is supposed to stand.

ABOVE: *The human cost of the Rwandan tragedy. UN forces could not cope with the scale of the slaughter which often included mothers and infants.* (DND PHOTO)

The trouble is that any set of ROE has the same potential. Such rules are necessarily based on speculation about future events. When the diplomats or the mandarins get it wrong, the first ones to find out are the guys on the ground. In Rwanda, it took nearly three weeks for it to be acknowledged by UNHQ that the old set of ROE were out of date and another six before the mandate could be officially changed.

The world we live in being what it is, it is far too easy for a ruthless warlord to adapt a strategy to the rules that restrain the UN forces in his area. Knowing the glacial speed with which decisions are made in UNHQ, any daring, would-be national hero can count on getting inside the UN decision-making cycle, of making tighter turns than is possible for the troops controlled from a distance by a bureaucracy that needs time to deliberate on any change of direction. In the short time I watched things unfold in Rwanda, there were probably six or seven such turns by the various factions. They played with us.

The whole idea of ROE in peacekeeping or peace enforcement ops is to make sure that the intervening force seizes and retains the moral high ground. By this I mean that ROE are designed to avoid the consequences of unrestrained action by the troops. But when ROE prevent troops from adapting to a changed situation that may require unanticipated action, as was the case in Rwanda, then the whole concept needs review.

Whatever else they are supposed to do, ROE tie the hands of soldiers who are often the only ones who can really tell what is going on and who know what is immediately available to deal with it. It could be argued that the Somalia murders prove the need for tighter ROE, but this argument fails to deal with the larger problem of needing freedom to act as quickly as the protagonists did in the case of Rwanda. That is not to say that leaders are not responsible for bad judgement or that soldiers are not morally responsible for individual acts; only that bureaucratic controls are an impediment to success in an arena where the odds are always high that the good guys will lose. Given the high cost of such impediments in Rwanda, surely it is time to rethink a procedure that puts far too much emphasis on negative control and far too little faith in the moral competence and military acumen of the officers and soldiers who are face-to-face with the problem and who consequently understand it in ways impossible for someone not there.

REPRINTED FROM:
Esprit de Corps, Volume 5 Issue 6
AUTHOR: *Phil Lancaster*

HAITI

In 1993, when a military coup seized power in Haiti, Canada supported the UN Security Council's arms and oil embargo on the impoverished Carribean island. When ousted President Aristide was restored to power, Canadian troops helped to police the transition peaceably.

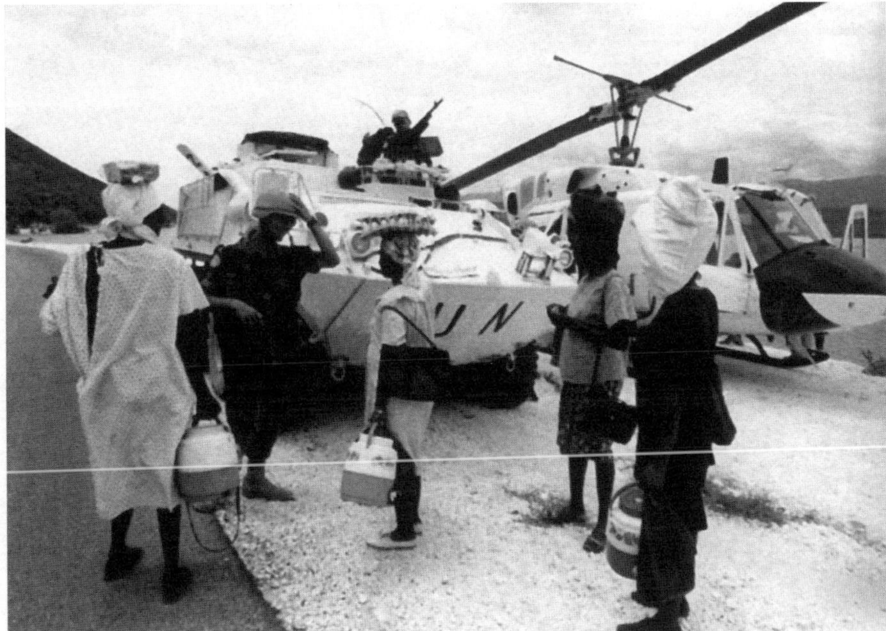

***ABOVE:** Local Haitian women, carefully balancing food and water,speak with Canadian peacekeepers as they stand next to a Bison and Twin Huey helicopter. They are part of the UN Quick Reaction Force (QRF) monitoring the border between Haiti and the Dominican Republic. (DND PHOTO)*

"AFTER CUBA, HAITI IS the largest of the Antilles,"Dr. J.C. Dorsainvil wrote in 1924 in his *Haitian History Primer*. "Four mountain chains run along it length. Its plains, covered with plantations are watered by numerous and abundant brooks, streams and rivers. Forests, coffee bushes, banana trees, and corn cover its mountains, their summits crowned with clouds. Because of its natural wealth, its fertility, the sweetness of its climate, and the incomparable beauty of its landscape, Haiti is worthy to be called "The Pearl of the Antilles."

Still used in Haitian schools, Dorsainvil's primer describes another world. Breaking through the cloud cover over the high peaks that back Port-au-Prince, one sees nothing flying into Haiti today but bare and eroded hillsides. The trees have long been felled for firewood and silt has turned the rivers the colour of café-au-lait as the last of Haiti's topsoil washes out to sea. Coffee, bananas and corn are only a memory. In downtown Port-au-Prince, Harry Truman Boulevard, once an elegant tropical thoroughfare leading to the harbour, has been reduced to a rutted dirt track by flash floods carrying rocks, boulders and debris. Mud slides during the rainy season regularly block other streets and knock down shanties in the city's teeming slums. The Haitian landscape increasingly resembles sub-Saharan Africa, those parched, scrubby regions where the edges of the desert are creeping southward. Haiti is dying and there is some doubt that anything can turn it around. Once the richest and most fertile colony in the New World, the "Pearl" is now the poorest country in the Western Hemisphere.

BLACK JACOBINS

The French had transformed the island, then known as Saint Domingue, into a vast and immensely profitable sugar plantation worked by harshly-regimented African slaves. The result was the great slave rebellion of 1791 which evolved into the Haitian revolution led by Toussaint L'Ouverture, a former cattle herder – a long and complex struggle among blacks, whites, mulattos and French, British and Spanish forces. After Napoleon's effort to reconquer the colony failed, Jean-Jacques Dessalines declared Haiti an independent state in 1804. But independence did little to improve the former slaves' lot. Repressed and exploited by a mulatto elite, Haiti's successive governments, military and civilian, have been preoccupied with staying in power and stealing public funds.

PAPA AND BABY DOC

The Duvaliers, father and son, were typical. A rural doctor with a shrewd understanding of peasant mentalities, "Papa Doc" used this knowledge to keep their support while ignoring their interests. Using the culture of Voodoo, a combination of Roman Catholic and African belief, for his political advantage, he claimed occult powers that few dared challenge. During his 14-year dictatorship, Haiti's poor were oppressed by his officials and terrorized by the paramilitary Tontons Macoutes. Less shrewd, his son Jean-Claude, "Baby Doc," became president at 19 and continued the family tradition of looting the country and perpetuating its poverty. By the time he boarded an American military transport to fly into exile in France in 1986, fewer than 40 per cent of Haitians had jobs and more than half were suffering from malnutrition. In the wretched bidonvilles of Cité Soleil, St. Martin, Fort National and La Saline, per capita income was $360 dollars a year and life expectancy 45.

The downfall of the Duvaliers changed little in Haiti and ushered in an era of political chaos. Four military juntas, three coup d'états, a state-of-siege and hundreds of deaths later, poor Haitians, virtually all Voodoo celebrants, elected the Catholic priest Jean-Bertrand Aristide to the presidency. Less than a year later, he was overthrown in a brutal military coup led by General RaoulCédras, the Commander-in-Chief of

ABOVE:
A Twin Huey helicopter is used to transport lumber to remote Haitian villages where new schools and medical facilities are being built with the assistance of non-government organizations (NGO).
(DND PHOTO)

the Haitian Armed Forces. In protest, the United Nations Security Council immediately imposed an oil and arms embargo.

GOVERNOR'S ISLAND

On 3 July 1993 ousted President Aristide and General Cédras were brought together in New York City and signed the Governor's Island Agreement which provided for Aristide's return to Haiti. The Agreement also called for the establishment of a United Nations Mission in Haiti (UNMIH) to supervise new elections and the modernization of the police and armed forces. Canada contributed a detachment of engineers and 100 RCMP officers who were to join a multinational UN civilian police force. However, after weeks of increasing violence and intimidation, armed gangs loyal to the regime expelled advance parties and would not allow the disembarkation of UNMIH personnel aboard the USS *Harlan County* at Port-au-Prince.

With the junta refusing to abide by the terms of the Agreement, the United Nations approved Resolution 875 calling for renewed sanctions. Fifteen Canadian military observers were dispatched to monitor the border between the Dominican Republic and Haiti and a Canadian Naval Task Group made up of the destroyers HMC Ships *Fraser* and *Gatineau* and the supply ship HMCS *Preserver* took up position offshore as part of a multinational Maritime Interdiction Operation. At the same time, an American-led force seized Haitian ports of entry and airports and fanned out into the countryside to enforce the provisions of the Governors Island Agreement and neutralize the Haitian Armed Forces. Mission accomplished, President Aristide was returned to power and an enlarged UNMIH was deployed under Canadian command.

FOR THE FIRST TIME IN HAITIAN HISTORY, THANKS TO UN PEACEKEEPERS, A PEACEFUL TRANSITION OF POWER BETWEEN TWO DEMOCRATICALLY-ELECTED PRESIDENTS, JEAN BERTRAND ARISTIDE AND RENÉ PREVAL, TOOK PLACE IN FEBRUARY 1996.

FORCE COMPOSITION

Garrisoned at Port-au-Prince and Cap Haitien, the two largest population centres, the 1200-strong force was made up of infantry battalions from Bangladesh and Pakistan. The Canadian Contingent in Haiti, operating from Camp Maple Leaf near the Port-au-Prince airport, numbered some 700 personnel and included a reconnaissance battalion from the Royal 22e Régiment, engineers, military police and a military information support team, a ground transportation platoon, the 408 Tactical Helicopter Squadron from Edmonton equipped with four CH-I35 Twin-Hueys, medical officers and an administrative and headquarters platoon. More than 100 civilian police and RCMP constables joined the contingent to provide field training for Haitian National Police recruits and to serve as advisors at the Haitian National Police Academy.

UNMIH MANDATE

The mandate of UNMIH was to assist the government of Haiti in maintaining a secure and stable environment in which free elections could be held. The Haitian Army and the dreaded Tonton Macoutes were disbanded and a National Police Force set up under civilian control. For the first time in Haitian history, thanks to UN peacekeepers, a peaceful transition of power between two democratically-elected Presidents, Jean Bertrand Aristide and René Preval, took place in February 1996.

Canada took a leading role in Haiti as there has been close political ties between the two countries since the turn of the century. Canadian missionaries and foreign aid workers have been active in Haiti for many years and there is a large Haitian-Canadian community in Canada. Moreover, instability in Haiti was seen as having a negative impact on the Dominican Republic and the Commonwealth Caribbean, a region where Canada has major political and economic interests. Canada's leadership was greatly appreciated by the Organization of American States and its member countries and by the Haitian people.

ABOVE:
A Canadian peacekeeper entertains Haitian orphans. Although politicians proclaimed the mission to Haiti to be a tremendous success, the massive UN intervention in the country provided little, real, long-term benefit. Rampant poverty and corrupt government institutions remain a reality in Haiti. (DND PHOTO)

DEMOCRACY IN HAITI HAS STUMBLED BADLY. PARLIAMENT HAS BEEN DISSOLVED LEAVING THE COUNTRY WITHOUT A FUNCTIONING GOVERNMENT. CORRUPTION REMAINS ENDEMIC AND FOREIGN AID HAS BEEN SUSPENDED.

FRIENDS AND PROTECTORS

Night after night, as Canadian patrols moved through the chaotic streets of Port-au-Prince they were greeted as protectors and friends. Many Canadian peacekeepers devoted their spare time to humanitarian projects, visiting orphanages and providing care and attention to sick children. Eighty homeless children at the World Harvest Mission near Camp Maple Leaf were unofficially adopted by the troops. Medical personnel helped Haitian women to give birth and tended to the elderly and accident victims. Engineers from the 4 Engineer Support Regiment at CFB Gagetown worked on construction projects for the benefit of the population and built a school at Non Pagnol. In September 1997, Canadian divers helped in the grisly task of recovering the bodies of drowning victims of the overturned ferry *Fierté GonÉvienne*. Canadians also took up guard duties at the Presidential Palace and assisted the movement of aid workers throughout the coutry.

SOMALIA'S SHADOW

The Somalia Inquiry cast a long shadow over the mission to Haiti. "We're doing good work here," a veteran peacekeeper complained. "But back in Canada all the public hears about are the bad things in the military." Morale suffered as the troops were continually lectured on the use of force in violent situations and issued wallet-sized cards reminding them not to abuse, torture or kill prisoners. "The cards weren't really for us," one soldier said. "They just want to cover their ass in Ottawa."

Military police photgraphed Haitian prisoners before turning them over to local authorities to prove that they had not been mistreated and many officers wrote down their orders to protect themselves in the event that misunderstandings or problems arose in the future. Strict rules on travel and alcohol consumption were enforced leading some to ridicule Camp Maple Leaf as "Camp Kindergarden."

The United Nations Mission in Haiti came to an end on 30 November 1997 and Canadian troops returned home with some sense of accomplishment. "The men and women of our Armed Forces were very successful in establishing and maintaining an environment in which the Haitian people could build democracy," Defence Minister Art Eggleton said as he welcomed the first contingent back at Jean-Lesage Airport in Quebec City.

But democracy in Haiti has stumbled badly. Parliament has been dissolved leaving the country without a functioning government. Corruption remains endemic and foreign aid has been suspended. Haiti remains a desperately poor country with deforestation and its inexorable companions, drought, famine and disease approaching apocalyptic proportions. And the soil continues to wash out to sea.

AUTHOR: *Bill Twatio*

RIGHT: *Corporal Jordie Yeo and Private Melchers under fire - their wounds were listed as accidental.* (ILLUSTRATION BY KATHERINE TAYLOR)

Despite what often seems an inflated bureaucracy and public affairs staff, DND does not record all the 'casualties of peace' incurred by our forces on UN missions. Also, DND has claimed some soldiers were wounded or killed in ways which they were not – as if some casualties are more politically acceptable than others.

CASUALTIES OF PEACE

IN JANUARY 1996, CBC International conducted a radio interview with Public Affairs Officer, Captain Bob Kennedy. One of the subjects covered in the discussion was the Defence Department's deliberate under-reporting of Canadian peacekeeping casualties. Kennedy gave a blunt and detailed rundown on the problems he had encountered in even trying to complete an official listing of our killed and wounded soldiers. In his opinion, there was no question that the policy to downplay casualty figures emanated from National Defence Headquarters. Although Kennedy's damning allegation did not spark any major media interest, it set off alarm bells in the offices of his immediate superiors. Colonel Geoff Haswell, then the branch head of public affairs, phoned Kennedy at his home in Toronto just after the radio interview. The little militia captain was shocked at Haswell's rage. "He was sputtering something about laying criminal charges against me." When the nonplussed captain asked Haswell, "What sort of crime is telling the truth?" his colonel slammed down the receiver. Just days later, Kennedy was advised that "his services were no longer required" by the Canadian military. He had struck a nerve, and he paid the price.

At the time of his dismissal, Kennedy was the military's undisputed authority on Canadian casualties. As the editor of the army's *Garrison* newspaper, Kennedy had published the first official list of soldiers killed or wounded while serving with UNPROFOR. From the time that initial edition hit the streets, it set off a wave of reaction throughout the Forces. Kennedy's office was soon flooded with calls and letters from soldiers whose injuries had either not been reported or were "sanitized." The young captain had then begun compiling an updated list, at the same time trying to determine how DND could not have kept accurate records of such statistics. Kennedy knew that "the military has long had a well-regulated system of reporting casualties: the detailed instructions are contained in Administrative Order 24-1, which was last revised in 1985." In response to his queries, DND had shrugged the issue off by claiming the reporting system had become "decentralized" over the years of peace. When things blew up in Yugoslavia in April 1992, "setting up a filing system for stats on the wounded wasn't at the top of their minds."

CONSISTENT PATTERN

Kennedy was a former correspondent with Canadian Press, and he had worked the other side of the fence long enough to know that this "bureaucratic slip-up" response did not wash; the pattern of "mistakes" and "omissions" was so consistently in favour of an image-conscious department that it had to be deliberate. Using subsequent issues of his *Garrison* newspaper to prompt responses, Kennedy's "unofficial" list of UNPROFOR casualties soon jumped from the original 84 to 116 soldiers. Letters to the editor indicated that this new total still did not reflect anywhere near the actual number of troops that had been injured on duty in the former Yugoslavia. One officer, writing of his own unrecorded wounds, noted that Lieutenant Colonel Michel Jones's First Battle Group alone had suffered 37 casualties. The official chart still showed just 24.

"WE WEREN'T PREPARED"

DND's original response had been that in the spring of 1992, when they first deployed into Yugoslavia, they had not been prepared to catalogue injuries and death statistics. However, as Kennedy compiled his data, it clearly showed that the military was just as "unprepared" to record the casualties when Canada pulled out of the UN mission in the fall of 1995. Captain David MacDonald, the first Canadian UN military observer in Croatia, had also been the first casualty. On 3 April 1992, MacDonald was hospitalized in Zagreb with mortar fragments in both his legs. He was not on the list.

Lieutenant Cam Ellis was with the detachment of peacekeepers who first entered the enclave of Srebrenica. His APC struck a landmine on 24 April 1993. The ensuing blast had thrust Ellis forward into the armoured cupola, crushing his face into a bloody pulp. He required an immediate medevac to the Canadian camp hospital in Visoko, from which he was transferred to the Franco-Spanish medical facility in Split, Croatia. From there Ellis was sent to the U.S. hospital at Ramstein, Germany, then on to the National Defence Medical Centre in Ottawa, where he underwent reconstructive surgery. He was not on the list.

NO RECORDS...

Neither were Sergeant D.L. Paris or Corporal T.J. Parcells, who took mortar shrapnel at the airfield in Srebrenica and were heroically rushed to safety by Sergeant Morrison.

On 12 August 1993, Captain Kevin Crowel took a .50 calibre round in the leg and was rushed to the hospital in Sarajevo. His injury was not officially recorded.

Corporal P. Desloges was hit in the hand by a rifle bullet after several bursts were fired at his APC just outside Visoko on 17 October 1993. No entry was made.

Two months later, Corporal Yan Davey was hit in the forearm by a sniper's bullet during a fire-fight in Srebrenica. It took seven days to arrange a medevac out of the besieged village, and Davey was eventually flown home to Canada. He did not make the casualty list.

When Private S.J. Bowen was blasted from his APC by a landmine on 8 April 1994, Corporal D.K. Konchuk was also badly injured in the explosion. Bowen's very serious injuries were tabled as "minor" and Konchuk's wounds were not officially recorded

Even as late as 2 July 1995, the mortar shrapnel injuries sustained by postal clerk Master Corporal C.S. Wray were not entered on the official casualty database.

TELL ONLY WHEN NECESSARY

Other soldiers' wounds were sometimes left unreported at the time they occurred. Troops would occasionally choose to patch themselves up and remain with their platoons. If, or when, complications developed, the injuries were not traced back to their origins. This was the case for Master Corporal Peter Vallée. The shots fired beside his head, outside the Sarajevo airport, had badly damaged his eardrum. At the time, Vallée had thought the ringing in his head would gradually disappear. Six months later he was not so sure. He had mentioned the ailment during his medical examination prior to his second tour and again prior to his third. The military doctors had all noted a partial deafness due to a damaged eardrum. No treatment was possible, and Vallée had been pronounced fit for duty. It was only in Camp Visoko during his final tour of Bosnia that a doctor had advised him that he was eligible for a disability pension and a wound stripe. His name was never added to the list.

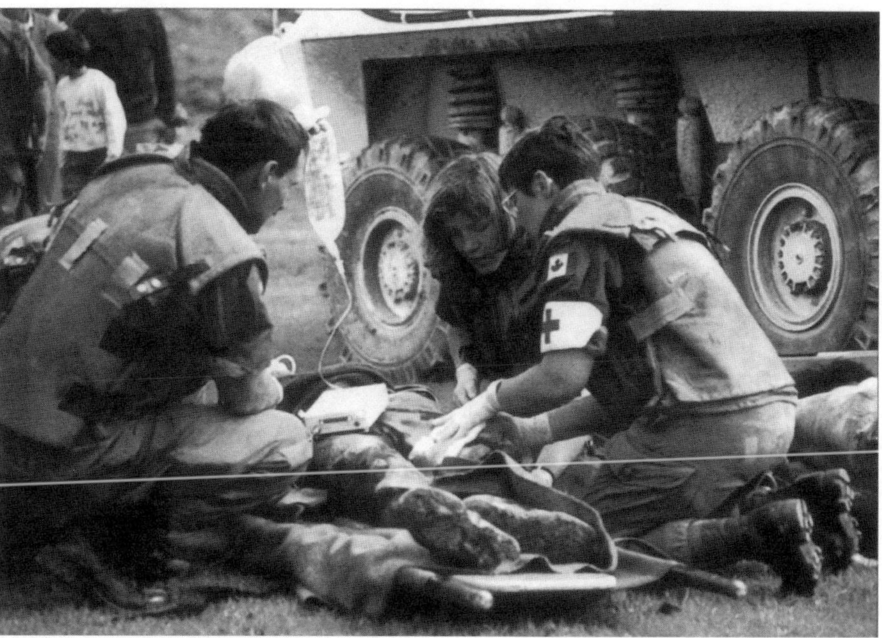

ABOVE:
Canadian medics frantically tend a wounded peacekeeper in Bosnia. Canadian officials routinely under-reported or 'sanitized' the casualty lists. (DND PHOTO)

SANITIZED LIST

In the case of many of the soldiers whose names did make it onto the official list, the cause of their wounds was often "sanitized" to reflect a reduced incidence of combat. For instance, the violent grenade ambush that had hospitalized Master Corporal Jordie Yeo and Private Jeff Melchers in Srebrenica was listed as an "accident" as opposed to "hostile fire." The same "accidental" reason was given for the injuries sustained by Private Fred Taylor, Master Corporal M.E. "Newf" Bennet, Corporals James MacPherson and M.E. Lapthorne. These were the four soldiers wounded during the artillery bombardment of the Medak Pocket. At the time of the incident, DND's official press response had almost blamed these individuals' lack of combat experience for their injuries: "Our soldiers just aren't used to the dangers of artillery fire, it's something we'll have to get used to...." No mention was made of the intense fire-fights or the 30 Croats killed by our peacekeepers during those fierce engagements.

Even when accidents did occur, the circumstances surrounding the incident were often 'cleaned up' to protect the families and to avoid enraging the Canadian public. Captain Jim Decoste's body was looted and his two badly injured comrades were similarly robbed by Serb soldiers whose truck collided with the Canadian jeep. Despite knowing of the theft and blatant violation of our injured soldiers, the Canadian government chose not to pursue the issue with the Serb authorities. Instead, it was decided to accept their version of the accident and to pay full restitution for the damaged truck.

For many of the soldiers who survived these traumatic incidents, their physical wounds were listed officially, but their emotional scars remained unrecorded. Lieutenant Rick Turner had broken his arm and suffered multiple lacerations in the Decoste jeep collision, yet, long after those fractures and cuts had mended, Turner still required psychotherapy to deal with the emotional trauma of seeing two close comrades die within a matter of days of each other.

Corporal Tim Thomas was unhurt in the vehicle accident that killed his friend, Master Corporal John Ternapolski. However, the horror of retrieving Ternapolski's severed head and the torment of lingering guilt at not having driven the APC himself that day, continue to haunt Thomas. Although diagnosed with post-traumatic stress disorder (PTSD), Tim Thomas's name is not on any casualty list.

There are countless numbers of peacekeeping veterans who fit into the same category as Thomas. They are the unseen casualties, those who bear no physical scars, but cannot put Yugoslavia behind them. Too many young soldiers have already chosen to end their mental anguish through suicide. Others are becoming increasingly vocal in demands for treatment and therapy.

PUGLIESE VS COLEMAN

On 24 April 1998, a delegation of soldiers from Jim Calvin's 2PPCLI battle group made a presentation to the parliamentary committee on defence. Over four years after the event had occurred, the Battle of the Medak Pocket was finally described to the government of Canada. Eighteen months earlier, *Ottawa Citizen* reporter David Pugliese had broken the story of *Canada's Secret Battle* in newspapers coast to coast. Up to the last minute, Colonel Ralph Coleman, then head of army public affairs, had tried to kill the story. He had even ordered Lieutenant Colonel Calvin to break off his promised interview with Pugliese, but the tactic had backfired. Pugliese threatened to change his story lead to *Army Officer Silenced Over Secret Battle*, and NDHQ had backed down. They need not have worried. Launched in the dog days of summer, with Parliament in recess and Defence Minister David Collenette fighting vainly to prop up his lame-duck Chief of the Defence Staff, Jean Boyle, the Liberal government had ignored the issue entirely.

ABOVE: *Captain Jim Decoste was killed in a vehicle accident in 1993. His body was looted by Serb soldiers.* (PHOTO BY KATHERINE L. TAYLOR)

When the full details were presented to the assembled politicians on the committee, nothing was more gripping or emotionally moving than the testimony of Sergeant Chris Byrne. A big, tough Newfoundlander, Byrne was built like a human freight train. In his years playing army league hockey, Byrne was a much-feared enforcer, graceless on skates, brutal with his fists. In contrast to his spit-and-polish dress uniform, Byrne's oft-broken nose and gnarled fists gave the tough veteran a look of disciplined ferocity. In addressing the parliamentarians, Byrne explained his personal reason for wanting to brief the committee. He had not been in the fire-fight. Instead, he had been part of the Medak Pocket clean-up crew:

"I was trained for war, but I wasn't trained for the result of war in my mind.... There has to be some kind of therapy in place for us when we get back to Canada. You can't just take soldiers out of a war-torn country, slam them back into a civilized world and expect that everything is going to be okay. There has to be a stand-off period, a gap. To be honest, there really isn't a lot of help for the soldier. The budget cuts have impacted hard and it's pathetic to hear somebody in a psychology department say, 'Well, we're just scraping by....' I am only the tip of the iceberg as to what is really out there in the Forces."

Through welling tears, Byrne continued to describe his own personal saga, and how love for his three-year-old daughter had finally pushed him to seek counselling:

"Emotionally, I was at the end of my rope. I had come home from work one day and my daughter came up to me and saw I was crying. She put her arm around me and said, 'Dad, it's going to be okay.' It was at that point that I looked at her and said, 'Yes, it will be okay.' The next morning, I went to work and asked for help. I asked, 'What is wrong with me?'"

There were few dry eyes in the room by the time Byrne had completed his presentation. The mood was lightened by a few muffled chuckles when one elected official asked why the big NCO had waited so long before seeking help. "I was afraid the guys would think I was a wimp," Byrne had replied, deadpan.

REPRINTED FROM: Tested Mettle: Canada's Peacekeepers at War
AUTHORS:
Scott Taylor & Brian Nolan

TOXIC WARFARE

LEFT: *Since poison gas was first introduced to the world's battlefields in 1915, soldiers have been exposed to an increasing number of toxic substances.*
(US DEPARTMENT OF DEFENCE)

From service in the Persian Gulf to the Balkans, veterans are falling ill at an alarming rate. There remains no clear conclusion as to the cause, but the toxic hazards of modern battlefields are taking their toll.

IN RECENT YEARS, SERVICE men and women seem as much at risk from the environment and their own ordnance and medical services as from hostile enemy action. Many Gulf War veterans have experienced a baffling combination of mood swings, memory loss, sleeplessness, headaches and anxiety. Veterans of Bosnia and Croatia display similar symptoms. Too often, their complaints have been ignored, or they were told "it's all in your head" by pension boards.

The debate about the effects of exposure to toxic substances and the use of experimental drugs is not limited to Canada. Questions have been raised in NATO councils, in Britain, France and the United States. In February 2000, a congressional committee of the U.S. House of Representatives issued a damning report on the continued use of a controversial anthrax vaccine.

Infectious, spread by a bacterium usually found in sheep and cattle but capable of transmission to humans, anthrax is usually fatal. Although it has never been used as a weapon, the Pentagon fears it might be; by Iraq, Iran, Libya, China, North Korea, or any of five other states it says are harbouring or working on such weapons. Taking no chances, it ordered the vaccination of all military personnel.

The vaccine, developed decades ago for workers handling animals and hides, was designed to cover contact with the skin and it is not known how well it would protect humans from airborne infection. Tests with rhesus monkeys have been inconclusive. Inoculation consists of three shots given two weeks apart, followed by more injections at six, 12 and 18 months. Immunization kicks in after the third shot. Nearly 400,000 soldiers have been inoculated with the vaccine since former U.S. Defence Secretary ordered the immunization of all active and reserve troops beginning with those in the Persian Gulf and South Korea.

ANTHRAX VACCINE AND THE HOUSE REPORT

Worried about hundreds of accounts of adverse reactions to the vaccine, the National Security Subcommittee of the House of Representatives recommended that its use be suspended. Vaccinated soldiers complained of fevers, muscle pain, vertigo, seizures and dizziness, as well as problems with the liver and immune system. In its 80-page report, the committee heard testimony of falling morale, resignations and recruitment difficulties over concerns about the effects of the vaccine.

"At best the vaccine provides some measure of protection to most who receive it," the report noted. "Just how much protection is acquired, by whom and for how long are questions the Defence Department answers with an excess of faith but a paucity of science." Committte chairman Chris Shays, a former military pilot, said that the vaccination program "is built on a dangerously narrow scientific and medical foundation." He told a press conference that the vaccine should be considered experimental because its effectiveness is still uncertain and the troops receiving it are not being monitored adequately. Shay claimed that the program was "plagued by uncertain supplies, uncertain safety and unproven efficacy against the anthrax threat." He and his colleagues concluded that use of the vaccine "should not be mandatory or force-wide."

In response, the Pentagon insisted that it had no plans to stop vaccinating soldiers. A spokesman noted that the U.S. Food and Drug Administration had repeatedly backed the vaccine's effectiveness. Serious allergic reactions to the vaccine occur about once in every 50,000 doses he said, compared with an average reaction rate for all vaccines of once in 100,000 doses. The assistant defence secretary for Heath Affairs reported fewer than 600 instances of flu-like symptoms or other adverse reactions to the vaccine, adding that only 26 people had required hospital treatment and only six of those appeared to have been directly related to the vaccine.

BAD MEDICINE

Canada, following the American example, ordered the innoculation of 576 military personnel bound for the Middle East in 1998. Unfortunately, they received doses of a stale-dated vaccine that was highly contaminated with gasket or stopper particles. DND had even planned to use a vaccine acquired from a British laboratory that may have been tainted with Creutzfeld-Jacob or Mad Cow Disease. Medical experts now believe that there is no evidences that the disease can be transmitted through a vaccine. At the time, however, concern about the quality of the vaccine was so great that the British army made the use of the vaccine voluntary. Two-thirds refused it and high-ranking defence officials were given a vaccine produced in the United States.

The British vaccine was never used as DND spoiled the entire shipment of 1600 doses when it was improperly stored in a refrigerator which was not monitored for temperature variations. Indeed, DND wasted more anthrax vaccine than it used. More than 3000 of the 12,000 doses purchased over a period of 18 months were either accidentally spoiled or passed the expiry date.

Spoiling the British batch left DND scrambling to obtain more vaccine. In February 1995 it secured a new supply from an American firm, Michigan Biologic, which was later cited for poor quality control, inadequate record keeping and substandard manufacturing practices. In 1997 the U.S. Food and Drug Administration (FDA) gave notice that it would revoke the firm's license if it did not comply with regulations. The Canadian military simply dismissed the notice. Between 1995 and 1997, Canadian United Nations inspectors in the Middle East were innoculated with lots of the vaccine that had failed potency testing and that the FDA had requested be pulled from distribution.

Mike Kipling, an Air Force sergeant serving in Kuwait, balked when ordered to take the vaccine. Vaccinated on an earlier tour of duty in the Persian Gulf, he had suffered six months of nausea, fatigue and aching joints. Many others reported similar symptoms but were reluctant to file official complaints fearing it might damage their military careers. Honourably discharged after 26 years of service, Kipling was subsequently charged with refusing a lawful order.

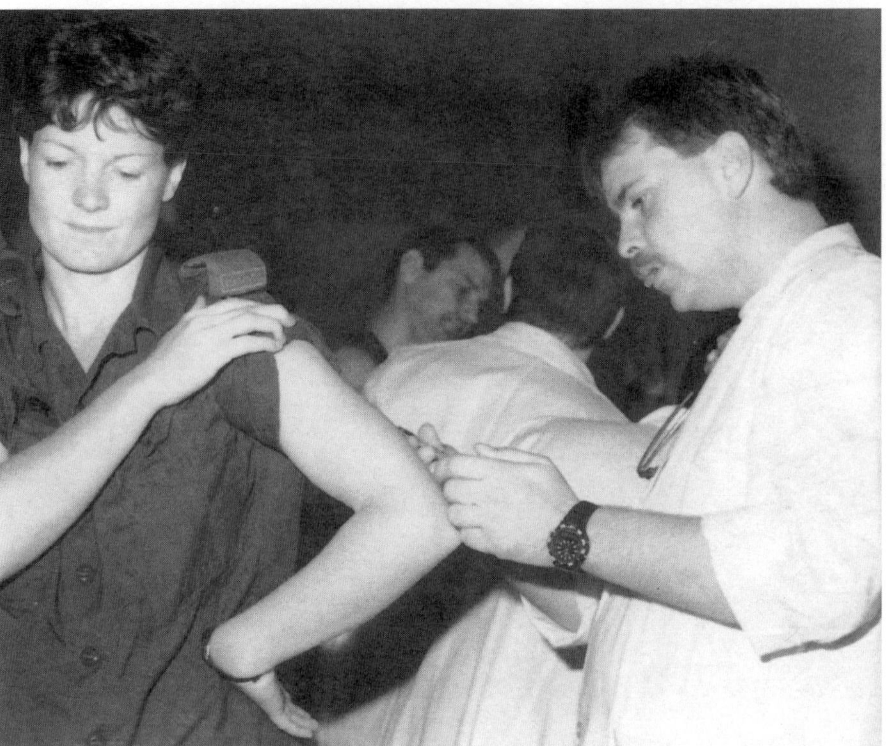

ABOVE: *A soldier receives an anthrax vaccination prior to departing for service in the Persian Gulf, 1990.*
(ILC 90-003-1, BY DANIELLE CAOUETTE)

DEPLETED URANIUM AND GULF WAR SYNDROME

The death of Captain Terry Riordan in April 1999 reopened the debate about the controversial illness known as Gulf War Syndrome. Riordan, a former military policeman, served in the Gulf in 1991 and then was beset by a wide range of mysterious and painful symptoms. An autopsy conducted by Dr. Asaph Durokavic, an expert on Gulf War Syndrome and a former research scientist with the U.S. Department of Veterans Affairs, found high levels of uranium isotopes in Riordan's bones nearly a full decade after the war. Dr. Durokavic also found traces of uranium in the urine of living veterans.

An estimated 320 tonnes of depleted uranium – a by-product of uranium 235 – was used for the first time during the Gulf War as a hardening agent on missiles and ammunition and to armour plate military vehicles. Declassified U.S. documents show that 944,000 rounds of DU ammunition were fired in Iraq and Kuwait during the war. DU shells were also used in Kosovo, mostly by A-10 "Warthog" aircraft. Depleted uranium is favoured as a tank and bunker-buster because its extreme density allows it to punch through armour and concrete.

The uranium coating on a DU shell is safe to the touch, but becomes dangerously radioactive inside the human body, according to some experts. They argue that when a shell explodes it creates a cloud of toxic particles that are sucked into the lungs. Over a long period of time, these heavy metal particles decompose internally and migrate to the bones. "The kind of radiation given off by U-235 is alpha radiation," says Gordon Edwards of the Canadian Coalition for Nuclear Responsibility and a consultant on radiation health issues. "It is recognized that it is dangerous inside the body, as much as 20 times more damaging on a per unit dose than gamma radiation or X-rays."

Roger Cognill, an experimental biologist, told a conference in London that "one single particle of depleted uranium lodged in a lymph node can devastate the entire immune system." Coghill had been studying the links between DU shels and cancers in Iraq. "We know that some million DU rounds were fired during the Persian Gulf War and many still lie in the desert, causing cancers and birth defects. The connection between the two is biologically extremely plausibe," he said. He also predicted up to 10,000 deaths in Kosovo as a result of immune-related disorders.

CLEARING THE AIR

Part of the problem with the debate about the use of anthrax vaccine and depleted uranium is a lack of scientific data. Critics argue that chemical weapons used by Iraqi forces in the 1990-1998 war with Iran and the firing of oil wells in Kuwait during the Gulf War are the real reasons for health problems in the region. Similar problems in Kosovo and the former Yugoslavia are attributed to the destruction of chemical plants and refineries during NATO's bombing campaign. Ailing veterans of both conflicts have been inundated with conflicting theories about the origins of their illnesses.

There is a complete lack of trust in DND which continues to insist that there is no problem with the anthrax vaccine and claims that there is no such thing as Gulf War Syndrome. As one embittered veteran said: "How many more Canadian soldiers must die before the government responds appropriately and tries to find out the answers." To its credit, DND has recognized Post-Traumatic Stress Disorder as a legitimate illness and has made it known that it is willing to test any member of the Canadian Forces who feels he or she may have been exposed to depleted uranium. Concern about the continued use of the anthrax vaccine is another matter, as Mike Kipling can well testify.

Service men and women understand that their service is an unlimited liability; that they serve the nation selflessly in return for assurance that they and their families will be treated decently in the event of a service-related illness or disability. To date, the Department of National Defence has not kept up its side of the bargain.

***AUTHOR**: Bill Twatio*

THE SOMALIA SCANDAL

ABOVE: *Canadian troops were given little preparation as to the culture and climate they would encounter in Somalia. Shortly after the Airborne Regiment arrived, tensions mounted between the locals and the paratroopers. (DND)*

In March 1993, The Defence Department's clumsy attempts to cover-up several atrocities perpetrated by Airborne soldiers in Somalia would result in the disbandment of a once-proud regiment. The public outrage and subsequent inquiry served to expose the military's senior leadership to a media scrutiny which they could not hope to survive.

THROUGHOUT THE FOUR-YEAR period that the Somalia scandal was locked in the national media spotlight, the senior commanders held fast to their claim that there had never been an orchestrated cover-up. Major General Romeo Dallaire went so far as to publicly state, "The possibility of there being a top level military conspiracy to protect individuals involved in Somalia is inconceivable." The main thrust of the top brass' hypothesis was that they would have had "no clear motive" for obfuscating about events in Somalia. However, as the complex trail of evidence and testimony would later unravel before a public inquiry, the senior management was implicated in the whole fiasco from the outset. While many warning signs of impending trouble had been duly reported, either no effort was made to correct the problems, or in some cases, key individuals were placed into positions where their noted shortcomings would only serve to exacerbate the breakdown in discipline.

PROBLEMS EXACERBATED

The case of Captain Michel Rainville was undoubtedly the clearest example of the senior brass' misjudgment and the primary motive for them to attempt a cover-up of the events which unfolded in Somalia. In February 1992, Rainville led a mock terrorist attack against the Citadel in Quebec City to "test the security" of this military facility. During the "training exercise," Rainville and his over-zealous accomplices would torture and anally rape (with weapons) two soldiers who were guarding the armoury that night. Neither of these young privates were aware this was not a real attack and both believed they would be killed by

Rainville. After two hours of brutality, one of the captives escaped and alerted the Quebec City police. As the details of Rainville's sadistic behaviour were revealed to his superiors, it was decided to protect the young Captain's career and to ignore the complaints of his victims. In the subsequent weeks, Rainville's sadism exploded in two additional incidents of assault – in one case a soldier was rendered unconscious by having his head held under water and in the second case, Rainville went berserk during an unarmed training demonstration. Still, the senior army officials chose to turn a blind eye to Rainville's activities. Rather than lay criminal or military charges against him, they chose instead to issue a verbal reprimand to Rainville and transfer him to the Airborne Regiment so that he could deploy to Somalia.

At that time, the Airborne Regiment had just been assessed by their Commanding Officer, Lieutenant Colonel Paul Morneault as not being fit to deploy. There had been several serious discipline problems – particularly in 2 Commando – during the pre-Somalia training sessions. Unfortunately, senior brass chose to ignore warnings and instead of replacing the troublesome 2 Commando (as had been suggested) they removed Morneault from command. The Army's top commanders knew that the best choice for Morneault's replacement would be the "tough-as-nails" Lieutenant Colonel Peter Kenward, but because of internal Anglo / Franco considerations the less-capable (but Quebec-born) Lieutenant Colonel Carol Mathieu was handed the responsibility of command. Mathieu did not take the time to weed out any of the noted troublemakers, but instead pleased his superiors by reversing Morneault's assessment and pronouncing his Regiment "fit to deploy." In mid-December 1992 the Airborne headed to Somalia.

Once in theatre, it did not take long for the ignored problems to emerge. Major Tony Seward – the commander of 2 Commando – was put on "recorded warning" for the repeated shortcomings of his troops (including Seward's own accidental discharge of his rifle). Mathieu had lost the respect of his regiment due to his frequent drunkenness – a glaring example of which occurred on 1 January 1993, when he was observed by his troops stumbling through the streets of Belet Uen, waving his pistol and shouting, "Happy f---ing New Year!"

As the local Somalis became accustomed to the newly arrived paratroopers, looting of the Canadian camp steadily intensified. Frustrated by the heat and the apparent futility of their mission, Airborne soldiers became less and less tolerant of the Somalis. One 2 Commando trooper expressed contempt for the whole UN operation, "All we were doing there was adding to the corruption."

FIRST COVER-UP

In mid-February, in an attempt to curtail the theft of supplies, Lieutenant Colonel Mathieu issued a directive that looters could be shot in the legs "between the skirt and the flip-flops." This was a major change in the original Rules of Engagement (ROEs) under which the Airborne had been deployed. The original ROEs had provided only for the use of firearms if Canadians had first been fired upon. While it is clearly evident that Mathieu's immediate superior in theatre – Colonel Serge Labbé was aware of this change, many senior officials in Ottawa later claimed they were never informed at the time.

Nevertheless, Mathieu's directive was clearly the cause for much consternation on the part of the senior brass on the morning of 5 March 1993. The previous evening, Captain Michel Rainville had led a patrol to ambush Somali looters. They had tried to lure two Somalis into the camp using food and water as bait. When the civilians sus-

__OPPOSITE PAGE, LEFT:__ Trooper Kyle Brown foiled the cover-up in Somalia when he came forward with the trophy photos. (KYLE BROWN) __OPPOSITE PAGE, RIGHT:__ Clayton Matchee was the main culprit in Shidane Arone's death. (KYLE BROWN) __RIGHT:__ General Jean Boyle was at the vortex of the Somalia cover-up from its inception until the Public Inquiry was shut down. Boyle was promoted twice as the scandal caught fire, and, as the Chief of Defence Staff, it ultimately burned his career. (DND) __FAR RIGHT:__ Colonel Serge Labbé was the Canadian contingent commander in Somalia. Records indicate that he reported the serious incident to his superiors, but then assisted in their cover-up by giving misleading interviews to the media. Labbé's promotion to general was quietly rescinded when the scandal broke. (DND)

pected the trap and fled into the desert, Rainville's men opened fire, wounding both Somalis. During the apprehension, Master Corporal Brent Countway shot one of the wounded at point blank range. Both unarmed Somalis were shot outside the Canadian camp. Major Barry Armstrong, the Airborne Regiment's surgeon, reported to Mathieu and Colonel Serge Labbé immediately that he believed the dead Somali had been "executed" after his capture.

In Ottawa, generals and bureaucrats were frantic upon learning of these events. Aware of Rainville's reputation, they knew that this incident could not withstand an outside investigation. After discussions with Ottawa, Labbé ordered Doctor Armstrong to dispose of any damaging evidence and Military Police in Ottawa were told *not* to prepare an investigation team. To divert any media attention, Labbé did a pre-emptive interview with CBC radio during which he misleadingly claimed that the two Somali "intruders" had been in fact "armed saboteurs."

While Rainville's shooting incident gathered no public interest in Canada, in Somalia it set the tone for a rapid escalation of Airborne violence towards the local thieves. On 16 March, Major Tony Seward countermanded Mathieu's "skirt and flip-flop" order by directing that looters were to be captured and "abused" so as to dissuade repeat offenders. That night, Captain Michael Sox led a "snatch" patrol to capture a looter and, just after nightfall, his men nabbed 16-year old Shidane Arone inside the neighbouring US compound. Following his capture, Arone was systematically tortured and beaten by the men of 4 Platoon, 2 Commando. The primary protagonist was Master Corporal Clayton Matchee who assaulted Arone with wild abandon over a three hour period. Initially Trooper Kyle Brown had participated in the assault during his shift, and when Trooper David Brocklebank replaced Brown on his guard shift, Matchee insisted that the three paratroopers should pose for some "trophy photos" beside the bloodied Arone. When Trooper Shawn Class arrived to replace Brocklebank, he could not stomach the sight of the battered Somali boy, so he left Matchee alone to continue the torture.

At approximately 01:00 hours, it was discovered that Arone had stopped breathing. Shortly thereafter, Captain Michael Sox organized Matchee and Kyle Brown to deposit the body at the civilian hospital in Belet Uen. Captain Neil Gibson was the doctor who had pronounced Arone dead, and he and Major Seward had a long conference before they notified Colonel Serge Labbé of the incident.

From the message which Labbé forwarded from Somalia to Ottawa later that night, it was clearly acknowledged that Arone had been killed while in captivity and it was noted that "photographs and statements" would be taken immediately.

SECOND COVER-UP

The fact that no such evidence was gathered during the next 36 hours clearly indicates that Labbé received contrary instructions from Ottawa. In the interim, Captain Gibson had issued a second report claiming he had found only "two small bruises" on Arone's body and that the death was "suspicious." In Ottawa, Defence Minister Kim Campbell was given a briefing based on this falsified input and the implication was that a sick Somali had just "expired" while in Canadian custody.

All would have remained covered up, had it not been for Kyle Brown's "trophy photos" and the integrity of the other soldiers in 2 Commando. Around noon on 18 March, Brown and several sergeants approached Major Seward to advise him that this murder would not be "covered up." Once the photos were presented, Seward had no option but to order Master Corporal Matchee arrested. Again Ottawa was informed of this development, but inexplicably, the senior brass refused to detail a military police investigation. Also unexplained was why no statements were taken from Matchee and no additional evidence was gathered at the camp. Clayton Matchee did write a long letter to his wife saying how much he was looking forward to seeing their child again and he took a number of photos of his makeshift jail. Within hours of sending off these messages, Matchee was found hanging from a wire in his cell. His guards were not present but by happenstance, several US Special Forces soldiers had spotted Matchee's limp form and cut him down. Major Armstrong was the first doctor on the scene and he successfully resuscitated Matchee. Armstrong was immediately suspicious about the wealth of bruises on the body. However, whether Matchee attempted to take his own life or was assaulted will forever remain a mystery – after 12 minutes without oxygen, the brain damage suffered prevented Matchee from recalling details of the incident.

When Labbé dutifully reported Matchee's "attempted suicide" on 19 March, he noted that journalists had been in the vicinity. In Ottawa, it was still believed that the top brass could keep the lid on the whole scandal. A Military Police team was finally dispatched to Somalia to probe the Arone death, but no public announcement was made.

Shortly after Master Warrant Officer Paul Dowd – the senior MP investigator – arrived in Belet Uen, a steady flow of "secret" reports were forwarded to the Operations Center at National Defence Headquarters. Colonel Mike O'Brien was the go-between for all this message traffic, and he would regularly update his carpool during the morning commute. Major Brian Reid recalled O'Brien discussing the torture death and the trophy photos and being shocked that nothing was being told to the media. O'Brien reportedly stated that "The Gang of Eight" (senior general and bureaucrats) had decide the "Somalia Scandal could never be made public."

Unfortunately for "The Gang," the journalist who had been "in the vicinity" had returned to Pembroke from East Africa and had begun putting two-and-two together. On 31 March, a hasty message was issued to Dowd instructing him to "prosecute quickly" as "Matchee's name is known" to the media. Just hours before the story broke in the press, Deputy Minister Bob Fowler, the senior bureaucrat at DND, had his assistant Richard Burton brief Minister Kim Campbell's staff as to the true story.

ABOVE: *Deputy Minister 'Teflon' Bob Fowler was the top bureaucrat at DND and he ran the department like his personal fiefdom. As the events in Somalia unfolded, he kept his political master – Defence Minister Kim Campbell (**LEFT**) in the dark until it was too late to prevent a scandal. The media mistakenly blamed Campbell for the cover-up.* (DND PHOTOS)

STORY BREAKS

As the media spotlight began to focus on the Arone death, the first editorial choruses of "cover-up" were being echoed across the country. The simplest assumption was that Kim Campbell had not wanted to jeopardize her bid for the leadership of the Progressive Conservative Party. However, before Campbell's staff could come to grips with the Arone revelation, the second shoe was about to drop.

Major Barry Armstrong had never destroyed the evidence of 4 March execution and after exhausting all avenues of achieving justice through the chain of command, he sent a detailed letter to his wife. On 21 April 1993, Jennifer Armstrong turned over her husband's startling claim of a second murder to the *Toronto Star*. When their story broke, the media embarked on a feeding frenzy aimed directly at the Airborne Regiment. Irrelevant claims of Neo-Nazism and white supremacy in the ranks clouded the whole issue and inadvertently allowed the senior managers at DND to avoid answering for the more damaging issue of a cover-up. To keep any additional revelations from surfacing, Deputy Minister Bob Fowler advised Kim Campbell to conduct a broad based Board of Inquiry to review the Airborne Regiment from "top to bottom." This effectively placed a gag order on all serving members and bought a relative 'grace period' from media scrutiny.

This internal BOI and the lengthy processing of the various courts martial served to mete out shocking details of the Somalia incidents over a long period of time. The public gradually became aware of the key players and DND senior brass were effectively able to control the media spin that this had been the work of "a few bad apples." The military justice system was complicit in protecting the senior officers. There was no attempt to probe the cover-up, despite ample evidence and as the courts martial concluded, it was readily apparent that the higher the rank the lighter the responsibility. Trooper Kyle Brown was convicted of torture and received a five year

sentence. Sergeant Mark Boland – who had simply not stopped Matchee – was convicted and sentenced to 90 days (later increased to one year). Captain Michel Rainville was convicted of possessing an illegal weapon and received a reprimand and a fine. Captain Michael Sox received a reprimand and a demotion to Lieutenant. Major Tony Seward – who had ordered his men to "abuse" the prisoners received a reprimand. The Commanding Officer, Carol Mathieu, was charged but found innocent and Colonel Serge Labbé walked away unscathed. Matchee himself was determined mentally unfit to stand trial.

In the fall of 1994, in response to a growing public sympathy for Trooper Kyle Brown, who was being seen increasingly as the "scapegoat" in this affair, DND decided to make public the shocking "trophy photos." The strategy almost worked, as the mainstream media plastered the graphic shots everywhere, sparking a tremendous backlash of outraged viewers. Rick Gibbons, editor of the *Ottawa Sun*, went so far as to proclaim that this public airing of the photos finally "closed the book" on the sordid Somalia Affair.

When the public relations plan backfired, Barry Armstrong wrote to Rick Gibbons advising him of the instructions he'd received to "destroy evidence." The *Ottawa Sun* launched an onslaught on the alleged cover-up and Dr. Armstrong found himself at the vortex of a media storm. The Liberal government, in particular Defence Minister David Collenette, initially resisted the calls to establish a public inquiry into the Somalia scandal. Just days later, Kyle Brown spoke-out publicly through interviews conducted inside the military detention barracks. After the *Sun* ran Brown's stories about the 4 March "Turkey Shoot," the public pressure was too great to resist. Collenette reluctantly announced the establishment of a Commission of Inquiry.

BEFORE THE PUBLIC INQUIRY "TRIAL" COULD EVEN COMMENCE, THE GOVERNMENT'S "SENTENCE" ON THE AIRBORNE REGIMENT WAS HANDED OUT AND FORMALLY EXECUTED.

PUBLIC INQUIRY

From the outset, the Liberal's Somalia Commission was plagued with controversy. One of the initial three commissioners, Anne-Marie Doyle, had to remove herself from the panel when the *Ottawa Sun* discovered she had close personal ties to Bob Fowler – one of the key witnesses. Even before the Inquiry could convene its hearings, a series of media revelations set in motion a domino effect which resulted in the Liberal government ordering the disbandment of the Airborne Regiment. A home video of Somalia, shot by members of 2 Commando around the time of Arone's murder was turned over to *Esprit de Corps* magazine and it was forwarded to CBC. On 15 January 1995 CBC reported Susan Harada aired a news story about the videotape which included several segments of soldiers uttering racist remarks. Within hours, every network in Canada was airing the same clips and DND was refusing to give any comment. On 18 January, the initial commotion was abating when CTV obtained a videotape showing members of 1 Commando engaging in an Airborne initiation. The graphic scenes of naked, drunken soldiers eating each others vomit and feces shocked the country when they aired that evening. Once again, senior

ABOVE: *Somalia Inquiry commissioners, from left: Peter Desbarats, Justice Gilles Letourneau, and Justice Robert Rutherford. They proclaimed DND to be "a culture of cover-up."*

officers failed to publicly defend their paratroops and Prime Minister Jean Chretien was already making noise in the media about, "dismantling if necessary." The Airborne was finished. On 23 January 1995 David Collenette announced that the regiment would be disbanded. Before the public inquiry "trial" could even commence, the government's "sentence" was handed out and formally executed.

The Public Commission of Inquiry would nonetheless continue for the next two years. During that time Justices Gilles Letourneau and Robert Rutherford, along with Peter Desbarats, would pore over thousands of documents and cross examine hundreds of witnesses. When it became apparent that the Defence Department was withholding and/or tampering with key documents, it became necessary to conduct a subinquiry into this manipulation of evidence. It was during this portion of the proceedings that Chief of Defence Staff, General Jean Boyle, a key Somalia player from the outset, was brought into the spotlight. The ensuing examination of Boyle resulted in not only the termination of the General's appointment but also it revealed that DND's senior offices pervaded "a culture of coverup."

The Commission was unearthing a steady stream of embarrassing information and by December 1996, the Liberal government lost their nerve. In an effort to protect several of their close political associates from further damage, Defence Minister Doug Young announced that the public inquiry was to be aborted. It was a tremendous risk to take, especially as the country was headed into an election, but the gamble paid off. Public apathy abounded despite furious attempts by the media and the Somalia Commissioners to decry this unprecedented act of termination.

When the Liberals coasted to an easy victory in the June election, Prime Minister Chretien and his Cabinet knew that they had weathered the political storm. As such, the reforms proposed in the final report from the Somalia Inquiry were initially denounced and subsequently ignored.

AUTHOR: *Scott Taylor*

AN ERA OF SCANDAL

While the Somalia affair was developing, DND was engulfed in an endless series of scandals which highlighted a corrupt senior management and a compromised military justice system. The result was a complete erosion of trust between the rank and file soldiers and their leadership, along with a number of sweeping reforms to the Judge Advocate General's empire.

IN FEBRUARY 1997, THE Conference of Defence Associations hosted a panel discussion entitled "Is there a leadership crisis in the Canadian Forces?" Given the composition of the DND-subsidized CDA – largely retired senior officers – the objective of the exercise was to try and shout down the mounting legion of critics. Unfortunately for the organizers, the weight of nearly 36 months of headline-garnering scandals had made questioning whether there was a CF leadership crisis completely rhetorical.

Since the spring of 1994 there had been a steady (at times almost daily) stream of embarrassing revelations in the mainstream media. At first, DND officials had tried to handle each issue independently but, by 1997, the sheer volume had overwhelmed the Public Affairs officers' feeble claims that these were "isolated incidents – only!" Tales of Florida golf junkets, and multi-million dollar fishing camps for senior officers were juxtaposed with internal reports of soldiers lining up at food banks and having to deliver pizza in their off hours simply to make ends meet.

The recurring theme was one of senior officers being caught defrauding the public purse and the military justice system turning a subsequent blind eye. In some cases, generals paid money back to the Crown without charges being laid, while in the remainder, plea bargains would garner a confession in exchange for nothing more than mild reprimands. All these officers would continue to serve in senior positions and/or collect their full pensions. The case of General Armand Roy was one of the most publicized, as he was fired from his post in December 1996. Roy had allegedly pocketed some $86,000 in unearned benefits, which he was obliged to reimburse to the Crown. However, without a conviction, he retained his lucrative, $100,000 a year, pension. High profile Generals Romeo Dallaire and Chief of Defence Staff John de Chastelain were likewise forced to return cash allowances which they had not been entitled to and, despite the evidence, neither were charged with criminal offences.

In the summer of 1996, Colonel Reno Vanier sparked a nationwide manhunt when he disappeared while being investigated by Military Police for fraud. Twelve days later he was found floating in Ottawa's Rideau River – alive and babbling in Creole. While Vanier was in fact charged and convicted of the fraud, he was never tried for being AWOL. Incredibly, he was not sentenced to any jail time, but simply reprimanded and demoted one rank to lieutenant colonel.

When the soldiers learned that Vanier had also received a $4,000 senior officer performance bonus that same year, there was a

tremendous internal backlash against both the brass and the military justice system.

Not until January 1996, was it first learned that in March 1994, members of the Royal 22nd Regiment (Vandoos) had conducted themselves inappropriately while stationed in Bosnia. Military police reports detailed a wide variety of serious misconduct ranging from the sexual abuse of mental patients to the loss of heavy machine guns. When the story first broke, DND tried to "categorically" deny the allegations, however, six months later, then-Army Commander General Maurice Baril was forced to publicly admit the wrongdoing at Bakovici. He ordered a full-blown (internal) inquiry.

Although heavily censored, the final Bakovici report detailed some serious criminal activity and implicated 32 soldiers and officers. Predictably, once again, DNDs internal investigation failed to probe the "cover-up" aspect of this affair. It has never been fully explained why, or on whose authority, the initial 1994 complaints to military police were ignored.

MILITARY INJUSTICE

Just prior to the 1997 CDA conference, the military justice system had been devastatingly torpedoed by Commander Dean Marsaw and the CBCs *Fifth Estate* investigative news show. In September 1996, the *Fifth Estate* had begun their season by running an entire episode on the court martial/conviction of Commander Marsaw.

The show detailed just how biased the military's judiciary had become, and exposed as corrupt a judicial system which appoints the prosecutor, defender and judges. It had been alleged that while in command Marsaw abused his submarine crew and had at one point sexually assaulted a sailor with a cigar tube. As the *Fifth Estate* explained, the prosecutor could not even identify an alleged victim –but Marsaw was convicted nevertheless.

When Commander Marsaw appealed his case, he also embarked on a hunger strike to draw attention to the injustice. As Marsaw hovered near death's door, the *Fifth Estate*, along with the mainstream media, focused their spotlight on the case just in time to watch the military justice system wither and collapse.

With the mounting public clamour rendering him unable to defend the indefensible, Defence Minister Doug Young called for an independent review of the entire military justice system. Led by former Supreme Court Justice Brian Dickson, this panel would recommend a number of radical reforms which proposed to repeal the *almost* absolute power heretofore enjoyed by the Judge Advocate General.

OPPOSITE PAGE: *General Armand Roy was ordered to repay the Crown $86,000 and fired from his post as Deputy Chief of Defence Staff. The Judge Advocate General (JAG) did not press criminal charges and Roy was thus allowed to keep his lucrative pension.* *(DND PHOTO)*

ABOVE LEFT: *General Romeo Dallaire was another senior officer who escaped conviction through "voluntary reimbursement" after being caught receiving benefits to which he was not entitled.* *(DND PHOTO)*

ABOVE MIDDLE: *General John de Chastelain twice had to pay money back to the Crown in order to avoid criminal charges.* *(DND PHOTO)*

ABOVE RIGHT: *General Maurice Baril had to publicly admit that his beloved Vandoos had committed a number of atrocious acts while stationed at a mental hospital in Bakovici, Bosnia.* *(DND PHOTO)*

Despite the government's acknowledgement of the problems, and DND's acceptance of the Dickson recommendations, little real change had been achieved by 2001. Abuses remained commonplace, and the JAG continued to resist relinquishing control of the military justice system.

AUTHOR: *Scott Taylor*

BACK INTO THE BALKANS WITH NATO

For a worn-out Canadian military, changing roles in the Balkans meant there would be no respite. Many soldiers simply changed their berets back from UN blue to standard green and soldiered on.

ABOVE: *A Canadian officer in Bosnia engages in a discussion with his NATO Implementation Force (IFOR) colleagues. One of their primary functions was to resettle the refugees, **(OPPOSITE PAGE)** into a " safe" environment.*

IN THE AUTUMN OF 1995 it was readily apparent that the United Nations Protection Force (UNPROFOR) was not up to the task of keeping the peace in the war torn former Yugoslavia. The atrocities and ethnic cleansing committed by Serb forces – such as those at Srebrenicia – and the seizure of the Krajina region by the Croatian Army demonstrated that, by the summer of 1995, the UN was unable to keep the peace on any level.

Numerous ceasefire agreements had been made, and then broken, by all sides. The world watched as the violence escalated and Yugoslavia continued to break apart. Tougher measures were required. European nations began to warm to the idea of turning the UN peacekeeping operation into a NATO peace enforcement operation. However, for this to actually succeed, the US would have to lead. Up until this time the US had avoided direct intervention.

The US would not intervene unless a peace agreement was in place and that the mission would be clearly defined and achievable. In mid November then President Clinton invited the belligerents and stakeholders to Dayton, Ohio to hammer out a deal all could live with. After much negotiating and arm twisting *The General Framework Agreement for Peace in Bosnia and Herzegovina – (GFAP)* (also known as the Dayton Accords) was initialed in Dayton on 21 November, and officially signed in Paris on 14 December 1995.

This then set the stage for the UN Security Counsel to provide NATO with a mandate. The North Atlantic Counsel then tasked NATO Supreme Allied Command Europe to deploy troops under the peace agreement. The task fell to Commander Allied Forces South who was to double as the Commander of the "Implementation Force" (IFOR). To ensure a robust force COMIFOR had elements of the 5th Allied Tactical Airforce flying fighter cover from Italy and a strong naval presence at sea in the Adriatic including aircraft carriers. The major task of providing security on the ground fell to the UK led Allied Rapid Reaction Corps.

The corps consisted of three major elements; 1st US Armor, 1st UK Armoured, and 1st FR divisions. During the planning phase Canada had decided that its best fit would be with the British contribution to be dubbed Multi-National Division South West (MNDSW). Canada's contribution would be a brigade headquarters based on 2nd Canadian Brigade Group HQ, a signals squadron, an armoured reconnaissance squadron, infantry company group, engineer squadron, and the requisite service support elements. As well, to fill out this small brigade, an infantry battalion – 6th Czech Mechanized Battalion, and a British armoured regiment– Queens Royal Hussars - were placed under operational control of the newly named and Canadian led 2nd Canadian Multi-National Brigade (2CAMNB).

The UN force and organization were becoming ever more ineffective in the fall of 1995. At this time it was just able to support itself and could not make any headway in the peace process. The anticipated change over to NATO had some contingents trying to leave to make way for the NATO forces, some simply changing hats and staying in location, some staying in-country but redeployed to new locations, and some conducting hand-overs. UNPROFOR services continued to be maintained such as the airport at Sarajevo and the UN flights. This proved to be very useful as the incoming NATO forces began to send in staff teams and commanders to conduct ground reconnaissance prior to the arrival or redeployment of troops. By mid-December this was very much under way. Incoming units looked for the best sites for their deployments. Prime real estate such as former UN camps were much sought after at the beginning of NATO's first ever-operational deployment.

Bosnia-Herzegovina (BH) is composed

of two entities; the Republika Srpska in the east populated Serbs, and the Federation of Bosnia-Herzegovina populated by Croatians and Muslims. The Canadians were assigned to the north west corner of Bosnia-Herzegovina, with an area of operations that included both entities and the Inter-Entity Boundary Line (IEBL) delineating the two.

Canadian troops first began changing over from UN to NATO operational control at the end of December 1995 with some support elements in Zagreb. Canadian officers, formerly UN Military Observers, began liaison and reconnaissance tasks and communications links with the brigade headquarters at CFB Petawawa. The first elements of the Brigade began to arrive early in January 1996, with the deployment complete by the end of the month.

Initially the major task of 2CAMNB was establishing itself on the ground in its area of operations. In order to establish well operated and secure camps the operation began with an "engineer surge," that is an additional squadron of engineers sent in theater for approximately a month to provide site construction and camp improvements. Coralici, the site of a former Bangladeshi battalion UN camp would be the brigade headquarters location, along with 2nd Signals Squadron, 2 Military Police Platoon, an Advanced Surgical Center (ASC) and a troop of engineers from 23 Field Squadron.

The main support base would be located at Velika Kladusa, inside Bosnia-Herzegovina but close to the Croatian border. This made for a secure line of support far from the Zone of Separation between the belligerents, and ensured security for troops and equipment coming from the arrival airport in Zagreb.

Meanwhile the remainders of the Canadian units were deployed to the southeast corner of the area of operations in the town of Kljuc. Located there were "A" Squadron the Royal Canadian Dragoons with 22 Cougar armoured vehicles, 23 Field Engineer Squadron from 2 Combat Engineer Regiment which in addition to its compliment of heavy engineer equipment had two Leopard mine roller/plow tanks. "G" Company of the Royal Canadian Regiment operating

under tactical control of the British armoured regiment – the Queen's Royal Hussars – conducted operations with its 16 Grizzly armoured vehicles.

The Queen's Royal Hussars had as its main camp and headquarters location the town of Bosanski Petrovac directly west of Kljuc. The regiment, as well as having a Canadian infantry company, had a troop of eight Scimitar armoured reconnaissance vehicles, a squadron of fourteen Challenger tanks, and "B" Company of the 2nd Light Infantry equipped with 17 Warrior armoured infantry fighting vehicles.

6th Mechanized Czech Battalion was the only unit located in the Republika Srpska, the camp was south east of the town of Prijedor. Equipped with 18 BVP-2 armoured infantry fighting vehicles, and nine OT-64 eight wheeled armoured vehicles the Czechs were anxious to show their skills to future NATO partners.

Some major services and assistance to 2 CAMNB came from the division level and higher. This included helicopter support, artillery located in the brigade's area of operation, explosive ordinance disposal, psychological operations, and tactical air support and secure tactical communications.

The conduct and the type of peace enforcement operations that had been authorized for NATO/IFOR were very different than those authorized for UNPROFOR. There was a more robust set of rules of engagement. There was a change in attitude. There would be no more instances of denial of movement, no threats and or attacks on peacekeeping forces. This was not to be UNPROFOR II. The GFAP authorized *"...the IFOR to take such actions as required, including the use of necessary force, to ensure compliance ...and to ensure its own protection..."*. In addition the GFAP made a clear distinction between what were military tasks and what were civilian tasks. The High Representative (senior ranked civilian in the GFAP) had no authority over the conduct of military operations.

The initial primary military task conducted by 2 CAMNB was the establishment, through the use of GPS, to site the Inter-Entity Boundary Line and Zone of Separation (ZOS). Belligerents were to move apart from each other and outside of the ZOS by D-Day +30. Next would be the transfer of areas designated under the GFAP that would occur on D-Day + 45. There could be no occupation of theses areas by military forces before D-Day + 91. Next came the cantonment of weapons. Both forces were required to move their heavy weapons to sites for storage designated by IFOR and to be completed by D-Day + 120. Non-compliance would be met by force if necessary. By D-DAY+ 183 Bosnia-Herzegovina would be ready for the election process to begin.

The first IFOR rotation of Canadian troops out of Bosnia-Herzegovina began in early July 1996. The brigade and its units would be replaced by the 5th Canadian Mechanized Brigade Group from Valcartier and it would be renamed 5th Canadian Multi-National Brigade. IFOR's mandate was for one year, however it became readily apparent that one year was not enough to ensure an end state. The UN Security Council would in December of 1996 renew the IFOR mandate for 18 more months and necessitate its name change to SFOR – Stabilization Force.

***AUTHOR:** Howard H Michitsch*

AID TO CIVIL POWER (AND AUTHORITY)

Never glorious, but always appreciated, Canadian soldiers are frequently called out to assist civilian authorities during domestic crises.

ABOVE: *Much to the amusement of the rest of Canada, Mayor Mel Lastman of Toronto called in the Army in the wake of a winter storm in January, 1999. Reservists from 32 Canadian Brigade Group shovel out a newspaper box.* (JON O'CONNOR)

ONE POPULAR IMAGE OF Canadian servicemen and women is that of heading off for some foreign location on a warlike or peacekeeping mission. Unlike many nations, especially among those of the Third World and repressive dictatorships, the function of the Canadian Armed Forces is not that of subduing the population and repressing potential or actual rebellion. However, at times forces have been called upon to assist in dealing with emergency situations at home.

THE MOST RECENT MAJOR EXAMPLE OF COMMUNITY ASSITANCE AROSE DURING THE SEVERE ICE STORMS WHICH PARTLY PARALYSED EASTERN ONTARIO AND QUEBEC IN EARLY 1998. THE CF SENT 16,000 MEMBERS TO ASSIST.

PREMIERS JUST HAVE TO ASK

The National Defence Act authorizes the Chief of the Defence Staff to assign members of the Canadian Forces to assist "on request of the Premier of a Province," should an emergency situation arise which is beyond the power of provincial resources to deal with it. This is in addition to other domestic functions which have been a traditional part of Canada's military activity – the most notable of these is perhaps the Search and Rescue role in which members of the Canadian Forces, often at great risk, have saved many lives on land and sea.

The presence of military and naval units in the communities across Canada has also resulted in a traditional ceremonial role. Openings of provincial legislatures, escorts for dignitaries (the Queen's Plate event in Toronto is invariably opened by the Vice-regal representative accompanied by an equestrian escort from the Governor General's Horse Guards) and fund-raising events and band concerts (especially by the local militia units) are all visible reminders of the Forces' presence and involvement in the community.

Sometimes assistance is provided for events of a more serious nature. With their readily-available pool of able-bodied human resources, it is not surprising that the Forces are called upon to provide their expertise, materiel and equipment and above all their people to respond to major natural and other disasters.

This is not always popular. During the years between the World Wars, troops had been called out to protect property and control unruly crowds in labour and social disputes. This ticklish job was usually handled with the aplomb characteristic of the Canadian serviceman – indeed on at least two occasions, in Nova Scotia and Ontario, the troops appeased the angry populace with sporting events and band concerts and when their tour of duty ended the local inhabitants were sorry to see them leave.

Another breakdown of law and order sometimes occurred during prison riots and disorders. Several times over the last half-century or so, provincial authorities have called on the Army for assistance, which involved helping to quell the riots and, until order was restored, acting a "jail warders." Other confrontations occurred some years ago when the Quebec government requested the help of The R22eR to assist in a stand-off situation at a Native People's reserve in Oka, Quebec.

More seriously was the "October" crisis in Quebec, when a separatist group began terrorist operations and Prime Minister Pierre Trudeau invoked the War Measures Act. In the same decade, Montreal was again the scene of high-profile activity by the Canadian Forces in support of the 1976 Summer Olympics. (In addition to excellent administrative support, security was a major factor in view of the assassination of Israeli athletes in Munich in 1972.)

Canadian Forces were most visible in their assistance the community in cases of natural disaters. The major flooding in the Winnipeg area in Spring of 1950 brought out over 12,000 helpers, whose tasks included evacuation, building sandbag dikes and levees and even underwater operations by frogmen flown in from Halifax. Four years

later, after Hurricane Hazel, the most severe inland storm to strike Canada, heavy personnel and material assistance was provided to the inhabitants of Toronto and central Ontario.

The most recent major example of community assitance arose during the severe ice storms which partly paralysed Eastern Ontario and Quebec in early 1998. In January of that year a devastating combination of snow and freezing rain isolated many communities, left over half a million homes without electric power, and rendered thousands of inhabitants homeless.

TOP LEFT: *Operation SAGUENAY. Soldiers of the 12e Régiment Blindé du Canada fill sandbags near Ville de la Baie, Quebec, as floods devastate the region in July 1996.* ***TOP RIGHT*** and ***LEFT:*** *Coming to the assistance of victims of Hurricane* Andrew, *which swept across south Florida in October 1992, a crewman unloads emergency supplies from HMCS* Protecteur *at the Port of Miami.* *(BOTH COURTESY DND)*

The Canadian Forces were asked to assist and on 9 and 10 January moved into Quebec and Ontario. A total of 16,000 regular and reserve service personnel took part in Operation RECUPERATION. Their tasks included provision and operation of emergency accommodation, and in some cases assisting the hard-pressed medical facilities. Engineers and other Forces members helped to reopen roads, removing thosands of fallen trees which had given way under the heavy ice coating, as well as helping out the overworked electricity workers in their task of restoring power.

HOMES EVACUATED

Communicators joined Bell Canada workers in an effort to restore communications, while the important function of providing security to the evacuated homes was carried out by reserbists under control of Military police. The Air element was not forgotten – fixed-wing airctaft and helicopters were active in transport and casualty evacuation. Logistical and supply assistance took the form of transportation (often the military all-terrain vehicles were the only ones able to reach some of the affected areas) and provision of a host of bedding and other materials for the shelters. Service cooks probably had more satisfied "clients" than ever before, as field kitchens were set up to feed the victims.

A severe shortage of electrical generators was partly alleviated by engineer supplies, who also turned up with chain saws and other essential equipment. The Canadian Forces worker earned a multitude of tokens of appreciation from provinces, municipalities and individuals, when normality was restored, sometimes within a week, in other areas several weeks later. What was perhaps a unique experience was the decision of the Operational Commander to make this a "dry" operation, partly because of the the dangerous conditions under which the troops worked. Despite many offers of liquid hospitality from grateful citizens, only four charges were laid for breach of this direction, during the whole operation.

Detractors of our serving men and women may not always appreciate the spending of their pitifully few tax dollars on the military – to many other Canadians, even in times of peace, it's money well spent.

AUTHOR: *Les Peate*

OPERATION DETERMINATION: THE SECOND GULF CRISIS

HMCS* Toronto *shown shortly after her commissioning ceremony. In 1998 she was deployed into the Persian Gulf in anticipation of renewed hostilities with Iraq.
(DND PHOTO)

In 1998, when the United States refused to lift crippling sanctions, Iraq ousted the international arms inspectors. Americans and Canadians were soon en route to the Persian Gulf to re-assert their military domination of the region.

ON 10 FEBRUARY 1998, THE Government of Canada announced that it had agreed to deploy HMCS *Toronto* and a detachment of two KCC-130 air to air refuelling Hercules refuelling tankers from 435 Squadron, Winnipeg to the Arabian Gulf. This mission, called Operation DETERMINATION, was intended to support a military coalition to conduct offensive action against Iraq to re-establish compliance with UN Security Council Resolution 687 dated April 1991.

HMCS *Toronto*'s original mission had been to support NATO's Standing Naval Force Atlantic. On 12 February, the ship was re-routed in the middle of its cold climate NATO exercise off the coast of Norway to the Arabian Gulf to assist in the US-led multinational effort to ensure that Iraq complies with the UNSC 687 and permit UNSCOM inspectors to monitor Iraqi sites.

On 20 February 1998, the United Nations had signed an agreement with Iraq on the subject of inspections and it quickly became clear that this operation had become redundant. So, on 3 March the mandate of the air assets was changed. Henceforth, the two KCC-130 air to air refuelling (AAR) aircraft were used to support Operation SOUTHERN WATCH (OSW) the coalition mission to enforce the no-fly zone in Iraq which was established shortly after the cessation of hostilities in Iraq in 1991. This mission would remain unchanged until the air assets ceased operation in the region on 16 May 1998. In all the AAR portion of Op DETERMINATION completed 142 missions, providing coalition fighters with more than three million pounds of jet fuel.

HMCS *Toronto,* for her part, arrived in theatre in early March. Although the operation had become redundant, it remained in the region to conduct a series of Maritime Interdiction Operations (MIO) in support of the UN embargo against Iraq. It ceased operations in the Arabian Gulf on 12 May. During this period, *Toronto* conducted approximately 75 hailings, boardings and inspections. The ship also participated in several naval exercises with other coalition warships in the Arabian Gulf. When the ship returned to Halifax on 16 June 1998.

***ABOVE:** Sergeant Mike Kipling (seen here with his daughter) gained national attention when he refused to be injected with a controversial anthrax vaccine.*
(WINNIPEG FREE PRESS)

Although this operation was stillborn, it gained considerable notoriety because it was during this operation that the issue surrounding the anthrax vaccine made national headlines. (Sergeant Mike Kipling was part of the 435 Squadron detachment that was deployed to the Arabian Gulf.) During this visit eyebrows were raised when Tim Horton's obtained what has arguably been called an endorsement of the product from the ship's crew. In exchange for several cans of coffee, Tim Horton's was able to produce a commercial using the testimony of CF personnel onboard HMCS *Toronto*.

AUTHOR: *G. Jaxon*

SHOWDOWN OVER KOSOVO

NATO officials proclaimed the necessity to bomb Yugoslavia was to "prevent a humanitarian disaster." However, the flood of refugees from Kosovo did not begin until after the bombing began. (SCOTT TAYLOR)

Serbia's refusal to sign the Rambouillet Accord cleared the way for NATO bombers.

BY 1990, THE FIRST armed clashes were taking place between the now Serbian Kosovar police and Albanian separatists.

Western Europe and the international media paid little attention to these internal developments. The situation in Kosovo was completely eclipsed by the fragmentation of Yugoslavia in June 1991. The split began with the proclamations of independence by Slovenia and Croatia (followed by Bosnia in April 1992). Four years of brutal civil war ensued, followed by ruthless campaigns to purify zones of control known as "ethnic cleansing." Serbia, while not directly involved in the conflict, supplied men and weapons to the Bosnian Serbs and the Krajina regions. Although the combined Serb forces achieved early successes, the imposition of international trade sanctions, coupled with the U.S. provision of military aid to the Croats and Muslims, reversed their fortunes. By the time the Dayton Peace Accord was enforced in 1996, the Serbs had suffered tremendous losses.

In addition to the estimated 20,000 soldiers killed, more than 750,000 Serbs had been cleansed from Croatia and Bosnia. Trade sanctions remained in place against the rump Republic of Yugoslavia, now comprised of only Serbia and Montenegro. The economy was in tatters.

During the 1996 municipal elections, the people had exercised their democratic right to send the Belgrade government a message. The opposition won an overwhelming majority over Milosevic's party at the ballot boxes. However, when these results were ignored, the electorate was outraged.

Hundreds of thousands of Serbs took to the streets night after night to protest the presidency of Slobodan Milosevic.

Milosevic's concerns over growing domestic unrest were compounded by steadily increasing Albanian terrorist activity in Kosovo. To cope with the flood of Serbian refugees displaced by the war, the Yugoslav government had initiated a resettlement program in Kosovo. Ethnic Albanians saw this as a deliberate ploy to alter the region's demographics, thereby precluding their eventual independence. The separatists stepped up their campaign of terror. Milosevic had responded by increasing both the number and capabilities of his security forces in Kosovo.

On 29 November 1997, a funeral was held in Drenica for an Albanian teacher who had been killed by Yugoslav police. When two masked, armed men appeared, the mourners began to chant U-C-K, the Albanian slogan for KLA. Soon the chant could be heard across the province.

As the KLA gained control of rural areas, Yugoslav police units were bolstered by elements of the Vojska Jugoslavije, the regular army and reservists. On 5 March 1998, a Serbian battle group surrounded Adem Jashari, the KLA commander, at his mountain outpost. Jashari and his followers refused to surrender and were killed. Jashari became a martyr, and the fighting intensified.

By July, the widening conflict drew the concern of the European community. Despite international pressure for a cease-fire, the Serb forces mounted a major offensive in August to reclaim the area previously seized by the KLA. Roughly 45 per cent of the province was under Albanian control and guerrillas were operating just five kilometres from Kosovo's capital, Pristina.

As Yugoslav troops regained the tactical initiative, the United Nations Security Council passed Resolution 1199. Both parties were to agree to an immediate cease-fire, and the Yugoslav security forces were to withdraw. Failure to comply with the directive would trigger "additional measures [being taken by the U.N.] to maintain or restore peace and stability."

There was always the likelihood of a Russian or Chinese veto, since NATO countries had been instrumental in pushing the Kosovo resolutions through the U.N. Security Council. However, NATO officials publicly declared they would ignore any veto. Their aircraft were poised to launch punitive airstrikes against the Serbs and, with or without U.N. approval, they intended to bomb.

Milosevic appeared to concede and, by 27 October 1998, his armoured forces were returning to their barracks. Part of the U.N. resolution called for the deployment of "unarmed international verifiers" to monitor the cease-fire in Kosovo. Throughout November, nearly 2000 observers arrived in the war-ravaged province to find that the firing had never really ceased. Since their setback at the hands of the Serbs in August, the KLA had been re-equipped and trained by international "advisors" in Albania.

As the Serb armour pulled back, the new, improved KLA renewed their guerrilla attacks on Serb police forces with a vengeance.

On the diplomatic front, things were also beginning to unravel. Milosevic had agreed to the concept of a U.N. Verification Force, but he balked at allowing Louise Arbour, the Canadian judge serving as the chief prosecutor for the U.N. War Crimes Tribunal, to conduct an investigation into alleged Serb atrocities.

For their part, the Albanian Kosovar delegation had split internally. Ibrahim Rugova, the pacifist delegate, was prepared to make several key concessions to the Serbs. From the outset, Rugova had been opposed to the use of KLA terrorism to achieve independence. Hashim Thaci, the KLA leader, was not so accommodating. Denouncing Rugova's conservative approach, and emboldened by his rising status within the NATO community, Thaci proclaimed the KLA to be the sole representative of the Albanian Kosovars. As Rugova appealed to the U.N. to deploy peacekeepers to Kosovo, Thaci ordered his men to resume the war.

On 16 January, after months of scattered fighting during which it became increasingly apparent that the KLA was being furnished with sophisticated weaponry by NATO sources, the crisis came to a head. At the village of Racak, U.N. verifiers discovered 40 Albanian corpses and evidence of torture. Serbian officials claimed the dead were KLA terrorists, but their protests fell on deaf ears.

Although heavily embroiled in the Monica Lewinsky impeachment scandal, American President Bill Clinton took to the airwaves to express his outrage over the Racak incident. NATO reiterated that they were prepared to impose a military settlement if an agreement could not be reached between the Serbs and the KLA.

Both warring factions were instructed to send delegates to Rambouillet, France to hammer out an accord by 19 February.

NATO instructed the Serbian government that failure to participate would result in airstrikes against Yugoslavia; the KLA was told that a lack of compliance would mean a suspension in provision of military aid. Even to the casual observer, it became evident that, despite claims of impartiality, NATO was clearly in the KLA camp.

***LEFT:** Canadian judge Louise Arbour was anxious to proclaim a "war crime" had occurred at Racak in Kosovo. This incident would later be proven to have been a staged hoax – but at the time, U.S. Secretary of State Madeleine Albright (**BELOW**) used Racak as an excuse for U.S. intervention in Kosovo.*
(AMEL EMRIC, AP/AFP)

As the peace talks got underway in Rambouillet, Serbian apprehension mounted. When negotiations stalled, U.S. Secretary of State Madeleine Albright met secretly with the Albanian delegation. She outlined three possible options: 1) they could refuse to sign the American draft proposal and thereby lose all NATO support; 2) they could sign the deal and, if the Serbs refused, NATO would bomb them into accepting the deal; and 3) both parties would agree to the conditions and NATO troops would enforce the agreement.

Under the terms of the Rambouillet Accord, there would be no referendum on Kosovo independence for at least three years. For KLA delegate Hashim Thaci, such a delay was unacceptable.

The Serbs had a number of objections to the proposal, not the least of which was the plan calling for NATO troops to be allowed free access to Yugoslavian airspace and land routes. Ostensibly, this was simply to facilitate the establishment of a NATO peacekeeping force in Kosovo. The Serbs saw it as an occupation of their homeland. The guarantee of an eventual referendum on Kosovar independence was another thing they were not prepared to accept.

When the original deadline passed with neither side having signed, Albright once again approached the Albanians. She advised them that she now had a fourth option: If both sides refused to sign, NATO would withdraw the threat of airstrikes against Yugoslavia. On 24 February, the Albanian delegates proposed a hasty compromise, suggesting a two-week delay, which would allow them time to consult with the residents of Kosovo.

Once again, heavy fighting erupted in the war-torn province. Serbian police forces were reinforced, and Yugoslav air defence units were reportedly deployed to strategic sites inside Kosovo.

On 15 March, the Albanians announced they would agree to the Rambouillet terms. As a matter of courtesy, the Serbs were given one last opportunity to sign the accord. Since no new concessions were being offered, they refused. On 18 March, at the Arc de Triomphe in Paris, the Albanian Kosovars signed sole approval of the peace deal. Madeleine Albright's second option, the bombing of Belgrade, was cleared for take-off.

REPRINTED FROM: INAT: Images of Serbia and the Kosovo Conflict
AUTHOR: *Scott Taylor*

CANADA'S AIR ATTACKS ON YUGOSLAVIA

Although Canada contributed only two per cent of the Allied air force, our pilots participated in ten per cent of the bombing attacks. No casualties were suffered during 78 days of continuous air strikes.

ABOVE:
Canadian pilots used "smart bombs" for the first time during the air assault against Yugoslavia. When Canada ran out of these weapons, America was able to sell us additional stocks. (DND PHOTO)

IN JUNE 1998, CANADA sent six CF-18 fighters and approximately 125 military personnel to Aviano, Italy to help enforce a no-fly zone over Bosnia-Herzegovina. This mission was called Operation ECHO. Between 24 March and 10 June 1999, Canadian Task Force Aviano changed its mandate and took part in the NATO air bombing campaign over the Federal Republic of Yugoslavia. The following is a brief look at Canada's participation in the 78-day NATO air bombing campaign and the NATO humanitarian effort associated with this same operation.

OPERATION ECHO DEPLOYMENT

Between 24 March - 3 April there were 6 CF-18s completing an average of four missions per day. During this period these missions were primarily air-to-ground missions.

Between 4 April and 2 May Task Force Aviano had 12 CF-18s. The Task Force then began flying between eight and 12 sorties per day. Missions were almost exclusively air-to-ground strikes, using precision-guided munitions.

Between 3 May and 10 June, Task Force Aviano had 32 pilots and 18 CF-18s and flew an average of 16 sorties per day. These pilots represented some 36 percent of the total number of combat ready fighter pilots available in the Canadian Forces (90). More than 300 Canadian aircrew, and ground support personnel were also deployed to Aviano at this juncture. During this period, Task Force Aviano was given an additional task - air interdiction.

Following the end of the NATO air bombing campaign in early June, eight CF-18s left Aviano on 27 June 1999 and arrived in Bagotville the following day. Another four left on 29 June. The remaining six CF-18s and 120 military personnel began returning to Canada in December 2000 when Operation ECHO was officially terminated.

SORTIES

During Operation ALLIED FORCE, the official designation for its air bombing campaign over the Federal Republic of Yugoslavia, Canadian CF-18s planned to fly some 945 sorties. However, six sorties were cancelled due to maintenance problems, 85 sorties were called off because of a variety of operational factors while another 176 sorties were cancelled due to bad weather. So, Canadian pilots actually flew a total of 678 sorties[1] out of a NATO total of 37,500 sorties. Some 558 of the Canadian sorties were air-to-ground and 120 were air-to-air. The 678 sorties represented approximately 2,547 flying hours.

MISSIONS

Seen from a different perspective, Canadian CF-18s flew a total of 224 missions,[2] or 167 air-to-ground missions (strike missions) and 57 air-to-air (air combat patrol) missions. In fact, while Canada only possessed some 2 percent of the combat aircraft involved in the campaign, Canadian Cf-18s flew about 10 percent of all NATO strike missions and Canadian pilots were the package commanders (leaders) on approximately 50 percent of the missions they were assigned.

Of the 167 air-to-ground missions, 82 managed to deliver their precision guided munitions. Nine delivered unguided bombs (Mark 82s). Seventy-two of the missions reported hits and all nine of the missions that delivered non-precision guided munitions delivered on target. Although the CF-18s were armed with sidewinders and sparrow air-to-air missiles, none were expended during the 57 air-to-air missions.

TARGETS

One new facet of this air bombing campaign was the process by which targets were assigned to Canadian pilots. For every Canadian mission flown, a Canadian Forces legal officer carefully examined the target that had been assigned with a view towards its legitimacy and relevance under Canadian and international legal standards.

According to the government spokespersons, the laser guided bombs used by the CF-18s experienced a 70 percent success rate. In other words, 70 percent of the laser guided bombs dropped hit their intended target(s). The remaining 30 percent did not hit their target for a variety of reasons. For example, Canadian pilots experienced smoke or cloud obscuration of the target at the last moment, sometimes the laser designation equipment failed after the release of the bomb release. Finally, there was the failure of the bomb to detonate on target.

Targets assigned to Task Force Aviano included army camps, airfields, radio relay stations, bridges, tunnels, industrial targets, fielded forces, fuel depots, and storage depots deployed in the Federal Republic of Yugoslavia and especially in the province of Kosovo. No Canadian bombs were dropped in circumstances acknowledged by NATO to have been *"errors"* resulting in civilian casualties.

ABOVE AND TOP:
With Serbian air defence only able to reach up to 10,000 feet, and the NATO aircraft operating at 22,000 feet, there was no 'hostile' threat to Canadian pilots, the most dangerous task faced by our pilots was during their air-to-air refueling.
(DND PHOTO)

MUNITIONS

During this air bombing campaign Canadian CF-18s dropped some 360 precision-guided munitions. Approximately 120 were laser guided GBU 10s (2000lbs gravity bombs outfitted with a laser kit that allowed it to travel down to a target highlighted by a laser). The remaining 240 were laser guided GBU 12s (500lbs gravity bombs also outfitted with a laser kit). In addition another 170 Mark 82 gravity bombs were delivered on their respective targets (500 lbs. Bombs with no laser guiding mechanism). Canada did not use either cluster bombs or depleted uranium munitions.

Approximately 35 C-130 Hercules and CC-150 Polaris sorties were required to support the Canadian participation in Op Allied Effort. In all, these transport aircraft delivered some 350,000 pounds – including 410 passengers to Aviano.

Another important facet of the support received by Task Force Aviano came from the NATO Airborne early Warning Force based in Geilenkirchen, Germany. Approximately 79 of the AWACS aircrew along with 40 support personnel based in Germany were Canadian. On average of two Canadians took part in each of the 497 sorties (4800 hours) flown by the AWACS over the Federal Republic of Yugoslavia during Operation Allied Effort.

HMCS *Athabaskan* took up position with the Standing NATO Force Atlantic (SNFL) ready to support the NATO operation should it be called upon.

The incremental cost associated with Task Force Aviano (excluding the AWACs, and HMCS *Athabaskan*) was in the neighbourhood of $26 million of which $18 million were for the costs of replacing the munitions.

In addition to the CF-18 contribution to Operation ALLIED FORCE, there was a humanitarian aide dimension to this NATO effort. Canadian participation in this NATO humanitarian effort was called Operation MIKADO. Essentially, it consisted of 20 C-130 Hercules sorties flown for a total of 151 hours of flying time to bring 284,000 pounds of humanitarian material from Norway and Denmark to their destination airports in Albania and the Former republic of Macedonia.

The incremental cost associated with Operation MIKADO was in the order of $1.2 million.

AUTHOR: *G. Jaxon*

OCCUPATION OF KOSOVO

Following the airstrikes and the withdrawal of Yugoslav forces, it was up to NATO troops to try and curtail the violence in Kosovo.

On guard in Mitrovica, Kosovo. Racial tension and ethnic violence continued even after the NATO occupation.
NEXT PAGE: General Baril made a brief visit to the embattled Balkan province. (DND PHOTO)

THE NATO-LED MISSION to Kosovo (Kosovo Force – KFOR) was made to ostensibly stop the ethnic cleansing of Kosovar Albanians by the ethnic Serbian Yugoslav government of Belgrade. The NATO mission, code named Operation ALLIED FORCE, was tasked with:

- creating a secure environment for the return of displaced persons and refugees as well as international and non-governmental organizations;
- providing immediate humanitarian assistance to displaced persons; and
- performing public security functions prior to and after the arrival of international organizations.

In response to the Belgrade operations in Kosovo, and intransigence during negotiations, NATO began an air campaign on 24 March 1999 to halt ethnic cleansing and to force the Yugoslav military from Kosovo.

The Canadian participation in the air portion of the operation was code-named Operation Echo. This consisted of – at its peak – 18 CF-18 fighter bombers stationed in Aviano Italy along with 300 air force personnel to provide air support as required. In addition there were also approximately 90 Forces members in Geilenkirchen, Germany, providing support and crew members for NATO Airborne Early Warning Force (NAEWF) aircraft, which were also operating in the Balkan region.

The Canadian contribution to the NATO ground operation was dubbed Operation KINETIC. The force aimed to create stable and safe conditions in Kosovo that enabled the return of hundreds of thousands of refugees and the reestablishment of a functioning economy.

Canada had, at its peak, approximately 1300 members serving in Kosovo and FYROM as part of Operation Kinetic. The Canadians formed part of a British brigade (4 Armoured Brigade) within the NATO-led force.

The Canadian contingent included an Armoured Reconnaissance Squadron, a Tactical Helicopter Squadron, a Combat Engineer Regiment and an Infantry Battle Group as well as a National Command Element and a National Support Element.

Approximately 170 members from 408 Tactical Helicopter Squadron Element from CFB Edmonton supplemented the British Armoured Brigade by carrying out airborne reconnaissance / surveillance, transport and medical evacuation missions. The eight CH-146 Griffon helicopters were equipped to carry out night and day surveillance.

The Lord Strathcona's Horse (Royal Canadians) Reconnaissance Squadron, from CFB Edmonton deployed with approximately 180 soldiers. Co-located with the Tactical Helicopter Squadron at an airstrip southwest of Pristina, they provided the 4 (UK) Armoured Brigade with detailed night and day surveillance. The Recce Squadron of the LdSH (RC) was equipped with the Coyote Light Armoured Vehicle-Reconnaissance (LAV-Recce), which had a combination of sights, radar, thermal imaging and laser range-finding equipment.

CFB Edmonton deployed 15 Engineer Squadron with approximately 160 sappers. Stationed in Pristina, the main functions of the squadron were to conduct mine clearance, construct camps for Canadian troops, and help restore civilian infrastructure.

The Canadian contingent also deployed a Battle Group of 600 soldiers, consisting of two infantry companies and a combat support company from 1st Battalion, Princess Patricia's Canadian Light Infantry (1PPCLI). Additional support was provided by an engineer troop from 1st Combat Engineer Regiment (1CER) and a Leopard I tank troop from the LdSH (RC) to provide additional firepower and mine clearance capability.

The mission of the Battle Group was to provide a secure environment while building confidence among the locals to encourage the return of refugees.

Located at Camp Maple Leaf in Skopje FYROM, the Canadian National Support Element (NSE) and the National Command Element (NCE) had approximately 275 troops and 95 troops respectively, including a National Command Control Information System Detachment.

Canada's operation code name Operation QUADRANT encompassed general participation in other international organization missions in Kosovo. This mostly involved mine clearance, investigation of war crimes and the establishment of an interim government administration, including participation in:

- the UN Mission Interim Administration

in Kosovo (UNMIK);

- the Mine Action Coordination Center (MACC);
- the International Criminal Tribunal for Yugoslavia (ICTY); and
- the Organization for Cooperation and Security in Europe (OSCE).

By spring 2001 there were nine CF members still deployed or earmarked for Operation QUADRANT.

CHRONOLOGY

NATO Secretary General Javier Solana on 23 March 1999, ordered the Supreme Allied Commander in Europe (SACEUR), General Wesley Clark, to begin air operations in Yugoslavia. This decision was taken after the failure of diplomatic negotiations.

24 March – NATO aircraft, including Canadian CF-18s, carried out the first wave of attacks.

2 April – the first Polaris (Airbus) aircraft of 437 Transport Squadron left 8 Wing at Trenton, Ontario carrying 14 metric tons of emergency relief supplies. On arrival at the RAF base at Brize-Norton, England, these supplies were transferred to Hercules transport aircraft and flown to Albania and FYROM. In all, more than 140 metric tons of supplies were flown in by 429 Transport.

7 April – Canada announced it would accept 5000 Kosovar refugees as a temporary measure. Canadian Forces Bases and training centres (including Trenton, Borden, Petawawa and Meaford in Ontario; Valcartier, Quebec; Gagetown, New Brunswick; and Halifax and Greenwood, Nova Scotia), were prepared to house them, under the name Operation PARASOL.

9 April – The refugee crisis easing, the UNHCR decided to allow displaced Kosovars to remain in the region. The CF however, remained ready to receive refugees at short notice, should the situation change.

Late April – Canada announced that ground troops would be dispatched to the Balkans. They were sent to Macedonia to join 12,000 NATO troops already in that region. This force would enter Kosovo with the full consent of all parties involved only after a peace agreement.

4 May – the first of 5000 Kosovar refugees begin arriving in Canada at the two Airbases in Trenton, Ontario, and Greenwood, Nova Scotia.

8 May – NATO apologized after some of its warplanes had accidentally bombed the Chinese Embassy in Belgrade.

10 May – the Yugoslav army announced a partial withdrawal of military and police forces from Kosovo. The verifiable withdrawal of Yugoslav units was among the key conditions set down by NATO for stopping the bombing campaign.

14 May – NATO accidentally and to much condemnation, bombed a convoy of Kosovar Albanian refugees.

18 May – two Serb prisoners of war headed back to Belgrade. NATO handed them over to the Yugoslav government while European leaders continued to lobby for a diplomatic solution to the crisis in Kosovo.

27 May – the first 140 Canadian troops departed from CFB Edmonton; 650 more would follow them in the next few days.

10 June – the North Atlantic Council approved the Military-Technical Agreement that was concluded between General Jackson and the Yugoslav authorities earlier that day. The North Atlantic Council suspended the air campaign.

12 June – KFOR began its deployment into Kosovo.

16 June – Canadian troops came face to face with the horror of the war in Kosovo when they discovered the graves of more than 65 bodies. The remains were believed to be ethnic Albanians who were apparently executed by Serbian police.

20 June – NATO Secretary General terminated the air campaign, which he had suspended ten days previous.

28 June – the first of a total of 12 CF-18s returned to Canada.

30 June – While flying in Kosovo a Canadian helicopter comes under fire from a lone sniper. The crew of the Griffon responded with machinegun fire. The sniper fled, but was eventually apprehended by British troops. There were no casualties and the helicopter was not damaged.

7 July – The first planeload of Kosovars leaves Canada . Despite warnings that it was not safe, the refugees were anxious to return to Kosovo.

May 2000 – stretched to its limit, the CF decided to focus its energy and resources on NATO's Stabilization Force (SFOR) operations in Bosnia. Various redeployments, which included Canada's withdrawal from Kosovo – with the exception of Operation QUADRANT – began at this time.

AUTHOR: *Howard Michitsch*

A TIMELY INTERVENTION IN EAST TIMOR?

The hastily-organized relief operation to East Timor highlighted how over-extended and ill-equipped the Canadian Forces were in 1999.

ON 30 AUGUST 1999, EAST TIMORESE PEOPLE WENT TO THE POLLS TO ASCERTAIN WHETHER THEY WOULD CHOOSE EITHER SPECIAL AUTONOMY FOR EAST TIMOR OR OUTRIGHT INDEPENDENCE. THEY CHOSE TO MOVE TOWARD INDEPENDENCE.

ABOVE:
Aging Hercules aircraft proved to be particularly embarrassing. A series of mechanized breakdowns en route and in-theatre were widely reported in the media. (DND PHOTO)

CANADA RESPONDED TO UNITED Nations Security Council Resolution 1264 (1999) adopted on 15 September 1999 and created Operation TOUCAN. The Operation in East Timor was divided into three parts. There was the Canadian Forces airlift component, designated as the Canadian Airlift Task Force – Darwin or ALTF Darwin. The second component was the land force composed of a light infantry company group along with a National Support Element (NSE) and a National Command Element (NCE). Finally, there was a sea component that consisted of HMCS *Protecteur* along with a Sea King helicopter detachment from 430 Squadron, Esquimalt. In all, more than 750 military personnel from all across Canada took part in this operation. The following is a statistical summary of the Canadian Forces contribution to the international military effort in East Timor in 1999.

Canada's bilateral military relations with Indonesia during the late 1990s were minimal. The last time a Canadian military presence was seen in Indonesia was in April 1997. HMCS *Vancouver* arrived in the Indonesian port of Surabaya as part of the Canadian navy's 1997 Operation WESTPLOY. Essentially, this three-month mission was aimed at increasing Canada's military role in Asia-Pacific to match its growing economic stake in the region.

On 30 August 1999, East Timorese people went to the polls to ascertain whether they would vote for either a special autonomy for East Timor or outright independence. Some 98 per cent or registered voters went to the polls deciding by a margin of 21.5 per cent to 78.5 per cent to reject the proposed autonomy and begin a process of transition towards independence.

Following the announcement of the results, pro-integration militias launched a campaign of violence. On 12 September, the Government of Indonesia agreed to accept the offer of assistance from the international community.

On 15 September 1999 the United Nations Security Council adopted Resolution 1264 (1999) which eventually led to the creation and deployment of the Australian-led coalition force known as the International Force for East Timor (INTERFET). The first members of INTERFET arrived in Dili, East Timor on 20 September 1999.

AIR COMPONENT

The mission of the ALTF Darwin was to provide tactical airlift, airdrop and medical evacuation capability between Australia and East Timor in support of INTERFET. The Canadian contribution to ALTF Darwin was two CC-130 Hercules air transport aircraft and approximately 103 military personnel from 8 Wing (429 and 436 Squadrons), Canadian Forces Base Trenton, Ontario.

ABOVE LEFT: *Although dispatched almost immediately after the Prime Minister announced Canada's participation, HMCS* Protecteur *would take over one month to arrive in East Timor.* (DND PHOTO)
ABOVE RIGHT: *Unloading humanitarian aid.*(DND PHOTO)

The ALTF Darwin carried a variety of military supplies and equipment to East Timor, including building material, armoured personnel carrier and other equipment in support of INTERFET. Military passengers also travelled on most fights.

The ALTF was part of a multinational coalition airlift force of 28 aircraft called the INTERFET Combined Airlift Wing (ICAW). This wing provided a combined airlift capability between Darwin and several locations in East Timor, particularly Dili and Bacau. The ICAW averaged about 25 flights per day. The Canadian component flew an average of approximately two flights per day.

After considerable delays, the ALTF completed its first airlift operation to Dili, East Timor from Darwin, Australia on 29 September.

The ALTF began to re-deploy its military personnel and air transport aircraft back to Canada between 26 November and 3 December 1999. While the ALTF was deployed in the region it flew approximately 130 missions in the operational theatre during which time it carried more than one thousand tons of cargo and 2100 passengers. These figures represented roughly 40 percent of the INTERFET cargo.

LAND COMPONENT

The strength of the land component was approximately 250 personnel, divided between the infantry company group based on A Company, 3rd Battalion, Royal 22e Régiment, the National Support Element and the National Command Element. The infantry company group was part of the First Battalion of the Royal New Zealand Regiment responsible for peacekeeping in the western portion of East Timor.

The Light Infantry Company Group arrived in Suai, East Timor on 29 October 1999. By mid-November the infantry company group concentrated their activities in the area around Zumalai, some 25 km east of Suai. The Infantry Company Group carried out a series of patrols in rural and urban areas, provided security as well as convoy escorts and supported humanitarian aid organisations inside a 10,000 km square area. The Canadian troops returned to Canada beginning on 19 March 2000.

SEA COMPONENT

The supply ship HMCS *Protecteur*, with her two CH-124 Sea King helicopters and a helicopter detachment from 443 Maritime Helicopter Squadron departed from its home port of Esquimalt, British Columbia for East Timor on 23 September. It arrived in theatre and commenced military operations on 24 October. HMCS *Protecteur* was relieved from operations on 25 January 2000 and began its return to its home port in Canada in early February. It eventually arrived in Esquimalt on 2 March 2000.

During its deployment to East Timor, the ship provided supplies to the coalition ships and land forces deployed in East Timor. The operational tasks consisted of moving ashore fuel, water, food, military stores, and building materials.

In fact, HMCS *Protecteur* provided every ounce of diesel fuel for the land force. In addition, the ship's complement also volunteered some 2700 hours to 18 different humanitarian projects in Dili and Suai.

The estimated cost of deploying this air, land and sea military force to east Timor for six months was approximately $33 million.

AUTHOR: *G. Jaxon*

THE NEW WORLD ORDER

WEAPONS AND UNIFORMS

LEFT: *An infantry master corporal of the 1980s carries a C7 5.56-mm fully automatic rifle with a 30-round magazine. (An optical scope would later become standard issue.) His load-bearing equipment includes a small pack in the rear (not shown) and a gas mask bag on the left side. Slung over his shoulder is an 84-mm Carl Gustav, a short-range anti-armour weapon (medium) (SRAAW-M) rocket launcher.* (ILLUSTRATION BY KATHERINE TAYLOR) **BELOW:** *Private Patrick Cloutier of the Royal 22e Regiment stood his ground while face to face with a Mohawk warrior. During Operation SALON (or the Oka Crisis), the discipline and restraint of the soldiers was absolutely necessary to ensure that there were no accidents. Indeed, after the military took control of the situation, there were no injuries or deaths during the standoff.* (CANAPRESS PHOTO SHANEY KOMULAILEN)

LEFT: *The belt-fed machine gun based on the FN MAG was originally purchased as an addition for the Leopard C1 tank in the role of coaxial MG. This machine gun was far superior to the C5 machine gun (which was a refurbished M1919 .30 calibre gun) in use by the rest of the army. In the early 1980s, the C5 gun was replaced by a modified FN MAG, dubbed the C6. Weighing in at 11 kilograms, the weapon, with its quick change barrel, is capable of a cyclic rate of fire of 650-1000 rounds per minute. Gas operated, belt-fed and air cooled, this 7.62-mm machine gun has an effective range of 800 meters on its bipod, and 1800 metres when mounted on a tripod with traverse and elevating mechanism.* (DND PHOTO)

LEFT: *Soldiers of the Royal 22e Regiment during Operation SALON, September 1990, maintain vigilance and communications. Most soldiers were deployed to "face down" the Mohawk warriors at Oka. However, soldiers fully camouflaged and armed were deployed to hidden positions, ready at a second's notice to use deadly fire. Note that the soldiers depicted are armed with both fragmentation grenades (baseball-sized) and smoke grenades (pop can-sized). (DND ISC 90-598)* ***BOTTOM RIGHT:*** *The role of the military combat engineers (or sappers) within the Land Force is to conduct specialized operations that contribute to the survivability, mobility and combat effectiveness of other arms and services, and disrupt enemy operations. Their duties include building bunkers, road and bridge construction, destruction of munitions and minefields – all with the goal of increasing mobility of friendly forces and to deny mobility to the enemy. This sapper prepares to detonate live Iraqi munitions discovered at the end of the Gulf War. Special materials are used to absorb the blast. (PHOTO BY SCOTT TAYLOR)*

RIGHT:
Javelin is a very short-range, surface-to-surface air defence artillery missile system employed to counter hostile aircraft at very low altitudes. This man-portable, 38 kg weapon can either be fired from the shoulder or mounted on a lightweight multiple launcher. With a range of 4.4 to 5.5 kilometres, it has high explosive impact and proximity missiles guided by an integral laser. There are 110 air defence artillery Javelin missile systems in service since 1990 in the Land Force.

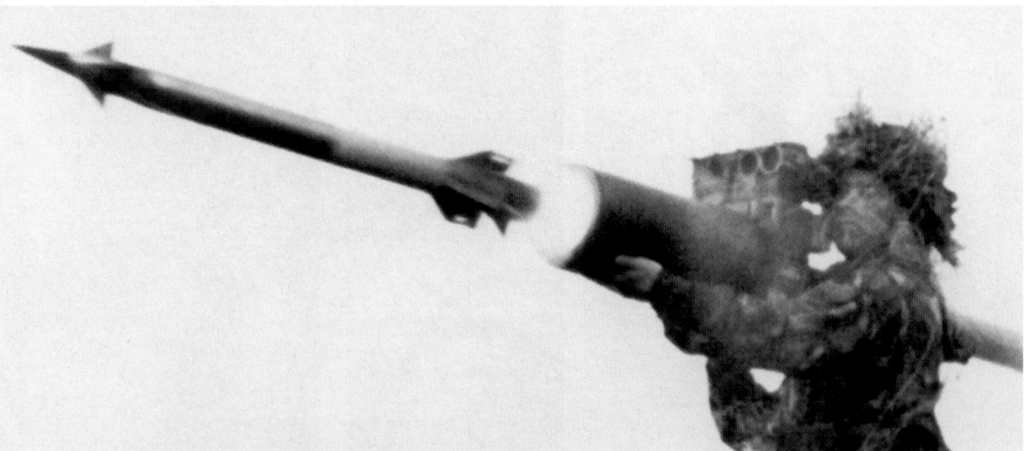

OPPOSITE PAGE, BOTTOM LEFT:
During the Gulf War of 1991, the potential for the enemy (Iraq) to use chemical or biological weapons was assessed as very high and considered a serious threat. The main method of delivery was believed to be by SCUD medium-range ballistic missile. All troops in theatre were equipped with the latest in Nuclear Biological Chemical Defence (NBCD), including protective gas masks, suits, antidotes and electro-chemical warning devices. The threat of chemical attacks was taken seriously and, climbing into full gear, Tactical Operations Protective Posture 3 (TOPP3) became a common occurrence.
(COURTESY TED ZUBER, DND)

BOTTOM:
The Sea King, a ship-based helicopter, has both day and night flight capabilities and is carried aboard most of Maritime Command's destroyers, frigates and replenishment ships. The Sea King employs detection, navigation and weapons systems as part of its primary role of searching for, locating and destroying submarines. With subsurface acoustic detection equipment and homing torpedoes, it is an aging but capable submarine-killer. Crewed by four airmen, it carries the MK46 Mod6 torpedo as its main armament. Purchased between 1963 and 1969, the CF currently has 29 in service.
(DND PHOTO)

The CF-18 is a twin-engined, supersonic tactical fighter jet that has engines which deliver 7290 kilograms of thrust and speeds of up to Mach 1.8. Canada purchased 122 of these aircraft between 1982 and 1988. The Hornet's primary roles include the air defence of North America, training with our allies, responding to situations anywhere in the world, providing combat air patrol cover, close air support or strategic bombing. Canadian CF-18s took part in the Gulf War and NATO's bombing of Yugoslavia in 1999. (DND PHOTO)

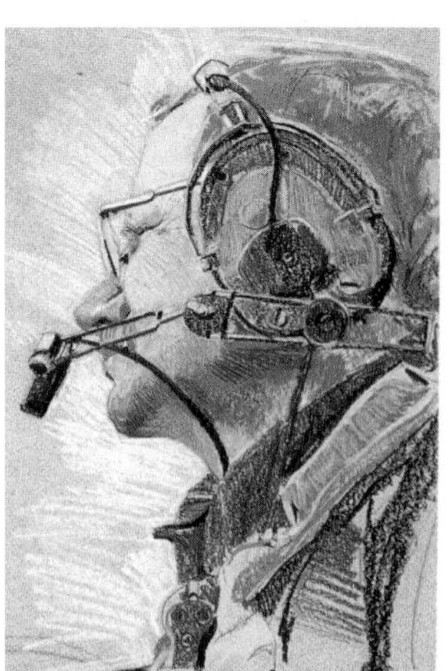

LEFT: *Major General Lewis Mackenzie, hero of Sarajevo (affectionately called General Lew by his troops), cared a great deal about the welfare of his soldiers. One of the few generals to speak his mind, Mackenzie was blunt in describing the situation in Bosnia to the media, resulting in threats against his life and rumours designed to impugn his reputation. (GEORGE REEKIE, TORONTO SUN)*
RIGHT: *Warrant Officer Matt Stopford, a dedicated soldier of the Princess Patricia's Canadian Light Infantry, has become the rallying force for new veterans. Stopford was made deathly ill by his service in Bosnia and Croatia in 1993. Unable to get the support he needed, he approached the press. This generated a media assault, culminating in a Board of Inquiry led by Brigadier General Joe Sharpe. Tasked with examining allegations that hundreds of soldiers who served in Croatia had been exposed to persistent toxic hazards, the board was unable to determine the cause of these mysterious illnesses, but eventually drew links between the sick soldiers and post-traumatic stress disorder (PTSD). (ILLUSTRATION BY KATHERINE TAYLOR)*

ABOVE:
On New Year's Eve 1994 in the Krajina, Croatia, Private Phillip Badani (of The Royal Canadian Regiment) and Private John Tescioni (of the 48th Highlanders of Canada) were on a routine escort mission when they were ambushed. In the town of Kolorina, 20 Serb soldiers had attempted to stop their jeep. The Serbs had left a slight gap in the roadway and Badani gunned the engine. The Serbs let loose a barrage of small arms fire, hitting the vehicle 53 times. Both men were hit half a dozen times. Tescioni, losing blood, managed to drive the vehicle back to camp, their jeep leaking fuel and with only two tires inflated. (ILLUSTRATION BY KATHERINE TAYLOR)
OPPOSITE PAGE, BOTTOM:
The wounding of Corporal Jordie Yeo and Private Jeff Melchers just south of Srebrenica in Bosnia demonstrated just how dangerous peacekeeping can be. A platoon believed to be Bosnian Muslims opened fire on the pair while they were on foot patrol in July 1993, ambushing them with grenades, small arms and a .50 calibre machine gun. The two Vandoos, Yeo and Melchers, took cover and returned fire. Both were wounded and losing blood. A radio call to the company HQ launched the immediate reaction rescue platoon. Upon its arrival, it too was engaged by fire. By alternately running and crawling, Yeo and Melchers eventually reached safety. They were evacuated to the unit medical station and then by French helicopter to a field hospital. The injuries sustained by these two Canadians were initially listed as being caused by an "accident." (ILLUSTRATION BY KATHERINE TAYLOR)

RIGHT: *On 18 June 1993, Corporal Daniel Gunther, along with Vandoos Sergeant Mario Roberts and Lieutenant Yuan Pichette, deployed with their APC to an observation post on the Visoko-Ksijelek patrol route in central Bosnia. After a quiet morning, Roberts and Pichette went behind as Gunther remained standing in the vehicle's driver hatch. Suddenly, Gunther observed a line of tracer arcing across the valley in front coming from the Muslim positions. Turning to call back a warning, there was a flash 700 metres to his left and an explosion lifted the APC off the ground. Pichette and Roberts jumped in the carrier and found Gunther's smouldering remains.*
(ILLUSTRATION BY KATHERINE TAYLOR)

LEFT: *The LAV III is the essential component of the army's leading-edge high tech battlefield systems. This state of the art Light Armoured Vehicle is a fast, well-armed, well-protected infantry troop carrier. It can be used in all weather conditions, in normal battlefield smoke, at night and on most types of terrain. The LAV III provides many options in both combat and non-combat situations. The troops may be kept mounted and protected while using the 25-mm stabilized cannon – an option not available in the past. The driver and commander have computer display terminals for the Tactical Navigation System (TACNAV), as well as thermal viewers. The TACNAV links a Global Positioning System (GPS) with a digital magnetic compass and laser range finder. Anti-mine protection and an automatic fire and explosion suppression system provide additional safety. Here are the ten soldiers of an Infantry Section Carrier with their full battleload, including the driver, vehicle commander, gunner and seven soldiers for dismount. Note the Eryx short range anti-armour weapons (heavy) (SRAAW-H) on the right, to centre right, ammunition, tools and other equipment. With a 350 horsepower diesel engine, an ability to cross a two-metre trench and climb a 60 per cent grade, the LAV III has a maximum speed of 100 kilometres per hour and a range of 500 kilometres. (DND PHOTO)*

MIDDLE: *Pioneers and their beards became part of a controversy on dress regulations in the fall of 1999 when some Canadians had the impression that the soldiers looked more like "bikers" than peacekeepers. Regulations were subsequently amended to ensure that soldiers maintained beards of one inch in length only, rather than the traditional untrimmed beard of the infantryman cum engineer. (DND PHOTO)*

BOTTOM: *Unbeknownst to Canadians in general, peacekeeping operations in the former Yugoslavia have often crossed the line and become combat operations. The Medak Pocket was a contested area between the Serbs and Croats. The Canadians came under Croat mortar and artillery fire numerous times in mid-September 1993. Such intense firefights and both defensive and offensive operations of the type experienced in the Medak Pocket had not been seen by Canadian soldiers since Korea. (ILLUSTRATION BY KATHERINE TAYLOR)*

RIGHT: *Canada's Utility Transport Tactical Helicopter (UTTH), the Griffon provides the army with a robust, reliable and cost-effective capability to conduct: airlift of equipment and personnel, command and liaison flights, surveillance and reconnaissance, casualty evacuation, and logistic transport. It is also used for search and rescue, counter-drug operations, and domestic relief operations. The workhorse of 1 Wing, the CH146 Griffon helicopter has participated in humanitarian relief operations at home and abroad, including the Saguenay area during the floods of 1996, in Manitoba during the floods of 1997, the ice storm in 1997 and in Honduras in 1998. Griffons were deployed to Haiti in 1996-97 as part of United Nations Support Mission in Haiti and in Kosovo in support of NATO. Griffons currently remain in Bosnia as part of NATO's Stabilization Force. Crewed by three personnel, the Griffon can carry nine passengers. With a cruising speed of 220 kilometres per hour and a range of 656 kilometres it is a flexible and essential part of military operations.* (DND PHOTO)

ABOVE LEFT:
Halifax class frigates carrry a powerful set of weapons and sensor systems that include eight Harpoon long-range, surface-to-surface missiles, 16 Sea Sparrow surface-to-air missiles, a Bofors 57-mm rapid-fire gun, a 20-mm Phalanx anti-missile close-in weapons system (CIWS), eight 12.7-mm machine guns and 24 anti-submarine homing torpedoes. Defensive measures include infra-red supression, shield decoys, chaff, flares, a towed acoustic decoy, and radar and sonar jamming devices. The ship's torpedo-carrying helicopter (at present, the Sea King CH-124) significantly extends the operational effectiveness due to the range of the aircraft. Displacing 4770 tons, with a speed of 29+knots, the Halifax-class frigates are fast, quiet and state of the art. Crewed by 225 sailors and powered by two GE gas turbine engines for acceleration and one 20 cylinder diesel engine for cruising, they have a range of 9500 nautical miles. (DND PHOTO)

ABOVE RIGHT:
The first of four British-built Victoria class diesel electric submarines was commissioned into the Canadian fleet in December 2000. Victoria class submarines are modern, and have far more hydrodynamic features, advanced marine engineering systems, better habitability, and endurance than previous Canadian boats. They are able to 'snort' (through an extendible air-breather) while at periscope depth and can remain deeply submerged for extended periods at slow speed. Operating at depths over 200 metres, the hulls are covered with anechoic rubber tiles designed to absorb sonar transmissions and make the submarines hard to detect. There is a five-person diver lockout chamber in the fin. Displacing 2400 tons submerged, it is considered a long-range patrol boat. The Victoria class boats have formidable defensive and offensive capabilities as they are extremely quiet and stealthy. (DND PHOTO)

The Coyote is a vital component of the army's high tech battlefield systems as it enters the 21st century. This highly-mobile, well-armed and well-protected reconnaissance variant of the Light Armoured Vehicle family is used for battlefield reconnaissance and surveillance missions. Equipped with a telescopic mast, incorporating radar and a variety of electro-optic sensors, the Coyote surveillance system provides an all-weather, day and night capability to the Army. Over 200 Coyotes are used by the Army's six mechanized infantry battalions, three armoured regiments, and armour and infantry schools. The 14.4-ton vehicle mounts a powerful 25-mm chain gun in an electrical and gyrostabilized turret which enables the gun to be fired accurately while on the move. With a maximum speed of 100 kilometres per hour and a range of 660 kilometres, this vehicle can cross a trench 2.06 metres wide, climb a 60 per cent grade and ford rivers 1.3 metres deep with no preparation. (DND PHOTO)

BOTTOM RIGHT:

After two years of war, in which more than 100,000 people died, Ethiopia and Eritrea signed a cessation of hostilities agreement on 18 June 2000, calling upon the UN to establish a peacekeeping mission to ensure observance of the security commitments. The UN Security Council passed Resolution 1312 establishing UNMEE with a proposed commitment of approximately 4000 military personnel, an observer force of about 220 personnel and associated support resources. The Standby High Readiness Brigade (SHIRBRIG), of which Canada is part, was approached by the UN to provide troops for UNMEE. The Netherlands indicated that it would provide one battalion on the condition that a reliable and experienced peacekeeping nation would participate in a significant way. The Dutch asked for Canada's participation and, on 19 September 2000, the CF issued a warning order for units to prepare equipment, and train for the mission. Canadian troops deployed early in 2001. This is the first operational deployment of the LAV III, depicted here in UN colours. (DND PHOTO)

BOTTOM LEFT:

Reservists participating in a "Fighting in a Built-up Area" (FIBUA) exercise. Note the use of laser sensors on the helmets and load-bearing equipment to simulate receiving fire. Weapons are equipped with a low-powered laser that initiates when a blank round is fired. The sensors then make a loud beeping noise indicating that the wearer has either been killed or wounded. It is not often that the Canadian militia has access to such sophisticated training sessions. Decades of fiscal neglect have once again rendered the Canadian Army a mere shell of its former glory. (CAPTAIN M. MURGOCI)

SITREP – INTO THE NEXT MILLENNIUM

Decades of neglect and political manipulation have left Canada's military in a tragic state. Unfortunately the future appears to be even bleaker.

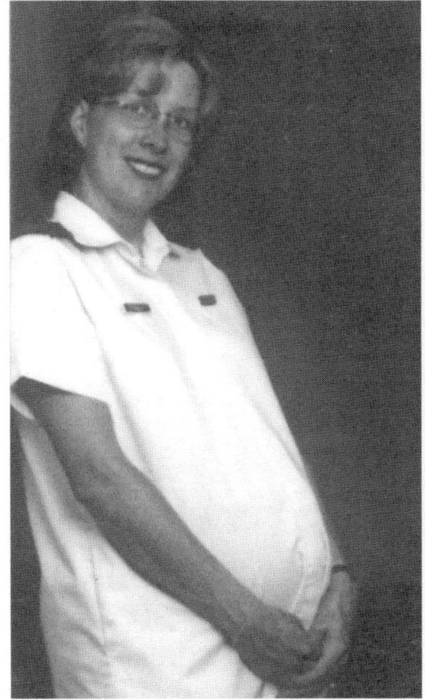

ABOVE LEFT: *In 1997 British General Sir Hugh Pike claimed that Canada's "politically correct policies" (such as producing combat maternity clothes) had left our military unfit as a fighting force. (DND PHOTOS)* ***ABOVE:*** *Defence Minister Art Eggleton (holding coffee) took offense to Pike's comments.*

PEERING OUT OF HIS pick-up truck, ex-airman Brian Isfeld had difficulty in identifying his former residence at Canadian Forces Base Comox on British Columbia's Vancouver Island. Structurally, the Personnel Married Quarters (PMQs) have remained unchanged since they were constructed in 1952, but the squalid similarity of these tiny, 800 square-foot homes made Isfeld's task a challenge. The tightly packed collection of drab, worn-out dwellings — festooned with colourful clotheslines and animated by groups of boisterous children at play — creates an impression of a run-down tenement.

Lieutenant Colonel Terry Leversedge, the deputy commander at Comox admitted that the housing situation on his base was "one of the worst" in the Canadian military. Leversedge noted that a plan to turn over the administration of the PMQs to the city of Comox had stalled. The local politicians were adamant, he said, that the Department of National Defence must first spend millions of dollars to upgrade this district's roads and sewers to what the city would consider an "acceptable level."

Operationally, this Air Force base is in even worse shape. As a proud, 32-year veteran, Isfeld is dismayed at the current state of his former squadron. The fleet of Aurora maritime patrol aircraft that he used to serve aboard is showing signs of aging. As reported in the Vancouver *Sun*, the Aurora's technology is now so old that its on-board computer has less memory than one of today's pocket-sized calculators. Working with their outmoded equipment means that the aircrews almost never have a problem-free flight. Equally plagued by age-related difficulties is Comox's fleet of Labrador search and rescue helicopters. Although destined to be replaced in 2001, the delay caused by the Liberal government's 1993 decision to cancel the EH101 helicopter contract means the 35-year-old Labradors are currently flying on borrowed time.

In addition to the stress placed on equipment and infrastructure, the service members themselves are being put to the test. A military policeman explained that he was pulling 72-hour work weeks at the Comox guard-hut to compensate for the vast number of his colleagues who are serving abroad on six-month long peacekeeping missions.

OVERSTRETCHED

The "rust-out" of equipment and "burnout" of personnel found at CFB Comox are mirrored throughout all three branches of the Canadian Forces. The Navy has been unable to launch emergency medical evacuation flights and were forced to cancel major training exercises due to the unserviceability of their ancient Sea King helicopters. The supply shortage and over-commitment of our troops forced the Army to take out newspaper ads asking for surplus uniforms to be returned in order to outfit a contingent bound for Bosnia. In 1998, the Air Force began offering $75,000 resigning bonuses in an effort to retain their CF-18 pilots.

The genesis for this deplorable state of affairs is not difficult to determine. Since the end of the Cold War, Canada has reduced its regular troop levels from 89,000 to a meagre 58,800. During that same time frame, the Canadian military has gone to war three times — in the Persian Gulf, Somalia and Yugoslavia — and has mounted six major peacekeeping operations around the globe — Croatia, Cambodia, Bosnia, Haiti, Kosovo and East Timor.

At the close of 1999, Canada had over 4400 personnel posted abroad on 22 separate missions — the most Canadian troops deployed since the Korean War. Given the reduced manpower pool from which to draw upon, this "mission creep" has caused concern among many defence analysts. Retired Brigadier General Jim Hanson explained that "the troops are stretched to the breaking point." In the past soldiers could expect up to 18 months at home between UN tours. With the current demand, these intervals have often been reduced to less than 12 months. During those periods soldiers are sent on training courses and are required to provide aid the civil powers (forest fire fighting, ice storm duty, etc.). "Even when you're in Canada you're not at home," Hanson said. "This puts an incredible strain on the families."

To compound matters the federal budget has failed to reflect the military's increased number of tasks. Since 1993, defence spending has been slashed by 23 per cent to the current $9 billion. This represents only 1.1 per cent of the GDP and ranks Canada just barely ahead of Luxembourg for the lowest such expenditure in NATO. On a November 1999 visit to Ottawa, George Robertson, the secretary-general of the 19-nation military alliance, described our defence policy as "languishing" and he warned that additional spending was required should Canada "actually want to take part in what will be the major crisis management situations in the future."

LEFT: *While our soldiers have been providing "care and comfort" to people in the world's war zones. DND has "failed miserably" to take care of their own troops. Casualties – both physical and mental – have been hard-pressed to receive adequate medical treatment from an unsympathetic and uncaring bureaucracy.* (DND PHOTO)

BREACH OF TRUST

For the rank and file, the Defence Department's fiscal crunch and disproportionate workload has manifested itself into personal hardship. In March 1999, following an extensive parliamentary committee study on the living conditions of our service members, the government authorized a $750 million "quality of life" improvement package. Unfortunately, all but $150 million of this funding is to be drawn from the existing budget. This means that either badly needed new equipment projects must be delayed or the already thin troop ranks must be further stretched in order to finance this new morale boosting program.

Ironically, a 1995 internal DND poll found that only 3.3 per cent of our soldiers felt that their pay was a major concern. The majority of those polled complained about equipment shortcomings and the erosion of both family life and operational capability due to their numerous peacekeeping duties. More importantly, a significant number cited the cause of the current malaise as being due to a lack of accountability among the military's senior leadership as fewer than 17 per cent polled claimed they still had faith in their top commanders.

This fundamental breach of trust between the ranks gained its foothold in the brass's attempted cover-up of a young boy's brutal death at the hands of Canadian paratroopers in Somalia. The rift was exacerbated by the ensuing Public Inquiry and the increased media spotlight which it attracted. A decorated World War II veteran, Somalia Inquiry Commissioner Justice Robert Rutherford was himself disillusioned with what his two-and-a-half-year probe uncovered. After tabling his final report, he described National Defence Headquarters as "a culture of cover-up."

The troops have been further disheartened by shocking media revelations of official neglect shown to soldiers who became casualties while on United Nations operations. Hundreds of soldiers who first complained of strange illnesses after returning from duty in Croatia had their medical files purged to remove a doctor's warning of possible exposure to toxic soil. Following sick soldiers complaining about denied pensions, public pressure forced the Defence Department to conduct a Board of Inquiry into the affair. In October 1999, Colonel Joe Sharpe, the Inquiry's president, admitted that DND had "made a mistake." This sentiment echoed a 1996 apology by then-Army Commander General Maurice Baril who acknowledged that the military had "failed miserably" to care for its wounded peacekeepers.

In October 1994, Warrant Officer Tom Martineau was shot by a Muslim sniper while on duty in Bosnia. The bullet lodged in his spine and left him permanently disabled. However, due to internal department bickering over which directorate should foot the bill, the badly injured Martineau had to wait over a year to get a wheelchair. "There should have been a system in place to take care of us *before* they sent us into harm's way," said Martineau bitterly.

PERPETUATING THE MYTH

During the NATO Defence Ministers' Summit in Toronto in September 1999, Canada's Air Force was tasked to send two Hercules transport aircraft to East Timor. Embarrassingly, it took four consecutive tries to get one aircraft en route due to repeated malfunctions, while the second plane was temporarily grounded in Fiji due to a loss of cabin pressurization.

In response to the public clamour, the deputy head of the Air Force, Major General Peter Gartenburg penned a number of angry letters to the editor. Although he acknowledged the 35-year-old Hercules aircraft would "some day" need to be replaced, Gartenburg levelled the blame for the Air Force's shortcomings on media criticism. He

RIGHT: *Prime Minister Jean Chretien listens intently as U.S. President Bill Clinton addresses NATO leaders. Canada's foreign policy is increasingly dictated by the U.S. State Department. With or without UN approval, Canada now provides tacit approval on all U.S. military interventions.* (NATO PHOTO)

wrote: "When people's self esteem is constantly chipped away, their morale will inevitably degrade. The result is that Canada gets less for the defence dollars it spends."

Unfortunately, the Defence Department's heavily politicized senior management have increasingly employed this public relations strategy of "shooting the messenger" rather than admit any shortcomings. In 1997, British Falkland war hero Lieutenant General Sir Hugh Pike created a controversy when he claimed that "politically correct policies" had eroded the Canadian Forces' combat capability. In response, Defence Minister Art Eggleton rose in the House of Commons to denounce this independent assessment with the short phrase, "Take a hike, Pike!"

Veteran peacekeeper Sergeant Tom Hoppe took exception to Eggleton's dismissal. With three medals for bravery, Hoppe is currently the most decorated Canadian soldier since the Korean War. "Pike is right," Hoppe said. "When you've got DND more concerned with paying for transsexual operations than taking care of combat stressed soldiers, and policy makers more concerned about body piercings and hair tinting than new armoured vehicles, we've got a serious problem."

AT WHAT COST

In his 1999 report to parliament, Auditor General Denis Desautels noted that while the Defence Department urgently required $11 billion in new equipment, their policy planners had only budgeted $5 billion for that purpose. Despite this sizeable shortfall, many analysts caution against massive increased spending without first implementing sweeping reforms. "It is too simplistic to believe that more money will solve all the problems," claims retired Colonel Michel Drapeau. "The Defence Department is currently gripped by a moral crisis. What they are lacking first and foremost is accountable leadership."

Comox resident Brian Isfeld is not just another ex-servicemember who is angered by the government's seeming indifference to the plight of our military. For him, it's much more personal. His son Mark, a combat engineer, was killed in a Croatian minefield on 23 June 1994. Upon hearing of the tragedy, Brian wrote an open letter to the Canadian public which read in part, "Who is in control here? Why are our people being sent into areas of high danger with inadequate, aged and obviously inferior equipment? Just who in hell's name is making the decisions that cost me a son and this country an excellent soldier?" Five years later, as he drives away from his dilapidated former airbase, he's still looking for the answers.

AUTHOR*: Scott Taylor*

PRO PATRI MORI

Canada's war dead are buried at home and in Commonwealth War Commission cemeteries in 70 countries... Remember them.

"IT WOULD BE A USEFUL lesson to cold-blooded politicians, who calculate on a war costing so many lives or so many limbs, or to the thoughtless at home if they would visit a military hospital for just one hour ...This simple truth was suggested to my mind by the exclamation of a poor woman. I had 220 wounded that morning and among them an American farmer nearly 60 years of age. One ball had shattered his thigh bone, and another lodged in his body, the last obviously mortal. His wife, a respectable elderly-looking woman, came under a flag of truce and made for the hospital where she found her husband lying on a truss of straw, writhing in agony, for his sufferings were dreadful. She sat down on the ground, and taking her husband's head on her lap and looking around wildly exclaimed: 'O that the King and President were both here this moment to see the misery their quarrels lead to - they would never go to war again without a cause that they would give as a reason to God at the last day, for thus destroying the creatures he hath made in his own image.' In half an hour the poor fellow ceased to suffer."

William "Tiger" Dunlop (Surgeon)
Lundy's Lane, 1814.

The War of 1812 was a mere skirmish in the wilderness by European standards. During the war 7738 Americans and 8774 British and Canadians lost their lives. By comparison, Napoleon lost 40,000 men at Leipzig in the "Battle of the Nations," in the same year that Tiger Dunlop was recording the above comments in his diary. The Russians lost an estimated 44,000 men, or

***RIGHT:** Beneath the maple trees of this Cemetery are buried the soldiers who died in the capture of Cambrai. Hundreds of cemeteries throughout the world commemorate Canadian soldiers, sailors and airmen who lost their lives in the struggle for peace.*
(GEORGE HUNTER, CWM)

one in three participants, in the Battle of Borodino, and 40,000 died at Waterloo.

With the exception of the American Civil War, in which 620,000 Union soldiers and Confederates were killed, the wars fought on the North American continent have been relatively bloodless; small consolation, however, to the dead and wounded and their grieving families.

On the Plains of Abraham, a mere 56 British soldiers were killed and 36 more died as a result of cannon fire from the city walls in the days before the city capitulated. French losses were estimated at around 700 dead and wounded. Mother St. Ignace at the General Hospital recalled that "we were surrounded by the dead and dying who were brought in by the hundreds and many of whom were closely connected with us, but we had to lay aside our grief and seek space in which to put them."

Although James Murray wrote to William Pitt that "our little army was in the habit of beating the enemy," he lost more than a thousand dead and wounded at the Battle of Ste. Foy. Scurvy then swept through the Quebec garrison. By Christmas 150 were dead, 700 were lost by the end of April and 1000 by May. Hundreds of bodies lay unburied, frozen to the ground.

Quebec would be attacked again in 1775 by Montgomery and Arnold in a wild winter storm on New Year's eve. Thirty Americans died and 450 were taken prisoner. The defenders' casualties were limited to seven dead and 11 wounded.

More than 500 Quebecois were killed during the Rebellion of 1837. Two died in Mackenzie's comic-opera uprising in Upper Canada. Nils von Schoultz and the Hunters posed a much more dangerous threat. At the Battle of the Windmill 13 were killed and 28 wounded. The Canadian Militia suffered 61 casualties, 13 of which were fatal.

The Fenians were responsible for fewer than 20 deaths and the First Riel Rebellion claimed three lives. The Northwest Rebellion resulted in some 85 fatal casualties. At Batoche, Middleton lost five dead and 25 wounded; the Métis 21 dead, although the parish priest reported that 51 had been killed.

IN FOREIGN FIELDS

Sir Garnet Wolseley, brave and capable, but also "vain, pompous, and scheming," masterminded the expedition up the Nile to rescue Gordon at Khartoum in 1885, recalling the abilities of Canadian voyageurs from his earlier military life in Canada. For the first time, Canadians would die in foreign fields. Sixteen of 386 voyageurs perished; eight from drowning, six from typhoid, and two from falls from a train.

Of the 7384 Canadians who served in the Boer War at least 270 were killed or died of diseaseand 250 were wounded. 112 of their dependents were obliged to seek assistance from the Patriotic Fund, a charity established to assist soldiers and their families.- The fund also received 712 applications from men whose earning power had been impaired due to wounds or disease.

In the new century, the century of total war, Canadian casualties would be horrendous. Of the 620,000 who served in the First World War, 59,444 were killed and another 172,950 wounded, a causalty rate of approximately 39 per cent. During the Second World War, 1.1 million Canadians answered the call to arms. The number killed was 42,042 with 54,414 wounded. The fighting in Korea brought the horror of war to 26,791 service personnel, claiming the lives of 516 and wounding another 1072. Peacekeeping operations since the Korean War, cost the lives of an additional 108 Canadian military personnel on 90 different missions. The lament of that American widow at Lundy's Lane has echoed in countless Canadian homes throughout the years.

Canada's war dead are buried at home and in 70 countries in Commonwealth War Graves Commission cemeteries. Some, like those ringing Vimy Ridge, are almost completely Canadian, others contain only one or two Canadian graves. They are buried near Yokohama, Pusan in Korea, at Sun Wan Bay overlooking Hong Kong harbour, in North Africa, Sicily and Italy, above the beaches at Dieppe, across Normandy and the bocage country, alongside Dutch polders and in Flanders' fields. Remember them.

***AUTHOR:** Bill Twatio*

GLOSSARY

Steeped in abbreviations, jargon and slang terms, the military environment can often be difficult for those unfamiliar with its terminology to comprehend. Following is a brief selection of frequently-used terms.

AA - Anti-aircraft

AAA - Anti-aircraft artillery

ACE - Fighter pilot with five or more victories.

ADC - Aide-de-camp

ADJUTANT - Officer, usually a captain, responsible for seeing that a senior officer's commands are carried out.

ADMIRALTY - Office responsible for administration of naval affairs, particularly the Royal Navy.

AEW - Airborne Early Warning.

AFV - Armoured Fighting Vehicle.

ANZAC - Australia and New Zealand Army Corps.

AP - Armour Piercing.

APC - Armoured Personnel Carrier

ARMY - A major military formation made up of at least two corps and commanded by a full general.

ARMY GROUP - The largest military command, comprising at least two armies.

ARTY - Artillery.

ASDIC - (from Allied Submarine Detection Committee) Early British term for SONAR.

ASW - Anti-submarine warfare.

BANGALORE - Exploding charge for destroying barbed wire.

BARBARROSA - German invasion of the Soviet Union (22 June 1941).

BARRAGE - Concentrated artillery fire or a large field of sea-mines.

BATTALION - Basic infantry administrative unit. In WWII a Canadian battalion consisted of 800 men organized into a headquarters company, 4 rifle companies, a carrier platoon, reconnaissance platoon and support company.

BATTLE DRESS - Working dress of the Canadian soldier. In WWII it consisted of a blouse or jacket and trousers made from coarse khaki serge.

BATTERY - Basic unit of artillery made up of 4-8 guns.

BATTLECRUISER - A large cruiser carrying the same calibre guns but not the armour of a battleship.

BATTLESHIP - The largest gun-firing warship.

BAZOOKA - American hand-held anti-tank rocket launcher.

BCATP - British Commonwealth Air Training Plan.

BEF - British Expeditionary Force.

BIG FOUR - WWII - The United States, Great Britain, the Soviet Union and China.

BIVOUAC - An encampment without tents or huts. Derived from German *Beiwacht*, meaning watch or guard.

BLIGHTY - England or home. A minor wound that would get a soldier there.

BLITZ - Term adopted by British to describe aerial bombardment of the United Kingdom by the Luftwaffe.

BLITZKRIEG - Literally "lightning war." German term to describe warfare utilizing massed armour and aircraft.

BLUE RIBAND - A nominal title awarded to the passenger ship recording the fastest passage of the Atlantic.

BOATSWAIN - (Bos'n) - Petty Officer in charge of rigging and all deck gear. Oldest naval title.

BOFORS - Swedish arms manufacturer famous for its 40-mm anti-aircraft gun used throughout WWII and up to the present.

BOCHE - French term for German.

BRASS HAT - Senior officer.

BREW UP - A tank that has been hit and set on fire. Also, preparing tea.

BRIG - A two-masted, square-rigged sailing ship. Also, a ship's jail.

BRIGADE - Formation of two or more battalions commanded by a Brigadier. In WWII it was made up of three infantry battalions and a heavy weapons company. Armoured brigades were made up of three armoured regiments.

BRIGANTINE - A two-masted sailing ship, square-rigged on the forward mast, fore-and-aft rigged on the main mast.

BULLY BEEF - Corned beef ration.

BUZZ BOMB - German V-1 flying bomb.

BYNG BOYS - Canadian troops in WWI. After General Sir Julian Byng.

CALUMET - Native peace pipe with clay bowl and reed stem.

CARRONADE - Short-barreled naval gun used for close-in fighting. Manufactured at Carron works in Scotland.

CGIS - Canadian Government Intelligence Service (U.S.).

CHAR - French for tank.

CIA - (U.S.) Central Intelligence Agency.

CIRCUS - WWI. Large formation of German aircraft.

CLIPPER - A full-rigged, fine-lined fast sailing ship.

COMBINED OPERATIONS - Joint operations conducted by forces of different services and/or nationalities.

COMMANDO - A body of troops, highly trained for specialized tasks or missions.

COMPANY - Basic sub-unit of an infantry battalion, 125-strong and commanded by a Captain. Organized into a HQ platoon and three rifle platoons.

CONCHIE - Conscientious objector.

CONTEMPTIBLES - Original BEF in WWI. From a speech by the Kaiser in which he dismissed the British army as a "contemptible little police force."

CONVOY - A fleet of merchant ships gathered together under naval escort.

CORPS - A formation of two or more divisions with artillery and support units, commanded by a Lieutenant General.

CORVETTE - A fast sailing ship, smaller than a frigate. A small WWII anti-submarine vessel modelled after commercial whalers.

COUNTER-BATTERY - Artillery fire intended to neutralize enemy artillery.

COXSWAIN - (Cox'n) - Senior non-commissioned officer on a ship, usually a Chief Warrant Officer.

CREEPING BARRAGE - Artillery term for advancing fire.

CROCODILE TANK - A Churchill tank equipped with a flamethrower.

CRUISER - Warship next in size to a battleship.

CWAC - Canadian Women's Army Corps.

D-DAY - Day on which an operation starts.

DEMS - Defensively Equipped Merchant Ships.

DEPTH CHARGE - Explosive device projected or dropped from air or surface craft detonated at predetermined depths by a hydrostatic mechanism.

DESTROYER - Fast anti-submarine ship, smaller than a cruiser.

DISPLACEMENT - Weight of water displaced by a ship.

DIVISION - Major operational and fighting formation commanded by a Major General. A WWII Canadian infantry division was made up of three brigades, each with three infantry battalions, reconnaissance, artillery, engineer and service components. Total strength: 18,200. An Armoured Division consisted of an armoured brigade of three regiments, an infantry brigade with three battalions, a reconnaissance regiment, artillery, engineers and support services.Total strength: 15,000 with 300 AFVs.

DOGFACE - Slang for American soldier.

DND - Department of National Defence.

DOGFIGHT - Confused air battle usually involving a large number of aircraft.

DOODLEBUG - German V-1 pilotless flying bomb.

DRAGOONS - Heavy cavalry.

E-BOAT - Fast German attack boat armed with guns and torpedoes.

ENFILADE - Fire which hits a formation on the flank.

ENIGMA - German encoding machine.

ENSA - Entertainment Services Association (Br.). Known to Canadian troops as "Every Night Something Awful."

FENCIBLES - Infantry trained and equipped as regulars enlisted only for defence of Canada. Hence the name.

FIELD REGIMENT - Artillery unit organized into three batteries, each with two troops of four guns.

FIREFLY - Sherman tank armed with a 17-pdr. (76.2-mm) gun.

FISH-HEAD - Slang for sailor.

FIVE NATIONS - Iroquois Confederacy, see Six Nations.

RIGHT: *A Pioneer of the Royal Canadian Regiment patrols the streets of Mitrovica, Kosovo.* *(DND PHOTO)*

FLAG OFFICER - An Admiral in command.

FLAGSHIP - A ship from which an Admiral or senior officer commanded, so called because it flew the Admiral's distinguishing flag.

FLAK - Anti-aircraft fire. From German abbreviation F.L.A.K. *Flugzeug-Abwehr-Kanon*.

FLANK - The side of a military formation.

FLEET - The largest naval formation. Commanded by an Admiral.

FLIGHT - A unit of three or four aircraft under single command.

FOIL - see window.

FOO - Forward Observation Officer. Artillery equipped with wireless operator who accompanied combat units to call down artillery fire.

FORECASTLE (Fo'c'sle) - Raised part of deck in the bow.

FLOTILLA - An operational formation of small vessels, destroyers and smaller.

FRIGATE - A sailing ship that was smaller than a ship-of-the-line but larger than a corvette. Today, ship next in size and speed after a destroyer.

FRONT - WWII Soviet army group. Also the major confrontation lines (ie: Western Front).

FUSILIER - Light infantry tasked with guarding artillery and entrenched battalions. Derived from French *fusil* (rifle).

GAULEITER - Nazi party regional leader.

GEE - Radio-aid to navigation target identification device.

GERRY - Slang for German.

GESTAPO - *Geheimstaatspolizei*. Nazi secret state police.

GLASS HOUSE - Slang for military prison.

GHQ - General Headquarters.

GI - Government issue. Slang for American soldier.

GONG - Slang for medal or decoration.

GOC - General Officer Commanding.

GRAND FLEET - British WWI battleship and battlecruiser fleet.

GRAPESHOT - Used in 19th century naval warfare. A canvas bag with wood or metal bottom holding iron balls of various sizes. When fired, the sack burst or burned releasing the balls.

GRENADIERS - Infantrymen trained and equipped to throw grenades. Grenadier company was made up of the tallest and most able men and was used as shock troops. Distinguished by high mitred head-gear.

GS - General Service.

GUIDON - Swallow-tailed pennon or flag flown by armoured regiments. Similar to infantry colours.

GUN - An artillery piece with high muzzle velocity and long range which fires at angles of 45 degrees or less.

H2S - WWII navigational aid used aboard bombers.

HALFTRACK - Lightly-armoured truck with rear wheels replaced by tracks.

HARDTACK - Biscuit ration.

HE - High Explosive.

HEADS - Naval term for toilets.

HEDGEHOG - Spigot mortar used to fire patterns of small (65lb.) contact-fused anti-submarine projectiles ahead of a ship.

HOOCHIE - Soldier's shelter made from materials found in the field.

HUFF-DUFF - HF/DF - High Frequency Direction Finding.

HUN - Slang for German.

HUSSAR - A light cavalryman originally recruited into western Europe from Hungary.

INTRUDER - RAF/RCAF night-fighters used to disrupt enemy airfields and communications.

IRON RATION - Emergency ration.

IVAN - Slang for Russian.

JABO - *Jagdbomber*. German term for Allied fighter-bomber.

JAG - Judge Advocate General.

JAGDSTAFFEL - German fighter squadron.

JEEP - A corruption of GP (General Purpose) quarter-ton vehicle.

JERRY - Slang for German soldier.

JOCK - A pilot, or more specifically, a jet pilot. Also, slang for members of a Highland regiment.

JOINT TASK FORCE II/JTFII - A top secret Canadian Forces anti-terrorism unit.

KGB - Soviet Committee for State Security.

KIA - Killed in action.

KNOT - A unit of speed equalling one nautical mile an hour.

K-RATIONS - U.S. Army field ration.

KUBELWAGEN - German equivalent of the jeep.

KYE - Hot chocolate served aboard warships.

LANCE JACK - Lance-corporal.

LANDSER - Common German soldier.

LAY - Align an artillery piece.

LICHTENSTEIN - German airborne interception radar.

LIMEY - Slang for British. Originated in 18th century when Royal Navy issued lime-juice to sailors to combat scurvy.

LINE - Military or naval formation greater in breadth than depth. Also, regular infantry and cavalry as opposed to light troops or the guard.

LINE OF BATTLE - Tactical formation with ships more or less in line ahead to bring broadsides to bear.

LORRY - British term for truck.

LUFTWAFFE- German air force. Literally, "air-weapon."

MAE WEST - Life-saving jacket. Named after buxom American actress.

MARQUEE - A large tent capable of sleeping 30-40 men.

MAYDAY - International distress signal. From French "m'aidez."

MEATHEAD - Slang for military police.

MESS - Military dining hall.

MIA - Missing in action.

MiG - Soviet aircraft designation. Mikoyan and Gurevich, MiG-15.

MILK RUN - Routine mission.

MOANING MINNIE - German trench mortar.

MONITOR - Coastal warship armed with battleship guns for shore bombardment.

MORTAR - Smooth-bore infantry support weapon firing explosive shells at a high angle.

MP - Military Police. British Provost or Red Cap.

MULE - Tractor for towing aircraft.

NAAFI - Navy, Army and Air Force Institute (Br.). Provided canteens for Commonwealth troops.

NAPALM - Jellied petroleum used as an anti-personnel weapon.

NATO - North Atlantic Treaty Organization.

NAZI - see NSDAP.

NEBELWERFER - German multi-barreled rocket launcher mounted on wheels and fired electrically.

NISSEN HUT - General purpose corrugated iron building.

NKVD - Soviet People's Commissariat for Internal Affairs.

NO-MAN'S-LAND - Strip of ground between opposing trenches.

NORAD - North American Air Defence.

NSDAP - *Nationalsozialistiche Deutsche Arbeiterpartei* (National Socialist German Worker's Party). The Nazi Party.

NULL TAG - (Zero Day). German equivalent of D-Day.

O-Group - Orders Group. A meeting of officers in which orders are given for a forth-coming operation.

ABOVE: *Bazooka team of a Canadian infantry battalion in Korea.* (DND PHOTO)

OBOE - Blind-bombing radar device.

OKH - *Oberkommando des Heeres* (German Army High Command).

OKL - *Oberkommmando der Luftwaffe* (German Air Force High Command.).

OKM - *Oberkommando der Kreigsmarine* (German Navy High Command).

OKW - *Oberkommando der Wehrmacht* (High Command of the German Army).

OERLIKON - Swiss armament manufacturer noted for 20-mm cannon.

ORDERLY OFFICER - Duty officer of junior rank in army or air force.

OR'S - Other Ranks (i.e. not officers).

OSS - (U.S.) Office of Strategic Services. Forerunner of CIA.

OVERLORD - Allied invasion of France, 6 June 1944.

PACE STICK - A highly-polished wooden measuring device one pace (2.5 feet) long with a hinge that allows it to be expanded to double pace length. Carried by a Warrant Officer.

PAK - *Panzerabwherkanone* - German anti-tank gun.

PANZER - German tank.

PANZERGRENADIER - German mechanized infantry.

Pdr. - Pounder. British projectile weight/gun-size measurement, for example 25-pdr.

PETROL - (Br.) Gasoline.

PHONEY WAR - Period of inactivity on the Western Front during WWII (1939-1940).

PIAT - (Br.) Projectile Infantry Anti-Tank.

PIONEER - Infantryman assigned to road building, mine-clearing and light construction duties.

PILLBOX - German ferro-concrete bunker.

PLATOON - Sub-unit of infantry

numbering about 35 men and commanded by a lieutenant.

POM-POM - First applied to 1-pdr. gun in Boer War. In naval context, the Vicker's 2-pdr. Supposedly after the sound of the gun firing.

POOP DECK - A raised deck aft.

PORT - Left side of a ship or aircraft when looking forward.

POTATO-MASHER - German hand grenade.

POW - Prisoner of war.

PRANG - Hit, damage, smash or crash an aircraft.

PRIVATEER - A privately-funded warship sailing under Letters of Marque licensed to attack enemy shipping.

PROVOST - Military policeman. See also MP and MEATHEAD.

PW - Prisoner of War. POW is an Americanism.

QM - Quartermaster. (Supply).

QUARTERDECK - Rear deck reserved for officers in command of a sailing ship.

RADAR - Radio Detection and Ranging.

RANGER - Light infantryman tasked with foraging, reconnaissance and harassing the enemy.

RAP - Regimental Aid Post.

RCAF - Royal Canadian Air Force.

RCEME - Royal Canadian Electrical and Mechanical Engineers.

RED CAP - (Br.) Military policeman.

REGIMENT - In most armies a military unit with two or more battalions commanded by a Colonel. Commonwealth equivalent is a Brigade. An armoured regiment consists of approximately 70-80 AFVs.

RIFLEMAN - Originally (c. 1800) a soldier equipped with a rifle rather than a smooth-bored musket.

RMC - Royal Military College, Kingston, ON.

RONSON - Nickname for Sherman tank after a popular cigarette lighter which lit "first-time every time."

RSM - Regimental Sergeant-Major.

ST. CYR - French army military academy.

SACHEM - The supreme chief of some North American Indian tribes.

SALVO - Artillery tactic similar to naval broadside where all guns fire at the same time for maximum impact.

SAM - Surface-to-air missile.

SAMURAI - Feudal warrior class of Japan.

SANDHURST - British military academy.

SAPPER - Lowest enlisted rank in Royal Engineers and generic term for all engineers. Term derived from specialized troops who constructed "saps" or approaches to enemy fortresses.

SAS - (Br.) Special Air Service.

SBS - (Br.) Special Boat Service.

SCHOONER - A fore-and-aft rigged sailing ship of three or more masts of equal size.

SCHRÄGE MUSIK - (Slanted or jazz music). Upward-firing cannon mounted on German night-fighters.

SCRAN - Slang for ship's food.

SCUTTLEBUT - Ship's rumour or gossip.

SECTION - Smallest infantry sub-unit consisting of 10 men commanded by a corporal.

SHELL - Hollow artillery projectile containing high explosive.

SHELL DRESSING - Thick bandage carried by soldiers and used for immediate first aid.

SHIP-OF-THE-LINE - In sailing days the principal vessel of war of 64, 74, 80, 90, 98 or100 guns arranged in broadside batteries. Ships were classified fourth to first rate, "Fit to lie in the line-of-battle." Nelson's *Victory* was a first-rate ship.

SHOT - Solid artillery projectile.

SHERIFF - Air force slang for Duty Officer.

SHRAPNEL - Spherical case shot. Used only by Royal Artillery. A shell loaded with lead bullets fired from both guns and howitzers against enemy personnel. Range: 800-1000 yards. Named after inventor.

SICK BAY - Space or quarters aboard ship for treating sick or wounded.

SIGINT - Signal Intelligence.

SITREP - Situation Report.

SITZKREIG - British term for PHONEY WAR of 1939/1940.

SIX NATIONS - Iroquois Confederacy of the Cayuga, Mohawk, Oneida, Onondaga, Seneca and Tuscorara. Known as the Five Nations prior to the Tuscoraras joining the Confederacy.

SLIT TRENCH - The proverbial "fox hole."

SLOOP - Naval vessel smaller than a corvette.

SORTIE - Operational flight by a single aircraft.

SPROG - Air force slang for student pilot.

SQUADRON - A formation of aircraft. Also, a sub-unit of an armoured regiment consisting of HQ troop and four fighting troops each of four tanks.

SQUID - (Br.) Three-barreled anti-submarine mortar firing ahead under ASDIC control.

SS - *Schulzstaffel* (Protective Bodies). Security arm of Nazi Party. Gradually became the most powerful organization in the Third Reich responsible for all police and intelligence services including the Gestapo, concentration and extermination camps.

STAFF - General or Admiral's assistants. In British Army their duties were organized into operations and intelligence (G), administration and personnel (A), and supply (Q). In the U.S. Army, staff is divided into G-1,2,3,4, and 5 categories, G-3 being the equivalent of British operations and intelligence.

STALAG - *Mannschafts-Stammlager* (Enlisted Men's PW Camp).

STARBOARD - Right side of a ship or aircraft when looking forward.

STAVKA - Soviet High Command.

STEN GUN - Manufactured by Sheppard and Turpin, hence the name. 9-mm submachine gun with a bad reputation for jamming. Crude but effective when it worked. Also known as "Plumber's Delight."

STICK - A formation of parachutists jumping from a single aircraft.

STOL- Short Take-off and Landing.

STONK - Quick, heavy bombardment by guns, howitzers or mortars on a target area.

SUNRAY - Wireless designation for commanding officer.

SWAGGER STICK - 18" leather-covered stick carried by officers in Commonwealth armies.

TACTICAL AIR - Aircraft devoted to ground support.

TASK FORCE - Military force organized to carry out a specific mission.

TIN HAT - Steel anti-shrapnel helmet issued to Commonwealth troops in 1916.

TOMMY - Slang for British soldier.

TOMMY COOKER - German slang for Sherman tank.

TOMMY GUN - Thompson submachine gun.

TROOP - Basic sub-unit of an armoured regiment. Four tanks commanded by a lieutenant.

U-BOAT - *Unterwaserboot*. German submarine.

ULTRA - Top secret intelligence source based on the ability to read German Enigma coding machine.

VAN - Head of a column of troops or ships.

V-E - Victory in Europe.

V-J - Victory over Japan.

ABOVE: *The Harrier jump-jef gained a formidable reputation during the Falklands War.* (AP)

V-WEAPONS - German vengeance weapons, V-1 (see DOODLEBUG) and V-2 rocket.

VOLKSGRENADIER - Hastily-assembled and poorly-trained German divisions at end of WWII.

VOLTIGEUR - French light infantryman.

WAMPUM - Beads or shells strung together for money, decoration or as a mnemonic device by North American Indians.

WAFFEN SS - Armed SS.

WAVY NAVY - Royal Canadian Navy Volunteer Reserve (RCNVR). After its irregular rank band.

WEHRMACHT - German armed forces.

WEST POINT - Principle cadet school of U.S. Army.

WHIZZ BANG - German field artillery shell.

WIA - Wounded in action.

WINDOW - Strips of aluminum foil dropped from bombers to disrupt enemy radar.

WING - A formation of two or more aircraft squadrons.

WIRELESS - (Br.) Radio designation.

WOLF PACK - An operational unit of German submarines deployed in an extended line to search for convoys. When found, ordered to concentrate for a night attack on the surface.

WOLSELEY HELMET - Type of white sun helmet still worn by some Canadian units as part of ceremonial dress.

WRENS - Women's Royal Canadian Naval Service.

YAK - Soviet aircraft designation, after manufacturer Yakolev, e.g. Yak-7.

ZEPPELIN - German airship.

ZIPPERHEADS - Slang for tank crews.

ZOMBIE - Derogatory term for those recruited under the National Resources Mobilization Act (1940). Required to serve in Canada only and could not be sent overseas.

FURTHER READING

There are, of course, hundreds of published works which relate to each section of *Canada at War and Peace*. For example, there are more than 60,000 titles referring to the American Civil War alone and the bibliography for the *Battle of Gettysburg* runs to 4000 pages. The following list is thus in no way comprehensive but should be of interest to students and the casual reader.

GENERAL

Finlay, J.L. and Sprague, D.M., *The Structure of Canadian History*, Toronto: Prentice-Hall, 1979.

German, Tony, *The Sea is at Our Gates*, Toronto: McClelland & Stewart, Toronto: 1990.

Greenhouse, Brereton & Halliday, Hugh, *Canada's Air Forces, 1914-1999*, Montreal: Art Global, 1999.

Marteinseon, John, *We Stand on Guard. An Illustrated History of the Canadian Army*, Montreal: Ovale Publications, 1992.

Milner, Marc, *Canada's Navy: The First Century*, Toronto: University of Toronto Press, 1999.

Morton, Desmond, *A Military History of Canada, From Champlain to Kosovo*, Toronto: McClelland & Stewart, 1999.

Stanley, G.F.G., *Canada's Soldiers: The Military History of an Unmilitary People*, Toronto: McClelland & Stewart, 1974.

Wise, Greenhouse et al., *The Official History of the RCAF*, Ottawa: Ministry of Supply & Services, 3 Volumes, 1980-1994.

THE FORMATIVE YEARS, 1000-1699

Armstrong, J.C.W., *Champlain*, Toronto: Macmillan, 1987.

Berkhofer, Robert F., *The White Man's Indian: Images of the American Indian from Columbus to the Present*, New York: Knopf, 1978.

Braudel, Fernand, *The World of Jacques Cartier*, Paris: Berger-Levrault, 1984.

Dickason, Olive Patricia, *Canada's First Nations: A History of Founding Peoples From the Earliest Times*, Toronto: McClelland & Stewart, 1992.

The Myth of the Savage, Edmonton: University of Alberta Press, 1977.

Eccles, W.J. *France in America*, New York: Putnam, 1972.

Jenness, Diamond, *The Indians of Canada*, Toronto: University of Toronto Press, 1977.

Josephy, Alvin M., *500 Nations: An Illustrated History of North American Indians*, New York: Knopf, 1994.

Le Fay, Howard, *The Vikings*, Washington: National Geographic Society, 1972.

Morison Samuel Eliot, *The European Discovery of America*, New York: Oxford University Press, 1971.

Rutledge, J.L., *Century of Conflict*, New York: Doubleday, 1957.

Syme, Ronald, *Frontenac of New France*, New York: William Morrow, 1969.

Trudel, Marcel, *The Beginnings of New France, 1524-1663*, Toronto: McClelland & Stewart, 1973

THE FIGHT FOR CONTROL, 1700-1774

Chartrand, René, *Canadian Military Heritage, 1000-1754*, Vol.1, Montreal: Art Global, 1993.

Canadian Military Heritage, 1755-1871, Vol. II, Montreal: Art Global, 1995.

Creighton, Donald, *Empire of the St. Lawrence*, Toronto:-Macmillan, 1956.

Downey, Fairfax, *Louisbourg: Key to a Continent*, New York: Englewood, 1965.

Eccles, W.J., *Canada Under Louis XIV 1663-1701*, Toronto: McClelland & Stewart, 1966.

The Canadian Frontier, 1534-1760, Albuquerque: University of New Mexico Press, 1983.

FréGault, Guy, *La Guerre de la Conquête,1754-1760*, Montreal: Fides, 1955.

1nnis, Harold, *The Fur Trade in Canada*, New Haven: Yale University Press, 1930.

Jennings, Francis, *Empire of Fortune: Crowns, Colonies & Tribes in the Seven Years War in America*, New York: Norton, 1988.

Kepperman, Paul, *Braddock at the Monongahela*, Pittsburgh: University of Pittsburg Press, 1977.

Leckie, Robert, *A Few Acres of Snow: The Saga of the French and Indian Wars*, Toronto: John Wiley & Sons, 1988.

Parkman, Francis, *Montcalm and Wolfe*, New York: Collier, 1996. First published in Boston in 1884.

Verney, Jack, *The Good Regiment: The Carignan-Salières Regiment in Canada 1665-1668*, Montreal & Kingston, McGill-Queen's, 1991.

BORDERS DEFINED, 1775-1815

Berton, Pierre, *The Invasion of Canada, 1812-13*, Toronto: McClelland & Stewart, 1980.

Flames Across the Border, 1813-14, Toronto: McClelland & Stewart, 1981.

Bradley, Arthur, *The United Empire Loyalists*, London: Macmillan, 1932.

Casselman, A., (ed.) *Richardson's War of 1812*, Toronto: Coles, 1974.

Dunlop, Dr., *Recollections of the American War, 1812-14*, Toronto: Bryant Press, 1906.

Eckert, Allan W., *A Sorrow in Our Heart: The Life of Tecumseh*, Toronto: Bantam, 1992.

Fleming, Thomas, *Liberty, The American Revolution*, New York: Viking, 1997.

Graves, Donald E., *The Battle of Lundy's Lane*, Baltimore: Nautical and Aviation Press, 1993.

Field of Glory: The Battle of Crysler's Farm, 1813, Toronto: Robin Brass Studio, 1999.

(ed.) *Merry Hearts Make Light Days: The War of 1812 Journal of Lt. John Le Couteur, 104th Foot*, Ottawa: Carleton University Press, 1993.

Guillet, Edwin C., *Early Life in Upper Canada*, Toronto: University of Toronto Press, 1963.

Hitsman, J. Mackay, *The Incredible War of 1812*, Toronto: University of Toronto Press, 1972.

Leckie, *Robert, George Washington's War*, New York: Harper-Collins, 1972.

Malcomson, Robert & Thomas, *HMS Detroit: The Battle for Lake Erie*, St. Catharines: Vanwell, 1990.

May, Robin, *The British Army in North America, 1775-1783*, London: Osprey, 1974.

Pockock, Tom, *Young Nelson in the Americas*, London: Collins, 1980.

Pope, Dudley, *Life in Nelson's Navy*, Annapolis: Naval 1nstitute Press, 1981.

Stanley, G.F.G., *The War of 1812: Land Operations*, Ottawa: Canadian War Museum, 1983.

Tebbel, John, *Turning the World Upside Down: Inside the American Revolution*, New York: Random House, 1993.

Tuckman, Barbara, *The First Salute: A View of the American Revolution*, New York, Random House, 1993.

SECURING THE DOMINION, 1816-65

Fryer, Mary Babcock, *Volunteers and Redcoats, Rebels and Raiders*, Toronto: Dundurn Press, 1987.

Greer, Allan, *The Patriots and the People: The Rebellion of 1837 in Rural Lower Canada*, Toronto: University of Toronto Press, 1993.

Guillett, Edwin C., *The Lives and Times of the Patriots*, Toronto: University of Toronto Press, 1963.

Kilbourn, William, *The Firebrand: William Lyon Mackenzie and the Rebellion in Upper Canada*, Toronto: Clarke, Irwin, 1956.

Lower, A.R..M., *Colony to Nation*, Toronto: University of Toronto Press, 1946.

New, C.W., *Lord Durham*, London: Oxford University Press, 1926.

Senior, Elinor Kyte, *Redcoats and Patriots.The Rebellion in Lower Canada, 1837-38*, Ottawa: Canadian War Museum, 1985.

Schull, Joseph, *Rebellion: The Uprising in French Canada, 1837*, Toronto: Macmillan, 1971.

THE AMERICAN CIVIL WAR, 1861-65

McPherson, James M., *Battle Cry of Freedom; The Civil War Era*, New York: Oxford University Press, 1968.

Oates, Stephen B., *Our Firey Trial*, Amherst: University of Massachusetts Press, 1979.

With Malice Toward None: The Life of Lincoln, New York: Harper & Row, 1977.

Wills, Garry, *Lincoln at Gettysburg*, New York: Simon & Schuster, 1992.

TAMING THE FRONTIERS, 1866-1899

Ahenakow, Edward, *Voices of the Plains Cree*, Toronto: McClelland & Stewart, 1973.

Beal, Bob & Macleod, Rod, *Prairie Fire: The 1885 North-West Rebellion*, Edmonton: Hurtig, 1984.

Cameron, W.B., *The War Trail of Big Bear*, Toronto: Coles, 1977.

Creighton, Donald, *John A. Macdonald: The Young Politician*, Toronto: Macmillan, 1952.

John A. Macdonald: *The Old Chieftan*, Toronto: Macmillan, 1955.

The Road to Confederation, Toronto: Macmillan, 1964.

Deane, R., *Mounted Police Life in Canada*, Toronto: Coles, 1973.

Erasmus, Peter, *Buffalo Days and Nights*, Calgary: Glenbow–Alberta Institute, 1979.

Flanagan, Thomas, *Louis David Riel: Prophet of the New World*, Toronto: University of Toronto Press, 1979.

Riel and the Rebellion of 1885 Reconsidered, Saskatoon: Western Producer Prairie Books, 1983.

McDougall, John, *Pathfinding on Plain and Prairie*, Toronto: Coles, 1971.

Morton, Desmond, *Ministers and Generals: Politics and the Canadian Militia*, Toronto: University of Toronto Press, 1970.

The Last War Drum: The North-West Campaign of 1885, Hakkert, 1972.

Newman, Peter C., *Canada - 1892: Portrait of A Promised Land*, Toronto: McClelland & Stewart, 1992.

Opening Up the West, North-West Mounted Police Reports, 1874-1881, Toronto: Coles, 1973.

Senior, Howard, *The Last Invasion of Canada: The Fenian Raids, 1866-1870*, Toronto: Dundurn Press, 1991.

Stanley, G.F.G., *The Birth of Western Canada: A History of the Riel Rebellions*, Toronto: University of Toronto Press, 1978.

Woodcock, George, *Gabriel Dumont*, Edmonton: Hurtig, 1975.

SOUTH AFRICA 1899-1902

Chapwell, Mike, *The Canadian Army at War*, London: Osprey, 1985.

Haycock, Ronald, *Sam Hughes, Waterloo*: University of Waterloo Press, 1986.

Miller, Carman, *Painting the Map Red.:Canada and the South African War, 199l-1902*, Montreal and Kingston: McGil-Queen's University Press, 1993

Morton, Desmond, *The Canadian General: Sir William Otter*, Toronto: Hakkert, 1974.

Packenham, Thomas, *The Boer War*, New York: Random House, 1979.

Ried, Brian A., *Our Little Army in the Field: The Canadians in South Africa, 1899-1902*, St.-Catharines: Vanwell, 1996.

Schull, Jospeh, *Laurier*, Toronto: Macmillan, 1965.

THE GREAT WAR, 1914-1918

Berton, Pierre, *Vimy*, Toronto: McClellan & Stewart, 1986.

Bishop, Arthur, *Courage in the Air*, Toronto: McGraw-Hill, 1992.

Borden, Robert Laird, *Robert Laird Borden: His Memoirs*, Toronto: McClelland and Stewart, 1969.

Cowley, Deborah, (ed.), *Georges Vanier: Soldier. The Wartime Letters and Diaries, 1915- 1919*. Toronto: Dundurn, 2000.

Dancocks, Daniel, *Welcome to Flanders Fields: The First Canadian Battle of the Great War, Ypres, 1915*, Toronto: McClelland & Stewart, 1988.

Spearhead to Victory, Edmonton: Hurtig, 1987.

Fitzsimons, Bernard, (ed.), *Warships & Sea Battles of World War 1*, New York: Beekman House, 1973.

Gwyn, Sandra, *Tapestry of War: A Private View of Canadians in the Great War*, Toronto: Harper Collins, 1992.

Hyatt, A.M.J., *General Sir Arthur Currie: A Military Biography*, Toronto: University of Toronto Press, 1987.

Keegan, John, *The First World War*, Toronto: Key Porter, 1988.

Livesay, Anthony, *Great Battles of World War One*, New York: Macmillan, 1989.

Morris, Grace, *But This Is Our War*, Toronto: University of Toronto Press, 1987.

Morton, Desmond, & Granatstein, J.L., *Marching to Armaggedon: Canadians and the Great War, 1914-1919*, Toronto: Lester & Orpen Dennys, 1989.

Nicholson, Col. G.W.L., *The Canadian Expeditionary Force, 1914-1919*, Ottawa: Department of National Defence, 1962.

Ralph, Wayne, *Barker VC: William Barker, Canada's Most Decorated War Hero*, Toronto: Doubleday, 1997.

Read, Daphne, (ed.), *The Great War and Canadian Society*, Toronto: New Hogtown Press, 1992.

Scott, Reverend, F.G., *The Great War As I Saw It*, Vancouver: Clark & Stuart, 1934.

Williams, Jeffery, *Byng of Vimy: General and Governor-General*, Toronto: University of Toronto Press, 1983.

BETWEEN THE ACTS, 1920-1939

Abraham, David, *The Collapse of the Weimer Republic*, Princeton: Princeton University Press, 1981.

Berton, Pierre, *The Great Depression*, Toronto: McClelland & Stewart, 1986.

Bullock, Alan, *Hitler: A Study in Tyranny*, Toronto: McClelland & Stewart, 1964.

Hitler and Stalin: Parallel Lives, Toronto: McClelland & Stewart, 1991.

Eayrs, James, *In Defence of Canada, Vol.11, Appeasement and Rearmament*, Toronto: University of Toronto Press, 1965.

Gilbert, Martin, *Marching to War, 1933-1939*, Toronto: Doubleday, 1989.

Mowat, Farley, *The Regiment*, Toronto: McClelland & Stewart, 1955.

Irving, David, *The War Path: Hitler's Germany 1933-39*, London: Macmillan, 1978.

Shirer, William L., *The Collapse of the Third Republic. An Inquiry Into the Fall of France, 1940*, New York: Simon & Schuster, 1967.

Thomas, Hugh, *The Spanish Civil War*, London: Macmillan, 1977.

Watt, D.Cameron, *How War Came: The Immediate Origins of the Second World War, 1938-39*, London: Macmillan, 1989.

Zuelke, Mark, *The Gallant Cause: Canadians in the Spanish Civil War*, Toronto: Stoddart, 1993.

1939 - WAR AGAIN!

Adachi, Ken, *The Enemy That Never Was: A History of the Japanese Canadians*, Toronto: McClelland & Stewart, 1976.

Bothwell, Robert & Killowin, *William C.D. Howe*, Toronto: McClelland & Stewart, 1989.

Copps, Terry and Vogel, Robert, *Maple Leaf Routes, 5 Volumes*, Alma, ON: *Maple Leaf Route, 1983-88*.

Copps, Terry and Nielsen, *Richard, No Price Too High: Canadians and the Second World War*, Toronto: McGraw-Hill Ryerson, 1996.

Dancocks, Daniel, *The D-Day Dodgers: The Canadians in Italy*, Toronto: McClelland & Stewart, 1991.

Dexter, Grant, *Ottawa at War*, Winnipeg: Manitoba Record Society, 1995.

Dunmore Spencer & Carter, William, *Reap the Whirlwind*, McClelland & Stewart, 1991.

Galloway, Colonel Strome, *With the Irish Against Rommel, A Diary of 1943,* Battleline Books

Granatstein, J.L., *The Generals: The Canadian Army's Senior Commanders in the Second World War*. Toronto: Stoddart, 1994.

Canada's War: The Politics of the Mackenzie King Government, 1939-1945, Toronto: University of Toronto Press, 1975.

Granatstein, J.L., and Morton, Desmond, *Bloody Victory: Canadians and the D-Day Campaign, 1944*, Toronto: Lester, 1994.

Victory, 1945, Toronto: Harper Collins, 1995.

Hadley, Michael L., *U-Boats Against Canada: German Submarines in Canadian Waters*, Kingston & Montreal: McGill-Queen's University Press, 1992.

Halford, Robert G., *The Unkown Navy: Canada's World War II Merchant Navy*, St. Catharines: Vanwell, 1994.

Hoyt, Edwin P., *The U-Boat Wars*, New York: Random House, 1984

Lawrence, Hal, *A Bloody War*, Toronto: Macmillan, 1966.

Levin, Nora, *The Holocaust: The Destruction of European Jewry, 1933-1945*, New York: Schocken Books, 1975.

Milberry, Larry & Halliday, Hugh, *The RCAF at War, 1939-1945*, Toronto: CANAV Books, 1996.

Milner, Marc, *The North Atlantic Run: The RCN and the Battle for the Convoys*, Toronto: University of Toronto Press, 1985.

The U-Boat Hunters, Toronto: University of Toronto Press, 1994.

Mowat, Farley, *And No Birds Sang*, Toronto: McClelland & Stewart, 1979.

Nicolson, G.W.L., *The Canadians in Italy, 1943-1945*, Ottawa: Queen's Printer, 1960.

Peden, Murray, *A Thousand Shall Fall*, Stittsville: Canada's Wings, 1979.

Pickersgill, J.W., & Forster, D., (ed.), *The Mackenzie King Record*, Toronto: University of Toronto Press, 1961-1970, 4 volumes.

Roskill, S.W., *The War at Sea, 1939-1945*, London: H.M.S.O., 1954-1961, 4 volumes.

Stacey, C.P.Arms, *Men and Governments: The War Policies of Canada, 1939-1945*, Ottawa: Department of National Defence, 1970.

Canada and the Age of Conflict: The Mackenzie King Era, Toronto: Macmillan, 1981.

Six Years of War, Ottawa: Queen's Printer, 1957.

The Victory Campaign: The Operations in North-West Europe, Ottawa: Queen's Printer, 1960.

Weinberg, Gerhard L., *A World At Arms*, London: Cambridge University Press, 1994.

Whitaker, Dennis & Shelagh, *Tug of War: The Canadian Victory That Opened Antwerp*, Toronto: Stoddart, 1984.

Rhineland: The Battle to End the War, London: Cooper, 1989.

Dieppe: Tragedy to Triumph, Toronto: McGraw-Hill Ryerson, 1992.

Williams, Jeffery, *The Long Left Flank: The Hard Fought Way to the Reich, 1944-45*. Toronto: Stoddart, 1988.

UNEASY AFTERMATH

AND THE KOREAN WAR, 1946-1953

Barris,Ted, *Deadlock in Korea: Canadians at War,*

1950-1953. Toronto: Macmillan, 1999.

Bercuson, David J., *Blood on the Hills: The Canadian Army in the Korean War,* Toronto: University of Toronto Press: 1999.

Bothwell, Robert, Drummond, Ian, & English, John, *Canada Since 1945*, Toronto: University of Toronto Press, 1981.

Broadfoot, Barry, *The Veterans' Years. Coming Home From the War*, Vancouver: Douglas & McIntyre, 1985.

Gardham, John, *Korea Volunteer: An Oral History From Those Who Were There*, Burnstown: General Store Publishing, 1994.

Hastings Max, *The Korean War*, London: Michael Joseph, 1987.

MacKay, R.A.(ed.), *Canadian Foreign Policy, 1945-1965*, Toronto: McClelland & Stewart, 1977.

Melady, John, *Korea: Canada's Forgotten War*, Toronto: McClelland & Stewart, 1983.

Meyers, Edward C., *Thunder in the Morning Calm, The Royal Canadian Navy in Korea, 1950-1955.*

Reid, Escott, *Time of Fear and Hope*, Toronto: McClelland and Stewart, 1977.

Wood, Herbert Fairlie, *Strange Battleground: The Official History of the Canadian Army in Korea*, Ottawa: Queen's Printer, 1966.

EAST VS WEST– COLD WAR, 1954-1989

Allan, Tony, *The Nuclear Age.Time Frame AD 1950-1990*, New York: Time-Life, 1990.

Bercuson, David & Granatstein, J.L., *War and Peacekeeping From South Africa to the Gulf: Canada's Limited Wars*, Toronto: Key Porter, 1991.

Clearwater, John, *Canadian Nuclear Weapons*, Toronto: Dundurn, 1998.

de Domenico, J.E.G., *Land of a Million Elephants: Memoirs of a Canadian Peacekeeper*, Burnstown: General Store, 1997.

Deere, David N., *Desert Cats:The Canadian Fighter Squadron in the Gulf War*, Stoney Creek: Fortress Books, 1991.

Dow, James, *The Arrow*, Toronto: Lorimer, 1997.

Gaffen, Fred, *Unkown Warriors. Canadians in the Vietnam War*, Toronto: Dundurn, 1990.

In the Eye of the Storm: A History of Canadian Peacekeeping Operations, Toronto: Deneau & Wayne, 1987.

Galen, Ted, (ed.), *NATO's Empty Victory. A Postmortem on the Balkan Wars*, Washington: The Cato Institute, 2000.

Gardham, John, *The Canadian Peacekeeper*, Burnstown: General Store, 1992.

Granatstein, J.L. & Lavender, D., *Shadows of War, Faces of Peace: Canada's Peacekeepers*, Toronto: Key Porter, 1992.

Hilsman, Roger, *The Cuban Missile Crisis*, Wesport: Praeger, 1996.

Isaacs, J.& Downing, T., *Cold War.An Illustrated History, 1945-l991*, New York: Little, Brown, 1998.

Karnow, Stanley, *Vietnam: A History*, New York: Viking, 1983.

Mackenzie, MGen., Lewis, *Peacekeeper: The Road to Sarajevo*, Vancouver: Douglas & McIntryre, 1993.

Maloney, Sean, *War Without Battles: Canada's NATO Brigade in Germany, 1951-1993.*

Melvan, L.R., *A People Betrayed.The Role of the West in Rwanda's Genocide*, London: Zed Books, 2000.

Miller, D.E., & Hobson, S., *The Persian Excursion.-The Canadian Navy in the Gulf War*, Toronto: Canadian Institute of Strategic Studies, l995.

Pimlot, John, *The Cold War*, New York: Aladdin, 1987.

Rohde, David, *Endgame: The Betryal and Fall of Srebrenica*, New York: Farrar, Strauss & Giroux, l997.

Ross, Douglas, *In the Interests of Peace:Canada and Vietnam, 1954-1973*, Toronto: University of Toronto Press, 1984.

THE POST COLD WAR DECADE

Abbot, Elizabeth, *Haiti: The Duvaliers and their Legacy*, New York: Touchstone, 1991.

Bercuson, David, *Significant Incident. Canada's Army, the Airborne and the Murder in Somalia*. Toronto: McClelland & Stewart, 1977.

Coulon, Jocelyn, *Soldiers of Diplomacy. The United Nations, Peacekeeping and the New World Order*, Toronto: University of Toronto Press, 1998.

Cribb, R., and Brown, B., *Modern Indonesia since 1945*, London: Longman, 1995.

Davis, James, *The Sharp End: A Canadian Soldier's Story*, Vancouver: Douglas & McIntyre, 1997.

Fortune's Warriors. Private Armies and the New World Order, Vancouver: Douglas & McIntyre, 2000.

Depleted Uranium Education Project, Metal of Dishonour, Depleted Uranium, New York: International Action Centre, 1997.

Desbarats, Peter, *Somalia Cover-Up: A Commissioner's Journal*, Toronto: McClelland & Stewart, 1977.

English, John A., *Lament for an Army. The Decline of Canadian Military Professionalism*, Toronto: Irwin, 1988.

Joksimovich, Vojin, *Kosovo Crisis,* Los Angeles: Graphics Management, 1999.

Moeller, Susan D., *Compassion Fatigue*, New York: Touchstone, 1991.

Off, Carol, *The Lion, the Fox, and the Eagle.A Story of Generals and Justice in Rwanda and Yugoslavia*, Toronto: Random House, 2000.

Taylor, Scott and Nolan, Brian, *Tarnished Brass: Crime and Corruption in the Canadian Forces*, Ottawa: Lester Publishing, 1996.

Taylor, Scott and Nolan, Brian, *Tested Mettle: Canada's Peacekeepers at War*, Ottawa: *Esprit de Corps* Books, 1998.

Taylor, Scott, *Inat: Images of Serbia and the Kosovo Conflict*, Ottawa: *Esprit de Corps* Books, 2000.

Worthington, Peter, and Brown, Kyle, *Scapegoat: How the Army Betrayed Kyle Brown,* Toronto: Seal Books, 1997.

Canadian Forces Table of Ranks

Modern military ranks derive from the titles of officers in medieval mercenary companies — the chief or captain, his deputy or lieutenant, and sergeants. When the companies were formed into a larger group or column, they were put under the authority or "regiment" of a colonel. When a number of regiments were grouped to form an army, its superior officers assumed "general" instead of "regimental" rank. Combinations of these titles, with the use of the suffix "major", yield most of the ranks of modern armies. It should be noted that a major general is junior to a lieutenant general as the rank was derived from "sergeant-major general."

Naval ranks derive from the ranks of soldiers aboard a ship — captain and lieutenant. Admiral comes from the Arabic *amir al bahr* (commander of the sea).

	NAVY	ARMY & AIR FORCE	PRE-UNIFICATION, 1967 ROYAL CANADIAN AIR FORCE
Commissioned Ranks	Admiral	General	Air Chief Marshal
	Vice Admiral	Lieutenant General	Air Marshal
	Rear Admiral	Major General	Air Vice Marshal
	Commodore	Brigadier General	Air Commodore
	Captain (N)	Colonel	Group Captain
	Commander	Lieutenant Colonel	Wing Commander
	Lieutenant Commander	Major	Squadron Leader
	Lieutenant (N)	Captain	Flight Lieutenant
	Sub-Lieutenant	Lieutenant	Flying Officer
	Acting Sub-Lieutenant	Second Lieutenant	Pilot Officer
	Naval Cadet	Officer Cadet	Officer Cadet
Non-Commissioned Ranks	Chief Petty Officer 1st Class	Chief Warrant Officer	Warrant Officer Class 1
	Chief Petty Officer 2nd Class	Master Warrant Officer	Warrant Officer Class 2
	Petty Officer 1st Class	Warrant Officer	Flight Sergeant
	Petty Officer 2nd Class	Sergeant	No equivalent
	Master Seaman	Master Corporal	No equivalent
	Leading Seaman	Corporal	Corporal
	Ordinary Seaman	Private	Aircraftsman

INDEX